Fifth Edition

CANADIAN BUSINESS ENGLISH

Fifth Edition

CANADIAN BUSINESS ENGLISH

Mary Ellen Guffey
Professor of Business Emerita
Los Angeles Pierce College

Patricia Burke
Professor of English
Humber Institute of Technology
& Advanced Learning

NELSON EDUCATION

Canadian Business English, Fifth Edition
by Mary Ellen Guffey and Patricia Burke

Associate Vice President, Editorial Director:
Evelyn Veitch

Editor-in-Chief:
Anne Williams

Publisher:
Cara Yarzab

Acquisitions Editor:
Bram Sepers

Marketing Manager:
Amanda Henry

Senior Developmental Editor:
Linda Sparks

Permissions Coordinator:
Vicki Gould

Senior Content Production Manager:
Natalia Denesiuk Harris

Production Service:
Graphic World Publishing Services

Copy Editor:
Wayne Herrington

Proofreader:
Graphic World Publishing Services

Indexer:
Graphic World Publishing Services

Production Coordinator:
Ferial Suleman

Design Director:
Ken Phipps

Managing Designer:
Katherine Strain

Cover Design:
Angela Cluer

Cover Images:
Centre: © Najlah Feanny/Corbis; clockwise, starting at top left: Kristian Sekulic/Shutterstock; © Tanya Constantine/Corbis; Stephen Coburn/Shutterstock; Mark Aplet/Shutterstock; © Jim Craigmyle/Corgis

Compositor:
Graphic World Inc.

Printer:
RR Donnelley

Printed and bound in Canada
4 5 6 12 11 10

For more information contact Nelson Education Ltd., 1120 Birchmount Road, Toronto, Ontario, M1K 5G4. Or you can visit our Internet site at http://www.nelson.com

Library and Archives Canada Cataloguing in Publication Data

Guffey, Mary Ellen
Canadian business English / Mary Ellen Guffey, Patricia Burke. — 5th ed.

Includes index.
ISBN 978-0-17-644026-8

1. English language—Business English. 2 English language—Grammar. I. Burke, Patricia II. Title.

PE1115.G83 2008a 808'.06665
C2008-904562-9

ISBN-13: 978-0-17-644026-8
ISBN-10: 0-17-644026-7

Contents

unit 5

Punctuating Sentences 307

unit 6

Writing With Style 373

appendices

self-help exercises

Preface

Canadian Business English, Fifth Edition, is the Canadian version of Mary Ellen Guffey's well-known and successful *Business English* text. The bold and innovative approach taken by Dr. Guffey in *Business English* continues to appeal to instructors and students in Canada and the United States. Since 1995 *Canadian Business English* has helped thousands of Canadian students improve their language skills. This edition of *Canadian Business English* continues to serve Canadian students in reaching excellence in language skills and incorporates changes that more accurately reflect the Canadian landscape and the new technologies and challenges facing students in the business community.

Revisions That Expand Job Skills

Although *Canadian Business English,* Fifth Edition, largely retains the content and sequencing of previous editions, it puts new emphasis on employment skills such as editing, proofreading, and writing skills. We also examined every sentence to be sure that we demonstrate awareness of the massive effects of technology in the field of business communication. Here are some of the most significant changes in the fifth edition.

Editor's Challenge Feature—Now two in each chapter!

Cumulative editing exercises in every chapter enable students to continuously review grammar and punctuation guidelines. Documents to be edited include email messages, memos, letters, and short reports. These realistic documents familiarize students with the forms of business writing they are likely to see on the job.

Learning Web Ways—More than 50 per cent new material!

These short exercises help students improve their Internet skills. Students learn about browsers, URLs, hotlinks, and many exciting tips for using the Web effectively.

Hotlinks—Fifty per cent have been updated!

These are references to websites of interest to business English students. These "hotlinks" show students that the Internet can be useful for their personal and professional benefit.

Textbook Features

Many unique features ensure that students will be successful with *Canadian Business English* in the classroom.

Writer's Workshops

Six workshops feature composition tips and techniques. These workshops begin with proofreading skills and progress through the writing of sentences, paragraphs, email messages, memos, letters, short reports, and internal proposals. Frequent skill checks allow students to apply writing principles immediately, and each workshop presents an optional writing assignment.

Pretest

Preceding Chapter 1 is a short pretest designed to help students assess their business English strengths and weaknesses. Answer keys for this test and for all chapter exercises are provided in the Instructor's Manual.

Three-Level Approach

Beginning with Chapter 4, language concepts appear in levels. These levels progress from fundamental, frequently used concepts in Level I to more complex concepts in Level III. Each level has its own trial exercises as well as numerous relevant student reinforcement drills.

The three-level approach has three distinct advantages. First, the overall organization of the complex subject of English is immediately recognizable. Second, the three-level approach facilitates comprehension and promotes student confidence by providing small, easily mastered learning segments. Third, this strategy provides convenient blocks of material that allow individual instructors to tailor the content of the course to fit student abilities, institutional goals, and time constraints.

Hotline Queries

One of the most popular features of *Canadian Business English* has been its questions and answers patterned on those from grammar hotline services. These questions—and the answers to them—illustrate everyday communication problems encountered in the work world. In easy-to-read question-and-answer format, important distinctions in English grammar, usage, style, and vocabulary are explained.

Pretests and Posttests

Each chapter includes a brief pretest to preview concepts and to pique student interest. Chapters also provide a posttest to enable students to evaluate their achievement.

Self-Check Exercises and Unit Reviews

The first student exercise in each level of each chapter is self-checked. Students are thereby able to determine immediately whether they comprehend the concepts just presented. At the end of each unit, a self-checked review exercise enables students to test their mastery of the unit.

Learning Objectives

Concisely stated learning objectives introduce each chapter. These overtly stated goals summarize the concepts to be presented and facilitate learning by stimulating a student mind-set favourable to the learning process.

Spelling and Vocabulary

For students who desire them and for instructors who can find time to include them, optional spelling and vocabulary development materials are provided in separate appendices.

Writing Component

Sentence-writing exercises conclude each chapter. These skill-building opportunities encourage students to apply chapter principles in forming complete sentences. Optional editing and composition unit tests are available in the Instructor's Manual, which also includes ideas for incorporating this writing program in the business English course.

Self-Help Exercises

Because business English students need many opportunities to try out their learning, additional self-paced exercises are supplied. Supplementary exercises for all levels of all chapters and the exercise answers are provided in the back of the text.

Marginal Annotations

The interesting marginal annotations continue to provide stimulus to our students.

Unparalleled Supplements and Instructor Support

Canadian Business English includes a number of supplements to help students learn and instructors teach. Nelson provides the best support for business communication in Canada.

Website for Students & Instructors. http://www.businessenglish5e.nelson.com This website provides chapter-specific quizzes for student review. Additional resources for students include Editor's Challenges, Skill Builders, Media and Study Resources, Career Tips, and Grammar Review modules. A password-protected Instructor's website includes downloadable Microsoft® PowerPoint® slides and the Instructor's Resource Manual. Instructors should request a password from their local sales representative.

Instructor's Resource Manual. (0-17-647461-7). Written by the authors, this valuable resource includes solutions, discussion of the Writer's Workshop features, and other features to assist instructors in making the most of their classroom time.

Test Bank. The Test Bank provides Unit Tests and Chapter Tests. Each Chapter Test includes at least fifty objective questions and an answer key.

Computerized Test Bank. The Computerized Test Bank provides the same questions and answers as the paper-based test bank. ExamView® is a test generator program that enables you to create tests, enter your own questions, and customize the content and appearance of the tests you create. It is compatible with both Windows® and Macintosh® platforms.

Microsoft® PowerPoint® Slides. The PowerPoint® slides feature important concepts in the text and are provided for classroom use.

Student Resources in the Text

Study Tip

Memory devices and learning suggestions appear as study tips. They help you understand and retain the many language principles you will be reviewing.

Career Tip

These tips suggest applications and practical career advice that relate language concepts you are learning to your needs on the job.

Spot the Blooper

To provide humorous relief from the sometimes heavy load of grammar and mechanics, these bloopers demonstrate common language errors and help you understand how faulty expression can destroy a message.

Did You Know?

These tidbits relate interesting trivia to *Canadian Business English* concepts.

Hotlink

Recommended websites help you learn more about the chapter.

Acknowledgments

Colleagues and students at Humber Institute of Technology & Advanced Learning have given me the experience necessary to appreciate and adapt Mary Ellen Guffey's excellent text. Sincere thanks go to all those many colleagues and students whom I have worked with in more than twenty-five years of teaching.

Special thanks are extended to Vaska Tumir for her invaluable work on the Hotlink and Learning Web Ways sections of the text. Numerous people at Nelson have worked on the Canadian editions of this text, and working with them has always been a pleasure. This time Cara Yarzab, Bram Sepers, Linda Sparks, and Natalia Denesiuk Harris in particular should be acknowledged for being helpful, considerate, and patient.

Thanks must also go to the reviewers for their thoughtful comments and suggestions: Rebecca Ranjan, Algonquin College; Lara Kirkpatrick, Vancouver Island University; Pat Squibb, SAIT; Peggy McGurran, Durham College; Gloria Cott, NAIT; Shauna MacDonald, NAIT.

Patricia Burke

NAME ____________________

PRETEST

In the following sentences, errors in grammar, punctuation, capitalization, or number expression may appear. For each sentence underline any inappropriate form(s). Then write a corrected form in the space provided. *Clue:* one sentence at each level is correct.

Example: The inheritance will be given to my brother and myself on our twenty-first birthdays. ____me____

LEVEL I

1. In today's organizations teams play an increasingly important role, employees must learn to work together. ____________
2. The software workshop scheduled for the fall in Saskatoon, Saskatchewan sounds as if it will be worthwhile. ____________
3. The announcement from our Human Resources Department surprised the secretaries as much as I. ____________
4. Jim and I certainly appreciate you answering the telephone when he and I are away from the office. ____________
5. A list with all our customers' names and addresses were given to the manager and her last week. ____________
6. Every field employee, as well as every management and certified employee, is eligible for sales discounts. ____________
7. For you Mrs. Alison, we have a one-year subscription to your favourite newspaper. ____________
8. Under the circumstances, we can give you only 90 days time in which to sell the house and its contents. ____________
9. We normally hire only experienced operators; but we occasionally consider well-trained individuals who lack experience. ____________
10. In the fall Lisa took courses in history, french, and accounting. ____________

LEVEL II

11. More than 500 customers names and confidential information were revealed when hackers broke into the computer records. __________

12. Either Martin or she will be working at the shop on the next two Sunday's. __________

13. Of the eighty-six email messages she received, Ellen Turner said that only nine were legitimate. __________

14. To arrange a three-week summer vacation, you must speak to the Manager before January 15. __________

15. You should have saw the warehouse before its contents were moved to Seneca Street. __________

16. Chapter 15, which is titled "Credit Buying," is one of the best chapters in *Today's Consumer.* __________

17. Before her trip to the East last summer, my mother bought a Sony Camera. __________

18. We need at least one hundred eighty-cent postage stamps. __________

19. Your account is now 90 days overdue, therefore, we are submitting it to an agency for collection. __________

20. I feel badly about your missing the deadline, but the application has been lying on your desk for 15 days. __________

LEVEL III

21. A cash bonus is always given to whomever has the best record. __________

22. All job applicants must comply to the rules printed in our employee handbook. __________

23. Montreal is larger than any city in Quebec. __________

24. The number of cheques with insufficient funds are causing the bank to tighten its cheque-cashing procedures. __________

25. The school's alumni are certainly different than its currently enrolled students. __________

26. Courtney is one of those efficient, competent managers who is able to give sincere praise for work done well. __________

27. Because she looks like her sister, Mary is often taken to be her. __________

28. If I was he, I would call the Harrises' lawyer at once. __________

29. Three employees were given merit raises, namely, Carol Chang, Tom Nelson, and Toni Simpson. __________

30. It was definitely she who left the package on the boss's desk. __________

U N I T 1

Laying a Foundation

Chapter 1
Reference Skills

Chapter 2
Parts of Speech

Chapter 3
Sentences: Elements and Patterns

C H A P T E R

Reference Skills

1

OBJECTIVES When you have completed the materials in this chapter, you will be able to do the following:

- *Describe several types of dictionaries.*
- *Use a dictionary confidently to determine spelling, meaning, pronunciation, accent, word usage, and word history.*
- *Select a dictionary to suit your needs.*
- *Anticipate what information is included in dictionaries and what information is not.*
- *Understand the value of reference manuals.*
- *Use an electronic dictionary with confidence.*

PRETEST

Each chapter begins with a brief pretest. Answer the questions in the pretest to assess your prior knowledge of the chapter content and also to give yourself a preview of what you will learn. Compare your answers with those at the bottom of the page. When you complete the chapter, take the posttest to measure your improvement.

Write *T* (true) or *F* (false) after the following statements.

1. Today's business and professional people use both print and online dictionaries. ________
2. Dictionary guide words help readers pronounce words correctly. ________
3. The usage label *archaic* means that a word is very old. ________
4. All dictionaries present word definitions (senses) in the same order. ________
5. A reader should not expect to find the spelling of the plural form of *business* in most dictionaries. ________

1.T 2.F 3.T 4.F 5.T

Just what is business English, and why should you study it? Business English is the study of language fundamentals. These basics include grammar, usage, punctuation, capitalization, and number style. Because business people must express their ideas clearly and correctly, such language basics are critical.

In today's workplace, you can expect to be doing more communicating than ever before. You will be participating in meetings, writing reports, and sending many email messages. Suddenly, English skills are becoming very important. Professional people who never expected to be doing much writing on the job are finding that the Internet forces everyone to exchange written messages. As a result, professional people are increasingly aware of their communication skills. Misspelled words, poor grammar, sloppy punctuation—all these faults stand out glaringly when printed. Not only are people writing more, but their messages are travelling farther and are being seen by larger audiences than ever before.

Because of the growing emphasis on exchanging information, language skills are increasingly relevant. As a professional person, you will want to feel confident about your writing skills. This textbook and this course can sharpen your skills and greatly increase your confidence in expressing ideas. Improving your language skills is the first step toward success in your education, your career, and your life.

When Jennifer S. enrolled in business English, she did not plan to become an expert in the subject. When she finished the course, she didn't think of herself as an expert. However, when she started to work, she discovered that many of her fellow workers considered her an English expert. Most of them had no specific training in grammar—or they had studied it long ago, and their skills were very rusty. Jennifer found that even her boss asked her questions like "What are they doing now about letter salutations?" or "Where do you think we should put that apostrophe?" Because she had just finished school, her co-workers assumed she knew all the answers. Jennifer didn't know all the answers, but she knew where to find them.

One of the goals of your education is to know where to find the answers, as well as how to interpret the information you find. Experts do not know *all* the answers. Lawyers refer to casebooks. Doctors consult their medical libraries. And you, as a student of the language, must develop skill and confidence in using reference materials. You can become an English expert not only by learning from this textbook but also by learning where to find additional information when you need it.

▶ Dictionaries

Using references should become second nature to you. Dictionaries and online resources are invaluable when you must verify word spellings and meanings, punctuation style, and usage. If you have your own personal library of reference materials, you can find information quickly. At a minimum you need a current desk or college dictionary and a good reference manual. Another helpful reference book is a **thesaurus.** This is a collection of **synonyms** (words with similar meanings) and **antonyms** (words with opposite meanings). Many helpful resources are now available digitally, whether online or in a software program such as MS Word.

A dictionary is an alphabetical list of words with their definitions. Most dictionaries contain pronunciation guides, parts of speech, word history or etymology, labels, and other information which you'll learn about in this chapter. You can purchase dictionaries in almost every language. Bilingual dictionaries, such as English-French and Italian-English, are increasingly popular in today's global marketplace. In addition, many fields, such as law and medicine, have specialized dictionaries that contain vocabulary specific to that field.

Professional people today make use of both print dictionaries and online dictionaries. Even with the availability of online dictionaries, many prefer to have a print dictionary handy to look words up quickly and easily. First, you'll learn about print dictionaries, including how to select one and how to use it. Then, you'll learn about using an electronic dictionary, such as the one that comes with your word processing software. Finally, you'll learn how to use online dictionaries.

Did You Know?

The English language has about three times as many words as any other language on earth. English is estimated to include at least 450,000 words. German has 185,000, Russian 130,000, and French 100,000.

Selecting a Print Dictionary

Not all dictionaries are the same, as you will doubtless notice when you shop for one. To make a wise selection, you should know how to distinguish among three kinds of print dictionaries: pocket, desk, and unabridged. You should also know when your dictionary was published (the copyright date), and you should examine its special features.

Pocket Dictionary. As its name suggests, a pocket dictionary is small. Generally, it contains no more than 75,000 entries, making it handy to carry to class and efficient to use. However, a pocket dictionary doesn't contain enough entries to be adequate for postsecondary or college reference homework.

Desk or College-Level Dictionary. A desk or college-level dictionary may contain as many as 200,000 entries plus extra features. For college work you should own a current desk dictionary, preferably Canadian. The following list shows some of the best-known desk dictionaries, including two Canadian dictionaries. Spelling, definitions, and usage in this textbook are based on *The Canadian Oxford Dictionary,* Second Edition (2004).

The Canadian Oxford Dictionary
Collins Gage Canadian Paperback Dictionary
The Concise Oxford Dictionary
Merriam-Webster's Collegiate Dictionary

Unabridged Dictionary. An unabridged dictionary is a complete dictionary. (Abridged dictionaries, such as pocket and desk dictionaries, are shortened or condensed.) Because unabridged dictionaries contain nearly all English words, they are large, heavy volumes. Schools, libraries, newspapers, and offices that are concerned with editing or publishing use unabridged dictionaries. One of the best-known unabridged dictionaries is *Merriam-Webster's Third New International Dictionary*, which has over 450,000 entries. The most famous unabridged dictionary is the *Oxford English Dictionary (OED)*. This 20-volume set shows the historical development of all English words; it is often used by professional writers, scholars of the language, and academics. CD-ROM versions are available for easy computer searching.

Study Tip

To *abridge* means to "shorten," as a bridge shortens the distance between two points. An "unabridged" book has not been shortened.

Copyright Date. If the copyright date of your current dictionary shows that the dictionary was published ten or more years ago, invest in a more recent edition. English is a responsive, dynamic language that admits new words and recognizes changes in meanings, spelling, and usage of familiar words. These changes are reflected in an up-to-date dictionary.

Features. In selecting a dictionary, check the features it offers in addition to its word definitions. Many editions contain biographical and geographical data, abbreviations, standard measurements, signs, symbols, foreign words and phrases, lists of colleges and universities, given names, and information about the language. Non-native users of English will find especially helpful features in dictionaries such as the *Oxford ESL*

Dictionary (which has Canadian content), *Oxford Advanced Learner's Dictionary,* or various other dictionaries published by Oxford, Longman, or Collins Cobuild.

Dictionary Entry. The following example from *The Canadian Oxford Dictionary** illustrates some of the points we will discuss here to help you use your dictionary more effectively.

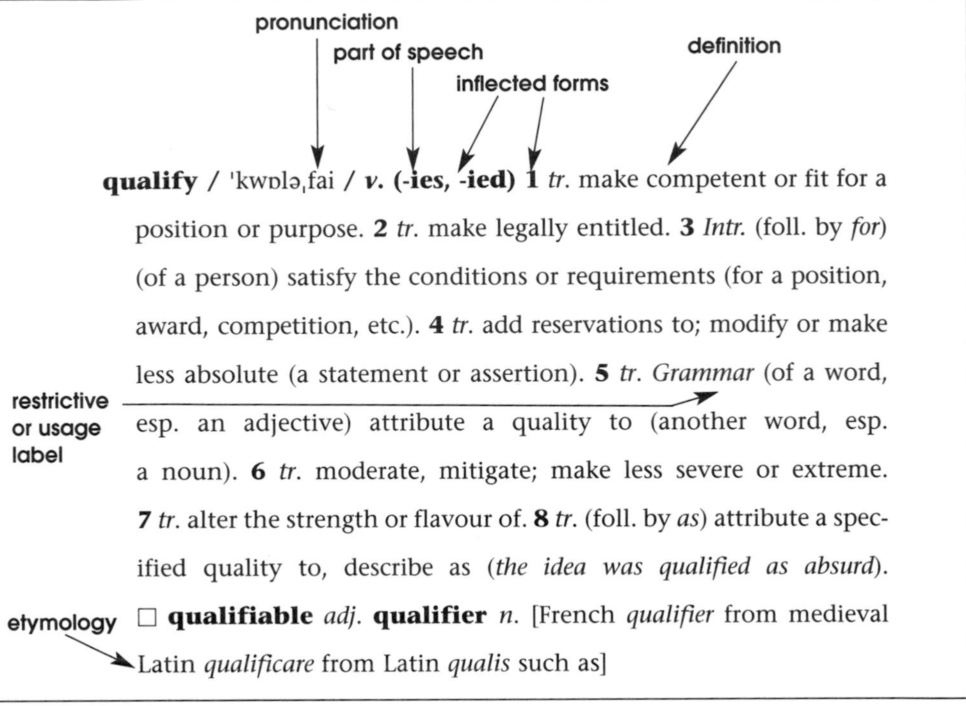

qualify / ˈkwɒləˌfai / ***v.*** **(-ies, -ied) 1** *tr.* make competent or fit for a position or purpose. **2** *tr.* make legally entitled. **3** *Intr.* (foll. by *for*) (of a person) satisfy the conditions or requirements (for a position, award, competition, etc.). **4** *tr.* add reservations to; modify or make less absolute (a statement or assertion). **5** *tr. Grammar* (of a word, esp. an adjective) attribute a quality to (another word, esp. a noun). **6** *tr.* moderate, mitigate; make less severe or extreme. **7** *tr.* alter the strength or flavour of. **8** *tr.* (foll. by *as*) attribute a specified quality to, describe as (*the idea was qualified as absurd*). □ **qualifiable** *adj.* **qualifier** *n.* [French *qualifier* from medieval Latin *qualificare* from Latin *qualis* such as]

Career Tip

Don't be ashamed to use a dictionary on the job. Such use signifies diligence and eagerness to improve, qualities that employers seek.

Using a Print Dictionary

Introduction. Before using your dictionary, take a look at the instructions for use that are located in the pages just before the beginning of the vocabulary entries. Pay particular attention to the order of definitions (senses). Some dictionaries show the most common definitions first. Other dictionaries develop meanings historically; that is, the first known meaning of the word is shown first.

Hotlink

To keep up with the constant innovation in language, a good dictionary regularly updates itself. Visit **<http://www.oup.com/ca/genref/vote/>** to check out the new words and phrases recorded by the *Canadian Oxford Dictionary* in the last year, and vote on the one you think most likely to stick around.

Guide Words. In boldface type at the top of each dictionary page are two words that indicate the first and last entries on the page. When searching for a word, look *only* at these guide words until you locate the desired page.

Pronunciation. Special symbols (diacritical marks) are used to help you pronounce words correctly. A detailed explanation of pronunciation symbols is found in the front pages of a dictionary; a summary of these symbols may appear at the bottom of each set of pages. If two pronunciations are possible, the preferred one is usually shown first.

Accent. Many dictionaries show accents with a raised stress mark preceding the accented syllable, as shown for the syllable *kwɒl* in our example. Other dictionaries use a raised stress mark immediately *following* the accented syllable (*kwɒl'ə fai).* Secondary stress may be shown with a lowered stress mark, as illustrated for the syllable *ˌfai* in our example, or it may be shown with a stress mark in lighter print *(kwɒl'ə fai')*.

Etymology. College-level dictionaries provide in square brackets [ ] or parentheses ( ) the brief history or etymology of the word. For example, the word *qualify* originated in

* From *The Canadian Oxford Dictionary, 2nd Edition,* edited by Katherine Barber. Copyright © 2004 Oxford University Press Canada. Reprinted by permission of the publisher.

Latin. Keys to etymological abbreviations may be found in the introductory notes in your dictionary. Do not confuse the etymological definition shown in brackets with the actual word definition(s).

Part of Speech. Following the phonetic pronunciation of an entry word is an italicized or boldfaced label indicating what part of speech the entry word represents. The most common labels are the following (sometimes followed by periods):

adj	(adjective)	*prep*	(preposition)
adv	(adverb)	*pron*	(pronoun)
conj	(conjunction)	*v* or *vb*	(verb)
interj	(interjection)	*vt* or *v tr*	(transitive verb)
n	(noun)	*vi* or *v int*	(intransitive verb)

Spelling, pronunciation, and meaning may differ for a given word when that word functions as different parts of speech. Therefore, check its grammatical label carefully. If the parts of speech seem foreign to you at this time, do not despair. Chapter 2 and successive chapters will help you learn more about the parts of speech.

Labels. Not all words listed in dictionaries are acceptable in business or other professional writing. Usage or register labels advise readers about the use of certain words. In the dictionary entry for *qualify*, one meaning is labelled *Grammar*, indicating that this meaning is restricted to a specific context. The following list defines some example usage labels. See the guide to your dictionary for more details.

Label	Example
archaic: from a previous period, now seldom used	*quittance* (meaning *release*)
dialect, Brit., US, Scot, Irish, etc.: used in certain regions	*gossoon* (Irish for *boy*)
informal or *colloquial:* used in casual writing or conversation	*rad* (meaning *radiator*)
offensive: insulting, whether intentionally or not	*mongolism* (meaning *Down's syndrome*)
slang: very informal but may be used sparingly for effect, mainly in speech	*skinny* (meaning *inside information*)

If no usage label appears, a word is considered standard; that is, it is acceptable for all uses. However, note that many lexicographers, those who make dictionaries, have substantially reduced the number of usage labels in current editions.

Inflected Forms. When nouns, verbs, adverbs, or adjectives change form grammatically, they are said to be *inflected,* as when *child* becomes *children.* Because of limited space, dictionaries usually show only irregular inflected forms. Thus, nouns with irregular or unusual plurals (*wife, wives*) will be shown. Verbs with irregular tenses or difficult spelling (*gratified, gratifying*) will be shown. Adverbs or adjectives with irregular comparatives or superlatives (*good, better, best*) will also be shown. However, regular noun plurals, verb tenses, and comparatives generally will *not* be shown in dictionaries. Succeeding chapters will elucidate regular and irregular parts of speech.

Synonyms and Antonyms. *Synonyms,* words having similar meanings, are often provided after word definitions. For example, a synonym for *elucidate* is *explain.* Synonyms are helpful as word substitutes. *Antonyms,* words having opposite meanings, appear less frequently in dictionaries; when included, they usually follow synonyms. One antonym for *elucidate* is *confuse.* The best place to find synonyms and antonyms is a thesaurus (see p. 10).

Career Tip

In the workplace people are judged by the words they use. Knowing the part of speech for a word helps you use it correctly. For example, if you discover that a word is a verb, you won't try to use it to describe a noun.

Spot the Blooper

In a Chinese fortune cookie: "You will gain admiration from your pears."

Using Electronic Dictionary Programs

Hotlink

Baffled by neologisms such as *freeganism* or *movieoke*? Looking for advice to improve your letter-writing skills? Or simply need some spelling and grammar tips? You can find answers to these and other language questions at **<http://www.askoxford.com/?view=uk>**.

Most word processing programs today come with a dictionary/thesaurus feature that helps you locate misspelled words as well as search for synonyms and antonyms. In addition, most email programs now include a spell-check feature that uses an electronic dictionary. You may even be able to program your email program to automatically spell-check your messages when you press the **Send** button.

Locating Misspelled Words. An **electronic dictionary,** also called a **spell checker,** compares your typed words with those in the computer's memory. MS Word uses a wavy red line to underline misspelled words as you type them. If you immediately recognize the error, you can quickly key in the correction. If you see the red wavy line and don't know what's wrong, you can right-click on the word. This pulls up a drop-down menu that generally shows a variety of options to solve your spelling problem. If one of the suggested spellings appears correct, you can click it and the misspelled word is replaced.

Many writers today rely heavily on their spell checkers; in fact, many may rely too much on them. The real problem is that spell checkers won't catch every error. For example, spell checkers can't always distinguish between similar words, such as *too* and *two*. That's why you should proofread every message carefully after running it through your spell checker. In addition, important messages should be printed out for proofreading.

Searching for Synonyms and Antonyms Electronic dictionary programs often include an online thesaurus showing alternative word choices. Let's say you are writing a report and you find yourself repeating the same word. With MS Word you can highlight the overused word and click *Tools, Language,* and *Thesaurus*. A number of synonyms appear in a dialogue box. If none of the suggested words seems right, you can change the search term by using a closely related word from the *Replace with Synonym* column. From the new *Meanings* list, you can also change the word or phrase to help you find the most precise word for your meaning. A good online thesaurus can be a terrific aid to writers who want to use precise language as well as increase their vocabularies.

Using Online and Other High-Tech Dictionaries

An increasing number of electronic resources are available on the Web, on CD-ROMs, and as handheld devices. The Web provides an amazing amount of information at little or no cost to users. Many excellent online resources, some of which are described in Figure 1.1, are similar to their print counterparts. The big differences, though, are that most of the online versions are free and many also provide audio pronunciations. Some even give hyperlinked cross-references. Online dictionaries are especially useful because they can be updated immediately when new words or meanings enter the language.

Online sites offer many features. The best-known site is *Merriam-Webster OnLine,* where you not only find authoritative definitions but also can play word games and increase your vocabulary with the *Word of the Day* feature. The site for *OneLook Dictionaries* provides over 1000 different dictionaries in various fields.

If you don't want to bother searching the Web to look up a word, you may purchase one of many CD-ROM dictionaries. Installed on your computer, products such as the *Random House Compact Unabridged Dictionary* or the *Oxford English Dictionary OED CD-ROM* give you access to a large database of words that can be easily searched electronically.

Handheld electronic dictionaries offer another efficient way to check spellings, find meanings, and look up synonyms. Many students and business people find handhelds easy to use. They are especially appealing to people struggling with a different language, such as tourists, interpreters, emigrants, and immigrants. Some are voice-enabled translation devices and even can talk. Two examples are the *Franklin Handheld Dictionary* and the *Merriam-Webster Collegiate Speaking Dictionary.*

Spot the Blooper

From a legal notice: "The case is now before the court and is awaiting a herring."

Figure 1.1
Notable Online Dictionaries

- **Merriam-Webster Online <http://m-w.com>.** Indicates the pronunciations, etymologies, and authoritative definitions of a vast number of words. Site also provides essays on the history of English and the processes involved in the making of dictionaries. Word of the Day feature defines an infrequently used word. Offers a thesaurus as well as a Spanish-English and a medical-terms dictionary.
- **Dictionary.com <http://dictionary.reference.com/>.** Provides links to a variety of references, including English dictionaries, foreign language dictionaries, thesauruses, online translators, and language-related articles. You can also access a Word of the Day feature and vocabulary games.
- **OneLook Dictionaries <http://www.onelook.com>.** Claims to index more than 12 million words in more than 1000 online dictionaries. Offers a Reverse Dictionary, which enables you to find a word by its definition.
- **Glossarist <http://www.glossarist.com/>.** A searchable directory of nearly 5,000 glossaries and topical dictionaries specializing in areas from arts and culture to health, medicine, and fitness.
- **Online Dictionary of the Social Sciences <http://bitbucket.icaap.org/>** and **<http://socialsciencedictionary.nelson.com/ssd/main.html>.** The entries cover basic concepts in anthropology, sociology, criminology, Canadian studies, political science, and women's studies, illustrated with Canadian examples.
- **WhatIs.com <http://whatis.techtarget.com/>.** A compendium of computer and other technical terms organized in easily searchable categories.
- **Technology Glossary <http://www.trinity.edu/~rjensen/245glosf.htm>.** Maintained by Bob Jensen at Trinity University, the page functions as a portal to various Internet glossaries of technology, accounting, finance, and business.

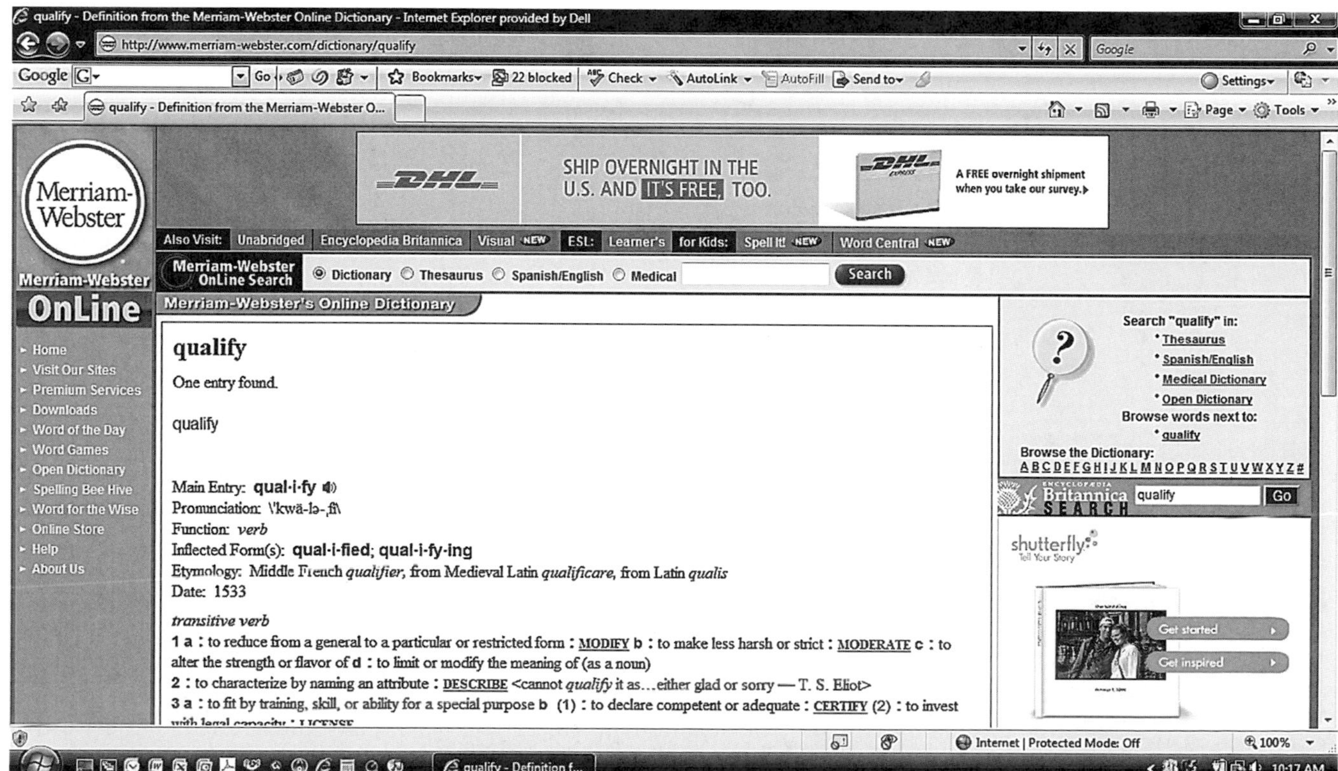

By permission. From Merriam-Webster Online © 2008 at www.Merriam-Webster.com.

Hotlinks

The Word Net facility at **<http://vancouver-webpages.com/wordnet/index.html>** offers an online dictionary that you can explore in different directions, finding words that mean the same, are more general, more specific—as well as getting a brief description.

Word lovers with online connection can check out Oxford Dictionary's Word of the Day feature at **<http://www.oed.com/cgi/display/wotd>.** Each day's entry comes with pronunciation tips, the etymology of the word, quotations of its use, and a date chart. You can also sign up to have the OED's word of the day emailed to you.

▶ Reference Manuals

Reference Manual Versus Dictionary

In addition to one or more dictionaries, every writer should have a good reference manual or handbook readily available. In it you can find helpful information not available in dictionaries. Most reference manuals provide information such as the following.

1. Punctuation. Detailed explanations of punctuation rules are presented logically. A well-written manual also provides ample illustrations of punctuation usage so that you can readily find solutions to punctuation dilemmas.

2. Hyphenation. Some dictionaries provide syllable breaks. Words cannot, however, be divided at all syllable breaks. A reference manual supplies rules for, and examples of, word division. Moreover, a good reference manual explains when compound adjectives should be hyphenated (as in *one-year-old child*).

3. Capitalization. Complete rules with precise examples illustrating capitalization style are shown.

4. Number Style. Deciding whether to write a number as a figure or as a word can be very confusing. A reference manual provides both instruction and numerous examples illustrating number and word styles.

Other topics covered in reference manuals are confusing words (such as *effect* and *affect*), abbreviations, contractions, literary and artistic titles, forms of address, and letter and report formats. In addition, some manuals contain sections devoted to English grammar, office procedures, and computers. This textbook is correlated with the widely used reference *The Gregg Reference Manual,* Seventh Canadian Edition, by William A. Sabin, et al.

Reference Manual Versus Textbook

You may be wondering how a reference manual differs from a business English textbook such as the one you are now reading. Although their content is similar, the primary difference is one of purpose. A textbook is developed *pedagogically* (that is, for teaching) so that the student understands and learns concepts. A reference manual is organized *functionally* so that the reader finds accurate information efficiently. A well-written reference manual is complete, coherent, and concise.

Most of the language and style questions that perplex business people and students could be answered quickly by a trained person using a reliable dictionary and a well-written reference manual.

Thesaurus

A thesaurus can be useful when you are composing your own documents. In book form, such as the famous *Roget's Thesaurus,* or in a word processing program, a thesaurus can help you avoid overrepetition of vocabulary items by listing related words that could be used as substitutes. It can also help you to remember a word that may have slipped your mind or to find a more precise word. If you do use a thesaurus, be careful not to use an unfamiliar synonym or antonym unless your dictionary indicates that the word is appropriate for your sentence.

Now complete the reinforcement exercises on the following pages.

Did You Know?

The World Wide Web is an exciting source of grammar and language services. Use a search engine such as *AltaVista* **<http://www.altavista.com>** or *Google* **<www.google.com>** to search for "grammar help" or similar terms.

NAME ______________________

CHAPTER 1 Reinforcement Exercises

Note: At the beginning of every set of reinforcement exercises, a self-check exercise is provided so that you will know immediately if you understand the concepts presented in the chapter. Do not look at the answers until you have completed the exercise. Then compare your responses with the answers shown at the bottom of the page. If you have more than three incorrect responses, reread the chapter before continuing with the other reinforcement exercises.

A. **(Self-check)** Write *T* (true) or *F* (false) after the following statements.

1. Students and office workers would find an unabridged dictionary handy to carry with them. ______

2. Guide words indicate the first and last words on a page. ______

3. Online dictionaries are generally more up to date than print dictionaries. ______

4. Online dictionaries may be fast and current, but they are also expensive to use. ______

5. All dictionaries show accented syllables with a raised stress mark preceding a syllable. ______

6. Dictionaries usually show noun plurals only if they are irregular. ______

7. Synonyms are words that are spelled alike or sound alike. ______

8. A thesaurus is a small dictionary. ______

9. Rules for hyphenating compound adjectives may be found in a reference manual. ______

10. Today's spell-check programs can be used to locate all misspelled words in a document. ______

Check your answers at the bottom of the page.

Use a *current* college-level or electronic dictionary to complete the following exercises. If you do not have a dictionary, use one at a library. The definitions, pronunciation, and usage in this book are based on *The Canadian Oxford Dictionary*.

B. Select the letter that provides the best definition or synonym for each word shown.

1. reticent (adj) (a) famous, (b) silent, (c) depressed, (d) emphatic ______

2. imminent (adj) (a) old, (b) famous, (c) impending, (d) stubborn ______

3. jeopardy (n) (a) game show, (b) adornment, (c) immunity, (d) danger ______

4. obtuse (adj) (a) dull, (b) old, (c) fixed, (d) stubborn ______

1. F 2. T 3. T 4. F 5. F 6. T 7. F 8. F 9. T 10. F

5. superficial (adj) (a) shallow, (b) managerial, (c) attractive, (d) elevated ____________

6. warrant (n) (a) caution, (b) rabbits, (c) authorization, (d) program ____________

C. Write the correct form of the following words. Use a current dictionary to determine whether they should be written as one or two words or should be hyphenated.

Example: print out (n) printout

1. street wise ____________
2. double check (v) ____________
3. in as much as ____________
4. work place ____________
5. old fashioned ____________
6. time clock ____________

D. For each of the following words, write the syllable that receives the primary accent. Then give a brief definition or synonym of the word.

	Word	Syllable	Definition or Synonym
Example:	judicious	di	prudent, exhibiting sound judgment
1.	posthumous		
2.	comparable		
3.	desert (n)		
4.	desert (v)		
5.	formidable		
6.	irrevocable		

E. If your dictionary shows usage labels for the following words, write them in the spaces provided. If no label appears for a word, which of the following labels would you consider giving it if you were a lexicographer? Put your initials next to the labels you suggest.

LABELS: archaic Canadian dialect informal or colloquial slang

Example: goo informal

1. anyways ____________
2. hadst ____________
3. ice road ____________

4. petrol ______

5. rain date ______

6. seat sale ______

7. dork ______

8. munchies ______

F. Select the letter that most accurately completes the sentence or answers the question.

1. A proposal to construct a shopping centre received *approbation* from city officials; therefore, the centre will probably be
   (a) rejected (b) delayed (c) constructed (d) modified ______

2. Which of the following is correctly written?
   (a) monarch butterfly (b) monarch Butterfly (c) Monarch butterfly (d) Monarch Butterfly ______

3. If an expression is *redundant,* it is
   (a) obsolete (b) repetitive (c) clever (d) awkward ______

4. To stage a *boycott,* individuals might follow which of the following actions?
   (a) withhold their services (b) refuse to buy a product (c) reduce their production (d) refuse to cross picket lines ______

5. The word *rapid* originated in which language?
   (a) Greek (b) Latin (c) French (d) Old English ______

6. Condominiums that provide more than one form of *egress* must have more than one
   (a) parking space (b) level (c) exit (d) mortgage ______

7. If you *encrypt* an email message, you are
   (a) preserving it (b) encoding (scrambling) it (c) erasing it (d) decoding (unscrambling) it ______

8. An office desk and chair that were *ergonomically* designed would
   (a) reduce fatigue and discomfort (b) improve office decor (c) save money (d) eliminate depreciation ______

9. The abbreviation *i.e.* stands for
   (a) for example (b) for instance (c) in earnest (d) that is ______

10. What professional would most likely hold the *D.D.S.* degree?
    (a) dentist (b) licensed broker (c) banker (d) surgeon ______

11. The word *spam,* which now means "unsolicited email," derives from
    (a) the canned meat product (b) *Monty Python's* comedy sketch (c) users who hate receiving it (d) senders who remain anonymous ______

12. *Nepotism* is derived from French and Italian words suggesting
    (a) pain (b) nephew (c) employment (d) parent ______

G. Optional Writing. Your instructor may ask you to complete this exercise on a separate sheet, typed, if possible.

Write eight complete sentences using the following words: *unabridged dictionary, abridged dictionary, synonym, antonym, hyphenate, archaic, dialect,* and *colloquial.* In at least two more sentences, tell whether you prefer a print or an electronic dictionary and explain why.

Editor's Challenge

The following email message contains 14 misspelled or misused words, some of which you looked up in earlier exercises. Underline any error, and write a correction above it. *Note:* The Editor's Challenge documents that you see in this book are double-spaced so that you can write in corrections. Actual business documents would be single-spaced.

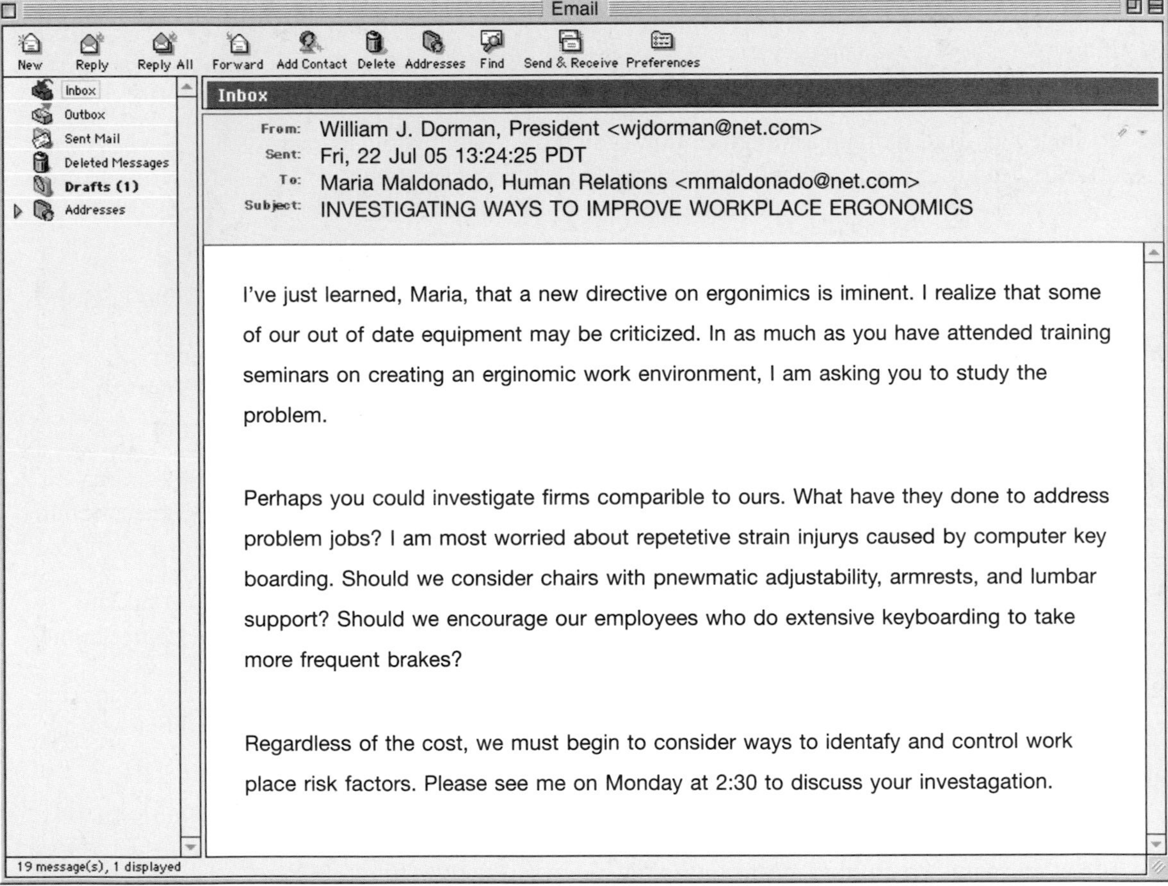

Email

New | Reply | Reply All | Forward | Add Contact | Delete | Addresses | Find | Send & Receive | Preferences

Inbox | Outbox | Sent Mail | Deleted Messages | Drafts (1) | Addresses

Inbox

From: William J. Dorman, President <wjdorman@net.com>
Sent: Fri, 22 Jul 05 13:24:25 PDT
To: Maria Maldonado, Human Relations <mmaldonado@net.com>
Subject: INVESTIGATING WAYS TO IMPROVE WORKPLACE ERGONOMICS

I've just learned, Maria, that a new directive on ergonimics is iminent. I realize that some of our out of date equipment may be criticized. In as much as you have attended training seminars on creating an erginomic work environment, I am asking you to study the problem.

Perhaps you could investigate firms comparible to ours. What have they done to address problem jobs? I am most worried about repetetive strain injurys caused by computer key boarding. Should we consider chairs with pnewmatic adjustability, armrests, and lumbar support? Should we encourage our employees who do extensive keyboarding to take more frequent brakes?

Regardless of the cost, we must begin to consider ways to identafy and control work place risk factors. Please see me on Monday at 2:30 to discuss your investagation.

19 message(s), 1 displayed

The following letter will afford you another chance to train your proofreader's eye. It contains 15 misspelled words and typographical errors (typos). Correct them with the help of your dictionary, if necessary, and consider whether all the errors would have been picked up by a spell checker.

LawnMaster
2330 Beaverhill Avenue
Winnipeg, MB R2H 4B1
February 7, 200x

Mrs. J. Ryan
1673 Dakota Street
Winnipeg, MB R2M 3M4

Dear Mrs. Ryan:

Thank you for being a value LawnMaster customer. We greatly apreciate that you have placed your confidance in us and our enviromentally friendly products. Continueing the progress we have made this year is critical to the health and vigour of your lawn. Therefore, we would like to give you an oppourtunity to save money on your 200x services.

Savings with prepayment
Prepay now for this season's services, and you'll receive a 10% discount off the application prizes for four applications of fertilizer (early and late spring, early summer, and fall) with oldfashioned manual weed removal at no additionnal charge. That is a savings of $22.83!

Convenient payment options
To prepay and recieve your special discount, just complete the reply card below and return it with your payment in the envelope provided. If you prefer to pay by credit card, complete the enclossed form and payment will be deducted automaticly from the account you indicate.

Thank you for your continued bussiness. We take pride in providing you with superior service and visable results. Please call us at (800) 565-5699 if you have any questions, requests, or concerns.

Sincerly,

Barry Keaton, Manager

POSTTEST

Write *T* (true) or *F* (false) after the following statements. Compare your answers with those at the bottom of the page.

1. The best dictionary for a college student's assignments is a pocket dictionary. ________
2. A reference manual is the best place to find synonyms. ________
3. The etymology of a word is usually contained within square brackets or parentheses. ________
4. The usage label *colloquial* means that the word may be used in certain regions only. ________
5. A dictionary user could expect to find the spelling of the past tense of an irregular verb such as *build*. ________

learning.web.ways

To make sure you enter the work world with good Internet skills, *Canadian Business English* provides a short web exercise in each chapter. If your instructor assigns this exercise, you will need access to a computer with an Internet connection. Additionally, your computer must have a web browser, such as Microsoft Explorer or Netscape. These programs enable you to see and use web pages.

All web pages have addresses called URLs (uniform resource locators). URLs must be typed exactly as they are shown, including periods (.), hyphens (-), underscores (_), slashes (/), tildes (~), and upper- or lower-case letters. URLs are often enclosed in angle brackets < >. You do not need to include the angle brackets when typing a URL.

The following exercise introduces you to an electronic dictionary. A major advantage of an online dictionary is that it presents the latest information. It also provides pronunciation if your computer has a sound card.

Goal: To gain confidence in using an online dictionary.

1. With your web browser on the screen, key the following URL in the location box: **http://www.m-w.com.** Press **Enter**.
2. Look over the **Merriam-Webster Online** home page. Move up and down the page by using the scroll bar at the right.
3. Scroll to the top, and move your cursor to the **Merriam-Webster Online Search** box.
4. Key the word *spam*. Click **Search**.
5. Scroll down to see the definition for *spam—noun*.

1.F 2.F 3.T 4.F 5.T

6. Print a copy of the definition page by clicking on **File** (upper left corner of your browser). Click **Print** and **OK**. Save all printouts to turn in.
7. Click **Back** (upper left corner of browser) to return to the search page.
8. In the **Merriam-Webster Online Search** box, delete *spam*. Key the word *firewall* and click **Search**. Read the definition and print a copy.
9. Click **Back**. Using the **Merriam-Webster Online Search** box, look up one word from Exercise F on p. 13. Print the definition.
10. Click **Word of the Day** (left navigation panel). Read about the word. Print a copy.
11. End your session by clicking the **X** box (upper right corner of browser).
12. Turn in all printed copies, properly identified; or send your instructor an email message summarizing what you learned.

C H A P T E R

Parts of Speech 2

OBJECTIVES When you have completed the materials in this chapter, you will be able to do the following:

- *Define the eight parts of speech.*
- *Recognize how parts of speech function in sentences.*
- *Compose sentences showing words playing more than one grammatical role.*

PRETEST

Study the following sentence and identify selected parts of speech. Underline the correct part of speech. Compare your answers with those at the bottom of the page.

The manager and I seriously examined all programs on office computers.

1. *and*	(a) preposition	(b) conjunction	(c) verb	(d) adverb
2. *seriously*	(a) preposition	(b) conjunction	(c) verb	(d) adverb
3. *examined*	(a) adjective	(b) conjunction	(c) verb	(d) adverb
4. *on*	(a) preposition	(b) pronoun	(c) noun	(d) adverb
5. *office*	(a) adjective	(b) pronoun	(c) noun	(d) adverb

As you learned in Chapter 1, business English is the study of the fundamentals of grammar, current usage, and appropriate business and professional style. Such a study logically begins with the eight parts of speech, the building blocks of our language. This chapter provides a brief overview of the parts of speech; the following chapters will deal with these topics more thoroughly.

---

1. (b) conj 2. (d) adverb 3. (c) verb 4. (a) prep 5. (a) adjective

▶ The Eight Parts of Speech

Learning the eight parts of speech helps you develop the working vocabulary necessary to discuss and study the language. You especially need to recognize the parts of speech in the context of sentences because many words function in more than one role. Only by analyzing the sentence at hand can you see how a given word functions.

Nouns

In elementary school you probably learned that *nouns* are the names given to persons, places, and things. In addition, though, nouns name qualities, concepts, and activities.

Study Tip

The adjectives *a, an,* and *the* are sometimes called "noun markers" because they identify or "mark" nouns.

Persons:	Maria, Mr. Hartman, president, Scott
Places:	Canada, Charlottetown, college, park
Things:	chair, computer, stationery, motorcycle
Qualities:	dependability, honesty, initiative, warmth
Concepts:	knowledge, freedom, friendship, happiness
Activities:	skiing, eating, reading, learning

Nouns are important words in our language. Sentences revolve around nouns since these words function both as subjects and as objects of verbs. To determine if a word is really a noun, try using it with the verb *is* or *are*. Notice that all the nouns listed here would make sense if used this way: *Maria is young, Charlottetown is in Prince Edward Island, honesty is important,* and so on. In Chapter 4 (pp. 55–61) you will learn four classes of nouns and rules for making nouns plural.

Hotlink

For an introduction to parts of speech, consult the materials prepared by Greg Dixon of North Vancouver and available at **<http://www.shared-visions.com/explore/english/parts.html>**.

Pronouns

As substitutes for nouns, *pronouns* are used in our language for variety and efficiency. Compare these two versions of the same sentence:

Without pronouns:	Elizabeth gave the book to John so that John could use the book to study.
With pronouns:	Elizabeth gave the book to John so that *he* could use *it* to study.

In sentences pronouns may function as subjects (for example, *I, we, they*) or as objects of verbs (*me, us, them*). They may show possession (*mine, ours, his*), and they may act as connectors (*that, which, who*). Only a few examples are given here. More examples, along with functions and classifications of pronouns, will be presented in Chapters 6 and 7 (pp. 91–115).

Study Tip

To test whether a word is truly a verb, try using it with a noun or pronoun, such as *George runs, she seems, it is. He food* doesn't make sense because *food* is not a verb.

Verbs

Verbs do two things: (a) they show the action of a sentence, or (b) they join or link to the subject of the sentence words that describe or rename it. Some action verbs are *runs, studies, works,* and *fixes*. Verbs that join descriptive words to the subject are called "state of being" or "linking" verbs. Some linking verbs are *am, is, are, was, were, be, being,* and *been*. Other linking verbs express the senses: *feels, appears, tastes, sounds, seems, looks,* and *smells*.

Verbs will be discussed more fully in Chapters 8 through 11 (pp. 139–203). At this point it is important that you be able to recognize verbs so that you can determine whether sentences are complete. All sentences have at least one verb; many sentences have more than one verb. Verbs may appear singly or in phrases.

Stacy *submitted* her application to become a management trainee. (Action verb)
It *is* a computer that *stores, processes,* and *retrieves* data. (Linking and action verbs)
I *feel* bad because Karen *worked* so late last night. (Linking and action verbs)
Our company *will be installing* a new computer system soon. (Verb phrase)

Note that the forms of the verbs indicate tense or time. For example, *submitted* shows past and *is* shows present time.

Study Tip

mWords such as *his, my,* and *its* are classified as adjectives when they describe nouns (*his car, my desk, its engine*).

Adjectives

Words that modify (describe or limit) nouns or pronouns are called *adjectives*. They usually answer the questions *what kind, how many,* or *which one*. The adjectives in the following sentences are italicized. Observe that the adjectives all answer questions about the nouns or pronouns that they describe.

Small, independent businesses can be *profitable*. (What kind of businesses?)
Fourteen franchises were granted in *four* provinces. (How many franchises? How many provinces?)
That chain of hotels started as *a small* operation. (Which chain? What kind of operation?)
He is *energetic* and *forceful* and she is *personable* and *deliberate*. (What pronouns do these adjectives describe?)

Did You Know?

Seventy per cent of the world's mail is written and addressed in English, and eighty per cent of the world's computer text is stored in English.

Adjectives usually precede nouns. They may, however, follow the nouns or pronouns they describe, especially when used with linking verbs, as shown in the first and last examples above.

Here are a few more examples of words often used as adjectives:

successful	sensitive	effective	new
terrific	bright	small	tall
helpless	long	wet	bad

Three words—*a, an,* and *the*—form a special group of adjectives called *articles*.

Adverbs

Words that modify verbs, adjectives, or other adverbs are *adverbs*. Adverbs usually answer the questions *when, how, where, to what extent,* or *why*.

Today we must begin work. (Must begin when?)
Jamie proceeded *rapidly* with the orders. (Proceeded how?)
He seemed *exceedingly* happy. (How happy?)
Did you see the schedule *there?* (Where?)
The prosecutor questioned him *further*. (Questioned him to what extent?)

Study Tip

To remember more easily what an *adverb* does, think of its two syllables: *ad* suggests that you will be adding to or amplifying the meaning of a *verb*. Hence adverbs often modify verbs—though they can also modify adjectives and other adverbs.

Here are additional examples of common adverbs:

carefully	evenly	quickly	sincerely
commercially	greatly	rather	too
easily	now	really	very

Most, but not all, words ending in *ly* are adverbs. Common exceptions are *friendly, costly,* and *ugly,* all of which are adjectives.

Prepositions

Prepositions join nouns and pronouns to other words in a sentence. As the word itself suggests (*pre* meaning "before"), a preposition is a word in a position *before* a noun or pronoun (called the *object* of the preposition). The term *prepositional phrase* signifies a group of two words or more that begins with a preposition and ends with its object, for example, *with Mr. Lee.* Prepositions are used in phrases to show a relationship between the object of the preposition and another word in the sentence. In the following sentence notice how the preposition changes the relation of the object (*Mr. Lee*) to the verb (*talked*):

> Marina often talked *with* Mr. Lee.
> Marina often talked *about* Mr. Lee.
> Marina often talked *to* Mr. Lee.

The most frequently used prepositions are *at, by, for, from, of, to,* and *with.* A more extensive list of prepositions can be found in Chapter 13 (on p. 246). Learn to recognize objects of prepositions so that you won't confuse them with sentence subjects.

Career Tip

To sound businesslike, credible, and objective, most writers avoid interjections and exclamation marks in professional messages.

Conjunctions

Words that connect other words or groups of words are *conjunctions.* The most common conjunctions are *and, or, but,* and *nor.* These are called *coordinating conjunctions* because they join equal (coordinate) parts of sentences. Other kinds of conjunctions will be presented in Chapter 15. Study the examples of coordinating conjunctions shown here:

> Koshi, Bill, *and* Amber are looking for jobs. (Joins equal words.)
> You may be interviewed by a personnel officer *or* by a supervising manager. (Joins equal groups of words.)

Interjections

Words expressing strong feelings are *interjections.* Interjections standing alone are followed by exclamation marks. When woven into a sentence, they are usually followed by commas.

> *Wow!* Did you see the total of our bill?
> *Gosh,* I hope I have my credit card!

Hotlink

Here's another online review of parts of speech: **<http://www.arts.uottawa.ca/writcent/hypergrammar/partsp.html>**.

▶ Summary

The sentence below illustrates all eight parts of speech.

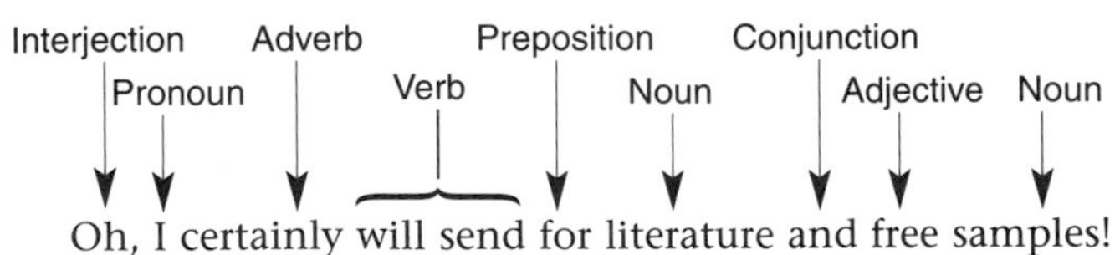

You need to know the functions of these eight parts of speech so that you will be able to understand the rest of this textbook and profit from your study of business English. The explanation of the parts of speech has been kept simple so far. This chapter is meant to serve as an introduction to later, more fully developed chapters. You should not expect to be able to identify the functions of *all* words in *all* sentences.

A word of caution: English is a wonderfully flexible language. As we noted earlier, many words in our language serve as more than one part of speech. Notice how flexible the word *mail* is in the sentences below:

Our *mail* is late today. (Noun—serves as subject of sentence.)
The knight's suit of *mail* protected him. (Noun—serves as object of preposition *of*.)
Mail the letter today. (Verb—serves as action word in sentence.)
Your *mail* slot is full. (Adjective—used here to describe *slot*, a noun which is the subject of sentence.)

Now complete the reinforcement exercises for this chapter on pp. 25–30.

Career Tip

"Whatever your program in college, be sure to include courses in writing and speaking. Managers must constantly write instructions, reports, memos, letters, and survey conclusions. If this comes hard to you, it will hold you back."—James A. Newman and Alexander Roy in *Climbing the Corporate Matterhorn*

HOTLINE QUERIES

Business and professional people are very concerned about appropriate English usage, grammar, and style. This concern is evident in the number and kinds of questions called in to grammar hotline services.

Among the callers are business supervisors, managers, executives, professionals, secretaries, clerks, administrative assistants, and word processing specialists. Writers, teachers, librarians, students, and other community members also request answers to language questions.

Selected questions and appropriate answers to them will be presented in the following chapters. In this way you, as a student of the language, will understand the kinds of everyday communication problems encountered in business and professional environments.

The representative questions in this text come from various hotlines. You can locate lists of grammar hotlines by using the search phrase *grammar hotline* in *Google* **<www.google.com>**. Many grammar hotlines have websites where you can browse questions and answers. Most grammar hotlines accept questions via both email and phone.

Question: Should an email message begin with a salutation or some kind of greeting?

Answer: When email messages are sent to company insiders, a salutation may be omitted. However, when email messages travel to outsiders, omitting a salutation seems curt and unfriendly. Because the message is more like a letter, a salutation is appropriate (such as *Dear Courtney, Hi Courtney, Greetings,* or just *Courtney*). Including a salutation is also a visual cue to where the message begins. Some writers prefer to incorporate the name of the recipient in the first sentence (*Thanks, Courtney, for responding so quickly*).

(Continued)

Question: I saw this sentence recently in the newspaper: *At the movie premiere the crowd scanned the limousines for glitterati.* Is *glitterati* a real word?

Answer: A recent arrival to our vocabulary, *glitterati* means "celebrities or fashionable, wealthy people." New words are generally considered legitimate when their use is clear and when they are necessary (that is, when no other words say exactly what they do). If educated individuals begin to use such words, the words then appear in dictionaries, and *glitterati* has made it.

Question: Which word should I use in this sentence? *Our department will* (disburse *or* disperse) *the funds shortly.*

Answer: Use *disburse. Disperse* means "to scatter" (*Police dispersed the unruly crowd*) or "to distribute" (*Information will be dispersed to all divisions*). *Disburse* means "to pay out." Perhaps this memory device will help you keep them straight: associate the *b* in *disburse* with *bank* (*Banks disburse money*).

Question: How should I address a person who signed a letter *J. R. Henderson*?

Answer: Use *Dear J. R. Henderson.*

Question: What's the difference between *toward* and *towards*?

Answer: None. They are interchangeable in use. However, it is more efficient to use the shorter word *toward.*

Question: Is *every day* one word or two in this case? *We encounter these problems every day.*

Answer: In your sentence it is two words. When it means "ordinary," it is one word (*She wore everyday clothes*). If you can insert the word *single* between *every* and *day* without altering your meaning, you should be using two words.

Question: What is the name of a group of initials that form a word? Is it an abbreviation?

Answer: A word formed from the initial letters of an expression is called an acronym (pronounced *ACK-ro-nim*). Examples: *snafu,* from ***s**ituation **n**ormal, **a**ll **f**ouled **u**p,* and *PIN,* from ***p**ersonal **i**dentification **n**umber.* Acronyms are pronounced as single words and are different from abbreviations. Expressions like *RCMP* and *dept.* are abbreviations, not acronyms. Notice that an abbreviation is pronounced letter by letter, whereas an acronym is pronounced as a word.

Question: My colleague insists that the word *his* is an adjective when it is used in an expression such as *his car.* I learned that *his* was a pronoun. What is it?

Answer: When words such as *his, her, our, your, their,* and *its* function as adjectives, they are classified as adjectives. Although most people consider them pronouns, when these words describe nouns, they are actually functioning as adjectives. Your colleague is right.

NAME ____________________

CHAPTER 2 Reinforcement Exercises

A. (**Self-check**) Complete these statements.

1. Words that substitute for nouns are
   (a) interjections (b) pronouns (c) adjectives (d) conjunctions ______

2. The part of speech that answers the question *what kind* is a/an
   (a) adverb (b) adjective (c) interjection (d) conjunction ______

3. Names for persons, places, things, qualities, concepts, and activities are
   (a) verbs (b) adjectives (c) nouns (d) pronouns ______

4. Words that answer the questions *how* and *to what extent* are
   (a) adverbs (b) adjectives (c) pronouns (d) conjunctions ______

5. *Me, us, you,* and *he* are examples of
   (a) nouns (b) pronouns (c) verbs (d) adverbs ______

6. Action words in sentences are
   (a) nouns (b) pronouns (c) adjectives (d) verbs ______

7. *Quickly, openly,* and *too* are examples of
   (a) adjectives (b) verbs (c) interjections (d) adverbs ______

8. Words that express strong feeling are
   (a) conjunctions (b) adverbs (c) pronouns (d) interjections ______

9. *And, or, nor,* and *but* are
   (a) conjunctions (b) verbs (c) interjections (d) adverbs ______

10. Words that join noun or pronoun objects to other words in sentences are
    (a) adverbs (b) prepositions (c) interjections (d) adjectives ______

Check your answers.

B. In each of the following groups of sentences, one word is used as an adjective, as a noun, and as a verb. For each sentence indicate the part of speech for the italicized word.

Example: Much *work* must be done. ____noun____

Can you *work* overtime? ____verb____

We need two *work* orders. ____adjective____

1. Factory workers must punch a *time* clock. ______
2. We have little *time* in which to make a decision. ______

1.b 2.b 3.c 4.a 5.b 6.d 7.d 8.d 9.a 10.b

3. The coach will *time* the runners. ____________

4. Put that desk in the *corner*. ____________

5. The new truck certainly does *corner* well. ____________

6. CEOs seem to prefer *corner* offices. ____________

7. Advertisements promised instruction from a *master* teacher. ____________

8. Few students can *master* web design in a short course. ____________

9. The pilot of a merchant ship is its *master*. ____________

Write complete sentences using the word *jet* as a noun, as an adjective, and as a verb.

10. (noun) ____

11. (adjective) ____

12. (verb) ____

C. The underlined words in the following sentences are either prepositions or conjunctions. Write *C* for conjunction or *P* for preposition.

	Sentence	Word	Answer
1.	Technical skills are important <u>for</u>	*for*	____________
	entry-level positions, <u>but</u> communication skills	*but*	____________
	are necessary for promotion <u>to</u> management.	*to*	____________
2.	Writing good letters <u>and</u> email messages	*and*	____________
	<u>to</u> clients creates goodwill	*to*	____________
	<u>for</u> business and professional organizations.	*for*	____________
3.	Neither large <u>nor</u> small service businesses	*nor*	____________
	maintain much merchandise <u>in</u> inventory because	*in*	____________
	selling goods <u>from</u> stock is not their function.	*from*	____________

D. Read the following sentences, and taking into account the function of each word within each sentence, identify the part of speech of each word shown. Use a dictionary if necessary.

She hurriedly scanned several email messages before the meeting.

she	____________	email	____________
hurriedly	____________	messages	____________
scanned	____________	before	____________
several	____________	meeting	____________

One email message contained a virus, but it was very soon deleted.

One	________	a	________	was	________
email	________	virus	________	very	________
message	________	but	________	soon	________
contained	________	it	________	deleted	________

E. Selected verbs in the following sentences have been italicized. Use check marks to indicate whether these verbs are linking or action verbs.

	Linking Verb	Action Verb
Example: Words *are* the most powerful drug used by mankind.	✓	________
1. The Chinese *are* major users of cellphones.	________	________
2. Our company *produces* components for computers.	________	________
3. The hotel manager *selected* four trainees from many applicants.	________	________
4. Her voice mail message *sounds* very professional.	________	________
5. We *borrowed* three-fourths of the necessary capital.	________	________
6. The manager and the personnel director *studied* all job descriptions carefully.	________	________
7. An optimist *is* a person who thinks a housefly is looking for a way out.	________	________
8. Please *deliver* the computers and printers before April 4.	________	________

F. Optional Writing. Your instructor may ask you to complete this exercise on a separate sheet.

Write eight sentences that illustrate the parts of speech: noun, pronoun, verb, adjective, adverb, conjunction, preposition, and interjection. Identify each part of speech by labelling it at the beginning of the sentence and underlining it within the sentence. If possible, type this exercise.

Example: Noun: I was asked to review the balance sheet.

Editor's Challenge

To develop your vocabulary skills, supply a single word for each blank in the following memo and letter. The word you supply should represent the part of speech shown.

Atlantic Industries
Interoffice Memo

TO: Allison Hever

FROM: Tran Nguyen

DATE: June 3, 200x

SUBJECT: JOB-SEARCH ADVICE

I'm sorry to learn that you have completed your internship with us and that you will be leaving, Allison. Since you (verb) _______________ advice in finding a job, I'd like to share with you a few pointers that I've learned.

My experience suggests that serious candidates will devote as much (noun) _______________ to job hunting as they do (preposition) _______________ working at a full-time job. If possible, hand-deliver your résumé (conjunction) _______________ your cover letter to the (noun) _______________ in charge of hiring.

Be sure that your (adjective) _______________ letter (verb) _______________ the requirements of the position advertised. If you send your résumé by mail, it's a(n) (adjective) _______________ idea to follow up with a telephone call in a few days. A(n) (adverb) _______________ high number of résumés are never received, are lost, or are thrown out.

You'll find that an interviewer often asks why (pronoun) _______________ want this particular job. In addition to answering (noun) _______________ , you should be prepared to ask (adjective) _______________ questions of your own. Try to remember that interviews are (adjective) _______________ learning experiences, whether (conjunction) _______________ not you get the job.

I hope this (noun) _______________ is helpful to you, and I wish you well in your (adjective) _______________ search.

Miss Alice Evans
Retail Credit Department
Union National Bank
P.O. Box 2051
Edmonton, AB T5W 4B3

Dear Miss Evans:

SUBJECT: Charges to Credit Account #4002-3422-8910-3299

Because of the wide acceptance of the Visa (adjective)_________ card and because (preposition)_________ your bank's low interest rate, my wife and I became cardholders two (noun)_________ ago. Recently, however, we had a charge to (adjective)_________ account that we would like to discuss (preposition)_________ you.

Between August 7 (conjunction)_________ September 17, we made 12 small purchases. Ten of (pronoun)_________ received telephone approval. When we (verb)_________ our October statement, we were surprised to see a $10 charge for each of these purchases because our account was over the limit. The total charge (verb)_________ $120.

We (adverb)_________ should have been more aware of the limit and the number of charges we made, (conjunction)_________ we assumed that if we received telephone approval, we were still within (adjective)_________ limit. Upon receiving our October statement, we (adverb)_________ called your (noun)_________ and were referred to Mr. Alan Moore. (Pronoun)_________ said he could do nothing because our purchases had been over the limit of the card.

Please (verb)_________ our account, Miss Evans, and reconsider this penalty. Since we have never before exceeded our credit limit and did receive approval for most of the charges, we (verb)_________ that the $120 charge should be removed. We look forward (preposition)_________ a speedy resolution of this problem.

POSTTEST

Identify selected parts of speech in the following sentence by underlining the correct choice. Compare your answers with those at the bottom of the page.

Greg recently installed two new printers in our department.

1.	*Greg*	(a) noun	(b) pronoun	(c) preposition	(d) conjunction
2.	*recently*	(a) verb	(b) adverb	(c) preposition	(d) conjunction
3.	*installed*	(a) adverb	(b) verb	(c) preposition	(d) conjunction
4.	*in*	(a) noun	(b) pronoun	(c) preposition	(d) conjunction
5.	*our*	(a) verb	(b) adverb	(c) adjective	(d) preposition

learning.web.ways

Many word processing software programs and online dictionaries include a thesaurus, a facility that allows you to look up word synonyms. This is especially useful if you are trying to avoid undue repetitiveness in your writing. However, most synonyms share only part of the meaning of the word you need to replace and cannot be used interchangeably with it. As a result, it is important to pay close attention to contextual word use, i.e., to how different synonyms function in context.

Goal: To learn to use an online thesaurus.

1. With your web browser on the screen, enter the following URL in the location box: **<http://www.yourdictionary.com>**.
2. In the Lookup box, key the word *obtain.*
3. Click on **GO**.
4. Note that the dictionary will first list the definition of *obtain,* followed by its related forms and a list of synonyms.
5. The note at the end of the entry is of particular importance as it explains the way *obtain* is used in the language. This explanation will help you select a synonym closest to the meaning you are looking for.

---

1. a 2. b 3. b 4. c 5. c

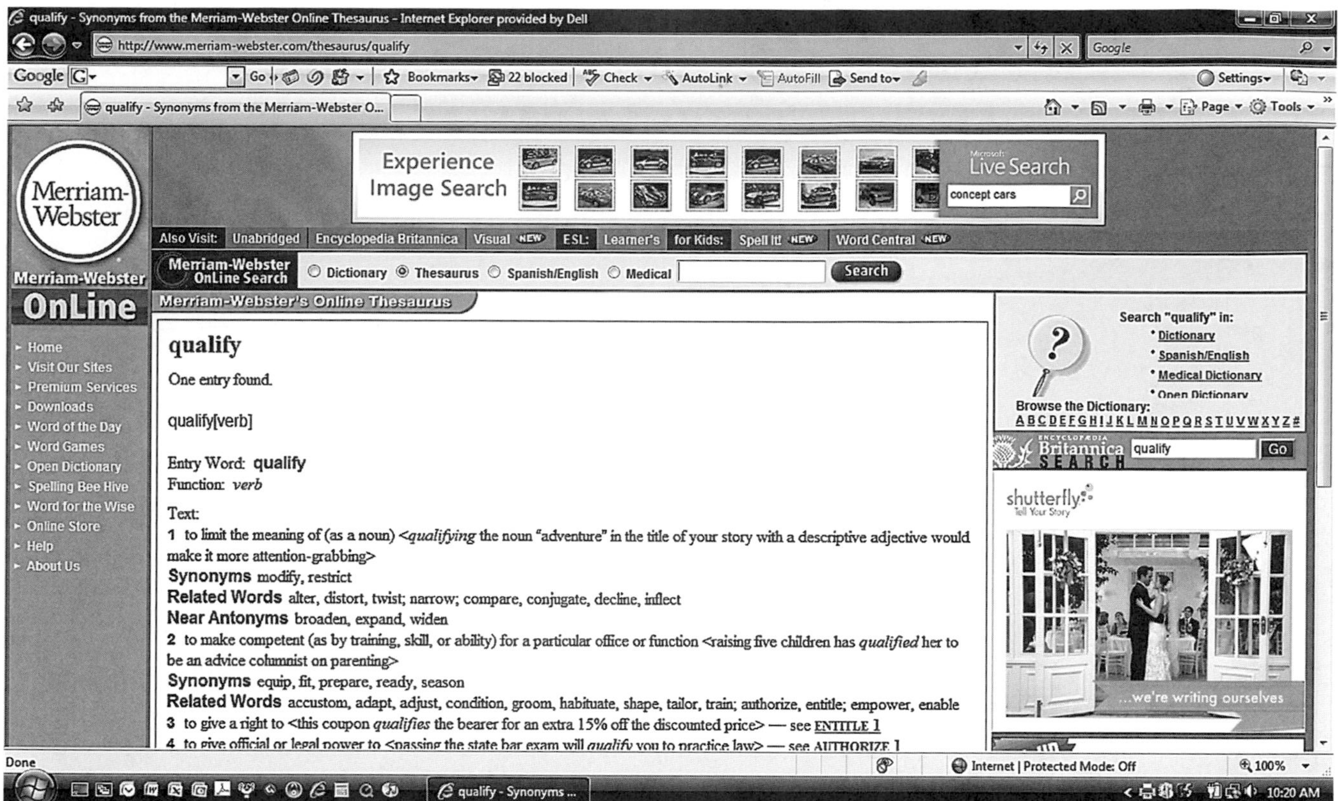

By permission. From Merriam-Webster Online © 2008 at www.Merriam-Webster.com.

C H A P T E R

Sentences: Elements and Patterns 3

OBJECTIVES When you have completed the materials in this chapter, you will be able to do the following:

- *Recognize subjects and predicates.*
- *Convert fragments into complete sentences.*
- *Recognize basic sentence faults such as comma splices and run-on sentences.*
- *Complete sentences in three basic sentence patterns.*

PRETEST

Write the correct letter after each of the numbered groups of words to identify it.

a = correctly punctuated sentence   c = comma splice
b = fragment   d = run-on sentence

1. Jessica, who was recently hired on a six-month contract. __________
2. John works 30 hours this week, Martha works 32. __________
3. Across the street are a copy shop and a convenience store. __________
4. Some employees filter their email however others do not want to bother. __________
5. Although some of our employees start at 8 a.m. and finish at 4 p.m. __________

---

1. b 2. c 3. a 4. d 5. b

Sentences are groups of words arranged to express complete thoughts. In this chapter you'll review the basic elements of every sentence. In addition, you'll learn to recognize sentence patterns. This knowledge will help you to use sentences correctly and to recognize and correct faulty sentences. This chapter also introduces proofreading marks, which are helpful in revising messages.

Career Tip

You may be worth an additional $5000 to your employer (and to yourself) if you have writing skills, says one communications expert. Because companies can no longer afford expensive on-site training, employees with already developed skills are much more valuable to employers.

▶ Sentence Elements

Sentences consist of two essential elements: subjects and predicates. In addition, sentences must make sense. When any one of these elements is missing, readers or listeners are confused. To help you better understand the structure of sentences, you'll learn to distinguish between simple and complete subjects and predicates.

Subjects and Predicates

The *subject* of a sentence is the person or thing being talked about; the *predicate* tells what the subject is, what the subject is doing, or what is being done to the subject. Study the following sentence:

The new manager of the office
received our co-operation.
complete subject
complete predicate

The *complete subject* of the preceding sentence includes the subject (in this case a noun) plus all the words that describe or limit the subject (its modifiers). The *complete predicate* includes the verb plus its modifiers.

The heart of the complete subject is the simple subject (*manager*), and the heart of the predicate is the simple predicate, the verb (*received*). The following sentences are divided into complete subjects and complete predicates. The simple subjects are underlined once, and the verbs (simple predicates) are underlined twice.

Hotlink

For an introduction to subjects and predicates, consult **<http://www.uottawa.ca/academic/arts/writcent/hypergrammar/subjpred.html>**.

Complete Subjects	**Complete Predicates**
All employees of the company	are linked by an intranet.
Our largest department store	will be having a sale.
An Alberta pilot program	will be launched next month.
Fast-food restaurant owners	conduct traffic counts.

Notice in the previous sentences that the verbs may consist of one word or several. In a verb phrase the principal verb is the final one; the other verbs are *helping* or *auxiliary* verbs. For example, in the verb phrase *will be having, having* is the principal verb and *will* and *be* are the helping verbs. The most frequently used helping verbs are *am, is, are, was, were, been, have, has, had, must, ought, might, can, could, would, should, will, do, does,* and *did.*

Study Tip

Many linking verbs also serve as helping verbs. Note that a verb phrase is *linking* only when the final verb is a linking verb, such as in the phrase *might have been.*

Locating Subjects

You can locate the subject in a sentence by asking, *Who or what is being discussed?*

> *Rebecca* wanted out of her dead-end job. (Who is being discussed? *Rebecca*)
>
> *Positions* in many companies are advertised online. (What is being discussed? *Positions*)

Don't be misled by prepositional phrases. Subjects are not found in such phrases.

In many companies *employees* must be promoted from within. (What is being discussed? *Employees.* Ignore the prepositional phrase *in many companies.*)

After January 1 *applicants* for all jobs must submit their résumés by email. (What is being discussed? *Applicants.* Ignore the prepositional phrases *After January 1* and *for all jobs.*

Sentences may have multiple subjects joined by the conjunctions *and* or *or.*

Either the *manager* or his *assistant* will conduct the training. (What two people are being discussed? *Manager* and *assistant*)

Artwork, paint, and *plants* are great ways to bring colour into an office. (What subjects are being discussed? *Artwork, paint,* and *plants*)

Although a sentence subject usually appears directly before a verb, in three instances the verb may precede the subject: (1) inverted sentences, (2) sentences beginning with *there* or *here,* and (3) questions.

First on the program was Jeffrey. (In this inverted sentence the verb *was* precedes the subject *Jeffrey.)*

There are many jobs listed online. (Ignore *There,* which cannot function as a sentence subject. Read the sentence as follows: *Many jobs are listed online.* Now the subject is obvious because the sentence is in its normal order.)

Are the best jobs listed online? (To locate the subject, reword this question: *The best jobs are listed online.*)

You'll learn more about locating subjects in Chapter 10.

Sentence Sense

In addition to a subject and a predicate, a group of words must possess one additional element to qualify as a sentence: *the group of words must make sense.* Observe that two of the groups of words that follow express complete thoughts and make sense; the third does not.

Bradley built his business through personal contacts. (Subject plus predicate making sense = sentence.)

Efficient service ensured return business. (Subject plus predicate making sense = sentence.)

When Bradley started his own business (Subject plus predicate but NOT making sense = no sentence.)

In the third case a reader or listener senses that the idea expressed is incomplete. We do not have a fragment; instead, we have a fragment.

▶ Sentence Patterns

Three basic word patterns express thoughts in English sentences.

Pattern No. 1: Subject–Verb

In the most basic sentence pattern, the subject is followed by its verb. The sentence needs no additional words to make sense and be complete.

Hotlink

The English Department at Acadia University also offers pointers on dealing with "The Grammar Outlaw. The Run-on Sentence" at: **<http://ace.acadiau.ca/English/grammar/runon.htm>**.

Subject	Verb
We	worked.
Everyone	is studying.
She	might have called.
All employees	should have been informed.

Pattern No. 2: Subject–Action Verb–Object

In this kind of sentence, the subject is followed by an action verb and its direct object. The object usually answers the question *what* or *whom.*

Spot the Blooper

The menu of a restaurant in Columbia, South Carolina, offers "A humongous baked potato, slightly hallowed and stuffed."

Subject	Action Verb	Object
Most students	brought	supplies.
The manager	praised	the employees.
Mrs. Chartrand	needed	a new car.
All proceeds	support	volunteers.

This basic sentence pattern may also employ an indirect object that usually answers the question *to whom.*

Subject	Action Verb	Indirect Object	Direct Object
Our company	offers	employees	excellent benefits.
Tiffany	gave	the manager	a cheque.
We	lent	a neighbour	our car.

Pattern No. 3: Subject–Linking Verb–Complement

In the third kind of sentence, the subject is followed by a linking verb and its complement. A *complement* is a noun, pronoun, or adjective that renames or describes the subject. A complement *completes* the meaning of the subject.

Hotlink

Another place for help with run-on sentences is the University of Victoria's Writer's Guide page at **<http://web.uvic.ca/wguide/Pages/SentRunons.html>**.

Subject	Linking Verb	Complement	
The author	was	Ms. Arnold.	
Our customers	are	friends.	(*Noun complements*)
Your supervisor	is	she.	
The callers	might have been	they.	(*Pronoun complements*)
These data	are	accurate.	
His report	is	excellent.	(*Adjective complements*)

The sentences shown here have been kept simple so that their patterns can be recognized easily. Although most speakers and writers expand these basic patterns with additional phrases and clauses, the basic sentence structure remains the same. Despite its length the following sentence follows the basic subject–action verb–object order:

> Many large *companies,* as well as small companies with sizable real estate holdings, *employ* specialized risk *managers* to handle their insurance problems. (The simple subject is *companies*, the verb is *employ*, and the object of the verb is *managers*.)

Inverted Order

Some sentences use inverted order, with the verb coming before the subject.

> Sitting in front is Doreen.
> Last came the school choir.

In questions the verb may come before the subject or may be interrupted by the subject.

> What is the shipment number?
> Have the bills been sent?

In sentences beginning with the adverbs *here* or *there,* the word order is also inverted.

> Here are the applications.
> There is a demand for accountants.

To locate the true subject in any inverted sentence, mentally rearrange the words. Place them in the normal subject–verb order.

> Doreen is sitting in front.
> The shipment number is what?
> The applications are here.

▶ Sentence Faults*

Three typical sentence faults are fragments, comma splices, and run-on sentences. You can eliminate these sentence faults by recognizing them and by applying revision techniques such as the ones described here.

Fragments

Fragments are most often groups of words that are broken off from sentences preceding or following them. They cannot function as complete sentences. Avoid fragments by making certain that each sentence contains a subject and a verb and makes sense by itself. In the following examples the fragments are italicized. Notice how they can be revised to make complete sentences.

Fragment: We're looking for a potential manager. *An individual who can accept responsibility and supervise other employees.*

Revision: We're looking for a potential manager who can accept responsibility and supervise other employees.

Fragment: My research report in business communication took a long time to prepare. *And then turned out badly.*

Revision: My research report in business communication took a long time to prepare and then turned out badly.

Career Tip

In workplace writing you'll most often use Patterns 1, 2, and 3 because readers want to know the subject first. For variety and emphasis, however, you can use introductory elements and inverted order.

Hotlinks

For further help with fragments, consult this page created by the Writing Centre at Memorial University, Newfoundland: **<http://www.mun.ca/writingcentre/frag.shtml>**.

For help with fragments, see this web page hosted by Acadia University **<http://ace.acadiau.ca/english/grammar/fragment.htm>**.

Spot the Blooper

From a set of bylaws: "Each condominium unit may have a reasonable number of household pets. Which at the desecration of the Association do not create a nuisance to other owners."

---

* *Refer also to Writer's Workshop for Unit 2, pp. 131–136.*

Hotlink

For material on fragments, see the Tidewater Community College grammar materials at **<http://www.tcc.edu/students/resources/writcent/HANDOUTS/GRAMMAR/FRAG.HTM>**.

Fragment: *To excel as a knowledge worker in today's digital workplace.* One must know how to find and evaluate information on the Internet.

Revision: To excel as a knowledge worker in today's digital workplace, one must know how to find and evaluate information on the Internet.

Occasionally, the omission of a small but essential word results in a fragment.

Fragment: We been looking for an administrative assistant for three weeks. (incomplete verb)

Revision: We have been looking for an administrative assistant for three weeks.

Fragment: Sometimes is too cold in our office. (subject missing)

Revision: Sometimes it is too cold in our office.

Note that commands (imperative sentences) such as *Turn off the photocopier* are not fragments, even though they seem at first glance to have no subject. The subject in all commands is understood to be *you* ([You] turn off the photocopier).

Run-on Sentences

A *run-on* (or fused) *sentence* joins two or more complete thoughts without punctuation. Notice how the run-on sentences below can be corrected by dividing the two thoughts into separate sentences.

Run-on Sentence: The work ethic in Canada is not dead it is deeply ingrained in most people.

Revision: The work ethic in Canada is not dead. It is deeply ingrained in most people.

Run-on Sentence: Gift certificates for courses are available prices range from $40 to $160.

Revision: Gift certificates for courses are available. Prices range from $40 to $160.

Run-on Sentence: Send an email message to all committee members tell them that our next meeting is planned for Friday.

Revision: Send an email message to all committee members. Tell them that our next meeting is planned for Friday.

You will usually recognize run-on sentences when you proofread because they are difficult to understand. If you are not sure that a group of words is a run-on sentence or are not sure how to correct it, identifying subjects and verbs can help.

Run-on Sentence: Every correct sentence must have a subject and verb it must also express a complete thought.

Revision: Every correct sentence must have a subject and verb. It must also express a complete thought.

Comma Splices

A *comma splice* results when two otherwise correct sentences are incorrectly joined or spliced together with a comma. Comma splices occur far more often than run-on sentences because the pause indicated by the comma makes them easier to read and, therefore, easier to miss during proofreading. Finding a subject and verb combination in each part of the comma splice will help you determine that the group of words contains two complete thoughts: *Legislation was enacted to protect homeowners, victims will receive compensation within 90 days.* The sentences below show how comma splices could be revised into acceptable sentences.

Comma Splice: Let us help you develop your online résumé, visit us at Resume.org.

Revision: Let us help you develop your online résumé. Visit us at Resume.org.

Comma Splice: You must fill one more purchase order, then your work is finished.

Revision: You must fill one more purchase order. Then your work is finished.

Comma Splice: Many applicants responded to our advertisement, however only one had the proper training.

Revision: Many applicants responded to our advertisement; however, only one had the proper training. (Semicolons will be discussed in Chapters 14 and 17.)

Hotlink

If your writing suffers from the infamous comma splice, here's another excellent Memorial University page to help you out: **<http://www.mun.ca/writingcentre/commasplices.shtml>**. For more exercises, click on the link at the bottom of the page.

Now complete the reinforcement exercises for this chapter on pp. 41–46.

HOTLINE QUERIES

Question: This sentence doesn't sound right to me, but I can't decide how to improve it: *The reason I'm applying is because I enjoy electronics.*

Answer: The problem lies in this construction: *the reason ... is because ....* Only nouns pronouns, or adjectives may act as complements following linking verbs. In your sentence an adverbial clause follows the linking verb *is* and sounds awkward. One way to improve the sentence is to substitute a noun clause beginning with *that: The reason I'm applying is that I enjoy electronics.* An even better way to improve the sentence would be to make it a direct statement: *I'm applying because I enjoy electronics.*

(Continued)

Question: My colleague says that this sentence is correct: *Please complete this survey regarding your satisfaction at our dealership, then return it in the enclosed addressed envelope.* I think something is wrong, but I'm not sure what.

Answer: You're right. This sentence has two short independent clauses, and some writers attempt to join them with a comma. However, this construction produces a comma splice. The adverb *then* cannot function as a conjunction, such as *but* or *and*, to join these two clauses. You can correct the problem by inserting *and* between the clauses, starting a new sentence, or using a semicolon between the clauses.

Question: My boss wrote a report with this sentence: *Saleswise, our staff is excellent.* Should I change it?

Answer: Never change wording without checking with the author. You might point out, however, that the practice of attaching *-wise* to nouns is frowned upon by many language experts. Such combinations as *budgetwise, taxwise,* and *productionwise* are considered commercial jargon. Suggest this revision: *On the basis of sales, our staff is excellent.*

Question: At the end of a letter, I wrote: *Thank you for recommending me.* Should I hyphenate *thank you*?

Answer: Do not hyphenate *thank you* when using it as a verb (*thank you for writing*). Do hyphenate it when using it as an adjective (*I sent a thank-you note*) or as a noun (*I sent four thank-yous*). Since *thank you* is used as a verb in your sentence, do not hyphenate it. Notice that *thank you* is never written as a single word.

Question: A fellow worker insists on saying, *I could care less.* It seems to me that it should be *I couldn't care less.* Who is right?

Answer: You are right. The phrase *I couldn't care less* has been in the language a long time. It means, of course, "I have little concern about the matter." Recently, though, people have begun to use *I could care less* with the same meaning. Most careful listeners realize that the latter phrase says just the opposite of its intent. Although both phrases are clichés, stick with *I couldn't care less* if you want to be clear.

NAME ______________________

CHAPTER 3 Reinforcement Exercises

A. (**Self-check**) Indicate whether the following statements are true (*T*) or false (*F*).

1. The verbs *is, can,* and *do* are examples of auxiliary or helping verbs. ________

2. A group of words with a subject and a predicate is automatically a complete sentence. ________

3. The complete subject of a sentence includes a noun or pronoun and all its modifiers. ________

4. Two complete sentences joined only by a comma create a *comma splice.* ________

5. In questions the verb may appear before the subject. ________

6. The complete predicate of a sentence tells what the subject is, what the subject is doing, or what is being done to the subject. ________

7. A run-on sentence can be corrected by inserting a comma. ________

8. The verb phrase *must have been* is considered to be a linking verb. ________

9. Sentences that begin with *here* or *there* follow normal subject–verb order. ________

10. Objects may follow either action verbs or linking verbs. ________

Check your answers.

B. Study the examples shown below. Then fill in the words necessary to complete the three sentence patterns.

Pattern No. 1: Subject–Verb

Example: The boss called.

1. The supervisor ____________.

2. Our computer ____________.

3. Students ____________.

4. My team ____________.

5. Our fax machine ____________.

6. Email messages ____________.

Pattern No. 2: Subject–Action Verb–Object

Example: Administrative assistants use software.

7. Patrick answered the ____________.

8. UPS delivers ____________.

9. Salespeople sold ____________.

10. The carpenter built a ____________.

11. Students threw a ____________.

12. Lawyers represent ____________.

1.T 2.F 3.T 4.T 5.T 6.T 7.F 8.T 9.F 10.F

Pattern No. 3: Subject–Linking Verb–Complement

Fill in noun or pronoun complements.

Example: The manager is John.

13. The applicant was ____________________.

14. Tina is the new ____________________.

15. The caller could have been ____________________.

16. The president is ____________________.

Fill in adjective complements.

Example: The salary is good.

17. My investment was ____________________.

18. Quebec City is ____________________.

19. The sales staff was ____________________.

20. The report could have been ____________________.

C. Underline the simple subject (noun or pronoun) once and the simple predicate (verb) twice.

Example: She is resigning for personal reasons.

1. The manuscript will be delivered by April 2.
2. Prince George is home to the University of Northern British Columbia.
3. Canada remains the United States' largest export market.
4. On October 26 this special offer will end.
5. The company has fired Vera Stewart.
6. Dynasty Motorcar was looking for new financing.
7. Andy preferred a handshake to a written contract.
8. The airline's president was highly unpopular with employees.

D. The following sentences display inverted word order. To help in locating subjects, revise these sentences so that the subject comes first. Then underline the simple subject once and the verb twice.

Example: Here are some of the materials we need.

Some of the materials we need are here.

1. There is no website listed for that organization. ____________________
2. Here are the minutes of the Tuesday board meeting. ____________________
3. Where is the Gibson contract? ____________________
4. Across from our office is the subway station. ____________________
5. Who is the leader in online shopping? ____________________

E. Expand the following sentence fragments into complete sentences.

Example: If I had seen the red light at the intersection ______, I could have stopped in time.______

1. If I had just won a lottery prize of $50 million ________________________________

____

2. My economics professor, although I promised to make up the work I missed ______________

____

3. All the helicopters, including those flying to Prince Edward Island ______________________

____

4. Although we have no openings for a person with your skills ___________________________

____

5. Since I am looking for a position in hotel management _______________________________

____

6. If there is mutual agreement to all contract terms __________________________________

____

7. ____

so that we will be able to write more effectively in the workplace.

8. ____

and left the office at 2:00 to meet a client.

F. Write the correct letter after each of the following groups of words to indicate whether it represents a fragment, a correctly punctuated sentence, a comma splice, or a run-on sentence.

a = correctly punctuated sentence c = comma splice
b = fragment d = run-on sentence

Example: Because the world seems to be getting smaller. ______b______

1. Anyone doing business in another country should learn what kinds of gifts are expected and when to give them. ______dA______
2. Gifts for the children of an Arab are welcome, however gifts for an Arab's wife are not. ______C______
3. Although we have a powerful printer capable of producing high-quality graphics. ______B______
4. Amina wanted a practical spreadsheet program, she just didn't know what to purchase. ______D______
5. In North America making eye contact is a sign of confidence and sincerity. ______D______
6. Mr. Harrington arrived at the airport on time, however, his flight was overbooked. ______C______
7. Some banks may require in-depth personal investigations. ______A______
8. Particularly if you are a married woman and want to open a credit account in your own name. ______B______

9. We have tried to collect this account in a friendly manner, our efforts, however, have failed to secure your co-operation. C

10. Being on time is important in North America in some other countries time is less important. R

11. Research suggests that job stress is linked to mental problems stress is also associated with ulcers and heart disease. R

12. Next Monday is Victoria Day, hence all branch offices will be closed. A

13. Mornings seem to be better than afternoons for catching business executives in their offices. A

14. Because Singapore flourishes as a centre of banking, shipbuilding, offshore-oil technology, refining, aircraft maintenance, electronics manufacturing, and international trade. B

15. The resources of that country, even though never fully developed. B

16. Council is finalizing a new street sign format it will be used across the city. R

17. Thank you for your support, the entire neighbourhood benefits from a strong community association. C

18. The next course focuses on ethical issues faced by individuals as citizens and professionals. A

For class discussion: In the preceding exercise, how could each of the incorrectly punctuated groups of words be made acceptable?

G. Optional Writing. Your instructor may ask you to complete this exercise on a separate sheet.

Write eight original sentences, two for each of the following patterns: sentence with action verb and object, sentence with linking verb and noun complement, sentence with adjective complement, and sentence in inverted order. Underline subjects once and verbs twice.

Editor's Challenge

The following email messages contain errors in sentence structure, spelling, and proofreading. Make corrections. Your instructor may ask you to read about proofreading marks on page 51 and to use those marks in noting your corrections.

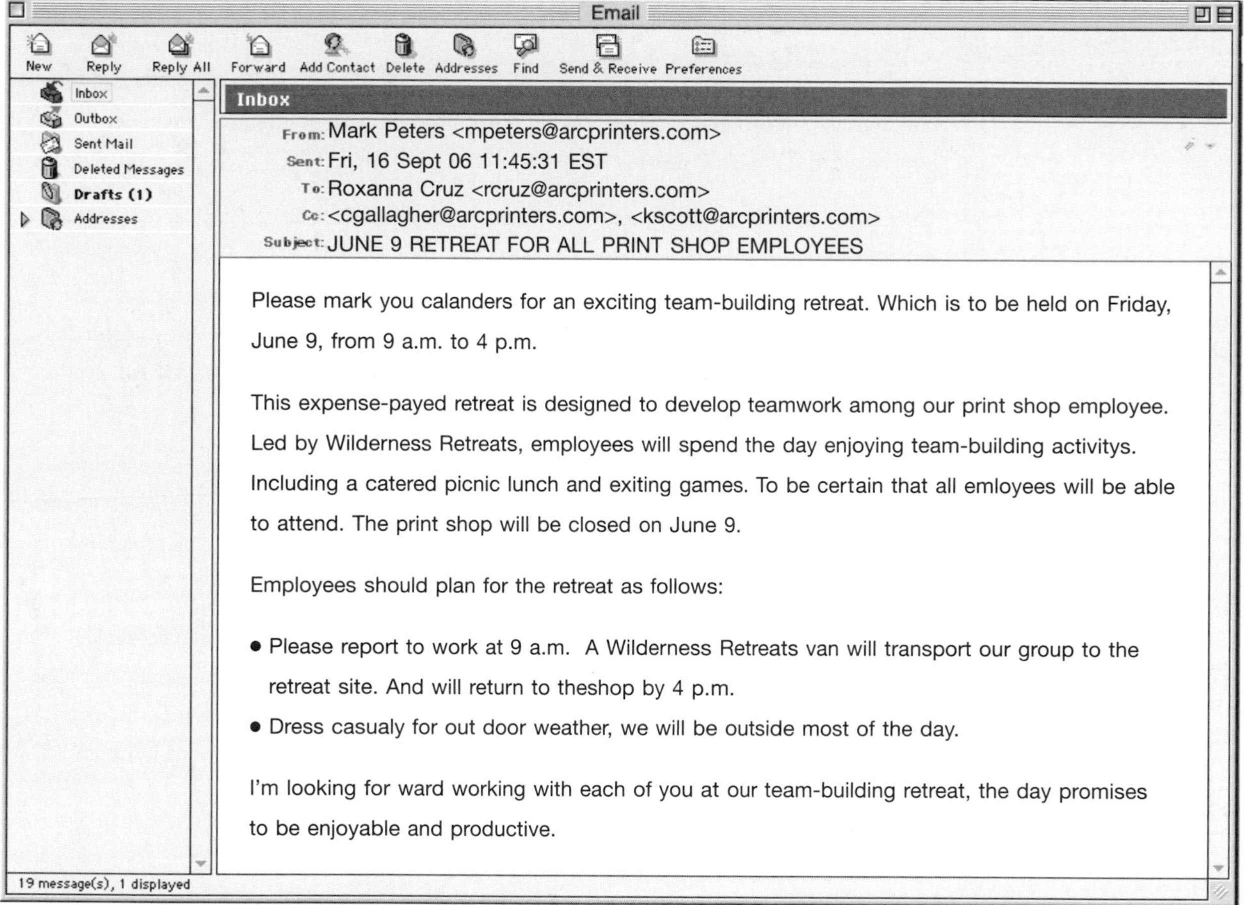

Inbox

From: Mark Peters <mpeters@arcprinters.com>
Sent: Fri, 16 Sept 06 11:45:31 EST
To: Roxanna Cruz <rcruz@arcprinters.com>
Cc: <cgallagher@arcprinters.com>, <kscott@arcprinters.com>
Subject: JUNE 9 RETREAT FOR ALL PRINT SHOP EMPLOYEES

Please mark you calanders for an exciting team-building retreat. Which is to be held on Friday, June 9, from 9 a.m. to 4 p.m.

This expense-payed retreat is designed to develop teamwork among our print shop employee. Led by Wilderness Retreats, employees will spend the day enjoying team-building activitys. Including a catered picnic lunch and exiting games. To be certain that all emloyees will be able to attend. The print shop will be closed on June 9.

Employees should plan for the retreat as follows:

- Please report to work at 9 a.m. A Wilderness Retreats van will transport our group to the retreat site. And will return to theshop by 4 p.m.
- Dress casualy for out door weather, we will be outside most of the day.

I'm looking for ward working with each of you at our team-building retreat, the day promises to be enjoyable and productive.

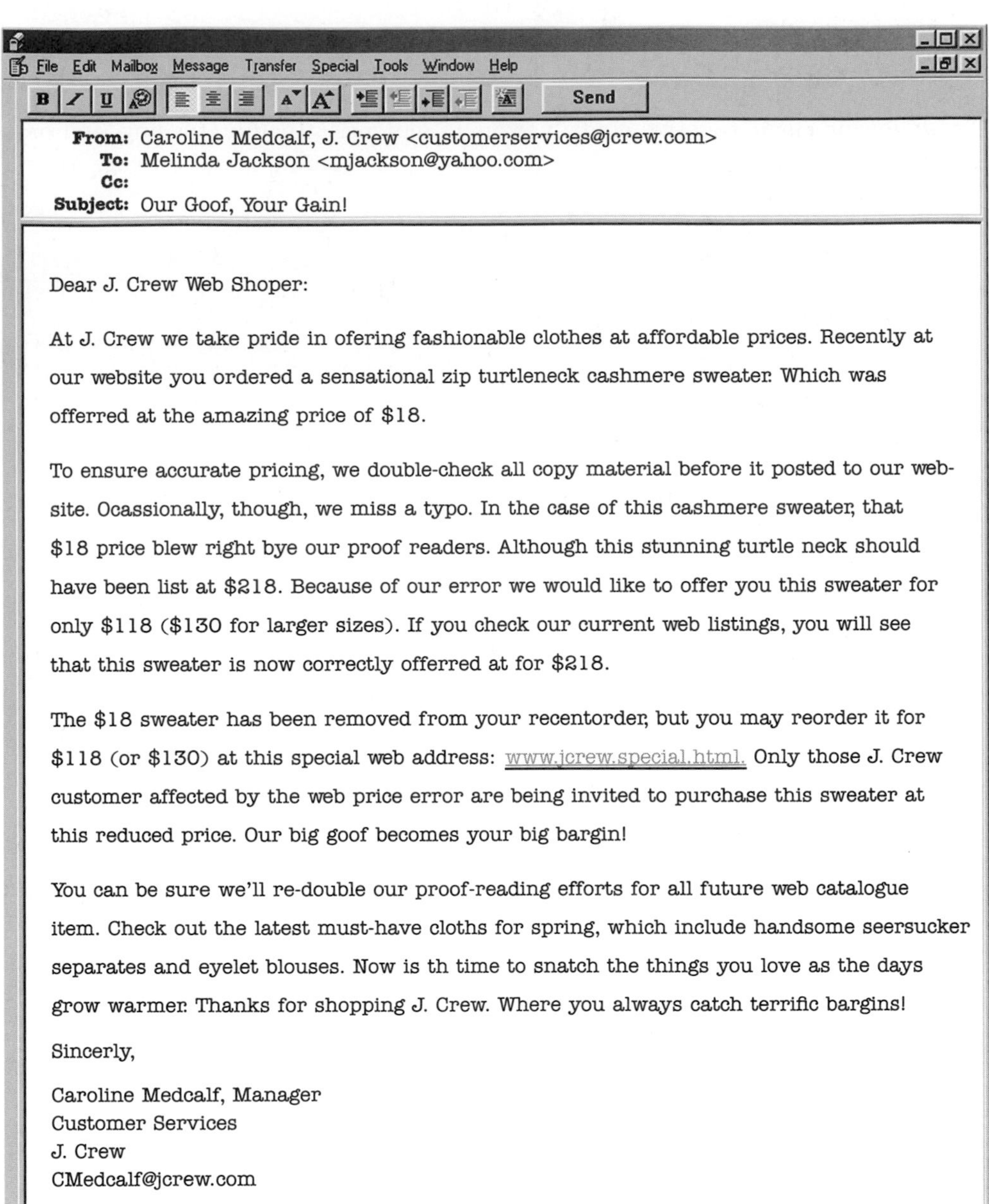

From: Caroline Medcalf, J. Crew <customerservices@jcrew.com>
To: Melinda Jackson <mjackson@yahoo.com>
Cc:
Subject: Our Goof, Your Gain!

Dear J. Crew Web Shoper:

At J. Crew we take pride in ofering fashionable clothes at affordable prices. Recently at our website you ordered a sensational zip turtleneck cashmere sweater. Which was offerred at the amazing price of $18.

To ensure accurate pricing, we double-check all copy material before it posted to our website. Ocassionally, though, we miss a typo. In the case of this cashmere sweater, that $18 price blew right bye our proof readers. Although this stunning turtle neck should have been list at $218. Because of our error we would like to offer you this sweater for only $118 ($130 for larger sizes). If you check our current web listings, you will see that this sweater is now correctly offerred at for $218.

The $18 sweater has been removed from your recentorder, but you may reorder it for $118 (or $130) at this special web address: www.jcrew.special.html. Only those J. Crew customer affected by the web price error are being invited to purchase this sweater at this reduced price. Our big goof becomes your big bargin!

You can be sure we'll re-double our proof-reading efforts for all future web catalogue item. Check out the latest must-have cloths for spring, which include handsome seersucker separates and eyelet blouses. Now is th time to snatch the things you love as the days grow warmer. Thanks for shopping J. Crew. Where you always catch terrific bargins!

Sincerly,

Caroline Medcalf, Manager
Customer Services
J. Crew
CMedcalf@jcrew.com

POSTTEST

Write the correct letter after each of the numbered items below.

a = correctly punctuated sentence c = comma splice
b = fragment d = run-on sentence

1. The computer arrived Monday the printer is expected shortly. ____________
2. Across the road from the hospital is a shopping mall. ____________
3. Since the contract was mailed Monday but not received until late Friday. ____________
4. On Monday my email box is overflowing, on Friday it is empty. ____________
5. Because Ahmed, who is one of our best employees, was ill last week. ____________

learning.web.ways

Many colleges and universities offer online writing labs (OWLs). These websites provide helpful resources for students and business people. You can either read online or download handouts providing help with punctuation, spelling, sentence construction, parts of speech, and writing in the job search.

Goal: To learn to use an online writing lab.

1. With your web browser on the screen, key the following URL in the location box: **<http://www.ccc.commnet.edu/grammar>**. Press **Enter**.
2. Look at the **Capital Community College Guide to Grammar and Writing**.
3. Scroll down to **Peripherals & PowerPoints**.
4. Select **PowerPoint Presentations**.
5. From the list of materials, click on the **Parts of Speech** presentation. Be patient while it loads because it's huge!
6. View the presentation.
7. Click back twice to return to the **Guide to Grammar and Writing** page.
8. From the **Ask Grammar, Quizzes, Search Devices** section, select **170+ Interactive Quizzes**.

1.d 2.a 3.b 4.c 5.b

9. Click on **Recognizing Nouns** and do the quiz.
10. Print the whole page, with the correct answers included.
11. End your session by clicking the **X** box in the upper right corner of your browser. Turn in your printout, or send an email message to your instructor summarizing what you learned.

NAME ______________________

UNIT 1 REVIEW Chapters 1–3 (Self-Check)

Begin your review by rereading Chapters 1 through 3. Then check your comprehension of those chapters by filling in the blanks in the exercises that follow. Compare your responses with those provided at the end of the book, p. 554.

Write *T* (true) or *F* (false) after the following statements.

1. All dictionaries use the same plan for showing the order of definitions. ______
2. Usage labels such as *archaic* and *informal* warn dictionary users about appropriate usage. ______
3. The etymology code helps you to pronounce a word correctly. ______
4. Because the English language changes very little, the publication date of a dictionary is unimportant. ______
5. Most dictionaries show verb tenses only if the forms are irregular, such as the past tense *taught.* ______
6. A thesaurus is a collection of words and their definitions. ______
7. A reference manual is organized functionally rather than pedagogically. ______
8. The usage label *obsolete* means that a word is considered indecent or coarse. ______
9. The terms *desk* and *college-level* refer to the same kind of dictionary. ______
10. A summary of diacritical marks is often found at the bottom of dictionary pages. ______

Read the following sentence carefully. Identify the parts of speech for the words as they are used in this sentence.

He glanced quickly at the page and then jotted down two answers.

11. *He*	(a) noun	(b) pronoun	(c) adj	(d) adverb	______
12. *glanced*	(a) conj	(b) prep	(c) verb	(d) adverb	______
13. *quickly*	(a) conj	(b) prep	(c) adj	(d) adverb	______
14. *at*	(a) conj	(b) prep	(c) adj	(d) adverb	______
15. *page*	(a) noun	(b) pronoun	(c) conj	(d) adverb	______
16. *and*	(a) noun	(b) pronoun	(c) conj	(d) prep	______
17. *then*	(a) noun	(b) adverb	(c) conj	(d) prep	______
18. *jotted*	(a) verb	(b) adverb	(c) conj	(d) prep	______
19. *two*	(a) verb	(b) adj	(c) adverb	(d) prep	______
20. *answers*	(a) noun	(b) pronoun	(c) adj	(d) prep	______

For each of the following statements, determine the word or phrase that correctly completes that statement and write its letter in the space provided.

21. In the sentence *Excellent communication skills can help you get a job,* the simple subject is (a) Excellent, (b) communication, (c) skills, (d) you. ______

22. In the sentence *Here are the contracts,* the simple subject is (a) Here, (b) are, (c) contracts, (d) you. ______

23. In the sentence *She looked unwell,* the word *looked* is considered a (a) linking verb, (b) helping verb, (c) action verb, (d) subject. ______

24. The sentence *She sent many email messages* represents what sentence pattern: (a) subject–verb, (b) subject–action verb–object, (c) subject–linking verb–complement, (d) subject–linking verb–object. ______

From the list below select the letter that describes each of the following groups of words.

a = complete sentence b = fragment c = comma splice d = run-on sentence

25. Ryan hates to receive spam, he uses filters to avoid unwanted email messages. ______

26. Whenever Mr. Jackson calls to confirm the shipping date. ______

27. We turned on our computers when we arrived, and we left them on all day. ______

28. That company's products are excellent its service is somewhat slow, however. ______

29. Many employees have signed up for the proposed in-service training. ______

30. Although you will be on vacation when your cheque is issued. ______

31. Complete the form and send it with your cheque. ______

32. Our corporate headquarters will be moved next year, then we expect to be transferred. ______

33. The letter arrived today the package should be here next week. ______

34. Some employers weigh education and grades heavily, they look at transcripts carefully. ______

35. After you read the contract, sign and return it. ______

Hotline Review

Select the word or phrase that correctly completes each statement, and write its letter in the corresponding blank.

36. (a) Thankyou, (b) Thank-you, (c) Thank you for submitting the report early. ______

37. We will (a) disperse (b) disburse informative literature and coupons at the beginning of our promotion. ______

38. We can have deliveries (a) everyday, (b) every day, (c) every-day if we make arrangements in advance. ______

39. The reason I am late is (a) because, (b) that my car stalled. ______

40. An email message should (a) always, (b) never, (c) sometimes begin with a salutation. ______

Developing Proofreading Skills

As you complete each set of chapters (a unit), you will find a workshop exercise that introduces various techniques to help you improve your writing skills. This first workshop emphasizes proofreading skills. You will learn about proofreading marks, which are often used to edit printed material. Study the basic symbols shown here. See the inside front cover of your textbook for a more comprehensive list.

≡ Capitalize	∨ Insert apostrophe	⊙ Insert period
ℓ Delete	∧ Insert comma	/ Lower-case
∧ Insert	= Insert hyphen	⊂ Close up space

Example:

Proof reading marks areused by writers an editors too make corrections and revisions in printed copy they use these Standard Marks for clarity and consistency. If you are revising your own work Youll probable use these mark only occasional. In many jobs today however you will be working in a team environment. Where writing tasks are shared. Thats when its important to able to aply these well known marks correctly.

Proofreading Tips

- Be sure to check spelling. If you have composed at a computer, use its spell checker, but do not rely on it totally. It can't tell the difference between *it's* and *its* and many other confusing words.
- Look for grammar and punctuation errors. As you complete this book, you'll be more alert to problem areas, such as subject–verb agreement and comma placement.
- Double-check names and numbers. Compare all names and numbers with their sources because inaccuracies are not immediately visible. Especially verify the spelling of the names of individuals receiving the message. Most people immediately dislike someone who misspells their name.
- For long or especially important documents, always print a copy (preferably double-spaced), set it aside for at least a day, and then proofread when you are fresh.
- Be prepared to find errors. One student confessed, "I can find other people's errors, but I can't seem to locate my own." Psychologically, we don't *expect* to find errors, and we don't *want* to find them. You can overcome this obstacle by anticipating errors and congratulating, not criticizing, yourself each time you find one.

Writing Application 1.1 After you read and edit the letter on the next page, your instructor may ask you to write a similar introductory personal business letter to her or him. On a separate sheet of paper, explain why you enrolled in this class, evaluate your present communication skills, name your field of study, describe the career you seek, and briefly tell about your current work (if you are employed) and your favourite activities. Your instructor may ask you to write a first draft quickly, print it, and then use proofreading marks to show corrections. Make a final copy. Double space the rough draft; single space the final copy. Turn in both copies. See Appendix C for a model personal business letter.

The following personal business letter contains intentional errors in typing, spelling, capitalization, and sentence punctuation. Use proofreading marks to edit this letter.

810 North Miller Road
Vancouver, BC V6B 4H3
September 8, 200x

Professor Margaret M. Sullivan
Department of Busness Administration
Schoolcraft College
Vancouver, BC V6B 5H6

Dear Professor Sulivan:

I enrolled this class to help me improve the way I use language I know that comunication skills are important, and Im afraid that my pre sent skills are below average. They're not good enough for me to get the kind of job I want I also enrolled in this class because its required in my program of study.

Accounting is my major I chose this field because I like working with figures. And because I know that many good jobs are available in accounting. Although I thought that accountants worked totaly with figures. My adviser tells me that accountants also need to be able to explain their work to management, to fellow employees, and to clients. My language skills are not terrific, and I want to improve. When I finish my accounting program, Ihope to get a job in the entertainment industry as a Junior Accountant.

I have a parttime job at Pizza Bob's. Where I deliver pizzas to campus dormitories or to apartments an homes. I like my job because I get to meet people and because it helps me pay for my car and it's insurance.

When I'm not studing or working, I like to surf the internet. My favourite places to visit are websites devoted to unusual hobbys and businesses. Right now I'm interested in "CyberSlice," a site showing the menus of participating pizzerias in a neighbourhood. May be I can get Pizza Bob to participate!

Sincerely,

U N I T 2

Knowing the Namers

Chapter 4
Nouns

Chapter 5
Possessive Nouns

Chapter 6
Personal Pronouns

Chapter 7
Pronouns and Antecedents

C H A P T E R

Nouns

4

OBJECTIVES When you have completed the materials in this chapter, you will be able to do the following:

LEVEL I

- *Recognize four kinds of nouns.*
- *Follow the basic rules for spelling plural nouns.*

LEVEL II

- *Spell challenging plural nouns ending in* y, o, *and* f.
- *Form the plurals of compound nouns, numerals, letters, degrees, and abbreviations.*

LEVEL III

- *Recognize and use correctly foreign plural nouns and selected special nouns.*
- *Use plural personal titles appropriately.*

PRETEST

Underline any incorrectly spelled noun in the following sentences. Spell the word correctly in the space provided.

1. We store infrequently used supplies on the top shelfs. ______________
2. He ordered 20 pounds of tomatoes and 50 pounds of potatos. ______________
3. Several Crown attornies requested tax write-offs for books. ______________
4. Our two RNs both asked for leave of absences in June. ______________
5. Based on all the criterion, several diagnoses were given. ______________

1. shelves 2. potatoes 3. attorneys 4. leaves of absence 5. criteria

This business English textbook treats the study of our language *selectively*. We will not consider *all* the rules and conventions of English. Instead, this book will focus on those aspects of the language that are often troublesome. Therefore, in this chapter on nouns, the principal concern will be the forming and spelling of plural nouns—an area of confusion for many business writers.

Beginning with this chapter, concepts are presented in levels, progressing from basic, frequently used concepts at Level I to more complex, less frequently used concepts at Level III.

LEVEL I

As you will recall from Chapter 2 (p. 20), nouns name persons, places, things, qualities, concepts, and activities.

▶ Kinds of Nouns

As the "namers" in our language, nouns perform an important function. They often serve as sentence subjects. To help you understand nouns better, we will first divide them into two categories: concrete and abstract.

Concrete and Abstract Nouns

Concrete nouns name specific objects that you can actually see, hear, feel, taste, or smell. Abstract nouns name qualities and concepts. Because concrete nouns are precise, they are more forceful and effective in writing and talking than abstract nouns.

Concrete Nouns		**Abstract Nouns**	
dictionary	valley	freedom	happiness
stapler	jasmine	success	accuracy
envelope	affidavit	memory	personality
dentist	coffee	truth	value

Career Tip

Successful job applicants fill their résumés with concrete expressions and quantifiable data rather than abstractions. Instead of *Worked as lab assistant,* try *Assisted over 300 students and 25 faculty members using Word, WordPerfect, and Excel in computer lab.*

Common and Proper Nouns

Common nouns name *generalized* persons, places, and things. Proper nouns, on the other hand, name *specific* persons, places, and things and are always capitalized. Rules for capitalization are presented in Chapter 19 (pp. 375–382).

Common Nouns		**Proper Nouns**	
document	dog	Charter of Rights and Freedoms	Labrador retriever*
organization	computer	United Nations	Dell computer*
student	telephone	Mark Montgomery	Nokia cellphone*
photocopier	company	Xerox machine*	Bata Shoes
candy	magazine	Aero candy bar*	*Canadian House & Home*

* *Note that common nouns following proper nouns or adjectives are not capitalized.*

▶ Basic Plurals

Singular nouns name *one* person, place, or thing. Plural nouns name *two* or more. At Level I you will learn basic rules for forming plurals. At Level II you will learn how to form the plurals of nouns that can create spelling problems.

Regular nouns form the plural with the addition of *s* or *es*.

Add s *to most nouns:*

password, passwords	advantage, advantages	graphic, graphics
merchant, merchants	house, houses	Tom, Toms*
passenger, passengers	issue, issues	Johnson, Johnsons*

Add es *to nouns ending in* s, x, z, ch, *or* sh:

brush, brushes	business, businesses	quartz, quartzes
tax, taxes	wrench, wrenches	Sanchez, Sanchezes*

Irregular nouns form the plural by changing the spelling of the word.

man, men	foot, feet	mouse, mice
goose, geese	child, children	ox, oxen

Because of space restrictions, most dictionaries do *not* show plurals of *regular* nouns. Thus, if you look up the plural of *ranch*, you probably will not find it. Dictionaries *do* show the plurals of nouns that might be confusing or difficult to spell.

Apostrophes (') are *not* used to form plural nouns. Reserve the apostrophe to show possession. (Chapter 5 discusses possessive nouns in detail.)

Wrong: Management *executive's* have excellent *salary's.*

Right: Management *executives* have excellent *salaries.*

Now complete the reinforcement exercises for Level I on pp. 63–64.

Spot the Blooper

Nabisco once introduced a new product as *Teddy Graham Bearwich's.* Not long after, it quietly gave the box a new design and new name, *T. G. Bearwiches.*

Hotlink

Additional material on irregular plurals of nouns can be found at this University of Victoria website: **<http://web2.uvcs.uvic.ca/elc/studyzone/330/grammar/irrplu.htm>**.

LEVEL II

▶ Challenging Noun Plurals

Your ability to spell certain troublesome noun plurals can be greatly improved by studying the following rules and examples.

1. *Common nouns ending in y* form the plural in two ways.

   a. When the *y* is preceded by a vowel (*a, e, i, o, u*), the plural is formed by the addition of *s* only.

valley, valleys	journey, journeys	buoy, buoys
turkey, turkeys	delay, delays	Garvey, Garveys

   b. When the *y* is preceded by a consonant (all letters other than vowels), the plural is formed by changing the *y* to *ies.*

country, countries	quality, qualities	luxury, luxuries
currency, currencies	company, companies	secretary, secretaries

Study Tip

In making family names plural, never change the original spellings. Adding *s* or *es* is acceptable, but changing *Kennedy* to *Kennedies* would change the original spelling.

---

* *Proper nouns are made plural in the same way that common nouns are made plural except for proper nouns ending in* y. *See the explanation in 1.b. in Level II.*

Did You Know?

English is the first language in history of which the majority of speakers are non-native. Of the 750 million people who use English regularly, only 300 million are native speakers. It is the universal language of scholarship, science, and trade.

Note: This rule does *not* apply to the plural forms of proper nouns: *Amy, Amys; Kelly, Kellys; Harry, Harrys.*

2. *Nouns ending in fe* or *f* follow no standard rules in the formation of plurals, though most simply add *s* to the singular form. Study the examples shown here, and use a dictionary when in doubt.

Add *s*	**Change to *ves***	**Both Forms Recognized***
brief, briefs	half, halves	dwarfs, dwarves
cliff, cliffs	knife, knives	scarves, scarfs
proof, proofs	leaf, leaves	wharves, wharfs
safe, safes	shelf, shelves	
sheriff, sheriffs	wife, wives	
tariff, tariffs	wolf, wolves	
Wolf, Wolfs		

Be careful not to confuse plural nouns with verb forms ending in *s*. He *saves* (verb) his money in two *safes* (noun). Be especially aware of the following words:

Nouns	**Verbs**
belief, beliefs	believe, believes
leaf, leaves (foliage)	leave, leaves (to depart)
loaf, loaves (of bread)	loaf, loafs (to be idle)
proof, proofs	prove, proves

3. *Nouns ending in o* may be made plural by adding *s* or *es*.

   a. When the *o* is preceded by a vowel, the plural is formed by adding *s* only.

studio, studios	curio, curios	radio, radios
patio, patios	ratio, ratios	portfolio, portfolios

   b. When the *o* is preceded by a consonant, the plural is formed by adding *s* or *es*. Study the following examples, and again use your dictionary whenever in doubt.

Add *s*	**Add *es***	**Both Forms Recognized***
auto, autos	echo, echoes	cargoes, cargos
Franco, Francos	embargo, embargoes	ghettos, ghettoes
logo, logos	hero, heroes	innuendoes, innuendos
memo, memos	potato, potatoes	mangoes, mangos
silo, silos	tomato, tomatoes	mosquitoes, mosquitos
typo, typos	veto, vetoes	mottoes, mottos

   c. Musical terms ending in *o* always form the plural with the addition of *s* only.

alto, altos	cello, cellos	piano, pianos
banjo, banjos	contralto, contraltos	solo, solos

* *More common form shown first.*

4. *Compound nouns* may be written as single (or solid) words, may be hyphenated, or may appear as separate words (open form).

   a. When written as single words, compound nouns form the plural by appropriate changes in the final element.

bookshelf, bookshelves	printout, printouts
footnote, footnotes	stepchild, stepchildren
photocopy, photocopies	walkway, walkways

   b. When written in hyphenated or open form, compound nouns form the plural by appropriate changes in the principal noun.

editors-in-chief	bills of lading
mayors-elect	boards of directors
mothers-in-law	leaves of absence
runners-up	paper clips

   c. If a hyphenated compound noun has no principal noun at all, the final element is made plural.

cure-alls	look-alikes	show-offs
go-betweens	no-shows	trade-ins
know-it-alls	run-ins	write-ups

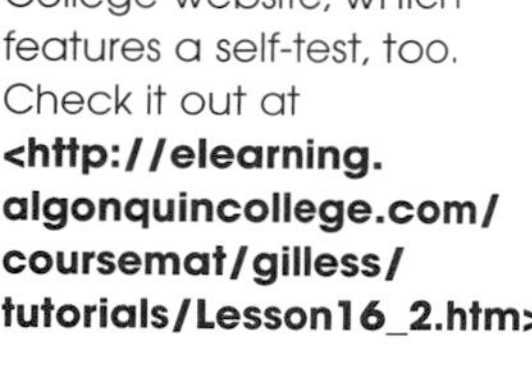

Hotlink

Irregular plurals also get attention at the Algonquin College website, which features a self-test, too. Check it out at **<http://elearning.algonquincollege.com/coursemat/gilless/tutorials/Lesson16_2.htm>**.

5. *Numerals, alphabet letters, isolated words,* and *degrees* are made plural by adding *s, es,* or *'s*. Use the *'s* only when necessary for clarity (see *d* below).

   a. Numerals and upper-case letters (with the exception of *A, I, M,* and *U*) require only *s* in plural formation.

   Price trends from the *1980s* continued through the *1990s*.
   Her new calculator was not printing *7s* and *9s*.
   Narinder received all *Bs* and *Cs* on his report card.

   b. Isolated words used as nouns are made plural with the addition of *s* or *es*, as needed for pronunciation.

   The Speaker of the House took a count of *yeses* and *noes* on the bill.
   Numerous *ands, ahs,* and *you knows* made his speech ineffective.
   She considered all the *pros* and *cons* before signing the contract.

   c. Degrees are made plural with the addition of *s*.

   Dr. Helstrum holds two *Ph.D.s* in related fields.
   Graduates with *M.B.A.s* are being heavily recruited.

   d. Isolated lower-case letters and the capital letters *A, I, M,* and *U* require *'s* for clarity.

   Unless she writes more legibly, her *o's* may be mistaken for *a's*.
   In preparing the notice for the marquee yesterday, we ran out of *A's* and *I's*.

Hotlink

For another look at irregular noun plurals, consult **<http://grammar.ccc.commnet.edu/grammar/plurals.htm>**.

6. *Abbreviations* are usually made plural by adding *s* to the singular form.

yr., yrs.	mgr., mgrs.	dept., depts.	wk., wks.
No., Nos.	CAAT, CAATs	DVD, DVDs	bldg., bldgs.

The singular and plural forms of abbreviations or symbols for units of measurement are, however, usually identical (*always* identical in the case of metric units of measurement).

g	(gram or grams)	L	(litre or litres)
km	(kilometre or kilometres)	deg.	(degree or degrees)
cm	(centimetre or centimetres)	ft.	(foot or feet)

Now complete the reinforcement exercises for Level II on pp. 65–67.

LEVEL III

▶ Special Plural Forms

Study Tip

Language purists contend that the word *data* can be only plural (*the data are*). However, see the Hotline Queries for another view.

Hotlink

Another place to consult for assistance with irregular plurals is this PDF document at **<www.athabascau.ca/html/services/write-site/documentation/Irregular-plurals-general.pdf>**.

Selected nouns borrowed from foreign languages and other special nouns require your attention because their plural forms can be confusing.

1. *Nouns borrowed from foreign languages* may retain a foreign plural. A few, however, also have an anglicized plural form, shown second below. Check your dictionary for the preferred or more frequently used form.

Singular	**Plural**
alga	algae
alumna (*feminine*)	alumnae (pronounced *a-LUM-nee*)
alumnus (*masculine*)	alumni (pronounced *a-LUM-neye*)
analysis	analyses
bacterium	bacteria
basis	bases
crisis	crises
criterion	criteria
curriculum	curricula
datum	data
diagnosis	diagnoses
erratum	errata
formula	formulae or formulas
hypothesis	hypotheses
larva	larvae
memorandum	memoranda or memorandums
parenthesis	parentheses
phenomenon	phenomena
stimulus	stimuli
thesis	theses

2. *Personal titles* may have both formal and informal plural forms.

Singular	**Formal Plural**	**Informal Plural**
Miss	the Misses Smith	the Miss Smiths
Mr.	Messrs.* Kahn and Lee	Mr. Kahn and Mr. Lee
Mrs.	Mmes.† Davis and Klein	Mrs. Davis and Mrs. Klein
Ms.	Mses.†† Freiden and Allen	Ms. Freiden and Ms. Allen

* *Pronounced MES-erz (abbreviation of* Messieurs*)*
† *Pronounced May-DAM (abbreviation of* Mesdames*)*
†† *Pronounced MIZ-ez (Ms. is probably a blend of Mrs. and Miss.)*

3. *Special nouns,* many of which end in *s,* may normally be *only* singular *or* plural in meaning. Other special nouns may be considered *either* singular *or* plural in meaning.

Usually Singular	**Usually Plural**	**May Be Singular or Plural**
economics	clothes	corps
genetics	goods	deer
mathematics	pants	politics
measles	scissors	sheep
news	thanks	Vietnamese

Study Tip

Practise these special nouns by using them with the singular verb *is* or the plural verb *are*. Genetics *is* fascinating (singular). Scissors *are* useful (plural).

4. *Single-letter abbreviations* may be made plural by doubling the letter.

pp. (pages)	See pp. 18–21. (pages 18 through 21)
ff. (and following)	See pp. 18 ff. (page 18 and following pages)

Now complete the reinforcement exercises for Level III on pp. 67–69.

HOTLINE QUERIES

Question: It seems to me that the meaning of the word *impact* has changed. I thought it meant "an effect." But now I hear this use: *How does this policy impact the Middle East?* What's happening to this word?

Answer: In our language nouns often become verbs (to *bridge* the gap, to *corner* a market, to *telephone* a friend). Whether a noun-turned-verb is assimilated into the language seems to depend on its utility, its efficiency, and the status of the individuals who use it. Transformation of the noun *impact* into a verb would appear to be unnecessary, since the word *affect* clearly suffices in most constructions (*how does this program affect the Middle East?*). Although we hear *impact* used frequently as a verb today, some language specialists find it offensive.

Question: Could you help me spell the plurals of *do* and *don't?*

Answer: In forming the plurals of isolated words, the trend today is to add *s* and no apostrophe. Thus we have *dos* and *don'ts.* Formerly, apostrophes were used to make isolated words plural. However, if no confusion results, make plurals by adding *s* only. Because of capitalization, the lower-case *dos* would not be confused with the upper-case *DOS (disk operating system).*

Question: One member of our staff consistently corrects our use of the word *data.* He says the word is plural. Is it never singular?

Answer: The word *data* is indeed plural; the singular form is *datum.* Through frequent usage, however, *data* has recently become a collective noun. Collective nouns may be singular or plural depending on whether they are considered as one unit or as separate units. For example, *These data are much different from those findings,* or *This data is conclusive.*

Question: I don't have a dictionary handy. Can you tell me which word I should use in this sentence: *A (stationary/stationery) circuit board will be installed.*

Answer: In your sentence use *stationary,* which means "not moving" or "permanent" (*the concrete columns are stationary*). *Stationery* means "writing paper" (*his stationery has his address printed on it*). You might be able to remember the word *stationery* by associating *envelopes* with the *e* in *stationery.*

(Continued)

Question: My mother is always correcting me when I say, *I hate when that happens.* What's wrong with this? I hear it on TV all the time.

Answer: Your mother wants you to speak standard English, the written and spoken language we need to use in order to make the best impression in school and work contexts. Hearing an expression on TV is no assurance that it's acceptable in all situations. The problem with an expression like *I hate when that happens* is that an adverbial phrase (*when that happens*) is used as the object of a verb (*hate*). Only nouns, noun clauses, or pronouns may act as objects of verbs. Correction: *I hate it when that happens,* or *I hate this to happen.*

Question: As a sportswriter, I need to know the plural of *hole-in-one.*

Answer: Make the principal word plural, *holes-in-one.*

Question: In email messages is it acceptable to use abbreviations such as *IMHO (in my humble opinion), ROTFL (rolling on the floor laughing),* and *TIA (thanks in advance)*?

Answer: Among close friends who understand their meaning, such abbreviations are certainly acceptable. But in business messages, these abbreviations are too casual and too obscure. Many readers would have no idea what they mean. Smileys such as :-) are also too casual for business and professional messages.

Question: In the sentence *Please read our FAQs,* does the abbreviation need an apostrophe?

Answer: No. The abbreviation for *Frequently Asked Questions* is *FAQs,* as you wrote it. Avoid using an apostrophe for plural forms.

Question: What is the plural of computer *mouse*?

Answer: *Mice* refers to both computer devices and rodents. However, some experts prefer *mouse devices,* which seems less confusing.

NAME ______________________

CHAPTER 4 Reinforcement Exercises

LEVEL I

Note: At the beginning of each level, a self-check exercise is provided so that you may immediately check your understanding of the concepts in that level. Do not look at the answers until you have finished the exercise. Then compare your responses with the answers shown at the bottom of the page. If more than three of your answers do not agree with those shown, reread the level before continuing with the other reinforcement exercises.

A. (**Self-check**) Write the plural forms of the singular nouns shown in parentheses.

Example: The (Cox) have purchased an office building on Lakeshore Boulevard. Coxes

1. Some (business) are formed as limited partnerships. ______
2. Many organizations have (virus) on their office computers. ______
3. Most toy manufacturers employ (child) to test new products. ______
4. After four lengthy (speech), boredom overcame the audience. ______
5. All (fax) in our office are printed on plain paper. ______
6. The condition will not change unless Parliament passes a law with (tooth) in it. ______
7. One administrative assistant may serve six (boss). ______
8. The (Finch) are planning to move to Saskatchewan at the end of the school year. ______
9. Tracy made two (batch) of cookies after school. ______
10. The cafeteria uses over a dozen (loaf) of bread every day. ______

Check your answers.

B. Write plural forms for the nouns listed.

1. employee ______
2. watch ______
3. Lynch ______
4. franchise ______
5. quartz ______
6. foot ______
7. mile ______
8. Ahmad ______
9. goose ______
10. Lorna ______
11. bias ______
12. sketch ______

1. businesses 2. viruses 3. children 4. speeches 5. faxes 6. teeth 7. bosses 8. Finches 9. batches 10. loaves

13. Banks ____________________

14. Lohman ____________________

15. service ____________________

16. gas ____________________

17. ____________________quota

18. ____________________absence

19. ____________________pamphlet

20. ____________________Peretz

C. Correct any errors in the use of plural nouns in the following sentences by underlining the incorrect form and writing the correct form in the space provided. If the sentence is correct as it stands, write *C*.

Example: The advertising agency submitted several <u>sketch</u> of the design. ___sketches___

1. More than twenty men and woman were interviewed for the vacant position. ____________
2. Anderson was one of the writer's working on the screenplay. ____________
3. After many delays the heavy box were delivered. ____________
4. Each year the Canadian Cancer Society sells bunchs of daffodils. ____________
5. Mrs. Hollingsworth secured the door with two latchs. ____________
6. Three Jennifer's are employed in that department, so we use surnames. ____________
7. Each employee received two free pass's to the exhibit. ____________
8. Kelly Jackson used two different lens for her photography assignment. ____________
9. The Williamses were the first sisters to play each other in a Grand Slam tennis tournament. ____________
10. Have the Welshs submitted this year's income tax return? ____________
11. The reception room has four benchs and two upholstered chairs. ____________
12. Mr. Burtness and his two stepchilds attended the reunion. ____________
13. Sharing ownership in the venture are the Joneses and the Harveys. ____________
14. Only two news dispatchs were released concerning the stock split. ____________
15. Ryan carefully placed all the dishs on the kitchen shelves. ____________

NAME ______________________________

LEVEL II

A. (**Self-check**) Provide the correct plural forms of the expressions shown in parentheses.

1. We have decided to close on (Sunday) during July and August. ______________
2. Upper (shelf) contain less frequently used company files. ______________
3. Our organization is prepared to deal in foreign (currency). ______________
4. For the past three (Tuesday), business has been slow. ______________
5. Students had to show their (ID) before they were admitted. ______________
6. Both (bill of lading) showed excessive shipping charges. ______________
7. Deciduous trees drop their (leaf) in the autumn. ______________
8. Both of her (sister-in-law) visited Mirella in the hospital. ______________
9. Few orchestras have seven (cello) in the string section. ______________
10. The committee debated the (pro and con) of decentralization. ______________

Check your answers.

B. Write the correct plural forms of the singular expressions shown in parentheses.

1. All that remained standing were two blackened (chimney). ______________
2. We compared liquidity (ratio) of the two companies. ______________
3. A total of 212 (MP) responded to the survey. ______________
4. President Farley wanted a manager with conservative (belief). ______________
5. Both (Lisa) are outstanding customer service representatives. ______________
6. Sales are increasing with all Pacific Rim (country). ______________
7. Do the (Wolf) subscribe to *Canadian Business*? ______________
8. City Council awarded medals to the fire (hero). ______________
9. After the lecture three (hanger-on) remained at the lectern. ______________
10. A worldwide economic depression occurred in the early (1890). ______________
11. Computer users must distinguish between zeros and (O). ______________
12. What percentage of (CEO) are women? ______________

1. Sundays 2. shelves 3. currencies 4. Tuesdays 5. IDs 6. bills of lading 7. leaves 8. sisters-in-law 9. cellos 10. pros and cons

13. The two (board of directors) voted to begin merger negotiations. ____________

14. The manager hired her two (daughter-in-law) as salesclerks. ____________

15. At least two employees have recently taken (leave of absence). ____________

C. Write plural forms for the nouns listed. Use a dictionary if you are unsure of the spelling.

1. editor-in-chief ____________
2. half ____________
3. bill of sale ____________
4. 1990 ____________
5. subsidiary ____________
6. TV ____________
7. Monday ____________
8. balance of trade ____________
9. Murray ____________
10. safe ____________
11. liability ____________
12. 7 ____________
13. valley ____________
14. banjo ____________
15. port of entry ____________
16. cure-all ____________
17. IPO* ____________
18. D ____________
19. No. ____________
20. mayor-elect ____________
21. if ____________
22. disk jockey ____________
23. RSVP ____________
24. dept. ____________
25. q ____________
26. Ph.D. ____________
27. Emory ____________
28. don't ____________
29. Fox ____________
30. in and out ____________

D. Writing Exercise. Write sentences using the plural forms of the nouns shown in parentheses.

1. (trade-in) ____________

2. (Oakley) ____________

3. (up and down) ____________

4. (RN)* ____________

5. (mm) ____________

** Check your dictionary if you are not sure of the meanings of abbreviations or symbols.*

NAME ______________________

6. (standby) ______________________

____

7. (hero)______________________

____

8. (business) ______________________

____

LEVEL III

A. (**Self-check**) Write the plural forms of the singular expressions in parentheses.

1. Moving lights and other (stimulus) affect the human eye. ________________
2. Black holes are but one of the (phenomenon) of astronomy. ________________
3. Art collections illustrate varying (emphasis) of museum directors. ________________
4. Fundraisers contacted all (alumnus) of the University of Manitoba. ________________
5. Formal invitations were sent to (Mrs.) Wagner, Phillips, and Wang. ________________
6. An appendix appears on (p.) 535–540. ________________
7. Experts presented conflicting (analysis) of the problem. ________________
8. Numerous (crisis) within education will only be worsened by budget cuts. ________________
9. The announcement reported that (Mr.) Spinello and Busch had formed a partnership. ________________
10. Many (Vietnamese) took part in the lunar new year celebration. ________________

Check your answers.

B. Write the correct plural forms of the expressions in parentheses.

1. Researchers collected substantial (datum) to support their hypothesis. ________________
2. The girls' school will honour its illustrious (alumna). ________________
3. References to videophones may be found on pp. 25 (and following pages). ________________
4. Dr. Hsu used several (criterion) to judge the success of her experiment. ________________
5. Translations of foreign words are enclosed in sets of (parenthesis). ________________
6. Galileo's (hypothesis) about the solar system were rejected by his peers. ________________
7. Jack asked for information about two related (curriculum). ________________
8. Improper temperature controls allowed (bacterium) to contaminate some of the restaurant's food. ________________
9. Her disorder has resulted in several different (diagnosis). ________________
10. Betty's master's and doctor's (thesis) are both in the library. ________________

C. Complete the sentences below, selecting the singular verb form *is* or plural verb form *are* to agree with the noun subject of each

1. Economics (is, are) a dynamic field of study. ________________
2. Curricula (is, are) currently being developed in office technologies. ________________

---

1. stimuli 2. phenomena 3. emphases 4. alumni 5. Mmes. 6. pp. 7. analyses
8. crises 9. Messrs. 10. Vietnamese

3. (Is, Are) the proceeds to be donated to charity? ____________

4. If the scissors (is, are) sharp, we can cut the ballots. ____________

5. Mathematics (is, are) feared by some female students. ____________

6. The statistics on violent crime (is, are) staggering. ____________

7. Thanks (is, are) due to our organizing committee. ____________

8. Several Taiwanese (is, are) enrolled in this class. ____________

9. News of the store's closing (is, are) worrying neighbouring retailers. ____________

10. Insect larvae (is, are) responsible for the damage. ____________

D. Review of Levels I, II, and III. (**Self-check**) In the following sentences underline any noun or noun-verb errors. For each sentence write a corrected form in the space provided. If a sentence is correct, write *C* in the space. Then check your answers at the bottom of the next page.

1. Many banks have installed multilingual ATMs to serve their customers. ____________

2. Few students in most colleges earn all As in their classes. ____________

3. The huge number of inquirys resulting from the announcement overwhelmed our two websites. ____________

4. Although many stimulus are being studied, scientists have not yet determined an exact cause of the bacterial mysteries. ____________

5. Unless Revenue Canada proves that the Kellys owe federal taxs, no penalty can be assessed. ____________

6. Leaves of absence for the week of June 7 were granted to both woman. ____________

7. Tomatoes are grown to perfection in the interior vallies. ____________

8. Our directory lists RN's and MD's separately. ____________

9. Physics are the most important subject in the second-semester curriculum. ____________

10. After numerous brushs with the law, Mark became a consultant to a security company. ____________

11. The Fitch's named three beneficiaries in their insurance policies. ____________

12. Attorneys and judges were advised to place their heaviest books on the lower shelfs. ____________

13. Because of numerous glitches in our software, email messages arrived in irregular batchs. ____________

14. Despite the new flexible hours for Mondays through Thursdays, all employees must put in a full workday on Fridays. ____________

15. The Harrises discussed all the in's and out's of the transaction before signing the contract. ____________

E. Optional Writing. Your instructor may ask you to complete this exercise on a separate sheet.

Write ten complete sentences using the plural forms of the following nouns: *belief, CEO, company, datum, delay, employee, father-in-law, Mr. and Mrs. Lopez, phenomenon, tooth.*

---

1. C 2. A's 3. inquiries 4. stimuli 5. taxes 6. women 7. valleys 8. RNs and MDs 9. Physics is 10. brushes 11. Fitches 12. shelves 13. batches 14. C 15. ins and outs

Editor's Challenge

The following letters contain intentional errors in spelling, noun plurals, sentence structure, and general proofreading. Use proofreading marks to correct them.

SHEARMAN BROTHERS
415 Yonge Street
Toronto, ON M5B 2E7

Phone: (416) 502-8694 *Fax: (416) 502-7619* *Web: http://www.shearmanbros.com*

April 5, 200x

Ms. Judy Bender Bachman
The Daily News
11 Thornhill Drive
Dartmouth, NS B3B 1R9

Dear Ms. Bachman:

Thanks for the oportunity to contribute to the article. That you are writting about fast-food promotions. As an analyst with Shearman Brothers, I specialize in the fast-food and beverage industrys.

You specifically wanted information about what sells fast food. Actually, competition among the fast food giants has always been as much about appearances as reality. Its a lot like a three-ring circus, with flashy new showstoppers needed to keep men, woman, and children coming back. Some promotions by companys have been fiascos. I assume, however, that you are most interested in sucessful stategies such as the following:

- **Giveaways**. Fast-food giants suchas McDonald's use movie tie-ins and toy promotions that appeal children, who then persuade their parents to come into the stores.
- **Advertising**. Companys spend million on ad campaigns promoting expressions that they hope will become part of everyone's speech, such as classics like "You deserve a break today."
- **Food**. Nothing else matters if the food doesn't taste good. McDonald's, for example, grows its own potatos and raises cattle to ensure that its french frys and sandwichs meet rigid specifications.
- **Price**. Cutting prices increases sale, but usually for a short time only. In the end, price-cutting erodes profites. Another strategy is the repackaging of popular items in "value" combinations. Which is an effort to boost sales.
- **Convenience.** People often go to a fastfood restaurant on impulse, the more restaurants that a company has, the likelier that it will make a sale.

I hope theseideas are helpful to you in prepareing your article. If you use any of this material, I must submit your article to our lawyers for approval. Call me when you would like to talk further about this article.

Sincerely,

Paul Lahijanian

Paul Lahijanian
Senior Analyst

FOREST COMMUNICATION SERVICES
259 Water Street, Suite 400
Vancouver, BC V6B 1A2
(604) 647-2250
conferencing@forest.com

April 12, 200x

Ms. Mary Lou Chau
Networking Voices
3540 Freeport Boulevard
Halifax, NS B3J 2N2

Dear Ms. Chau:

We apreciate this opportunity to contribute to the magazine article. That you are writing about web conferencing for *Networking Voices.* My specialty here at Forest Communication is conferening services for North America.

Online meetings are becoming more frequent. And more necessary. Many companys find that such meetings save time and money. Participants can hold live, interactive meetings and share documents and presentations. With out ever leaving their offics or homes. Conferencing is simply more conveneint then having to attend meeting in person. Nearly all web conferencing providers offer a common set of user features that increase productivity and collaborative sucess. Let me summarize a few of these features:

- **Participant ID.** This feature displays on your screen the name of all attendees and indicates who are talking over the phone line.
- **PowerPoints/Document Sharring.** Presenters can show web-based visuals and describe them by talking on the telephone.
- **Polling/Surveys.** A virtual "show of hands" can speed consensus and shorten a meeting. Because these conferencing polls are anonymous, they are less intimidating then those taken in live meetings.
- **Whiteboard.** Just as in physical meetings, a whiteboard is handy for jotting down key points and recording brain storming ideas.
- **Archive.** If requested, all content can be archived so that participants who could not join can catch up as their schedule permit.

Web conferencing eliminates the need for travelling to meetings. And is especially effective for global teams and large groupes. If you would like a list of do's and don't's for web conferencing, please call me at (604) 647-2250.

Cordially,

Anderson M. Copley

Anderson M. Copley
Director, Conferencing Services

POSTTEST

Underline any incorrectly spelled nouns. Write the correct forms.

1. All the children were warned to be careful of the sharp knifes. ____________
2. These bunches of red tomatos look ripe enough to eat. ____________
3. Coyote's have been seen in the two valleys. ____________
4. In the 1990s many companys were searching for graduates with M.B.A.s. ____________
5. After several business crisis, we hired two troubleshooters. ____________

learning.web.ways

Many websites provide summaries of information about well-known companies. Some sites, such as Hoovers.com, allow you to see a capsule of information at no charge. For more extensive information, you must subscribe. You can find information such as a company's addresses (web and land), the names of its current officers, its subsidiary locations, its products, and its competition. You can even find out its annual revenue and other financial information. In this exercise you will search for information about the Hudson's Bay Company.

Goal: To learn to search for company data on the Web.

1. With your web browser on the screen, key the following URL: <**http://www.hoovers.com**>. Press **Enter**.
2. Ignore the advertising clutter, and place your cursor in the **Search Now** box.
3. Key in **Hudson's Bay** and click on the **Search Now** button.
4. When the **Company Search Results** page is fully loaded, you will see a heading in green print: **Hoover's Company Name Matches**. The first link, for Hudson's Bay Company, will get you the Hoover's free **Factsheet** on Hudson's Bay. On the Factsheet page, under **Competition,** click on **Read More about Hudson's Bay's competition**.
5. Scroll down the new page, and look for "Compare Hudson's Bay to its competition." This will yield a drop-down list of items you can choose from. Select **Department Stores & Discount Stores**. Click on **Update View**.
6. Scroll down the new page, and look for the **Recent Developments** section in the rightmost column. Under the heading *Canadian Retail Sales Grow,* study the information on the types of sales that have increased in the most recent period

---

1. knives 2. tomatoes 3. Coyotes 4. companies 5. crises

presented here. Which types of items have seen the sharpest rise in sales? Which have registered the slowest rate of growth?

7. In the same section, **Recent Developments**, find some of the promotional strategies the retail industry has used in the last year. Which ones strike you as potentially most effective?

End your session by clicking the **X** in the upper right corner of your browser. Your instructor may ask you to report on your findings.

C H A P T E R

Possessive Nouns

5

OBJECTIVES When you have completed the materials in this chapter, you will be able to do the following:

LEVEL I

- *Distinguish between possessive nouns and noun plurals.*
- *Follow five steps in using the apostrophe to show ownership.*

LEVEL II

- *Use apostrophe construction for animate nouns.*
- *Distinguish between descriptive nouns and possessive nouns.*
- *Make compound nouns, combined ownership nouns, organization names, and abbreviations possessive.*
- *Understand incomplete possessives.*
- *Avoid awkward possessives.*

LEVEL III

- *Make proper nouns possessive.*

PRETEST

Underline any incorrect possessive forms of nouns. Write correct versions in the spaces provided.

1. Some students loans carried lower interest rates than yours. ______________
2. Because of his training, Michael's salary is greater than Alans. ______________
3. Most landlords require two months rent in advance. ______________
4. Mr. Ross real talent lies in the electronics field. ______________
5. The Horowitzes real estate holdings are in the Eastern Townships. ______________

Thus far you have studied four kinds of nouns (concrete, abstract, common, and proper), and you have learned how to make nouns plural. In this chapter you will learn how to use the apostrophe to make nouns possessive.

LEVEL I

Hotlink

Here's another brief introduction to the apostrophe: **<http://www2.actden.com/writ_den/tips/sentence/puctuate.htm>**.

▶ Showing Possession With Apostrophes

Notice in the following phrases how possessive nouns show ownership, origin, authorship, or measurement:

Jack's computer (ownership)
Saskatchewan's citizens (origin)
Atwood's writings (authorship)
three years' time (measurement)

In expressing possession, speakers and writers have a choice. They may show possession with an apostrophe construction, or they may use a prepositional phrase with no apostrophe:

the computer of Jack
the citizens of Saskatchewan
the writings of Atwood
the time of three years

The use of a prepositional phrase to show ownership is more formal and tends to emphasize the ownership word (the object of the preposition). The use of the apostrophe construction to show ownership is more efficient and more natural, especially in conversation. In writing, however, placing the apostrophe can be perplexing. Here are five simple but effective steps that will help you write possessives correctly.

1. students' 2. Alan's 3. months' 4. Mr. Ross' or Ross's 5. Horowitzes'

Five Steps in Using the Apostrophe Correctly

1. *Look for possessive construction.* Usually two nouns appear together. The first noun shows ownership of (or a special relationship to) the second noun.

   the man['s] book
   the children['s] games
   a year['s] rent
   both doctors['] offices
   the musicians['] instruments

2. *Reverse the nouns.* Use the second noun to begin a prepositional phrase. The object of the preposition is the ownership word.

   book of the *man*
   games of the *children*
   rent of a *year*
   offices of both *doctors*
   instruments of the *musicians*

3. *Examine the ownership word.* To determine the correct placement of the apostrophe, you must know whether the ownership word is singular or plural.

4. *If the ownership word is singular, add apostrophe and* s.

   the man's book
   a year's rent

5. *If the ownership word is plural, you have two choices:*

   a. *If it ends in* s, *add only an apostrophe.*

      both doctors' offices
      the musicians' instruments

   b. *If the ownership word is plural but does not end in* s, *add an apostrophe and s.*

      the children's games
      men's health

A word of caution. Once people begin to study apostrophes, they sometimes use a shotgun approach on passages with words ending in *s*, indiscriminately peppering them with apostrophes. Do *not* use apostrophes for nouns that simply show more than one of something. In the sentence *These companies are opening new branches in the West,* no apostrophes are required. The words *companies* and *branches* are plural; they are not possessive. In addition, be careful to avoid changing the spelling of singular nouns when making them possessive. For example, the *secretary's* desk (meaning the desk of one secretary) is *not* spelled *secretaries'*.

Pay particular attention to the following possessive constructions. Perhaps the explanations and hints in parentheses will help you understand and remember these expressions.

a day's work (the work of one single day)
three days' work (the work of three days)
a dollar's worth (the worth of one single dollar)
your money's worth (the worth of your money)
today's weather (there can be only one *today*)
tomorrow's work (there can be only one *tomorrow*)
the shareholders' meeting (we usually assume that a meeting involves more than one person)

Spot the Blooper

From Lois and Selma DeBakey's collection of bad medical writing: "The receptionist called the patients names." (How does the omitted apostrophe alter the meaning?)

Hotlink

A brief overview of how to show possession correctly using the apostrophe is hosted by Hot Potato Grammar at **<http://xnet.rrc.mb.ca/leshanson/Hot_Potato/Grammar_PPT/Using_Apostrophes.doc>**.

Study Tip

Whenever you have any doubt about using an apostrophe, always put the expression into an "of" phrase. You'll immediately recognize the ownership word and see whether it is singular or plural and whether it ends in *s*.

The guides for possessive construction presented thus far cover the majority of possessives found in professional writing.

Complete the reinforcement exercises for Level I on pp. 82–84.

LEVEL II

▶ Challenging Possessive Constructions

You can greatly improve your skill in using apostrophes by understanding the following especially challenging possessive constructions.

1. *Animate versus inanimate nouns.* As a matter of style, some writers prefer to reserve the apostrophe construction for nouns that represent people, animals, and other living entities (such as trees or organizations). For other nouns they use prepositional phrases or simple adjectives.

   roof of the car or car roof (better than *car's roof*)
   colour of the desk or the desk colour (better than *desk's colour*)
   heat of the motor or motor heat (better than *motor's heat*)

Study Tip

To identify descriptive nouns, ask if ownership is involved. Is *industry* possessed by *electronics*? Does *record* belong to *earnings*? When the answer is no, omit the apostrophe.

2. *Descriptive versus possessive nouns.* When nouns are used as adjectives to provide description or identification only, the possessive form is *not* used. Writers have most problems with descriptive nouns ending in *s*, such as *Claims* Department. No apostrophe is needed, just as none is necessary in *Legal* Department.

   Human Resources Department (*not* Resources' Department)
   the electronics industry (*not* electronics' industry)
   earnings record (*not* earnings' record)

3. *Compound nouns.* Make compound nouns possessive by adding an apostrophe or an *'s* to the final element of the compound.

   his father-in-law's property
   onlookers' interest
   notary public's seal

4. *Incomplete possessives.* When the second noun in a possessive noun construction is unstated, the first noun is nevertheless treated as possessive.

   You'll find bond paper at the stationer's [store].
   Let's meet at Patrick's [home] after the game.
   This year's sales are higher than last year's [sales].

Study Tip

Look at the object owned (*rights, business,* etc.). If that object is singular, ownership is usually combined.

5. *Separate or combined ownership.* When two nouns express separate ownership, make both possessive. When two nouns express combined ownership, make only the second one possessive.

Separate Ownership	**Combined Ownership**
landlords' and tenants' rights	the husband and wife's business
Mike's and Sam's cellphones	my aunt and uncle's house

6. *Names of organizations.* Organizations with possessives in their names may or may not use apostrophes. Follow the style used by the individual organization. (Consult the organization's stationery or a directory listing.)

Metro Tenants Legal Services	Harvey's Restaurants
Ontario Secondary School Teachers' Federation	Sears

Spot the Blooper

From a Sears advertisement: "Are you giving away your kids old clothes as fast as you're buying them new ones?"

7. *Abbreviations.* Make abbreviations possessive by following the same guidelines as for animate nouns.

the CMA's ruling	All Ph.D.s' dissertations
the CBC's coverage	Ticketmaster Canada Inc.'s sales

8. *Awkward possessives.* When the addition of an apostrophe results in an awkward construction, show ownership by using a prepositional phrase.

Awkward	**Improved**
my brothers-in-law's opinions	opinions of my brothers-in-law
your neighbour's doctor's telephone number	telephone number of your neighbour's doctor
my professor, Dr. Aller's, office	office of my professor, Dr. Aller

Study Tip

To avoid an awkward possessive, use an *of* phrase starting with the object owned, such as *the advice of my sister's lawyer.*

Complete the reinforcement exercises for Level II on pp. 84–85.

LEVEL III

▶ Additional Guideline

You have learned to follow five steps in identifying possessive constructions and in placing the apostrophe correctly. The guides presented thus far cover most possessive constructions. Determining the possessive form of a few proper nouns, however, requires a refinement of Step 4.

Let us briefly review the five-step plan for placing the apostrophe in noun possessives, adding a refinement to the fourth step.

1. Look for possessive construction. (Usually, though not always, two nouns appear together.)
2. Reverse the nouns.
3. Examine the ownership word.
4. If the ownership word is singular, add an apostrophe and *s*. *However, if the ownership word is a name ending in an s sound, you may choose to add only an apostrophe* (see next page).
5. a. If the ownership word is plural and ends in *s*, add only an apostrophe.
   b. If the ownership word is plural but does not end in *s*, add an apostrophe and *s*.

Hotlink

The University of Victoria has an excellent web page that offers a series of links to its materials on the use of the apostrophe at **<http://web.uvic.ca/wguide/Pages/MasterToc.html>**.

Spot the Blooper

Announcement pasted on top of each Domino's pizza box: "We accept all competitors coupons."

Study Tip

The word *the* preceding a name is a clue that the name is being used in a plural sense. For example, *the Rosses* means the entire Ross family.

▶ Making Difficult Proper Nouns Possessive

Of all possessive forms, individuals' names—especially those ending in *s* sounds—are the most puzzling to students, and understandably so. Even experts don't always agree on the possessive form for singular proper nouns.

Traditionalists, as represented in *The Chicago Manual of Style* and *The Modern Language Association Style Manual,* prefer adding *'s* to troublesome *singular proper* nouns that end in *s* sounds. On the other hand, writers of more popular literature, as represented in *The Associated Press Stylebook and Libel Manual,* prefer the simpler style of adding just an apostrophe to singular proper nouns. You may apply either style, but be consistent. Please note in the examples below that the style choice applies *only* to singular names ending in *s* sounds. Plural names are always made possessive with the addition of an apostrophe only. Study the examples shown.

Singular Name	Singular Possessive—Traditional	Singular Possessive—Popular	Plural Possessive
Mrs. Jones	Mrs. Jones's	Mrs. Jones'	the Joneses'
Mr. Morris	Mr. Morris's	Mr. Morris'	the Morrises'
Mrs. Lopez	Mrs. Lopez's	Mrs. Lopez'	the Lopezes'
Miss Schwartz	Miss Schwartz's	Miss Schwartz'	the Schwartzes'

Complete the reinforcement exercises for Level III on pp. 86–87.

HOTLINE QUERIES

Question: Where should the apostrophe go in *employee's handbook*?

Answer: This is tricky because the writer of that phrase must decide whether he or she considers the handbook from one employee's point of view or from all employees' points of view. Depending upon the writer's intention, the apostrophe could be justified for either position. The trend seems to favour the singular construction (*employee's handbook,* one handbook per employee). Likewise, we write *owner's manual, seller's market,* and *writer's cramp.* You should also know that a few organizations prefer to use these terms as adjectives: *employee handbook, driver license, owner manual.*

Question: I'm addressing a letter to the Canadian Nurses Association. What salutation shall I use? One person in our office suggested *Gentlewomen.* Is this being used?

Answer: I recommend that you use *Ladies and Gentlemen* since both male and female nurses are members of the association. In fact, this salutation is appropriate for any organization in which men and women may be represented in management. I would not use *Gentlewomen* because it sounds artificial.

Businesses and individuals can avoid sexism in language without using stilted constructions. Salutations such as *Dear Sir* and *Gentlemen* are no longer used. Today we are more sensitive to women as employees, managers, and executives. The use of awkward terms like *Gentlewomen* or *Gentlepersons,* however, is an overreaction and should be avoided. Probably the best approach is to address specific people. Try to find the name of the individual you should be addressing.

Question: Should *underprepared* be hyphenated? I can't find it in my dictionary.

Answer: The prefixes *under* and *over* are not followed by hyphens. These prefixes join the main word: *underpaid, underprivileged, undersecretary, overbook, overeager, overnight,* and so forth.

Question: My boss is ready to send out a letter that says, *I respectfully call you and your client's attention to* .... What's wrong with this? How can I make *you* possessive?

Answer: The best way to handle this awkward wording is to avoid using the possessive form. Use a prepositional phrase instead (*I respectfully call to the attention of you and your client* ...).

Question: Here at the Cancer Society we have a bureau of speakers. Where should the apostrophe go when we use the possessive form of the word *speakers*?

Answer: *Speakers' bureau.*

Question: As the holiday season approaches, I'm wondering whether it's *Season's Greetings* or *Seasons' Greetings.*

Answer: Because you are referring to one season, it's *Season's Greetings.*

Question: I have a problem with the following sentence from a legal document involving a restaurant chain called Denny's: *The plaintiff was in fact fired ostensibly for violating Denny's alcoholic beverage service policy.* How do I make possessive a proper name that is already possessive?

Answer: As you suspected, you can't add another apostrophe. In the interests of clarity, consider the name descriptive, thus avoiding an additional *'s,* and write *Denny's alcoholic beverage service policy.* By the same reasoning, you would not add another apostrophe to anything possessed by *McDonald's.*

Question: In preparing an announcement for sales reps, our sales manager wrote about a *two months' training period.* I wanted to make it a *two-month training period.* Who is right?

Answer: Actually, you are both correct! The expression *two months' training period* is possessive (training period of two months). If the expression is *two-month training period,* it is descriptive and no apostrophe is required. Only a slight difference in wording distinguishes a descriptive phrase from a possessive phrase, and sometimes it is hard to tell them apart.

NAME ______________________

CHAPTER 5 Reinforcement Exercises

LEVEL I

A. (Self-check) Rewrite the following phrases without apostrophes. Use prepositional phrases instead.

	Revision
Example: the trainee's hours	hours of the trainee
1. the defendant's pleas	pleas of the defendant
2. this client's email message	email message of this client
3. three women's ideas	ideas of three woman
4. our company's policy	policy of our company
5. your money's worth	worth of your money
6. a beginner's luck	luck of a beginner
7. two years' time	time of two years
8. her parents' wishes	wishes of her parents
9. the children's education	
10. six months' interest	

Check your answers.

B. Using apostrophes, change the following prepositional phrases into possessive constructions. Ownership words are underlined.

Example: compensation of <u>men</u>	men's compensation
1. questions of the job <u>candidate</u>	candidate's' questions
2. rights of <u>patients</u>	Patients' rights
3. permit for a <u>learner</u>	learner's permit
4. interest of ten <u>months</u>	months' interest
5. addresses of <u>customers</u>	customers' addresses
6. advertisement of the <u>agency</u>	agency's advertisement
7. prices of <u>competitors</u>	competitors' prices.
8. duties of the <u>treasurer</u>	treasure's duties

1. pleas of the defendant 2. email message of this client 3. ideas of three women 4. policy of our company 5. worth of your money 6. luck of a beginner 7. time of two years 8. wishes of her parents 9. education of the children 10. interest of six months

9. delay of a <u>month</u> ______

10. meeting of <u>shareholders</u> ______

C. In the following sentences, use the appropriate possessive form of the word in parentheses.

1. Success depends on a (company) capacity to deliver. ______
2. Search engines can find only a fraction of the (Web) vast contents. ______
3. Customers expect a (dollar) worth of value for a dollar spent. ______
4. In just one (day) email, the manager receives as many as 250 messages. ______
5. Both (clerk) salaries will be reviewed next quarter. ______
6. Most (student) difficulties lie in recognizing possessives. ______
7. Many management firms will tailor their services and charges to a (client) needs. ______

D. Underline the errors in possessive construction in the following sentences. Write the correct form at the right. If the sentence is correct as it stands, write *C*.

Example: Some <u>students</u> cars were ticketed. students'

1. Every passengers bags must be X-rayed and some will be opened. ______
2. Three months interest will be due in four days. ______
3. Success depends on a companies capacity to deliver. ______
4. The four astronomers theories created international news. ______
5. A customers credit card may be used as safely on the Internet as in a restaurant. ______
6. Some companies are cutting expenses by requiring employees, customers, and vendors to communicate by email. ______
7. An inventors patent protects an invention for seventeen years. ______
8. At each buyers expense, quality upgrades may be substituted. ______
9. You have exactly four days in which to find new fire and liability insurance policies for the buildings. ______
10. All taxpayers returns are checked by computer. ______
11. Many of Disneys animated films are made in Vancouver, North America's second-largest film production centre. ______
12. David Lees salary is higher than that of the other clerks because he has greater responsibilities. ______
13. Camille could not find her name on the voters list. ______
14. A number of changes have occurred in the composition of our Board of Trustees. ______
15. Police officers checked all drivers licenses at two checkpoints. ______

NAME ______________________________

LEVEL II

A. **(Self-check)** For each of the following sentences, underline any possessive construction that could be improved. Write an improved form in the space provided. If the sentence is acceptable as it stands, write *C*.

Examples: Our office's roof is leaking. — The roof of our office

The meeting Friday is at Ellens. — Ellen's

1. The car's brakes are worn. ____________
2. The Jones' brothers both play hockey. ____________
3. Lisa's and Jason's new car is very expensive. ____________
4. This company's product line is superior to that companys. ____________
5. The first runner-ups prize of $200 went to Chandra Lewis. ____________
6. Sales of shares were stimulated by the CRTC's ruling. ____________
7. She was elected by members of the Ontario Secondary School Teacher's Federation. ____________
8. A notary publics seal is required on these documents. ____________
9. Most ladies and mens raincoats are reduced in price. ____________
10. Is your sister-in-laws job downtown? ____________

Check your answers.

B. For each of the following sentences, underline any possessive construction that could be improved. Write an improved form in the space provided. If the sentence is acceptable as it stands, write *C*.

1. What is that sticky substance on the computer's keys? ____________
2. The King and Queen's limousine approached slowly. ____________
3. Web graphics must be designed with the audience's browsers in mind. ____________
4. On the second floor is the chief of staffs office. ____________
5. All beneficiaries names must be submitted when we issue policies. ____________
6. NATOs member countries include Canada and France. ____________
7. They took their complaint to small claim's court. ____________
8. This year's computer sales outdistanced last years. ____________
9. Numerous employees personnel folders will be reviewed. ____________

1. The brakes of the car or The car brakes 2. Jones 3. Lisa 4. company's 5. runner-up's 6. C
7. Teachers' 8. notary public's 9. ladies', men's 10. sister-in-law's

10. Several new roses were described in news releases. ________________

11. Both the husband's and wife's signatures must be secured before the sale is valid. ________________

12. The human resource's manager commanded the group's attention. ________________

13. At least a dozen buyers and sellers finances were scrutinized. ________________

14. The last power failure happened on New Years' Eve. ________________

15. Your totals for the last three columns are certainly different from Carols. ________________

16. Because of the gravity of the offence, the Crown attorneys staff is investigating. ________________

17. Lyon & Co.s annual sale is scheduled to begin in three days. ________________

18. Two of the table's legs were damaged in transit. ________________

19. Although I'm interested in the electronics' field, I have not settled on a definite career. ________________

20. Were they at Marions last Saturday night? ________________

C. Rewrite these sentences to remedy awkward or incorrect possessives. (*Hint:* Start your sentence with the word that is owned.)

Example: My brother's friend's car is available. ____The car of my brother's friend is available.____

1. My cousin's friend's cellphone was lost.

____

____

2. Brent Harris, my dentist's, practice is flourishing.

____

____

3. Were both your sisters-in-law's cars ticketed on the same day?

____

____

4. The engineer's assistant's computer held all the necessary equations.

____

____

5. My boss's friend's motorhome is always parked in the company lot.

____

____

NAME ______________________________

LEVEL III

A. (**Self-check**) Select the acceptable possessive form(s).

1. Several of the (a) seamstresses', (b) seamstress's machines were broken. ________
2. We can't locate (a) Francises', (b) Francis' or Francis's file. ________
3. Is that a realtor's sign on the (a) Harrises's, (b) Harrises' home? ________
4. Only one (a) waitress's, (b) waitresses' service was criticized. ________
5. Cheryl took Dr. (a) Fox' or Fox's, (b) Foxes' prescription to a pharmacy. ________
6. All (a) creditor's, (b) creditors' claims will be honoured. ________
7. Have you seen Annie (a) Leibovitz' or Leibovitz's, (b) Leibovitzes' photographs? ________
8. Please verify Mrs. (a) Davises', (b) Davis's or Davis' hours. ________
9. Have you noticed that the (a) Horowitzes, (b) Horowitzes' have a new car? ________
10. Are you using the computer to schedule your (a) bosses', (b) boss's appointments? (One boss) ________

Check your answers.

B. Fill in the singular possessive forms for the two styles shown below.

Name	Traditional Style	Popular Style
Example: [Mr. Jones] suit	Mr. Jones's suit	Mr. Jones' suit
1. [Ms. Reis] purse		
2. [Chris] motorcycle		
3. [Dr. Cortez] office		
4. [Miss Mertz] letter		
5. [Lois] computer		

1. a 2. b 3. b 4. a 5. a 6. b 7. a 8. b 9. a 10. b

C. Review of Levels I, II, and III. Correct any errors in possessives in the following sentences. Write the corrected forms in the space provided.

1. I believe that Russ letter is on the top of the pile. __________
2. His landlord said that four months rent was due. __________
3. Mrs. Otis paycheque did not reflect the deduction. __________
4. We were all invited to the party at the Thomas. __________
5. Despite a weeks delay the package finally arrived. __________
6. I can find other peoples errors but not my own. __________
7. All city council representatives were invited to the homeowners meeting. __________
8. Our records show that Mr. Murray account has an error. __________
9. In seven years time the loan will be repaid in full. __________
10. One witnesses testimony was questioned. __________
11. The Moskowitz two sons are enrolled in a Saskatchewan college. __________
12. Do you feel that you got your moneys worth? __________
13. After three days practice all trainees qualified. __________
14. Today's weather is much better than yesterday. __________
15. Elvis home, Graceland, is located in Memphis, Tennessee. __________
16. If our departments had been aware of each others needs, we could have shared our inventories. __________
17. Although Arthur's car was only slightly damaged, Mrs. Lopezes required major repairs. __________
18. Our mens team placed second in the hockey championship. __________
19. Many artists works will be on display at the exhibit. __________
20. You must examine a contractors licence before agreeing to any work. __________

D. Optional Writing. Your instructor may ask you to complete this exercise on a separate sheet.

Write ten original sentences to illustrate the possessive forms of the following words: *Tiffany, two years, driver, Jason and Ann, waitress, a week, customers, host, editor-in-chief, the Cosbys.* Underline the possessive form in each sentence.

Editor's Challenge

The following personal business letter and community announcement contain intentional errors in sentence structure, plural nouns, possessive nouns, and general proofreading. Use standard proofreading marks (see the inside front cover) to show your corrections.

2320 Centennial Road
Oshawa, ON L1G 8K7
February 9, 200x

Mr. Jonathon Benson
Benson Brothers Management Services
368 Glenlake Ave.
Toronto, ON M9B 2B4

Dear Mr. Bensen:

SUBJECT: MANAGING APARTMENT COMPLEX IN DON MILLS

Please send me more information about your companys managment service for apartment owners' I especially would like answers to the following questions.

What are your fees to manage an apartment complex with six unit? Do you take care of renting the units when they become vacant? What percentage of all renters payments do you keep?

Will you enforce a list of do's and don't's that the owner provides? Do you require the last months rent in advance, do you maintain lawyers to handle legal problems?

Its now my responsibility to care for my father-in-laws six-unit apartment complex in Don Mills. This complex is 23 years old with all units occupied. Although we expect to have two vacancys in April. Your firms management services' may be exactly what I need. Since I do not live near the apartment complex. Please respond to my questions before March 1. So that I may evaluate the pro's and con's of your services.

Sincerely,

Laura W. Stephens

Laura W. Stephens

GYPSY MOTHS

We have receive some updated information about the gypsy moth problem in the province, and the citys Forrestry Department has again identified a gypsy moth infestation in certain part's of our area.

Last year an airal application of Btk, a biological pest control agent, was organized in the neighbourhoods immediately surrounding St. Georges' Golf Club, this year another aerial spraying is being recomended further out.

The gypsy moth caterpillar is a devastating pest. And left unchecked could cause severe damage to the tree canopy in our neighborhood's. Oak trees and maple tress are favourite targets, but in an infestation the caterpillers will attack other trees as well.

Recently the Cities Parks and Environment Comittee approved a staff report that outlines a proposal to control the gypsy moths. To learn more about the the problem orto obtain a copy of the Forestry Department's report on it, call the Urbane Forestry Department at (416) 338-TREE.

POSTTEST

Underline any incorrect possessive forms. Write correct versions.

1. New dividends were announced at the shareholders meeting. ________
2. This month's sales figures were better than last months. ________
3. Three companys tax returns were audited. ________
4. Mrs. Holtz secretary located all the accounts receivable. ________
5. The three witnesses testimonies required seven court days. ________

1. shareholders' 2. last month's 3. companies' 4. Holtz' or Holtz's 5. witnesses'

learning.web.ways

Your boss is irritated by unwanted email messages, such as "Earn Big Money Working at Home!" She asks you to use the Web to find a way to stop this misuse of her computer. You decide to use a well-known search engine, Google.

Goal: To learn to refine search terms.

1. With your web browser on the screen, key the following URL in the Search box: **<http://www.google.ca>**.
2. Look at the Google opening page and locate the **Search** box.
3. Key in the following search term: **email**. Press **Enter** or click **Search**.
4. Note how many results were obtained. You will see that over 3,430,000 pages include the word *email*. Scan over the site titles presented. See any relevant sites?
5. To reduce the number of "hits," you must refine your search term. In the **Search** box, key a new search term: **"unwanted email**." Make sure to enclose the words in quotation marks.
6. Check the number of hits. This refined search term still brings up over 1,410,000 items.
7. Go back to the **Search** box and insert a new search item. Include quotation marks: **"unwanted email/spam**." This time Google will find only those sites that include this whole phrase as a unit.
8. Although you will again see a large number of hits, some of them will certainly look promising. Scan over the first page of Google results and click on a page that seems to offer the answer to this question: What can an email user do to stop unwanted email and spam?
9. Print one or two pages with advice on how to deal with unwanted email.
10. End your session by clicking on the **X** in the upper right corner of your browser. Send your instructor an email message summarizing what you have learned.

C H A P T E R

Personal Pronouns

6

OBJECTIVES When you have completed the materials in this chapter, you will be able to do the following:

LEVEL I

- *Use personal pronouns correctly as subjects and objects.*
- *Distinguish between personal possessive pronouns (such as* its*) and contractions (such as* it's*).*

LEVEL II

- *Choose the correct pronoun in compound constructions, comparatives, and appositives.*
- *Use reflexive pronouns correctly.*

LEVEL III

- *Use subjective-case pronouns with subject complements.*
- *Select the correct pronouns for use with the infinitive* to be.

PRETEST

Underline the correct pronouns.

1. Please send the completed form to (I, me, myself) by Friday.
2. (Us, We) employees receive additional benefits in September.
3. No one in the office deserved the award more than (her, she).
4. Are you sure it was (her, she) who called me yesterday morning?
5. Reliable managers like you and (he, him) are difficult to retain.

As you will remember from Chapter 2 (p. 20), pronouns are words that substitute for nouns and other pronouns. They enable us to speak and write without awkward repetition. Grammatically, pronouns may be divided into seven types (personal, relative, interrogative, demonstrative, indefinite, reflexive, and reciprocal). Rather than consider all seven pronoun types, this textbook will be concerned only with those pronouns that cause difficulty in use.

---

1. me 2. We 3. she 4. she 5. him

LEVEL I

Spot the Blooper

From Marilyn Monroe in *Seven-Year Itch*: "A girl like I hardly ever gets to meet interesting men."

Hotlink

For another introduction to the objective or accusative versus subjective or nominative forms and uses of personal pronouns, see **<http://www.writersblock.ca/tips/monthtip/tipoct98.htm>**.

Spot the Blooper

From a commercial greeting card: "If the stars were champagne bubbles spilled across the sky . . . that enchanted night would be a toast to you and I. Happy Anniversary!"

▶ Personal Pronouns

Personal pronouns indicate the person speaking, the person spoken to, or the person or thing spoken of. Notice in the following table that the personal pronouns change their form (or *case*) depending upon who is speaking (called the *person*), how many are speaking (the *number*), and the sex (or *gender*) of the speaker. For example, the third person feminine singular objective case is *her*. Most personal pronoun errors by speakers and writers involve faulty usage of case forms. Study this table to avoid errors in personal pronoun use, and be sure that you understand how these pronouns function in sentences.

	Subjective Case*		Objective Case		Possessive Case	
	Singular	**Plural**	**Singular**	**Plural**	**Singular**	**Plural**
First person (person speaking)	I	we	me	us	my, mine	our, ours
Second person (person spoken to)	you	you	you	you	your, yours	your, yours
Third person (person or thing spoken of)	he, she, it	they	him, her, it	them	his, her, hers, its	their, theirs

Basic Use of the Subjective Case

Subjective-case pronouns are used primarily as the subjects of verbs. Every verb or verb phrase, regardless of its position in a sentence, has a subject. If that subject is a pronoun, it must be in the subjective case.

I thought *he* was texting someone.
They asked if *we* had valid passports.

Basic Use of the Objective Case

Objective-case pronouns are used most commonly as objects of verbs or objects of prepositions.

Object of a Verb. When pronouns act as direct or indirect objects of verbs, they must be in the objective case.

Bob asked *her* for help. (direct object)
The manager gave *them* a building map. (indirect object)

Object of a Preposition. The objective case is used for pronouns that are objects of prepositions.

Just between *you* and *me,* profits are slipping.
A letter signed by all of *us* was sent to *him.*

When the words *between, but, like,* and *except* are used as prepositions, errors in pronoun case are likely to occur. To avoid such errors, isolate the prepositional phrase, and

* *Some authorities prefer the term* nominative case.

then use an objective-case pronoun as the object of the preposition. Example: *Every employee [but Tom and her] completed the form.*

Basic Use of the Possessive Case

Possessive pronouns show ownership. Unlike possessive nouns, possessive pronouns require no apostrophes. Study these five possessive pronouns: *hers, yours, ours, theirs, its.* Notice the absence of apostrophes. Do not confuse possessive pronouns with contractions. Contractions are shortened (contracted) forms of subjects and verbs, such as *it's* (for *it is* or *it has*), *there's* (for *there is* or *there has*), *they're* (for *they are*), and *you're* (for *you are*). In contractions the apostrophes indicate omitted letters.

Possessive Pronouns	**Contractions**
Theirs are the first few seats.	*There's* not an empty seat left.
The cat is cleaning *its* fur.	*It's* a household pet.
Your presentation will be excellent.	*You're* the next speaker.
Their anniversary is tomorrow.	*They're* going to have a party.

Study Tip

Never use *it's* unless you can substitute *it is* or *it has;* if you cannot, use the pronoun *its.*

As you learned in Chapter 2, some possessive forms function as adjectives when they describe nouns (*its fur, your presentation,* for example).

Complete the reinforcement exercises for Level I on pp. 98–99.

▶ Challenges in Using Personal Pronouns

LEVEL II

Compound Subjects and Objects

When a pronoun appears in combination with a noun or another pronoun, special attention must be given to case selection. Use this technique to help you choose the correct pronoun case: Ignore the extra noun or pronoun and its related conjunction, and consider separately the pronoun in question to determine what the case should be.

[Larry and] *he* enrolled in the class. (Ignore *Larry and.*) (compound subject)
Will you permit [Tony and] *them* to join you? (Ignore *Tony and.*) (compound object)
Laura asked [you and] *me* for advice. (Ignore *you and.*) (compound object)

Hotlink

A page at **<http://www.world-english.org/pronouns.htm>** lists possessive and reflexive pronouns and offers two user-friendly quizzes on them.

Notice in the first sentence, for example, that when *Larry and* is removed, it is much easier to recognize that the pronoun *he* must be selected because it functions as the subject of the verb.

Comparatives

In statements of comparison, words are often implied but not actually stated. To determine pronoun case in only partially complete comparative statements introduced by *than* or *as,* always mentally finish the comparative by adding the implied missing words.

Jon earns as much as *they.* (Jon earns as much as *they* [not *them*] earn.)
Lisa spells better than *he.* (... better than *he* [not *him*] spells.)
Tardiness annoys Mr. Britton as much as *me.* (... as much as it annoys *me* [not *I*].)

Spot the Blooper

Paris Hilton wore a T-shirt that said "Thats hot" on the front and "Your not" on the back.

Appositives

Appositives explain or rename previously mentioned nouns or pronouns. A pronoun appositive takes the same case as the noun or pronoun with which it is in apposition. In order to determine more easily what pronoun case to use for a pronoun in combination with an appositive, temporarily ignore the appositive.

> *We* [consumers] are protected by laws. (Ignore *consumers.*)
> Precautions were taken by *us* [neighbours]. (Ignore *neighbours.*)

Spot the Blooper

From the side of a General Mills Cinnamon Toast Crunch cereal box: "What gives Cinnamon Crunch it's totally intense taste?"

Reflexive Pronouns

Reflexive pronouns end in *-self* or *-selves* and emphasize or reflect on their antecedents (the nouns or pronouns previously mentioned).

> The president *himself* presented the award. (Emphasizes *president.*)
> We hope the matter will resolve *itself.* (Refers to *matter.*)

Errors result when reflexive pronouns are used instead of personal pronouns. If a sentence has no previously mentioned noun or pronoun, use a personal pronoun instead of a reflexive pronoun.

> Send the proposed agenda to either Bradley or *me.* (Not *myself*)
> Bill Stewart and *I* analyzed the numerous possibilities. (Not *myself*)

Complete the reinforcement exercises for Level II on pp. 100–101.

LEVEL III

▶ Advanced Uses of Subjective-Case Pronouns

Although the following applications appear infrequently, careful speakers and writers try to understand why certain pronoun forms are used.

Subject Complement

As we saw earlier in this chapter, subjective-case pronouns usually function as subjects of verbs. Less frequently, subjective-case pronouns also perform as subject complements. A pronoun that follows a linking verb and renames the subject must be in the subjective case. Be especially alert to the linking verb forms *am, is, are, was, were, be, being,* and *been.*

> It *was I* who placed the order. (Not *me*)
> I'm sure it *is she* who usually answers the telephone. (Not *her*)
> If you *were I,* what would you do? (Not *me*)

Study Tip

Whenever a pronoun follows a linking verb, that pronoun should be in the subjective case.

When a verb of several words appears in a phrase, look at the final element of the verb phrase. If it is a linking verb, use a subjective pronoun.

> It *might have been they* who made the bid. (Not *them*)
> The driver *could have been he.* (Not *him*)
> If the manager *had been she,* your money would have been refunded. (Not *her*)

In conversation it is common to say, *It is me,* or more likely, *It's me.* Careful speakers and writers, though, normally use subjective-case pronouns after linking verbs. If the resulting constructions sound too "formal," revise your sentences appropriately. For example, instead of *It is I who placed the order,* use *I placed the order.*

Infinitive *To Be* Without a Subject

Infinitives are the present forms of verbs preceded by *to;* for example, *to sit, to run,* and *to walk.* Subjective pronouns are used following the infinitive *to be* when the infinitive has no subject. In this instance the infinitive joins a complement (not an object) to the subject.

Her twin sister was often taken to be *she.* (The infinitive *to be* has no subject; *she* is the complement of the subject *sister.*)
Darrell was mistakenly thought to be *I.* (The infinitive *to be* has no subject; *I* is the complement of the subject *Darrell.*)
Why would Jennifer want to be *she?* (The infinitive *to be* has no subject; *she* is the complement of the subject *Jennifer.*)

Hotlink

For more advanced work on pronouns—and helpful review/quiz material—look at Chapter 13 of this online grammar "book" prepared by Capital Community College: **<http://www.ccc.commnet.edu/sensen/>**.

Infinitive *To Be* With a Subject

When the infinitive *to be* has a subject, any pronoun following it will function as an object. Therefore, the pronoun following the infinitive will take the objective case. Note: the subject immediately precedes the infinitive as in the following examples.

The interviewer believed the best candidate to be *her.* (The subject of the infinitive *to be* is *candidate;* therefore, the pronoun functions as an object. Try it another way: *The interviewer believed her to be the best candidate.* You would not say, *The interviewer believed she to be the best candidate.*)
John expected the callers to be *us.* (The subject of the infinitive *to be* is *callers;* therefore, the pronoun functions as an object.)
Colonel Dunn judged the winner to be *him.* (The subject of the infinitive *to be* is *winner;* therefore, use the objective-case pronoun *him.*)

Spot the Blooper

From *The Province* [North Vancouver]: "Dr. Ivan Rebeyka sees the day when surgeons like he will repair tiny hearts in the womb."

Whenever you have selected a pronoun for the infinitive *to be* and you want to test its correctness, try reversing the pronoun and its antecedent. For example, *We thought the winner to be her* (We *thought her* [not *she*] *to be the winner*) or *Cheryl was often taken to be she* (*She* [not *her*] *was often taken to be Cheryl).*

Summary of Pronoun Cases

The following table summarizes the uses of subjective- and objective-case pronouns.

Subjective Case	
Subject of the verb:	*They* are skydivers.
Subject complement:	That is *he.*
Infinitive *to be* without a subject:	Ed pretended to be *he.*
Objective Case	
Direct or indirect objcct of a verb:	We interviewed *her.*
	Give *him* another chance.
Object of a preposition:	Send the order to *him.*
Object of an infinitive:	Jane promised to call *us.*
Infinitive *to be* with subject:	We thought the guests to be *them.*

▶ Types of Pronouns

For those of you interested in a total view, here is a summary of the seven types of pronouns, with sentences illustrating each type. This list is presented only for your interest, not for potential testing.

1. **Personal pronouns** replace nouns or other pronouns.

Subjective case:	I, we, you, he, she, it, they
Objective case:	me, us, you, him, her, it, them
Possessive case:	my, mine, our, ours, your, yours, his, her, hers, its, their, theirs

Dr. Benton said *she* put *her* signature on *it* yesterday.

2. **Relative pronouns** join subordinate clauses to antecedents. Examples: who, whose, whom, which, that, whoever, whomever, whichever, whatever.

He is the candidate *whom* we all admire.

3. **Interrogative pronouns** replace nouns in a question. Examples: who, whose, whom, which, what.

Who is sitting here?

4. **Demonstrative pronouns** designate specific persons or things. Examples: this, these, that, those.

This must be the work request we need.

5. **Indefinite pronouns** replace nouns: everyone, anyone, someone, each, everybody, anybody, somebody, one, none, some, most, all.

Everybody needs adequate nourishment.

6. **Reflexive pronouns** emphasize or reflect on antecedents. Examples: myself, yourself, himself, herself, itself, oneself, ourselves, yourselves, themselves.

The CEO *himself* answered that letter.

7. **Reciprocal pronouns** indicate mutual relationship. Examples: each other, one another.

The three chief executive officers consulted *one another* before making the announcement.

Complete the reinforcement exercises for Level III on pp. 102–104.

Career Tip

"Whatever your program in college, be sure to include courses in writing and speaking. Managers must constantly write instructions, reports, memos, letters, and survey conclusions. If this comes hard to you, it will hold you back."
—James A. Newman and Alexander Roy in *Climbing the Corporate Matterhorn*

Spot the Blooper

Advice from a Canadian telephone company booklet: "Hang up if the caller ... doesn't identify themself to your satisfaction."

HOTLINE QUERIES

Question: On the radio I recently heard a talk-show host say, *My producer and myself.* A little later the same host said, *Send any inquiries to the station or myself at this address.* This sounded half right and half wrong, but I would have trouble explaining the problem. Can you help?

Answer: The problem is a common one: use of a reflexive pronoun *(myself)* when it has no preceding noun on which to reflect. Correction: *My producer and I* and *Send inquiries to the station or me.* Reflexive pronouns like *myself* should be used only with obvious antecedents, such as *I, myself, will take the calls.* Individuals in the media often misuse reflexive pronouns, perhaps to avoid sounding egocentric with overuse of *I* and *me*.

Question: I have a question about the use of *etc.* in this sentence: *We are installing better lighting, acoustical tile, sound barriers, and etc.* Should I use two periods at the end of the sentence, and does a comma precede *etc.*?

Answer: Although the use of *etc.* (meaning "and so forth") is generally avoided, do not, if it is to be used, include the redundant word *and.* When *etc.* is found at the end of a sentence, one comma should precede it. When *etc.* appears in the middle of a sentence, two commas should set it off. For example, *Better lighting, acoustical tile, sound barriers, etc., are being installed. Never* use two periods at the end of a sentence, even if the sentence ends with an abbreviation, such as *etc.*

Question: Should a hyphen be used in the word *dissimilar*?

Answer: No. Prefixes such as *dis* and *un* do not require hyphens. Even when the final consonant of a prefix is repeated in the initial letter of the root word, no hyphens are used: *disspirited, misspell, unnamed.*

Question: I thought I knew the difference between *to* and *too,* but could you provide me with a quick review?

Answer: *To* may serve as a preposition (*I'm going to the store*), and it may also serve as part of an infinitive construction (*to sign his name*). The adverb *too* may be used to mean "also" (*Andrea will attend too*). In addition, the word *too* may be used to indicate "to an excessive extent" (*the letter is too long*).

Question: I have a lot of trouble with the word *extension,* as in the terms *extension* cord and telephone *extension.* Is the word ever spelled *extention*?

Answer: You are not alone in having trouble with *extension.* No, it is never spelled with the familiar suffix *tion.* Perhaps you could remember it better if you associate the word *tension* with *extension.*

Question: My son is studying a foreign language; and he asked me, a teacher of business English, why we capitalize the personal pronoun *I* in English when we don't capitalize other pronouns.

Answer: That's a fascinating topic, and a little research on the Web revealed that linguists ponder the same question. In a linguistic journal, some relevant theories were discussed. One linguist thought that perhaps the lower-case *i* was too easily confused with the number *1* or with similar looking *i*'s, *u*'s, and *v*'s in medieval handwriting. Another attributed the word's capital letter to our egocentric nature. Another suggested that since the pronoun *I* usually appeared as the first word in a sentence, it was capitalized for that reason. In earlier centuries before the language was standardized, most nouns and pronouns were capitalized haphazardly. One linguist thought that a better question to ask would be why all of the other pronouns lose their capital letters and *I* retains its.

Question: My supervisor told me that when I answer the telephone, I should say *This is she.* However, this sounds unnatural to me. How can I answer the phone naturally but still sound professional?

Answer: To sound natural and professional, try saying *This is . . .* followed by your name.

NAME ______________________________

CHAPTER 6 Reinforcement Exercises

LEVEL I

A. (**Self-check**) Select the correct form.

1. We are sure that (he, him) graduated from Queen's University. ____________
2. Everyone except (she, her) prefers to use instant messaging. ____________
3. Send the letter to (they, them) at their Florida address. ____________
4. (They, Them), as well as some other employees, volunteered for the project. ____________
5. We're not surprised that someone like (he, him) was nominated for the award. ____________
6. I have a lunch meeting today with Michael Scott and (she, her). ____________
7. Purchases made by (she, her) were billed incorrectly. ____________
8. Are you sure (there's, theirs) time to complete the form? ____________
9. Miriam said that (its, it's) your turn next. ____________
10. Don is certain that nobody but (he, him) can access these files. ____________

Check your answers.

B. In the spaces provided, list five personal pronouns that can be used as subjects of verbs and five that can be used as objects of verbs or objects of prepositions.

As Subjects	As Objects
1. ____________	1. ____________
2. ____________	2. ____________
3. ____________	3. ____________
4. ____________	4. ____________
5. ____________	5. ____________

C. In the spaces provided, write *a, b,* or *c* to indicate how the italicized pronouns function in these sentences.

a = subject of a verb b = object of a verb c = object of a preposition

Example: Please tell *her* that the refund is being processed. ____________

1. Ms. Larsen asked *me* for my cellphone number. ____________
2. Cheryl and *she* were late for their counselling appointments. ____________

1. he 2. her 3. them 4. They 5. him 6. her 7. her 8. there's 9. it's 10. him

3. After Mike finished his presentation, the supervisor praised *him*. ____________

4. The secret agreement between Hana Harper and *him* was not revealed. ____________

5. *They* made a good impression on the board of directors. ____________

6. Sitting next to *us* were several recent graduates. ____________

7. Without his support *I* wouldn't be here today. ____________

8. Pina enjoyed telling *us* the good news. ____________

D. In the following all omitted pronouns serve as subjects of verbs. Write the correct pronoun for each sentence.

1. The project director and (she, her) worked on the program budget. ____________

2. I know that James Naylor and (he, him) will be purchasing the franchise together. ____________

3. To prepare for their trip, Emil and (she, her) will take a conversational Italian class. ____________

4. Last month other salespeople and (they, them) attended four training sessions. ____________

5. We are pleased to learn that (he, him) will be transferred to our division. ____________

In the next set of sentences, all the omitted pronouns serve as objects of verbs or as objects of prepositions. (Selected prepositions have been underlined to help you recognize them.) Write the correct pronoun for each sentence.

6. Mr. Jacobson asked whether the terms of the agreement were satisfactory <u>to</u> (we, us). ____________

7. A substantial investment in the Tim Hortons franchise was made <u>by</u> (he, him). ____________

8. Send Elena Jordan and (I, me) information about Bluetooth technology. ____________

9. Everyone <u>but</u> (they, them) invested in technology stocks. ____________

10. When you finish with it, please give the video <u>to</u> (we, us). ____________

E. Select the correct pronoun.

1. Please have (he, him) notarize this document. ____________

2. The city is proud of (it's, its) recycling record. ____________

3. Nobody but (he, him) has been authorized to use the premises. ____________

4. Are you sure that this apartment is (there's, theirs, their's)? ____________

5. Between you and (I, me), I think Paula Bernhardt is most qualified. ____________

6. We have already sent the parts to (they, them) for inspection. ____________

7. (Your, You're) new office is on the third floor. ____________

8. As Mr. Hadley and (she, her) discussed the matter, new information came to light. ____________

NAME ______________________________

A. (**Self-check**) Select the correct pronoun, and write it in the space provided.

LEVEL II

1. A profit-sharing plan was offered to (we, us) employees in place of cost-of-living raises. ____________
2. No one knows technical jargon better than (he, him). ____________
3. His counsellor and (he, him) worked out a schedule of classes. ____________
4. Both programmers, Alicia and (she, her), are testing spam-blocking software. ____________
5. (Us, We) delegates stayed at the Hotel Dupar during the convention. ____________
6. Catherine Ferguson and (myself, I, me) received new job classifications. ____________
7. Proposals submitted by (her and me, her and I, she and I) were considered. ____________
8. No one but my friend and (myself, I, me) spoke up during the discussion. ____________
9. Separate planes were taken by the business manager and (he, him). ____________
10. The tragedy shocked Dr. Callihan as much as (myself, I, me). ____________

Check your answers.

B. Write the correct pronoun in the space provided.

1. (Her, She) and a colleague plan to take a writing course at night. ____________
2. Carrie is much taller than (she, her). ____________
3. A lawyer is in charge of (we, us) trainees. ____________
4. No other employees are quite like Steve and (he, him). ____________
5. The presentation on social responsibility inspired him as much as (I, me). ____________
6. He has no one but (he, him, himself) to blame. ____________
7. It's interesting that (us, we) accountants were audited this year. ____________
8. Will you and (he, him) have time to meet with the delegates? ____________
9. The co-pilots, Turner and (he, him, himself), requested permission to land. ____________
10. A serious disagreement between Nikki and (he, him, himself) caused problems in the office. ____________
11. Mr. Jefferson and (I, me, myself) will make the announcement very soon. ____________

1. us 2. he 3. he 4. she 5. We 6. I 7. her and me 8. me 9. him 10. me

12. Believe me, no one knows that problem better than (I, me, myself). ____________

13. News of the merger upset President Linda Davis as much as (I, me, myself). ____________

14. All employees but Dan Herzog and (I, me, myself) agreed to the economy measures. ____________

15. Several of (we, us) candidates plan to visit local colleges. ____________

16. Do you think Melanie can complete the work more quickly than (he, him)? ____________

17. Campaign literature was sent to (we, us) homeowners prior to the elections. ____________

18. The signatures on the letter appear to have been written by you and (she, her, herself). ____________

19. The authors typed the manuscripts (themself, themselves). ____________

20. Everyone except two drivers and (he, him) has checked in with the dispatcher. ____________

C. Write complete sentences that begin with the words shown. Supply a pronoun where indicated.

Example: Dana Paulson and (pronoun) *Dana Paulson and he agreed to market their invention.*

1. My supervisor and (pronoun) ____

2. The two sales reps, Don and (pronoun), ____

3. Just between you and (pronoun), ____

4. Except for Mr. Sanders and (pronoun), ____

5. The manager expected Yumiko and (pronoun) ____

6. Ours ____

NAME ______________________________

LEVEL III

A. (**Self-check**) Select the correct pronoun, and write it in the space provided.

1. Was it (they, them) who suggested a merger? ____________

2. If you were (she, her), would you have sent that email message? ____________

3. Ramco asked my partner and (I, me) to design a logo. ____________

4. If I were (he, him), I would withdraw my endorsement. ____________

5. Gilbert said that it was (he, him) who used the printer last. ____________

6. We all assumed the new president would be (her, she). ____________

7. It might have been (she, her) who called in the alarm. ____________

8. The audience didn't discover that Marcelle was (she, her) until the final act. ____________

9. They thought Marcelle to be (she, her). ____________

10. I'll forward the message to you and (they, them) immediately. ____________

Check your answers.

B. Write the correct pronoun in the space provided.

1. When Frank answered the telephone, he said, "This is (he, him)." ____________

2. If you were (I, me), would you take an internship? ____________

3. The committee chair asked Emma and (I, me) to serve on a special task force. ____________

4. Nearly everyone mistook the statuesque blonde to be (her, she). ____________

5. Do you think it was (they, them) who arrived late for the meeting? ____________

6. An attempt was made to reach (he and she, him and her) in Geneva. ____________

7. We are unsure whether the supervisor will be (he, him). ____________

8. I'm sure that it was (she, her) who called this morning. ____________

9. The lifeguard credited with the rescue was thought to be (he, him). ____________

10. If the newly elected council member had been (he, him), our worst fears might have been realized. ____________

11. The committee declared the scholarship recipient to be (her, she). ____________

1. they 2. she 3. me 4. he 5. he 6. she 7. she 8. she 9. her 10. them

12. The student association invited Professor Basil and (he, him) to speak at a campus event. ________________

13. Adam and Tanisha were certain it was not (they, them) who created the shortage. ________________

14. The intruder was taken to be (he, him). ________________

15. When Lakshmi opened the door, she expected to see you and (he, him). ________________

16. It must have been (they, them) who reported the missing funds. ________________

17. We hope to include Russ McGovern and (she, her) in our next series of interviews. ________________

18. If the caller is (he, him), please get his telephone number. ________________

19. The office staff expected the new manager to be (she, her). ________________

20. Are you certain it was (she, her) who created the website? ________________

C. **Review of Levels I, II, and III.** Select the correct pronoun.

1. His mentor and (he, him) plan to meet weekly. ________________

2. If the task had been given to anyone but (she, her) to do, I would have less apprehension. ________________

3. Do you know (whose, who's) working on the final version of the Jet Com proposal? ________________

4. A convincing sales talk was given by (she, her) when she met with their chief executive officer. ________________

5. One of our principal concerns about the motor is (it's, its) tendency to overheat. ________________

6. The wage discussions between Mr. O'Donnell and (they, them) appear to be progressing smoothly. ________________

7. I'm not sure whether this ruler is (yours, your's) or mine. ________________

8. We believe that no one is more familiar with the situation than (he, him). ________________

9. (We, Us) investors, of course, expect to make at least a minimal profit. ________________

10. No one could have been more surprised at the announcement than (we, us). ________________

11. Jensen assumed it was (they, them) who made the initial report. ________________

12. It's strange that Martin is sometimes taken to be (he, him). ________________

13. The insurance salespeople, Mr. Stalls and (her, she), made several appointments for evening interviews. ________________

14. Everyone except (he, him) took part in the videoconference. ________________

15. The inventor credited with the idea was thought to be (he, him). ________________

16. All software technicians except Fatima and (she, her) were transferred. ________________

17. Our student business club is having (its, it's) annual banquet in May. ________________

18. Jean Powers and (I, me) completed our project on time. ________________

D. Review of Chapter 5 (Possessive Nouns) and Chapter 6 (Personal Pronouns). Underline any errors in possessive nouns or personal pronouns in the following sentences. For each sentence write a corrected form in the space provided. Be alert! Some sentences have more than one correction. If a sentence is correct, write *C* in the space.

1. Many small business owners', like Deborah and I, must equip offices in our homes. ________________
2. On the way to the airport, Stacy and me passed a white stretch limousine that was stalled at the side of the road with it's hood up. ________________
3. Our Accounting Department processed expense claims for Hillary and I, but Hillaries claim was rejected. ________________
4. Although I'm sure it was him who sent the email announcement, the CEO doesn't seem to remember it at all. ________________
5. Our companys website describing our new graphic's design capabilities stimulated many inquiries. ________________
6. Just between you and me, I think all passengers luggage except our's will be opened and inspected. ________________
7. If chocolate could teach, Marta and me would now be extremely well educated. ________________
8. Since the envelope was addressed to Mark and I, he and I should receive the free gift. ________________
9. Theirs just one problem: neither Craig nor me have credit cards. ________________
10. All our customers names and addresses are stored in Mr. Betz database. ________________
11. Neither Mr. Persaud nor I could believe that Jeff was taken to be him. ________________
12. Although Tonya and me agreed to pay two months rent in advance, the landlord would not rent to us. ________________
13. No one makes more use of the Web than me. ________________
14. Us programmers are concerned with the security of customers names and addresses. ________________
15. After reviewing our insurance policy and the companys explanation, my wife and I are certain their is a mistake in the reimbursement amount. ________________
16. Some people think vacations are a necessary evil, but we in management believe that recharging one's batteries away from the office really works wonders. ________________
17. The board has voted to give all employee's a retroactive pay increase. ________________
18. If you were me, would you step into the managers shoes at this time? ________________
19. Please send all RSVP's to Jamilah or I before December 1. ________________
20. Although Anne Manzo protested, I'm convinced it was her who sent the gift to Robert and I. ________________

E. Optional Writing. Your instructor may ask you to complete this exercise on a separate sheet.

Write four original sentences that illustrate pronouns with the following functions: subject of verb, object of verb, object of preposition, and complement of subject. Label each pronoun and its function. In addition, write sentences using these six words: *there, theirs, there's, its, it's,* and *yours.*

Editor's Challenge

The following memos have intentional errors related to principles you have studied thus far, as well as general proofreading errors. Use proofreading marks to make corrections. Your instructor may ask you to print the revised memo on your computer printer or to write it by hand on a separate sheet. Leave side margins of about 1 1/4 inches and a top margin of at least 1 inch. Double space if your instructor directs.

DATE: July 25, 200x

TO: Anita Musto, Vice-President

FROM: Rick Juarez, Research Analyst

SUBJECT: ANALYSIS OF PEPSI XL

Here is a summary of the research project assigned to David Quimby and I regarding Pepsi XL this is the reduced-sugar cola drink being introduced by our companies No. 1 competitor.

In just under a years time, Pepsi-Cola developed this new drink. Containing a mix of 50 per cent sugar (high-fructose corn syrup) and 50 per cent artificial sweetener (aspartame). Apparently, Pepsi-Colas plan is to spend over $8 million to introduce the drink and to assess consumers reactions to it. It will be tested on the shelfs of grocerys, mass merchants, and convenience stores in five citys in Florida.

The companys spokesperson said, "The 'X' stands for excelent taste and the 'L' for less sugar." Aimed at young adult's who don't like the taste of aspartame but who want to control calories, the new cola is a hybrid sugar and diet drink. Our studys show that similar drinks tried in the U.S. in the 1990's were unsuccessful. On the other hand, a 50-calorie low-sugar cola introduced in Canada two year ago was well received, and a 40-calorie soda is now marketed sucessfully by Coca-Cola in Japan.

However, neither Mr. Quimby nor myself believe that theres any reason for this countrys consumers to be interested in a midcalorie cola. In fact, all of we analysts in the lab were surprised at Wall Streets favourable response to Pepsis announcement of it's new drink Pepsi-Colas stock value rose slightly.

If the decision were up to Mr. Quimby or I, him and I would take a wait-and-see attitude. Toward the interduction of our own low-sugar drink.

MEMORANDUM

DATE: November 15, 200x

TO: Maria S. Damen, Vice-President, Marketing *MSD*

FROM: Ryan Jenkins, Exhibit Manager

SUBJECT: REDUCING A MAJOR EXPENSE AT TRADE SHOWS

As you suggested, Matthew Chavez and myself have been searching for ways to reduce our trade show exhibition costs'. One of our companys major expenses at these shows is the visitors gift that we present.

At last years show we gave away a nine colour, silk-screened T-shirt. Which was designed by a high-priced designer. Each shirt cost $15 to produce locally, however, I've located a Chinese supplier who can produce good-looking T-shirts. For the low cost of only $4 each. Look at the savings we can make:

2000 silk-screened T-shirts @$15	$30,000
2000 cheaper T-shirts @$4	8,000
SAVINGS	$22,000

This major saving was immediatley apparent to Matthew and I as we studied the problem. Please examine the enclosed T-shirt sample. If you compare T-shirts, you might expect a cheaper shirt to be dis-similar; but as you can see, this shirt is quiet presentable. What's more, it advertises our name just as well as the more expensive silk-screened T-shirts. If the decision were up to Matthew or I, we would be happy to wear the cheaper shirt.

With increasing travel costs and de-creasing trade show budgets, us in marketing must look carefully at how we spend the companies limited funds for exhibitions. Over the last several years,' we have de-creased the number of shows in which we participate, we have also taken fewer booth staffers then in the passed. This outsourcing is a significant reduction in expenses.

For our next major trade show, please authorize the purchase of 2000 T-shirts. Which can save us $22,000 in exhibition costs. With managements approval before December 1, we can be sure to receive supplys from our Chinese manufacturer for the spring Las Vegas trade show. Matthew and myself look forward to your quick response. If your worried about this suggestion or need more details, please call me at Ext. 480.

Enclosure

POSTTEST

Underline the correct pronouns.

1. My friend and (I, me, myself) are attending the conference together.
2. An email outlining the new procedure was sent to (we, us) employees.
3. I'm convinced that no one will try harder than (she, her).
4. James said it was (they, them) who picked up the order today.
5. Just between you and (I, me), which is the better investment?

learning.web.ways

When you are working on your own computer, you will want to *bookmark* or save the URLs of your favourite web pages.

Goal: To learn to bookmark favourite pages.

1. With your web browser on the screen, key the following URL in the location box and press **Enter: <http://www.refdesk.com>**.
2. This website claims to be the Fact Checker for the Internet. Scroll down and scan the various columns. What kind of information is available?
3. Bookmark this page.
4. Locate the **Reference Desk** link in the rightmost column, and from the drop-down menu select Grammar/Style.
5. Scan the entries listed under **Grammar Sites**. How many are there? Are any Canadian sites represented here? Which ones?
6. Click on the link for the **Basic Elements of English**, hosted by the University of Calgary.
7. Bookmark this page.
8. End your session and send an email to a classmate summarizing what you have learned.

---

1. I 2. us 3. she 4. they 5. me

C H A P T E R

Pronouns and Antecedents

7

OBJECTIVES When you have completed the materials in this chapter, you will be able to do the following:

LEVEL I

- *Make personal pronouns agree with their antecedents in number and gender.*
- *Understand the traditional use of common gender and be able to use its alternatives with sensitivity.*

LEVEL II

- *Make personal pronouns agree with subjects joined by* or *or* nor.
- *Make personal pronouns agree with indefinite pronouns, collective nouns, and organization names.*

LEVEL III

- *Understand the functions of* who, whom, whoever, *and* whomever.
- *Use the possessive pronoun* whose *correctly.*

PRETEST

Underline the correct word.

1. The office manager, along with her staff, submitted (her, their) time sheet.
2. Before voting, the committee took a poll of (its, their) members.
3. Either of the branches may send (its, their) manager to the meeting.
4. (Who, Whom) did you select for the management trainee position?
5. Send the brochures to (whoever, whomever) placed the order.

1. her 2. its 3. its 4. whom 5. whoever

Pronouns enable us to communicate efficiently. They provide short forms that save us from the boredom of repetitious nouns. But they can also get us in trouble if the nouns to which they refer—their *antecedents*—are unclear. This chapter shows you how to avoid pronoun–antecedent problems. It also presents solutions to a major problem for sensitive communicators today—how to handle the *his/her* dilemma.

LEVEL I

▶ Fundamentals of Pronoun–Antecedent Agreement

When pronouns substitute for nouns, the pronouns must agree with their antecedents in number (either singular or plural) and gender (either masculine, feminine, or neuter). Here are suggestions for using pronouns effectively.

Hotlink

University of Ottawa's HyperGrammar at **<http://www.arts.uottawa.ca/writcent/hypergrammar/pronref.html>** offers a thorough introduction to pronoun-antecedent agreement.

Make Pronoun References Clear

Do not use a pronoun if your listener or reader might not be able to identify the noun it represents.

Unclear:	Nathalie told Lisa that *she* should verify the balance.
Clear:	Nathalie told Lisa to verify the balance.
Unclear:	Ms. Harrison heard Luke tell Anthony that *he* would be late.
Clear:	Ms. Harrison heard Luke tell Anthony that Luke would be late.
Unclear:	*They* consider 60 per cent a passing grade at this college.
Clear:	This college considers 60 per cent a passing grade.
Or:	A passing grade at this college is 60 per cent.
Unclear:	In that restaurant *they* do not allow *you* to smoke.
Clear:	The restaurant management does not allow its patrons to smoke.
Or:	Smoking is not allowed in that restaurant.

Spot the Blooper

Sign in on Office Depot restroom: "Employees must wash your hands."

Make Pronouns Agree With Their Antecedents in Number

Pronouns must agree in number with the nouns they represent. For example, if a pronoun replaces a singular noun, that pronoun must be singular.

Michelangelo felt that *he* was a failure. (Singular antecedent and pronoun)

Great *artists* often doubt *their* success. (Plural antecedent and pronoun)

If a pronoun refers to two nouns joined by *and*, the pronoun must be plural.

The *president* and the *shareholders* discussed *their* differences. (Plural antecedent and pronoun)

Warren and *Jerome* asked that suggestions be sent to *them*. (Plural antecedent and pronoun)

Did You Know?

Despite efforts for the past 140 years, no one has yet come up with an acceptable multipurpose, unisex pronoun. Suggested replacements: *ne* (1850), *le* (1884), *se* (1938), *ve* (1970), *e* (1977), and *ala* (1988). What would you suggest to fill the void in our language?

Pronoun–antecedent agreement can be complicated when words or phrases come between the pronoun and the word to which it refers. Disregard phrases such as those introduced by *as well as, in addition to,* and *together with*. Find the true antecedent, and make the pronoun agree with it.

The *general,* together with the chiefs of staff, is considering *his* strategy carefully. (Singular antecedent and pronoun)

The *chiefs* of staff, along with the general, have submitted *their* plans. (Plural antecedent and pronoun)

A female *member* of the group of protesting students demanded that *she* be treated equally. (Singular antecedent and pronoun)

Make Pronouns Agree With Their Antecedents in Gender

Pronouns exhibit one of three genders: masculine (male), feminine (female), or neuter (neither masculine nor feminine). Pronouns must agree with their antecedents in gender.

John read *his* assignment. (Masculine gender)

Nancy studied *her* notes. (Feminine gender)

The idea had *its* limits. (Neuter gender)

Choose Alternatives to Common-Gender Pronouns

The English language has no all-purpose singular pronoun that can represent or refer to nouns of unclear gender such as *student* or *employee.* For this reason writers and speakers in the past used masculine, or common-gender, pronouns to refer to nouns that might be either masculine or feminine. For example, in the sentence "A student has *his* rights," the pronoun *his* referred to the word *student,* which might name either a female or male person.

Communicators today, however, avoid masculine pronouns (*he, his*) when referring to indefinite nouns that could be either masculine or feminine. Critics call these pronouns "sexist" because they exclude women. To solve the problem, sensitive communicators rewrite sentences that use such pronouns. Although many alternatives exist, here are three options:

Common gender:	An employee has *his* job to do.
Alternative No. 1:	Employees have *their* jobs to do.
Alternative No. 2:	An employee has *a* job to do.
Alternative No. 3:	An employee has *his* or *her* job to do.
Wrong:	An employee has *their* job to do.

In Alternative No. 1 the subject has been made plural to avoid the need for a singular common-gender pronoun. In Alternative No. 2 the pronoun is omitted, and an article is substituted for it, although at the cost of making the original meaning less emphatic. In Alternative No. 3 both masculine and feminine references (*his* or *her*) are used. Because the latter construction is wordy and rather clumsy, avoid frequently using it. Substituting the plural pronoun *their* is incorrect since it does not agree with its singular antecedent, *employee.*

Now complete the reinforcement exercises for Level I on pp. 117–119.

Career Tip

Business and professional people strive to avoid "sexist" and biased language. For example, use parallel terms (instead of *men and ladies,* say *men and women*). Use neutral titles (*salesperson* instead of *salesman, server* instead of *waitress*). Avoid implied gender (instead of *managers and their wives,* say *managers and their spouses*).

Spot the Blooper

Television commercial for *Encyclopedia Britannica:* "Every parent has a wish list for their child."

▶ Special Pronoun-Antecedent Agreement Challenges

LEVEL II

Antecedents Joined by *or* or *nor*

When antecedents are joined by *or* or *nor,* the pronoun should agree with the antecedent closer to it.

Either Alice or *Vicki* left *her* coat in the office.

Neither the manager nor the *employees* objected to *their* salary cuts.

Spot the Blooper

From an American Express print ad: "Every ten minutes someone travelling in America loses their cash."

Study Tip

When *either* or *neither* is followed by an "of" phrase, it's functioning as a singular pronoun. For example, *either of the books is available.*

Hotlink

Another website to consult if you're having trouble making your pronoun antecedents clear is this University of Calgary page: **<http://www.ucalgary.ca/UofC/eduweb/grammar/course/speech/1_2b.htm>**. Scroll down to the bottom of the page for an interactive quiz on pronoun antecedents.

You may be wondering why antecedents joined by *and* are treated differently from antecedents joined by *or* or *nor*. The conjunction *and* joins one plus one to make two antecedents; hence a plural pronoun is used. The conjunctions *or* or *nor* require a choice between Antecedent No. 1 and Antecedent No. 2. Always match the pronoun to the closer antecedent.

Indefinite Pronouns as Antecedents

Pronouns such as *anyone, something,* and *anybody* are called *indefinite* because they refer to no specific person or object. Some indefinite pronouns are always singular; others are always plural.

Always Singular		**Always Plural**
anybody	everything	both
anyone	neither	few
anything	nobody	many
each	no one	several
either	nothing	
everybody	somebody	
everyone	someone	

When indefinite pronouns function as antecedents of pronouns, make certain that the pronoun agrees with its antecedent. Do not let prepositional phrases obscure the true antecedent.

Somebody in the men's league left *his* lights on.

Each of the corporations had *its* own home office.

Few of the vendors missed the opportunity to demonstrate *their* equipment.

Several of our branches list *their* job openings on the company intranet.

The words *either* and *neither* can be confusing. When these words stand alone and function as pronoun subjects, they are always considered singular. When they are joined with *or* or *nor* to form the conjunctions *either/or* and *neither/nor,* however, they may connect plural subjects. These plural subjects may act as antecedents to plural pronouns.

Has *either* of the women made *her* selection? (*Either* is a singular pronoun and functions as the subject of the sentence.)

Either the woman *or* her friends left *their* packages. (*Either/or* is used as a conjunction joining the two subjects, *woman* and *friends*. The pronoun *their* agrees with the closer antecedent, *friends*.)

Collective Nouns as Antecedents

Words such as *jury, faculty, committee, staff, union, team,* and *group* are called *collective* nouns because they refer to a collection of people, animals, or objects. Such words may be either singular or plural depending on the mode of operation of the collection to which they refer. When a collective noun operates as a unit, it is singular. When the elements of a collective noun operate separately, the collective noun is plural.

Our *staff* reaffirmed *its* position on bargaining. (*Staff* operating as one unit.)
The *jury* rendered *its* verdict. (*Jury* operating as one unit.)
The *jury* were divided in *their* opinions. (*Jury* operating as individuals.)

However, if a collective noun is to be used in a plural sense, the sentence can often be made to sound less awkward by the addition of a plural noun (*The jury members were divided in their opinions*).

Spot the Blooper

From *The New York Times*: "Neither Gore nor Bush could bring themselves to utter a word in defense of scientific truth." (Are there *two* mistakes here?)

Company and Organization Names as Antecedents

Company and organization names are generally considered singular. Unless the actions of the organization are attributed to individual representatives of that organization, pronouns referring to organizations should be singular.

> Sears is having *its* biggest annual sale ever.
> The United Nations, in addition to other organizations, is expanding *its* campaign to fight hunger.
> Maclean Hunter Limited can trace *its* roots back to the nineteenth century.

Hotlink

For more help with pronoun–antecedent agreement, check out this *Horn Book* page at **<http://www.nipissingu.ca/english/hornbook/proant.htm>**.

The Antecedents *each, every,* and *many a*

When the limiting adjectives *each, every,* or *many a* describe either noun or both nouns in a compound subject, that compound subject is considered singular.

> *Every* player and coach on the men's team has *his* assigned duties.
> *Many a* daughter and mother will receive *her* award at the banquet.

Complete the reinforcement exercises for Level II on pp. 120–121.

LEVEL III

▶ Advanced Pronoun Use

The Problem of *who* and *whom*

The use of *who* and *whom* presents a continuing dilemma for speakers and writers. In conversation the correct choice of *who* or *whom* is often especially difficult because of the mental gymnastics necessary to locate subjects and objects. In writing, however, an author has ample time to analyze a sentence carefully and make a correct choice—if the author understands the traditional functions of *who* and *whom.*

Who is the subjective-case form. Like other subjective-case pronouns, *who* may function as the subject of a verb or as the subject complement of a noun following a linking verb. *Whom* is the objective-case form. It normally functions as the object of a verb or as the object of a preposition.

> *Who* do you think will be chosen to direct the play?
> (*Who* is the subject of *will be chosen.*)
> Jerry asked *who* your friend is. (*Who* is the complement of *friend.*)
> *Whom* should we hire? (*Whom* is the object of *should hire.*)
> Alicia is the one to *whom* I spoke. (*Whom* is the object of *to.*)

Spot the Blooper

Heading in the [Cleveland] *Browns News/Illustrated:* "Whom Will It Be?"

How to Choose Between *who* and *whom*

The choice between *who* and *whom* becomes easier if the sentence in question is approached according to the following procedure:

1. Isolate the *who/whom* clause.

2. Invert the clause, if necessary, to restore normal subject–verb–object order.

3. Substitute the subjective pronoun form *he* (or *she* or *they*) for *who.* Substitute the objective pronoun *him* (or *her* or *them*) for *whom.* If the sentence sounds correct

with *him*, replace *him* with *whom*. If the sentence sounds correct with *he*, replace *he* with *who*.

Study the following sentences, and notice how the choice of *who* or *whom* is made:

Here are the records of those (who/whom) we have selected.

Isolate: ________ we have selected
Invert: we have selected ________
Substitute: we have selected __him__
Equate: we have selected __whom__
Complete: Here are the records of those *whom* we have selected.

Do you know (who/whom) his doctor is?

Isolate: ________ his doctor is
Invert: his doctor is ________ (*or* ________ is his doctor)
Substitute: his doctor is __he__ (*or* __he__ is his doctor)
Equate: his doctor is __who__ (*or* __who__ is his doctor)
Complete: Do you know *who* his doctor is?

Spot the Blooper

Famous singer on NBC's *Today* show: "I began to recognize whom I am, and I wasn't afraid of whom I was."

In choosing *who* or *whom*, ignore parenthetical expressions such as *I hope*, *we think*, *I believe*, and *you know*.

Edward is the candidate (who/whom) we believe is best.

Isolate: ________ we believe is best
Ignore: ________ [we believe] is best
Substitute: __he__ is best
Equate: __who__ is best
Complete: Edward is the candidate *who* we believe is best.

Examples:

Whom do you think we should call? (Invert: you do think we should call her/*whom*)
The person to *whom* the article referred was Mr. Stein. (Invert: the article referred to him/*whom*)
Do you know *who* the manager is? (Invert: the manager is she/*who*)
Whom would you like to see appointed to that position? (Invert: you would like to see him/*whom* appointed to that position)

The Use of *whoever* and *whomever*

Whoever, of course, is subjective and *whomever* is objective. The selection of the correct form in clauses is sometimes complicated. These clauses may act as objects of prepositions, objects of verbs, or subjects of verbs. Within the clauses, however, you must determine how *whoever* or *whomever* is functioning in order to choose the correct form (either subject or object). Study the following examples and explanations:

Give the surplus to *whoever needs it.* (The clause *whoever needs it* is the object of the preposition *to;* but within the clause itself, *whoever* acts as the subject of *needs* and is therefore in the subjective case.)

Special provision will be made for *whoever* meets the conditions. (The clause *whoever meets the conditions* is the object of the preposition *for.* Within the clause, *whoever* acts as the subject of *meets* and is therefore in the subjective case.)

We will accept the name of *whomever they nominate.* (The clause *whomever they nominate* is the object of the preposition *of.* Within the clause, *whomever* is the object of *they nominate* and is therefore in the objective case.)

Hotlink

Another tip for dealing with *who* and *whom* (and a review exercise to help you master their use) can be found at **<http://www.grammarbook.com/grammar/whoVwhom.asp>**.

Complete the reinforcement exercises for Level III and the review exercises on pp. 122–125.

HOTLINE QUERIES

Question: My friend insists that the combination *all right* is shown in her dictionary as one word. I say that it's two words. Who's right?

Answer: *All right* is the only acceptable spelling. The listing *alright* is shown in many dictionaries to guide readers to the acceptable spelling, *all right.* Do not use *alright.* By the way, some individuals can better remember that *all right* is two words by associating it with *all wrong.*

Question: I don't seem to be able to hear the difference between *than* and *then.* Can you explain it to me?

Answer: The two words sound similar in ordinary speech, but they function quite differently. The conjunction *than* is used to make comparisons (*your watch is more accurate than mine*). The adverb *then* means "at that time" (*we must complete this task; then we will take our break*) or "as a consequence" (*if all the angles of the triangle are equal, then it must be equilateral as well*).

Question: Why can't I remember how to spell *already*? I want to use it in this sentence: *Your account has <u>already</u> been credited with your payment.*

Answer: You—and many others—have difficulty with *already* because two different words (and meanings) are expressed by essentially the same sounds. The adverb *already* means "previously" or "before this time," as in your sentence. The two-word combination *all ready* means "all prepared," as in *The club members are all ready to board the bus.* If you can logically insert the word *completely* between *all* and *ready,* you know the two-word combination is needed.

Question: If I have no interest in something, am I *disinterested?*

Answer: No. If you lack interest, you are *uninterested.* The word *disinterested* means "unbiased" or "impartial" (*disinterested judges are necessary for the cause of justice*).

(Continued)

Question: I'm disgusted with and infuriated at a New York University advertisement I just saw in our newspaper. It says, *It's not just* <u>*who*</u> *you know ....* Why would a leading institution of learning use such poor grammar?

Answer: Because it sounds familiar—but familiarity doesn't make it correct. You're right in recognizing that the proper form is *whom* (isolate the clause *you know him* or *whom*). The complete adage—or more appropriately, cliché—correctly stated is, *It's not what you know but* <u>*whom*</u> *you know.*

Question: Can you please explain something that is puzzling me? I thought that inanimate objects were not supposed to show possession, but how about the expression *a stone's throw*? A stone is certainly not alive!

Answer: Some common expressions are personified; that is, the nouns in these expressions are thought of as if they had human qualities. Here are a few examples: *at arm's length, for heaven's sake, in today's world,* and *a stone's throw.*

NAME ______________________________

CHAPTER 7 Reinforcement Exercises

LEVEL I

A. (**Self-check**) Select the correct word(s) to complete the following sentences.

1. When a lawyer appears in court, (he, she, he or she, they) should dress professionally. ____________
2. In addition to other family members, each winner was sent tickets for (his, her, its, his or her, their) personal use. ____________
3. The visiting scientist and our resident engineer had (his, her, his or her, their) problems finding the control centre. ____________
4. No veterinarian's assistant will be assigned to that task until (he is, she is, he or she is, they are) trained. ____________
5. One of the members of the boys' choir lost (his, his or her, their) robe. ____________
6. (They, Researchers) report that the rate of deforestation in Brazil's Amazon rainforest has increased sharply. ____________
7. One of the women asked how many sick days (she, he or she, they) had accumulated. ____________
8. All flight attendants must have (her, his, his or her, their) uniforms cleaned regularly. ____________
9. Miss Simon, after consulting the production staff and others, made (her, his or her, their) pricing decision. ____________
10. No employee must automatically retire when (he reaches, it reaches, he or she reaches, they reach) the age of 65. ____________

Check your answers.

B. Select the correct word(s) to complete the following sentences.

1. Workers in the largest plant asked that (his, his or her, their) working conditions be improved. ____________
2. An office manager, as well as the other members of management, must do (his, her, his or her, their) best to promote good employee relations. ____________
3. A judge often feels that (he, she, he or she, they) should review the charges for the jury. ____________
4. Both Dr. Alonzo and Dr. Reese submitted (his, her, his or her, their) registration forms for the convention. ____________
5. Lisa Lee, one of the clerks in the front office, asked that (her, their) vacation be changed. ____________
6. (You, Shoppers) aren't allowed to smoke in the mall. ____________

1. he or she 2. his or her 3. their 4. he or she is 5. his 6. Researchers 7. she 8. their 9. her 10. he or she reaches

7. An employee should know what rights (he has, she has, he or she has, they have) in the workplace. ____________

8. Mr. Tomkins and Mr. Ramos had already discussed the matter with (his, their) lawyers. ____________

9. If the insured party causes an accident, (he, she, it, he or she, they) will be charged an additional fee in future premiums. ____________

10. The human resources manager advised each candidate of (his, her, his or her, their) opportunities for advancement within the organization. ____________

C. Rewrite the following sentences to avoid the use of common-gender pronouns. Show three versions of each sentence.

1. Every resident must display his parking permit.

   a. ____

   b. ____

   c. ____

2. Be sure that each new employee has received his orientation packet.

   a. ____

   b. ____

   c. ____

3. A patient who doesn't accurately report his history to the doctor runs the risk of misdiagnosis.

   a. ____

   b. ____

   c. ____

4. Every nurse in the hospital is required to carry her ID at all times.

   a. ____

   b. ____

   c. ____

D. Rewrite these sentences to make the pronoun references clear.

1. They require you to make dinner reservations in that restaurant.

   ____

   ____

2. Mr. Redman told Mr. Vaccaro that he needed to take a vacation.

3. Speer was Hitler's companion until the final days of the war when he turned against him.

4. Mrs. Hartmann talked with Courtney about her telecommuting request, but she needed more information.

5. Recruiters like to see job objectives on résumés; however, it may restrict their chances.

NAME ____________________

LEVEL II

A. (**Self-check**) Select the correct word(s) to complete the following sentences.

1. Anyone at the meeting can share (his, her, his or her, their) opinion on the issue. ____________
2. Apparently, neither the memorandum nor the letters had (its, their) contents proofread very carefully. ____________
3. Gold, Steinmetz & Burns Inc. held an open house in honour of (its, their) anniversary. ____________
4. Someone on the girls' team lost one of (her, their) shoes. ____________
5. Each man, woman, and child in the club made (his, her, his or her, their) own contribution to the food drive. ____________
6. Either Mrs. Wall or Mrs. Snyder will offer (her, their) home for the meeting. ____________
7. Nobody in the boisterous crowd could hear (his, her, his or her, their) name when it was called. ____________
8. The International Olympic Committee indicated (its, his or her, their) concern about possibly misleading advertisements. ____________
9. Neither of the men would admit (his, their) part in causing the accident. ____________
10. The Coast Guard has five regional offices, but (its, his or her, their) headquarters is in Ottawa. ____________

Check your answers.

B. Select the appropriate pronoun(s) to complete the following sentences.

1. Every employee and manager was notified when (his, her, his or her, their) annual performance review would be held. ____________
2. Dun and Bradstreet bases (its, their) financial ratings on accounting reports. ____________
3. The Supreme Court will announce (its, their) decision in June. ____________
4. Not one of the creditors would allow (his, her, his or her, their) claims to be decreased. ____________
5. Someone in this office reported that (his, her, his or her, their) computer had a virus. ____________
6. The CRTC can use (its, their) power to increase the amount of Canadian content in the media. ____________
7. Every one of the cars had (its, their) suspension damaged by driving over potholes. ____________
8. The inspection team will have (its, their) decision on your desk Monday. ____________

1. his or her 2. their 3. its 4. her 5. his or her 6. her 7. his or her 8. its 9. his 10. its

9. Neither the glamour nor the excitement of the job had lost (its, their) appeal. ____________

10. Any new subscriber may cancel (his, her, his or her, their) subscription within the first ten days. ____________

11. Union members elected (its, their) officers by electronic ballot. ____________

12. Has everybody on the girls' team had (her, its, their) picture taken? ____________

13. Either of the companies may move (its, their) headquarters to Calgary. ____________

14. Every renter and every homeowner should exercise (his, her, his or her, their) right to vote. ____________

15. If anyone needs assistance, Mr. Torres will help (him, her, him or her, them). ____________

16. Our staff agreed that (its, their) stand must be unified. ____________

17. *Consumer Reports* announced a plan to change (its, their) method of distribution. ____________

18. Each of the supermarkets featured (its, their) advertisements on Thursday. ____________

19. Every one of the girls was pleased with (her, their) internship program. ____________

20. Neither the father nor his sons wanted (his, their) shares to be sold. ____________

NAME ______________________

LEVEL III

A. (**Self-check**) Select the correct word, and write it in the space provided.

1. I know perfectly well (who, whom) you are. who
2. This is the applicant (who, whom) impressed the hiring committee. who
3. The contract will be awarded to (whoever, whomever) submits the lowest bid. whoever
4. (Who, Whom) do you think we should elect as our new chairperson? whom
5. Jacquie Carrier is the investment counsellor of (who, whom) I spoke. whom
6. When I return the call, for (who, whom) should I ask? whom
7. (Who, Whom) did you say would drop by? who
8. Will you recommend a lawyer (who, whom) can handle this case? who
9. To (who, whom) were these messages sent? whom
10. The grand prize will be given to (whoever, whomever) the judges select. whomever

Check your answers.

B. Write the correct word in the space provided.

1. Carmen, (who, whom) left last week, was our most experienced web designer. ______
2. He is the graphics designer (who, whom) we believe developed our competition's prize-winning website. ______
3. Please tell us the name of (whoever, whomever) you recommend for the position. ______
4. Nadine King, (who, whom) recently passed the bar exam, immediately hung out her shingle. ______
5. (Who, Whom) have you asked to research promotion of our products on the Internet? ______
6. For (who, whom) does the bell toll? ______
7. I have a pizza for (whoever, whomever) placed the telephone order. ______
8. The "Father of Accounting" to (who, whom) the professor referred was Luca Pacioli. ______
9. Ms. Stewart is the one (who, whom) we think should be made supervisor. ______
10. Rob Evans is the player against (who, whom) offensive interference was called. ______

1. who 2. who 3. whoever 4. Whom 5. whom 6. whom 7. Who 8. who 9. whom 10. whomever

11. You'll never guess (who, whom) we saw in town. __________

12. Do you know (who, whom) will be taking your place? __________

13. Hamid will help (whoever, whomever) is next in line. __________

14. In making introductions, who should be introduced to (who, whom)? __________

15. Mrs. Silver asked us (who, whom) we think should train Kelly. __________

16. Please put the call through to (whoever, whomever) is in charge of the project. __________

17. Tom Garcia is the graduate (who, whom) applied first. __________

18. (Who, Whom) shall I say is calling? __________

19. Charles Gennaro, (who, whom) we thought should be appointed, was not among the final candidates. __________

20. For (who, whom) is this book being ordered? __________

C. Review of Levels I, II, and III. Underline any errors, and write a correction in the space provided. Write *C* if the sentence is correct.

1. The CEO told each member of their voting rights. __________

2. Whomever is in charge of finances should receive the bill. __________

3. Someone on the men's team left their soccer shoes on the bus. __________

4. Have you decided whom the winner is? __________

5. Every man, woman, and child in the country is expected to make their contribution. __________

6. Patricia Best, whom we think will be at the meeting, is a magazine editor. __________

7. Our entire staff agreed that their response must be unified. __________

8. To whom should I speak about my claim? __________

9. Neither the professor nor the student knew their rights. __________

10. General Motors reported that their sales increased in June. __________

11. Either of the possible lottery winners must present his winning ticket by the end of the month. __________

12. Whom is sending all these email messages? __________

13. Any taxpayer may ask to have his property reassessed. __________

14. None of us could believe whom the new manager is. __________

15. Each of the supermarkets featured their advertisements on Friday. __________

D. Cumulative Review. (Self-check) These sentences review Chapters 1 through 7. Underline any errors. Then write corrected forms in the spaces provided. Be alert! Some sentences contain more than one correction. If a sentence is correct, write *C* in the space. Then check your answers below.

1. Pfizer Canada hired a Toronto ad agency to create there TV campaign for Viagra. ____________

2. In a progressive company, a CEO is able to act on his believes. ____________

3. Itinerarys of all employees travel plans must be sent to Rick or myself before any reservations are made. ____________

4. The manager just assumed it was them because of there numerous earlier calls. ____________

5. How many faxs do you and her normally receive in a day? ____________

6. Advocates for both tenants and landlords rights brought their arguments to the city councils weekly meeting. ____________

7. Because us renters demanded our rights', a mayors committee was appointed to study the matter further. ____________

8. Two lawyers were necessary to handle my father's-in-laws business transactions. ____________

9. Every dentist knows that he is feared by some patients. ____________

10. Kim said that her childrens needs always came before her companys demands on her time. ____________

11. If you were him, would you disregard five years experience and switch careers? ____________

12. Before going over your bosses head, be sure to ask her permission. ____________

13. Because Lisa is more productive than him. She will certainly receive the promotion. ____________

14. In some companys its standard practice to distribute a months pay at Christmas as a bonus. ____________

15. Just between you and I, whom do you think will be named CEO? ____________

16. Drug maker Bayer cut 6100 jobs, half were in Europe. ____________

17. Todays companies will generally send employment applications to whomever requests them. ____________

18. Neither of the men had their seat belt on. ____________

19. Jeff James, whom was interviewed by Mr. Woo and I, is our best candidate. ____________

20. Nearly all libraries offer computerized indexes and databases to whoever needs it. ____________

Check your answers.

---

1. its TV campaign 2. his or her beliefs 3. Itineraries employees' Rick or me 4. it was they because of their 5. faxes you and she 6. tenants' landlords' council's 7. we renters rights mayor's 8. father-in-law's 9. he or she 10. children's company's 11. you were he years' 12. boss's his or her 13. than he, she 14. companies it's month's 15. you and me, who 16. jobs. Half 17. Today's whoever 18. his seat belt 19. who Mr. Woo and me 20. needs them.

E. Optional Writing. Your instructor may ask you to complete this exercise on a separate sheet.

Write seven original sentences in which the following words function as subjects: *either, everybody, many, someone, staff, committee,* and *McDonald's*. In each of the sentences, the verb should be either *is* or *are*. You may add phrases for clarity, such as *Either of the two choices....* In addition, write sentences showing *who* as the subject of a verb, *whom* as the object of a preposition, and *whoever* as the subject of a clause. Label each sentence.

Editor's Challenge

The following business letter and email message contain errors reflecting the concepts you have studied thus far, as well as general proofreading errors. Use standard proofreading marks (see the inside front cover) to show your corrections.

❖ BENSON BROTHERS MANAGEMENT SERVICES ❖

368 Glenlake Ave.
Toronto, ON M9B 2B4

(416) 358-2249 Email: bensonbros@world.com Web: www.bensonbros.com

February 9, 200x

Ms. Laura W. Stephens
2320 Centennial Road
Oshawa, ON L1G 8K7

Dear Ms. Stephens:

My partner and myself are certain that our rental management service can help you care for your fathers-in-law apartment complex in Don Mills, here are answers to you're questions.

To manage a clients rental units, we charge 10 per cent of all fees' collected, we will advertise whenever a unit becomes vacant. We charge an additional 10 per cent on the first years rent whenever we fill a vacant unit. Whether we charge the last months rent in advance is between you and I. Our firms two lawyers are available to assist you and I. If necessary.

During the 1990's we expanded, our's is now the only firm to offer maintenance and cleaning services to their customers.

Ms. Stephens, we now manage over 75 rental propertys in the greater Toronto area. We are available to whomever needs rental assistance. Either for private residences or for multiple unit. One client wrote to us saying, "You've managed my units much better than I, and you're firm has made life much easier for my husband and I." Not one of our costumers has ever cancelled their contract with us, and we are convinced that we can ease the burden of your responsibilitys also, please call my partner or I at 416-358-2249 to arrange an appointment this week.

Sincerely yours,

Jonathon Benson

Jonathon Benson

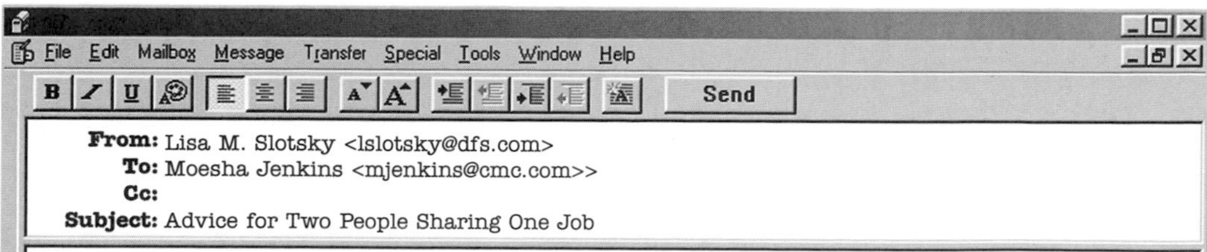

From: Lisa M. Slotsky <lslotsky@dfs.com>
To: Moesha Jenkins <mjenkins@cmc.com>>
Cc:
Subject: Advice for Two People Sharing One Job

I'm happy to hear, Moesha, that you and Sherisa Baldwin plan to ask your manger whether you may share a job. Susan Caminiti and me have had ten years experience in sharing a job here at Deerfield Financial Services, and the arrangement has worked quit well. As you requested, I'll tell you about our arrangement.

Susan and myself share an office, a desk, a computer, a phone (including an out going voice mail message), and even a monthly parking pass. I'm in the office Monday and Tuesday, Susan is in on Thursday and Friday. We alternate Wednesday's. Communication and organization skills are extremely important to Susan and I. On Sunday afternoon Susan delivers to my home a big manila envelope containing a detailed list of meeting, projects, conferences, and phone calls that took place on my days off. At our mid-week switch, I do the same for her. We strive to insure that our staff has no trouble in it's assignments.

Job sharing, however, can work only when you find the right partner, then it requires a seamless blend of work ethics, personality traits, and egos. During the first year Susan and myself found that we were often both in the office on Wednesdays. I think her and me did more for our boss's then we did for ourselfs. Over the years, however, our arrangement has worked so well that our department now has a staff of 20, and we have earned many bonus.

Of course, an employee who wants to share a job must check with there manager before proceding. We would advice whomever wants to share a job to write a formal proposal that details the division of responsibilitys, schedules, game plans for emergency situations, and so forth. Consider a "two-headed" résumé that explains how your strengths mesh with your partners.

Point out that by sharring a demanding job, two people can work the equivalent of a 60-hour week—without burning out. If you want additional advise, just call Susan or I at 443-6630.

Lisa Slotsky
Investor Relations Department
lslotsky@dfs.com

POSTTEST

Underline the correct word.

1. Did anyone on the women's softball team leave (her, their) glove on the bus?
2. The entire faculty voted to give (its, their) support to the president.
3. Neither of the companies could identify (its, their) equipment.
4. (Who, Whom) would you like to see as the next department manager?
5. We will give a bonus to (whoever, whomever) reaches the sales goal first.

learning.web.ways

As you become more familiar with the Web, you may begin to think that the Web is the perfect place for all research. Wrong! The Web does not include all useful data, and what it does contain is not always accurate. The following exercise helps you learn to think more critically about what you find on the Web.

Goal: To learn to evaluate website credibility.

1. Open your web browser, and type this URL in the location box: **<http://www.library.dal.ca/how/criteval.htm>**.
2. This website, maintained by Dalhousie University, has a series of links to web pages that will help you learn how to search the Internet and evaluate the material you find on it.
3. Click on **Criteria for Evaluating Web Sites**. Read the six criteria recommended, and test some of the sites linked on the page to assess them for the specific criterion listed.
4. Copy down some of the questions you might ask in deciding whether a website is reliable.
5. Scroll back up the page, and click on **Checklist for Evaluating Web Sites**.
6. Print the **Checklist**.
7. End your session by clicking the **X** in the upper right corner. Turn in your list of questions.

1. her 2. its 3. its 4. Whom 5. whoever

NAME ______________________

UNIT 2 REVIEW Chapters 4–7 (Self-Check)

LEVEL I

Begin your review by rereading Chapters 4 through 7. Then test your comprehension of those chapters by filling in the blanks in the exercises that follow. Compare your responses with the key at the end of the book.

1. The home of the (a) Lutzes, (b) Lutz, (c) Lutz's is located near the bike path. ______

2. Every political campaign is filled with wordy (a) speechs, (b) speeches, (c) speech's. ______

3. Each summer I search the farmers' market for the best (a) peachs, (b) peaches. ______

4. In seven (a) days, (b) day's, (c) days' time, Maxwell will retire. ______

5. We are giving careful consideration to each (a) company's, (b) companies', (c) companys shares. ______

6. Many of our (a) students', (b) students, (c) student's have difficulty with possessive constructions. ______

7. The committee completed (a) it's, (b) its work last week. ______

8. Let's keep this news between you and (a) me, (b) I. ______

9. All employees except Paul and (a) he, (b) him agreed to the reorganization. ______

10. Ask both of the designers when (a) she, (b) he, (c) he or she, (d) they can give us estimates. ______

11. When a customer complains, (a) he, (b) she, (c) he or she, (d) they must be treated courteously. ______

LEVEL II

12. Parking is not allowed in the back (a) alleys, (b) allies, (c) alleys', (d) alley's. ______

13. Adrienne Hale consulted her three (a) sister-in-laws, (b) sister-in-law's, (c) sisters-in-law before making her decision. ______

14. Brian Mulroney and Jean Chrétien both served as prime minister during the (a) 1990s, (b) 1990's, (c) 1990s'. ______

15. (a) Steve and Leslie's, (b) Steve's and Leslie's new home is in Clarenville. ______

16. I certainly hope that today's weather is better than (a) yesterdays, (b) yesterday's, (c) yesterday. ______

17. How did the (a) Sale's, (b) Sales, (c) Sales' Department manage to avoid layoffs? ______

18. Insincerity irritates Mr. Sanchez as much as (a) I, (b) me, (c) myself. ______

19. The president and (a) I, (b) me, (c) myself will answer all questions. ________

20. Neither the foreman nor the jury members wanted (a) his name, (b) their names to be released by the media. ________

21. Every clerk and every administrative assistant elected to exercise (a) his, (b) her, (c) his or her, (d) their voting rights. ________

22. Marsten, Davis, and Jackson Inc. plans to move (a) it's, (b) its, (c) their offices in September. ________

LEVEL III

23. Following several financial (a) crisis, (b) crises, (c) crisises, the corporation was forced to declare bankruptcy. ________

24. Because of its excellent work, thanks (a) is, (b) are in order for our organizing committee. ________

25. We read an announcement that the (a) Harris', (b) Harris's, (c) Harrises, (d) Harrises' son won a scholarship. ________

26. I'm certain that my (a) bosses, (b) boss's, (c) bosses' signature will be forthcoming. ________

27. Tom (a) Hanks' or Hanks's, (b) Hanks, (c) Hankses' new film is doing well at the box office. ________

28. The employee credited with the suggestion was thought to be (a) he, (b) him. ________

29. If I were (a) her, (b) she, I would decline the offer. ________

30. To (a) who, (b) whom did you send your application? ________

31. (a) Who, (b) Whom has been asked to head the commission? ________

32. Give the extra supplies to (a) whoever, (b) whomever needs them. ________

33. (a) Who, (b) Whom would you prefer to see in that job? ________

34. You'll never guess (a) who, (b) whom I saw today. ________

35. It could have been (a) her, (b) she who called you. ________

Hotline Review

36. Professor Breuer said it was (a) to, (b) too early to sign up for these classes. ________

37. Check your (a) owner's, (b) owners' warranty carefully. ________

38. Because the apartments are so (a) dis-similar, (b) dissimilar, we cannot make exact comparisons. ________

39. We have (a) all ready, (b) already, (c) allready called the technician. ________

40. Shorter, rather (a) then, (b) than longer, training sessions are preferable. ________

Techniques for Effective Sentences

The basic unit in writing is the sentence. Sentences come in a variety of sizes, shapes, and structures. As business and professional communicators, we are most interested in functional sentences that say what we want to say correctly and concisely. In this workshop you'll concentrate on two important elements: writing complete sentences and writing concise sentences.

Writing Complete Sentences

To be complete, a sentence must have a subject and a predicate and must make sense. As you learned in Chapter 3, incomplete sentences are fragments. Let's consider four common fragment errors you'll want to avoid.

1. The fragment contains a subject and a predicate, but it begins with a subordinate word (such as *because, as, although, since,* or *if*) and fails to introduce a complete clause. You can correct this problem by joining the fragment to a relevant main clause.

   Fragment: Because world markets and economies are becoming increasingly intermixed.

   Revision: Because world markets and economies are becoming increasingly intermixed, Canadians are doing more business with people from other cultures.

   Fragment: Although North Americans tend to come to the point directly.

   Revision: Although North Americans tend to come to the point directly, people from some other cultures prefer indirectness.

2. The fragment does not contain a subject and a predicate, but a nearby sentence completes its meaning.

   Fragment: In the spring of every year in Las Vegas. That's when computer vendors stage a huge show.

   Revision: In the spring of every year in Las Vegas, computer vendors stage a huge show.

3. The fragment starts with a relative pronoun such as *which, that,* or *who.* Join the fragment to a main clause to form a complete sentence.

   Fragment: Which is a precious item to North Americans and other Westerners.

   Revision: Concise business letters save time, which is a precious item to North Americans and other Westerners.

4. The fragment starts with a noun followed by a *who, that,* or *which* clause. Add a predicate to form a complete sentence.

   Fragment: The visiting Asian executive who was struggling to express his idea in English.

   Revision: The visiting Asian executive who was struggling to express his idea in English appreciated the patience of his listener.

Skill Check 2.1 Eliminating Sentence Fragments

Each of the following consists of a fragment and a sentence, not necessarily in that order. Use proofreading marks to eliminate the fragment.

Example: Speak in short sentences and use common words. If you want to be understood abroad.

1. Although you should not raise your voice. You should speak slowly and enunciate clearly.
2. A glazed expression or wandering eyes. These alert a speaker that the listener is lost.
3. In speaking with foreign business people, be careful to avoid jargon. Which is special terminology that may confuse listeners.
4. Kevin Chambers, who is an international specialist and consultant. He said that much of the world wants to like us.
5. Graciously accept the blame for not making your meaning clear. If a misunderstanding results.

Skill Check 2.2 Completing Sentences

Expand the following fragments into complete sentences, adding your own ideas. Be ready to explain why each fragment is incomplete and what you did to remedy the problem.

Example: If we keep in mind that North Americans abroad are often accused of talking too much.

Revision: If we keep in mind that North Americans abroad are often accused of talking too much, we'll become better listeners.

1. The business person who engages a translator for important contracts ____________

____

2. Assuming that a nod, a yes, or a smile indicates agreement ____________

____

3. If you learn greetings and a few phrases in the language of the country you are visiting

____

____

4. Although global business transactions are often conducted in English ____________

____

5. Which is why we sometimes put words in the mouths of foreign colleagues struggling to express an idea ____________

____

Avoiding Run-on (Fused) Sentences and Comma Splices

In Chapter 3 you also learned to recognize run-on sentences and comma splices. Remember that locating subjects and verbs may help in identifying and correcting run-ons and comma splices.

A run-on sentence consists of two or more complete thoughts without punctuation to separate them. A comma splice consists of two or more complete thoughts with only a comma between them. The simplest way to correct these errors is to separate complete thoughts.

Run-on sentence: Profit for the second quarter rose to $24.1 million sales rose to $151.9 million.

Revision: Profit for the second quarter rose to $24.1 million. Sales rose to $151.9 million.

Comma splice: Analysts expected a decline of 2.3 per cent in sales, the decline was actually 5 per cent.

Revision: Analysts expected a decline of 2.3 per cent in sales. The decline was actually 5 per cent.

Note that other methods of correcting run-ons or comma splices can be used.

Analysts expected a decline of 2.3 per cent in sales, but the decline was actually 5 per cent. (Coordinating conjunctions are discussed in Chapter 14.)

Analysts expected a decline of 2.3 per cent in sales; the decline was actually 5 per cent. (Semicolons are discussed in Chapter 17.)

Skill Check 2.3 Correcting Comma Splices and Run-on Sentences

Use proofreading marks to correct any comma splices or run-ons in the following items.

1. Internet companies now provide listings of available vacation homes these services reduce the risks of long-distance renting.

2. The Ontario government will probably build a new highway in the Niagara Region, the location of the new road has not been announced.

3. Although Singapore Airlines announced that it was the first airline to offer in-flight web browsing, it had to admit that the service was initially quite limited.

4. The tour operator offers motor coach tours throughout Europe participants choose from a variety of itineraries, activities, and accommodations.

5. Quebec City was founded by Champlain in 1608, its historic district was named a UNESCO World Heritage Site in 1985.

6. After September 11, 2001, tourism fell sharply in the U.S. capital, and within two months an estimated 17,000 Washington residents had lost jobs related to the tourist industry.

7. *Mrs. Miniver* is the title of a British bestseller from 1939 it is also the title of an extremely popular American movie from 1942.

8. Munich is Germany's Silicon Valley, it is a cultural centre as well.

9. Nicholas checked his email then he checked his voice mail.

10. The Japanese delicacy *fugu,* or blowfish, is known for its exhorbitant price, furthermore, it is well known for being extremely poisonous.

11. One minute he was there the next minute he was gone.

12. Thailand offers many adventures, more than 157,000 Canadians visited the country last year.

Writing Concise Sentences

Business and professional people value concise, economical writing. Wordy communication wastes the reader's time and sometimes causes confusion. You can make your sentences more concise by avoiding opening fillers, revising wordy phrases, and eliminating redundant words.

Avoiding Opening Fillers

Openers such as *there is, it is,* and *this is to inform you that* fill in sentences but generally add no meaning. These fillers reveal writers spinning their wheels until deciding where the sentence is going. Train yourself to question these constructions. About 75 per cent can be eliminated, almost always resulting in more concise sentences.

Wordy: *There are* three students who volunteered to help.
Revised: Three students volunteered to help.

Wordy: *This is to inform you that* our offices will be closed on Monday.
Revised: Our offices will be closed on Monday.

Revising Wordy Phrases

Some of our most common and comfortable phrases are actually full of "word fat." When examined carefully, these phrases can be pared down considerably.

Wordy Phrases	Concise Substitutes
as per your suggestion	as you suggested
at this point in time	now
due to the fact that	because, since
for the purpose of	to
give consideration to	consider
in all probability	probably
in spite of the fact that	even though
in the amount of	for
in the event that	if
in the near future	soon
in the neighbourhood of	about
in view of the fact that	because, since
with regard to	about

Notice how you can revise wordy sentences to make them more concise:

Wordy: *Due to the fact that* fire damaged our distribution centre, we must delay some shipments.
Revised: *Because* fire damaged our distribution centre, we must delay some shipments.

Wordy: The cost for the entire system is *in the neighbourhood of* $18,000.
Revised: The cost for the entire system is *about* $18,000.

Eliminating Redundant Words

Words that are needlessly repetitive are said to be "redundant." Writers must be alert to eliminating redundant words and phrases, such as the following:

advance warning
assemble together
basic fundamentals
collect together
consensus of opinion
contributing factor
dollar amount
each and every
end result
exactly identical
few in number
free and clear
grateful thanks
great majority
integral part
last and final
midway between
new changes
past history
perfectly clear
personal opinion
positively certain
potential opportunity
proposed plan
reason why
refer back
today's modern world
true facts
very unique
visible to the eye

Wordy:	We studied the *past* history of *each and every* potential donor.
Revised:	We studied the history of every potential donor.
Wordy:	Please collect *together* all the *true* facts before proceeding.
Revised:	Please collect all the facts before proceeding.

Skill Check 2.4 Writing Concise Sentences

In the space provided, rewrite the following sentences to make them more concise.

1. There is a free booklet that shows all the new changes in employee benefits.

   There is a free booklet that shows new changes in employee benefit

2. In view of the fact that health care benefits are being drastically altered, this is to inform you that an orientation meeting will be scheduled in the near future.

3. A great majority of students will in all probability support the proposed satellite parking plan.

4. In the event that McDonald's offers new menu items for the purpose of increasing sales, experts think that there is every reason to believe that the effort will be successful.

5. There will be a second showing of the orientation training film at 10 a.m. due to the fact that there were so few in number who were able to attend the first showing.

6. The reason why we are attending the protest is to make our opinion perfectly clear.

Skill Check 2.5 Proofreading a Memo

In the following memo, we have deliberately introduced sentence fragments and wordy writing. Use proofreading marks to make all sentences complete and concise.

Becktelman Worldwide Contractors

Interoffice Memo

TO: Marcia Murphy
FROM: Jason Corzo
DATE: August 20, 200x
SUBJECT: CONGRATULATIONS ON YOUR ASSIGNMENT TO JAPAN

Your assignment to Kansai, Japan, as office manager of our International Business Relations Department. That's cause for celebration! This is to inform you that although I'm a little late in responding to your request, I have assembled together some experiences and advice that may interest you.

When I was on assignment for our firm in Japan. My job was to help us break into the construction business. I found it very difficult to locate a Japanese construction firm. That would act as a subcontractor for us. In time I did find a company, and eventually we began to win contracts. In spite of the fact that the process was slow and frustrating.

Despite the slow pace of qualifying for and winning contracts. I am optimistic with regard to expanding our business in Asian countries. In my personal opinion, an important contributing factor in our successful entrance into Pacific Rim markets is how willing we are to play the game according to Asian rules. In the event that we are willing to work from the inside and show our long-term commitment. I am positively certain that we can succeed in gaining a great majority of Asia's construction business in the near future.

On a personal level, Marcia, there are a few things that really helped me in communicating with the Japanese. I learned to smile a lot due to the fact that a smile is perfectly clear to everyone. I also learned to listen without interrupting, and I learned to accept blame each and every time a communication misunderstanding occurred.

Due to the fact that you are in all probability midway between assignments. This message may take a while to catch up with you. Regardless, I congratulate you on this promotion, Marcia. It is the consensus of opinion in our office that you will be very successful in managing our Kansai office in Japan.

Writing Application 2.1 After you edit the memo, your instructor may ask you to respond to it. In a memo on a separate sheet, assume that you have received this memo. Show your appreciation to Jason Corzo for his advice. Explain that you are both excited and worried about your new assignment. Use your imagination to tell why. Describe how you expect to prepare for the new assignment. You might say that you plan to start learning the language, to read about the culture, and to talk with colleagues who have worked in Japan. Put this in your own words and elaborate.

U N I T 3

Showing the Action

C H A P T E R

Verbs: Kinds, Voices, Moods

8

OBJECTIVES When you have completed the materials in this chapter, you will be able to do the following:

LEVEL I

- *Distinguish between transitive and intransitive verbs.*
- *Identify at least eight linking verbs.*

LEVEL II

- *Recognize active- and passive-voice verbs.*
- *Convert sentences written in the passive voice to sentences in the active voice.*

LEVEL III

- *Recognize sentence constructions requiring the subjunctive verb mood.*
- *Use subjunctive forms correctly.*

PRETEST

Underline the appropriate answers.

1. In the sentence *Maria scheduled a web conference,* the verb *scheduled* is (a) transitive, (b) intransitive, (c) linking.
2. In the sentence *Written instructions were provided,* the verb phrase *were provided* is in the (a) active voice, (b) passive voice, (c) subjunctive mood.
3. In the sentence *Barbara Benesch taught the class,* the verb *taught* is in the (a) active voice, (b) passive voice, (c) subjunctive mood, (d) intransitive mood.
4. Jackie acts as if she (a) was, (b) were the manager.
5. Della Jones moved that a vote (a) is, (b) be taken.

1.a 2.b 3.a 4.b 5.b

Verbs express an action, an occurrence, or a state of being.

> Alexandra wrote an excellent proposal. (Action)
> The winter holidays end the fall term. (Occurrence)
> Sandee is the new technical writer. (State of being)

In relation to subjects, verbs generally tell what the subject is doing or what is being done to the subject. Verbs may also link to the subject words that describe the subject or identify it.

The verb is the most complex part of speech. A complete treatment of its forms and uses would require at least a volume. Our discussion of verbs will be limited to practical applications for business people and professionals.

In this chapter you'll learn about kinds of verbs, verb voices, and verb moods.

LEVEL I

▶ Kinds of Verbs

We'll begin our discussion of verbs by focusing on verbs that express action. These verbs may be divided into two categories: transitive or intransitive.

When a verb directs its action toward an object, it is *transitive*. When the action is complete in itself and requires no object, the verb is *intransitive*. Some verbs may be either transitive or intransitive, depending on how they function in a sentence.

Hotlink

To check your knowledge of transitive and intransitive verbs, use this short quiz at **<http://www.uottawa.ca/academic/arts/writcent/hypergrammar/trnsintr.html>**

Transitive Verbs

A verb expressing an action directed toward a person or thing is said to be *transitive*. An action verb used transitively needs, in addition to its subject, a noun or pronoun to complete its meaning. This noun or pronoun functions as the direct object of the transitive verb. Notice in the following sentences that the verbs direct action toward objects (shown in italics).

> The directors demanded improved *profits*.
> Yesterday the president called *him*.
> We sold the *shares* at a profit.

Objects usually answer the questions *what*? or *whom*? In the first example, the directors demanded *what*? The object is *profits*. In the second example, the president called *whom*? The object is *him*.

Intransitive Verbs

An action verb that does not require an object to complete its action is said to be *intransitive*.

> Ralph worked in our Human Resources Department last summer.
> E-commerce grows rapidly because of the Internet.
> Tanya Asper listened carefully to the directions.

Spot the Blooper

From a card sent by a Saturn dealer to customers: "Thank you... Your Special!"

Notice that the verbs in these sentences do not express actions directed toward persons or things. Prepositional phrases (*in our Human Resources Department, because of the Internet, to the directions*) and adverbs (*rapidly, carefully*) do not receive the action expressed by the verbs, nor do they answer the questions *what*? or *whom*? In other words, prepositional phrases and adverbs do not function as objects of verbs.

Linking Verbs

You will recall that linking verbs *link* to the subject words that rename or describe the subject. A noun, pronoun, or adjective that renames or describes the subject is called a *complement* because it *completes* the meaning of the subject.

> Angie is the *manager*. (*Manager* is a noun complement that completes the meaning of the sentence by renaming *Angie,* the subject.)
>
> Her salary is *excellent*. (*Excellent* is an adjective complement that completes the meaning of the sentence by describing *salary*, the subject.)
>
> The caller was *he*. (*He* is a pronoun complement that completes the meaning of the sentence by identifying *caller*, the subject.)

Spot the Blooper

Advice in Harvard Medical School's *Heart Letter*: "Do not feel too badly about missing dosages of your pills."

Notice in the preceding sentences that the noun, pronoun, or adjective complements following the linking verbs do not receive action from the verbs; instead, the complements *complete* the meaning of the subject.

You are already familiar with those linking verbs that are derived from the verb *to be*: *am, is, are, was, were, be, being, been.* Other words that often serve as linking verbs are *feel, appear, taste, seem, sound, look,* and *smell.* Notice that many of these words describe sense experiences. Verbs expressing sense experiences may be followed by complements just as the *to be* linking verbs often are.

> They feel *bad* about the sale of the company. (*Bad* is an adjective complement following the linking verb *feel*. An adjective—not the adverb *badly*—is needed here to describe the senses.)
>
> Jay appears *sad*. (*Sad* is an adjective complement following the linking verb *appears*.)

Study Tip

Here's a mnemonic (memory) device to help you remember the verbs of the senses. Call them the FATS verbs, an acronym (word formed of initials) made from the first letters of *feel, appear, taste,* and *seem.*

The use of adjectives following such verbs is discussed more completely in Chapter 12.

The function of a verb in a sentence determines its classification. The action verb *write,* for example, is intransitive when it has no object (*Ernie writes*). The same verb is transitive when an object follows (*Ernie writes email*). The verb *felt* is linking when it is used to connect a complement describing the subject (*Geoff felt marvellous*). The same verb is transitive when it directs action to an object (*Geoff felt the wet desk*). To distinguish between classifications, study carefully the constructions in which the verbs appear.

To review briefly:

1. Action Verbs—two kinds:
    a. Transitive: need objects to complete their meaning.
    b. Intransitive: do not need objects to complete their meaning.
2. Linking Verbs: form a link to words that rename or describe the subject.

Complete the reinforcement exercises for Level I on pp. 145–147.

▶ Verb Voices

LEVEL II

You will recall that a verb expressing an action directed toward a person or thing is said to be transitive. Transitive verbs fall into two categories depending upon the receiver of the action of the verbs.

Hotlink

These Grammar Tutorials **<http://www.ucalgary.ca/UofC/eduweb/grammar/course/speech/1_3f.htm>** created by the University of Calgary offer a thorough overview of the active and passive voices. For an interactive quiz, scroll down to the bottom of the page.

Active Voice

When the verb expresses an action directed by the subject toward the object of the verb, the verb is said to be in the *active voice.*

> Alison answered the telephone. (Subject directs action to the object, *telephone.*)
> Our department uses Excel. (Subject directs action to the object, *Excel.*)

Verbs in the active voice are direct and forceful; they clearly identify the doer of the action. For these reasons, writing that frequently uses the active voice is vigorous and effective. Writers of business and professional communications strive to use the active voice; in fact, it is called the *voice of business.*

Passive Voice

When the action of the verb is directed toward the subject, rather than by the subject, the verb is said to be in the *passive voice*. Compare the two groups of sentences below:

Passive Voice	Active Voice
The figures are totalled daily.	We total the figures daily.
The machines are being sold by Mr. Chavez.	Mr. Chavez is selling the machines.
Three errors were made in the report.	The accountant made three errors in the report.
The order was submitted after the deadline.	You submitted the order after the deadline.

Study Tip

In the passive voice, verbs always require a *helper*, such as *is, are, was, were, being,* or *been*. For example, *Repairs were made by the manufacturer.*

Because the passive voice can be used to avoid mentioning the performer of the action, the passive voice is sometimes called the *voice of tact.* Notice how much more tactful the passive versions of the last two examples are. Although directness in business writing is generally preferable, in certain instances the passive voice is used because indirectness is desired.

Complete the reinforcement exercises for Level II on pp. 148–150.

LEVEL III

▶ Verb Moods

Three verb moods are available to enable a speaker or writer to express an attitude toward a subject: (1) the *indicative mood* is used to express a fact (*We need the contract*); (2) the *imperative mood* is used to express a command (*Send the contract immediately*); (3) the *subjunctive mood* is used to express a doubt, a conjecture, or a suggestion (*If the contract were here, we'd be pleased*). The subjunctive mood usually causes speakers and writers difficulty and therefore demands special attention.

Career Tip

To be an effective communicator, use the subjunctive correctly. A business person would avoid saying *if I was you,* for example.

Subjunctive Mood

Although the subjunctive mood is seldom used today, it is still employed by careful individuals in the following constructions.

1. ***If* and *wish* clauses.** When a statement that is doubtful or contrary to fact is introduced by *if, as if, as though,* or *wish,* the subjunctive form *were* is substituted for the indicative form *was.*

   > If Lori *were* here, we could proceed. (Lori is *not* here.)
   > She acts as if she *were* the boss. (She is *not* the boss.)

He spends money as though he *were* a millionaire. (He is *not* a millionaire.)
George wishes he *were* able to snowboard. (George is *not* able to snowboard.)

But if the statement could possibly be true, use the indicative form.

If Chris *was* in the audience, I missed him. (Chris might have been in the audience.)

Spot the Blooper

From an advertisement for the Egyptian Tourist Authority appearing in *The Boston Globe*: "I wish I was in Egypt."

2. ***That* clauses.** When a *that* clause follows a verb expressing a command, recommendation, request, suggestion, or requirement, the subjunctive verb form *be* is used for *to be* verbs. For third-person singular verbs the *s* or *es* is dropped.

   The doctor recommended that everyone *be* [not *is*] inoculated.
   Our manager ordered that all reports *be* [not *are*] proofread twice.
   Test Centre rules require that every student show [not *shows*] photo ID.

3. **Motions.** When a motion is stated, a subjunctive verb form should be used in the following *that* clause.

   Sheldon moved that a vote *be* taken.
   It has been seconded that the meeting *be* adjourned.

   Caution: In a sentence without *that* clauses, do not mix subjunctive and indicative verbs.

   Right: If she *were skilled,* she *would receive* job offers. (Both verbs subjunctive)
   Right: If she *is skilled,* she *will receive* job offers. (Both verbs indicative)
   Wrong: If she *were skilled,* she *will receive* job offers. (One subjunctive verb and one indicative verb)

Hotlink

For more illustrations of the use of the subjunctive, consult **<http://www.writersblock.ca/tips/monthtip/tipsep96.htm>**.

Complete the reinforcement exercises for Level III on pp. 151–152.

HOTLINE QUERIES

Question: Which is better: *The truck carried canisters of highly* *<u>flammable</u>* *or* *<u>inflammable</u>* *liquid?*

Answer: Actually, both *flammable* and *inflammable* mean "easily set on fire." Either would be correct in your sentence. However, *flammable* is preferable because its meaning is less likely to be confused. Since the prefix *in* often means "not," the word *inflammable* could be misunderstood. Therefore, use *flammable* in technical matters, particularly if you wish to suggest a warning. You may use *inflammable* or its derivatives for non-technical descriptions, such as *Her words were* *<u>inflammatory</u>*.

Question: I have a sentence that begins *Beside(s) providing financial aid ....* Is there any real difference between *beside* and *besides*?

Answer: Yes, indeed! *Beside* is a preposition meaning "by the side of" (*come sit* *<u>beside</u>* *me*). *Besides* is an adverb meaning "in addition to" (*<u>besides</u>* *paper we must order cartridges*). In your sentence use *besides*.

Question: I have looked and looked, but I cannot find this word in a dictionary. I'll pronounce it phonetically for you: *per-rog-a-tive.* I know it exists. What am I doing wrong?

(Continued)

Answer: Like many other people, you are mispronouncing it. The word is *pre-rog-a-tive,* meaning "a right or privilege" (*it is your prerogative to join a union*).

Question: I received a magazine advertisement recently that promised me a *free gift* and a *15 per cent off discount* if I subscribed. What's wrong with this wording?

Answer: You have a double winner here in the category of redundancies. The word *gift* suggests *free;* therefore, to say *free gift* is like saying *I'm studying English English.* It would be better to say *special gift.* In the same way, *15 per cent off discount* repeats itself. Omit *off.*

Question: When do you use *may,* and when do you use *can*?

Answer: Traditionally, the verb *may* is used in asking or granting permission (*Yes, you may use that desk*). *Can* is used to suggest ability (*You can succeed in business*). In informal writing, however, authorities today generally agree that *can* may be substituted for *may.*

Question: On my computer I'm using a program that checks the writer's style. My problem is that it flags every passive-voice verb and tells me to consider using an active-voice verb. Are passive-voice verbs totally forbidden in business and professional writing?

Answer: Of course not! Computer style checkers capitalize on language areas that can be detected mechanically, and a passive-voice verb is easily identified by a computer. Although active-voice verbs are considered more forceful, passive-voice verbs have a genuine function. Because they hide the subject and diffuse attention, passive verbs are useful in sensitive messages where indirect language can develop an impersonal, inconspicuous tone. For example, when a lower-level employee must write a persuasive and somewhat negative message to a manager, passive-voice verbs are quite useful.

Question: What's the correct verb in this sentence? *Tim recognized that, if his company (was* or *were) to prosper, it would require considerable capital.*

Answer: The verb should be *were* because the clause in which it functions is not true. Statements contrary to fact that are introduced by words like *if* and *wish* require subjunctive-mood verbs.

NAME ______________________________

CHAPTER 8 Reinforcement Exercises

LEVEL I

A. (**Self-check**) In the spaces provided, indicate whether the italicized verbs are transitive (*T*), intransitive (*I*), or linking (*L*).

Example: Elvira *is* our team leader. ____L____

1. Ann *seems* happier in her new position. __________
2. Canada *exports* products to numerous foreign countries. __________
3. Before the conference, delegates *met* in the foyer. __________
4. Brian Rose *is* the one on whom we all depend. __________
5. Rachel *expects* Ms. Partington to return to the office soon. __________
6. It *was* he who devised the current work schedule. __________
7. The production manager *called* over four hours ago. __________
8. Shari Adams *feels* certain that the calendar date is clear. __________
9. Well-written business letters *get* results. __________
10. The Chungs *auctioned* their car on eBay. __________

Check your answers.

B. Each of the following sentences contains a verb that is either transitive or intransitive. If the verb is intransitive, underline it and write *I* in the space provided. If the verb is transitive, underline it, write *T* in the space provided, and also write its direct object.

Examples: After her presentation the salesperson <u>left</u>. ____I____

Employees <u>brought</u> their lunches. ____T (lunches)____

1. Rich Royka scheduled a meeting to discuss health care issues. __________
2. The network failed. __________
3. FedEx maintains a busy website for its customers. __________
4. Our suppliers raised their prices. __________
5. Storm clouds gathered. __________
6. Over the years our assets increased. __________
7. Bill Gates receives many email messages. __________

1. L 2. T 3. I 4. L 5. T 6. L 7. I 8. L 9. T 10. T

8. The telephone rang. ____________

9. Gregory answered it. ____________

10. Many employees take the subway to work. ____________

Linking verbs are followed by complements that identify, rename, or describe the subjects. The most common linking verbs are the forms of *be* (*am, is, are, was,* etc.) and the verbs of the senses (*feel, appear, taste, smell,* etc.). The following sentences all contain linking verbs. For each sentence underline the linking verb or verb phrase and write its complement in the space provided.

Examples: Joanna <u>feels</u> confident in her abilities. confident

Our current director <u>is</u> Ms. Abzug. Ms. Abzug

11. Employees are happy about pay increases. ____________

12. His presentation was professional and convincing. ____________

13. That pizza smells fantastic! ____________

14. Over the telephone his voice sounds resonant. ____________

15. It was she who called you earlier. ____________

16. Mr. Flores has been the committee representative for two years. ____________

17. She feels comfortable buying items online. ____________

18. The manager of that department might be Mr. Dorsey. ____________

19. That table would have been fine. ____________

20. It seems unusually cold in here today. ____________

C. In the following sentences selected verbs have been italicized. For each sentence indicate whether the italicized verb is transitive (*T*), intransitive (*I*), or linking (*L*). In addition, if the verb is transitive, write its object. If the verb is linking, write its complement.

Examples: The new sales rep *is* Janet Oso. L (Janet Oso)

Our computer *prints* the mailing list. T (list)

1. The chair of the committee *is* Margaret McHenry. ____________

2. Traffic *moves* from the suburbs along three major arteries. ____________

3. General Motors *offered* a warranty on certain engine parts. ____________

4. It *is* he who is responsible for processing all equipment requests. ____________

5. Please *lay* the keys on the desk when you finish with them. ____________

6. Her report *does appear* accurate, but we must verify some data. ____________

7. Mitchell *feels* marvellous about his recent promotion. ____________

8. Producers *move* goods to market to meet seasonal demands. ____________

9. It *must have been* they who made the anonymous gift. ________________

10. The economy *appears* bright despite interest rate increases. ________________

11. Daniel Borman *is* the person whom you should call. ________________

12. Although consumers protested, the airline *ended* its meal service. ________________

13. Please *raise* the window before you leave. ________________

14. Your report *is lying* on the boss's desk. ________________

15. All of us *feel* bad about her transfer. ________________

16. Our website *generates* many hits each day. ________________

17. Fibromyalgia *affects* 3 in 100 Canadians. ________________

18. The world's highest tides *happen* twice a day in the Bay of Fundy. ________________

19. We *listened* to the presentation with great interest. ________________

20. The manager's frown *seemed* permanent. ________________

NAME ______________________________

LEVEL II

A. (**Self-check**) Transitive verbs in the following sentences have been italicized. For each sentence write *active* or *passive* to indicate the voice of the italicized verb.

Example: Several building code violations *were found* by inspectors. passive

1. The Internet activity of all employees *is monitored* by our company. ________
2. Our company *monitors* the Internet activities of all employees. ________
3. Computer and communication skills *are required* by many hiring companies. ________
4. Many hiring companies *require* computer and communication skills. ________
5. Our insurance company *is* now *offering* a new method of premium payment on life insurance. ________
6. The new plan *was devised* to make premium payment completely automatic. ________
7. Mark Messenger prepared the certified cheque. ________
8. The certified cheque was prepared by Mark Messenger. ________
9. Funds for the youth campaign *were collected* from private donors. ________
10. Private donors *made* contributions to the campaign because they believed in the merit of the project. ________

Check your answers.

B. In the spaces provided, write *active* or *passive* to indicate the voice of the italicized verbs.

1. Many Canadians *see* American TV advertisements. ________
2. American TV advertisements *are seen* by many Canadians. ________
3. Intranets and wireless devices *are being used* in many companies. ________
4. You *withdrew* the funds in question on May 29. ________
5. From his gross income, Harrison *deducts* medical expenses and contributions. ________
6. Arthur Haig *was told* to submit the expense claim by Friday. ________
7. Contract arbitration *will be conducted* by the union and the manufacturer. ________
8. Thom *married* a woman he met at the gym. ________
9. The Infiniti *had been stolen* from a city parking lot. ________
10. Steinberg *is being held* for questioning. ________

1. passive 2. active 3. passive 4. active 5. active 6. passive 7. active 8. passive 9. passive 10. active

C. Careful writers strive to use the active voice in business and professional communications. This is an important skill for you to develop. To give you practice in developing this skill, rewrite the following sentences, changing their passive-voice verbs to active voice. Normally you can change a verb from passive to active voice by making the doer of the action—usually contained in a *by* phrase—the subject of the sentence.

Example: *Passive:* Production costs must be reduced *by manufacturers.*
Active: Manufacturers must reduce production costs.

1. Pollution was greatly reduced by Chrysler Canada when the company built its new plant. (*Hint: Who* greatly reduced pollution? Start your sentence with that name.)

____

____

____

2. The documents were carefully reviewed by investigators during the audit.

____

____

____

3. Massive short-term financing is used by Nike to pay off its production costs during its slow season.

____

____

____

D. Some sentences with passive-voice verbs do not identify the doer of the action. Before these sentences can be converted to active voice, a subject must be provided.

Example: *Passive:* New subscribers will be offered a bonus.
(By whom?—let's say by *Macleans*)
Active: *Maclean's* will offer new subscribers a bonus.

In each of the following sentences, first answer the question *by whom*? Then rewrite the sentence, beginning with your answer as the subject.

1. Our website was recently redesigned to increase its attractiveness and effectiveness.

(By whom?) ______________________________

____

____

2. Net income before taxes must be calculated carefully when you fill out your tax return.

(By whom?) ______________________________

____

____

3. Only a few of the many errors and changes were detected during the first proofreading.

(By whom?) ______________________________

____

____

NAME ____________________

LEVEL III

A. (**Self-check**) Select the correct word, and write it in the space provided.

1. If Ray Cortez (was, were) our manager, he would not approve these work rules. ____________
2. Do we have a motion that the meeting (is, be) adjourned? ____________
3. If I (was, were) Mrs. Prashad, I'd buy medical insurance for the trip abroad. ____________
4. Did your doctor advise that you (be, are) excused from heavy duty? ____________
5. If Mr. McHenry (was, were) at the opening session, he did not announce himself. ____________
6. The supervisor suggested that everyone (is, be) informed of the availability of the training seminar. ____________
7. If you were in my place, I'm sure you (will, would) agree. ____________
8. Sandi Woodruff recommended that additional chairs (are, be) set up for the afternoon session. ____________
9. He acts as if he (was, were) the only employee who had to work overtime. ____________
10. It is extremely important that all applications (are, be) completed by the 15th of the month. ____________

Check your answers.

B. Underscore verbs that are incorrectly used in the following sentences. Write correct forms in the spaces provided. Write *C* if correct.

1. William Harris wished that he was able to retire at age forty. ____________
2. I move that Natalie is appointed chair of our Grievance Committee. ____________
3. President Atkins recommended that each employee is given full benefits. ____________
4. If a better employee benefit program was available, recruiting would be easier. ____________
5. A shareholder moved that dividends are declared immediately. ____________
6. If he were in my place, he will be more understanding. ____________
7. I wish that our server was working so that I could read my mail. ____________
8. Lianne McGinley advised that antiglare shields are installed. ____________

1. were 2. be 3. were 4. be 5. was 6. be 7. would 8. be 9. were 10. be

9. Henri said he wished that you were able to accompany him. ____________

10. If Sam were in the office that day, I did not see him. ____________

C. Choose the correct verb forms, and complete the following sentences.

1. I wish that I (was, were)____________________

2. If my boss (was, were)____________________

3. If you (was, were) in my position, ____________________

D. Optional Writing. Your instructor may ask you to complete this exercise on a separate sheet.

Write ten sentences to illustrate the following: two transitive verbs, two intransitive verbs, a linking verb, two active-voice verbs, two passive-voice verbs, and a verb in the subjunctive mood. Label each sentence.

Editor's Challenge

The following email message and memo contain intentional errors in spelling, proofreading, and grammar principles you have studied thus far. Use proofreading marks to correct the errors.

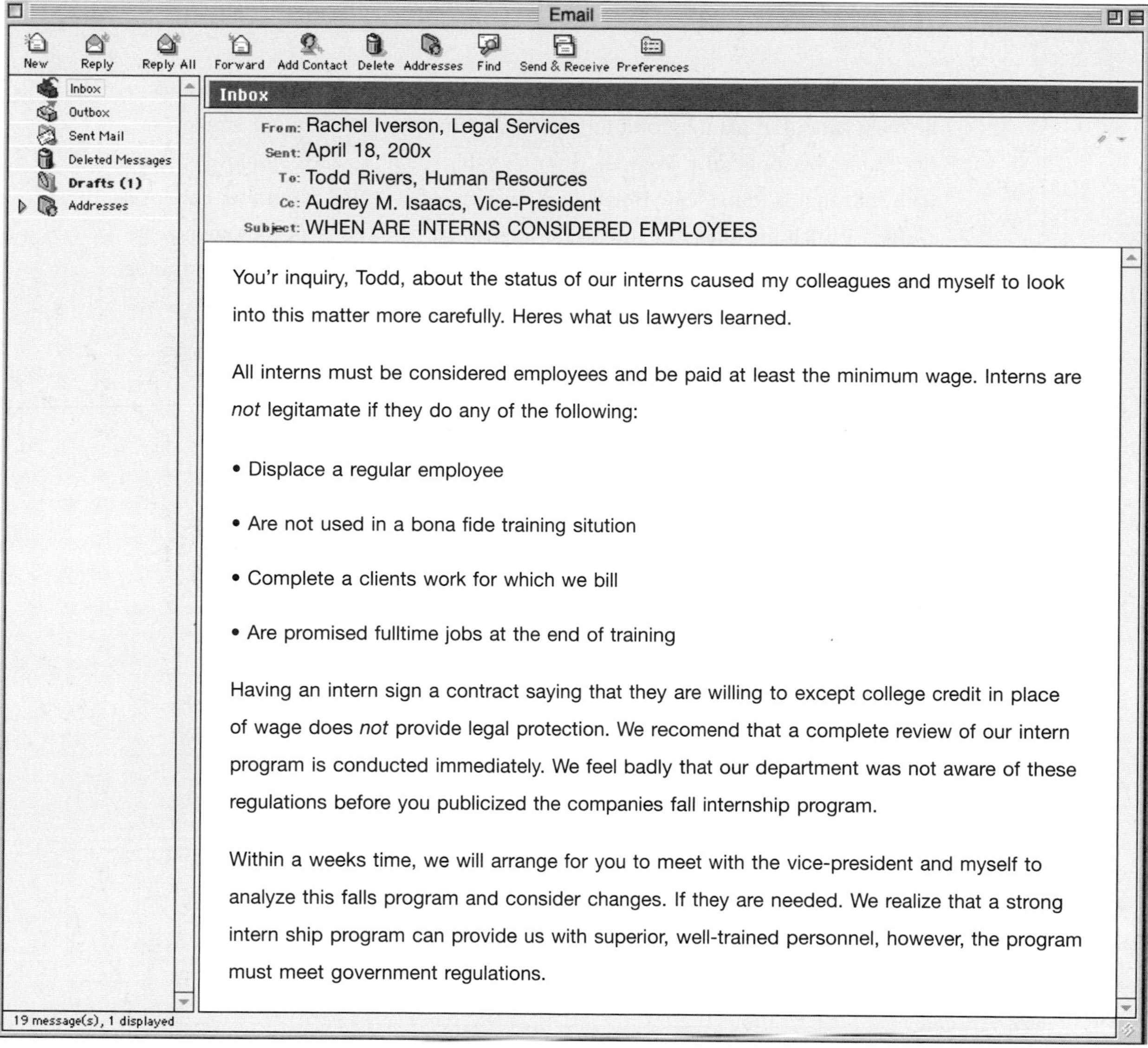

From: Rachel Iverson, Legal Services
Sent: April 18, 200x
To: Todd Rivers, Human Resources
Cc: Audrey M. Isaacs, Vice-President
Subject: WHEN ARE INTERNS CONSIDERED EMPLOYEES

You'r inquiry, Todd, about the status of our interns caused my colleagues and myself to look into this matter more carefully. Heres what us lawyers learned.

All interns must be considered employees and be paid at least the minimum wage. Interns are *not* legitamate if they do any of the following:

- Displace a regular employee
- Are not used in a bona fide training sitution
- Complete a clients work for which we bill
- Are promised fulltime jobs at the end of training

Having an intern sign a contract saying that they are willing to except college credit in place of wage does *not* provide legal protection. We recomend that a complete review of our intern program is conducted immediately. We feel badly that our department was not aware of these regulations before you publicized the companies fall internship program.

Within a weeks time, we will arrange for you to meet with the vice-president and myself to analyze this falls program and consider changes. If they are needed. We realize that a strong intern ship program can provide us with superior, well-trained personnel, however, the program must meet government regulations.

GRADIENT RESEARCH, INC.
INTEROFFICE MEMORANDUM

TO: Josh Hernandez, Production Manager

FROM: Edward J. Juralski, CEO

DATE: February 16, 200x

SUBJECT: TELECOMUTING EMPLOYEES' GUIDE

Because telecommuting is becomming increasingly popular, its neccesary for us to be more careful in planing for information security. As well as for our employees health and personal safty. We wish it was possible to talk to each employee individually, but that is impossible. Instead, we have prepared a "Telecommuter Employees Guide." Which includes structured agreements that specify space, equipment, scheduling, communications, and conditions of employment. The complete guide should be given to whomever is about to begin a telecommuting assignment. We appreciate you discussing the following recomendations with any of your staff members whom are considering telecommuting.

Arranging the Home Workspace

- Create a space where you can expect minimal traffic and distraction.
- Make it comfortable but with suficient space for computer, printer, and fax.
- Make your workspace off-limits to family and friend's.
- Provide proper lighting and telephone service.

Ensuring Information Security

- Remember that you're home office is an extension of the company office.
- Be carful to protect information and avoid computer virus's.
- Be sure to backup and store data and other information in a safe place.

We do not recommend at-home meetings for telecommuters. By the same token, we suggest using postal boxes rather then home addresses. We also require smoke detector's in home work areas.

To have any questions answered, my assistant or me can be reached at Ext. 310.

POSTTEST

Underline the appropriate answers.

1. In the sentence *Billie Scott released the report,* the verb *released* is (a) transitive, (b) intransitive, (c) subjunctive, (d) passive.
2. In the sentence *Lucy Williams hired four employees,* the verb *hired* is in the (a) active voice, (b) passive voice, (c) subjunctive mood, (d) intransitive mood.
3. In the sentence *Angela Clouse was given the award,* the verb phrase *was given* is in the (a) active voice, (b) passive voice, (c) subjunctive mood, (d) intransitive mood.
4. If Clara Smith (a) was, (b) were the instructor, the class would be full.
5. Professor St. Clair recommended that students (a) are, (b) be admitted free.

learning.web.ways

Colleges and universities now routinely provide grammar help in writing centres or writing labs. You should check the hours when the writing centre is open so that you can make an appointment with a tutor. You should also check whether your college offers a grammar hotline service, since you'd like to telephone or email a language specialist with a question.

Goal: To learn about the writing centre at your college.

1. With your web browser on the screen, enter the URL of your college. (Do you have it bookmarked?)
2. Find the **Search** box, and enter "Writing Centre" as your search term. Remember to include the quotation marks.
3. Find the web page that belongs to your college's writing centre (or lab), and print out the timetable that shows its hours of operation.
4. Jot down the contact telephone number you will need to call in order to make an appointment with a tutor.
5. Go back to the college home page, and do another search, this time for "grammar hotline."
6. Note the name, telephone number, and/or email address. If your college doesn't offer this service, you can locate lists of grammar hotlines by using the search phrase *grammar hotline* in *Google* **<www.google.com>**.
7. End your session and submit your printed page and listing.

1.a 2.a 3.b 4.b 5.b

C H A P T E R

Verb Tenses and Parts 9

OBJECTIVES When you have completed the materials in this chapter, you will be able to do the following:

LEVEL I

- *Write verbs in the present, past, and future tenses correctly.*
- *Understand how helping verbs function in verb phrases.*

LEVEL II

- *Recognize and use present and past participles.*
- *Write the correct forms of irregular verbs.*

LEVEL III

- *Recognize and supply correct verb forms in the progressive and perfect tenses.*

PRETEST

Underline the correct verb.

1. Anthony and she (came, come) over last night to use my computer.
2. After they had (gone, went), I was able to do my own homework.
3. The year-end financial statements are (laying, lying) on your desk.
4. Because prices are (raising, rising), we should look for an apartment immediately.
5. The condominium project has (set, sat) there untouched for a year.

English verbs change form (inflection) to indicate number (singular or plural), person (first, second, or third), voice (active or passive), and tense (time). In contrast to verbs in languages like French and German, English verbs are no longer heavily inflected; that is, our verbs do not change form extensively to indicate number or person. To indicate precise time, however, English employs three rather complex sets of tenses: primary tenses, perfect tenses, and progressive tenses. Level I will focus on the primary tenses. Level II will consider participles and irregular verbs. Level III will treat the progressive and perfect tenses.

---

1. came 2. gone 3. lying 4. rising 5. sat

LEVEL I

Hotlink

A good guide to the use of verb tenses, with the accompanying time clues to help you decide the correct tense, is presented by Athabasca University at **<http://www.athabascau.ca/courses/engl/155/support/verb_tenses.htm>**.

Spot the Blooper

In a job applicant's cover letter: "I had strong interpersonal and communication skills."

▶ Primary Tenses

Present Tense

Verbs in the present tense express current or habitual action and facts that are true at all times. Present tense verbs may also be used in constructions showing future action.

> We *order* office supplies every month. (Current or habitual action)
> Water *boils* at 100°C. (Fact)
> He *flies* to St. John's tomorrow. (Future action)

Past Tense

Verbs in the past tense show action that has been completed. Verbs that form the past tense with the addition of *d* or *ed* are called regular verbs.

> Mr. Pasternak *needed* the forms yesterday.
> Our vendor *provided* toner cartridges.
> She *used* to have a Japanese car.

Future Tense

Verbs in the future tense show actions that are expected to occur at a later time. Traditionally, the helper verbs *shall* and *will* have been joined with principal verbs to express future tense. Today, however, the verb *will* is generally used as the helper to express future tense. Some writers continue to use *shall* in appropriate first-person constructions (*I/we shall attend the meeting*).

> Andy *will need* office supplies next week.
> You *will receive* your order on Thursday.

Summary of the Primary Tenses

The following table summarizes the various forms employed to express the primary tenses:

	Present Tense		**Past Tense**		**Future Tense**	
	Singular	**Plural**	**Singular**	**Plural**	**Singular**	**Plural**
First person:	I need	we need	I needed	we needed	I will need	we will need
Second person:	you need	you need	you needed	you needed	you will need	you will need
Third person:	he, she, it needs	they need	he, she, it needed	they needed	he, she, it will need	they will need

Challenges Using Primary Tenses

Most adult speakers of our language have few problems using present, past, and future tense verbs. A few considerations, however, merit mention.

Spelling Verbs That Change Form

A dictionary should be used to verify spelling of verbs that change form. One must be particularly careful in spelling *y*-ending verbs (*hurry, hurries, hurried*) and verbs for which the final consonant is doubled (*occurred, expelled*). (Guidelines 4 and 5 in Appendix A discuss these changes.)

Using the *-s* Verb Ending

Third-person singular verbs require an *-s* ending in the present tense (*he needs*). Even if you might drop the *-s* or *-es* in speaking, be sure to include it in writing.

This equipment *breaks* down too often. (Not *break*)
Matt *drives* a pickup truck. (Not *drive*)

Expressing "Timeless" Facts

Present tense verbs may be used to express "timeless" facts, even if these verbs occur in sentences with other verbs in the past tense.

What did you say his duties *are*? (To indicate he continues to perform these duties)
We were often told that a penny saved *is* a penny earned. (To emphasize that this is a general truth)
What did you say the caller's name *is*? (To indicate the name hasn't changed)

Hotlink

Following a brief review of verb tenses, this page at **<http://www.ucalgary.ca/UofC/eduweb/grammar/course/speech/1_3c.htm>** also offers you an interactive quiz on the same.

▶ Helping (Auxiliary) Verbs

A verb that combines with a main verb to convey information about tense, mood, or voice functions as a helping or auxiliary verb. The most common helping verbs are forms of *be (am, is, are, was, were, being, been)*, forms of *do (does, did, done)*, and forms of *have (has, had)*. As you will recall, the verb *be* and all its forms also function as linking verbs.

Study Tip

In the present tense singular third person, verbs require an *s* ending (*he helps*); plural third person verbs do *not* (*they help*).

Our manager *is* a funny guy. (The linking verb *is* joins the complement *guy* to the subject.)
Our manager *is using* his computer. (The helping verb *is* combines with the main verb *using* to form a verb phrase whose object is *computer*.)
Our manager *has hired* a new assistant. (The helping verb *has* combines with the main verb *hired* to form a verb phrase.)
Our manager *was chosen* by a committee. (The helping verb *was* combines with the main verb *chosen* to form a passive-voice verb.)

Complete the reinforcement exercises for Level I on pp. 167–168.

LEVEL II

▶ Present and Past Participles

To be able to use all the tenses of verbs correctly, you must understand the four principal parts of verbs: present, past, present participle, and past participle. You have already studied the present and past forms. Now let's consider the participles.

Present Participle

The present participle of a regular verb is formed by adding *ing* to the present form of the verb. When used in a sentence as part of a verb phrase, the present participle is generally preceded by some form of the helping verb *to be* (*am, is, are, was, were, been).*

Betty *is changing* jobs. (Helping verb *is*, present participle *changing*)
You *are doing* a fine job.

Spot the Blooper

From a CNN interview: "The warden has came out and gave us his view of the execution."

Hotlink

To practise your mastery of irregular verbs, use the series of exercises available from **<http://www.chompchomp.com/handouts.htm#Irregular_Verbs>**.

Career Tip

In employment interviews, recruiters listen carefully to a candidate's spoken English. One quick way to be eliminated is to use a past participle in the place of a past tense. WRONG: *He come over last night* or *I seen them.*

Past Participle

The past participle of a regular verb is usually formed by adding a *d* or a *t* sound to the present form of the verb. Like present participles, past participles may function as parts of verb phrases, preceded by one or more helping verbs.

> Ryan *has checked* his homework. (Helping verb *has*, past participle *checked*)
> The homework *has been checked* by Ryan.
> Ms. Melchiori *should have built* the factory earlier.
> New roads to the building *should have been built.*

▶ Irregular Verbs

Up to this point, we have considered only regular verbs. Regular verbs form the past tense by the addition of *d* or *ed* to the present tense form. Many verbs, however, form the past tense and the past participle irregularly. (More specifically, irregular verbs commonly form the past tense by a variation in the root vowel and the past participle by the addition of an *en* sound.) A list of frequently used irregular verbs follows. Learn the forms of these verbs by practising them aloud in patterns such as the following:

Present tense:	Today I ___drive___ .
Past tense:	Yesterday I ___drove___ .
Past participle:	In the past I have ___driven___.

Frequently Used Irregular and/or Problematic Verbs

Present	Past	Past Participle
arise	arose	arisen
be (am, is, are)	was, were	been
bear (to carry)	bore	borne
become	became	become
begin	began	begun
bite	bit	bitten
blow	blew	blown
break	broke	broken
bring	brought	brought
build	built	built
buy	bought	bought
choose	chose	chosen
come	came	come
do	did	done
draw	drew	drawn
drink	drank	drunk
drive	drove	driven
eat	ate	eaten
fall	fell	fallen
fly	flew	flown
forbid	forbade	forbidden
forget	forgot	forgotten *or* forgot
forgive	forgave	forgiven
freeze	froze	frozen

Present	Past	Past Participle
get	got	gotten *or* got
give	gave	given
go	went	gone
grow	grew	grown
hang (to suspend)	hung	hung
hang (to execute)	hanged	hanged
hide	hid	hidden *or* hid
know	knew	known
lay (to place)	laid	laid
lead	led	led
leave	left	left
lie (to rest)	lay	lain
lie (to tell a falsehood)	lied	lied
lose	lost	lost
pay	paid	paid
prove	proved	proved *or* proven
raise (to lift)	raised	raised
ride	rode	ridden
ring	rang	rung
rise (to move up)	rose	risen
run	ran	run
see	saw	seen
set (to place)	set	set
shake	shook	shaken
shrink	shrank	shrunk
sing	sang	sung
sink	sank	sunk
sit (to rest)	sat	sat
speak	spoke	spoken
spring	sprang	sprung
steal	stole	stolen
strike	struck	struck *or* stricken
swear	swore	sworn
swim	swam	swum
take	took	taken
teach	taught	taught
tear	tore	torn
throw	threw	thrown
wear	wore	worn
write	wrote	written

Spot the Blooper

From Walt Disney Company: *Honey, I Shrunk the Kids.*

Spot the Blooper

From *The Times-Union* [Albany, NY]: "Jane Fonda's Beverly Hills hairdresser sweared the thick blond braid she's been sporting ... is her real hair."

▶ Three Pairs of Frequently Misused Verbs

The key to the correct use of the following pairs of verbs lies in developing the ability to recognize the tense forms of each and to distinguish transitive verbs and constructions from intransitive ones.*

* *Transitive and intransitive verbs were explained in Chapter 8, Level I, and are identified in some dictionaries.*

Lie–Lay

These two verbs are confusing because the past tense of *lie* is spelled in exactly the same way the present tense of *lay* is spelled. Memorize these verb forms.

Study Tip

Whenever you use *lay* in the sense of "placing" something, you must provide a receiver (object) of the action: *Please lay the* book *down.* If nothing receives action, you probably want the verb *lie*, which means "resting."

	Present	Past	Past Participle	Present Participle
Intransitive:	lie (to rest)	lay	lain	lying
Transitive:	lay (to place)	laid	laid	laying

The verb *lie* is intransitive; in other words, it requires no direct object to complete its meaning.

> I *lie* down for a nap every afternoon. (Note that *down* is not a direct object.)
> "*Lie* down," he told his dog. (Commands are given in the present tense.)
> Yesterday I *lay* down for a nap. (Past tense)
> They have *lain* there for some time. (Past participle)
> The papers are *lying* on the desk. (Present participle)

The verb *lay* is transitive and must have a direct object to complete its meaning.

> A bricklayer *lays* bricks. (*Bricks* is the direct object.)
> *Lay* the bricks over there. (Command in the present tense)
> He *laid* the bricks in a row. (Past tense)
> He has *laid* bricks all his life. (Past participle)
> The mason is *laying* bricks. (Present participle)

Spot the Blooper

From a Dunkin' Donuts advertisement: "The trouble with supermarket doughnuts is there's no telling how long they've been laying around."

Sit–Set

Less troublesome than *lie–lay*, the combination of *sit–set* can nevertheless be perplexing because the sound of the verbs is similar. The intransitive verb *sit* (past tense, *sat;* past participle, *sat*) means "to rest" and requires no direct object.

> Do you *sit* here often? (Note that *here* is not an object.)
> *Will* you *be sitting* here tomorrow? (Present participle)

The transitive verb *set* (past tense, *set*; past participle, *set*) means "to place" and must have a direct object.

> Letty usually *sets* her books there. (*Books* is the direct object.)
> She is *setting* her books here today. (Present participle)

Rise–Raise

The intransitive verb *rise* (past tense, *rose;* past participle, *risen*) means "to go up" or "to ascend" and requires no direct object.

> The sun *rises* every morning in the east. (*Every morning* is an adverbial phrase, not an object.)
> Yesterday the bread dough *rose* nicely. (Past tense)
> Prices have *risen* substantially. (Past participle)
> Our elevator is *rising* to the seventh floor. (Present participle)

The transitive verb *raise* (past tense, *raised*; past participle, *raised*) means "to lift up" or "to elevate" and must have a direct object.

Study Tip

To help you remember that these verbs are intransitive, look at the second letter of each:

l*i*e
s*i*t
r*i*se

Associate *i* with *i*ntransitive.

Please *raise* the window. (*Window* is the direct object.)
Apple Canada Inc. may *raise* prices next month. (*Prices* is the direct object.)

Complete the reinforcement exercises for Level II on pp. 169–171.

▶ Progressive and Perfect Tenses

LEVEL III

So far in this chapter, you have studied the primary tenses and irregular verbs. The remainder of this chapter focuses on two additional sets of verb tenses: the perfect tenses and the progressive (or continuous) tenses. Most native speakers and writers of English have little difficulty with these verb forms (although the names of these forms are probably unfamiliar) because they have frequently heard them used correctly. This largely descriptive section is thus presented for those who are not native speakers and for those who are eager to study the entire range of verb tenses.

Hotlink

You can find review material on verb tenses at **<http://www.arts.uottawa.ca/writcent/hypergrammar/rvtense.html>** and a variety of quizzes at **<http://langues.cmaisonneuve.qc.ca/clakoff/GRAMMAR%20LINKS/verbtenses.htm>**.

Progressive Tenses

Progressive tenses consist of a present participle and appropriate helping verbs as shown below. These tenses indicate action in progress now, in progress in the past, or in progress in the future.

Present Progressive Tense

	First Person	Second Person	Third Person
Active:	I am hearing we are hearing	you are hearing	he, she, it is hearing they are hearing
Passive:	I am being heard we are being heard	you are being heard	he, she, it is being heard they are being heard

Past Progressive Tense

	First Person	Second Person	Third Person
Active:	I was hearing we were hearing	you were hearing	he, she, it was hearing they were hearing
Passive:	I was being heard we were being heard	you were being heard	he, she, it was being heard they were being heard

Future Progressive Tense

	First Person	Second Person	Third Person
Active:	I will be hearing we will be hearing	you will be hearing	he, she, it will be hearing they will be hearing
Passive:	I will be being heard we will be being heard	you will be being heard	he, she, it will be being heard they will be being heard

Hotlink

If you'd like a really exhaustive reference site with "all about verbs," visit and bookmark this Capital Community College web page **<http://grammar.ccc.commnet.edu/grammar/verbs.htm>**.

Examples:

We *are exporting* grain to numerous countries. (Present progressive tense expresses action currently in progress.)
The bungalow down the street *is being sold* by the owner. (Present progressive, passive voice)

Many textile companies *were sending* delegates to the government conference. (Past progressive tense indicates action in the past.)
The sun *was shining* on the day of the company golf tournament. (Past progressive)
They *will be receiving* the announcement shortly. (Future progressive indicates action in the future.)
We expect that the Bank of Canada *will be raising* interest rates. (Future progressive)

Perfect Tenses

Perfect tenses consist of a past participle and appropriate helping verbs as shown below. The present perfect tense indicates an action begun in the past and continuing to the present or an action recently completed. The past perfect indicates an action completed before another past action. The future perfect indicates an action that will be completed before a specific time in the future.

Present Perfect Tense

	First Person	Second Person	Third Person
Active:	I have heard we have heard	you have heard	he, she, it has heard they have heard
Passive:	I have been heard we have been heard	you have been heard	he, she, it has been heard they have been heard

Study Tip

If you are an ESL student, you may need considerable work on verb tenses and other grammar points. Grammar books for you are widely available and include the *Grammar in Context* series by Sandra Elbaum et al. and the texts by Betty Schrampfer Azar.

Past Perfect Tense

	First Person	Second Person	Third Person
Active:	I had heard we had heard	you had heard	he, she, it had heard they had heard
Passive:	I had been heard we had been heard	you had been heard	he, she, it had been heard they had been heard

Future Perfect Tense

	First Person	Second Person	Third Person
Active:	I will have heard we will have heard	you will have heard	he, she, it will have heard they will have heard
Passive:	I will have been heard	you will have been heard	he, she, it will have been heard they will have been heard

Spot the Blooper

From a Fox News ad for a new book by Donald Trump: "Read my new book or your fired."

Examples:

He *has* just *heard* the news. (Present perfect tense expresses action just completed or *perfected*.)
We *have had* an office in North Bay since 1998. (Present perfect expresses action begun in the past and continuing in the present.)
The cheque *had cleared* the bank before I cancelled payment. (Past perfect tense shows an action finished before another action in the past.)

Jacob *had* already *paid* for a ticket when the concert was postponed. (Past perfect)

The polls *will have been* closed two hours when the results are telecast. (Future perfect tense indicates action that will be completed before another future action.)

The report *will have been released* by the time of our next meeting. (Future perfect, passive voice)

Summary of Verb Tenses

Primary Tenses	**Progressive Tenses**	**Perfect Tenses**
Present	Present progressive	Present perfect
Past	Past progressive	Past perfect
Future	Future progressive	Future perfect

Complete the reinforcement exercises for Level III and reviews on pp. 172–174.

HOTLINE QUERIES

Question: We have a new electronic mail system, and one of its functions is "messaging" people. When folks say, *I'll message you,* it really grates on my nerves. Is this correct?

Answer: "Messaging" is certainly a hot term with the explosion of email and instant messaging. As to its correctness, I think we've caught language in the act of evolving. What's happened here is the reinstitution of a noun (*message*) as a verb. Converting nouns into verbs is common in English (he *cornered* the market, we *tabled* the motion, I *pencilled* it in on my calendar, the farmer *trucked* the vegetables to market). Actually, *message* was sometimes used as a verb a century ago (in 1896 *the bill was messaged over from the house*). However, its recent use has been almost exclusively as a noun. Today it is increasingly being used again as a verb. New uses of words usually become legitimate when the words fill a need and are immediately accepted. Some word uses, though, appear to be mere fads, like *The homeless child could not <u>language</u> her fears.* Forcing the noun *language* to function as a verb is unnecessary since a good word already exists for the purpose: *express.* But other "nouns-made-verbs" have been in use long enough to sound reasonable: I *faxed* the document, he *videotaped* the program, she *keyed* the report.

Question: I'm embarrassed to ask this because I should know the answer—but I don't. Is there an apostrophe in this: *its relevance to our program?*

Answer: No. Use an apostrophe only for the contraction *it's,* meaning *it is* (*it's a good plan*) or *it has* (*it's been a long time*). The possessive pronoun *its,* as used in your example, has no apostrophe (*the car had its oil changed*).

Question: How do you spell *Moosonee?* I looked in the dictionary, but it isn't there.

Answer: *Moosonee* and other names are not in all dictionaries and this name is likely to be found only in a Canadian dictionary. Some dictionaries include proper nouns in the main entries; others have separate sections with biographical and geographical entries. You might also look up place names in a postal code directory or a telephone book if you have no other reference book handy.

(Continued)

Question: I thought I knew the difference between *principal* and *principle,* but now I'm not so sure. In a report I'm typing I find this: *The principal findings of the market research are negative.* I thought *principal* always meant your "pal," the school principal.

Answer: You're partly right and partly wrong. *Principal* may be used as a noun meaning "chief" or "head person." In addition, it may be used as an adjective to mean "chief" or "main." This is the meaning most people forget, and this is the meaning of the word in your sentence. The word *principle* means a "law" or "rule." Perhaps it is easiest to remember *principle* = *rule*. All other uses require *principal*: the *principal* of the school, the *principal* of the loan, the *principal* reason.

Question: Even when I use a dictionary, I can't tell the difference between *affect* and *effect.* What should the word be in this sentence? *Changes in personnel (affected/effected) our production this month.*

Answer: No words generate more confusion than do *affect and effect.* In your sentence use *affected.* Let's see if we can resolve the *affect/effect* dilemma. *Affect* is a verb meaning "to influence" (*smoking affects health; government policies affect citizens*). *Affect* may also mean "to pretend or imitate" (*he affected a British accent*). *Effect* can be a noun or a verb. As a noun, it means "result" (*the effect of the law is slight*). As a verb (and here's the troublesome part), *effect* means "to produce a result" (*small cars effect gasoline savings; GM effected a new pricing policy*).

Question: I'm editing a screenplay for a studio, and I know something is grammatically wrong with this sentence: *The old man left the room hurriedly after discovering a body laying near the window.*

Answer: As you probably suspected, the verb *laying* should be *lying. Lay* means "to place" and requires an object (*he is laying the report on your desk now*). *Lie* means "to rest" and requires no object (*the document is lying on your desk*).

Question: I learned that the verb *set* requires an object. If that's true, how can we say that the sun *sets* in the west?

Answer: Good question! The verb *set* generally requires an object, but it does have some standardized uses that do not require one, such as the one you mention. Here's another: *Glue sets quickly.* I doubt that anyone would be likely to substitute *sit* in either of these unusual cases. While we're on the subject, the verb *sit* also has some exceptions. Although generally the verb *sit* requires no object, *sit* has a few uses that require objects: *Sit yourself down* and *The waiter sat us at Table 1.*

NAME ______________________________

CHAPTER 9 Reinforcement Exercises

LEVEL I

A. (**Self-check**) Select the correct verb. Use your dictionary to verify spelling if necessary.

1. Workers (applyed, applied) two coats of paint. ____________

2. What (is, was) the name of the sales rep who stopped by yesterday? ____________

3. The machine (jamed, jammed) when conflicting instructions were entered. ____________

4. Mr. Milne said that the distance between Calgary and Edmonton (is, was) 300 kilometres. ____________

5. We (hurryed, hurried) through the rehearsals. ____________

6. What (is, was) your maiden name? ____________

7. He was (refered, referred) to an orthopedic surgeon. ____________

8. The researcher (tried, tryed) to get her findings published. ____________

9. The associate dean announced yesterday that all professors (are, were) now required to teach five classes. ____________

10. He (write, writes) dozens of emails every day. ____________

Check your answers.

B. In the following sentences, provide three tenses for each verb.

Example: She (arrive) at the office at 7:45 a.m.

Past *arrived* Present *arrives* Future *will arrive*

1. The nation's tax system (need) to stimulate investment.

Past ____________ Present ____________ Future ____________

2. Our supervisor (copy) us on every email message related to the pending merger.

Past ____________ Present ____________ Future ____________

3. Lori (hurry) to catch the bus.

Past ____________ Present ____________ Future ____________

4. The Royal Bank (open) its new branch office downtown today.

Past ____________ Present ____________ Future ____________

1. applied 2. is 3. jammed 4. is 5. hurried 6. is 7. referred 8. tried 9. are 10. writes

5. Professor Darlene Williams (cover) the same material in her class.

Past ______________ Present ______________ Future ______________

6. Monsanto (label) its plastic soft-drink bottle.

Past ______________ Present ______________ Future ______________

7. Donald (plan) to major in finance.

Past ______________ Present ______________ Future ______________

8. The local community college (invest) in child care facilities for student parents.

Past ______________ Present ______________ Future ______________

9. The Prime Minister (announce) the appointments today.

Past ______________ Present ______________ Future ______________

10. Questionnaires (sample) customers' reactions to our new products.

Past ______________ Present ______________ Future ______________

C. Compose sentences using the verbs shown.

1. (Past tense of *bury*) ____

____

____

2. (Present tense of *fly*) ____

____

____

3. (Past tense of *study*) ____

____

____

4. (Past tense of *cancel*) ____

____

____

5. (Future tense of *learn*) ____

____

____

NAME ______________________________

LEVEL II

A. (**Self-check**) Write the correct verb form. Do not add a helper verb.

Example: He should have (eat) before he left. eaten

1. Several of his friends (come) over yesterday. ________
2. Has she (see) the changes we made to the website? ________
3. That helicopter has (fly) over the intersection twice. ________
4. Yesterday Lon (swim) the length of the pool. ________
5. Our email manual was (write) by Lisa Shapiro. ________
6. The mild earthquake (shake) the windows in the conference room. ________
7. Last year Dr. Crowley (give) a substantial donation to UNICEF. ________
8. Have you (speak) with the supervisor yet? ________
9. I wish Scott had (know) about the scholarship earlier. ________
10. All employees should have (go) to the emergency procedures demonstration. ________

Check your answers.

B. Underline any verb errors you find in the following sentences. Write the correct forms in the spaces provided. Do not add helper verbs. Write *C* if the sentence is correct as it stands.

Example: Janet claimed that she <u>seen</u> the accident. had seen

1. Because of advances in technology, the world has shrank considerably. ________
2. Maureen set a record when she swam the Channel. ________
3. The office staff must chose new letterhead stationery. ________
4. Fibreglass was blown into the ceiling for insulation. ________
5. Omar and Ross have went to the lecture in Massey Hall. ________
6. Her friend asked if Marta had ate dinner yet. ________
7. His car was stole over the weekend. ________
8. We should have thrown out that old printer long ago. ________
9. Why wasn't our electric bill payed last month? ________
10. Is that the dog that has bit two passersby? ________

---

1. came 2. seen 3. flown 4. swam 5. written 6. shook 7. gave 8. spoken 9. known 10. gone

11. I can't believe Claudia brang her dog to work. ____________

12. The telephone has rang only twice in the past hour. ____________

13. In lieu of the month's vacation to Tahiti, Mrs. Ferguson choose a foreign sports sedan. ____________

14. Prices on the stock exchange sunk to a new low. ____________

15. The first pitch of the season was thrown out by the Prime Minister. ____________

C. *Lie–lay.* Write the correct verb forms.

Present	Past	Past Participle	Present Participle
lie (to rest):	____________	____________	____________
lay (to place):	____________	____________	____________

Select the correct verb.

1. Norma had to (lay, lie) down until the dizziness passed. ____________
2. Stacy (layed, laid) the mail on Mrs. Maracle's desk. ____________
3. The contracts have been (lying, laying) in her in-box for some time. ____________
4. In fact, they have (laid, lain) there for more than a week. ____________
5. Every day at 2 p.m., Arnold (lies, lays) down to rest. ____________
6. Yesterday, however, he (lay, laid) down at 3 p.m. ____________
7. Her clothes were (laid, lain) out on the bed. ____________
8. Fred was (laying, lying) in the sun without sunscreen. ____________
9. Iain Grant (lay, laid) some of the blame on management policies. ____________
10. He was accused of (lying, laying) down on the job. ____________

D. *Sit–set; rise–raise.* Write the correct forms of the verb.

Present	Past	Past Participle	Present Participle
sit (to rest):	____________	____________	____________
set (to place):	____________	____________	____________
rise (to go up):	____________	____________	____________
raise (to lift):	____________	____________	____________

Select the correct verb.

1. We'll need to (raise, rise) prices to cover our higher insurance costs. ____________
2. How can we finish if Roland (sits, sets) there all day? ____________

3. Close the windows if you want to (raise, rise) the temperature in the room. ____________

4. The temperature (raises, rises) rapidly in a room filled with people busy working at computers. ____________

5. Managers are (sitting, setting) goals for the production and sales staffs. ____________

6. I (sat, set) my books on the table when I came home. ____________

7. Miss Tibari (raised, rose) the question of retroactive benefits. ____________

8. Julie and Tom Kokales always (sit, set) near the door. ____________

9. Our office building (sits, sets) at the corner of Front and Pine. ____________

10. Consumer prices have (raised, risen) faster than consumer income. ____________

E. Compose original sentences using the verb forms shown.

1. choose ____

2. blown ____

3. shrank ____

4. lead ____

5. rose ____

6. sat ____

7. grown ____

8. lay ____

NAME ______________________________

LEVEL III

A. (**Self-check**) Verbs in the following sentences have been italicized. In the space provided, indicate the tense of each of these verbs. Indicate also if any verbs are in the passive voice. Refer to the text to guide you.

Example: Your credit cards *had been recovered* by the time you reported the loss. ___past perfect, passive___

1. The media *will have gotten* news of the layoffs before the employees. ______________
2. Those orders *are being sent* to your Oshawa branch. ______________
3. Mr. Adams' case *will have been heard* in six weeks. ______________
4. I cannot believe what I *am hearing*. ______________
5. Charles *had been told* to send the payroll reports to the auditor. ______________
6. We *have* just *seen* your product advertised on television. ______________
7. The manager's suggestions for reduced paper use *have been followed* by all employees. ______________
8. We *will be seeing* increased security measures at the airport. ______________
9. The Birches *have lived* in that neighbourhood for years. ______________
10. We *are* now *experiencing* the effects of the last cutback. ______________

Check your answers.

B. Write the proper verb forms according to the specifications in parentheses.

Example: They (drive) all night before they found a motel. (Past perfect) ___had driven___

1. Before the office announcement was made, we (hear) rumours about layoffs. (Past perfect) ______________
2. When her supervisor called, Natasha (get) ready to give her presentation. (Past progressive) ______________
3. By next April, RamCo (open) four branch outlets. (Future perfect) ______________
4. I'm sure they (tell) us about their trip when they return. (Future progressive) ______________
5. Plans (develop) to reduce administrative costs. (Present progressive, passive) ______________

1. future perfect 2. present progressive, passive 3. future perfect, passive 4. present progressive 5. past perfect, passive 6. present perfect 7. present perfect, passive 8. future progressive 9. present perfect 10. present progressive

6. Our company (think) about adopting a tuition reimbursement program. (Present progressive) ______________________

7. Check to see whether they (receive) the signed contracts. (Present perfect) ______________________

8. By 5 p.m. the contract (finish) and faxed to our client. (Past perfect, passive) ______________________

9. Before next Monday he (paint) all the exterior and trim on the house. (Future perfect) ______________________

10. Is it true that you (live) in the same house all your life? (Present perfect) ______________________

11. By the time the sun came up, William (do) four laps around the track. (Past perfect) ______________________

12. The company spokesperson says that the computer purchase (cancel) because of "the difficult economic environment." (Present perfect, passive) ______________________

13. Geac (sell) two money-losing divisions recently. (Present perfect) ______________________

14. Ford (offer) no-interest financing on its vehicles since the beginning of the month. (Present perfect progressive) ______________________

15. The CEO said that the corporation (lose) money in six divisions. (Past progressive) ______________________

16. We (hang) the new blinds in your office. (Present perfect) ______________________

17. The company's new policy (pay) off. (Present progressive) ______________________

18. The tide (begin) to turn. (Past progressive) ______________________

19. Record earnings (report) by Maersk. (Present progressive, passive) ______________________

20. Landlords found that rising vacancy rates (give) more leverage to renters. (Past perfect) ______________________

C. Cumulative Review. These sentences review Chapters 1 through 9, as well as general proofreading skills. Underline any errors. Then write corrected forms in the spaces provided. Some sentences require more than one correction. If a sentence is correct, write *C* in the space.

1. Fees for visits to a doctors office have rose steadily over the decade. ______________________

2. Although some policys allow you to chose any doctor, the plan selected for us office workers offers less freedom. ______________________

3. Steve and me could have forgave her if she had softened her tone. ______________________

4. The company hided it's losses by inflating sales. ______________________

5. Every employee must name a beneficiary on their life insurance forms. ______________________

6. During it's first month of operation, the recycling program has broke records for reducing waste. ______________________

7. You and me need to work hard to make sure that we don't loose this opportunity. __________

8. Many larger facilitys can recycle at no net cost because there haulers are taking away less trash. __________

9. Has anyone on the womens team submitted their doctor's release form yet? __________

10. Mr. Sanchez contract, which is laying on the desk, must be delivered immediately. __________

11. The vice-president has swore that no one would work harder than him to meet the deadline. __________

12. Not one of the job candidates who we interviewed has wrote a thank-you letter. __________

13. Although I told James dog to lay down, it jumped up and knocked me over. __________

14. Because it has took two hours to complete the test, I will be late. __________

15. Next Monday is Labour Day, hence we won't need the ride you offered to Beth and I. __________

16. The meeting begun before the CEOs staff arrived. __________

17. Our research shows that the average part-time retail employee will have stole over $300 worth of merchandise in a years time. __________

18. You may set the printer on this desk until a better location is found. __________

19. Cheryl said she seen you and him at Omars party. __________

20. Because to many computers were running, the room temperature had raised to 27°C. __________

D. Optional Writing. Your instructor may ask you to complete this exercise on a separate sheet.

Write ten original sentences, one for each of the following verb forms: *begun, chose, comes, driven, drunk, given, lying (resting), raise, seen,* and *spoke.*

Editor's Challenge

The following memo and letter contain errors reflecting the concepts you have studied thus far, as well as general proofreading errors. Use standard proofreading marks to show your corrections.

DATE: January 21, 200x

TO: All Employees

FROM: Vice-President, Human Resources

SUBJECT: CHANGE IN FLOATING HOLIDAY POLICY

The senior executive staff has approve a change in the companys floating holiday plan. Employees in the past vote on a single date to be took by all workers as there floating holiday, now, however, each employee will be allowed to chose the date that they wish to use as a floating holiday.

To reserve your floating holiday. Please notify your supervisor or I. Approval will be base on your units staffing needs. If a supervisor or myself receive several requests for the same date, employment seniority will govern.

A question has arose about how to record these holidays. I have spoke to Payroll, and they say you should use the Attendance Bonus code on your time card. This method will be used until Payroll has went over all employees records and modified it.

We wish it was possible for everyone to have their holiday exactly when desired, but we must urge you to be flexible. Our principle concern is that a reduced workforce may have a negative affect on our service. Because your supervisor has all ready began a schedule of employees floating holidays. It's not too early for you to submit your request.

Training Massage Wellness

June 4, 200x

Mr. Allen C. Fineberg
3250 Maple Way
Surrey, BC V4A 5G4

Dear Mr. Fineburg:

You probably choose Body Fitness because it has became one of the top-rated gyms in the Surrey area. Making your workout enjoyable has always been our principle goal. To continue to provide you with the best equipment and programs, my partner and myself need your feedback.

We have build an outstanding program with quality equipment, excellent training programs, and helpful support staff. We feel, however, that we could have a more positive affect and give more individual attention if we could extend our peak usage time. You have probable noticed that attendance at the gym raises from 4 p.m. to 8 p.m. We wish it was possible to accommodate everyone on their favourite equipment during those hours. Although we can't stretch an hour. We would like to make better use of the time between 8 p.m. and 11 p.m. With more members' coming later, we would have less crush from 4 to 8 p.m. Exercise machines that lay idle and strength-training equipment that sets empty could see action.

To encourage you to stay later, security cameras for our parking area are being considered by us. Cameras for some inside facilitys may also be added. We have gave this matter a great deal of thought. Although Body Fitness has never had an incident that endangered a member. We have went to considerable trouble to learn about security cameras because we think that you will feel all together more comfortable with them in action.

Please tell us what you think, fill out the enclosed questionnaire, and drop it the ballot box at the front desk during next weeks visit. We're asking for your feed back. Because we're devoted to serving you better. If you have any other suggestions for reducing the crush at peak times or other ideas that effect our members, please tell us on the enclosed form.

Cordially,

Nicolas Barajas

Nicolas Barajas, Manager

Enclosure

10500 North Military Trail Surrey, BC V3R 9P1 250.798.5302 bodyfitness.surrey.com

POSTTEST

Underline the correct verb.

1. After we (saw, seen) the advertisement, we bought the machine.
2. Your telephone has (rung, rang) only twice while you were gone.
3. The report has (laid, lain) on your desk for over a week.
4. Soil temperatures will slowly (raise, rise) during the spring.
5. Mr. Freeman has (worn, wore) the same suit every day this week.

learning.web.ways

Assume you're on the job and a new employee needs a little instruction in the use of email. You decide to use the Web to provide a quick tutorial.

Goal: To learn to use an email tutorial.

1. With your web browser on the screen, key the following URL for Fraser Valley Regional Library: **<http://www.fvrl.bc.ca/learn/tutorial/e-mail.html>**.
2. Read the five sections on this page.
3. How does email save natural resources?
4. How are multiple addresses entered in the "**Cc**" field?
5. This site provides a quick online tutorial for introducing email, but it suffers from some writing lapses. Can you find two comma splices?
6. Print two pages from this site, underline the answers to our questions, submit your printouts, and end your session.

---

1. saw. 2. rung 3. lain 4. rise 5. worn

C H A P T E R

Verb and Subject Agreement

10

OBJECTIVES When you have completed the materials in this chapter, you will be able to do the following:

LEVEL I

- *Locate the subjects of verbs despite intervening elements and inverted sentence structure.*
- *Make verbs agree with true subjects.*
- *Make verbs agree with subjects joined by* and *and with company names and titles.*

LEVEL II

- *Make verbs agree with subjects joined by* or *or* nor.
- *Select the correct verbs to agree with collective nouns and indefinite pronouns.*

LEVEL III

- *Make verbs agree with* the number/a number, *quantities and measures, fractions and portions, and clauses.*
- *Achieve subject–verb agreement with phrases and clauses as subjects and with subject complements.*

PRETEST

Underline the correct verb.

1. One of the plant supervisors (plan, plans) to implement a new safety program.
2. The head surgeon, along with her entire operating room team, (was, were) given training on the newest laser technology.
3. Neither the supervisor nor the members of his team (is, are) satisfied with the level of service.
4. Behind this building (lies, lie) the parking lot and swimming pool.
5. The number of email messages (is, are) increasing daily.

---

1. plans 2. was 3. are 4. lie 5. is

Subjects must agree with verbs in number (singular or plural) and person. Beginning a sentence with *He don't* damages a speaker's credibility and limits a communicator's effectiveness.

If an error is made in subject–verb agreement, it can generally be attributed to one of three lapses: (1) failure to locate the subject, (2) failure to recognize the number of the subject after locating it, or (3) failure to recognize the number of the verb. Suggestions for locating the true subject and determining the number of the subject and its verb follow.

LEVEL I

Hotlink

Athabasca University provides a good overview of sentence subjects and points on subject recognition at **<http://www.athabascau.ca/courses/engl/egh/recognition_of_sentence_parts.php#subject_recognition>**.

Spot the Blooper

On the label of Heinz 57 sauce: "Its' unique tangy blend of herbs and spices bring out the natural taste of steak." (Did you spot two bloopers?)

Spot the Blooper

From the Inmac computer catalogue: "WORD is full of new automatic features that really does simplify your workday."

▶ Locating Subjects

All verbs have subjects. Locating these subjects can be difficult, particularly when (a) a prepositional phrase comes between the verb and its subject, (b) an intervening element separates the subject and verb, (c) sentences begin with *there* or *here*, and (d) sentences are inverted. You practised locating subjects in Chapter 3, but because this is such an important skill, we provide additional instruction here.

Prepositional Phrases

Subjects of verbs are not found in prepositional phrases.* Therefore, you must learn to ignore such phrases in identifying subjects of verbs. Some of the most common prepositions are *of, to, in, from, for, with, at,* and *by*. Notice that the italicized prepositional phrases in these sentences do not contain the subjects of the verbs:

> Only one *of the company executives* has insurance. (The verb *has* agrees with its singular subject *one*, not with *executives*, the object of the preposition.)
> We wonder if the invoice *for the two shipments* is lost. (The verb *is* agrees with its subject *invoice*.)
> The range *of tasks and skill requirements* allows for upward growth potential. (The verb *allows* agrees with the subject *range*.)

Some of the less easily recognized prepositions are *except, but, like,* and *between*. In the following sentences, distinguish the subjects from the italicized prepositional phrases:

> All employees *but Tom* are to report early. (The verb *are* agrees with its plural subject *employees*.)
>
> Everyone *except the Harrises* is able to attend. (The verb *is* agrees with its subject *everyone*.)

Intervening Elements

Groups of words introduced by *as well as, in addition to, such as, including, plus, together with,* and *other than* do *not* contain sentence subjects.

> The priceless book, *as well as other valuable documents,* was lost in the fire.

In this sentence the writer has elected to emphasize the subject *book* and to de-emphasize *other valuable documents*. The writer could have given equal weight to these elements by writing *The priceless book and other valuable documents were lost in the fire.*

---

* *Occasionally a prepositional phrase may help to determine whether an indefinite pronoun, portion, or fraction is singular or plural; but the object of the preposition does not function as the subject of a verb. These points are discussed later in this chapter on pages 183 and 184.*

Notice that the number (singular or plural) of the verb changes when both *book* and *documents* are given equal emphasis. Here are additional examples involving intervening elements:

> Our president, *together with her entire staff of nine employees*, sends her greetings. (The singular subject *president* agrees with the singular verb *sends*.)
> Other pianists, *such as Pennario*, appear on the program. (The plural subject *pianists* agrees with the plural verb *appear*.)

Career Tip

Skilful writers avoid starting sentences or clauses with the unnecessary filler *there*. Usually sentences can be rewritten without it.

The Adverbs *there* and *here*

In sentences beginning with *there* or *here*, look for the true subject *after* the verb. As adverbs, *here* and *there* cannot function as subjects.

> There are four candidates for the position. (The subject *candidates* follows the verb *are*.)
> Here is the fuel oil consumption report. (The subject *report* follows the verb *is*.)

Be especially careful when using contractions. Remember that *here's* is the contraction for *here is*; therefore, it should be used only with singular subjects. Likewise, *there's* is the contraction for *there is* and should also be used only with singular subjects.

Incorrect: Here's the documents you requested. (The plural subject *documents* does not agree with the verb *is*.)

Correct: Here are the documents you requested. (The plural subject *documents* agrees with the verb *are*.)

Incorrect: There's three reasons you should hire me for the proofreader position. (The plural subject *reasons* does not agree with the verb *is*.)

Correct: There are three reasons you should hire me for the proofreader position. (The plural subject *reasons* agrees with the verb *are*.)

Study Tip

Remember that, although the ending -s makes a noun plural, it makes a verb singular (*The students come from Alberta; the student comes from Alberta*).

Inverted Sentence Order*

In inverted sentences and in questions, look for the subject after the verb or after the first element of a verb phrase.

> Have the product specifications been submitted? (The subject interrupts the verb phrase.)
> How important are salary, benefits, and job security? (The verb precedes the subjects.)
> On our board of directors are three prominent scientists. (The verb precedes the subject.)

Hotlink

The PowerPoint presentation on subject–verb agreement at **<http://xnet.rrc.mb.ca/leshanson/Writing_Resources.htm>** also contains a link to an interactive quiz on the same. Make sure to activate the link on the last slide.

▶ Basic Rules for Verb–Subject Agreement

Once you have located the sentence subject, decide whether the subject is singular or plural and select a verb that agrees in number. The chart on p. 158 of Chapter 9 will remind you that the third person singular form of most present tense verbs requires an *s*.

* *See also Chapter 3, p. 37.*

Subjects Joined by *and*

When one subject is joined to another by the conjunction *and*, the result is a compound subject; the subject is plural and requires a plural verb.

> Carolyn and her brother work at Baker's. (*Carolyn* and *brother* = they)
> The proposed law and its amendment are before the legislature. (*law* and *amendment* = they)

Company Names and Titles

Even though they may appear to be plural, company names and titles of publications are singular; therefore, they require singular verbs.

> *Seven Secrets to Successful Investing* was an instant bestseller. (one book = it)
> Thai Airways connects with Air Canada in Los Angeles. (one company = it)
> Richards, Bateman, and Richards is offering the bond issue. (one company = it)

Complete the reinforcement exercises for Level I on pp. 187–188.

LEVEL II

▶ Special Rules for Verb–Subject Agreement

Making sure your subjects agree with your verbs sometimes requires the application of special rules. This is especially true when dealing with subjects joined by *or* or *nor*, indefinite pronouns as subjects, and collective nouns as subjects.

Subjects Joined by *or* or *nor*

When two or more subjects are joined by *or* or *nor*, the verb should agree with the closer subject.

> Neither the supervisor nor the clerks know the order number.
> Either Leslie or you are in charge of ordering supplies.
> The manufacturer or the distributors carry spare parts.

Study Tip

Unlike subjects joined by *and*, subjects joined by *or* or *nor* require a choice between Subject No. 1 and Subject No. 2. Always choose the subject closer to the verb to determine the correct verb form.

Indefinite Pronouns as Subjects

As you may recall from Chapter 7 (p. 112), some indefinite pronouns are always singular, whereas some indefinite pronouns are always plural. In addition, some may be either singular or plural, depending on the words to which they refer.

Always Singular	Always Plural	Singular or Plural
anyone, anybody, anything,	both	all
each, either, every, everyone,	few	more
everybody, everything, many a,	many	most
neither, nobody, nothing, someone,	several	some
somebody, something		any
		none*

* *See discussion in Hotline Queries on p. 185.*

Either of the two applicants *is* qualified.
Everybody in the lottery *has* an equal chance.
A *few* of the employees *are* applying for shares.
Neither of the websites *is* particularly helpful.

Hotlink

A thorough guide to subject-verb agreement issues can be found at **<http://www.ccc.commnet.edu/sensen/part1/three/index.html>**.

Indefinite pronouns such as *all, more,* and *most* provide one of the few instances when prepositional phrases become important in determining agreement. Although the prepositional phrase does not contain the subject of the sentence, it may contain the noun to which the indefinite pronoun refers.

Most of the letters *are* finished. (*Most* is plural because it refers to the plural noun *letters*.)
Most of the work *is* completed. (*Most* is singular because it refers to the singular noun *work*.)

If *each, every,* or *many a* is used to describe two or more subjects joined by *and*, the subjects are considered separate. Therefore, the verb is singular.*

Many a semicolon and colon *is* misused.
Every man, woman, and child *is* affected by the tax cut.

Anyone, everyone, and *someone* are spelled as two words when followed by *of* phrases.

Any one of those websites can be used to book hotel reservations.
Every one of the candidates has a campaign committee.

Spot the Blooper

From *The St. John's Evening Telegram*: "It's important that we have in that position someone who's judgment, integrity, and incompetence is beyond question." (Did you spot three bloopers?)

Collective Nouns as Subjects

Nouns that are singular in form but represent a group, such as *faculty, committee,* and *council,* may be singular or plural, depending on their mode of operation. Usually a collective noun operates as a single unit, so its verb should be singular. If the elements of a collective noun operate separately, the verb should be plural.

Our faculty *has* unanimously approved the proposal. (*Faculty* has operated as a single unit.)
The council *were* sharply divided over appropriations. (*Council* members were acting separately. While technically correct as it stands, the sentence would be less awkward if it read, "The council *members* were sharply .... ")
The council *has* voted in favour of the zoning change. (*Council* is operating as a single unit.)
Our faculty *disagree* on the need for a strike. (*Faculty* members are acting separately.)

Spot the Blooper

From the *Evansville* (Indiana) *Press*: "Although a large crowd were gathered..."

Complete the reinforcement exercises for Level II on pp. 189–190.

LEVEL III

▶ Additional Rules for Verb–Subject Agreement

In some instances it is difficult to know whether a subject is singular or plural. Here are a few additional rules to guide you in selecting appropriate verbs for such subjects.

* *This use of a singular verb for two or more subjects joined by* and *is the only exception to the general rule presented in Level I.*

Spot the Blooper

Radio ad: "A new block of tickets are now on sale for *The Phantom of the Opera.*"

Study Tip

To determine the correct verb in *one of those who* clauses that do not include the word *only*, begin reading with the word *of*: *Of those people who are late sleepers,* John is one.

Hotlink

For extra help on special and additional rules for subject-verb agreement, don't miss Martine Johnson's advice and explanations on this University of Toronto web page **<http://www.utoronto.ca/writing/l2agr.html>**.

The Distinction Between *the number* and *a number*

When the word *number* is the subject of a sentence, its article (*the* or *a*) becomes significant. *The* is specific and therefore implies *singularity*; *a* is general and therefore implies *plurality*.

> *The number* of managers *is* declining. (Singular)
> *A number* of orders *were* lost. (Plural)

Quantities, Measures

When they refer to *total* amounts, quantities and measures are singular. If they refer to a number of individual units, quantities and measures are plural.

> Three years *is* the period of the loan. (Quantity as a total amount)
> Three years *were* spent on a complete renovation of the museum. (Quantity as individual units)

Fractions, Portions

Fractions and portions may be singular or plural, depending on the nouns to which they refer.

> Only a *third* of the students' reading scores are satisfactory.
> Over *half* of the contract was ratified.
> A *majority* of employees agree with the proposal.
> A *minimum* of work is required to receive approval.
> A small *percentage* of the delegates are in favour of the plan.
> *Part* of the proposal is ambiguous.

Who Clauses

Verbs in *who* clauses must agree in number and person with the nouns to which *who* refers. In *who* clauses introduced by *one of*, the verb is usually plural because *who* refers to a plural antecedent. In *who* clauses introduced by *the only one of*, the verb is singular because *who* refers to *one*.

> Mrs. Stephens is *one of* those managers who always support the employees.
> John is *one of* those people who are late sleepers.
> Margaret is *the only one of* the girls who is prepared.

Verbs must agree in person with the nouns or pronouns to which *who* refers.

> It is you who are responsible for security.
> Could it be I who am to blame?

Phrases and Clauses as Subjects

Use a singular verb when the subject of a sentence is an entire phrase or clause.

> *Learning about the stock market* is fascinating.
> *That verbs must agree with subjects* is accepted.

Subject Complements

In Chapter 8 you learned that linking verbs are followed by complements. Although a complement may differ from the subject in number, the linking verb should always agree with the subject.

> The best part of the show is the *singing and dancing*. (The singular subject *part* agrees with the singular verb *is* despite the plural complement *singing and dancing*.)
>
> The reason for his bankruptcy is poor *investments*.

If such a sentence seems awkward, you may reconstruct it so that the plural element is first: *Poor investments are the reason for his bankruptcy*. Or reword the sentence so that the subject is plural: *The best parts of the show are the singing and dancing.*

Spot the Blooper

From an Associated Press article: "Education and employer training is often the biggest need in an independently owned business."

Complete the reinforcement exercises for Level III on pp. 191–192.

HOTLINE QUERIES

Question: My uncle insists that *none* is singular. My English book says that it can be plural. Who's right?

Answer: Times are changing. Thirty years ago *none* was almost always used in a singular sense. Today, through usage, *none* may be singular or plural depending on what you wish to emphasize. For example, you may write *None are more willing than we*. On the other hand, you may say *None of the students is failing,* to emphasize *not even one*.

Question: When should I use *all together,* and when should I use *altogether*? I can never remember whether it's one word or two.

Answer: *All together* means "collectively" or "all the members of a group" (*we must work all together to reach our goal*). *Altogether* means "entirely" (*he was altogether satisfied*).

Question: Please help me with this sentence that I'm transcribing for a medical laboratory: *A copy of our analysis, along with our interpretation of its results, (has* or *have) been sent to you.*

Answer: The subject of your sentence is *copy*; thus the verb must be *has*. Don't let interrupting elements obscure the real sentence subject.

Question: After looking in the dictionary, I'm beginning to wonder about this: *We have alot of work yet to do*. I can't find the word *alot* in the dictionary, but it must be there. Everyone uses it.

Answer: The two-word phrase *a lot* is frequently used in conversation or in very informal writing (*the copier makes a lot of copies*). *Alot* as one word does not exist. Don't confuse it with *allot* meaning "to distribute" (*the company will allot to each department its share of supplies*).

(Continued)

Question: I'm totally confused by job titles for women today. What do I call a woman who is a *fireman*, a *policeman*, a *chairman*, or a *spokesman*? And what about the word *mankind*?

Answer: As more and more women enter non-traditional careers, some previous designations are being replaced by neutral, inclusive titles. Here are some substitutes:

actor	for *actress*
firefighter	for *fireman*
mail carrier	for *mailman*
police officer	for *policeman*
flight attendant	for *steward* or *stewardess*
reporter or journalist	for *newsman*

Words like *chairman, spokesman,* and *mankind* have traditionally been used to refer to both men and women. Today, however, sensitive writers strive to use language that cannot be considered sexist. Possible substitutes are *chair, spokesperson,* and *humanity.*

Question: I'm never sure how to handle words that are used to represent quantities and proportions in sentences. For example, what verb is correct in this sentence: *A large proportion of voters (was* or *were) against the measure?*

Answer: Words that represent fractional amounts (such as *proportion, fraction, minimum,* and *majority*) may be singular or plural, depending on the words they represent. In your sentence *proportion* represents *voters,* which is plural. Therefore, use the plural verb *were.*

NAME________________________________

CHAPTER 10 Reinforcement Exercises

LEVEL I

A. (**Self-check**) Select the correct word to complete each sentence below. Write it in the space provided.

1. Everyone except Jan and two other workers (is, are) parking in the company lot. ____________
2. One desk in our department, along with several on the second and third floors, (is, are) equipped with special ergonomic features. ____________
3. There (is, are) three primary reasons to invest in foreign securities. ____________
4. (Has, Have) the title page and bibliography been completed yet? ____________
5. No one but Nina and her cousins (has, have) seen the ranch. ____________
6. The computer and the monitor, along with the printer, (was, were) less expensive than we had expected. ____________
7. Addressing the graduating class (is, are) members of the class of '80. ____________
8. We understand that British Airways (is, are) interviewing flight attendants. ____________
9. A set of guidelines to standardize input and output (was, were) developed. ____________
10. *Freakonomics* by Steven D. Levitt and Stephen J. Dubner (appear, appears) to be one of the bestselling economics books of all time. ____________

Check your answers.

B. Assume that the following phrases serve as sentence subjects. Underline the simple subject(s) in each item. Then indicate if the subject is singular or plural.

	Singular	Plural
Example: the controller and the treasurer of the county		✓
1. a list of website addresses		
2. the office manager, together with his staff		
3. other services such as HTML coding and graphics		
4. the production cost and the markup of each item		
5. one of the most interesting websites on the Internet		
6. current emphasis on product safety and consumer protection		

1. is 2. is 3. are 4. Have 5. has 6. were 7. are 8. is 9. was 10. appears

7. Madison, Lee & Cassidy, an executive placement service ____________ ____________

8. the anger and frustration of the passengers ____________ ____________

C. For each of the following sentences, cross out any phrases that separate the verb from its subject. Underline the subject. Then choose the correct verb, and write it in the space provided.

Examples: The <u>supervisor</u>, ~~together with two of his assistants~~, (is, are) here. ____is____

Our <u>catalogue</u> ~~of gift ideas~~ (is, are) being sent to you. ____is____

1. Our company's full range of products and services (is, are) available through our local dealers. ____________
2. A description of the property, along with several other legal documents, (was, were) filed with my lawyer. ____________
3. Everyone except temporary workers employed during the last year (has, have) become eligible for retroactive benefits. ____________
4. The wingspan on each of Boeing's latest passenger planes (is, are) longer than the Wright brothers' first flight. ____________
5. All co-operatives except one (has, have) been able to show a profit for participating members. ____________
6. The use of cellphones and pagers (is, are) not allowed during meetings. ____________
7. Outstanding salespeople like Mrs. Love (has, have) helped make our company a leader in the field. ____________
8. One of your duties, in addition to the tasks already described, (is, are) the budgeting of funds for both departments. ____________

D. Select the correct verb, and write it in the space provided.

1. Here (is, are) a complete list of product features. ____________
2. Seated next to the Alvarados (is, are) Joe Miranda. ____________
3. There (is, are) two things you must do immediately. ____________
4. How essential (is, are) experience and education in this field? ____________
5. Our president, along with the general manager and three salespeople, (plan, plans) to attend the conference. ____________
6. Not one of our four service representatives (is, are) available. ____________
7. Cisco Systems (has, have) found a way to restructure its finances. ____________
8. Lying on my desk (is, are) my itinerary and plane tickets. ____________
9. Kerr, McClellan, and Horn, a legal firm in Halifax, (specializes, specialize) in corporate law. ____________
10. Considerable time and money (was, were) spent on the final product. ____________

NAME ______________________

LEVEL II

A. (**Self-check**) Write the correct form.

1. A task force of four men and five women (is, are) to be appointed. ____________
2. Either Eric Leibeler or Lily Chow (has, have) the room key. ____________
3. The inventory and the report (is, are) being prepared. ____________
4. Each of the websites (provide, provides) live support. ____________
5. All union members (has, have) to vote on the proposed contract. ____________
6. Nothing but catalogues and bulletins (is, are) in this box. ____________
7. Many a server and busser (has, have) complained about rude customers. ____________
8. (Everyone, Every one) of the sales reps made quota this month. ____________
9. All that work (is, are) yet to be logged in. ____________
10. Each clerk, administrative assistant, and word processing specialist (was, were) asked to complete a questionnaire. ____________

Check your answers.

B. Write the correct form.

1. The National Council of Jewish Women (has, have) taken a firm position. ____________
2. Neither Sergio Pelligrino nor Bonnie Hahn (is, are) afraid of hard work. ____________
3. (Everyone, Every one) of the résumés contained grammatical errors. ____________
4. Several of the proposals (contain, contains) complex formulas. ____________
5. Either the owner or her partners (is, are) responsible for the taxes. ____________
6. The group of players, coaches, and fans (plan, plans) to charter a plane. ____________
7. Either of the two solutions that you propose (is, are) satisfactory. ____________
8. Something about these insurance claims (appear, appears) questionable. ____________
9. Neither the president nor the faculty members (favour, favours) a tuition increase. ____________
10. Abstracts and affidavits (is, are) the principal work in this office. ____________

1. is 2. has 3. are 4. provides 5. have 6. is 7. has 8. Every one 9. is 10. was

11. (Was, Were) any of the members of the organization present that afternoon? ____________

12. (Is, Are) either of the clients satisfied with our marketing campaign? ____________

13. The jury (has, have) announced its verdict. ____________

14. Preservation of the ocean and its creatures (is, are) a major concern. ____________

15. Every one of the employees who attended the meeting (was, were) opposed to the reductions in benefits. ____________

16. A map showing campgrounds and picnic areas (is, are) provided at the gas station. ____________

17. Either a book or an article (has, have) to be read as part of the assignment. ____________

18. Our program, along with the efforts of other civic-minded businesses, (is, are) aimed at urban renewal. ____________

19. Any one of the shareholders (has, have) the right to delegate his or her proxy. ____________

20. Some of the handwriting in the sales reports (is, are) illegible. ____________

C. Use your imagination to complete the sentences started below, after choosing the correct verb from the choices in parentheses.

1. The staff (is, are) ____________

____

2. Our city council (has, have) ____________

____

3. Not one of the plans (was, were) ____________

____

4. Some of the jury members (believe, believes) ____________

____

5. Somebody in the theatre filled with patrons (was, were) ____________

____

6. The audience (was, were) ____________

____

NAME ____________________

LEVEL III

A. (**Self-check**) For each sentence write the correct verb in the space provided.

1. The number of companies performing background checks (is, are) greater than expected. ____________
2. Part of the loss of customers (is, are) the result of poor service. ____________
3. Laurie McDonough is one of those accountants who (has, have) earned the respect of their clients. ____________
4. Fourteen metres of pipe (is, are) exactly what was specified. ____________
5. Didn't you know it is you who (is, are) to be honoured at the ceremony? ____________
6. A number of problems (is, are) yet to be resolved. ____________
7. She is the only one of the service reps who (speak, speaks) three languages. ____________
8. Whoever is named for the job (has, have) my approval. ____________
9. About one-third of the records (is, are) stored on microfiche. ____________
10. The hardest part of the job (is, are) the bending and lifting. ____________

Check your answers.

B. Select the correct verb.

1. Five hundred dollars (is, are) required as a damage deposit on the conference facility. ____________
2. Our latest advertisements featuring our spring clothing line (is, are) an example of the campaign. ____________
3. Is it he who (is, are) the new account representative? ____________
4. Carole is the only one of the lab assistants who (was, were) able to repair the malfunctioning machine. ____________
5. Vacations for employees who are entitled to three or more weeks (is, are) the next item on the agenda. ____________
6. Sixty days (is, are) the period of the loan. ____________
7. In our agency the number of highly successful realtors (is, are) steadily increasing. ____________
8. Only a fraction of the conference delegates (was, were) unable to find accommodations at the Royal Manor. ____________

1. is 2. is 3. have 4. is 5. are 6. are 7. speaks 8. has 9. are 10. is (Even better: *The hardest parts of the job are* ....)

9. Serving on the student council (is, are) a representative from each of the 20 departments on campus. ____________

10. Over 80 per cent of the individuals attending the lecture series (is, are) residents of nearby communities. ____________

11. Michael is one of those people who always (get, gets) along well with fellow workers. ____________

12. The primary reason for his wealth (is, are) wise investments in oil. ____________

13. Keeping your skills up to date (is, are) important in today's economy. ____________

14. Representing our office (is, are) several men and women with many years of experience. ____________

15. Trimark Mutual Funds, with headquarters in Toronto, often (advertise, advertises) in *The Globe and Mail.* ____________

16. Mr. Gouveia is one of the executives who (is, are) being investigated. ____________

17. A chart showing all staff positions and responsibilities (was, were) prepared by the vice-president. ____________

18. Taking night classes while working (is, are) challenging. ____________

C. Review of Levels I, II, and III. Underline any subject–verb agreement problem, and write an improved form or forms in the space provided. Write *C* if the sentence is correct.

1. The reason for her many absences are severe headaches. ____________

2. One of the great places to visit, in addition to all the other destinations in New Brunswick, is historic St. Andrews By-The-Sea. ____________

3. With fewer than 1000 panda bears left in the wild, the visiting bear's conception and development was closely monitored. ____________

4. Was any of the members of the organization present for the final vote? ____________

5. After several days of deliberation, the jury has announced its verdict. ____________

6. Are either of the applicants available to interview on Friday? ____________

7. Persistent inflation and interest rate worries often causes share prices to drop. ____________

8. Globalization and the changing ethnic composition of Canada is causing more and more organizations to embrace diversity programs. ____________

D. Optional Writing. Your instructor may ask you to complete this exercise on a separate sheet.

Write ten original sentences using the following words as subjects of *present tense* verbs: *anyone, any one, everyone, every one, committee, the number, a number, everything, some,* and *one of the assistants.*

Editor's Challenge

The following letter proposal and email message contain intentional errors in spelling, proofreading, and grammar principles you have studied thus far. Use standard proofreading marks to show your corrections.

Wright Research Consultants

385 Eglinton Ave. West
Toronto, ON M4T 2H9
Web: http://www.wrightresearch.com Phone: (416) 220-9184 Email: rwright@wrightresearch.com

April 15, 200X

Mr. Morris Edelson
Consumer Credit Service
1021 Birchmount Road
Toronto, ON M1K 5G3

Dear Mr. Edelson:

At your request my staff and myself is submitting the following proposal regarding a survey of university students credit habits in southern Ontario.

Problem

As you point out, credit purchase's among university students is burdening them with to much debt, more than half of full-time undergraduate students now has at least one major credit card. Although students account for less than 3 per cent of the domestic credit card business, a significant number of these students is having more trouble than other borrowers in repaying. Credit card use among students has rose dramatically in the past decade.

Background

We understand that your non-profit organizations principle goal is to open a credit counselling service aimed at university students in southern Ontario. Specifically, you want to investigate (1) credit card habit's among university students in general, (2) credit card habits among students in your area, and (3) the affectiveness of student counselling services in other parts of the country.

Proposed Plan

On the basis of our experience in conducting many local and national surveys. Wright Research propose to develop a short but thorough questionnaire probing the data you desire. We will submit the questionnaire for you approval, and we will consult with you regarding the exact sample and it's demographics. Data from the surveywill be analyze by our experienced team of experts. Using the latest computer systems and advanced statistical measures.

Consumer Credit Service Page 2 April 15, 200X

Staffing and Budget

Wright Research Consultants are a nationally recognized, experienced research consulting firm specializing in survey investigation. My staff and myself has assigned your survey to Dr. Rebecca Horne, whom is our director of research. Dr. Horne was trained at the University of Alberta and has successfully supervise our research program for the past nine years. Further information about her qualifications and our staffs training are provided in the attached brochure. Everyone of the members of our staff are experienced in survey research. Budget figures for this proposed survey is shown in the attach brochure.

Authorization

My staff and myself sincerely believe that our profesionally designed and administered survey are exactly what you need to enable you to make a decision about the establishment of a student credit counselling service in southern Ontario. Wright Research can have the results for you by July 2. If you sign the enclosed duplicate copy of this letter and return them immediately to Dr. Horne or I with a retainer of $3000. The prices in this offer is in affect only until September 1.

Sincerely,

Lawrence R. Wright

Lawrence R. Wright
President

Enclosure

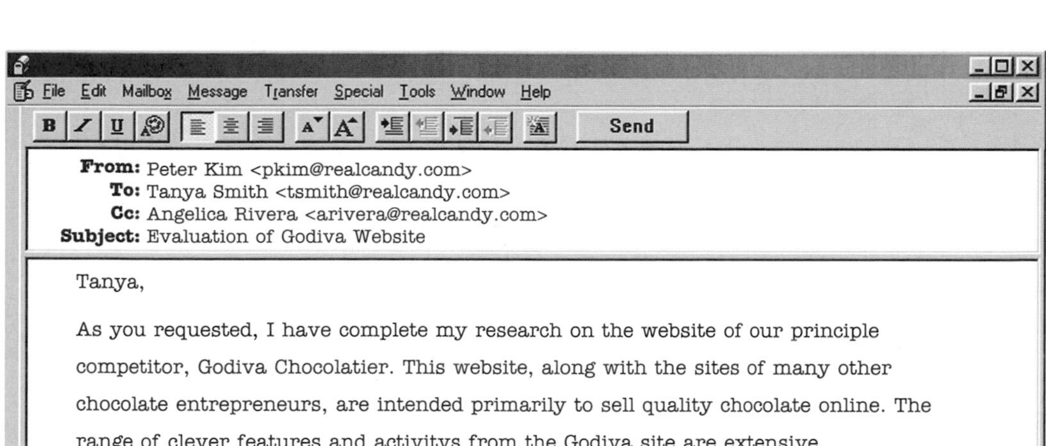

File Edit Mailbox Message Transfer Special Tools Window Help

Send

From: Peter Kim <pkim@realcandy.com>
To: Tanya Smith <tsmith@realcandy.com>
Cc: Angelica Rivera <arivera@realcandy.com>
Subject: Evaluation of Godiva Website

Tanya,

As you requested, I have complete my research on the website of our principle competitor, Godiva Chocolatier. This website, along with the sites of many other chocolate entrepreneurs, are intended primarily to sell quality chocolate online. The range of clever features and activitys from the Godiva site are extensive.

Although selling chocolates online are very important, advertising and customer service is also important at *Godiva.com*. Stylish graphics and a gold back ground reminiscent of Godivas gold packaging makes the site one of the most attractive I have saw.

Navigating the site seems easy. Clear links take visitors to different parts of the site, allowing them to order chocolate, learn about Godiva products, or work with a customer service representative. Although the link's change frequently. Here is a few typical links:

- **Shopping Online.** This link enables the web cruiser to search for and purchase Godiva chocolates via an online catalogue. Customers may search for chocolates by price, by type, or even by holiday. The selections they have chose are collected in a shopping basket and purchase with a credit card.
- **Recipes.** A number of mouth-watering recipes featuring Godiva chocolates are posted on this link. However, if you have ever ate Godiva chocolates, you would wonder why any one would ever ruin them by cooking them!
- **Business Gift Giving.** One of the best links for companys describe corporate incentive programs, custom packaging, and volume discounts.
- **What's New?** A collection of new items are featured, including Godiva biscuits, gifts, recipes, and new products. Although prices are raising, Godiva's seems reasonable.

The **Spotlight** feature describes an online sweepstakes, a soap opera, Godiva kosher products, and *Chocolatier Magazine.* I will send printouts of several of *Godiva.coms* best web pages. Visitors' may also access the site directly at **www.godiva.com**.

If you have began to think seriously about launching our companys website, I am eager to help sit it up. Please write or call me at Ext. 388 to let me know how I may assist.

Peter

POSTTEST

Underline the correct verb.

1. At least one of our accountants (suggest, suggests) using a tax-deferred plan.
2. The cost of supplies, along with service and equipment costs, (is, are) a major problem.
3. Either the administrative assistant or the engineers (has, have) to find the original copy.
4. There (is, are) many firms we can use to design our new website.
5. A number of surprising events (is, are) creating spikes in the stock market.

learning.web.ways

"Netiquette" is network etiquette covering the dos and don'ts of online communication. To become familiar with some of the informal "rules of the road" in cyberspace, you will visit the "Business Netiquette International" site.

Goal: To learn about netiquette.

1. With your web browser on the screen, enter the following URL: **<http://www.bspage.com/1netiq/Netiq.html>** (that's a number "1" preceding "netiq").
2. If this URL doesn't work, find the site by using a search engine **<www.google.com>** with the term **Business Netiquette International**.
3. Scroll through the Business Netiquette International site. Don't click any links.
4. What is the basic rule of etiquette in any circumstance?
5. When is it permissible to send attachments to email messages?
6. Should you use first names in email messages?
7. Print the first page of this site.
8. End your session, and submit your printed page and written answers.

1. suggests 2. is 3. have 4. are 5. are

C H A P T E R

Verbals

11

OBJECTIVES When you have completed the materials in this chapter, you will be able to do the following:

LEVEL I

- *Recognize gerunds and supply appropriate modifiers of gerunds.*
- *Identify and remedy split infinitives that result in awkward sentences.*

LEVEL II

- *Correctly punctuate introductory and other verbal phrases.*
- *Avoid writing awkward participial phrases.*

LEVEL III

- *Spot dangling verbal phrases.*
- *Rewrite sentences to avoid misplaced verbal phrases.*

PRETEST

Write *a, b,* or *c* to describe the following sentences.

a = contains no errors
b = contains error in use of verbal form
c = contains error in punctuation of verbal form

1. When preparing my report, the Web provided me with the best information. __________
2. After considering the project carefully the vice-president gave his approval. __________
3. To register by mail, return the enclosed application form. __________
4. Announced in August, CEO Milton explained details of the payout plan. __________
5. To be finished on time the report required many hours of extra effort by the staff. __________

1. b 2. c 3. a 4. b 5. c

As you learned earlier, English is a highly flexible language in which a given word may have more than one grammatical function. In this chapter you will study verbals. Derived from verbs, verbals are words that function as nouns, adjectives, or adverbs. Three kinds of verbals are gerunds (verbal nouns), infinitives, and participles (verbal adjectives).

LEVEL I

Hotlink

For further help with gerunds and infinitives, followed by an online quiz, visit Grammar Goblins at **<http://langues.cmaisonneuve.qc.ca/sbeller/quizzes/Grammar_Goblins/GGvger-infinExplan.html>**.

▶ Gerunds

A verb form ending in *ing* and used as a noun is called a *gerund.*

Advertising is necessary. (Gerund used as subject)
Dale enjoys *skiing.* (Gerund used as direct object)

Using Gerunds Correctly

In using gerunds, follow this rule: Make any noun or pronoun modifying a gerund possessive, as *Karen's keyboarding* or *her computing.* Because we sometimes fail to recognize gerunds as nouns, we fail to make their modifiers possessive.

Wrong: The staff objects to *Kevin smoking.*
Right: The staff objects to *Kevin's smoking.*

The staff does not object to Kevin, as the first version states; it objects to his smoking. If we substitute a more easily recognized noun for *smoking,* the possessive form seems more natural: *The staff objects to Kevin's behaviour. Behaviour* is a noun, just as *smoking* is a noun; the noun or pronoun modifiers of both must be possessive.

Mr. Drake resented *my* calling during lunch. (The gerund *calling* requires the possessive pronoun *my,* not the objective-case pronoun *me.*)
We appreciate *your* bringing this matter to our attention. (Not *you bringing*)

Of course, not all verb forms ending in *ing* are gerunds. Some are participles acting either as elements in verb phrases or as adjectives. Compare these three sentences:

I saw Monica programming. (The word *programming* functions as an adjective describing Monica.)
I admired Monica's programming. (As the object of the verb, *programming* acts as a gerund.)
Monica is programming. (Here, *programming* is part of a verb phrase.)

Hotlink

Getting a headache over split infinitives? To ease your mind, read this intriguing CBC article on the subject at **<http://www.cbc.ca/news/indepth/words/infinitives.html>**.

▶ Infinitives

When the simple present form of a verb is preceded by *to,* the most basic verb form results: the *infinitive.* The sign of the infinitive is the word *to.*

Try *to sign* the papers immediately.
To write gracefully requires great skill.

Using Infinitives Correctly

In certain expressions infinitives may be misused. Observe the use of the word *to* in the following infinitive phrases. Do not substitute the conjunction *and* for the *to* of the infinitive.

Try *to call* when you arrive. (Not *try and call*)
Be sure *to speak* softly when you use your cellphone in public. (Not *Be sure and speak*)
Check *to see* when your appointment is. (Not *check and see*)

When any word appears between *to* and the verb (*to* carefully *prepare*), an infinitive is said to be split. At one time split infinitives were considered great grammatical sins. Today most authorities agree that infinitives may be split if necessary for clarity and effect. However, avoid split infinitives that result in awkward sentences.

Awkward: Mr. Stokes wanted *to*, if he could find time, *recheck* his figures.
Better: If he could find time, Mr. Stokes wanted *to recheck* his figures.

Awkward: Our company has *to*, when the real estate market returns to normal, *consider* purchasing an office building.
Better: Our company has *to consider*, when the real estate market returns to normal, purchasing an office building.

Acceptable: *To* wilfully *lie* under oath is perjury. (No awkwardness results from split infinitive.)
Acceptable: Mrs. Higgins expects you *to* really *concentrate* when you proofread. (No awkwardness results from split infinitive.)

Complete the reinforcement exercises for Level I on pp. 204–206.

Spot the Blooper

Headline from *The Urbana* [Ohio] *Daily Citizen:* "Volunteers Use Sandbags to Try and Save Water Plant."

Hotlink

Help with using gerunds is available on this University of Toronto web page: **<http://www.utoronto.ca/writing/l2ger.html>**.

▶ Participles

LEVEL II

In Chapter 9 you studied the present and past forms of participles functioning as parts of verb phrases. You will recall that in such constructions present and past participles always require helping verbs: *is typing, was seen, has been, had broken.*

In this chapter we will be concerned with a second possible function of participles. Participles can function as adjectives. As adjectives, participles modify nouns or pronouns and do not require helping verbs. Here are sentences that illustrate the five forms of the participle.

Present participle, active: *Helping* William with the proposal, we are staying late. (The participle *Helping* modifies *we.*)

Present participle, passive: William McCain, *being helped* by his colleagues, is completing the proposal. (*Being helped* is a participle that describes *William McCain.*)

Past participle, passive: Although *helped* by three others, William found it difficult to admit their assistance. (The participle *helped* functions as an adjective to describe *William.*)

Study Tip

To distinguish between *ing* forms used as nouns and those used as adjectives, try the *what?* question approach. In the sentence *I admired Monica's programming,* say to yourself, "I admired *what?*" Answer: "I admired Monica's *programming,* not Monica." Therefore, *programming* is the object and functions as an *ing* noun.

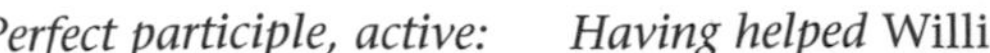

Perfect participle, active: *Having helped* William on many previous occasions, his colleagues were accustomed to his inability to thank them. (The participle *Having helped* describes *his colleagues.*)

Perfect participle, passive: William, *having been helped* on many big projects, was deeply indebted to his colleagues. (The participle *having been helped* functions as an adjective to describe *William.*)

Hotlink

For a good overview of verbal phrases (and some interactive exercises on verbals), visit this University of Calgary website **<http://www.ucalgary.ca/UofC/eduweb/grammar/>**. First click on Sentence Elements; then scroll down to the link for Verbal Phrases.

Using Participles Correctly

Avoid using participles that sound awkward, such as the following:

Awkward: Pam's having been promoted to office manager was cause for celebration.
Better: Pam's promotion to office manager was cause for celebration.

Awkward: Being as you have arrived early, may I leave now?
Better: Since you have arrived early, may I leave now?

▶ Punctuating Verbal Forms

Determining whether verbal forms require commas sometimes causes difficulty. Let's try to clear up this difficulty with explanations and examples.

Punctuating Introductory Verbal Forms

When verbal forms are used in introductory words or expressions, there's no question about punctuating them. A comma should be placed between an introductory verbal form or phrase and the main clause of a sentence.

Astonished, the lawyer turned to the jury. (Introductory verbal form)
To improve product distribution, Burke hired a traffic manager. (Introductory verbal phrase)
Receiving too many email messages, Andy established filters. (Introductory verbal phrase)
Having completed forty-three years with the company, Betty Bond retired. (Introductory verbal phrase)

Career Tip

You'll win the respect of your colleagues if you avoid using *being, being as,* or *being that* when you mean *since* or *because (Being it was hot* ...). These substandard usages create the impression of poor English skills and can limit a career.

Not all verbal phrases that begin sentences, however, are introductory. If the verbal phrase represents the subject or part of the predicate of the sentence, *no* comma should separate it from the rest of the sentence.

Preparing a budget is Al's responsibility. (Verbal phrase used as subject; no comma)
To change our budget at this time is almost impossible. (Verbal phrase used as subject; no comma)
Located in the other building is our Shipping Department. (Verbal phrase used as part of predicate; no comma)

Punctuating Non-Essential Verbal Phrases

Essential (restrictive) information is needed for the reader to understand the sentence. Verbal phrases often help identify the subject; these phrases require no commas. Non-essential (non-restrictive) information could be omitted without altering the basic meaning of the sentence, so non-essential phrases are set off by commas.

Mrs. Lanier, *working late at the office,* was able to meet the deadline. (The verbal phrase *working late at the office* adds additional information, but it is not essential. The subject is fully identified by name. Use commas to set off the non-essential phrase.)

The woman *working late at the office* was able to meet the deadline. (In this sentence the verbal phrase *working late at the office* is essential; it is needed to identify the subject. *Which* woman was able to meet the deadline? The woman *working late at the office.* No commas set off this essential verbal phrase.)

TD-Canada Trust, *opening a new branch in St. John's,* offered gifts to attract customers. (The verbal phrase is not essential because there is only one TD-Canada Trust, and it has been identified. Commas enclose this non-essential verbal phrase.)

A company *opening a new branch in St. John's* offered gifts to attract customers. (This verbal phrase is essential to identify *which* company offered gifts. No commas are needed. *Note:* Even if you pause when you reach the end of the verbal phrase, don't be tempted to add a comma.)

Study Tip

To help you understand the use of commas in dealing with non-essential information, think of a window shade. Use commas to lower the window shade and cover the words enclosed. If words in a verbal phrase are not essential to the meaning of a sentence, use a "comma window shade" to obscure them.

Notice in the preceding sentences that whenever a non-essential verbal phrase interrupts the middle of a sentence, *two* commas set it off.

Complete the reinforcement exercises for Level II on pp. 207–209.

▶ Avoiding Misplaced Verbal Modifiers

LEVEL III

Used correctly, verbal modifiers and phrases add clarity and description to your writing. Let's consider the best way to position them within sentences.

Introductory Verbal Phrases

Introductory verbal phrases must be followed by words they can logically modify. Such phrases can create confusion or unintended humour when placed incorrectly in a sentence. Consider this sentence: *Sitting in the car, the mountains were breathtaking.* The introductory participial phrase in this sentence is said to *dangle* because it is not followed immediately by a word it can logically modify; this phrase is called a *dangling modifier*. The sentence could be improved by revising it to read: *Sitting in the car, we saw the breathtaking mountains.* (*We*, a word logically modified by the verbal phrase, has been placed directly after the phrase.) See how the following illogical sentences have been improved:

Illogical:	Slipping on the ice, his back was injured.
Logical:	Slipping on the ice, *he* injured his back.
Illogical:	Turning on the fan, papers flew about the office.
Logical:	Turning on the fan, *I* caused papers to fly about the office.
Illogical:	After answering the telephone, the doorbell began to ring insistently.
Logical:	After answering the telephone, *Jeremy* heard the doorbell ring insistently.
Illogical:	Skilled with computers, the personnel director hired Kay.
Logical:	Skilled with computers, *Kay* was hired by the personnel director.

Spot the Blooper

From *Country Collectibles*: "Sitting by a blazing fire, reading a good mystery novel, a dog can jump into your lap and beg for a few playful pats on the head."

Hotlink

University of Acadia's *Grammar Outlaw* offers additional hints on how to handle misplaced and dangling modifiers at **<http://ace.acadiau.ca/english/grammar/mmodifier.htm>**.

But:	To master a language, listen carefully to native speakers. (In commands, the understood subject is *you*. Therefore, this verbal phrase is correctly followed by the word to which it refers: To master a language, [you] listen carefully to native speakers.)

Study Tip

After reading an introductory verbal phrase, ask the question *who?* The answer to that question must immediately follow the introductory phrase. For example, *To find a good job, who?* Answer: To find a good job, *Derek* wrote to many companies.

Verbal Phrases in Other Positions

In other positions within sentences, verbal phrases must also be placed in logical relation to the words they modify—in other words, as close as possible to those words.

Illogical:	The missing purchase orders were found by Mrs. Seldon's assistant lying in the top desk drawer.
Logical:	Mrs. Seldon's assistant found the missing purchase orders lying in the top desk drawer.
Illogical:	Emma met many women who were planning weddings while working at Sunnylea Bridal.
Logical:	While working at Sunnylea Bridal, Emma met many women who were planning weddings.

Complete the reinforcement exercises for Level III on pp. 210–212.

HOTLINE QUERIES

Question: Are there two meanings for the word *discreet*?

Answer: You are probably confusing the two words *discreet* and *discrete. Discreet* means "showing good judgment" and "prudent" (*The witness gave a discreet answer, avoiding gossip and hearsay*). The word *discrete* means "separate" or "non-continuous" (*Alpha Inc. has installed discrete computers rather than a network computer system*). You might find it helpful to remember that the *e*'s are separate in *discrete*.

Question: Should I use *complimentary* or *complementary* to describe free tickets?

Answer: Use *complimentary,* which can mean "containing a compliment, favourable, or free" (*the dinner came with complimentary wine; he made a complimentary remark*). *Complementary* means "completing or making perfect" (*the complementary colours enhanced the room*). An easy way to remember *compliment* is by thinking "*I* like to receive a *compliment*."

Question: I confuse *i.e.* and *e.g.* What's the difference?

Answer: The abbreviation *i.e.* stands for the Latin *id est,* meaning "that is" (*the package exceeds the weight limit, i.e., 3 kilos*). The abbreviation *e.g.* stands for the Latin *exempli gratia,* meaning "for the sake of example" or "for example" (*the manufacturer may offer a purchase incentive, e.g., a rebate or discount plan*). Notice the use of commas before and after *i.e.* and *e.g.*

Question: We're having an argument in our office about abbreviations. Can *department* be abbreviated as *dep't*? How about *manufacturing* as *mf'g*? Where could we find a correct list of such abbreviations?

Answer: In informal writing or when space is limited, words may be contracted or abbreviated. If a conventional abbreviation for a word exists, use it instead of a contracted form. Abbreviations are simpler to write and easier to read. For example, use *dept.* instead of *dep't;* use *natl.* instead of *nat'l;* use *cont.* instead of *cont'd.* Other accepted abbreviations are *ins.* for *insurance; mfg.* for *manufacturing; mgr.* for *manager;* and *mdse.* for *merchandise.* Notice that all abbreviations end with periods. Some dictionaries show abbreviations within the main entries so that a reader must know how to spell the word in full in order to be able to locate the abbreviation. Other dictionaries alphabetize abbreviations as separate entries. Reference manuals often have helpful lists of abbreviations.

Question: I'm not sure which word to use in this sentence: *They have used all (they're, their, there) resources in combatting the disease.*

Answer: Use *their,* which is the possessive form of *they.* The adverb *there* means "at that place or at that point" (*we have been there before*). *There* is also used as an expletive or filler preceding a linking verb (*there are numerous explanations*). *They're* is a contraction of *they are (they're coming this afternoon).*

Question: A sentence in a letter written by my boss reads, *We do not want an open invoice without there being justifiable reasons.* How should we spell *there*?

Answer: *There* is spelled correctly, but its use creates an awkward verbal form. If your boss agrees, revise the sentence to read, *We do not want an open invoice without justification.*

Question: I saw this in an auction announcement for a Beverly Hills home: *Married to interior decorator Dusty Bartlett, their home saw many of the great Hollywood parties with friends such as Ingrid Bergman and Katharine Hepburn setting by the pool on weekends.* Am I just imagining, or does this sentence say that the home was married to the interior decorator?

Answer: Amazing, isn't it! But that's what the sentence says. This is a classic dangling modifier. An introductory verbal phrase must be immediately followed by words that the phrase can logically modify. This sentence doesn't give us a clue. Did you also notice another problem? The verb *setting* should be *sitting.*

NAME ______________________________

CHAPTER 11 Reinforcement Exercises

LEVEL I

A. (**Self-check**) In the following sentences gerunds are italicized. Other *ing* words that are not italicized are not functioning as gerunds. Select appropriate modifiers.

1. She is unhappy with (you, your) *handling* of the order.
2. I saw (Mardi, Mardi's) *leaving* the office early.
3. (His, Him) *travelling* first class was questioned by the auditor.
4. Did Gene tell you about (Gail, Gail's) *moving* to Yellowknife?
5. The manager was upset about (Steve, Steve's) *leaving* early.
6. The (clerk, clerk's) making the sale receives the commission.
7. Renate suggested (you, your) *making* reservations early.
8. I recognized Mrs. (Lee, Lee's) *handwriting* on the invoice.
9. I appreciate (them, their) *responding* to my emails so quickly.
10. The (salesperson, salesperson's) making the appointment is here.

Check your answers.

B. Gerunds are again italicized. Choose the correct modifier.

1. Randy's hiring depends on (him, his) *making* a good impression in the interview.
2. The (executive, executive's) submitting four disks forgot to sign his work request.
3. The accuracy of this report depends on (him, his) *proofreading*.
4. They said (you, your) *printing* of the brochures was excellent.
5. The (firm, firm's) printing the forms went out of business.
6. Our success depends on (you, your) *choosing* the best investments.
7. The (customer, customer's) paying his bill complimented the service.
8. We are incredulous at (them, their) *winning* the series.
9. The (person, person's) picking up the check gets to choose the restaurant.
10. (Him, His) *being* on time for the appointment is very important.

1. your 2. Mardi 3. His 4. Gail's 5. Steve's 6. clerk 7. your 8. Lee's 9. their 10. salesperson

C. From each of the pairs of sentences that follow, select the more acceptable version, and write its letter in the space provided.

1. (a) Emilio Aguilar was asked to, as soon as possible, develop a website.
(b) Emilio Aguilar was asked to develop a website as soon as possible. ________

2. (a) Happily, Mrs. Nasrin began to open her birthday cards.
(b) Mrs. Nasrin began to happily open her birthday cards. ________

3. (a) Be sure and say hello for me.
(b) Be sure to say hello for me. ________

4. (a) Our team celebrated his winning the award.
(b) Our team celebrated him winning the award. ________

5. (a) The secretary started to, as the deadline approached, check the names and addresses.
(b) As the deadline approached, the secretary started to check the names and addresses. ________

6. (a) Try to find out when the meeting is scheduled.
(b) Try and find out when the meeting is scheduled. ________

7. (a) Did the boss recommend their attending the demonstration?
(b) Did the boss recommend them attending the demonstration? ________

8. (a) Please check to see if the contract is ready.
(b) Please check and see if the contract is ready. ________

9. (a) You may wish to, if you have time, contact your broker.
(b) You may wish to contact your broker if you have time. ________

10. (a) The travel counsellor recommended our travelling by train.
(b) The travel counsellor recommended us travelling by train. ________

D. Rewrite the following sentences to remedy any gerund or infinitive faults.

1. We plan to, if all the papers have been signed, initiate proceedings tomorrow.

____

____

____

2. Be sure and call to, if you haven't changed your mind, make your plane reservations.

____

____

____

3. I hope that you will inform your two agents that I appreciate them listening to my complaints.

4. When you are in Montreal, try and visit the art gallery.

5. David's promotion depends largely on him doing a good job on this report.

NAME ____________________

LEVEL II

A. (**Self-check**) Verbal phrases in the following sentences are shown in italics. All the sentences have been punctuated correctly. Study each sentence, and select the letter that explains the reason for including or omitting commas.

a = Introductory verbal phrase, comma necessary
b = Essential verbal phrase, no commas necessary
c = Non-essential verbal phrase, commas necessary
d = Verbal phrase used as a subject, no commas necessary

Examples: To *settle the matter* is extremely difficult. ____d____

Vince Manning, *to settle the matter,* flipped a coin. ____c____

1. *In preparing copies of her résumé,* Terri Mays used a laser printer. ________
2. Terri Mays, *preparing copies of her résumé,* used a laser printer. ________
3. The student *looking for a parking place* was late to class. ________
4. *Finding an earlier class* is very unlikely. ________
5. *Preparing copies of a résumé* is easy when one uses a laser printer. ________
6. *According to the report,* the investigation found proof of more than $15 million in illegal profits. ________
7. The person *consulting her astrologer* refused to set foot outside her front door. ________
8. *Reporting a sharp climb in quarterly earnings,* the bank greatly exceeded analysts' expectations. ________
9. Anyone *looking at a class schedule* can see what classes are available. ________
10. Professor Kathleen Allix, *looking at a class schedule,* announced a time change. ________

Check your answers.

B. Selected verbals and verbal phrases have been italicized in the sentences below. Insert commas if needed. In the space provided at the right, write the number of commas that you insert for each sentence. If no commas are needed, write *0*.

Example: *To complete the job before the deadline*, we worked late. ____1____

1. *To introduce a new product successfully* manufacturers often depend on advertising. ________
2. *Trading in options to buy TXU shares* surged more than sevenfold before the announcement. ________

1.a 2.c 3.b 4.d 5.d 6.a 7.b 8.a 9.b 10.c

3. *After making money from inside tips* investors paid cash to Mr. Collotta. ____________

4. *Perplexed* the new owner of the retail outlet hired a financial expert for advice. ____________

5. *Working in another office* are the legal secretaries who specialize in contracts. ____________

6. *Sending frequent email messages and writing reports* the manager could not get along without her laptop. ____________

7. *To improve the writing of government employees* we hired consultants. ____________

8. *Startled* Jane Juralski dropped the letter folder. ____________

9. *Beginning as a sole proprietor* H. J. Heinz eventually built a large corporation. ____________

10. *Breaking down a job cycle into separate units of work* is the first task in a time-and-motion study. ____________

C. Selected verbal phrases in the following sentences have been italicized. Insert commas if the phrases are nonessential. In the space provided, write the number of commas that you insert for each sentence. If you add no commas, write *0*.

1. Tommy Porter *sitting in the first seat of the third row* is next. ____________

2. The student *sitting in the first seat of the third row* is next. ____________

3. Sales Manager Everett *accessing her email network daily* was able to stay in contact with her clients and her office while travelling. ____________

4. You may be interested to know that any student *enrolled in the fourth year of this degree program* will have a 14-week paid work term. ____________

5. The latest company contract enables employees *participating in our profit-sharing plan* to benefit from the stock split. ____________

6. Kim Odjig *striving to qualify for a promotion* enrolled in a Saturday course. ____________

7. Anyone *striving to qualify for a promotion* should consider enrolling in college courses. ____________

8. The clerk *keyboarding at her computer for as many as 14 hours a day* developed repetitive stress injury. ____________

D. If necessary, insert commas to punctuate verbal forms in the following sentences. In the space provided, indicate the number of commas added.

1. To plan effectively management must have a realistic picture of production. ____________

2. General Motors facing unexpected competition from foreign suppliers decided to close the small fabrication plant. ____________

3. Having completed 20 years of service Mr. Pelletier was awarded a gold watch. ____________

4. Explaining the failure of the merger negotiations proved a difficult task for the business reporters. ____________

5. Anyone working for more than six months is eligible for benefits. ____________

6. Our CEO facing another year of intense pressure resigned his post. ____________

7. Reducing safety and health hazards our division recently set a record for consecutive accident-free workdays. ________________

8. Human Resources Director Higgins hoping to help employees improve their job skills organized an in-service training class. ________________

9. All employees interested in improving their job skills are invited to attend the in-service programs. ________________

10. To enrol in any of the programs employees must sign up immediately. ________________

NAME ______________________________

LEVEL III

A. (**Self-check**) From each of the pairs of sentences that follow, select the sentence that is stated in the more logical manner. Write its letter in the space provided.

1. (a) To locate precisely the right word, a thesaurus may be used.
(b) To locate precisely the right word, one may use a thesaurus. ____________

2. (a) Sealed in an airtight crock, the Joneses savoured the fine cheese.
(b) Sealed in an airtight crock, the fine cheese was savoured by the Joneses. ____________

3. (a) To complete the accounting equation, one must add liabilities to equity.
(b) To complete the accounting equation, it is necessary to add liabilities to equity. ____________

4. (a) Before crossing the border, identification must be shown.
(b) Before crossing the border, one must show identification. ____________

5. (a) In sorting the names and addresses, Gilda discovered an error.
(b) In sorting the names and addresses, an error was discovered by Gilda. ____________

6. (a) To graduate early, carry more credits.
(b) To graduate early, more credits must be carried. ____________

7. (a) After collecting author references on note cards, write the bibliography.
(b) After collecting author references on note cards, the bibliography should be written. ____________

8. (a) Having graduated at the top of his class, Randall was given numerous job interviews.
(b) Having graduated at the top of his class, numerous job interviews were given to Randall. ____________

9. (a) After seeing the job advertisement, a letter was sent by Miss Bruner.
(b) After seeing the job advertisement, Miss Bruner sent a letter. ____________

10. (a) To qualify for the certificate, perfect attendance must be maintained.
(b) To qualify for the certificate, students must maintain perfect attendance. ____________

Check your answers.

B. Each of the following sentences has an illogical introductory verbal phrase. Rewrite each sentence using that introductory phrase so that it is followed by a word it can logically modify. Adding a subject may be necessary. Keep the introductory verbal phrase at the beginning of the sentence.

Example: Driving through the hills, the city came into view.

Driving through the hills, we saw the city come into view.

1.b 2.b 3.a 4.b 5.a 6.a 7.a 8.a 9.b 10.b

1. Answering the telephone on the first ring, goodwill is created by our staff.

2. Completing her post-diploma program, her dream came true.

3. To be binding, a consideration must support every contract.

4. Repainted and completely reconditioned in every part, Laura was amazed at her old Volkswagen.

5. Selected as Employee of the Year, the CEO presented an award to Cecile Chang.

6. After breaking into the building, the police heard the alarm set off by the burglars.

7. To be promoted, your performance appraisal must be excellent.

The preceding sentences had misplaced introductory verbal phrases. The next sentences have misplaced verbal phrases in other positions. Rewrite these sentences so that the verbal phrases are close to the words they can logically modify.

8. An autopsy revealed the cause of death to be strangulation performed by the coroner.

9. His wallet was found by Dave Evola lying under the front seat of his car.

10. Agnes Macphail became the first female parliamentarian in the British Empire elected to the House of Commons in 1921.

11. The brochure states that the Ambassador Bridge is the world's longest international suspension bridge stretching between terminals in Windsor, Ontario, and Detroit, Michigan.

12. Officials did not disclose the name of the man who died at the request of his family.

C. Write an appropriate sentence to follow each introductory verbal phrase below.

1. In order to hear better, ________________
2. While studying for final exams, ________________
3. Applauding wildly, ________________
4. Written by a well-known journalist, ________________
5. To obtain a package of tourist information, ________________
6. Playing in her first international competition, ________________

D. Optional Writing. Your instructor may ask you to complete this exercise on a separate sheet.

Write ten original sentences, two for each of the following verb forms: gerund, infinitive, present participle, past participle, and perfect participle. Label each sentence.

Editor's Challenge

The following letter and memo contain errors in spelling, proofreading, and language principles covered thus far. Use standard proofreading marks to show your corrections.

Mr. Michael K. Topton
455 Zionsville Road
Corner Brook, NL A2H 4G1

Dear Mr. Toptan:

At the suggestion of your former partner, Ms. Molly Harned. I am submiting this application for the position of legal secertary in your office. I understand that you are seeking an individual whom has communication, transcription, and microcomputer skills. Both my education and my experience, I believe, qualifies myself for this position.

Having finish two years' of schooling at Valley Community College. My skills include word processing, machine transcription, and business letter writing. To learn about working for a lawyer, a course in legal procedures was completed. Being that we studied personal injury, dissolution, and unlawful detainer procedures, I now have skill in these areas. Moreover, I have took a course in legal terminology.

In addition to my education, I have complete a six-month internship with two lawyers, Mr. Ronald W. Schultz and Ms. Robin Sawicki, in Halifax. Keyboarding legal documents and updating a client database in Mr. Schultz office has helped me learn current computer software program.

Please study the enclosed résumé to review my complete educational and employment background. Ms. Harned said that you needed some one immediately, if I was hired for this position, I would be able to start in June. I must give at least two weeks notice to my present employer. If I meet your requirements, I would appreciate you calling me at 389-5910 to arrange a interview at a time convenent to you.

Sincerely,

Michelle A. Robinson

Michelle A. Robinson

Enclosure

From: Marissa Pelham <mpelham@zyt.net>

To: Heather Martinez <hmartinez@horizonschool.ca>

Subject: Thanks for Considering ZyTec Software

Cc:

We are happy to learn from your recent massage that Horizon School is considering ZyTec Software Systems as it's source for educational software.Designed to be especially user-friendly many schools and businesses are successfully using our software.

When we sell a software system to a school, we take great care to provide suitable training for the school staff. Some companys provide a short training course for there school staff; however, we recognize that most questions arise long after training sessions are completed. Rather than providing the the superficial training that has become common in the industry, we've learned that the best way to train school staff is to provide in-depth training for two teachers from each school. After these two teachers work with our training consultant, they are formerly equip to act as teacher-trainers who can expertly train you teachers and staff.

Unlike trainers who are available for only a few ours, your teacher-trainers would be able to, whenever questions and concerns arise, deal with them. Furthermore, ZyTec establish ongoing relationships with teacher-trainers so that your teachers will always have the software support they need.

You will soon be receiving a copy of ZyTecs educational software training program guide, as well as a copy of one of our training CD's. I hope you will find these recources helpful as you consider our educational software. Inasmuch as a number of neighbouring schools is using ZyTec software, you might find it useful to speak with a teacher-trainer from a near by school district. To let me know whether such a meeting is feasible please call or write me.

All the best,

Marissa Pelham
Senior Marketing Manager
ZyTec Software Systems
Phone: (514) 921-1489
Email: mpelham@zyt.net

POSTTEST

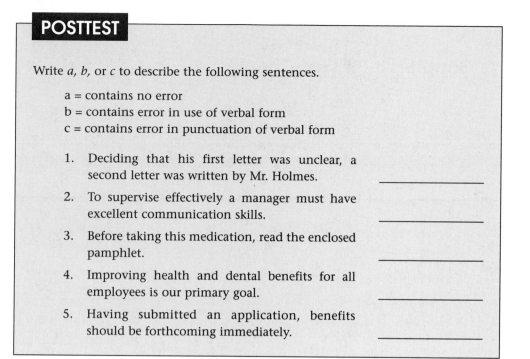

Write *a, b,* or *c* to describe the following sentences.

a = contains no error
b = contains error in use of verbal form
c = contains error in punctuation of verbal form

1. Deciding that his first letter was unclear, a second letter was written by Mr. Holmes. ______
2. To supervise effectively a manager must have excellent communication skills. ______
3. Before taking this medication, read the enclosed pamphlet. ______
4. Improving health and dental benefits for all employees is our primary goal. ______
5. Having submitted an application, benefits should be forthcoming immediately. ______

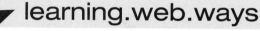

learning.web.ways

You've been asked to make a presentation on personal finance and credit debt. You decide that you need a good Canadian (and perhaps humorous) quotation on money. Many websites provide free quotations.

Goal: To find a Canadian quotation.

1. With your web browser on the screen, enter **<http://northernblue.ca/hconline/canquotes/canquote.php>**.
2. Click on **Your Canadian Quote of the Day,** and copy and paste it into a document.
3. Now click on the bottom arrow button for another Canadian quotation. Copy and paste this, too, into a document.
4. Use Google.com **<http://www.google.com>**, and enter "Canadian quotations" in the search box.
5. Select a site and print a selection, circling the quotation you like best.
6. End your session, and submit your printed pages.

1. b 2. c 3. a 4. a 5. b

NAME ____________________

UNIT 3 REVIEW Chapters 8–11 (Self-Check)

Begin your review by rereading Chapters 8 through 11. Then test your comprehension of those chapters by completing the exercises that follow. Compare your responses with those provided at the end of the book.

LEVEL I

In the blank provided, write the letter of the word or phrase that correctly completes each of the following sentences.

1. In the sentence *Maggie framed her diploma,* the verb *framed* is (a) transitive, (b) intransitive, (c) linking. ________

2. In the sentence *She is the president,* the word *president* is a(n) (a) object, (b) linking verb, (c) complement. ________

3. There (a) is, (b) are many kind words we'll be able to say about him at his retirement dinner. ________

4. The president, together with all the employees, (a) send, (b) sends greetings to you. ________

5. The president and her entire staff (a) send, (b) sends greetings to you. ________

6. Be sure (a) and write, (b) to write the name and address legibly. ________

7. We certainly appreciate (a) him, (b) his handling of the program. ________

8. Davis, Crowley, and Kovacs, Inc., (a) is, (b) are expecting an increase in profits this quarter. ________

9. The shipping statement for the equipment and supplies (a) was, (b) were delayed. ________

10. Is there any possibility of (a) you, (b) your coming early? ________

11. How effective (a) is, (b) are the company guidelines on Internet use? ________

12. Downsizing could result in (a) me, (b) my losing my job. ________

LEVEL II

Write the letter of the word or phrase that correctly completes each of the following sentences.

13. When converting a verb from the passive to the active voice, the writer must make the doer of the action the (a) subject, (b) object of the active-voice verb. ________

14. In the sentence, *Construction will be completed next month,* the verb is in the (a) active, (b) passive voice. ________

15. Many letters and packages have (a) laid, (b) lain, (c) lay on that desk for the past week. ________

16. If she had (a) took, (b) taken the subway to work, she would have been on time. ________

17. The contract (a) laying, (b) lying on your desk must be signed. ________

18. Neither the computer nor the printers (a) is, (b) are working. ________

19. We think that (a) anyone, (b) any one of the finalists could win the competition. ________

Insert commas where necessary in the next group of sentences. Indicate the number of commas added. Write *0* for none.

20. We were very pleased to see that Rebecca working until 10 p.m. was able to complete the job. ________

21. Storing thousands of customer files became physically possible when we installed an electronic database. ________

22. Working until 10 p.m. Rebecca was able to complete the job. ________

LEVEL III

In the blank provided, write the letter of the word or phrase that correctly completes each sentence.

23. He acts as if he (a) was, (b) were the only employee who had to work overtime. ________

24. She suggested that everyone (a) meet, (b) meets at the café after work. ________

25. The number of employees participating in elective classes (a) is, (b) are steadily increasing. ________

26. It is you who (a) is, (b) are to do the judging tomorrow. ________

27. It looks as if three-fourths of the brochures (a) has, (b) have yet to be assembled. ________

28. She is one of those executives who always (a) tell, (b) tells the truth. ________

For each sentence below, indicate whether (a) the sentence is written correctly or (b) the sentence has a verbal phrase placed illogically. Rewrite illogical sentences.

29. To qualify for a full scholarship, applications must be made by January 1. ________

____

____

30. Using two search engines, the website was finally located.____________________

31. Skilled at troubleshooting network problems, the human resources manager hired Hans instantly.

32. Driving to the office, two accidents were seen by Debbie. ____________________

33. Although her mother was in it, thieves stole a suitcase containing jewellery and clothing from the car of Mrs. Mercier. ____________________

Hotline Review

Select the word or phrase that correctly completes each statement, and write its letter in the corresponding blank.

34. Karen Kain was promoted to (a) principal, (b) principle dancer within one year of joining The National Ballet of Canada. __________

35. A great deal of research is being done on the (a) affects, (b) effects of food additives. __________

36. Human resources staff members are required to be (a) discreet, (b) discrete when dealing with employees' files. __________

37. We attract many customers by offering a (a) free gift, (b) valuable gift with a minimum purchase of $40. __________

38. Both plaintiffs and defendants were (a) all together, (b) altogether pleased with the out-of-court settlement. __________

Techniques for Effective Paragraphs

As you learned in the Writer's Workshop for Unit 2, the basic unit in writing is the sentence. The next unit is the paragraph. Although no rule regulates the length of paragraphs, business writers recognize the value of short paragraphs. Paragraphs with fewer than eight printed lines look inviting and readable, whereas long, solid chunks of print appear formidable. In this workshop you will learn writing techniques for organizing sentences into readable, coherent, and clear paragraphs. The first very important technique involves topic sentences.

Organizing Paragraphs Around Topic Sentences

A well-organized paragraph has two important characteristics. First, it covers just one subject. For example, if you are writing about your booth at a computer show, you won't throw in a sentence about trouble with your taxes. Keep all the sentences in a paragraph related to one topic. Second, a well-organized paragraph begins with a topic sentence that summarizes what the paragraph is about. A topic sentence helps readers by preparing them for what follows.

Consider the following scenario. Let's say your company promotes an extensive schedule of team sports for employees after hours. One group enjoys weekend bicycling. You've been assigned the task of writing a memo to the members of this group stating that they must wear helmets when cycling. One paragraph of your memo covers statistics about cycling accidents and the incidence of brain injury for unhelmeted riders. Another paragraph discusses the protection offered by helmets:

> *Helmets protect the brain from injury.* They spread the force of a crash from the point of impact to a wider area. When an accident occurs, an unhelmeted head undergoes two collisions. The first occurs when the skull slams into the ground. The second occurs when the brain hits the inside of the skull. A helmet softens the second blow and acts as a shock absorber. Instead of crushing the brain, the impact crushes the foam core of the helmet, often preventing serious brain injury.

Notice how the preceding paragraph focuses on just one topic: how helmets protect the brain from injury. Every sentence relates to that topic. Notice, too, that the first sentence functions as a topic sentence, informing the reader of the subject of the paragraph.

The best way to write a good paragraph is to list all the ideas you may include. Here's a rough draft of ideas for the preceding paragraph. Notice that the fourth item doesn't relate to the topic sentence. By listing the ideas to be included in a paragraph, you can immediately see what belongs—and what doesn't. Once the list is made, you can easily write the topic sentence.

Paragraph Idea List

1. Helmets spread force of impact.
2. Crashes cause two collisions, the first when skull hits ground and the second when brain hits skull.
3. Foam core of helmet absorbs impact.
4. ~~The federal government has issued biking regulations requiring helmets.~~

Topic Sentence: Helmets protect the brain from injury.

Skill Check 3.1 Organizing a Paragraph

In a memo to the college president, the athletic director is arguing for a new scoreboard in the gym. One paragraph will describe the old scoreboard and why it needs to be replaced. Study the following list of ideas for that paragraph.

1. The old scoreboard is a tired warhorse originally constructed in the 1970s.
2. It's now hard to find replacement parts for it when something breaks.
3. The old scoreboard is not energy efficient.
4. Coca-Cola has offered to buy a new sports scoreboard in return for exclusive rights to sell soft drinks on campus.
5. The old scoreboard should be replaced for many reasons.
6. It shows only scores for basketball games.
7. When we have soccer games or track meets, we're without any functioning scoreboard.
    - **a.** Which sentence should be the topic sentence? ______________
    - **b.** Which sentence(s) should be developed in a different paragraph? ______________
    - **c.** Which sentences should follow the topic sentence? ______________

Writing Coherent Paragraphs

Effective paragraphs are coherent; that is, they hold together. Coherence is a quality of good writing that doesn't happen accidentally. It is consciously achieved through effective organization and through skilful use of three devices. These writing devices are (a) repetition of key ideas or key words, (b) use of pronouns that refer clearly to their antecedents, and (c) use of transitional expressions.

Repetition of Key Ideas or Key Words. Repeating a key word or key thought from a preceding sentence helps guide a reader from one thought to the next. This redundancy is necessary to build cohesiveness into writing. Notice how the word *deal* is repeated in the second sentence below.

> For the past six months, college administrators and Coca-Cola have been working on a *deal* in which the college would receive a new sports scoreboard. The *deal* would involve exclusive rights to sell non-alcoholic beverages on the 12,000-student campus.

Use of Pronouns That Refer Clearly to Their Antecedents. Pronouns such as *this, that, they, these, those,* and *it* help connect thoughts in sentences; but these pronouns are useful only when their antecedents are clear. Often it's better to make the pronoun into an adjective joined with its antecedent to ensure that the reference is absolutely clear. Notice how the pronoun *this* is clearer when it is joined to its antecedent *contract.*

Confusing: The Coca-Cola offer requires an exclusive contract committing the college for ten years without any provision preventing a price increase. *This* could be very costly to students, staff, and faculty.

Improved: The Coca-Cola offer requires an exclusive contract committing the college for ten years without any provision preventing a price increase. *This contract* could be very costly to students, staff, and faculty.

Avoid vague pronouns, such as *it* in the following example.

Confusing: Both Coca-Cola and Pepsi offered to serve our campus, and we agreed to allow *it* to submit a bid.

Improved: Both Coca-Cola and Pepsi offered to serve our campus, and we agreed to allow Coca-Cola to submit a bid.

Use of Transitional Expressions. One of the most effective ways to achieve paragraph coherence is through the use of transitional expressions. These expressions act as road signs. They indicate where the message is headed, and they help the reader anticipate what is coming. Some common transitional expressions follow:

also	hence	moreover
as a result	however	nevertheless
consequently	in addition	of course
for example	instead	on the other hand
for this reason	in this way	therefore
furthermore	meanwhile	thus

Other words that act as connectives are *first, second, finally, after, next, after all, although, specifically, likewise, as,* and *as if.*

The following paragraph achieves coherence through use of all three techniques. (1) The key idea of *surprising battle* in the first sentence is echoed in the second sentence with repetition of the word *battle* coupled with *unexpected,* a synonym for *surprising.* (2) The use of a pronoun, *This,* in the second sentence connects the second sentence to the first. (3) The transitional expressions *however* and *as a result* in the following sentences continue to build coherence.

> A *surprising battle* between two global cola giants was fought in Venezuela. *This battle* was *unexpected* because Venezuelans had always been loyal Pepsi drinkers. *However,* when the nation's leading bottler sold half of its interest to Coca-Cola, everything changed. *As a result,* Coca-Cola turned the Pepsi-drinking nation of Venezuela into Coke drinkers almost overnight.

Skill Check 3.2 Improving Paragraph Coherence

On a separate sheet of paper, use the information from Skill Check 3.1 to write a coherent paragraph about replacing the sports scoreboard. Remember that this paragraph is part of a memo from the athletic director to the college president. Include a topic sentence. Strive to illustrate all three techniques to achieve coherence.

Developing Parallel Construction

Paragraph clarity can be improved by using similar grammatical structures to express similar ideas. For example, if you are listing three ideas, do not use *ing* words for two of the ideas and a *to* verb with the third idea: *reading, eating, and studying* (not *to study*). Use adjectives with adjectives, verbs with verbs, phrases with phrases, and clauses with clauses. In the following list, use all verbs: the *machine sorted, stamped, and counted* (not *and had a counter*). For phrases, the wording for all parts of the list should be matched; *safety must be improved in the home, in the classroom, and on the job* (not *for office workers*).

Poor: Miss Tanaga is energetic, resourceful and she can be relied on.

Improved: Miss Tanaga is energetic, resourceful, and reliable. (Matches adjectives.)

Poor: The new shredder helped us save money, reduce pollution, and paper could be recycled.

Improved: The new shredder helped us save money, reduce pollution, and recycle paper. (Matches verb–noun construction.)

Skill Check 3.3 Improving Parallel Construction

Revise each of the following sentences to improve parallel construction.

1. Your job is to research, design, and the implementation of a diversity program.

   ____

   ____

2. Few managers are able to write letters accurately, concisely, and with efficiency.

   ____

   ____

3. The new software totals all balances, gives weekly reports, and statements are printed.

   ____

   ____

4. She proofread for errors in spelling, punctuation, and the use of capital letters.

   ____

   ____

For further practice, see Chapter 21 (Exercise B on pp. 425–426).

Writing Application 3.1 On a separate sheet, revise the following paragraph. Add a topic sentence and improve the organization. Correct unclear pronouns, wordiness, and misplaced verbal modifiers (which you learned about in Chapter 11). Add transitional expressions if appropriate.

> You may be interested in applying for a new position within the company. The Human Resources Department has a number of jobs available immediately. The positions are at a high level. Current employees may apply immediately for open positions in production, for some in marketing, and jobs in administrative support are also available. To make application, these positions require immediate action. Come to the Human Resources Department. We have a list showing the open positions, what the qualifications are, and job descriptions are shown. Many of the jobs are now open. That's why we are sending this now. To be hired, an interview must be scheduled within the next two weeks.

Writing Application 3.2 On a separate sheet, revise the following poorly written paragraph. Add a topic sentence and improve the organization. Correct misplaced modifiers, unclear pronouns, wordiness, and any other writing faults. Add transitional expressions if appropriate.

> As you probably already know, this company (Lasertronics) will be installing new computer software shortly. There will be a demonstration April 18, which is a Tuesday. We felt this was necessary because this new software is so different from our previous software. It will be from 9 to 12 a.m. in the morning. This will show employees how the software programs work. They will learn about the operating system, and this should be helpful to nearly everyone. There will be information about the new word processing program, which should be helpful to administrative assistants and product managers. For all you people who work with payroll, there will be information about the new database program. We can't show everything the software will do at this one demo, but for these three areas there will be some help at the Tuesday demo. Oh yes, Paula Roddy will be presenting the demonstration. She is the representative from Quantum Software.

Writing Application 3.3 Assume you work in the Human Resources Department of Imperial Trust. You must write an announcement describing a special program of classes for your employees. Use the following information to write a well-organized paragraph announcement. Explain that Imperial Trust will reimburse any employee the full cost of tuition and books if that employee attends classes. Describe the plan. Skyline Community College, in co-operation with Imperial Trust, will offer a group of courses for college credit at very convenient locations for our employees. Actually, the classes will be offered at your downtown and East Bay branches. Tell employees that they should call Jean Fujimoto at Ext. 660 if they are interested. You'd better mention the tuition: $180 for a semester course. Explain that we (Imperial Trust) are willing to pay these fees because we value education highly. However, make it clear that employees must receive a grade of C or higher before they are eligible for reimbursement of course and book fees. It might be a good idea to attach a list of the courses and the times that they will be offered. Include a deadline date for calling Jean.

U N I T 4

Modifying and Connecting Words

C H A P T E R

Modifiers: Adjectives and Adverbs

12

OBJECTIVES When you have completed the materials in this chapter, you will be able to do the following:

LEVEL I

- *Form the comparative and superlative degrees of regular and irregular adjectives and adverbs.*
- *Use articles and demonstrative adjectives correctly and avoid double negatives.*

LEVEL II

- *Employ adjectives after linking verbs and use adverbs to modify verbs, adjectives, and other adverbs.*
- *Punctuate compound and successive independent adjectives correctly.*

LEVEL III

- *Compare degrees of absolute adjectives and make comparisons within a group.*
- *Place adverbs and adjectives close to the words they modify.*

PRETEST

Underline the correct word.

1. This is the (worse, worst) business report I've ever read.
2. (A, An) exceptional job was done on the website redesign.
3. If you did (good, well) in the interview, you will be hired.
4. Our (six-year-old, six year old) lease must be renegotiated.
5. The (newly repaired, newly-repaired) copier seems to be working well.

1. worst 2. An 3. well 4. six-year-old 5. newly repaired

Both adjectives and adverbs act as modifiers; that is, they describe or limit other words. Since many of the forms and functions of adjectives and adverbs are similar and since faulty usage often results from the confusion of these two parts of speech, we will treat adjectives and adverbs together in this chapter.

LEVEL I

▶ Basic Functions of Adjectives and Adverbs

Adjectives describe or limit nouns and pronouns. As you have already learned, they often answer the questions *what kind? how many?* or *which one?* Adjectives in the following sentences are italicized.

> *Short* visits are *the best* visits. (Adjectives answer *What kind?*)
> *Large government* grants were awarded to *the eight top* institutions. (Adjectives answer *what kind?* and *how many?*)

Adverbs describe or limit verbs, adjectives, or other adverbs. They often answer the questions *when? how? where?* or *to what extent?*

> *Yesterday* our work went *slowly*. (Adverbs answer *when?* and *how?*)
> He answered *fully*. (Adverb answers *to what extent?*)

Hotlink

The parts of speech section of **<http://www.ucalgary.ca/UofC/eduweb/grammar/>** has an excellent page that will help you practise distinguishing between adjectives and adverbs.

Comparative and Superlative Forms

Most adjectives and adverbs have three forms, or *degrees*: positive, comparative, and superlative. The examples below illustrate how the comparative and superlative degrees of regular adjectives and adverbs are formed.

	Positive	**Comparative**	**Superlative**
Adjective:	warm	warmer	warmest
Adverb:	warmly	more warmly	most warmly
Adjective:	careful	more careful	most careful
Adverb:	carefully	more carefully	most carefully

Career Tip

Good writers avoid vague and overworked adverbs and adjectives (such as *interesting, good, nice, great, really,* and *bad*). Strive to use precise words that say exactly what you mean.

The positive degree of an adjective or an adverb is used in simply describing or in limiting another word. The comparative degree is used to compare two persons or things. The superlative degree is used to compare three or more persons or things.

The comparative degree of short adjectives (nearly all one-syllable and most two-syllable adjectives ending in *y*) is formed by adding *r* or *er* (*warmer*). The superlative degree of short adjectives is usually formed by the addition of *st* or *est* (*warmest*). Long adjectives, and those difficult to pronounce, form the comparative and superlative degrees, as do adverbs, with the addition of *more* and *most* (*more careful, most careful*). The following sentences illustrate degrees of comparison for adjectives and adverbs.

Adjectives:	Sales are unusually *high*.	(Positive degree)
	Sales are *higher* than ever before.	(Comparative degree)
	Sales are the *highest* in years.	(Superlative degree)
Adverbs:	He drives *carefully*.	(Positive degree)
	He drives *more carefully* now.	(Comparative degree)
	He drives *most carefully* at night.	(Superlative degree)

Spot the Blooper

From an editorial in *U.S. News & World Report*: "Of two interpretations of conduct, they prefer the worst."

Do *not* create a double comparative form by using *more* and the suffix *er* together (such as *more neater*) or by using *most* and the suffix *est* together (such as *most fastest*).

A few adjectives and adverbs form the comparative and the superlative degrees irregularly. Common irregular adjectives include *good* (*better, best*), *bad* (*worse, worst*), *little (less, least*), and *many (more, most)*. Common irregular adverbs include *well* (*better, best*) and *much* (*more, most*).

Study Tip

The sound, not the spelling, of a word governs the choice between *a* and *an*. When the letter *u* sounds like a *y*, it is treated as a consonant: a *u*tility, a *u*sed car.

Modifiers That Deserve Special Attention

A few adjectives and adverbs require special attention because they can cause difficulty for writers and speakers.

Adjectives as Articles. The articles *a, an,* and *the* merit special attention. When describing a specific person or thing, use the definite article *the*, as in *the* film. When describing persons or things in general, use the indefinite articles *a* or *an,* as in *a film* (meaning *any* film). The choice of *a* or *an* is determined by the initial sound of the word modified. Use *a* before consonant sounds; use *an* before vowel sounds.

Before Vowel Sounds		Before Consonant Sounds	
an operator an executive		a shop a plan	
an hour an honour	*h* is not voiced; vowel is heard	a hook a hole	*h* is voiced
an office an onion	*o* sounds like a vowel	a one-man show a one-week trip	*o* sounds like the consonant *w*
an understudy an umbrella	*u* sounds like a vowel	a union a unit	*u* sounds like the consonant *y*
an X-ray an M.D.	*X* and *M* sound like vowels ("ex" and "em")	a xylophone a meteor	*x* sounds like the consonant *z*; *m* consonant sound is heard

Hotlink

This extensive University of Western Ontario article on articles, downloadable from **<www.sdc.uwo.ca/writing/handouts/Articles.pdf>**, will answer most of your questions about them.

Adverbs and Double Negatives. When a negative adverb (*no, not, scarcely, hardly, barely*) is used in the same sentence with a negative verb (*didn't, don't, won't*), a substandard construction called a *double negative* results. Such constructions are considered illogical. In the following examples, notice that eliminating one negative corrects the double negative.

Incorrect: Calling her *won't* do *no* good.
Correct: Calling her will do no good.
Correct: Calling her won't do any good.

Incorrect: We *couldn't hardly* believe the news report.
Correct: We could hardly believe the news report.
Correct: We couldn't believe the news report.

Incorrect: Drivers *can't barely* see in the heavy fog.
Correct: Drivers can barely see in the heavy fog.
Correct: Drivers can't see in the heavy fog.

Did You Know?

At one time in the history of the English language (going back farther than Chaucer), multiple negatives were used to emphasize an idea. (*Don't never say nothing wicked!*) But in the 18th century, grammarians adopted Latin logic and decreed that two negatives created a positive.

The Demonstrative Adjectives *this/that* and *these/those*. The adjective *this* and its plural form *these* indicate something nearby. The adjective *that* and its plural form *those* indicate something at a distance. Be careful to use the singular forms of these words with singular nouns and the plural forms with plural nouns: *this shoe, that road, these accounts, those records.* Pay special attention to the nouns *kind, type,* and *sort.* Match singular adjectives to the singular forms of these nouns and plural adjectives to the plural forms.

Incorrect: Job candidates should be prepared for *these type questions.*
Correct: Job candidates should be prepared for this type of question.
Correct: Job candidates should be prepared for these types of questions.

Complete the reinforcement exercises for Level I on pp. 235–236.

LEVEL II

▶ Adjective and Adverb Challenges

In the following discussion you will learn not to confuse adjectives with adverbs. You will also learn to express compound adjectives and independent adjectives.

Career Tip

The misuse of *badly* for *bad* is one of the most frequent errors made by educated persons. Following the linking verb *feel,* use the adjective *bad,* not the adverb *badly.*

Confusion of Adjectives and Adverbs

Because they are closely related, adjectives are sometimes confused with adverbs. Here are guidelines that will help you avoid common adjective–adverb errors.

1. Use adjectives to modify nouns and pronouns. Note particularly that adjectives (not adverbs) should follow linking verbs.

   This orange tastes *sweet.* (Not *sweetly*—adjective modifies the noun *orange*)
   I feel *bad* about the loss. (Not *badly*)
   He looks *good* in his uniform. (Not *well*)

2. Use adverbs to describe verbs, adjectives, or other adverbs.

   The engine runs *smoothly.* (Not *smooth*)
   It runs *more smoothly* than before. (Not *smoother*)
   Listen *carefully* to the directions. (Not *careful*)
   He listened *really well.* (Not *real good*)

Note that a few adverbs have two acceptable forms: *slow, slowly; deep, deeply; direct, directly; close, closely.* Check your dictionary for the uses of such forms.

Drive *slowly.* (Or, less formally, *slow*)
You may dial us *directly.* (Or, less formally, *direct*)

Spot the Blooper

From a full-page IBM advertisement: "Can you really buy a computer that makes someone feel differently about their job?" (Do you see two problems?)

Compound Adjectives

Writers may form their own adjectives by joining two or more words. When these words act as a single modifier preceding a noun, they are temporarily hyphenated. If these same words appear after a noun, they are generally not hyphenated. (A reference manual can provide more guidance than we have space for in this text.)

Words Temporarily Hyphenated Before a Noun	Same Words Not Hyphenated After a Noun
never-say-die attitude	attitude of never say die
eight-storey building	building of eight storeys
a case-by-case analysis	analysis that is case by case
four-year-old child	child who is four years old
out-of-warranty repair	repair that is out of warranty
follow-up appointment	an appointment to follow up

Spot the Blooper

Headline in a Florida newspaper: "Man Eating Piranha Sold as Pet Fish."

Compound adjectives shown in your dictionary with hyphens are considered permanently hyphenated. Regardless of whether such a compound appears before or after a noun, it retains the hyphens. Use a current dictionary to determine what expressions are always hyphenated. Be sure that you find the dictionary entry that is marked *adjective*. Here are samples:

Permanent Hyphens Before Nouns	Permanent Hyphens After Nouns
old-fashioned attitude	attitude that is old-fashioned
short-term loan	loan that is short-term
well-behaved child	child who is well-behaved
well-rounded program	program that is well-rounded
first-class service	service that is first-class
part-time worker	worker who is part-time

Spot the Blooper

Newspaper headline: "Squad Helps Dog Bite Victim."

Don't confuse adverbs ending in *ly* with compound adjectives: *newly decorated office* and *highly regarded architect* would not be hyphenated.

In some cases hyphens are not used. When familiar compound nouns, written as separate words (e.g., *income tax, community college*), are used as adjectives, they are not hyphenated. Proper names used as adjectives are not hyphenated either. Here are some examples:

car insurance policy	real estate agent
charge account customer	St. Lawrence Seaway locks
home office staff	Royal Bank account
data processing centre	Wayne Gretzky poster

Independent (Coordinate) Adjectives

Study Tip

To determine whether successive adjectives are independent, mentally insert the word *and* between them. If the insertion makes sense, the adjectives are probably independent and require a comma.

Two or more successive adjectives that independently modify a noun are separated by commas. No comma is needed, however, when the first adjective modifies the combined idea of the second adjective and the noun.

Two Adjectives Independently Modifying a Noun	First Adjective Modifying a Second Adjective Plus a Noun
confident, self-reliant individual	efficient administrative assistant
attractive, efficient car	dark blue sports car
stimulating, provocative book	luxurious mobile home

Commonly Confused Adjectives and Adverbs

The following adjectives and adverbs cause difficulty for many writers and speakers. With a little study, you can master their correct usage.

almost (adv.—nearly):	Almost (not *Most*) everybody wants to work.
most (adv.—greatest in amount):	*Most* people want to work.

Spot the Blooper

From a radio advertisement for an Internet Service Provider (ISP): "With our Internet service, you'll get less annoying pop-up ads."

Hotlink

If you need some help with the use of hyphens, consult this University of Victoria page at **<http://web.uvic.ca/wguide/Pages/SenthyphWords.html>**.

farther (adv.—actual distance):	How much *farther* is the airport?
further (adv.—additionally):	I won't argue the matter *further*.
sure (adj.—certain):	He is *sure* of victory.
surely (adv.—undoubtedly):	He will *surely* be victorious.
later (adv.—after expected time):	The contract arrived *later* in the day.
latter (adj.—the second of two things):	Of the two options, I prefer the *latter*.
fewer (adj.—refers to number, used with plural noun):	*Fewer* requests for tours were granted this year.
less (adj.—refers to amount, used with singular noun):	*Less* time remains than we anticipated.
real (adj.—actual, genuine):	The *real* power in the company lies with the treasurer.
really (adv.—actually, truly):	Jan wondered if she could *really* learn the system in five hours.
good (adj.—desirable):	His is a *good* plan.
well (adv.—satisfactorily)	Robert did *well* on her performance evaluation.
well (adj.—healthy)	Deborah feels *well* enough to return to work.

Complete the reinforcement exercises for Level II on pp. 237–239.

LEVEL III

Hotlink

For a thorough overview of adjective and adverb use, download this PowerPoint Presentation at **<http://xnet.rrc.mb.ca/leshanson/Writing_Resources.htm>**.

Spot the Blooper

Advertisement in a national magazine: "Quaker Oats is one of nature's most perfect foods."

▶ Other Uses of Adjectives and Adverbs

In this section you will learn how to use absolute modifiers, how to make comparisons within a group, and how to place adjectives and adverbs appropriately in sentences.

Absolute Modifiers

Adjectives and adverbs that name perfect or complete (absolute) qualities cannot logically be compared. For example, to say that one ball is *more round* than another ball is illogical. Here are some absolute words that should not be used in comparisons:

complete	perfect	straight
correct	perpendicular	true
dead	right	unanimous
endless	round	unique

Authorities suggest, however, that some absolute adjectives may be compared by the use of the words *more nearly* or *most nearly*. Study the following sentences for various alternatives:

Illogical:	This rose is the most perfect flower in our garden.
Logical:	This rose is the most nearly perfect flower in our garden.
Illogical:	A straighter route through the Prairies is the Trans-Canada Highway.
Logical:	A more nearly straight route through the Prairies is the Trans-Canada Highway.

Comparisons Within a Group

When the word *than* is used to compare a person, place, or thing with other members of a group to which it belongs, be certain to include the words *other* or *else* in the comparison. This inclusion ensures clarity by separating the person or thing being compared from the group with which it is compared.

Illogical:	Calgary is larger than any city in Alberta. (This sentence suggests that Calgary is larger than itself or that it is not a city in Alberta.)
Logical:	Calgary is larger than any *other* city in Alberta.
Illogical:	Our team had more points than any league team. (Implies that our team does not belong to the league.)
Logical:	Our team had more points than any *other* league team.
Illogical:	Alex works harder than anyone in the office.
Logical:	Alex works harder than anyone *else* in the office.

Placing Adverbs and Adjectives

The position of an adverb or adjective can seriously affect the meaning of a sentence. Study these examples:

Only I can program this computer. (No one else can program it.)
I can *only* program this computer. (I can't do anything else to it.)
I can program *only* this computer. (I can't program any other computer.)

To avoid confusion, adverbs and adjectives should be placed close to the words they modify. In this regard, special attention should be given to the words *only, merely, first,* and *last.*

Confusing:	He *merely* said that all soldiers couldn't be generals.
Clear:	He said *merely* that all soldiers couldn't be generals.
Confusing:	Seats in the five *first* rows have been reserved.
Clear:	Seats in the *first* five rows have been reserved.

Complete the reinforcement exercises for Level III on pp. 240–241.

Spot the Blooper

From a radio commercial for The Club, a device to prevent auto theft: "The Club works where other cheap imitations fail." (Does this statement say that The Club is a cheap imitation?)

Hotlink

This online handout from the English Commons at the University of Guelph **<http://www.lib.uoguelph.ca/assistance/writing_services//components/documents/grammar.pdf>** has an excellent section on the placement of modifiers.

Spot the Blooper

Headline from *The Concord* [NH] *Monitor.* "How Can You Expect a Child Who Can't Tell Time to Only Get Sick During Office Hours?"

HOTLINE QUERIES

Question: One of my favourite words is *hopefully,* but I understand that it's often used improperly. How should it be used?

Answer: Language purists insist that the word *hopefully* be used to modify a verb (*we looked at the door hopefully, wishing that Mr. Gross would return*). The word *hopefully* should not be used as a substitute for *I hope that* or *We hope that* in formal English. Instead of saying, *Hopefully, interest rates will decline,* one should say, *I hope that interest rates will decline.*

(Continued)

Question: Is it necessary to hyphenate a *25 per cent discount*?

Answer: No. Per cents are not treated in the same way that numbers appearing in compound adjectives are treated. Thus, you would not hyphenate a *15 per cent loan*, but you would hyphenate a *15-year loan*.

Question: Should hyphens be used in *a point-by-point analysis?*

Answer: Yes. When words are combined in order to create a single adjective preceding a noun, these words are temporarily hyphenated *(last-minute decision, two-semester course, step-by-step procedures).*

Question: In my writing I want to use *firstly* and *secondly*. Are they acceptable?

Answer: Both words are acceptable, but most good writers prefer *first* and *second* because they are more efficient and equally accurate.

Question: How many hyphens should I use in this sentence? *The three, four, and five year plans continue to be funded.*

Answer: Three hyphens are needed: *three-, four-,* and *five-year plans*. Hyphenate compound adjectives even when the parts of the compound are separated or suspended.

Question: Why does the sign above my grocery store's express checkout say *Ten or less items*? Shouldn't it read *Ten or fewer items*?

Answer: Right you are! *Fewer* refers to numbers, as in *fewer items*. *Less* refers to amounts or quantities, as in *less food*. Perhaps the stores prefer *less* because it has fewer letters.

Question: I never know how to write *part time*. Is it always hyphenated?

Answer: The dictionary shows all of its uses to be hyphenated. *She was a part-time employee* (used as adjective). *He worked part-time* (used as adverb).

Question: Here are some expressions that caused us trouble in our business letters. We want to hyphenate all of the following. Right? *Well-produced play, awareness-generation film, decision-making tables, one-paragraph note, swearing-in ceremony, commonly-used book.*

Answer: All your hyphenated forms are correct except the last one. Don't use a hyphen with an *ly*-ending adverb.

Question: Why are these two expressions treated differently: *two-week vacation* and *two weeks' vacation*?

Answer: Although they express the same idea, they represent two different styles. If you omit the *s*, *two-week* is hyphenated because it is a compound adjective. If you add the *s*, as in *two weeks' vacation*, the expression becomes possessive and requires an apostrophe. Just don't use both styles together (not *two-weeks' vacation*).

NAME ______________________________

CHAPTER 12 Reinforcement Exercises

LEVEL I

A. **(Self-check)** Write the correct forms in the spaces provided.

1. This is undoubtedly the (worse, worst) movie I've ever seen. ______
2. This is certainly (worse, worst) than yesterday's coffee. ______
3. (This, These) types of computer viruses can be difficult to detect. ______
4. I can't think of a (better, more better) plan. ______
5. We (can, can't) hardly work in this room without air conditioning. ______
6. This is the (coldest, most cold) day we've had all year. ______
7. Examine closely the blades on (this, these) pair of scissors. ______
8. Driving to the bank and back requires at least (a, an) hour's time. ______
9. Rainfall for this year (has, hasn't) been barely 22 centimetres. ______
10. The outcome of the race between Connors and Morelli will determine the (faster, fastest) driver. ______

Check your answers.

B. Write the correct form in the spaces provided.

1. (That sort, Those sorts) of businesses have been asked to restrict exports. ______
2. Bill Gates is the (more, most) powerful of the software manufacturers. ______
3. Numerous plant workers are considering joining (a, an) union. ______
4. Ask the tailor whether (this, these) pair of pants is ready. ______
5. After paying his taxes, Gunther complained that he (has, hasn't) barely a dollar left. ______
6. The biotechnology industry is growing at (a, an) unusually fast pace. ______
7. Of the four brothers and sisters, he is the (younger, youngest). ______
8. Which of these two colours is (better, best) for the hall? ______
9. Susan said she couldn't see (no, any) other way to install the program. ______
10. The mortgage company doesn't have (no, any) reason to deny the loan. ______

1. worst 2. worse 3. These 4. better 5. can 6. coldest 7. this 8. an 9. has 10. faster

C. Can you find and correct 12 errors in this paragraph? *Hint:* eight errors involve adverbs and adjectives from Level I.

In Winnipeg a officer of a bank was involved in one of the worse embezzlement schemes in the banks history. Because of lax bank controls, the embezzler was able to withdraw hundreds of thousands of dollars in a unprecedented banking loss. To avoid detection by the banks computer fraud defences, the embezzler took advantage of his position as an bank officer. The scheme involved making debit and credit transactions in two offices, but the embezzler found the Winnipeg office was best for withdrawals. As the size of the theft grew, the bank officer couldn't hardly conceal it any longer. The bank discovered it's loss when the embezzler made a error in filling out a credit slip instead of a debit slip. Embarrassed bank officials have announced there intention to set up new operational controls to prevent these kind of fraudulent scheme in the future.

D. Supply the proper article (*a* or *an*) for the following words:

Example: ___an___ adjustment

1.	________ number	**7.**	________ warehouse	**13.**	________ insult
2.	________ honour	**8.**	________ agency	**14.**	________ X-ray
3.	________ inventory	**9.**	________ hour	**15.**	________ illegible letter
4.	________ pattern	**10.**	________ idea	**16.**	________ one-year lease
5.	________ hammock	**11.**	________ utility	**17.**	________ eight-year lease
6.	________ orange	**12.**	________ airplane	**18.**	________ oil embargo

E. In the space provided, write the correct comparative or superlative form of the adjective shown in parentheses.

Example: Of the three software packages, which is (good)? ___best___

1. Craig was the (smart) member of the team. ____________
2. She did (well) on the certification exam than she had expected. ____________
3. Please send me the (current) figures you can find. ____________
4. The new accounting software is (easy) to master than the software we were using. ____________
5. It appears that this plan is (costly) than our previous insurance coverage. ____________
6. Of all the employees, Richard is the (little) talkative. ____________
7. Ms. Hansen is (businesslike) than the office manager she replaced. ____________
8. Have you ever met a (kind) individual than Warren Stevenson? ____________
9. This is the (bad) winter we've had in years. ____________
10. Which is the (interesting) of the two novels? ____________

NAME ____________________

LEVEL II

A. (**Self-check**) Write the correct forms in the spaces provided.

1. Brendan looked (calm, calmly) as the verdict was read. ______
2. The lighthouse is (farther, further) away than it first appeared. ______
3. Better service is ensured if a purchaser has (face-to-face, face to face) dealings with the manufacturer. ______
4. Companies have reported (fewer, less) security breaches this year. ______
5. Unless sales data can be processed (quicker, more quickly), we will lose business to our competitors. ______
6. Mr. Burton (sure, surely) made his personal feelings apparent when he announced the policy change. ______
7. Matthew felt (bad, badly) that he forgot to return your message. ______
8. Of probationary and permanent employees, only the (later, latter) are eligible for tuition reimbursement. ______
9. Some small businesses barely exist from (year-to-year, year to year). ______
10. Asked about her health, Aunt Edna said she felt (good, well). ______

Check your answers.

B. Write the correct words in the spaces provided. Be prepared to explain your choices.

1. Politicians are finding that blogs work (beautiful, beautifully) for campaigning. ______
2. Because of the construction decline, (fewer, less) housing is available. ______
3. Lee thought that she did (good, well) in her interview. ______
4. Apples and brie cheese taste (good, well) on pizza. ______
5. Our office manager will (sure, surely) call for repairs. ______
6. Since its tune-up, the engine runs (smoother, more smoothly). ______
7. Lavonda wasn't (real, really) sure she could attend the meeting. ______
8. Please don't take her comments (personal, personally). ______
9. Do these peaches taste (bitter, bitterly) to you? ______
10. Your new suit certainly fits you (good, well). ______

1. calm 2. farther 3. face-to-face 4. fewer 5. more quickly 6. surely 7. bad 8. latter
9. year to year 10. well

11. The new suit looks very (good, well) on you. ____________

12. She wanted to debate the question (further, farther). ____________

13. He completed the aptitude test (satisfactory, satisfactorily). ____________

14. In an effort to reduce expenses, New Tech will offer employees (fewer, less) benefit options next year. ____________

15. Henry feels (sure, surely) that part-time salaries will improve. ____________

16. (Most, Almost) everyone agreed that work is the price one pays for money. ____________

17. Having prepared for months, we won the bid (easy, easily). ____________

18. To reduce legal costs, they pressed for a settlement (quick, quickly). ____________

19. Our ergonomically designed office furniture should keep employees working (comfortable, comfortably). ____________

20. Recovering from his illness, Luis said he felt (good, well). ____________

C. Select the correct group of words below. Write its letter in the space provided.

1. (a) coast to coast broadcast
   (b) coast-to-coast broadcast ____________

2. (a) well-documented report
   (b) well documented report ____________

3. (a) child who is ten-years-old
   (b) child who is ten years old ____________

4. (a) ten-year-old child
   (b) ten year old child ____________

5. (a) fully certified nurse
   (b) fully-certified nurse ____________

6. (a) state of the art technology
   (b) state-of-the-art technology ____________

7. (a) data-processing service
   (b) data processing service ____________

8. (a) strong-arm tactics
   (b) strong arm tactics ____________

9. (a) last-minute preparations
   (b) last minute preparations ____________

10. (a) widely-acclaimed cure
    (b) widely acclaimed cure ____________

11. (a) Red-River cart
    (b) Red River cart ____________

12. (a) tongue-tied child
(b) tongue tied child ______________

Are any of the above in your dictionary?

D. Place commas where needed in the following groups of words.

1. little red truck
2. narrow winding path
3. concise courteous letter
4. snug cheerful apartment
5. imaginative daring designer
6. efficient clerical employee
7. disappointing quarterly results
8. skilled financial analyst

E. Write sentences using the following words as compound adjectives. Be sure that the compound adjectives precede nouns.

Example: (on the spot) *We offer on-the-spot appraisals.*

1. (two year old) ______________________________

____

2. (once in a lifetime) ______________________________

____

3. (up to the minute) ______________________________

____

4. (work related) ______________________________

____

5. (first time) ______________________________

____

6. (community college) ______________________________

____

NAME ______________________________

LEVEL III

A. (**Self-check**) Underline any errors in the following sentences, and write their corrected forms in the spaces provided. If a sentence is correct as it is written, write *C*.

Example: Elwood is the <u>most unique</u> individual I know. most nearly unique

1. Because he used a ruler, his line is more straight than mine. ____________
2. Professor Anita Fugi is the most conscientious teacher I have. ____________
3. She is more conscientious than any teacher I've ever had. ____________
4. We were told to answer the ten last questions. ____________
5. That software company claims to have the most perfect web browser available. ____________
6. We are only concerned with your welfare and happiness. ____________
7. He merely thought you wanted one page copied. ____________
8. Mountains in the West are more perpendicular than those in the East. ____________
9. Tourists often say that Quebec City is the most fascinating city in Canada. ____________
10. Milan is more cosmopolitan than any city in Italy. ____________

Check your answers.

B. Underline errors, and write corrected forms in the spaces provided. If correct, write *C*.

1. The *Times* story about the embezzlement is more accurate than the *Globe* article. ____________
2. For rapid sale, the 15 last homes were drastically reduced. ____________
3. I would rather sell property for Doris than for any broker in the area. ____________
4. Is this the most correct answer among all the applicants' tests? ____________
5. I only have one idea for solving the security problem. ____________
6. Halifax is the largest city in Nova Scotia. ____________
7. Halifax is larger than any city in Nova Scotia. ____________
8. That encyclopedia is only sold by door-to-door salespeople. ____________
9. Kinko's offers the most complete office service in town. ____________
10. The two first applicants presented excellent résumés. ____________

---

1. more nearly straight 2. C 3. any other teacher 4. last ten questions 5. most nearly perfect
6. with only 7. wanted merely one 8. more nearly perpendicular 9. C
10. any other city

C. Review of Levels I, II, and III. For each sentence below, underline any error. Then write a corrected form in the space provided. If a sentence is correct, write *C* in the space.

1. It took us over a hour to decipher a nearly unreadable handwritten memo. ________________
2. Which of the three advertising campaigns do you like better? ________________
3. Sandy said that she couldn't barely hear you on your cellphone. ________________
4. Because of excessive costs, designer Donna Karan made less trips to the Far East and Africa in search of "creative inspiration." ________________
5. Hawkins interviewed a Canadian official and an European diplomat concerning the proposed two-year trade program. ________________
6. If deliveries can't be made more quicker, we will change carriers. ________________
7. Their daughter, who is only three-years-old, is already reading. ________________
8. One applicant felt that he had done good on the skills test. ________________
9. I like this job better than any job I've ever had. ________________
10. We can better judge our inventory once we have conducted our end of the year stock count. ________________
11. The designer attempted to create an attractive functional working environment. ________________
12. We only try to file necessary paperwork. ________________
13. Did you say that the two first rows had empty seats? ________________
14. The city council thought most everyone would vote in favour of protecting the open space. ________________
15. Dana made a point by point comparison of the programs. ________________

D. Optional Writing. Your instructor may ask you to complete this exercise on a separate sheet.

Write five original sentences using the following words as adjectives: *state of the art, step by step, federally funded, fast moving,* and *fewer.* In addition, write five sentences using the following words as adverbs: *well, farther, further, already,* and *only.*

Editor's Challenge

The following memo proposal and letter contain intentional errors in language principles covered thus far, as well as in spelling and proofreading. Use standard proofreading marks to show your corrections.

Rawlinson Enterprises
Interoffice Memo

DATE: June 5, 200x

TO: Larry LaGrange, Vice-President, Operations

FROM: Elyse Ellerman, Manager, Accounting

SUBJECT: INSTALLATION OF UNDERCARPET WIRING

Proposal

Because the Accounting Department needs a flexible economical wiring system that can acommodate our ever changing electrical needs. I propose that we install a flat undercarpet wiring system.

Present System

At this time the Accounting Department has an out of date system of floor wiring and power poles that limit us to surface wiring. This network of surface wiring appear to be totally overwhelmed by the demands we are now placing on them. The operation of 27 pieces of equipment in addition to 34 telephone lines require extensive electrical circuits and cabling. Moreover, our overhead lighting, which consist of fluorescent fixtures in a suspended egg-crate structure, contains excessive wiring above the ceiling. Technicians whom have came to our office have said that its the worse system theyve ever saw.

Advantages of Proposed System

Cabling for telephone, power, and data are now available in a flat form only 1 mm thick. This flat flexible cable can be install underneath existing carpeting. Thus preventing costly and disruptive renovation. Undercarpet wiring would mean less office power poles. Moreover, flat cables can be moved easy, giving we accountants greater flexibility when we need to add equipment. Having a undercarpet wiring system all ready installed in the Accounting Department would also enable the company to evaluate the systems affectiveness before considering it for other departments.

Cost and Savings

Suppliers and consultants estimates that an undercarpet wiring system for the Accounting department would cost about $75,000. If we was to use conventional methods to install round wiring, we would have to renovate our entire department, costing over $300,000. Equally important, however, is the savings in terms of productivity and employee satisfaction. Which would decline if renovation was required.

Please let me know by June 10 whether you want me to proceed with this project.

Elite Tropical Cruise Lines

8567 West Broadway
Suite 2398
Miami Beach, FL 3313

Phone: 305-555-5555
Fax: 305-222-2222
Website: http://www.elitetropical.com

November 2, 200x

Ms. Jessica Stoudenmire
Holiday Travel Agency
520 West Hickmore
St. Laurent, QC H3T 1K2

Dear Ms. Stoudemire:

At Elite Tropical Cruise Lines, my colleagues and myself genuinely appreciate the loyalty of Holiday Travel Agency and its continuing use of the "Voyager Ship" line for your holiday tour packages for travellers' of all ages. As our customers know, the "Voyager Ship" is more luxurious than any cruise ship in the world, offering the enjoyablest activities on the seas.

A wide range of guests have experienced unforgettable cruises to unique and exotic ports of call. These type of positive experiences have inspired our guests to return year after year. It is our long standing policy to try and offer fun, sun, and exciting tours to these guests, including high school and college students. Recently, however, some of our younger guests has been loud and disruptive. Last year we raised the drinking age from 18 to 21, but this plan didn't work very good. Because of unruly young people, some passengers couldn't barely enjoy their travel aboard our cruise ships.

As a result, we are now instituting a new policy. Effective immediately, any passenger under the age of 21 will be excepted only when accompanied by a adult over 25. If this new policy will effect your student tour packages, we hope you will agree that the reasons behind us instituting this new policy required serious action. Elite Tropicals goal is to provide a real relaxing environment for all its passengers. Promoting family packages are one way in which we help high-school and college students join their family's for vacation fun away from the stresses of every day life.

Expecting carefree fun filled vacations, your customers will not be dissappointed by Elite Tropical. We attract more guests then any cruise line in the world, and 98 per cent of our guests reports that they are very satisfied. If you would be willing to work with me to plan new packages for your customers. My staff and I will call you during the week of January 5.

Sincerely,

Stephanie Carroll

Stephanic Carroll
Vice-President, Customer Service

POSTTEST

Underline the correct word.

1. Gelato has (fewer, less) calories than ice cream.
2. It would be (a, an) honour to meet the author.
3. Mrs. Sherman said she felt (good, well) following her surgery.
4. Yusef completed a (page by page, page-by-page) check of the book.
5. The employees liked their (completely-redecorated, completely redecorated) office.

learning.web.ways

Your company is thinking of using blogs for research purposes, and you want to learn more about this Internet resource.

Goal: To learn about weblogs (blogs).

1. With your web browser on the screen, go to **<http://technorati.com/about/>**.
2. Read the brief article to learn about what blogs are and how they are used. Take notes of any interesting fact you learn about blogs.
3. Now go to **<http://blogs.canadianbusiness.com/advansis>** to find business-related blogs in Canada.
4. Once you find a blog that interests you, read some of its more recent entries. List three interesting facts you learned from those entries.
5. Print one page from the blog.
6. End your session, and turn in all printed pages and the notes you've made.

1. fewer 2. an 3. well 4. page-by-page 5. completely redecorated

C H A P T E R

Prepositions 13

OBJECTIVES When you have completed the materials in this chapter, you will be able to do the following:

LEVEL I

- *Use objective-case pronouns as objects of prepositions.*
- *Avoid using prepositions in place of verbs and adverbs.*

LEVEL II

- *Use nine troublesome prepositions correctly.*
- *Omit unnecessary prepositions and retain necessary ones.*
- *Construct formal sentences that avoid terminal prepositions.*

LEVEL III

- *Recognize words and constructions requiring specific prepositions (idioms).*
- *Use idioms involving prepositions correctly.*

PRETEST

Underline the correct word.

1. Lydia is frustrated because she receives (to, too) much spam.
2. She feels (as if, that) these spam messages are affecting her productivity.
3. Do you plan (on taking, to take) a two-week vacation?
4. Management and workers alike agreed (to, with) the contract.
5. The printer should be placed (beside, besides) the computer.

1. too 2. as if 3. to take 4. to 5. beside

Prepositions are connecting words that show the relationship of a noun or pronoun to another word in a sentence. This chapter reviews the use of objective-case pronouns following prepositions. It also focuses on common problems that communicators have with troublesome prepositions. Finally, it presents many words in our language that require specific prepositions (idiomatic expressions) to sound "right."

LEVEL I

Career Tip

"You are the same today that you are going to be five years from now except for two things: the people with whom you associate and the books you read."
—Charles Jones

Hotlink

The University of Victoria provides a basic overview of prepositions at **<http://web2.uvcs.uvic.ca/elc/studyzone/200/grammar/prepo.htm>**.

Spot the Blooper

Colorado Springs trafffic sign: "Following to close." (City officials blamed the sign company, which had shortened "Following too closely" because it didn't fit.)

▶ Common Uses of Prepositions

In this list of commonly used prepositions, notice that prepositions may consist of one word or several.

about	beside	in addition to	since
according to	between	in spite of	through
after	but	into	to
along with	by	like	under
among	during	of	until
around	except	off	upon
at	for	on	with
before	from	on account of	within
below	in	over	without

Objective Case Following Prepositions

As you will recall from Chapter 6, pronouns that are objects of prepositions must be in the objective case.

Marian, *along with* Jan and *her*, arrived later.
We received pledges *from him* and *her* for the charity bike ride.
Give the account balances *to* Mr. Love and *him*.

To review further, recall that some prepositions—such as *like, between, but,* and *except*—are particularly likely to lead to confusion in determining pronoun case. Consider the following examples.

Strictly *between* you and *me* (not *I*), the contract is already signed.
Applications from individuals *like* Mr. Sheldon and *him* (not *he*) are rare.
Recommendations from everyone *but them* (not *they*) have arrived.

Fundamental Problems With Prepositions

In even the most casual speech or writing, the following misuses of prepositions should be avoided.

***Of* for *have*.** The verb phrases *should have, would have,* or *could have* should never be written as *should of, would of,* or *could of.* The word *of* is a preposition and cannot be used in verb phrases.

Jeremy *should have* (not *should of*) called first.
He *could have* (not *could of*) given some advance notice.

***Off* for *from*.** The preposition *from* should never be replaced by *off* or *off of.*

My friend borrowed money *from* (not *off* or *off of*) me.
Doreen said she got the book *from* you.

***To* for *too*.** The preposition *to* means "in a direction toward." Do not use the word *to* in place of the adverb *too*, which means "additionally," "also," or "excessively."

Dividends are not distributed *to* shareholders unless declared by the directors.
No dividends were declared because profits were *too* small.
Contributions of services will be accepted *too.*

You will recall that the word *to* may also be part of an infinitive construction.

She is learning *to* program in HTML.

Complete the reinforcement exercises for Level I on pp. 252–253.

▶ Troublesome Prepositions

LEVEL II

Be particularly careful to use the following prepositions properly.

Among, between. *Among* is usually used to speak of three or more persons or things; *between* is usually used for two.

The disagreement was *between* Stipchek and his partner.
Profits were distributed *among* the four partners.

Spot the Blooper

From a job applicant's cover letter: "I would be prepared to meet with you at your earliest convenience to discuss what I can do to your company."

Beside, besides. *Beside* means "next to"; *besides* means "in addition to."

Please sit *beside* me at the assembly.
Besides a preface, you must write an introduction.

Except. The preposition *except,* meaning "excluding" or "but," is sometimes confused with the verb *accept,* which means "to receive."

Everyone *except* Melanie was able to come.
Please *accept* this gift as a token of our appreciation.

In, into, in to. *In* indicates a position or location. *Into* can mean several things, including (1) entering something, (2) changing form, or (3) making contact. Some constructions may employ *in* as an adverb preceding an infinitive.

We store copy paper *in* the supply cabinet. (The preposition *in* indicates location.)
Bring the boxes *into* the storeroom. (Preposition *into* indicates movement to an interior location.)
They went *in* to see the manager. (Adverb *in* precedes infinitive *to see.*)

Like. The preposition *like* should be used to introduce a noun or pronoun. Do not use *like* to introduce a clause (a group of words with a subject and a predicate). Use a conjunction like *as* to introduce clauses. (Conjunctions will be discussed further in Chapters 14 and 15.)

The copy looks very much *like* the original. (*Like* is used as preposition introducing the noun *original.*)
It looks *as if* (not *like*) it may rain soon. (*As if* is used to introduce the clause *it may rain soon.*)
As (not *like*) I said earlier, the order was sent. (Do not use *like* to introduce the clause *I said earlier.*)

Study Tip

Look at the word(s) following *like.* If many words follow, chances are they function as a clause; use *as, as if,* or *as though* instead of *like.*

Hotlink

For a quick overview of the basic uses of prepositions, have a look at this University of Ottawa web page **<http://www.uottawa.ca/academic/arts/writcent/hypergrammar/preposit.html>**.

▶ Using Prepositions Efficiently

Necessary Prepositions

Don't omit those prepositions necessary to clarify a relationship. Be particularly careful when two prepositions modify a single object.

We have every desire *for* and hope *of* an early settlement. (Do not omit *for*.)
What type *of* coupler do you need? (Do not omit *of*.)
Mr. Munoz is unsure *of* where to place the machine. (Do not omit *of*.)
Salaries for temporary positions seem to be higher than *for* permanent positions. (Do not omit *for*.)
When did you graduate *from* high school? (Do not omit *from*.)

Unnecessary Prepositions

Omit unnecessary prepositions, particularly *of*.

The book fell *off* the desk. (Not *off of*)
Leave the package *inside* the door. (Not *inside of*)
Both websites are useful. (Not *of the* websites)
All the letters require stationery. (Not *of the* letters)
Where is the meeting? (Not meeting *at*)
She could not help laughing. (Not *help from*)
Keep the paper *near* the printer. (Not *near to*)

Spot the Blooper

From an Ann Landers column: "...[They] might get their eyes opened up." (Is "up" needed?)

Ending a Sentence With a Preposition

In the past, language authorities warned against ending a sentence (or a clause) with a preposition. In formal writing today, most careful authors continue to avoid terminal prepositions. In conversation, however, terminal prepositions are acceptable.

Informal Usage	**Formal Usage**
What organization is he a member *of*?	*Of* what organization is he a member?
What is the medicine prescribed *for*?	*For* what is the medicine prescribed?
We don't know whom you spoke *to* when you called.	We don't know *to* whom you spoke when you called.
We missed the television news program she appeared *on*.	We missed the television news program *on* which she appeared.

Complete the reinforcement exercises for Level II on pp. 254–256.

▶ Idiomatic Use of Prepositions

Every language has idioms, which are word combinations peculiar to that language. These combinations have developed through usage and often cannot be explained rationally. A native speaker usually is unaware of idiom usage until a violation jars his or her ear, such as "He is capable *from* (rather than *of*) violence."

The following list shows words that require specific prepositions to denote precise meanings. This group is just a sampling of the large number of English idioms involving prepositions. Consult a dictionary when you are unsure of the correct preposition to use with a particular word.

acquaint with	Are you *acquainted with* the new president?
adept in (*or* at)	Are you *adept in* negotiation tactics?
adhere to	All employees must *adhere to* certain office rules.
agree to (a proposal)	Did they *agree to* the plan for splitting shifts?
agree with (a person)	In this matter I certainly *agree with* you.
angry at (a thing)	Customers are understandably *angry at* the delay.
angry with (a person)	How can you be *angry with* the child?
bored with (*not* of)	Terry became *bored with* his repetitive duties.
buy from	You may *buy from* any one of several wholesalers.
capable of	She is *capable of* remarkable accomplishments.
comply with	We must *comply with* government regulations.
concur in (an action)	Four countries *concur in* the plan to reduce oil production.
concur with (a person)	Do you *concur with* Andrew in the need for economy?
conform to	These machine parts do not *conform to* the specifications.
contrast with	The white boat *contrasts* sharply *with* the blue ocean.
correspond to (match)	A bird's wing *corresponds to* a man's arm.
correspond with (write)	We *correspond with* our clients regularly.
desire for	A *desire for* wealth may create greed.
desirous of	Rogers was *desirous of* acquiring blue-chip investments.
differ from (things)	Debit cards *differ from* credit cards.
differ with (a person)	I *differ with* you in small points only.
different from (not *than*)	This product is *different from* the one I ordered.
disagree with	Do you *disagree with* him?
expert in	Dr. Rand is an *expert in* electronics.
guard against	*Guard against* infection by covering wounds.
identical with (*or* to)	Our strategy is *identical with* our competitor's.
independent of	Living alone, the young man was *independent of* his parents.
infer from	I *infer from* your remark that you are dissatisfied.
interest in	Jan has a great *interest in* the bond market.
negligent of	*Negligent of* his diet, the old man became ill.
oblivious to *or* of	McClain was *oblivious to* (or *of*) his surroundings.
plan to (*not* on)	We *plan to* expand our target market.
prefer to	Do you *prefer to* work a four-day week?
reason with	Mr. Miller tried to *reason with* the unhappy customer.
reconcile with (match)	Chequebook figures must be *reconciled with* bank figures.
reconcile to (accept)	He has never become *reconciled to* retirement.
responsible for	William is *responsible for* locking the building.
retroactive to	The salary increase is *retroactive to* last July 1.
sensitive to	Mrs. Choy is unusually *sensitive to* her employees' needs.
similar to	Your term paper topic is *similar to* mine.
stand in (*not* on) line	How long have you been *standing in* line?
talk to (tell something)	The speaker *talked to* the large group.
talk with (exchange remarks)	After his lecture, the speaker *talked with* club members informally.

Hotlink

This overview of prepositions, available at **<http://ucalgary.ca/UofC/eduweb/grammar/course/speech/1_5a.htm>**, also carries an interactive quiz, that will help you check your mastery of this subject.

Hotlink

An excellent place to learn more about prepositions is Capital Community College's site **<http://grammar.ccc.commnet.edu/grammar/prepositions.htm>**.

Hotlink

For an exhaustive list of prepositions and the verbs or objects they go with, consult **<http://ess.nrcan.gc.ca/pubs/scipub/guide/gramm/prepos_e.php>**.

tired of	The receptionist gets *tired of* hearing the telephone ring.
wait for (expect)	Mark is *waiting for* the bus.
wait on (serve)	We left a tip for the person who *waited on* us at the restaurant.

Complete the reinforcement exercises for Level III on pp. 257–258.

HOTLINE QUERIES

Question: What's wrong with saying *Lisa graduated college last year?*

Answer: The preposition *from* must be inserted for syntactical fluency. Two constructions are permissible: *Lisa graduated from college* or *Lisa was graduated from college.* The first version is more popular; the second is preferred by traditional grammarians.

Question: Another employee and I are collaborating on a report. I wanted to write this: *Money was lost due to poor attendance.* She says the sentence should read *Money was lost because of poor attendance.* My version is more concise. Which of us is right?

Answer: Most language authorities agree with your co-author. *Due to* is acceptable when it functions as an adjective, as in *Success was due to proper timing.* In this sense, *due to* is synonymous with *attributable to.* However, *because of* should introduce adverbial phrases and should modify verbs: *Money was lost because of poor attendance. Because of* modifies the verb phrase *was lost.*

Question: Should *sometime* be one or two words in the following sentence? *Can you come over (sometime) soon?*

Answer: In this sentence you should use the one-word form. *Sometime* as an adverb means "an indefinite time" *(the convention is sometime in December).* The two-word combination means "a period of time" *(we have some time to spare).*

Question: I saw this printed recently: *Some of the personal functions being reviewed are job descriptions, job specifications, and job evaluations.* Is *personal* used correctly here?

Answer: Indeed not! The word *personal* means "private" or "individual" (*your personal letters are being forwarded to you).* The word *personnel* refers to employees *(all company personnel are cordially invited).* The sentence you quote requires *personnel.*

Question: Is there any difference between *proved* and *proven*?

Answer: As a past participle, the verb form *proved* is preferred *(he has proved his point).* However, the word *proven* is preferred as an adjective form *(that company has a proven record). Proven* is also commonly used in the expression *not proven.*

Question: We're writing a letter to our subscribers, and this sentence doesn't sound right to me: *Every one of our subscribers benefit* . . . .

Answer: As you probably suspected, the verb *benefit* does not agree with the subject *one.* The sentence should read as follows: *Every one of our subscribers benefits* . . . . Don't let intervening phrases obscure the true subject of a sentence.

Question: How should I write *industry wide*? It's not in my dictionary.

Answer: A word with the suffix *wide* is usually written solid: *industrywide, nationwide, countrywide, statewide, worldwide* (but *province-wide*).

Question: I'm writing a sentence that reads *Please proceed to the podium* . . . . Is this correct, or should I use *precede* instead of *proceed*?

Answer: You're correct to use *proceed,* which means "to go forward or continue," in this sentence. The word *precede* means "to go before" (*a discussion will precede the final vote*).

NAME ______________________________

CHAPTER 13 Reinforcement Exercises

LEVEL I

A. (**Self-check**) Select the correct word, and write it in the space provided.

1. Let's keep this news between you and (I, me). ____________
2. Thomas thought that he (should of, should have) been allowed extra time. ____________
3. Bernstein has (to, too) little patience for that job. ____________
4. Everyone received the announcement but (I, me). ____________
5. You might be able to get the lecture notes (off of, from) Kathleen. ____________
6. Should a photocopy be made for Mrs. Korkis or (her, she)? ____________
7. Government has (to, too) consider the effects of inflation. ____________
8. Can you borrow a tent (off, from) the Bouchers? ____________
9. With more experience Gregory (would of, would have) landed the job. ____________
10. No one in the group except her and (I, me) will miss the field trip. ____________

Check your answers.

B. Underline any errors you find in the following sentences. Write the correct forms in the spaces provided. Write *C* if the sentence is correct as written.

Example: Performers like Mervin and she are crowd-pleasers. her

1. Everyone in the office except he uses instant messaging. ____________
2. Bill Gates could of kept his fortune, but he chose to give much of it to a charitable foundation. ____________
3. We got her email address off of Tony. ____________
4. Many customers are eager to make appointments with Mr. Jerome or him. ____________
5. Our union said that management's offer was "too little and to late." ____________
6. Diana Bowman told Andrew and me that we should have read the directions more carefully. ____________
7. It's to soon to tell whether voice recognition will become standard. ____________
8. Along with Tim and I, Mr. De la Torre will check the computer printout. ____________

1. me 2. should have 3. too 4. me 5. from 6. her 7. to 8. from 9. would have 10. me

9. Just between you and me, the difference between a job and a career is the difference between 40 and 60 hours a week. ____________________

10. You could of attended the premier showing last evening. ____________________

11. Our manager, together with Tanya and he, helped to close the sale. ____________________

12. You should of attended the sales training session last week. ____________________

13. You can always rely on co-workers like Renée and she when you need help to meet a deadline. ____________________

14. Everyone except him and I received the announcement too late to respond. ____________________

15. To address the letter properly, you must use information off of their stationery. ____________________

16. If you could have seen the shipment when it arrived, you would of refused it too. ____________________

17. All the checkers except she and he have the holiday off. ____________________

18. Some of the paper is to long for our everyday use. ____________________

19. Last year we tried to order supplies off of them too. ____________________

20. CEO Christine Gerbig spoke with the marketing manager and I about sales. ____________________

NAME ______________________________

LEVEL II

A. (**Self-check**) Select the correct word(s).

1. The inheritance will be divided (between, among) all the heirs. ____________
2. Robert Whitmore moved (in, into) the office next door. ____________
3. We engraved identification serial numbers (inside, inside of) all new equipment. ____________
4. The office suite (beside, besides) ours has been vacant for months. ____________
5. It looks (like, as if) we'll be working late tonight. ____________
6. Have you decided whether you will (accept, except) the position? ____________
7. Despite her salary and new title, Helen feels (as, like) a technician. ____________
8. Differences (between, among) the two brothers affected their management styles. ____________
9. The contracts blew (off, off of) the desk when the door was opened. ____________
10. In her job search, Marcia used many resources (beside, besides) the Web. ____________

Check your answers.

B. In the following sentences cross out unnecessary prepositions and insert any necessary ones.

Examples: What type ^of wheel bearings are needed?
Where are you going ~~to~~?

1. The time for submitting entries is over with.
2. A new shopping centre is being built opposite to the college.
3. Who can tell me where the meeting is scheduled at?
4. Dr. Forward had a great interest and an appreciation of all applications of computerization.
5. Do you know if all of the orders have been filled?
6. Special printing jobs must be done outside of the office.
7. Only Mr. Larsen knows where those supplies might be stored at.
8. What type smart card does Infineon manufacture?
9. Where shall we move the extra desks and chairs to?

1. among 2. into 3. inside 4. beside 5. as if 6. accept 7. like 8. between 9. off 10. besides

10. Daniel's love and interest in photography led to a gratifying career.

11. Leah couldn't help from laughing when Noah spilled his latte as he walked into the conference room.

12. Where shall I send the cheque to?

13. Please place the new directories inside of the office.

14. We have been informed that the claim is due on April 15.

15. Jill Montgomery graduated college with a diploma in graphic design.

C. Select the correct word(s).

1. Relief funds were divided (among, between) all flood victims. ____________
2. (As, Like) we discussed last week, Friday will be a half day. ____________
3. The new research specialist will move into the office (beside, besides) mine. ____________
4. All three candidates have gone (in, into) the conference room. ____________
5. Your laptop computer looks just (like, as) mine. ____________
6. The advertising campaign looks (like, as if) it will be quite successful. ____________
7. Has anyone been (in to, into) see me this morning? ____________
8. We cannot (accept, except) the shipment without an invoice. ____________
9. After the interview, Lee felt (like, as if) he would be offered the position. ____________
10. If he (accepts, excepts) the position, he will have to move to Calgary. ____________
11. (Beside, Besides) Randy and Tyler, whom have you invited? ____________
12. Employees are required to turn expense reports (in to, into) their supervisors within one week. ____________

D. Write original sentences using these prepositions correctly.

1. (among) ____

____

2. (into) ____

____

3. (except) ____

____

4. (like) ____

____

5. (between) ____

____

E. The following sentences have prepositions that end clauses. Rewrite the sentences so that the prepositions come before their objects.

Example: Here is the information you asked about.

Here is the information about which you asked.

1. Whom did you send payment to? ____

____

2. Please locate the file you put the contract in. ____

____

3. What did I come into this room for? ____

____

4. We have a number of loyal members we can rely on. ____

____

5. What company did you purchase these supplies from? ____

____

NAME ____________________

LEVEL III

A. (**Self-check**) Underline any errors in the use of prepositions in the following sentences, and write a correct form in the space provided. Write *C* if the sentence is correct as written.

1. Al Fisher is exceptionally adept with troubleshooting. ________
2. We find it impossible to comply to the latest safety regulations. ________
3. In a televised address, the Prime Minister will talk with the nation at 6 p.m. ________
4. How long do you plan on staying at the conference? ________
5. Mrs. Reich's management philosophy is quite different than mine. ________
6. Ray is very angry at David for divulging the secret. ________
7. How can one reconcile this new business venture with their recent bankruptcy? ________
8. Isolated from neighbours, the hermit was independent with local laws. ________
9. A car very similar with yours is for sale. ________
10. Jordan is an expert at bioengineering. ________

Check your answers.

B. Underline any errors in the use of prepositions in the following sentences, and write a correction in the space provided. Write *C* if the sentence is correct as written.

1. It was a pleasure talking to you yesterday during the interview. ________
2. Mr. Colotti described how common stock differs with preferred stock. ________
3. Because she was negligent to her duties, she received a poor performance review. ________
4. Does Mr. Brady concur with other board members in raising tuition? ________
5. Customers were upset after standing on line for an hour. ________
6. All procedures must adhere with company policies. ________
7. The light background on the web page contrasts to the font colour. ________
8. Do you hire a translator when your company corresponds to Chinese customers? ________
9. Because the franchise is completely standardized, a fast-food restaurant in California may be identical to one in Saskatchewan. ________

1. adept in *or* at 2. comply with 3. talk to 4. plan to stay 5. different from 6. angry with 7. C 8. independent of 9. similar to 10. expert in

10. A firewall will help guard against unauthorized access to our intranet. ____________________

11. To conform with departmental procedures, all work must be logged in. ____________________

12. We cannot possibly agree with a contract that we have not yet read. ____________________

13. He's become bored of working at an office job. ____________________

14. Her son graduated Camosun College last spring. ____________________

15. We had to wait on two reports before we could make our decision. ____________________

C. Optional Writing. Your instructor may ask you to complete this exercise on a separate sheet.

Write ten original sentences using the following expressions: *oblivious to, adhere to, retroactive to, independent of, agree with, identical with, differ from, prefer to, contrast with,* and *was graduated from.* Use a dictionary if necessary.

Editor's Challenge

The following report and memo contain intentional errors in spelling, proofreading, and concepts you have studied thus far. Use standard proofreading marks to show your corrections.

RESULTS OF SMOKING POLICY SURVEY

by Craig Abrams, Human Resources

Background

A number of requests has been received from employees asking that smoking be banned in all areas of our buildings. Second hand smoke represent a health risk with significant compensation implications for our company and it's shareholders. To gather information, Human Resources distributed a questionnaire to 58 managerial and supervisory personnel, a total of 52 responses were received.

Findings

A tally of the returned surveys show that a clear majority of our managerial employees favours a complete non-smoking policy. A total of 42 employees, or nearly 80 per cent of the total survey, indicated there approval of such a policy. To implement this policy, excellent suggestions were made by respondents. Which are discussed from the attached printouts.

Conclusion

The results of this survey suggests that our managers and supervisors would support an non-smoking policy. They feel that a carefully planned sensitively implemented non-smoking policy could be successful about our organization.

Recommendations

A well managed cessation program should offer support and practical advice to those who want to use the opportunity to quit. Employees should be allowed sometime to take part in group counselling activitys. High visibility displays should promote participation. Whether to provide outdoor smoking areas for those employees who do not stop are a matter a committee must work on.

HIGH TECH SOLUTIONS
INTEROFFICE MEMO

DATE: July 1, 200x
TO: All Employees
FROM: Craig Abrams, Human Resources
SUBJECT: New Email and Web Policy

Over the past few month's, supervisors have provided datum about email and web use to top management and I. Beside using email and the Web for work related purposes, some employees are useing these tools for personal bussiness. This, of course, is having serious implications for our company and its productivity. Improper use can also led to larger problems such as lawsuits. We have, therefore, hired two lawyers who is expert at writing email and web policies to help write a policy for our firm. We plan on implementing the policy on September 1.

During the month of August, workshops will be given by my staff and I to help employees learn how to comply to the new policy. You can also schedule an appointment with your immediate supervisor to talk to them about the new policy. In addition, you can turn any comments or suggestions into me before September 1. Finally, you can obtain a rough draft of the policy off of my receptionist after July 31. She can also let you know where training sessions will be held at.

I think we can all understand that to much personnel email and web use can negatively effect our company. Thats why this policy is needed, and we are confident that you will all except it's provisions. The policy we develop will be similar with policies used by other company's in our industry. As we develop the policy, we will remain sensitive of the needs of all employees to make sure that the policy is something to which everyone can agree. If you have an interest in assisting us with this important task, please contact my assistant or I at Ext. 452 before August 15.

POSTTEST

Underline the correct word.

1. Her presentation is still three minutes (to, too) long.
2. It looks (like, as if) we will be able to avoid layoffs.
3. Is it necessary for all documents to comply (to, with) the new guidelines?
4. Dividends will be distributed (between, among) shareholders.
5. (Beside, Besides) Ann, who is able to work Saturday?

learning.web.ways

Your advertising company has been asked to create promotional material for a hotel in St. John's, Newfoundland. You want to get some basic facts about the province first.

Goal: To use an online encyclopedia.

1. With your web browser on the screen, go to the Canadian Encyclopedia site **<http://www.thecanadianencyclopedia.com>**. Enter the English version of the site.
2. In the search box in the upper right corner of the screen, key your search term, **Newfoundland**.
3. Read the entry about **Newfoundland and Labrador**, and print one page of the article.
4. When did Newfoundland officially join the confederation? What is its largest mountain system? Which two provincial institutes are located in St. John's?
5. To select another online encyclopedia, go to **<http://www.refdesk.com/topency.html>**.
6. From the list of encyclopedias, click on one, and compare the findings for Newfoundland. Print one page.
7. End your session, and turn in all printed pages and your answers to the questions.

1. too 2. as if 3. with 4. among 5. Besides

C H A P T E R

Conjunctions to Join Equals 14

OBJECTIVES When you have completed the materials in this chapter, you will be able to do the following:

LEVEL I

- *Distinguish between simple and compound sentences.*
- *Punctuate compound sentences joined by* and, or, nor, *and* but.

LEVEL II

- *Punctuate compound sentences using conjunctive adverbs such as* therefore, however, *and* consequently.
- *Punctuate sentences using parenthetical (interrupting) adverbs such as* therefore, however, *and* consequently.

LEVEL III

- *Recognize correlative conjunctions such as* either ... or, not only ... but also, *and* neither ... nor.
- *Use parallel construction in composing sentences with correlative conjunctions.*

PRETEST

Insert commas and semicolons to punctuate the following sentences correctly.

1. All employees must be able to communicate effectively therefore we evaluate communication skills during employment interviews.
2. It is important however that we also continue to cover all other sales territories adequately.
3. Eleanor Uyeda prefers to remain in Kitchener but Wanda Deen is considering the Windsor area.
4. As many as 20 agents will move nevertheless the transition must be made smoothly.

Circle the letter of the sentence that is more effective.

5. (a) Not only is this wireless service more reliable, but it is also cheaper than the other.
   (b) This wireless service is not only more reliable but also cheaper than the other.

1. effectively; therefore, 2. important, however, 3. Kitchener, 4. move; nevertheless, 5. b

Conjunctions are connecting words. They may be separated into two major groups: those that join grammatically equal words or word groups and those that join grammatically unequal words or word groups. This chapter will focus on those conjunctions that join equals. Recognizing conjunctions and understanding their patterns of usage will, among other things, enable you to use commas and semicolons more appropriately.

LEVEL I

Hotlink

Additional help on the use of coordinating conjunctions can be found at **<http://palc.sd40.bc.ca/palc/feature/2006/coordconjunctions.htm>**.

▶ Coordinating Conjunctions

Coordinating conjunctions connect words, phrases, and clauses of equal grammatical value or rank. The most common coordinating conjunctions are *and, or, but,* and *nor.* Notice in these sentences how coordinating conjunctions join grammatically equal elements.

We think your action is *illogical, unfair,* and *arbitrary.* (Here the conjunction *and* joins equal words.)

Give serious thought *to your letters* and *to reader reaction.* (Here *and* joins equal phrases.)

Mr. Freeman opens the mail, but *Miss Dunaway fills the orders.* (Here *but* joins equal clauses.)

Phrases and Clauses

A group of related words without a subject and a verb is called a *phrase*. You are already familiar with verb phrases and prepositional phrases. It is not important that you be able to identify the other kinds of phrases (infinitive, gerund, participial), but it is very important that you be able to distinguish phrases from clauses.

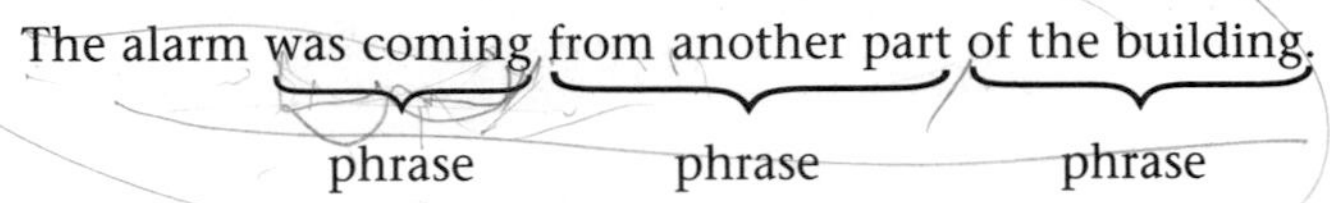

The alarm was coming from another part of the building.

Study Tip

Clauses have both subjects and verbs. Phrases do not. Clauses may have phrases within them.

A group of related words including a subject and a verb is a *clause*.

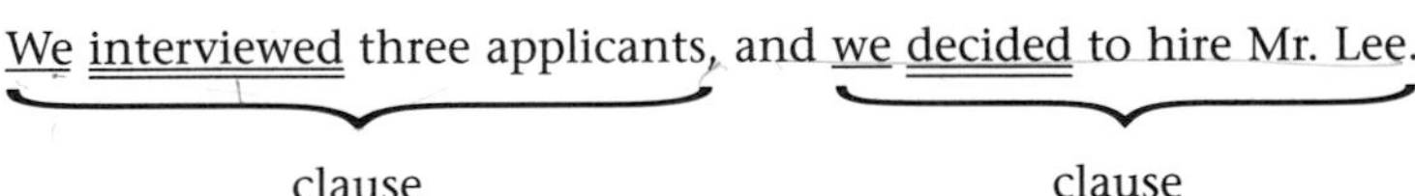

We interviewed three applicants, and we decided to hire Mr. Lee.
clause
clause

Karen is interested in a job in accounting, but she wants to travel also.

clause　　　　clause

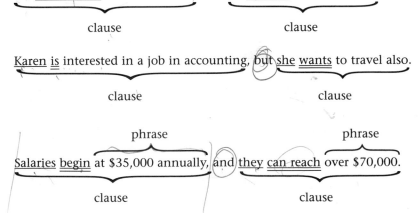

Hotlink

For a thorough overview of phrases and clauses, check out this Trent University handout **<http://www.trentu.ca/academicskills/unit9.htm>**.

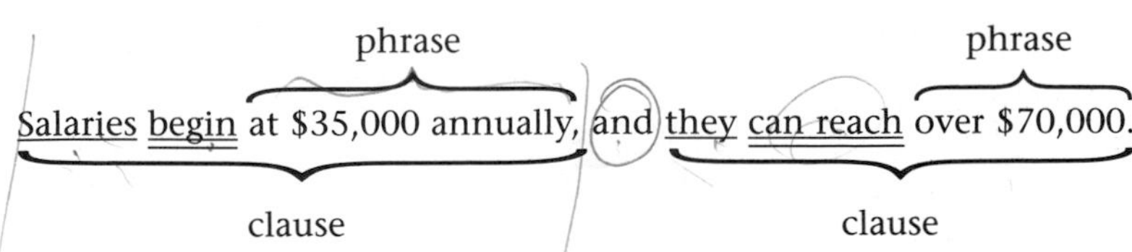

phrase
phrase
Salaries begin at $35,000 annually, and they can reach over $70,000.
clause
clause

Clauses often contain phrases, as illustrated in the last sentence.

Simple and Compound Sentences

A *simple* sentence has one independent clause, that is, a clause that can stand alone. A *compound* sentence has two or more independent clauses.

> We agreed to lease the equipment. (Simple sentence)
>
> Our Travel Services Department planned the sales trip, but some salespeople also made private excursions. (Compound sentence)

Spot the Blooper

From a Hewlett-Packard contest form: "If you would like the name of the winner ... send a elf-addressed stamped envelope."

Punctuating Compound Sentences Using Coordinating Conjunctions

When coordinating conjunctions join clauses in a compound sentence, a comma precedes the conjunction, unless the clauses are very short (six or fewer words in each clause).

> We can handle our employee payroll internally, *or* we can outsource it to a reputable firm.
>
> Ship by air *or* ship by rail. (Clauses are too short to require a comma.)

Do not use commas when coordinating conjunctions join compound verbs, objects, or phrases.

> The bank will notify you of each transfer, or it will send you a monthly statement. (Comma used because *or* joins two independent clauses.)
>
> The bank will notify you of each transfer or will send you a monthly statement. (No comma needed because *or* joins the compound verbs of a single independent clause.)
>
> Thomas Edison said that colleges should not have to choose between lighting their buildings *and* enlightening their students. (No comma needed because *and* joins the compound objects of the prepositional phrase beginning with *between*.)
>
> Shareholders are expected to attend the meeting *or* to send in their proxies. (No comma needed because *or* joins two infinitive phrases.)

Hotlink

To test your knowledge of coordinating conjunctions, visit **<http://web2.uvcs.uvic.ca/elc/studyzone/330/grammar/coconj1.htm>**.

Complete the reinforcement exercises for Level I on pp. 269–270.

▶ Conjunctive Adverbs — LEVEL II

Conjunctive adverbs may also be used to connect equal sentence elements. Because conjunctive adverbs are used to effect a transition from one thought to another and because they may consist of more than one word, they have also been called *transitional expressions*. The most common conjunctive adverbs and adverb phrases follow.

accordingly	however	on the other hand
consequently	in fact	otherwise
for example	in the meantime	that is
for instance	moreover	then
furthermore	nevertheless	therefore
hence	on the contrary	thus

Study Tip

Some authorities call a conjunctive adverb a "conjunctive joiner." Such a term may help you remember its function.

Hotlink

Also known as transitions, conjunctive adverbs get a full airing in the Transitional Words and Phrases handout prepared by Memorial University and posted at **<http://www.mun.ca/writingcentre/transword.shtml>**.

In the following compound sentences, observe that conjunctive adverbs join clauses of equal grammatical value. Note that semicolons (*not* commas) are used before conjunctive adverbs that join independent clauses. Commas should immediately follow conjunctive adverbs of two or more syllables. Note also that the word following a semicolon is not capitalized—unless, of course, it is a proper noun.

> Electricians rewired the equipment room; *nevertheless,* fuses continued to blow.
>
> Some equipment requires separate outlets; *consequently,* we installed new outlets.
>
> Equipment expenditures are high this quarter; *on the other hand,* the new equipment will reduce labour costs.
>
> Competition among computer manufacturers is intensive; *hence* prices have decreased sharply.
>
> The use of handheld phones in cars endangers safety; *thus* several communities are giving away bumper stickers that say "Drive Now, Talk Later."

Generally, no comma is used after one-syllable conjunctive adverbs such as *hence, thus,* and *then* (unless a strong pause is desired).

▶ Distinguishing Conjunctive Adverbs From Parenthetical Adverbs

Many words that function as conjunctive adverbs may also serve as *parenthetical* (interrupting) *adverbs.* Use semicolons only with conjunctive adverbs that join independent clauses. Use commas to set off parenthetical adverbs that interrupt the flow of a sentence.

> Mr. Jackson is, *however,* a fine administrator. (Adverb used parenthetically.)
>
> Mr. Jackson is a fine administrator; *however,* he is a poor fundraiser. (Adverb used to join two independent clauses.)
>
> The discount will, *furthermore,* be increased after six years.
>
> Policyholders are eligible for a discount after only three years; *furthermore,* the discount will be increased after six years.
>
> We believe, *on the other hand,* that cellular phone sales will continue to grow.
>
> We believe that cellphones are convenient; *on the other hand,* they must be used responsibly.

Study Tip

Use a semicolon with a conjunctive adverb only when you are joining two sentences.

Complete the reinforcement exercises for Level II on pp. 271–273.

LEVEL III

▶ Other Conjunctions

So far we have studied two kinds of conjunctions used to join grammatically equal sentence elements: coordinating conjunctions (used to join equal words, phrases, and clauses) and conjunctive adverbs (used to join grammatically equal clauses in compound sentences). *Correlative conjunctions* form the third and final group of conjunctions that join grammatically equal sentence elements.

Correlative Conjunctions

Correlative conjunctions are always paired: *both ... and, not only ... but (also), either ... or, neither ... nor.* When greater emphasis is desired, these paired conjunctions are used instead of coordinating conjunctions.

> Your PDA is on the counter *or* on the desk.
> Your PDA is *either* on the counter *or* on the desk. (More emphatic)

In using correlative conjunctions, place them so that the words, phrases, or clauses being joined are parallel in construction (have the same grammatical form).

Parallel:	He was working *either* in Victoria *or* in Nanaimo.
Not parallel:	*Either* he was working in Victoria *or* in Nanaimo.
Parallel:	She was *not only* gracious *but also* kind.
Not parallel:	She was *not only* gracious, *but* she was *also* kind.
Parallel:	I have *neither* the time *nor* the energy for this.
Not parallel:	I *neither* have the time *nor* the energy for this.

Spot the Blooper

From a New York sports columnist: "While checking my bags at the counter, Magic Johnson arrived in a stretch limo."

Additional Coordinating Conjunctions

At Level I we studied four commonly used coordinating conjunctions: *and, or, nor,* and *but.* Three other coordinating conjunctions should also be mentioned: *yet, for,* and *so.*

The words *yet* and *for* may function as coordinating conjunctions, although they are infrequently used as such.

> We use email extensively, *yet* we still prefer personal contact with our customers.
> The weary traveller was gaunt and ill, *for* his journey had been long and arduous.

Hotlink

To get a shorter overview of conjunctive adverbs, download the University of Western Ontario handout from **<http://www.sdc.uwo.ca/writing/handouts/Coordination.pdf>**.

The word *so* is often informally used as a coordinating conjunction. In more formal contexts, the conjunctive adverbs *therefore* and *consequently* are recommended as substitutes.

Informal:	The plane leaves at 2:15 *so* they still have time to pack.
Formal:	The plane leaves at 2:15; *therefore,* they still have time to pack.

If you wish to avoid using *so* as a conjunction, try starting your sentence with *because* or *although.*

Informal:	Cellphone calls in public can be intrusive, *so* they are banned in some places.
Improved:	*Because* cellphone calls in public can be intrusive, they are banned in some places.

Complete the reinforcement exercises for Level III on pp. 274–275.

HOTLINE QUERIES

Question: Please help me decide which *maybe* to use in this sentence: *He said that he (maybe, may be) able to help us.*

Answer: Use the two-word *may be,* which is a verb phrase. The single word *maybe* is an adverb that means "perhaps" *(maybe she will call).*

(Continued)

Question: Is it acceptable to key part of an individual's name at the end of one line and carry the rest to the next line?

Answer: Full names may be divided between the first and the last names or after the middle initial. For example, you could key *John R.* on one line and *Williamson* on the next line. Do not, however, separate a short title and a surname (such as *Mr./Williamson*), and do not divide a name (such as *William/son*). By the way, many computer programs make unacceptable line-ending decisions. Be sure to inspect your copy, either on the screen or on the printout, so that you can correct poor hyphenation and unacceptable word separations.

Question: What should the verb in this sentence be? *There (has, have) to be good reasons ...*

Answer: Use the plural verb *have,* which agrees with the subject *reasons.* In sentences that begin with the word *there,* look for the subject after the verb.

Question: Does *Ms.* have a period after it? Should I use this title for all women in business today?

Answer: *Ms.* is probably a blend of *Miss* and *Mrs.,* and it is written with a period following it. Some women in business prefer to use *Ms.,* presumably because it is a title equal to *Mr.* Neither title reveals one's marital status. Many other women, however, prefer to use *Miss* or *Mrs.* as a title. It's always wise, if possible, to determine the preference of the individual.

Question: I just typed this sentence for my boss: *He was given a new title <u>in lieu of</u> a salary increase.* I went to my dictionary to check the spelling of *in lieu of,* but I can't find it. How is it spelled and what does it mean?

Answer: The listing in the dictionary is under *lieu,* and the phrase means "in place of" or "instead of." Many authorities today recommend avoiding such foreign phrases. It's easier and clearer to say "instead of."

Question: Can you help me with the words *averse* and *adverse?* I've never been able to straighten them out in my mind.

Answer: *Averse* is an adjective meaning "disinclined" or "reluctant" and is generally used with the preposition *to (the little boy was averse to bathing; she is averse to statistical keyboarding). Adverse* is also an adjective, but it means "hostile" or "unfavourable" *(adverse economic conditions halted the company's growth; the picnic was postponed because of adverse weather conditions).* In distinguishing between these two similar words, it might help you to know that the word *averse* is usually used to describe animate (living) objects.

Question: What should I write: *You are our No. 1 account,* or *You are our number one account?* Should anything be hyphenated?

Answer: Either is correct, but I prefer *No. 1* because it is more easily recognizable and because figures are generally used to express numbers referred to as numbers. No hyphen is required.

Question: A friend of mine gets upset when I say something like, *I was so surprised by her remark.* She thinks I'm misusing *so.* Am I?

Answer: Your friend is right, if we're talking about formal expression. The intensifier *so* requires a clause to complete its meaning. For example, *I was so surprised by her remark that I immediately protested.* It's like waiting for the other shoe to drop when one hears *so* as a modifier without a qualifying clause. *He was so funny.* So funny that what? *He was so funny that he became a stand-up comedian.*

NAME ______________________________

CHAPTER 14 Reinforcement Exercises

LEVEL I

A. (Self-check) Select *a, b,* or *c* to identify the sentences below.

a. A comma correctly punctuates a compound sentence.
b. The sentence is not compound; thus the comma should be omitted.
c. Although the sentence is compound, the clauses are too short to require a comma.

Example: It rained most of the morning, but stopped in the afternoon when the sun began to shine. ___b___

1. Heated competition will drive down prices on flat-screen TVs, and the prices of DVD recorders will also fall. ______
2. I did not expect a profit, and did not fear a loss. ______
3. Listen well, and watch carefully. ______
4. Word processing specialists must possess excellent English skills, and they must be skilled at keyboarding. ______
5. Thank you for applying for admission, and for sending us your résumé. ______
6. The concert did not begin until 8 p.m., but a large crowd began to gather at noon. ______
7. Email your résumé or fax it. ______
8. Albert Einstein was four years old before he could speak, and seven years old before he could read. ______
9. A New York restaurant received so many complaints about cellphone use that it set up a cellphone lounge, and banished the phones' use elsewhere. ______
10. The city of Bombay originally rested on seven islands, but the islands were joined by landfill long ago. ______

Check your answers.

B. A simple sentence has one independent clause. A compound sentence has two or more independent clauses. Indicate with a check mark whether the following sentences, all of which are punctuated correctly, are simple or compound. *Hint:* A sentence is not compound unless the words preceding and following a conjunction form independent clauses. If these groups of words could not stand alone as sentences, the sentence is not compound.

	Simple	Compound
1. James Thomas conducted research on blogs, and he shared his findings with other department members.	______	______

1. a 2. b (not compound because no subject follows *and*) 3. c 4. a 5. b (no comma is needed because this is a simple sentence with two prepositional phrases joined by *and*) 6. a 7. c 8. b (the words following *and* do not form an independent clause) 9. b 10. a

	Simple	Compound
2. James Thomas conducted research on blogs and shared his findings with other department members.	______	______
3. We will allow you our discount of 10 per cent and also a cash rebate of $50 for each purchase.	______	______
4. The recently constructed corporate headquarters contained attractive executive offices, but the structure had few support facilities for employees.	______	______
5. The recently constructed corporate headquarters contained attractive executive offices but few support facilities for employees.	______	______
6. Management trainees are sent to all our branch offices in this country and to some of the branch offices in South America and Europe.	______	______
7. The best companies embrace their mistakes and learn from them.	______	______
8. Fill in all answer blanks on the application, and send the completed form to the human resources director.	______	______
9. Send copies of the project report to me and to other management personnel in our three subsidiaries.	______	______
10. Supplies for three offices arrived today, but most of our order will not arrive until later.	______	______

C. Insert commas where appropriate in the following sentences. Then, in the space provided, indicate the number of commas you have added for each sentence. If no comma is needed, write *0*.

Example: Kevin attended classes on Monday, but he went to the beach on Tuesday. ____1____

1. Some employees think their email should be confidential but courts generally uphold an employer's right to monitor messages. ________

2. Women are outpacing men on university campuses and now earn the majority of diplomas in fields once dominated by men. ________

3. Mr. Peterson was not pleased with the delay but he did not seem to be angry with the vendor. ________

4. Please copy this letter and fax it immediately. ________

5. Today's software can detect potentially troublesome words or identify high-pressure sales tactics in email messages. ________

6. Annuities for all contributors may accumulate yearly or may be withdrawn at regular intervals over a five-year period. ________

7. Periods of stock market growth are called *bull markets* and periods of stock market decline are known as *bear markets*. ________

8. Raw materials and supplies are available but machinery and equipment must be replaced before production can begin. ________

9. Consider the alternatives and act accordingly. ________

10. Charles Goodyear invented a process leading to the manufacture of rubber but he failed to benefit from it and died in poverty. ________

NAME ______________________

LEVEL II

A. (**Self-check**) Selected adverbs and conjunctions have been italicized in the following sentences. Insert commas and semicolons where appropriate. In the space provided, indicate the number of punctuation marks added to each sentence. Be prepared to explain your choices.

Example: Some loans must be secured; *therefore,* the borrower must supply collateral. ___2___

1. Click fraud has become a huge problem *thus* many companies no longer advertise on websites such as Google. ______
2. We are *however* able to make single copies quickly. ______
3. The bill of lading did not match the order *consequently* the shipment was refused. ______
4. Many people fear becoming victims of identity theft *however* identity theft rarely results in actual financial loss for consumers. ______
5. Kelly did *nevertheless* pick up the printed copies she needed immediately. ______
6. Ellen Arnold appears to be the best qualified *on the other hand* Diana Percy has excellent recommendations. ______
7. Jeanette considered the possibility of changing jobs *but* was unwilling to accept the risks involved. ______
8. Liam *on the other hand* changed jobs whenever the urge impelled him. ______
9. Our Accounts Receivable Department has written to you three times *however* we have had no response to our letters. ______
10. Your account is now three months overdue *hence* we have only one alternative left open to us. ______

Check your answers.

1. (1) problem; thus 2. (2) are, however, 3. (2) order; consequently, 4. (2) theft; however, 5. (2) did, nevertheless, 6. (2) qualified; on the other hand, 7. (0) 8. (2) Liam, on the other hand, 9. (2) times; however, 10. (1) overdue; hence

B. Insert commas and semicolons where appropriate. Indicate in the space provided the number of punctuation marks added to each sentence. Be prepared to explain your choices.

Example: Too many staff members missed the seminar; therefore, attendance will be mandatory in future. 2

1. The capital of Canada has changed several times in fact Kingston, Ontario, was capital from 1841 to 1843. ________
2. Microwave relay stations have reduced telephone costs moreover cable and satellite circuits reduce costs even more. ________
3. We are faced nevertheless with unusually expensive communication costs. ________
4. We submitted a low bid but did not get the contract. ________
5. Insurance works according to the law of averages thus increased losses send the average cost of premiums upward. ________
6. The car came with an automatic transmission nevertheless it provided better-than-average gas mileage. ________
7. We are moreover pleased with its manoeuvrability and handling. ________
8. A new directory will be released later in the month in the meantime use the old book and the information service. ________
9. Automobile repair costs are skyrocketing consequently car insurance costs are rising sharply. ________
10. Please place your order immediately or you will not be eligible for the discount. ________
11. Members of our management staff moreover are interested in hiring a consultant to train customer service personnel on the new equipment. ________
12. Nokia needed data concerning cellphone use therefore the company conducted a survey. ________
13. We were late for the meeting thus we did not hear the introductions. ________
14. We are currently using envelopes made from kraft paper and find that some of our deliveries are arriving in damaged condition. ________
15. ColorImage for example has registered two complaints and has required replacements because of damage. ________
16. The company gave each employee a holiday bonus therefore Christmas cheques were considerably larger this year. ________
17. Raises on the other hand have been limited. ________
18. The sessions for business managers start on Tuesday but the seminars for sales associates do not begin until Wednesday. ________

C. Write compound sentences using the conjunctions and conjunctive adverbs shown below.

1. *consequently* ______

______

2. *but* ______

______

3. *nevertheless* ______

______

4. *otherwise* ______

______

5. *and* ______

______

6. *moreover* ______

______

7. *or* ______

______

8. *then* ______

______

NAME ______________________________

LEVEL III

A. (**Self-check**) Select the more effective version of each of the following sentence pairs. Write its letter in the space provided.

1. (a) Either she sent the letter on Monday or Tuesday.
(b) She sent the letter on either Monday or Tuesday. ______

2. (a) Alex Kinsman is not available to conduct the meeting, and neither is Cindy Bragg.
(b) Neither Alex Kinsman nor Cindy Bragg is available to conduct the meeting. ______

3. (a) Our objectives are both to improve customer relations and increasing sales.
(b) Our objectives are both to improve customer relations and to increase sales. ______

4. (a) She neither called nor explained her absence.
(b) Neither did she call nor explain her absence. ______

5. (a) This work order must be completed by Friday, so you may have to work late Thursday.
(b) This work order must be completed by Friday; therefore, you may have to work late Thursday. ______

6. (a) The new network is not only faster but also more efficient.
(b) Not only is the new network faster, but it is also more efficient. ______

7. (a) Neither did the staff finish the proposals nor the contracts.
(b) The staff finished neither the proposals nor the contracts. ______

8. (a) He has no formal education, yet he appears to be quite well-read.
(b) He has no formal education; yet he appears to be quite well-read. ______

9. (a) Cheryl needed more time for her studies, so she asked for a part-time assignment.
(b) Because Cheryl needed more time for her studies, she asked for a part-time assignment. ______

10. (a) You must either email or fax the proposal quickly.
(b) Either you must email or fax the proposal quickly. ______

Check your answers.

B. Which of these sentence pairs is more effective?

1. (a) Either send the proposal to Tina Chang or to me.
(b) Send the proposal either to Tina Chang or to me. ______

2. (a) Our travel counsellor will both plan your trip and make your reservations.
(b) Our travel counsellor will both plan your trip and reservations will be made. ______

1.b 2.b 3.b 4.a 5.b 6.a 7.b 8.a 9.b 10.a

3. (a) We have checked every figure carefully; yet the totals do not balance.
(b) We have checked every figure carefully, yet the totals do not balance. __________

4. (a) Not only does a product carry an expressed warranty, but it also carries an implied warranty.
(b) A product carries not only an expressed warranty but also an implied warranty. __________

5. (a) We must receive either your payment or a reason for nonpayment.
(b) Either we must receive your payment, or you must give us a reason why you cannot pay. __________

C. Rewrite the following sentences to make them more effective.

1. Either shares can be purchased online, or they can be purchased from a broker.

____

____

2. Neither the staff was happy with the proposed cutbacks in class offerings, and nor were the students.

____

____

3. Not only do banks use computers to sort cheques, but they also use computers for disbursing cash automatically.

____

____

4. Users of cellphones are often guilty of boorish behaviour, so many restaurants and other public places have imposed cellphone bans.

____

____

5. Old computer hardware creates hazardous dump sites, so computer manufacturers are starting recycling programs.

____

____

D. **Optional Writing.** Your instructor may ask you to complete this exercise on a separate sheet.

Write four original sentences, one to illustrate each of the following: *a simple sentence, a compound sentence, a parenthetical adverb,* and *a pair of correlative conjunctions.* Label each sentence. Then write six compound sentences using different conjunctive adverbs.

Editor's Challenge

The following email message and memo contain intentional errors in spelling, proofreading, punctuation, and language principles covered thus far. Use standard proofreading marks to show necessary corrections.

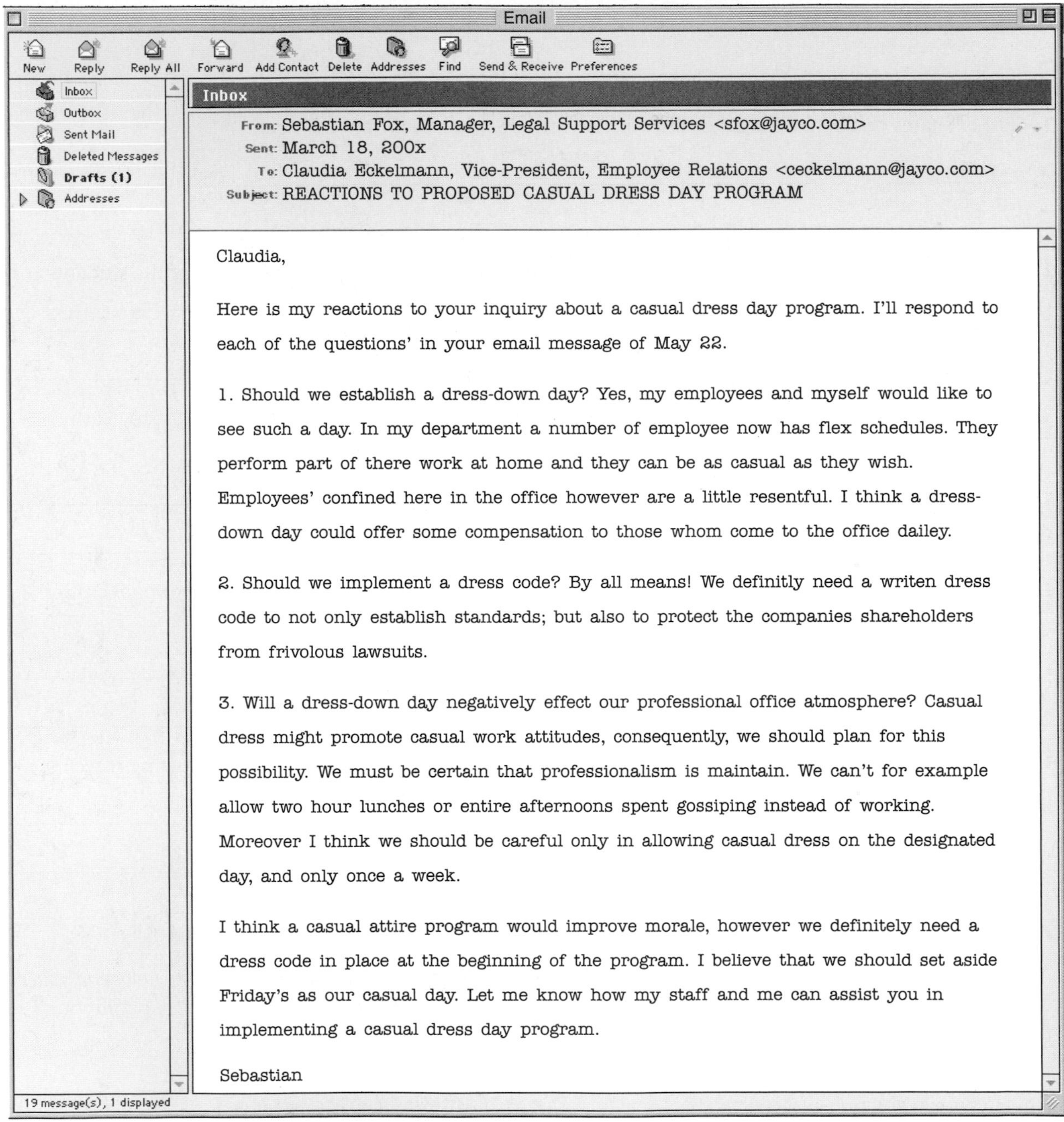

Email

New Reply Reply All Forward Add Contact Delete Addresses Find Send & Receive Preferences

Inbox
Outbox
Sent Mail
Deleted Messages
Drafts (1)
Addresses

Inbox

From: Sebastian Fox, Manager, Legal Support Services <sfox@jayco.com>
Sent: March 18, 200x
To: Claudia Eckelmann, Vice-President, Employee Relations <ceckelmann@jayco.com>
Subject: REACTIONS TO PROPOSED CASUAL DRESS DAY PROGRAM

Claudia,

Here is my reactions to your inquiry about a casual dress day program. I'll respond to each of the questions' in your email message of May 22.

1. Should we establish a dress-down day? Yes, my employees and myself would like to see such a day. In my department a number of employee now has flex schedules. They perform part of there work at home and they can be as casual as they wish. Employees' confined here in the office however are a little resentful. I think a dress-down day could offer some compensation to those whom come to the office dailey.

2. Should we implement a dress code? By all means! We definitly need a writen dress code to not only establish standards; but also to protect the companies shareholders from frivolous lawsuits.

3. Will a dress-down day negatively effect our professional office atmosphere? Casual dress might promote casual work attitudes, consequently, we should plan for this possibility. We must be certain that professionalism is maintain. We can't for example allow two hour lunches or entire afternoons spent gossiping instead of working. Moreover I think we should be careful only in allowing casual dress on the designated day, and only once a week.

I think a casual attire program would improve morale, however we definitely need a dress code in place at the beginning of the program. I believe that we should set aside Friday's as our casual day. Let me know how my staff and me can assist you in implementing a casual dress day program.

Sebastian

19 message(s), 1 displayed

CONSOLIDATED INDUSTRIES
Interoffice Memo

DATE: January 28, 200x
TO: All Employees
FROM: Brandon George, Manager
SUBJECT: Reducing Overnight Delivery Costs

Overnight delivery services are speedy but they costing us too much money. Here at Consolidated we have see our use of these services increasingly devour a major portion of our shipping budget. It seems that any one who wants to send something to a customer or a vendor automatically send it by FedEx. We have corporate rates with FedEx, however, we are still spending too much on overnight deliveries.

To avoid future restrictions imposed by the CEO I'm asking you to voluntarily reduce your use of these delivery services by 50 per cent in the next two month.

Rather than face a ban on all delivery services, let's work together to reduce our costs. Here is some suggestions:

1. Ask yourself weather the recipient will require the material immediately. If not, use a cheaper method.

2. Send messages either by fax or email. A long distance fax costs only about 35 cents and local messages and email messages cost nothing.

3. Use the FedEx or UPS account number off the recipient whenever possible.

4. Plan ahead so that you can use FedEx, or UPS ground service. These ground services usually take three to five days.

Some overnight shipments, of course, are critical. However to retain our budget for those essential shipments, we must reduce our overall use by one half before April 1. If you can think of other ways to reduce overnight shipments, please call me at Ext. 213. I appreciate you helping to solve this problem.

POSTTEST

Add commas or semicolons to the following sentences.

1. The cost of our raw materials is increasing consequently the price of our product must also increase.
2. We are convinced nevertheless that our products will continue to be competitive in today's market.
3. We are searching for other suppliers and we are also trying to reduce transportation costs.
4. Technology is changing rapidly therefore most employees need regular retraining.

Circle the letter of the sentence that is more effective.

5. (a) Neither can we ship the printer or the computer until April 1.

   (b) We can ship neither the printer nor the computer until April 1.

learning.web.ways

Goal: To learn about spyware.

1. With your web browser on the screen, go to this page at the Microsoft site: **<http://windowshelp.microsoft.com/Windows/en-US/internet.mspx>**.
2. Scroll down the page to the **Surfing Safety** section, and click on **Spyware: FAQ**.
3. Read each entry listed. What is spyware? What are the signs of spyware infection? How can you prevent spyware from getting to your computer? How can you get rid of it?
4. Now go to the CA Security Advisor Research Blog at **<http://community.ca.com/blogs/securityadvisor/archive/2007/06/06/who-can-you-trust-to-remove-spyware.aspx>**.
5. What advice on removing spyware can you find there? What warnings do you find especially useful?
6. End your session by clicking the **X** in the upper right corner of your browser. Turn in your answers to the questions.

---

1. increasing; consequently, 2. convinced, nevertheless, 3. suppliers, 4. rapidly; therefore, 5. b

CHAPTER

Conjunctions to Join Unequals

15

OBJECTIVES When you have completed the materials in this chapter, you will be able to do the following:

LEVEL I

- *Distinguish among dependent clauses, independent clauses, and phrases.*
- *Recognize subordinating conjunctions and relative pronouns functioning as conjunctions.*

LEVEL II

- *Punctuate introductory and terminal dependent clauses.*
- *Punctuate parenthetical, essential, and non-essential dependent clauses.*

LEVEL III

- *Recognize simple, compound, complex, and compound–complex sentences.*
- *Convert simple sentences into a variety of more complex patterns.*

PRETEST

Insert appropriate commas in the following sentences. Mark *C* if correct.

1. When you receive an email attachment be sure to check it for a virus.
2. If possible you should check every one of your files for viruses.
3. The man who wrote that play must be a genius.
4. Sherilyn said that Kala Jones who works in our Marketing Department will be leaving next month.
5. Although several applicants passed the test no one has been hired yet.

1. attachment, 2. possible, 3. C 4. Jones, Department, 5. test,

In Chapter 14 we studied conjunctions that joined equal sentence elements such as words, phrases, and clauses. These equal sentence parts were joined by coordinating conjunctions (such as *and, or, but*), conjunctive adverbs (such as *therefore, however, consequently*), and correlative conjunctions (such as *either ... or*). Now let's look at a group of conjunctions that join unequal sentence parts.

LEVEL I

▶ Subordinating Conjunctions

To join unequal sentence elements such as independent clauses and dependent clauses, we use subordinating conjunctions. A list of the most common subordinating conjunctions follows.

after	because	since	until
although	before	so that	when
as	if	that	where
as if	in order that	though	whether
as though	provided (that)	unless	while

Spot the Blooper

From a sales brochure for New Life Health Center: "We have every day low prices on hundreds of products. Here's a few to peak your interest!" (Can you spot three errors?)

You should become familiar with this list of conjunctions, but do not feel that you need to memorize all of them. Generally, you can recognize a subordinating conjunction by the way it limits or subordinates the clause it introduces. In the clause *because he always paid with cash,* the subordinating conjunction *because* limits the meaning of the clause it introduces. The clause beginning with *because* is incomplete and could not stand alone as a sentence.

▶ Independent and Dependent Clauses

Main clauses that can stand alone are said to be *independent.* They have subjects and verbs and make sense by themselves.

> Business writing should be concise. (One main clause.)
> Business writing should be concise, and it should be clear as well. (Two main clauses.)
> Shauna Cox writes many email messages, but Kathleen Young writes more letters. (Two main clauses.)

Spot the Blooper

Bank of Montreal advertising slogan: "Get the card that thinks like you."

Clauses that cannot stand alone are said to be *dependent.* They have subjects and verbs, but they depend upon other clauses for the completion of their meaning. Dependent clauses are often introduced by subordinating conjunctions and may either precede or follow independent clauses.

> When Ms. Cox wants a quick reply, she sends an email message. (Dependent clause precedes the main clause.)
> Since Ms. Young writes many letters, she keeps her address file current. (Dependent clause precedes the main clause.)
> Business letters are important because they represent the company. (Dependent clause, *because they represent the company*, comes after the main clause.)

Hotlink

You can get more on dependent clauses at **<http://www.uottawa.ca/academic/arts/writcent/hypergrammar/claustyp.htm/#dependent%20clauses>**.

▶ Relative Clauses

The relative pronouns *who, whom, whose, which,* and *that* actually function as conjunctions when they introduce dependent clauses. *Who* is used to refer to persons. It may introduce essential or non-essential clauses. *That* refers to animals or things and should be used to introduce essential clauses. *Which* refers to animals or things and should introduce non-essential clauses.

The tricky part is deciding whether a clause is essential or non-essential. An essential clause is needed to identify the noun to which it refers. Therefore, no commas should separate this clause from its antecedent. Non-essential clauses contain information that the reader does not need to know; the main clause is understandable without this extra information. In some cases only the writer knows whether a clause is intended to be essential or non-essential. If a clause is non-essential, it should be set off from the rest of the sentence by commas. You'll learn more about punctuating these sentences in Level II.

Study Tip

Dependent clauses should never be written or punctuated as if they were complete sentences.

> Anyone *who* (not *that*) has a computer can create a website. (The relative pronoun *who* refers to a person, and it introduces an essential clause.)
>
> A company *that* (not *who* or *which*) values its employees is likely to succeed. (The relative pronoun *that* introduces an essential clause.)
>
> Software giant Microsoft, *which* is headquartered in Redmond, has many other offices in the state of Washington. (The relative pronoun *which* introduces a non-essential clause and is set off by commas.)
>
> Microsoft is the company *that* is headquartered in Redmond. (The relative pronoun *that* introduces an essential clause and requires no commas.)
>
> Lisa Meyers, *who has excellent recommendations*, is applying for a position in our department. (The relative pronoun *who* introduces a non-essential clause and is set off by commas.)

Hotlink

Here's another look at relative pronouns and clauses from Langara College in B.C.: **<http://www.langara.bc.ca/writingcentre/handouts/sentences.html#7>**.

Complete the reinforcement exercises for Level I on pp. 286–288.

LEVEL II

▶ Punctuation of Sentences With Dependent Clauses

Business writers are especially concerned with clarity and accuracy. A misplaced or omitted punctuation mark can confuse a reader by altering the meaning of a sentence. The following guidelines for using commas help ensure clarity and consistency in writing. Some professional writers, however, take liberties with accepted conventions of punctuation, particularly in regard to comma usage. These experienced writers may omit a comma when they feel that such an omission will not affect the reader's understanding of a sentence. Beginning writers, though, are well advised to first develop skill in punctuating sentences by following traditional guidelines.

Introductory Dependent Clauses

Use a comma after a dependent (subordinate) clause that precedes an independent clause.

> *Before* they left the office, they finished the proposal.
> *Until* he returns, we cannot continue.
> *When* you are ready to start, let me know.

Spot the Blooper

From classified ads in local newspapers: "LAWNMORE SHOP" and a house for sale with "walking closets."

Use a comma after an introductory dependent clause even though the subject and verb may not be stated.

> *As* [it is] expected, the shipment is overdue.
> *If* [it is] possible, send a replacement immediately.
> *When* [they are] printed, your brochures will be distributed.

Terminal Dependent Clauses

Generally, a dependent clause introduced by a subordinating conjunction does not require a comma when the dependent clause falls at the end of a sentence.

> They finished the proposal *before* they left the office.
> We cannot continue *until* he returns.
> Let me know *when* you are ready to start.

If, however, the dependent clause at the end of a sentence interrupts the flow of the sentence and contains additional information that is not essential, a comma should be used.

> I know the cancelled cheque was returned, *although* I cannot find it now.
> We will ship the goods within the week, *if* that is satisfactory for you.

Hotlink

Get another look at essential and non-essential relative clauses at this University of Victoria page: **<http://web2.uvcs.uvic.ca/elc/studyzone/410/grammar/adj.htm>**. Note also the link to an exercise at the bottom of the page.

Parenthetical Clauses

Within a sentence, dependent clauses that interrupt the flow of the sentence and are unnecessary for the grammatical completeness of the sentence are set off by commas.

> The motion, *unless* you want further discussion, will be tabled until our next meeting.
> At our next meeting, *provided* we have a quorum, the motion will be reconsidered.

Relative Clauses

You learned earlier that dependent clauses introduced by relative pronouns such as *who, that,* and *which* may be essential (restrictive) or non-essential (non-restrictive).

An *essential clause* is needed to identify the noun to which it refers; therefore, no commas should separate this clause from its antecedent.

> Any student *who missed the test* must make it up. (Dependent clause needed to identify which students must make up the test.)
> Parking permits *that were issued in the fall* must be validated for the spring. (Dependent clause needed to identify which parking permits must be validated.)

Study Tip

Since relative clauses introduced by *that* are always essential, they require no commas.

A *non-essential clause* supplies additional information that is not needed to identify its antecedent; therefore, commas are used to separate the non-essential information from the rest of the sentence. Notice that two commas are used to set off internal non-essential dependent clauses.

> Amy Kertesz, *who missed the exam,* must make it up. (Dependent clause not needed; the antecedent of the clause, Amy Kertesz, is clearly identified.)
> Lot C parking permits, *which were issued in the fall,* must be validated for the spring. (Dependent clause not needed; the antecedent of the clause, Lot C parking permits, is clearly identified.)

Punctuation Review

The following three common sentence patterns are very important for you to study and understand. Notice particularly how they are punctuated.

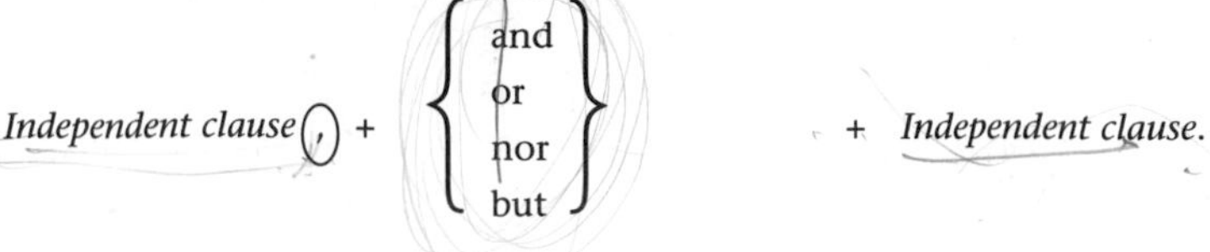

(Comma used when a coordinating conjunction joins independent clauses.)

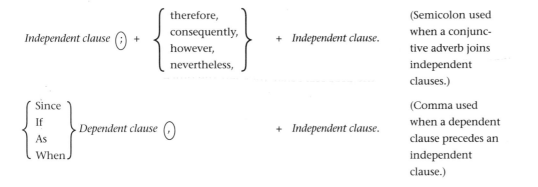

Independent clause (;) + {therefore, / consequently, / however, / nevertheless,} + *Independent clause.* (Semicolon used when a conjunctive adverb joins independent clauses.)

{Since / If / As / When} *Dependent clause* (,) + *Independent clause.* (Comma used when a dependent clause precedes an independent clause.)

Complete the reinforcement exercises for Level II on pp. 289–290.

Hotlink

More help with identifying and punctuating relative clauses is available from this Ryerson University handout, which you can download at **<http://www.ryerson.ca/studentservices/learningsuccess/pdf/unit5.pdf>**.

▶ Sentence Variety

To make their messages more interesting, good writers strive for variety in sentence structure. Notice the monotony and choppiness of a paragraph made up entirely of simple sentences:

> The United States purchased Alaska from Russia in 1867. The exact boundary of the "panhandle" strip of coastline seemed fairly unimportant. The 1898 Gold Rush made this boundary significant. Both Canadians and Americans wanted to profit from the prospectors and their gold. The boundary dispute became extremely serious. A court of six judges was chosen. It decided 4 to 2 against Canada's version of the boundary. The decision outraged Canadians. One good consequence of this controversy was the International Joint Commission. It was set up in 1909 to settle boundary disputes.

Compare the following version of this paragraph, which uses dependent clauses and other structures to achieve greater sentence variety:

> When the United States purchased Alaska from Russia in 1867, the exact boundary of the "panhandle" strip of coastline seemed fairly unimportant. However, the 1898 Gold Rush made this boundary significant since both Canadians and Americans wanted to profit from the prospectors and their gold. After the boundary dispute had become extremely serious, a court of six judges was chosen and decided 4 to 2 against Canada's version of the boundary. Although the decision outraged Canadians, one good outcome of this controversy was the International Joint Committee, which was set up in 1909 to settle boundary disputes.

Spot the Blooper

From *The Ft. Lauderdale Sun Sentinel:* "Architect Barry Sugerman of North Miami designed this pergola to divert attention from the garage, which is seen walking up to the house from the motorcourt."

Hotlink

The handout prepared by the Wilfrid Laurier Writing Centre, **<http://www.wlu.ca/forms/919/Subordination.pdf>**, gives extensive coverage to subordination.

Hotlink

Cambrian College offers additional help with sentence fragments and the use of subordinating conjunctions to correct them. Go to **<http://homepages.cambrianc.on.ca/tutorial/thetutorialcentre/writing/identifying_sentence_fragments.htm>**, and do the exercises at the bottom of the page.

Recognizing the kinds of sentence structures available to writers and speakers is an important step in achieving effective expression. Let's review the three kinds of sentence structures that you have been studying and include a fourth category as well.

Kind of Sentence	**Minimum Requirement**	**Example**
Simple	One independent clause	The United States purchased Alaska from Russia in 1867.
Compound	Two independent clauses	The exact boundary of the "panhandle" strip of coastline seemed fairly unimportant, but the 1898 Gold Rush made this boundary significant.
Complex	One independent clause and one dependent clause	After the boundary dispute had become extremely serious, a court of six judges was chosen.
Compound–complex	Two independent clauses and one dependent clause	When the United States purchased Alaska from Russia in 1867, the exact boundary of the "panhandle" strip of coastline seemed fairly unimportant; however, the 1898 Gold Rush made this boundary significant.

Developing the ability to use a variety of sentence structures to facilitate effective communication takes practice. Start sharpening your skills with the reinforcement exercises for Level III on pp. 291–293.

HOTLINE QUERIES

Question: Can the word *that* be omitted from sentences? For example, *She said [that] she would come.*

Answer: The relative pronoun *that* is frequently omitted in conversation and casual writing. For absolute clarity, however, skilled writers include it.

Question: Is there some rule about putting periods in organization names that are abbreviated? For example, does *IBM* have periods?

Answer: When the names of well-known business, educational, governmental, labour, and other organizations or agencies are abbreviated, periods are normally not used to separate the letters. Thus no periods would appear in IBM, YWCA, CMA, UAW, UN. The names of radio and television stations and networks are also written without periods: CNN, CFRB, CBC, PBS. Geographical abbreviations and the two-letter state and province abbreviations used in computerized address systems require no periods: US, UAE, UK, NF, ON, SK, CA, NY.

Question: As a command, which is correct: *lay down* or *lie down*?

Answer: Commands are given in the present tense. You would never tell someone to *closed the door* because commands are not given in the past tense. To say *lay down* (which is the past tense form of *lie*) is the same as saying *closed the door.* Therefore, use the present tense: *lie down.*

Question: In this sentence which word should I use? *Your order will be sent to you in the (later* or *latter) part of the week.*

Answer: Use *latter.* The word *latter* designates the second of two persons or things. In addition, *latter* can be used to mean "further advanced in time or sequence," or *latter* can be used to contrast with *former.* In your sentence, the *latter* part of the week contrasts with the *former* part of the week.

Question: I have a lot of trouble with verbs in sentences like this: *She was one of approximately 20,000 Canadian women who (was* or *were) diagnosed with breast cancer last year.*

Answer: You're not alone. Make your verb agree with its antecedent (*women*). One easy way to work with sentences like this is to concentrate on the clause that contains the verb: *Of those Canadian women who were diagnosed with breast cancer last year, she was one.*

Question: In a *New York Times* article about singer Michael Jackson and his fight with Sony Music Group, I saw this sentence: *Owning those rights are valuable because once Mr. Jackson owns them outright, he does not have to split royalty payments with Sony as he does now.* It seems to me the phrase *owning those rights* is singular and the verb should be *is.* Am I right?

Answer: Absolutely! When they act as sentence subjects, phrases and clauses are singular. You deserve a good grammar award!

NAME ______________________________

CHAPTER 15 Reinforcement Exercises

LEVEL I

A. (**Self-check**) Indicate whether the following word groups are phrases (*P*), independent clauses (*I*), or dependent clauses (*D*). (Remember that phrases do not have both subjects and verbs.)

Example: in the spring of the previous year ____P____

1. when you account for cultural differences ________
2. Microsoft and Google approved of the new Internet regulations ________
3. at the crack of dawn to finish studying ________
4. as he stated earlier in the lecture ________
5. she answered immediately ________
6. recently they acquired an option to purchase the property ________
7. before anyone had an opportunity to examine it carefully ________
8. in the middle of the five-year fiscal period from 2005 to 2010 ________
9. unless the human resources department rejects his application ________
10. our new pricing schedule takes effect January 1 ________

Check your answers.

B. Indicate whether the following word groups are phrases (*P*), independent clauses (*I*), or dependent clauses (*D*). For the clauses underline the subjects once and the verbs twice, and circle any subordinating conjunctions.

Example: (until) we are able to assess the damage ____D____

1. as you prepare for a behavioural employment interview ________
2. in order that employees may attend ________
3. many businesses sell services rather than products ________
4. on the first page of the website ________
5. after he complimented Maureen Ross's work ________
6. she laid the contract on the desk ________
7. might have been considered ________
8. since Charles began working as a marketing representative ________

1. D 2. I 3. P 4. D 5. I 6. I 7. D 8. P 9. D 10. I

9. Division Manager Kelsey analyzed the data ____________

10. during the final briefing last week ____________

C. After each sentence write the correct word in the space provided. Use the relative pronoun *which* only to introduce non-essential clauses (clauses that require commas).

1. We're shopping for software (who, which, that) we can use without customizing. ____________
2. Is this the horse (who, which, that) broke its leg? ____________
3. Revenue Canada, (who, which, that) processes our income tax returns, is choked with paperwork at the end of April. ____________
4. The Bank of Montreal is known as a company (who, which, that) emphasizes customer service. ____________
5. Are you the one (who, which, that) handles employee grievances? ____________
6. Any bank (who, that, which) adds an outside ATM can reduce the number of its inside tellers. ____________
7. Our team, (who, that, which) has authority to set its own work schedules, tries to rotate the hardest jobs. ____________
8. The ruby-throated hummingbird, (who, which, that) measures less than ten centimetres in length, migrates great distances to wintering grounds in the southern U.S. and Mexico. ____________
9. The city council needs to come up with a plan (who, which, that) will satisfy all residents. ____________
10. Employers are looking for workers (who, that, which) have good vocabularies, grammar, and manners. ____________

D. Sort this group of words into three lists, and write them below: *although, and, because, but, consequently, however, if, moreover, nor, or, since, thus.*

Coordinating Conjunctions	Conjunctive Adverbs	Subordinating Conjunctions
____________	____________	____________
____________	____________	____________
____________	____________	____________
____________	____________	____________

E. Use your imagination to write complete sentences according to the following directions. Remember that clauses must contain subjects and verbs.

1. A sentence using *and* to connect two independent clauses. ____________

____

____

2. A sentence using *but* to connect two independent clauses. ____________________

____

____

3. A sentence using *because* to introduce a dependent clause. ____________________

____

____

4. A sentence using *although* to introduce a dependent clause. ____________________

____

____

5. A sentence using *after* to introduce a dependent clause. ____________________

____

____

6. A sentence using *so that* to introduce a dependent clause. ____________________

____

____

7. A sentence using *until* to introduce a dependent clause. ____________________

____

____

8. A sentence using *and* to join two phrases. ____________________

____

____

NAME ______________________________

LEVEL II

A. (**Self-check**) Where appropriate, insert commas in the following sentences. In the space provided after each sentence, indicate the number of commas you have added to that sentence. Do not add any commas that you cannot justify.

Example: After we hiked to the summit, we pitched our tent. ____1____

1. Tony Molino who recently took out a life insurance policy wanted more security for his family. ________
2. As predicted the Bank of Canada raised interest rates. ________
3. The CEO of Research in Motion which makes the BlackBerry email devices said that he was not concerned about the competition. ________
4. A magazine that is featuring the 100 best places to work is now on the newsstands. ________
5. Annette Ridgeway who was the top salesperson in the country received a car as a bonus. ________
6. Any salesperson who sells more than the weekly quota will receive a bonus. ________
7. If possible send the report that shows this year's sales figures compared with last year's. ________
8. The latest production model unless it is altered drastically looks as if it will be a winner. ________
9. Please consider our budget deficit before you make a decision. ________
10. A profit-sharing plan for employees is now available although I believe the announcement will not be made until next week. ________

Check your answers.

B. Where appropriate, insert commas in the following sentences. In the space provided after each sentence, indicate the number of commas that you added. Be prepared to discuss the reasons for the commas you use.

1. Joseph Farrell who has just accepted a transfer to our Calgary office has been with us for almost ten years. ________
2. The man who accepted the transfer to our Calgary office has been with us for almost ten years. ________
3. Since Camille graduated from college she has been busy paying off thousands of dollars in student loans. ________
4. We have received a directive to hold all shipments although I do not know why. ________

1. (2) Molino, policy, 2. (1) predicted, 3. (2) Motion, devices, 4. (0) 5. (2) Ridgeway, country, 6. (0) 7. (1) possible, 8. (2) model, drastically, 9. (0) 10. (1) available.

5. I will edit and process the Microsoft order tomorrow morning if that meets with your approval. ____________________

6. When completed the newly created website will enable customers to track shipments. ____________________

7. All the information on my personal résumé which I wrote and formatted myself fills just one page. ____________________

8. Although you said my order was shipped ten days ago I have not yet received it. ____________________

9. The warranty that you refer to in your recent letter covers only merchandise brought to our shop for repair. ____________________

10. Ray Rampersad who works in the Traffic Department received last month's merit award. ____________________

11. A secretary who joined our staff only two months ago received this month's merit award. ____________________

12. Zone Improvement Program codes which are better known as zip codes were designed in the United States to expedite the sorting and delivery of mail. ____________________

13. I would like to give your suggestion more thought when I am not quite so preoccupied. ____________________

14. Parliament will surely when it convenes in its regular session discuss defence spending. ____________________

15. Before you make a decision consider our strained financial condition. ____________________

16. No additional tuition increases can be made if I understand the legislation correctly. ____________________

17. In order that we may complete the mailing quickly the address list is being printed from our database. ____________________

18. In the coming fiscal year provided that enough funds are available we hope to expand our employee fitness program. ____________________

19. Drivers who don't search online may have a hard time finding the best car insurance rate. ____________________

20. Individuals who are interested in applying for the supervisory position at Devon Canada must have at least five years of relevant experience. ____________________

NAME ______________________________

LEVEL III

A. (**Self-check**) Indicate the structure of the following sentences by writing the appropriate letter in the spaces provided:

a = Simple sentence b = Compound sentence
c = Complex sentence d = Compound–complex sentence

Example: Because the systems were not connected and could not share information with each other, data had to be entered many times. ____c____

1. Our project manager suggested a new marketing campaign. __________
2. Since it passed the controversial ordinance, the city council has been besieged by calls. __________
3. A decision had to be made soon; therefore, a managers' meeting was scheduled for Monday. __________
4. We have no supplies, and other departments face a similar problem. __________
5. Allen was offered a sales position in Fredericton; therefore, he eagerly made plans to travel to New Brunswick, where he looked forward to beginning his sales career. __________
6. We will be able to contact you only if you are selected for an interview. __________
7. The cost of the product increased, but sales continued to climb. __________
8. Although the letter was concise, its message was clear; moreover, it promoted goodwill. __________
9. Titles of essays, songs, and short stories are enclosed in quotation marks. __________
10. Because pictures are worth a thousand words, your report should include photos or graphics. __________

Check your answers.

1. a 2. c 3. b 4. b 5. d 6. c 7. b 8. d 9. a 10. c

B. Rewrite the following groups of simple sentences into *one* sentence for each group. Add coordinating conjunctions, conjunctive adverbs, and subordinating conjunctions as needed to create more effective complex, compound, and compound–complex sentences.

Example: Canadian Tire needed an executive assistant. It advertised in local newspapers. It finally hired a recent graduate. The graduate had excellent skills.

After advertising for an executive assistant in local newspapers, Canadian Tire finally hired a recent graduate who had excellent skills.

1. Joan Wallace is a registered nurse. Joan has just accepted a job at Kingston General Hospital. She will have to move to Kingston, Ontario.

2. Each intern is assigned to a senior staff member. The staff member acts as a mentor. The staff member assists the intern with eventual job placement.

3. The makers of Rolls-Royce cars plan to open showrooms in Shanghai and Hong Kong. The world's largest market for Rolls-Royce is China.

4. Jerry Eichorn recently graduated with a marketing diploma. He is looking for a job in Saskatchewan. Jerry grew up in Saskatchewan.

5. Nancy Burnett is a single parent. She has merchandising experience. Nancy started a mall-based chain of stores. These stores sell fashionable, durable children's clothing.

6. Skilled writers save time for themselves. They also save time for their readers. They organize their ideas into logical patterns. They organize their ideas before sitting down at their computers.

____

____

____

7. Cows will respond to beeps. Some Japanese ranchers learned of this phenomenon and equipped their cattle with pagers. Now they herd cattle with beepers. These ranchers need fewer workers as a result.

____

____

____

C. Optional Writing. Your instructor may ask you to complete this exercise of ten sentences on a separate sheet.

Write four original sentences that illustrate the following: a simple sentence, a compound sentence, a complex sentence, and a compound–complex sentence. Write four original sentences that begin with the following subordinating conjunctions: *if, when, as,* and *since.* In addition, write sentences in which *who* is used to introduce an essential clause and again to introduce a non-essential clause. Label each sentence.

Editor's Challenge

The following memo and email message contain intentional errors in spelling, proofreading, punctuation, and language principles covered thus far. Use standard proofreading marks to show all necessary corrections.

Dee Kirkland Modelling and Dance Studios

MEMORANDUM

DATE: February 21, 200x

TO: Karen Archer, Stacy Janisse, Eduardo Solano, Robin Haynes, Mayer Rubin, Tom Winters

FROM: Dee Kirkland

SUBJECT: MARCH 1 FASHION SHOW AT WESTLAND PLAZA HOTEL

Thanks to you acceptional students for agreeing to participate in this years fashion show at the Westland Plaza Hotel.

Show time is 8:15 p.m., if possible you should be there at 6:30 to prepare. Rehearsals is scheduled for Tuesday, February 25, and Thursday, February 27, from 5 to 6:15 p.m. Its important for you to be promp!

Participants in the fashion show will not be payed but we have a bonus for you. Mr. Lon McHenry who is this years sponsor is one of those people who likes to encourage young models, therefore he will allow you to by any of the item in the show at 20 per cent below his cost.

The cloths are all from CAL SPORT. Which specializes in informal fashions. Since shoes are not supplied everyone should bring there own casual shoes or running shoes.

Of all the students in the school, you were choosen to participate in the show because you have exhibit excellent potential and professionalism. I want you to treat this show like it was any professional paid job. This fashion show is bigger then any show in the area, please consider it a extension of your training. If you succeed here you can count on farther success as you grow in your career.

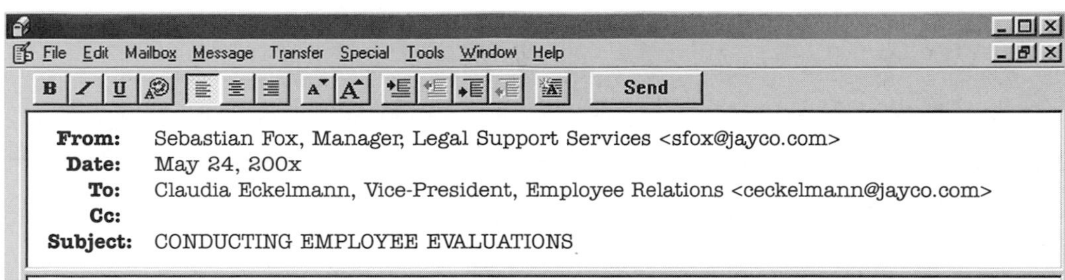

From: Sebastian Fox, Manager, Legal Support Services <sfox@jayco.com>
Date: May 24, 200x
To: Claudia Eckelmann, Vice-President, Employee Relations <ceckelmann@jayco.com>
Cc:
Subject: CONDUCTING EMPLOYEE EVALUATIONS

Claudia,

I recently learn that one of our employee's has filed a law suit against the company because of comments a supervisor made during a performance evaluation. This is a unfortunate event that could of been prevented. Here are a list of tips that you should share with all manager's.

1. Before you can accurately evaluate an employees performance you need to establish a system to measure that performance. Therefore; you need to develop performance standards and goals for each employee. Remember to remain sensitive of the employees needs. Plan on sharing these standards and goals in writeing with the employee.

2. Monitor the preformance of each employee throughout the year. Keep a log for each worker and note memorable incidents or projects involving that worker. Although many managers are understandably adverse to placing negative comments in files, such comments must be included as part of the evaluation process. Any employee, who does something exceptional, should be given immediate feed back. If you give this feedback orally make a written note of the conversation for the employees personnell file.

3. At least once a year, formally evaluate the worker by writing a performance appraisal and by meeting with the worker. At the meeting let your employee know what you think they did good, and which areas the employee maybe able to improve. Be sure and discuss the standards and goals you set earlier. Listen carefully to your employee's comments and take good notes.

Giving evaluations can be difficult, however, careful planning and preparation is necessary to make the process go smooth. Be specific, give deadlines, be honest, and be realistic. Following these steps is an excellent way to help the company avoid legal problems. Please email me with any questions.

Sebastian

POSTTEST

Insert appropriate commas in the following sentences. Mark *C* if the sentence is correct.

1. If your organization requires real-time communication try instant messaging. ____________
2. When necessary we make rush shipments of products that we have in our immediate inventory. ____________
3. The software demonstration by Jeremy Jenkins who represents DataTech Products will be Friday. ____________
4. Any manager or employee who is unable to attend the Friday demonstration should call me. ____________
5. Since many employees are interested in spreadsheet programs they will be discussed first. ____________

learning.web.ways

Goal: To learn about privacy policies.

1. With your web browser on the screen, go to the PC World article on privacy policies, available at **<http://www.pcworld.com/article/id,16274-page,1/article.html>**.
2. Read the article, and take note of what elements a privacy policy should include.
3. Inspect the privacy policies at three sites, such as Canada's flagship retailer the Hudson's Bay Company **<http://www.hbc.com/hbc/>**, leading financial institution Toronto Dominion Bank **<http://www.td.com/>**, and software giant Corel Corporation **<http://www.corel.com>**. Look carefully to find a reference to each site's privacy policy. Which company seems to have the most effective policy? Print two pages of the policy you like best.
4. End your session, and submit your printout along with your answers.

---

1. communication, 2. necessary, 3. Jenkins, Products, 4. C 5. programs,

NAME ________________

UNIT 4 REVIEW Chapters 12–15 (Self-Check)

Begin your review by rereading Chapters 12 through 15. Then test your comprehension of those chapters by completing the exercises that follow. Compare your responses with those provided at the end of the book.

LEVEL I

In the blank provided, write the letter of the word or phrase that correctly completes each of the following sentences.

1. I've never read a (a) worse, (b) worst executive summary. ________

2. In comparing the three shipping companies, we decided that DHL is (a) fastest, (b) faster. ________

3. If you need (a) a, (b) an example of her work, take a look at her e-portfolio. ________

4. The board members (a) would have, (b) would of been impressed with your presentation. ________

5. The service contract is (a) to, (b) too expensive. ________

6. We are fortunate to have exceptional employees like Thomas and (a) him, (b) he. ________

7. We're seeking a bright young person (a) which, (b) whom we can train. ________

8. The group of words *if you will write us* is a(n) (a) phrase, (b) independent clause, (c) dependent clause. ________

Insert commas where necessary. In the space provided, indicate the member of commas you added, if any.

9. Fran came to Moose Jaw in May but moved to Regina in July. ________

10. Jeffrey might be assigned to work in our legal office or he might be assigned to our administrative headquarters. ________

11. Stop at the crosswalk and look both ways. ________

12. WestJet scheduled new flights on its Vancouver–Edmonton route and also lowered Calgary–Vancouver fares. ________

13. Canadian women have made significant progress climbing the corporate ladder but a lot of work remains to be done. ________

LEVEL II

Write the letter of the word or phrase that correctly completes each sentence.

14. Let's discuss these ideas (a) further, (b) farther over lunch. ______

15. The search was conducted (a) house to house, (b) house-to-house. ______

16. If you have (a) less, (b) fewer than ten items, you may use the express checkout. ______

17. Mr. Jefferson agreed that the contract was written (a) satisfactorily, (b) satisfactory. ______

18. What paper is left must be divided (a) among, (b) between the three offices. ______

19. You must turn your paperwork (a) in to, (b) into me by Monday. ______

In the following sentences, selected words have been underscored. Using the letters below, indicate what punctuation should precede and what should follow the underscored words.

(a) , ______ (c) ______ , (e) no punctuation

(b) , ______ , (d) ; ______ ,

20. Miss Daily's payroll service was a huge success consequently she is opening a second office. ______

21. In the meantime we learned that many others felt the same way. ______

22. The employee who asked for a transfer will be moving to Sudbury. ______

23. Send all your cheques to Jerry Daniels who is in charge of contributions. ______

24. As reported our division shows declining sales and dwindling profits. ______

25. Mr. Hill who was named as a defendant resigned as vice-president. ______

26. Some foreign airlines threatened to divert traffic away from Canadian airports if fees were not lowered. ______

27. Ms. Ramden's statement is what annoyed a number of those who attended the lunch. ______

LEVEL III

Write the letter of the word or phrase that correctly completes each sentence.

28. Vancouver is larger than (a) any other city, (b) any city on the West Coast. ______

29. Examine carefully the (a) 50 first, (b) first 50 pages of the booklet. ______

30. Despite her meagre income, Sally remained independent (a) of, (b) from her parents. ______

31. The approved contract is not very different (a) than, (b) from the first version. ______

32. The union asked that the salary increase be retroactive (a) to, (b) from the first of the year. ______

In the following sentences, selected words have been underscored. Using the letters below, indicate what punctuation should precede and follow the underscored words.

(a) , ______________ (c) ______________ , (e) no punctuation

(b) , ______________ , (d) ; ______________ ,

33. When you called our office last week I was unable to locate the figures you requested. ______________

34. Sales increased immediately after Pat Cramer joined our Edmonton office. ______________

35. Sales in your district have risen markedly moreover service requests are decreasing. ______________

Hotline Review

Select the word or phrase that correctly completes the statement, and write its letter in the corresponding blank.

36. Of the two options the (a) later, (b) latter seems preferable. ______________

37. The enclosed text (a) maybe, (b) may be appropriate for your proposed course. ______________

38. She has (a) all ready, (b) already handled the customer inquiry. ______________

39. Gerald missed the luncheon (a) due to, (b) because of a prior appointment. ______________

40. (a) I hope that, (b) Hopefully, you now have a better understanding of English grammar. ______________

Email Messages and Memos

Email messages and memos are increasingly important forms of internal communication for most companies today. Organizations are downsizing, flattening chains of command, forming work teams, and empowering rank-and-file employees. Given more power in making decisions, employees find that they need more information. They must collect, exchange, and evaluate information about the products and services they offer. Management also needs input from employees to respond rapidly to local and global market actions. This growing demand for information results in an increasing use of memos and especially email. That's why anyone entering the business world today should know how to write good email messages and memos.

Characteristics of Email Messages and Memos

Email messages and memos have a number of characteristics in common:

- They begin with *To, From, Date,* and *Subject.*
- They generally cover just one topic.
- They are informal.
- They are concise.

Email messages and memos use efficient standard formats, such as you see in Figure 15.1 (page 301). So that they can be acted on separately, email messages and memos should discuss only one topic. Let's say you send your supervisor an email message requesting a copier repair. You also tack on a comment about an article you want to appear in the company newsletter. The supervisor may act on one item and overlook the other. He might also want to forward your request for a copier repair directly to the operations manager, but he has to edit or rekey the message because of the second topic. Thus email messages and memos are most helpful when they cover just one subject.

Because they replace conversation, these messages tend to be informal. They may include first-person pronouns, such as *I* and *me,* as well as occasional contractions, such as *can't* or *haven't.* The tone, however, should not become familiar or unbusinesslike. Moreover, email messages and memos should not be wordy. Concise messages save time and often are more easily understood than longer documents.

Writing Plan

For most informational and procedural messages, follow a direct writing plan that reveals the most important information first. Here are specific tips for writing the subject line, first sentence, body, and closing of email messages and memos.

Subject Line. Summarize the message in the subject line. Although brief, a subject line must make sense and should capture the reader's interest. Instead of *Meeting,* for example, try *Meeting to Discuss Hiring Two New Employees. A* subject line is like a newspaper headline. It should snag attention, create a clear picture, and present an accurate summary. It should not be a complete sentence and should rarely occupy more than one line.

First Sentence. Although an explanation may occasionally precede the main idea, the first sentence usually tells the primary idea of the message. For example, an appropriate first sentence in a memo announcing a new vacation procedure follows:

Figure 15.1
Comparing Email Messages and Memos

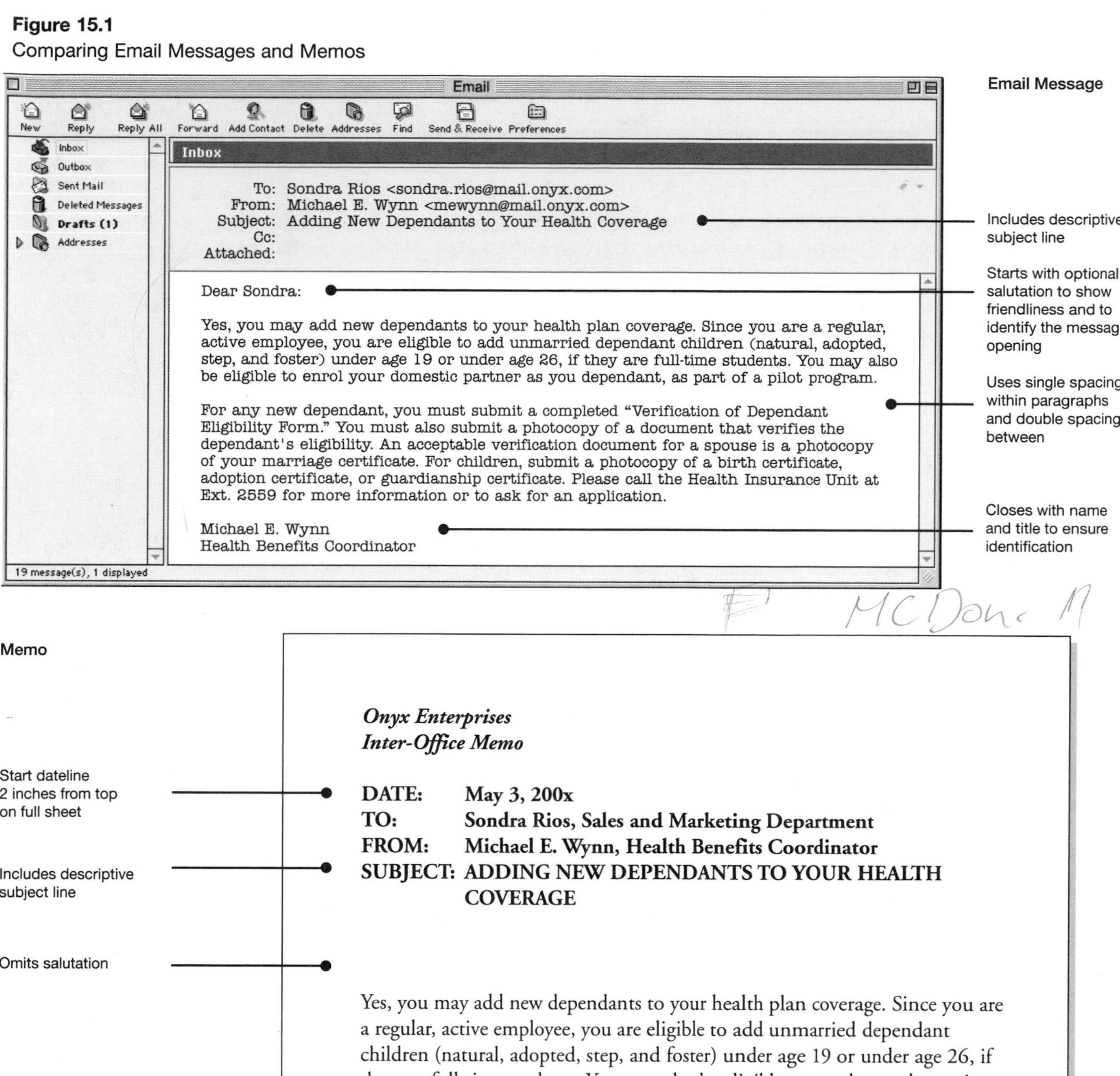

Email Message

Email

New | Reply | Reply All | Forward | Add Contact | Delete | Addresses | Find | Send & Receive | Preferences

Inbox
Outbox
Sent Mail
Deleted Messages
Drafts (1)
Addresses

Inbox

To: Sondra Rios <sondra.rios@mail.onyx.com>
From: Michael E. Wynn <mewynn@mail.onyx.com>
Subject: Adding New Dependants to Your Health Coverage
Cc:
Attached:

Dear Sondra:

Yes, you may add new dependants to your health plan coverage. Since you are a regular, active employee, you are eligible to add unmarried dependant children (natural, adopted, step, and foster) under age 19 or under age 26, if they are full-time students. You may also be eligible to enrol your domestic partner as you dependant, as part of a pilot program.

For any new dependant, you must submit a completed "Verification of Dependant Eligibility Form." You must also submit a photocopy of a document that verifies the dependant's eligibility. An acceptable verification document for a spouse is a photocopy of your marriage certificate. For children, submit a photocopy of a birth certificate, adoption certificate, or guardianship certificate. Please call the Health Insurance Unit at Ext. 2559 for more information or to ask for an application.

Michael E. Wynn
Health Benefits Coordinator

19 message(s), 1 displayed

Includes descriptive subject line
Starts with optional salutation to show friendliness and to identify the message opening
Uses single spacing within paragraphs and double spacing between
Closes with name and title to ensure identification

Memo

Onyx Enterprises
Inter-Office Memo

DATE: **May 3, 200x**
TO: **Sondra Rios, Sales and Marketing Department**
FROM: **Michael E. Wynn, Health Benefits Coordinator**
SUBJECT: **ADDING NEW DEPENDANTS TO YOUR HEALTH COVERAGE**

Yes, you may add new dependants to your health plan coverage. Since you are a regular, active employee, you are eligible to add unmarried dependant children (natural, adopted, step, and foster) under age 19 or under age 26, if they are full-time students. You may also be eligible to enrol your domestic partner as your dependant, as part of a pilot program.

For any new dependant, you must submit a completed "Verification of Dependant Eligibility Form." You must also submit a photocopy of a document that verifies the dependant's eligibility. An acceptable verification document for a spouse is a photocopy of your marriage certificate. For children, submit a photocopy of a birth certificate, adoption certificate, or guardianship certificate. Please call the Health Insurance Unit at Ext. 2559 for more information or to ask for an application.

Start dateline 2 inches from top on full sheet

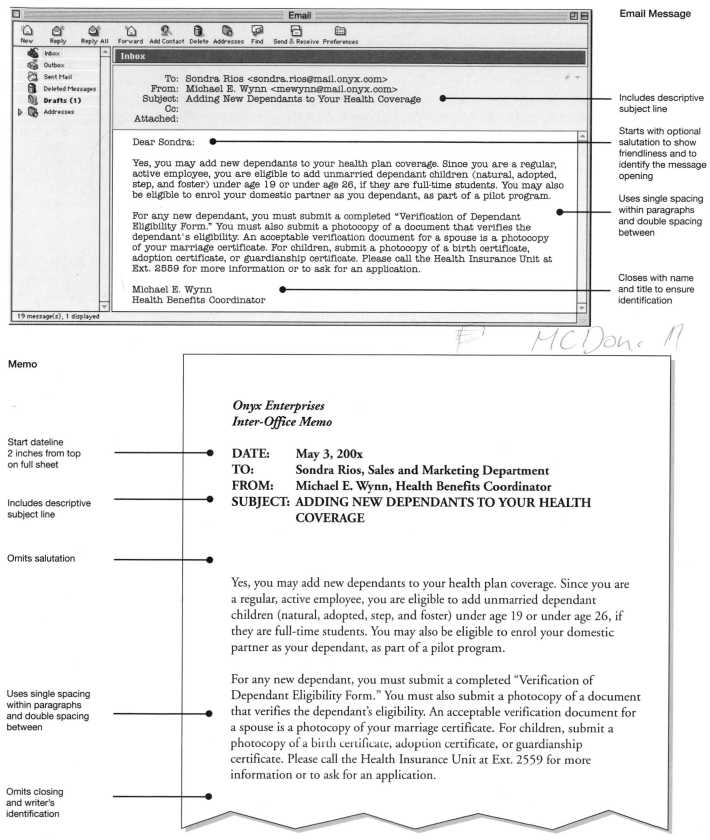

Includes descriptive subject line

Omits salutation

Uses single spacing within paragraphs and double spacing between

Omits closing and writer's identification

Here are new guidelines for employees taking two- or three-week vacations between June and September.

The opening of the message may issue a polite command *(Please answer the following questions about . . .),* make a request (*Please begin research on a summer internship program*), or ask a question (*Can your department complete the printing of a . . .*). Try not to begin with a lengthy explanation. Get to the point as quickly as possible.

Skill Check 4.1 Openings for Email Messages and Memos

Which subject line is better? Circle its letter.

1. **a.** SUBJECT: Inventory
   b. SUBJECT: Annual Pharmacy Inventory Scheduled for June 2
2. **a.** SUBJECT: This Memo Announces Revised Procedures for Applying for Dental Benefits
   b. SUBJECT: Revised Procedures for Dental Benefits Applications

Which opening sentence is better?

3. **a.** Employees interested in learning about new communication technologies are invited to a workshop on October 4.
   b. For some time now we have been thinking about the possibility of holding a workshop about new communication technologies for some of our employees.
4. **a.** We have noticed recently a gradual but steady decline in the number of customers purchasing items from our website.
   b. Please conduct a study and make recommendations regarding the gradual but steady decline of online customer purchases.
5. Write a subject line that describes the possibility of a new sports scoreboard sponsored by Coca-Cola, a topic to be discussed at the next management council meeting.

   ____

   ____

6. Write a subject line announcing a demonstration of new software for all employees to be given Thursday, November 16.

   ____

   ____

Body of Message. Provide details of the message in the body. If you are asking for information, arrange your questions in a logical order. If you are providing information, group similar information together. Think about using headings in bold print, such as you see in these paragraphs. They help readers understand, locate, and reference information quickly. You can also improve the readability of any message by listing items with numbers or bullets. Compare the two sets of instructions that follow:

Hard to Read
The instructions for operating our copy machine include inserting your meter in the slot, loading paper in the upper tray, and then copies are fed through the feed chute.

Improved

Here are instructions for using the copy machine:

- Insert your meter in the slot.
- Load paper in the upper tray.
- Feed copies through the feed chute.

Notice that all the items in the preceding bulleted list are parallel in construction, meaning that each item uses the same form. All begin with verbs. This kind of balanced writing helps readers anticipate and understand information more readily.

Skill Check 4.2 Listing Information

In the space provided, revise the following paragraph so that it includes an introductory sentence and a list of four items.

We are trying to improve budget planning, and we'd also like to control costs. To accomplish these goals, we must change our procedures for submitting requests in the future for outside printing jobs. The new procedures include first determining your exact printing specifications for a particular job. Then we want you to obtain two estimates for the job. These estimates should be submitted in writing to Kelly. Finally, you may place the outside print order—but only after receiving approval.

Closing an Email Message or a Memo. Email messages and memos frequently end with a (a) request for action, (b) summary of the message, or (c) closing thought. If action on the part of the reader is sought, be sure to spell out that action clearly. A vague request such as *Drop by to see this customer sometime* is ineffective because the reader may not understand exactly what is to be done. A better request might be worded as follows: *Please make an appointment to see Rebecca Johnson before June 2, when she will be leaving.* Notice that an *end date* is given. This technique, particularly when coupled with a valid reason, is effective in prompting people to act.

Another way to close an internal message is by summarizing its major points. A closing summary is helpful if the message is complicated. When no action request is made and a closing summary is unnecessary, the writer may prefer to end the memo with a simple closing thought, such as *I'll appreciate your assistance, What do you think of this proposal?* or *Call me if I may answer questions.* Avoid tired, mechanical phrases such as *Don't hesitate to call on me* or *Thank you for your cooperation.* If you wish to express these thoughts, find a fresh way to say them.

Figure 15.1 (p. 301) shows how the four parts of a writing plan combine to create readable, efficient email messages and memos. For more information on email and memo formats, see Appendix C.

Special Tips for Sending Email Messages

Instead of using paper to send memos, increasing numbers of business people have turned to email to send internal and external messages. To make the best use of email, you may wish to implement the following suggestions:

Compose off-line. Instead of dashing off hasty messages online, take the time to compose off-line. Consider using your word processing program and then uploading your message to the email network. This avoids "self-destructing" online (losing all your writing through some glitch or pressing the wrong key).

Get the address right. Email addresses are sometimes complex, often illogical, and always unforgiving. Omit one character or misread the letter *l* for the number *1*, and your message bounces. Solution: Use your electronic address book for people you write to frequently, and double-check every address that you key in manually. Also, be sure that you don't reply to a group of receivers when you intend to answer only one.

Keep lines, paragraphs, and messages short. Try to keep your lines under 65 characters in length and your paragraphs no longer than eight lines. Above all, keep your message short. If it requires more than three screens, consider sending it in hard-copy form.

Care about correctness. Senders and receivers of email tend to be casual about spelling, grammar, and usage. However, people are still judged by their writing, and you never know how far your message will travel. Read and edit any message before hitting the "Send" button!

Don't send anything you wouldn't want published. Because email seems like a telephone call or a person-to-person conversation, writers sometimes send sensitive, confidential, inflammatory, or potentially embarrassing messages. Beware! Email creates a permanent record that often does not go away even when deleted, and every message is a corporate communication that can be used against you or your employer. Don't write anything that you wouldn't want your boss, your family, or a judge to read.

Special Tips for Replying to Email Messages

Before replying to an email message, think about some of the suggestions provided here. You can save yourself time and heartache by developing good reply procedures.

Scan all messages in your inbox before replying to each individually. Because subsequent messages often affect the way you respond, read them all first (especially all those from the same individual).

Don't automatically return the sender's message. When replying, cut and paste the relevant parts. Avoid irritating your recipients by returning the entire "thread" (sequence of messages) on a topic.

Revise the subject line if the topic changes. When replying or continuing an email exchange, revise the subject line as the topic changes.

Never respond when you're angry. Always allow some time to cool down before shooting off a response to an upsetting message. You often come up with different and better alternatives after thinking about what was said. If possible, iron out differences in person.

Finally, remember that office computers are meant for work-related communication. Unless your company specifically allows it, never use your employer's computers for personal messages, personal shopping, or entertainment. Assume that all email is monitored. Employers legally have the right to eavesdrop on employee email messages, and many do.

Writing Application 4.1. On a separate sheet of paper or, preferably, at a computer, revise the following poorly written message. It suffers from wordiness, indirectness, and confusing instructions. Include a numbered list in your revised memo, and be sure to improve the subject line. Prepare this as an email message or as an internal memo.

TO: All Staff Members
FROM: Roy Minami, Manager
DATE: July 11, 200x
SUBJECT: COPIER RULES

Some of you missed the demonstration of the operation of our new Turbo X copier last week. I thought you might appreciate receiving this list of suggestions from the salesperson when she gave the demonstration. This list might also be helpful to other employees who saw the demo but didn't take notes and perhaps can't remember all these pointers. It's sometimes hard to remember how to operate a machine when you do it infrequently. Here's what she told us to do. There are two paper loading trays. Load 8 1/2-×-11-inch or 8 1/2-×-14-inch paper in the two loading trays. The paper should curve upward in the tray. You should take your copy and feed it into the machine face up. However, if you have small sheets or book pages or cut-and-pasted copy, lift the copier door and place your copy face down on the glass.

Before you begin, select the number of copies to be made by pressing the touch selector panel. Don't push too hard. If copies become jammed, open the front door and see where the paper got stuck in the feed path. Remove jammed paper. Oh yes, your meter must be inserted before the machine will operate. We urge you, of course, to make only as many copies as you really need. Keep this list to use again.

Don't hesitate to call on me if you need a private demonstration.

Writing Application 4.2. As the manager of Reprographic Services, write an email message to Kevin Suzuki, manager, Technical Services. You are very worried that the computer of one of your operators may be infected with a virus. The computer belongs to Jackie Jimenez. Jackie says that each time she opens a previously stored document in her Word program, the contents of the document are immediately deleted. Fortunately, because Jackie has backup files, she hasn't lost anything yet; but obviously she can't go on using this computer. You plan to assign Jackie some temporary tasks for the rest of the day; however, she must have her computer up and running by tomorrow. You want a technician to inspect her machine before 5 p.m. today. You know that Kevin likes to learn as much about a computer problem as possible before he sends a technician, so include sufficient details to help him identify the problem.

Writing Application 4.3. As the manager of the Customer Services Division, Molson Breweries, write an email message to Melissa Miller, supervisor, Customer Services. Ask Melissa to draft a form letter that can be sent to groups requesting plant tours. In your memo, explain that the brewery has always encouraged tour groups to see your home plant brewery. However, you cannot sponsor tours at this time because of extensive remodelling. You are also installing a new computer-controlled bottling system. Tours are expected to resume in September. You need a form letter that can be sent to all groups but that can be personalized for individual responses. You want the letter draft by Monday, April 6. The letter should build good customer relations, a primary goal of your tour policy. The letter might enclose a free product coupon and a brochure picturing your operations. Tell Melissa to add any information that she feels would improve the letter.

UNIT 5

Punctuating Sentences

Chapter 16
Commas

Chapter 17
Semicolons and Colons

Chapter 18
Other Punctuation

C H A P T E R

Commas 16

OBJECTIVES When you have completed the materials in this chapter, you will be able to do the following:

LEVEL I

- *Place commas correctly in series, direct address, and parenthetical expressions.*
- *Use commas correctly in punctuating dates, addresses, geographical items, and appositives.*

LEVEL II

- *Place commas correctly in punctuating independent adjectives, verbal phrases, and prepositional phrases.*
- *Use commas correctly in punctuating independent, introductory, terminal, and non-essential clauses.*

LEVEL III

- *Use commas correctly in punctuating degrees, abbreviations, and numerals.*
- *Use commas to indicate omitted words and contrasting statements, for clarity, and with short quotations.*

PRETEST

Insert appropriate commas in the following sentences.

1. Your interview Ms. Daw will take place Tuesday June 9 at 10 a.m.
2. We have suppliers in Oshawa Ontario and in Montreal Quebec.
3. The lawyer had reason to believe by the way that the judge was not impartial and might even be biased against this case.
4. The information revolution began about three decades ago and it has brought us into an age of digital interconnectivity.
5. Although tired employees preferred the evening not the morning in-service training programs.

1. interview, Ms. Daw, Tuesday, June 9, 2. Oshawa, Ontario, Montreal, 3. believe, way, 4. ago,
5. tired, evening, morning,

Did You Know?

Some writers of other languages envy those who write in English. Our systematic use of commas and other punctuation makes it easy to signal pauses, to emphasize ideas, and to enhance readability.

When you talk with a friend, you are probably unaware of the "invisible" commas, periods, and other punctuation marks that you are using. In conversation your pauses and voice inflections punctuate your thoughts and clarify your meaning. In writing, however, you must use a conventional set of symbols—punctuation marks—to help your reader understand your meaning.

Over the years we have gradually developed a standardized pattern of usage for all punctuation marks. This usage has been codified (set down) in rules that are observed by writers who wish to make their writing as precise as possible. As noted earlier, some professional writers may deviate from conventional punctuation practices. In addition, some organizations, particularly newspapers and publishing houses, maintain their own style manuals to establish a consistent "in-house" style.

The punctuation guidelines presented in this book represent a consensus of punctuation styles that are acceptable in business and professional writing. Following these guidelines will help you to write with clarity, consistency, and accuracy.

LEVEL I

▶ Basic Guidelines for Using Commas

The most used and misused punctuation mark, the comma, indicates a pause in the flow of a sentence. *Not all sentence pauses, however, require commas.* It is important for you to learn the standard rules for the use of commas so that you will not be tempted to clutter your sentences with needless, distracting commas. Here are the guidelines for basic comma usage.

Study Tip

As you begin to learn about commas, try to name a rule or guideline for every comma you insert. For example, *comma/series, comma/parenthetical,* and so forth.

Series

Commas are used to separate three or more equally ranked (coordinate) elements (words, phrases, or short clauses) in a series. A comma before the conjunction ensures separation of the last two items. No commas are used when conjunctions join all the items in a series.

Only in June, July, and August is a lifeguard on duty. (Series of words. Notice that a comma precedes *and* but no comma follows the last item, *August.*)

Marvella conducted the research, organized the data, and wrote the report. (Series of phrases)

Mrs. Horton is the president, Mr. Travis is the marketing manager, and Miss Zavala is the executive assistant. (Series of short clauses)

We need wireless access to email and websites and the home office. (No commas needed when conjunctions are repeated.)

Hotlink

Basic comma rules are also covered in this handout prepared by the University of Toronto and posted at **<http://web2.uvcs.uvic.ca/elc/studyzone/330/grammar/comma.htm>**.

Direct Address

Words and phrases of direct address are set off with commas.

You must agree, *Mr. Lee,* that Ingrid has done outstanding work.
I respectfully request, *sir,* that I be transferred.

Parenthetical Expressions

Parenthetical words, phrases, and clauses may be used to create transitions between thoughts. These expressions interrupt the flow of a sentence and are unnecessary for its grammatical completeness. These commonly used expressions, many of which are listed below, are considered non-essential because they do not specifically answer questions such as *when? where? why?* or *how?* Set off these expressions with commas when they are used parenthetically.

accordingly	furthermore	moreover
after all	hence	namely
all things considered	however	needless to say
as a matter of fact	in addition	nevertheless
as a result	incidentally	no doubt
as a rule	in conclusion	of course
at the same time	in fact	on the contrary
by the way	in my opinion	on the other hand
consequently	in other words	otherwise
finally	in the first place	therefore
for example	in the meantime	under the circumstances

Hotlink

The four basic comma rules are clearly and briefly explained by the Memorial University Writing Centre at **<http://www.mun.ca/writingcentre/commarules.shtml>**. The link at the bottom of the page will take you to an online exercise that offers a possible solution for each case.

In addition, your computer skills are excellent. (At beginning of sentence)
This report is not, *however,* one that must be classified. (Inside sentence)
You have checked with other suppliers, *no doubt.* (At end of sentence)

The words in question are set off by commas only when they are used parenthetically and actually interrupt the flow of a sentence. Study the following examples.

However the vote goes, we will abide by the result. (No comma needed after *however*, which introduces dependent clause.)
We have *no doubt* our selling techniques must be revamped. (No commas needed to set off *no doubt*, which is object of verb.)

Study Tip

Phrases are essential (no commas) when they answer the questions *when? where? why?* or *how?*

Don't confuse short introductory essential prepositional phrases functioning as adverbs with parenthetical expressions. Notice that the following short phrases are essential and, therefore, require no commas.

In the summer more rental units become available. (No comma is needed because the short prepositional phrase answers the question *when*?)
In Windsor we will hire additional personnel. (No comma is needed because the short prepositional phrase answers the question *where*?)
For this reason we will be lowering our wholesale prices. (No comma is needed because the short prepositional phrase answers the question *why*?)
With your help our production team can meet its goal. (No comma is needed because the short prepositional phrase answers the question *how*?)

Dates, Addresses, and Geographical Items

When dates, addresses, and geographical items contain more than one element, the second and succeeding elements are normally set off by commas. Study the following illustrations.

Study Tip

In separating cities and provinces and dates and years, many writers remember the initial comma but forget the final one, as in *My friend from Sherbrooke, Quebec, called.*

Dates

On January 3 we opened for business. (No comma needed for one element.)
On January 3, 2001, we opened for business. (Two commas set off second element.)
On Monday, January 3, 2001, we opened for business. (Commas set off second and third elements.)
In June 2003 the reorganization was effected. (Commas are not used when writing the month and year only.)

Addresses

Send the software to Mr. Chun Wong, 1639 Carling Avenue, Ottawa, Ontario K1A 0G5, before Tuesday. (Commas are used between all elements except the province and postal code, which are considered a single unit in this special instance.)

Spot the Blooper

From *The Union-Leader* [Manchester, NH] "Prince Louis Ferdinand of Prussia, a grandson of Germany's last emperor who worked in a Detroit auto plant in the 1930s and later opposed Nazi dictator Adolf Hitler, has died at age 86." (Could a comma help clarify who worked in the auto plant? Would the idea be better expressed in two sentences?)

Geographical Items

He moved from St. John's, Newfoundland, to Sydney, Nova Scotia. (Two commas set off the name of a province (or a state) unless it appears at the end of the sentence.)

Appositives

You will recall that appositives rename or explain preceding nouns or pronouns (Chapter 6). An appositive that provides information not essential to the identification of its antecedent should be set off by commas.

Debbie Robinson, *the DataMax sales representative,* is here. (The appositive adds non-essential information; commas set it off.)

The sales representative *Debbie Robinson* is here to see you. (The appositive is needed to identify which sales representative has arrived; therefore, no commas are used.)

Closely related one-word appositives read as a unit with the preceding item do not require commas.

My husband *Kevin* sometimes uses my computer.

Complete the reinforcement exercises for Level I on pp. 317–318.

LEVEL II

▶ Special Guidelines for Using Commas

At this level we will review comma usage guidelines that you studied in previous chapters, and we will add one new guideline for the punctuation of prepositional phrases.

Hotlink

Algonquin College offers a series of web pages on comma use. Start from **<http://elearning.algonquincollege.com/coursemat/gilless/tutorials/Lesson10_1.htm>** and continue your review clicking on the right arrow at the top of the page.

Independent Adjectives

Separate two or more adjectives that equally modify a noun (Chapter 12).

We're looking for an *industrious, ambitious* person to hire.

Online customers can conduct *secure, real-time* banking transactions.

Introductory Verbal Phrases

Verbal phrases that precede main clauses should be followed by commas (Chapter 11).

To qualify for the position, you must have two years' experience. (Infinitive verbal phrase)

Climbing quickly, the hikers reached the summit by noon. (Participial verbal phrase)

Prepositional Phrases

One or more introductory prepositional phrases totalling four or more words should be followed by a comma.

In the spring of the year, our thoughts may be diverted from academics.
During the winter months, production usually declines.

Introductory prepositional phrases of fewer than four words require *no* commas.

In August that stock reached its highest price. (Short prepositional phrase requiring no comma)
In some instances it will be necessary to increase our price. (Short prepositional phrase requiring no comma)

Do *not* use commas to set off prepositional phrases in other positions when they contain essential information and do not interrupt the sentence.

Sales for our branches *in the province of British Columbia* have improved. (No commas needed because prepositional phrases tell *where* sales improved and do not interrupt the flow of the sentence.)
We do not *at this time* anticipate any unusual expenses. (No commas needed because prepositional phrase tells *when* no unusual expenses are expected.)

Spot the Blooper

Poster for a university departmental event: "Door prizes will include lab equipment, books written by members of the department and a fruitcake."

Independent Clauses

When a coordinating conjunction joins independent clauses, use a comma before the coordinating conjunction, unless the clauses are very short, that is, six or fewer words in each (Chapter 14).

In Japan the wireless Internet has become wildly successful, and companies are pushing for even more sophisticated services.
James uses his cellphone and Jan prefers her BlackBerry. (No comma needed since both clauses are short.)

Study Tip

The comma after an introductory clause is probably the most frequently missed comma in student writing. Be sure to insert a comma after a clause beginning with *If, When, As, Since,* and so forth.

Introductory Clauses

Dependent clauses that precede independent clauses are followed by commas (Chapter 15).

When you have finished, please return the style manual.
If you need help, please call me at Ext. 306.
Since we need more clerks, we will begin advertising.

Terminal Dependent Clauses

A dependent clause at the end of a sentence is usually not preceded by a comma. Whether to use a comma to separate a dependent clause at the end of a sentence depends on whether the added information is essential. Generally, terminal clauses add information that answers questions such as *when?, why?,* and *how?* Such information is essential; thus no comma is necessary. A comma should be used only when a terminal clause adds unnecessary information or an afterthought.

Please return the style manual *when you have finished with it.* (No comma needed because the terminal dependent clause provides essential information and answers the question *when?*)
I plan to leave at 3:30, *although I could stay if you need me.* (A comma is needed because the terminal clause provides additional and unnecessary information.)

Non-Essential Clauses

Use commas to set off clauses that are used parenthetically or that supply information not needed for the grammatical completeness of a sentence.

> An increase in employee salaries, *as you can well understand,* must be postponed until profits improve.
> We received a letter from Anne Diga, *who is now living in Red Deer, Alberta.*

Do *not* use commas to set off clauses that contain essential information.

> A student *who is studying English* certainly needs an up-to-date dictionary. (No commas are necessary because the italicized clause is essential; it tells which student needs an up-to-date dictionary.)

Complete the reinforcement exercises for Level II on pp. 319–321.

LEVEL III

▶ Additional Guidelines for Using Commas

Degrees and Abbreviations

Degrees and professional designations following individuals' names are set off by commas. The abbreviations *Jr.* and *Sr.* are not set off by commas unless the individual prefers to use commas.

> Judith Lounsbury, Ph.D., applied for the position of college president.
> Elizabeth Trues, M.D., had a flourishing practice in Kelowna.
> John T. O'Dell Jr. is frequently confused with John T. O'Dell Sr.
> Only Gregory Stoddard, Jr., is unable to participate. (Individual prefers having *Jr.* set off by commas.)

Hotlink

For a thorough overview of comma use, go to the Red River College page at **<http://xnet.rrc.mb.ca/leshanson/Writing_Resources.htm>** to access a PowerPoint presentation on the same.

The abbreviations *Inc.* and *Ltd.* are not set off by commas (unless the company's legal name includes the commas).

> DMR Group Inc. is based in Montreal. (Canadian companies' legal names do not as a rule include commas before *Inc.* or *Ltd.*)
> The U.S. firm of Blackstone & Smythe, Inc., exports goods worldwide. (Since this company name includes a comma before *Inc.,* a second comma must follow *Inc.* when it appears in the middle of a sentence.)

Numerals

Unrelated figures appearing side by side should be separated by commas.

> A total of 150, 1990 graduates attended the reception.
> By 2010, 2.3 billion subscribers will be using wireless devices worldwide.

Spot the Blooper

Sign outside a restaurant in Grenada, Mississippi: "LETS EAT SENIOR CITIZENS."

Numbers of more than four digits require commas. Four-digit numbers require commas only when they occur together with larger numbers that must be written with commas.*

> 2760 47,950 6,500,000

* *A commonly accepted alternative style is to use spaces rather than commas. Spaces* must *be used when metric quantities are expressed.*

However, calendar years, house numbers, decimals, serial numbers, contract numbers, and US zip codes are written without commas within the numerals.

1867	(Calendar year)
20586 Victory Avenue	(House number)
.98651	(Decimal)
36-5710-1693285763	(Serial number)
No. 359063420	(Contract number)
02116	(Zip code)

Omitted Words

A comma is used to show the omission of words that are understood.

Last summer we hired 12 interns; this summer, 3 interns. (Comma shows omission of *we hired* after *summer*.)

Spot the Blooper

From a newspaper ad for HarrisDirect: "There's not one single reason to pick HarrisDirect online investing. There's a dozen."

Contrasting Statements

Commas are used to set off contrasting or opposing expressions. These expressions are often introduced by such words as *not, never, but,* and *yet.*

The nominating committee selected Mr. Cardinal, not Mr. Monroe, as its representative. (Two commas set off contrasting statement that appears in the middle of sentence.)

The harder our staff works, the further behind we seem to get. (One comma sets off contrasting statement that appears at the end of a sentence.)

Our budget for equipment this year is reduced, yet quite adequate.

Clarity

Commas are used to separate words repeated for emphasis and words that may be misread if not separated.

Susan Long said it was a very, very complex contract.
Whoever goes, goes at his or her own expense.
No matter what, you know you have our support.
In business, time is money.

Study Tip

Here's a good rule to follow in relation to the comma: *When in doubt, leave it out!*

Short Quotations

A comma is used to separate a short quotation from the rest of a sentence. If the quotation is divided into two parts, two commas are used. (Quotation marks are discussed in Chapter 18, Level III.)

Mrs. Lara said, "The deadline for the McBride contract is June 6."
"The deadline for the McBride contract," said Mrs. Lara, "is June 6."

Complete the reinforcement exercises for Level III on pp. 321–323.

HOTLINE QUERIES

Question: My boss always leaves out the comma before the word *and* when it precedes the final word in a series of words. Should the comma be used?

Answer: Although some writers omit this comma, present practice favours its use so that the last two items in the series cannot be misread as one item. For example, *The departments participating are Engineering, Accounting, Marketing,* and *Advertising.* Without that final comma, the last two items might be read as being one item.

Question: Should I use a comma after the year in this sentence? *In 1999 we began operations.*

Answer: No. Commas are not required after short introductory prepositional phrases unless confusion might result without them. If two numbers, for example, appear consecutively, a comma would be necessary to prevent confusion: *In 1999, 156 companies used our services.*

Question: Are these three words interchangeable: *assure, ensure,* and *insure*?

Answer: Although all three words mean "to make secure or certain," they are not interchangeable. *Assure* refers to persons and may suggest setting someone's mind at rest *(let me assure you that we are making every effort to locate it). Ensure* and *insure* both mean "to make secure from loss," but only *insure* is now used in the sense of protecting or indemnifying against loss *(the building and its contents are insured).* Use *ensure* to mean "to make certain" *(the company has ensured the safety of all workers).*

Question: It seems to me that the word *explanation* should be spelled as *explain* is spelled. Isn't this unusual?

Answer: Many words derived from root words change their spellings in their various grammatical forms. Consider these: *maintain, maintenance; repeat, repetition; despair, desperate, desperation; pronounce, pronunciation.*

Question: Is *appraise* used correctly in this sentence? *We will appraise shareholders of the potential loss.*

Answer: No, it's not. Your sentence requires *apprise,* which means "to inform or notify." The word *appraise* means "to estimate" (*he will appraise your home before you set its selling price*).

Question: Is an apostrophe needed in this sentence? *The supervisor('s) leaving early on Thursday prevented us from finishing the job by Friday.*

Answer: Yes, the apostrophe is needed *(the supervisor's leaving).* The word *leaving* is a verbal noun (a gerund), and its modifier must be possessive. Other examples of this are *the boy's whistling, the lion's roaring, my friend's driving.*

Question: Which word is correct in this sentence? *The officer (cited, sited, sighted) me for speeding.*

Answer: Your sentence requires *cited,* which means "to summon" or "to quote." *Site* means "a location," as in *a building site,* or "to choose a position for," as in *site the proposed school building. Sight* means "a view," as in *the building was in sight,* or "to see," as in *a ship was sighted.*

Question: When the word *too* appears at the end of a sentence, should it be preceded by a comma?

Answer: When the adverb *too* (*meaning "also"*) appears at the end of a clause, it requires no comma (*his friend is coming too*). However, when *too* appears in the middle of a sentence, particularly between the subject and the verb, it requires two commas to set it off (*his friend, too, is coming*). When *too* means "to an excessive extent," it requires no commas (*the speech was too long*).

NAME ______________________________

CHAPTER 16 Reinforcement Exercises

LEVEL I

A. (**Self-check**) Insert necessary commas in the sentences below. Indicate in the space provided the number of commas that you insert. Be prepared to explain the reason for any comma you use.

Example: He stated, on the contrary, that he would decline the offer. 2 (parenthetical)

1. Monday February 5 2001 is the most important date in the history of our company. ________
2. Hong Kong is on the other hand one of the most densely populated areas in the world. ________
3. Please see the large selection of trunks briefcases airplane luggage and other travel items in our store. ________
4. Patti lived in Kingston Ontario before she began working in Hull Quebec. ________
5. Your student Jim Farwell called this morning. ________
6. Judith Simpson your business English student also called. ________
7. In the winter we always hire additional personnel in the warehouse and in the office. ________
8. Your reservation Mr. Takeda has not been confirmed. ________
9. We have no doubt that such practices are widespread. ________
10. Organize your thoughts and jot down some notes and then keyboard the message from your notes. ________

Check your answers.

B. Insert necessary commas in the sentences below. Indicate in the space provided the number of commas that you insert. Be prepared to explain the reason for any comma you use.

1. As a matter of fact several students asked the same question. ________
2. Send the software to Mrs. J. D. McKay 4692 Oak Drive Etobicoke Ontario M9B 1L8 before January 1. ________
3. Cynthia Felix the former office manager now has a similar job in Winnipeg Manitoba. ________
4. We would like of course to have personal letters sent to all the donors. ________
5. The document was recorded on Tuesday March 21 1993 in Calgary Alberta. ________
6. We feel however that a job transfer would be appropriate. ________

1. (3) Monday, February 5, 2001, 2. (2) is, hand, 3. (3) trunks, briefcases, airplane luggage, 4. (3) Kingston, Ontario, Hull, 5. (0) 6. (2) Simpson, student, 7. (0) 8. (2) reservation, Mr. Takeda, 9. (0) 10. (0)

7. I see that your brother Keith is pleased with his new cellphone. ________________

8. With my new wireless phone I can download store and play songs from the Internet. ________________

9. Please tell us Mr. Trump what it's like to produce and star in *The Apprentice.* ________________

10. *The Apprentice* has had contestants work for such companies as Gillette Norwegian Cruise Line Arby's and General Motors. ________________

11. It is necessary consequently for you to pay the return postage. ________________

12. Terry Thomas who is a student at Mohawk College is studying office information systems. ________________

13. In the meantime we must make flight reservations immediately. ________________

14. Most people by the way don't like the idea that passengers might use cellphones while flying on planes. ________________

15. Tanya Collins is president Troy Schumacher is vice-president and Robert Chevrier is secretary. ________________

C. Insert necessary commas. Indicate in the space provided the number of commas you use.

1. I wonder Ms. Gilford when we may visit the Digby Nova Scotia resort hotels. ________________

2. My cousin Paul will arrive Monday July 17 from Chicoutimi Quebec. ________________

3. Bennie Porter the chief security officer responded to a disturbance that awoke nearly everyone in the building at 1:30 a.m. ________________

4. We must as a matter of fact analyze the entire document cycle. ________________

5. I have no doubt in my mind about his competency and integrity. ________________

6. Members may choose from many martial arts Pilates aqua fitness and salsa classes offered at Bally Total Fitness. ________________

7. Incidentally I feel that we should get an outside opinion. ________________

8. Our analysis Mr. and Mrs. Ford shows that you owe additional taxes for 2004 2005 and 2006. ________________

9. I noticed on our company website by the way that your friend Charles was promoted. ________________

10. Adam Adler the eminent Toronto architect studied our needs developed a plan and designed our office complex. ________________

11. The architect Adam Adler was recently featured in *Architectural Digest.* ________________

12. With your assistance we should be able to finish the report by Friday April 4. ________________

13. Popular places for destination weddings include Hawaii Mexico and the Caribbean because of their warm weather. ________________

14. Sam Walton the founder of Wal-Mart started out by opening a small store in Arkansas. ________________

15. Wal-Mart opened its first store in Shanghai on July 28 2005 in the Pudong area. ________________

NAME ______________________________

LEVEL II

A. (**Self-check**) Insert any necessary commas. In the space provided, indicate briefly the reason for the comma(s). Write *C* if the sentence is correct.

Example: If I were you, I would take a part-time job and continue school. ___intro. dependent clause___

1. We expect honest thorough answers during the interview process. ____________
2. To communicate effectively you must be able to express your ideas clearly. ____________
3. In 1983 the company enacted a program of energy conservation. ____________
4. As soon as Anna keyboarded the letter I proofread it and mailed it. ____________
5. By November we are able to predict with considerable accuracy the year's profits. ____________
6. Beginning June 15 the interest on your savings account will be non-taxable. ____________
7. Dr. Johnson plans to attend the conference in London and later he expects to vacation in Europe. ____________
8. The work in this office is strictly confidential as I am sure you are well aware. ____________
9. The person who designed your website is talented. ____________
10. When you complete this exercise you should check your answers immediately. ____________

Check your answers.

B. Insert any necessary commas. In the space provided, indicate briefly the reason for the comma(s). Write *C* if the sentence is correct.

1. If we reorganized several branches we could develop a more productive operation. ____________
2. The happy carefree students celebrated the completion of their examinations although many had to leave immediately for their jobs. ____________
3. Whether you do or do not buy we will be happy to advise you. ____________
4. The sportswriter charged that professional football players are overpaid overprivileged athletes. ____________
5. In the winter Susan Madarieta who was recently hired away from CyberVision will join the executive staff as chief information officer. ____________

---

1. honest, (independent adjectives) 2. effectively, (intro. verbal phrase) 3. C (no comma after short prep. phrase)
4. letter, (intro. dependent clause) 5. C (no comma after short prep. phrase) 6. June 15, (intro. verbal phrase)
7. London, (independent clauses with coord. conj.) 8. confidential, (non-essential dependent clause)
9. C (no commas in simple sentence with essential clause) 10. exercise, (intro. dependent clause)

6. Renouncing her wealthy social background Florence Nightingale became a nurse and is considered the founder of modern nursing. ____________________

7. Our current liability insurance in view of the new law that went into effect April 1 needs to be increased. ____________________

8. Some companies have excellent voice mail systems but other organizations use impersonal systems that frustrate and irritate callers. ____________________

9. It was a privilege to show you our new offices and we look forward to serving you in the near future. ____________________

10. In the fall the sports scene is dominated by football. ____________________

11. Having been selected to serve as our chair Patrick Leong made valuable contributions to our committee's work. ____________________

12. You have purchased from us often and your payments in the past have always been prompt. ____________________

13. Before a policy is issued a prospective policyholder is thoroughly investigated. ____________________

14. In our company a prospective policyholder is thoroughly investigated before a policy is issued. ____________________

15. The energetic resourceful sales representative was most successful. ____________________

C. Insert necessary commas. In the space provided, indicate briefly the reason for the comma(s).

1. Although it represents a small share of our total sales the loss of the Regina territory would negatively affect our profits. ____________________

2. Antonio Perez who is the chief executive of Eastman Kodak said that Kodak must change further if it hopes to survive the advent of digital imaging. ____________________

3. Before we announce this sale to the general public we are inviting our charge account customers to a one-day presale. ____________________

4. You were probably concerned about your increased insurance rates but you didn't know where to find adequate coverage at reduced rates. ____________________

5. The contracts that were finished during the early summer must be revised and resubmitted for consideration at the fall board meeting. ____________________

6. Planning for the cold months ahead your gas company has developed a plan to equalize your monthly bills. ____________________

7. We hope that the new year will be prosperous for you and that we may have many more opportunities to serve you. ____________________

8. At a meeting of our advertising committee we decided to renew our contract for one-page advertisements in your magazine. ____________________

9. We do not at this time see any reason for continuing this inefficient profitless practice. ____________________

10. When you send an email message remember that it may be forwarded to someone else. ____________________

11. We risk lost sales if the telephone is not answered by the third ring. ____________________

NAME ______________________

12. In 2006 The Oxford English Dictionary database reached 1 billion words and it now contains words like *inner-child* and *wiki*. ______________

13. If you look up the meaning of *wiki* in an online dictionary you learn that it is a type of website that allows users to quickly add and edit information. ______________

14. Agreeing to serve as our leader Frances Sheppard worked with students and faculty to devise an online learning program. ______________

15. Any increase in salaries as you might have expected is presently impossible because of declining profits. ______________

LEVEL III

A. (**Self-check**) Insert necessary commas. Indicate briefly in the space provided the reason(s) for the comma(s). Write *C* if the sentence is correct.

1. What it is is a matter of principle. ______________
2. The first loan was made February 3; the second September 1. ______________
3. "I am having your policy amended" said Mrs. Bennet "and you will receive the paperwork soon." ______________
4. In the fall we will need six operators; in the spring eight. ______________
5. Mark Simonton C.A. listed the firm's assets at $873500. ______________
6. In December 2001 286 Enron employees received bonuses totalling $72 million. ______________
7. We are issuing Policy No. 2176800394 in your name. ______________
8. We were expecting Miss Weber not Mr. Allen to conduct the audit. ______________
9. "A résumé is a balance sheet without any liabilities" said personnel specialist Robert Half. ______________
10. The octogenarians had known each other for a long long time. ______________

Check your answers.

B. Insert necessary commas. Indicate briefly in the space provided the reason(s) for the comma(s). Write *C* if the sentence is correct.

1. "Nothing you can't spell" said humorist Will Rogers "will ever work." ______________
2. Did you know that on July 23 16 additional workers will be hired? ______________
3. On January 1 your Policy No. 8643219 will expire. ______________

---

1. it is, (clarity) 2. second, (omitted words) 3. amended," Bennet, (short quotation) 4. spring, (omitted words) [*Note:* Do not use a comma after a short introductory prepositional phrase.] 5. Simonton, C.A., (professional designation) $873,500 (numeral more than four digits) or $873 500 6. 2001, (adjacent numerals) 7. C 8. Weber, Allen, (contrasting statement) 9. liabilities," (short quotation) 10. a long, (clarity)

4. Francisco Torres Sr. was born in 1917 and died in 2000. ____________

5. On paper diets often sound deceptively simple. ____________

6. The better we treat our customers the more loyal they will be to our company. ____________

7. Major responsibility for the loan lies with the signer; secondary responsibility with the co-signer. ____________

8. That task must be reserved for experienced never inexperienced employees. ____________

9. Motion-picture producer Samuel Goldwyn said "A verbal contract isn't worth the paper it's written on." ____________

10. In short employees must be more considerate of others. ____________

11. Jeff Brady Ph.D. specializes in information management. ____________

12. Toyota management was worried because 231 2003 sedans had to be recalled. ____________

13. It was Ford Motor Co. not General Motors Corp. that had the most recalls in 2005. ____________

14. What it was was an international power struggle. ____________

15. Half of the payment for the shipment is due on delivery; the balance in six weeks. ____________

16. Although bored students managed to stay awake during the lecture. ____________

17. Whatever it is it is not very amusing. ____________

18. In Room 201 32 computers and 16 printers are operating. ____________

19. Co-operation not criticism is what is needed. ____________

20. "Those who cannot remember the past" said George Santayana "are condemned to repeat it." ____________

21. The government has announced repairs to more than 21 000 km of highway. ____________

22. Lynn Craig D.C. and Annette Bellotti M.D. both have offices in the Queensland Medical Building. ____________

23. Level 6 secretaries are eligible for promotion after 12 months of probation; Level 5 secretaries after 18 months. ____________

24. The number of workers this year will not be reduced but only if sales remain good. ____________

25. "Coming together is a beginning staying together is progress and working together is success" said Henry Ford. ____________

C. Review of Levels I, II, and III. To make sure you have mastered the use of commas, try your skill on these challenging sentences that cover all levels. Insert needed commas, and write the number that you added in the space provided. Write *C* if the sentence is correct. Be prepared to discuss the rule for each comma you add.

1. On October 24 1901 Annie Taylor at the age of 64 became the first person to go over Niagara Falls in a barrel. ____________

2. John D. Rockefeller Sr. who founded Standard Oil was known as a driven determined and philanthropic man. ____________

3. Rockefeller by the way was born in Richland New York in July 1839. ______________

4. Denise Minor who was our first team leader moved to Barrie Ontario. ______________

5. The person who became our next team leader was from Oshawa Ontario. ______________

6. At a recent meeting of our team we decided that members should at their convenience complete an online training module. ______________

7. Although *National Geographic* prints only about 30 photographs for each article the photographer takes about 14,000 images. ______________

8. If you work in an office with open cubicles it is rude to listen to web radio any kind of streaming audio or your iPod without headphones. ______________

9. For three years you have worked here during the summer and you have always been an asset to the firm. ______________

10. Our yearly budget was over $2 000 000 for equipment supplies and utilities. ______________

11. "There is no such thing" said Tom Peters "as a minor lapse in integrity." ______________

12. We are looking for stable not risky stocks in which to invest. ______________

D. Optional Writing. Your instructor may ask you to complete this exercise on a separate sheet.

This chapter presents many guidelines for using commas. Select ten guidelines that you consider most important, and write original sentences to illustrate their use. Identify each guideline.

Editor's Challenge

The following letters contain intentional errors in spelling, proofreading, punctuation, and language principles covered thus far. Use standard proofreading marks to make all necessary corrections.

Adventure Sports, Inc.

8550 Old Dairy Road
Juneau, AK 99801

Email: troy@alaska.net
FAX: 907-789-2319

March 7, 200x

Mr. Kevin M. Simpson
433 East Albert
Edmonton, AB T9E 7X5

THANKS FOR YOUR INTEREST IN KAYAK TOURS

Enclosed is a list of current trips and other information, that you requested about our Kayak tours in Alaska. To ensure a quality wilderness experience the number of guests on a tour are limited to six people. No special experience is neccesary. Many of our guests have never been in a sea kayak, and are surprised to find that they are very stable. Moreover we teach you safe efficient operation of a kayak.

All equipment, meals, and safety gear is included in the trip price. We provide charter transportation from Juneau to the trip location, however you are responsible for getting to Juneau, and for your meals and lodging before and after the trip. To reserve a trip you must make a 50 per cent deposit. We will hold reservations for your party for two weeks. Anyone who must request a refund, will be charged a $50 handling fee. In some instances, we must cancel a trip because of to few participants, or dangerous weather. If we must cancel a full refund will be made.

Our most popular trip is whale watching and kayaking at Pt. Adolphus. This four day trip costs US$750 which includes boat charter and fairy. We also recommend the glacier tour at Tracy Arm, and our island tour of Pt. Couverdon. By the way custom dates is available for familys or group's of three or more.

Call, write or fax to make your reservations. We look forward to providing you with the wilderness adventure of a lifetime!

Troy M. Donohue

TROY M. DONOHUE, ADVENTURE SPORTS INC.

Enclosure

Briggs Mills Inc.

440 Vine Street
Fredricton, NB E3C 5G7

www.briggsmills.com
506-579-3100

May 12, 200x

Ms. Julie Perzel
Director Human Resources
Clayton Manufacturing
10001 East Industrial Park Road
Fredricton, NB G2B 4B8

Dear Ms. Pretzel:

Mr. Martin A. Anderson whom is applying for the position of manger of manufacturing support at your organization requested that I write this confidential letter of reccommendation. Mr. Anderson has worked under my supervision as a manufacturing support supervisor for three year's at Briggs Mills Inc.

As a supervisor of manufacturing support Mr. Anderson helped to hire, evaluate and supervise a team of four machine technicians. Him and his team was responsible for the preventive maintance, troubleshooting and repair of machines on three production lines. Because of his strong interpersonal skills Mr. Anderson expected and obtained high performance from his machine technicians. Each technician whom was evaluated ranked in the upper two levels of performance for the past three year's. In addition Mr. Andersons own performance was evaluated at our highest level for the last two year's.

Mr. Andersons team developed a highly-effective maintenance and calibration program, that reduced line shutdowns by 10 per cent. Furthermore, in addition to his supervisory work Mr. Anderson initiated improvements in machine documentation.

These changes enabled support personal to repair machines without relying on production engineers. Although documentation changes were cumbersome for our engineers Mr. Anderson brang about needed change without alienating engineers or technicians. His enthusiastic upbeat personality has had a positive affect on the entire organization.

Im sorry that Mr. Andersen may leave Briggs Mills but I am confident that his technical, interpersonal and leadership skills will serve you well in your organization. I recommend him highly, and would be happy to have him return to us in the future.

Sincerly,

Mark A. Summers

Mark A. Summers
Vice-President, Operations

POSTTEST

Insert appropriate commas in the following sentences.

1. Please let us know Mrs. Youngblood what we can do to ensure a pleasant smooth transition.
2. The manager thinks on the other hand that all service calls must receive prior authorization and that current service contracts must be honoured.
3. Professor Connie Jo Clark Ph.D. and Pat King M.B.A. have been asked to speak at our Banff Alberta conference.
4. When trained all employees in this company should be able to offer logical effective advice to customers.
5. If you are unsure you may ask Mrs. Carlson not Mr. Ray for additional information.

learning.web.ways

Soon you will be looking for a job. You decide to learn as much as possible about trends in your career area.

Goal: To gather job-search and career information.

1. With your web browser on the screen, go to the Workopolis site **<http://www.workopolis.com/index.html>** and bookmark it.
2. Familiarize yourself with Workopolis by exploring its **Career Resources** in the frame on the right.
3. Start by clicking on the **Researching a Company or Industry** link.
4. Note the information Workopolis gives you on how to obtain basic corporate information from the links provided on its website.
5. Scroll down the same page, and click on the **Business Information by Sector** link. Study the list of industries, and select the one you expect to join after graduating. What information can you find on this industry? Jot down the key points of interest to you.
6. Using your bookmarks, return to Workopolis. Find the **Keywords** box in the **Quick Job Search** column on the right, and enter the title of the job you will eventually seek. In the **City** box below it, enter the city where you would like to work, and click on the **Search** button below.
7. Print out a page showing information about your job choice in that city.
8. End your session, and submit your printouts and answers.

---

1. know, Mrs. Youngblood, pleasant, 2. thinks, hand, 3. Clark, Ph.D., King, M.B.A., Banff, Alberta, 4. trained, logical, 5. unsure, Carlson, Ray,

C H A P T E R

Semicolons and Colons 17

OBJECTIVES When you have completed the materials in this chapter, you will be able to do the following:

LEVEL I

- *Use semicolons correctly in punctuating compound sentences.*
- *Use semicolons when necessary to separate items in a series.*

LEVEL II

- *Distinguish between the proper and improper use of colons to introduce listed items.*
- *Correctly use colons to introduce quotations and explanatory sentences.*

LEVEL III

- *Distinguish between the use of commas and semicolons preceding expressions such as* namely, that is, *and* for instance.
- *Understand why semicolons are sometimes used to separate independent clauses joined by coordinating conjunctions.*
- *Use colons appropriately and be able to capitalize words following colons when necessary.*

PRETEST

Insert appropriate semicolons, colons, and commas in the following sentences.

1. "Green" technologies have been gaining a strong following consequently many industries are introducing green products and recycling programs.
2. The following experts were invited to speak Tom Woods Mount Royal College Beverly Linnell Southern Alberta Institute of Technology and Judy O'Shea Lethbridge Community College.
3. Speakers for the morning session are now scheduled speakers for the afternoon session have not yet been arranged.

continued

PRETEST

4. The programming committee however must proceed with plans for the entire conference.
5. Although the committee had many cities from which to choose it decided to limit the selection to the following namely Vancouver, Toronto, or Montreal.

Skilled writers use semicolons and colons to signal readers about the ideas that will follow.

The semicolon is a stronger punctuation mark than a comma, which signifies a pause; but the semicolon is not as strong as a period, which signifies a complete stop. Understanding the use of the semicolon will help you avoid fundamental writing errors, such as the *comma splice* (separating two independent clauses with a comma) and the *run-on sentence* (running two independent clauses together without punctuation).

WARNING! Don't overuse the semicolon. Most independent clauses will end with periods. Join clauses together only when combining ideas improves comprehension.

LEVEL I

▶ Basic Uses of the Semicolon

Semicolons tell readers that two closely related ideas should be thought of together. The most basic use of the semicolon occurs in compound sentences. Many business and professional communicators mistakenly use a comma when they should be using a semicolon. Study the following examples to make sure you don't make this error.

Independent Clauses Separated by Conjunctive Adverbs

Semicolons are used primarily when two independent clauses are separated by a conjunctive adverb or a transitional expression (Chapter 14). Here are some review examples.

Companies make no profits until they recover costs; *therefore*, most companies use a cost approach in pricing. (Semicolon separates two independent clauses joined by the conjunctive adverb *therefore*.)

Advertising is aimed at increasing sales; *thus* an advertising policy must be formulated with that objective. (Semicolon separates two independent clauses joined by the conjunctive adverb *thus*.)

Study Tip

Remember that a comma is used only after a conjunctive adverb of two syllables or more. And don't capitalize the word following a semicolon unless it's a proper noun.

Independent Clauses Without a Coordinating Conjunction or a Conjunctive Adverb

Two or more closely related independent clauses not separated by a conjunctive adverb or a coordinating conjunction *(and, or, nor,* etc.) may be joined by a semicolon.

The licensing company is called the *franchisor*; the dealer is called the *franchisee*.

1. following; consequently, 2. speak: Woods, College; Linnell, Technology; O'Shea, 3. scheduled; 4. committee, however, 5. choose, following; namely,

Our inside teller service closes at 4 p.m.; outside ATM service is available 24 hours a day.

As you learned in Chapter 3, a serious punctuation error results if separate independent clauses are joined by only a comma (a comma splice) or without any punctuation whatsoever (a run-on sentence).

Comma splice: Our inside teller service closes at 4 p.m., outside ATM service is available 24 hours a day.

Run-on sentence: Our inside teller service closes at 4 p.m. outside ATM service is available 24 hours a day.

Hotlink

For a quick overview of basic colon and semicolon rules, visit **<http://web2.uvcs.uvic.ca/elc/studyzone/410/grammar/colons.htm>**.

Series Containing Internal Commas or Complete Thoughts

Semicolons are used to separate items in a series when one or more of the items contain internal commas.

Only the company branches in St. John's, Newfoundland; Sherbrooke, Quebec; and Mississauga, Ontario, are showing substantial profits.

Attending the conference were Teresa Caruana, executive vice-president, Cabrillo Industries; Martin Manheim, president, Servex Corporation; and Joyce Moran, program director, Club Mediterranean.

Semicolons are used to separate three or more serial independent clauses.

The first step consists of surveying all available information related to the company objective so that an understanding of all problems can be reached; the second step consists of interviewing consumers, wholesalers, and retailers; and the third step consists of developing a research design in which the actual methods and procedures to be used are indicated.

Career Tip

Using the semicolon skilfully is one mark of an educated writer.

A series of short independent clauses, however, may be separated by commas (Chapter 16).

Amazon.com was founded in 1994, it unveiled its website in 1995, and it went public in 1997.

Complete the reinforcement exercises for Level I on pp. 335–336.

▶ Basic Uses of the Colon

LEVEL II

The colon is most often used to introduce lists, quotations, and explanatory sentences.

Formally Listed Items

Use a colon after an independent clause introducing one item, two items, or a formal list. A list may be shown vertically or horizontally and is usually introduced by such words as *the following, as follows, these,* or *thus.* A colon is also used when such words are implied but not stated.

Creating a company website offered the following advantage: improved customer service. (Independent clause introduces single item.)

Some of the most commonly used manufacturers' discounts are *the following*: trade, cash, quantity, and seasonal. (Formal list with introductory expression stated)

Hotlink

You will find guidance on the use of the colon at **<http://www.plainlanguage.mb.literacy.ca/resource/style.htm>**.

Spot the Blooper

From a student paper: "The three kinds of blood vessels are: arteries, vanes, and caterpillars."

Our business uses several delivery services: UPS, Purolator, and Federal Express. (Formal list with introductory expression only implied)

These are a few of the services that a correspondent bank performs for other banks:

1. Collecting cheques and payments
2. Accepting letters of credit and travellers' cheques
3. Making credit investigations (Formal list shown vertically)

Do not use a colon unless the list is introduced by an independent clause. Lists often function as sentence complements or objects. When this is the case and if the statement introducing the list is not complete, no colon should be used. It might be easiest to remember that lists introduced by verbs or prepositions require no colons (because the introductory statement is incomplete).

Three courses in this program are Accounting 103, Business English 210, and Computer Science 220. (No colon is used because the introductory statement is not complete; the list is introduced by a *to be* verb and functions as a complement.)

Awards of merit were presented to Professor Loncorich, Ms. Harned, and Dr. Konishi. (No colon is used because the introductory statement is not an independent clause; the list functions as the object of the preposition *to*.)

Do not use a colon when an intervening sentence falls between the introductory statement and the list.

According to a recent survey, these are the top convention cities in North America. The survey was conducted by *Tradeshow Week*.

Las Vegas	New York
Toronto	Chicago

Quotations

Use a colon to introduce long one-sentence quotations and quotations of two or more sentences.

Consumer advocate Sandra Hersh said: "Historically, in our private-enterprise economy, consumers determine what and how much is to be produced through their purchases in the marketplace; hence the needs of consumers are carefully monitored by producers."

Spot the Blooper

Advertisement for a car wash: "We do not scratch your paint finish with machinery, we do it by hand." (Do you see two errors?)

Incomplete quotations not interrupting the flow of a sentence require no colon, no comma, and no initial capital letter.

The columnist described the new Jackson-Triggs winery as "a vintner's heaven."

Explanatory Sentences

Use a colon to separate two independent clauses if the second clause explains, illustrates, or supplements the first.

The company's newly elected directors immediately faced a perplexing dilemma: they had to choose between declaring bankruptcy and investing additional funds in an attempt to recoup previous losses.

The applicants for the position all exhibited one common trait: they were achievers who accepted nothing less than success.

Complete the reinforcement exercises for Level II on pp. 337–338.

▶ Special Uses of Semicolons and Colons

LEVEL III

You've just studied basic uses for semicolons and colons. Occasionally, though, these punctuation marks are used in circumstances demanding special attention.

Introductory Expressions Such as *namely*, *for instance*, and *that is*

When introductory expressions (such as *namely, for instance, that is,* and *for example*) immediately follow independent clauses, they are preceded by either commas or semicolons. Generally, if the words following the introductory expression appear at the end of the sentence and form a series or an independent clause, use a semicolon before the introductory expression. If not, use a comma.

Use semicolons

Numerous fringe benefits are available to employees; *namely*, stock options, life insurance, health insurance, dental care, and vision care. (A semicolon is used because *namely* introduces a series at the end of the sentence.)

We offer outstanding prices on flights to Europe; *for example*, flights to Glasgow and Belfast begin at $469. (A semicolon is used because *for example* introduces an independent clause.)

Use commas

Our company is considering better ways to evaluate employees, *for example,* an objective performance appraisal system. (A comma is used because *for example* introduces neither a series nor an independent clause.)

These same introductory expressions (*namely, for instance,* etc.) may introduce parenthetical words within sentences. Usually, commas punctuate parenthetical words within sentences. If the introductory expression introduces several items punctuated by internal commas, however, use dashes or parentheses. (Dashes and parentheses are treated in detail in Chapter 18.)

Use commas

The biggest health problems facing workers, *namely,* drug abuse and alcoholism, cost industry over one billion dollars a year. (Parenthetical words contain only two items joined by *and.*)

Use dashes

The pursuit of basic job issues—*for instance,* wages, job security, and working conditions—was the main concern of workers. (Dashes are used because the introductory expression introduces several items punctuated with internal commas.)

Independent Clauses With Coordinating Conjunctions

Normally, a comma precedes a coordinating conjunction (*and, or, but,* etc.) when it joins two independent clauses. If either of the independent clauses contains an additional comma, however, the reader might be confused as to where the second independent clause begins. For this reason a semicolon may be used instead of the normally expected comma.

Use comma

We have considered your suggestions carefully, and it appears that they have considerable merit. (Comma precedes coordinating conjunction because no additional punctuation appears within either clause.)

Study Tip

Notice that a comma follows *namely, for instance, that is,* and *for example* when these words are used as introductory expressions.

Hotlink

An excellent *Hot Potato* PowerPoint on the use of the semicolon can be downloaded from the Red River Writing resources page at **<http://xnet.rrc.mb.ca/leshanson/writing_Resources.htm>**.

Hotlink

To check your skill in using colons and semicolons, try this quiz at **<http://www.mun.ca/writingcentre/colonquiz.shtml>**.

Use semicolon

The first three cities recommended by the relocation committee were Atlanta, Dallas, and Detroit; but Miami, San Diego, and Seattle were also mentioned. (Semicolon precedes coordinating conjunction to show where the second independent clause begins and to prevent confusion.)

Special Uses of Colons

Study Tip

Generally, no punctuation follows incomplete statements listed vertically.

- After the salutation of a business letter with mixed punctuation
  Dear Mr. Jameson: Dear Mike: Dear Customer Service:
- In expressions of time to separate hours from minutes
  2:45 p.m. 12:01 a.m.
- Between titles and subtitles
  HOW: A Handbook for Office Professionals (Book title)
  "Oil Prices: How High Can They Go?" (article title)
- Between place of publication and name of publisher
  Choy, Wayson. *The Jade Peony*. Vancouver: Douglas & McIntyre, 1995.

Capitalization Following Colons

Do not capitalize the initial letter of words or of phrases listed following a colon unless the words so listed are proper nouns.

The four Cs of effective letter writing are the following: clarity, courtesy, conciseness, and correctness.

These cities will receive heavy promotional advertising: Dauphin, Portage la Prairie, and Selkirk.

Do, however, capitalize the initial letters of words or phrases in a vertical list.

To be legally enforceable, a contract must include at least three elements:

1. Mutual assent of competent parties
2. A consideration
3. A lawful purpose

The listening comprehension section of the test has three parts:

- Question and response
- Short conversations
- Short talks

Hotlink

The online quiz on the use of colons and semi-colons provided by Memorial University at **<http://www.mun.ca/writingcentre/colonquiz.shtml>** will help you determine your mastery of these punctuation marks.

Do not capitalize the first letter of an independent clause following a colon if that clause explains or supplements the first one (unless, of course, the first word is a proper noun).

You will be interested in our credit card for one special reason: we offer you the opportunity of a full refund of the low annual fee.

Capitalize the first letter of an independent clause following a colon if that clause states a formal rule or principle.

Experienced negotiators adhere to this principle: Never cut what you can untie.

For a quotation following a colon, capitalize the initial letter of each complete sentence.

> Commenting on the importance of incorporation, historians Krooss and Seropian said: "A strong case can be made for the proposition that the increased use of the corporation was the most important institutional innovation of the century. The corporate form permeates American business."

Hotlink

Check your knowledge by using this interactive online quiz on commas, periods, colons, and semicolons at **<http://xnet.rrc.mb.ca/leshanson/Hot_Potato/comma.htm>**.

▶ A Final Word

Semicolons are excellent punctuation marks when used carefully and knowingly. After reading this chapter, though, some students are guilty of semicolon overkill. They begin to string together two—and sometimes even three—independent clauses with semicolons. Remember to use semicolons in compound sentences *only* when two ideas are better presented together.

Complete the reinforcement exercises for Level III on pp. 339–340.

HOTLINE QUERIES

Question: Here's a sentence we need help with: *We plan to present the contract to whoever makes the lowest bid.* My supervisor recommends *whoever* and I suggest *whomever.* Which of us is right?

Answer: Your supervisor. The preposition *to* has as its object the entire clause (*whoever makes the lowest bid*). Within that clause *whoever* functions as the subject of the verb *makes;* therefore, the subjective-case form *whoever* should be used.

Question: When I list items vertically, should I use a comma or semicolon after each item? Should a period be used after the final term? For example,

Please inspect the following rooms and equipment:

1. *The control room*
2. *The power transformer and its standby*
3. *The auxiliary switchover equipment*

Answer: Do not use commas or semicolons after items listed vertically, and do not use a period after the last item in such a list. However, if the listed items are complete sentences or if they are long phrases that complete the meaning of the introductory comment, periods may be used after each item.

Question: Is there a plural form of *plus and minus*?

Answer: The plural form is *pluses and minuses (consider all the pluses and minuses before you make a decison).*

Question: I'm setting up advertising copy, and this sentence doesn't look right to me: *This line of fishing reels are now priced ...*

Answer: Your suspicion is correct. The subject of the verb in this sentence is *line;* it requires the singular verb *is.*

(Continued)

Question: I wonder if the possessive is correctly expressed in this sentence that I'm transcribing: *I appreciate the candour of both you and Neil in our conversation.* Shouldn't both *you* and *Neil* be made possessive?

Answer: No. It would be very awkward to say *your and Neil's candour.* It's much better to use the *of* construction, thus avoiding the awkward double possessive.

Question: Is this a double negative: *We <u>can't</u> schedule the meeting because we have <u>no</u> room available?*

Answer: No, this is not regarded as a double negative. In grammar a double negative is created when two negatives appear in a single clause such as *I can't hardly…* or *We don't have nothing.* Avoid such constructions. Your sentence has two negatives, but they are quite acceptable as they are in separate clauses.

Question: A memo from our vice-president reads, *The new benefit package is equally as good as the previous package.* Is *equally as* correct English?

Answer: Writers should use *equally* or *as* but not both together. *The new benefit package is as good as the previous package,* or *The new benefit package equals the previous package,* or *The new benefit package and the previous package are equally good.*

Question: I've been told that I should spell *judgment* without the *e.* Why, then, do I sometimes see this word spelled *judgement*? Are both spellings acceptable?

Answer: Most dictionaries will give both the preferred and any alternate spellings of a word. The preferred spelling will always be listed first. Although *judgement* is included in many dictionaries as an alternate spelling, it should not be used in business or any other type of writing because most people would identify it as being misspelled. If you use this spelling in Word, it will be flagged as being misspelled. In addition, if you look this word up in any law dictionary using this spelling, you won't find it because *judgment* is the only accepted spelling in the legal field.

NAME ______________________________

CHAPTER 17 Reinforcement Exercises

LEVEL I

A. (**Self-check**) For each of the following sentences, underline any errors in punctuation. Then in the space provided, write the correct punctuation mark plus the word preceding it. Write *C* if the sentence is correct.

Example: Breeding and raising horses can be profitable, consequently, large sums are being invested. — profitable;

1. Jeff Bezos worked for years to build Amazon.com, it was years before the company made a profit. ______
2. Many people buy and sell items on eBay, it is the most widely used online auction site. ______
3. Investors' expectations were high consequently, competitive bidding for the new IPO was brisk. ______
4. Our equipment costs have tripled in the last five years, salary expenses have increased even more. ______
5. E-business has always been a risky undertaking, online companies seem to disappear as quickly as they appear. ______
6. According to Red Herring, four of the top European entertainment companies are Double Fusion, Jerusalem, Israel; Echovox, Geneva, Switzerland; IceMobile, Amsterdam, The Netherlands; and Mobix Interactive, London, United Kingdom. ______
7. The United Kingdom has the most companies on the list; and France and Israel tie for second place. ______
8. Communications is the largest sector on the list Internet services make up the second-largest sector. ______
9. One of the hottest areas is mobile communications, a number of companies offer chipsets and software to manage the downloading of video and other rich media to handsets and mobile phones. ______
10. Consumers are also looking for alternative sources of power, thus some companies are offering such products as paper-thin batteries for compact devices. ______

Check your answers.

B. Add any necessary commas or semicolons to the following sentences. (Do not add periods.) In the spaces provided, write the number of punctuation marks you inserted. Write *C* if a sentence is correct as written.

Example: New equipment was ordered eight weeks ago ; delivery is expected within two weeks. — 1

1. Amazon.com; 2. eBay; 3. high; 4. years; 5. undertaking; 6. C 7. list, 8. list; 9. communications; 10. power;

1. Toyota wants to expand beyond automobiles hence the company has moved into health care support, consulting, prefab houses, advertising, and sweet potatoes. ______

2. Dr. Paulson scheduled appointments every 30 minutes he was assisted by an experienced nurse. ______

3. Buildings swayed lights flickered and dishes rattled. ______

4. Serving on the panel are Pam Rippin marketing director Trinity Sales Evelyn Katusak sales supervisor Broome Products and Timothy Miank market analyst Lansing Enterprises. ______

5. Several members of the staff are near the top of their salary ranges we may have to reclassify their jobs before recommending them for increases. ______

6. Your account is now several months past due consequently it is not possible for us to grant you further extensions. ______

7. The shortest recorded reign of any monarch was that of Louis XIX of France it lasted only 15 minutes. ______

8. Every Christmas we hire a number of temporary office workers hence I am writing to ask you to make this announcement about job openings to your students. ______

9. Jeremy worked Jennifer supervised and Jean entertained. ______

10. Web advertising attempts to reach large international audiences television advertising is aimed at national or local audiences. ______

11. Dawson City was full of fortune hunters at the turn of the century it is now full of tourists, at least during the summer. ______

12. Computer hackers can easily decode short passwords thus passwords should be at least six to eight characters long and be a mix of letters and numerals. ______

13. We are opening a branch office in Drumheller and we hope we will be able to serve you from that office in the future. ______

14. Smart companies assume their computer networks will be broken into consequently they develop computer-use policies to limit the damage. ______

15. Some of the cities expected to bid on the 2016 Summer Olympics are Cape Town South Africa New Delhi India Lisbon Portugal Havana Cuba and San Francisco USA. ______

16. London England will host the 2012 Summer Olympics London was chosen over Paris New York Moscow and Madrid. ______

17. We have hired "white hat" hackers their job is to test how well our computer systems withstand assaults by real hackers. ______

18. Our training can usually be completed in six to ten months thus you can begin earning wages in less than a year. ______

19. If you open your account immediately your first 500 cheques will be supplied free you will moreover receive a bonus gift if you are among our first 50 customers. ______

20. Three participating institutions are Nova Scotia Community College Halifax Nova Scotia Keewatin Community College The Pas Manitoba and Red Deer College Red Deer Alberta. ______

NAME ______________________________

LEVEL II

A. (**Self-check**) For each of the following sentences, underline any errors in punctuation. Then in the space provided, write the correct punctuation plus the preceding word. If a colon should be omitted, write *Omit colon.* Write *C* if the sentence is correct.

Example: Special invitations were sent to: President Owens, Vice-President Spears, and Treasurer Avery. — Omit colon

1. Three factors on which auto insurers frequently base rates are: a driver's safety record, miles driven, and years of driving experience. ______

2. The educational trip through Ontario included visits to the following: Black Creek Pioneer Village, Toronto; Old Fort Henry, Kingston; and the Canadian Museum of Civilization, Ottawa. ______

3. Smart phones are available from the following three companies. Please check on prices:

   Motorola
   Nokia
   Samsung ______

4. During the presentation the realtor explained; "If you purchase before the start of construction, you can choose from 20 suite layouts; you can also customize your suite. Best of all, you can still take advantage of pre-construction prices." ______

5. The head of the computer security firm admitted one big problem: finding good people without criminal records. ______

6. Four of the worst computer passwords are: your first name, your last name, *Password,* and the name of a sports team. ______

7. We have requests for information from three local companies: Pharma Plus, Waldorf Inc., and Data Control. ______

8. Because of the urgency of the problem, we have sent fax messages to: Evelyn Dobson, Mary Ringle, and Connie Clark. ______

9. The most commonly observed holidays are the following: Thanksgiving, Remembrance Day, Christmas, Boxing Day, and New Year's Day. ______

10. Shane proposed a solution to our daycare problem: open a home office and share child care duties. ______

Check your answers.

1. Omit colon 2. C 3. prices. 4. explained: 5. C 6. Omit colon 7. C 8. Omit colon 9. C 10. C

B. For the following sentences add any necessary but missing punctuation marks. For each sentence indicate in the space provided the number of additions you have made. Write *C* if the sentence is correct as it stands.

Example: Shipments of computer components will be sent to Dallas, Vancouver, Barcelona, and Zurich. ___3___

1. Three similar types of tropical storms with different names are cyclones typhoons and hurricanes. ________
2. Japan faces a serious economic threat its dependence on oil imports endangers its future economic growth. ________
3. Polygraph examinations generally consist of four elements a pre-examination interview, a demonstration, questioning of the examinee, and a postexamination interview. ________
4. Speaking at the convention, humorist Lawrence Peter said "Most hierarchies were established by men who now monopolize the upper levels. This deprives women of their rightful share of opportunities for incompetence." ________
5. The records of the following employees will be reviewed for salary evaluation Please send the records by October 1

   Vicky Peck　　　　Julie Mauer
   Tony Watkins　　　Ivan Krakowski ________
6. Each balance sheet is a statement of assets liabilities and owner's equity. ________
7. The following scams are most likely to arrive in your email box business opportunities chain letters work-at-home schemes and investment opportunities. ________
8. Energy in this country is supplied from a number of sources oil natural gas coal nuclear fission and hydropower. ________
9. Of all the discoveries and inventions in human history, the four greatest are said to be these speech, fire, agriculture, and the wheel. ________
10. The law of supply and demand can function only under the following condition producers must know what consumers want. ________
11. Professor Charlotte Cohen asked that research reports contain the following parts introduction body summary and bibliography. ________
12. Additional costs in selling a house are title search, land transfer tax, preparation of documents, and closing fee. ________
13. Warren Bennis said "The factory of the future will have only two employees, a man and a dog. The man will be there to feed the dog. The dog will be there to keep the man from touching the equipment." ________
14. Google's many services include the following Google Maps Google Finance Google News Gmail Google Talk and Froogle. ________
15. Business letters generally include four parts date, inside address, body, and closing. ________

NAME ______________________________

LEVEL III

A. (**Self-check**) Insert necessary punctuation. In the space provided, write the number of punctuation marks that you inserted. Write *C* if the sentence is correct.

1. The local community youth program attracted several employees as volunteers; namely, Pam Wheeler, Benita Washington, Sid Daily, and Samar Hillo. ________
2. Sales personnel may be assigned to a number of countries; for example, India, Brazil, France, and South Africa. ________
3. If she accepts the transfer to Calgary, she will have a better chance of promotion; but if she declines the transfer, her family will not be uprooted. ________
4. The meeting started promptly at 1:15 p.m. and ended at 3:45 p.m. ________
5. Many banks now offer automated transfers from savings to chequing accounts that is money may be kept in an interest-bearing savings account until needed. ________
6. All employees are urged to observe the following rule: When in doubt, consult the company style manual. ________
7. The writer of a research report should include a variety of references; for example, books, periodicals, government publications, and newspapers. ________
8. A must-read book for investors is *Against the Gods The Remarkable Story of Risk*. ________
9. For the opening session of the convention, the keynote speaker will be systems analyst Norma Patterson; and for the afternoon general membership meeting, the speaker will be union representative Judith R. Rice. ________
10. You may pay your deposit using any of the following methods: credit card, cheque, or wire transfer. ________

Check your answers.

B. For the following sentences add any necessary but missing punctuation marks. For each sentence indicate in the space provided the number of additions you have made. Mark *C* if correct.

Example: If she completes the proposal, Ms. Upchurch will fly to Ottawa on Tuesday; if not, she will leave on Thursday. ___3___

1. When completing your résumé be sure to include relevant activities for example intern experience work-study experience and volunteer work. ________
2. Because of his extended service abroad Edward Mautz was selected to head the export division and because of her outstanding sales experience Barbara Malom was selected to head the marketing division. ________

1. C 2. C 3. C 4. C 5. (2) accounts; that is, 6. C 7. C 8. (1) *Gods:* 9. C 10. C

3. Karen Epstein remarked that she always found whatever she was looking for in her favourite dictionary namely the *Gage Canadian Dictionary.* ____________

4. One of the titles I'm considering for my book is *Your First Résumé A Complete Guide to Strategies and Techniques.* ____________

5. Some punctuation marks require a great deal of instruction and practice for example commas colons and semicolons. ____________

6. Three times have been designated for the interviews Thursday at 630 p.m. Friday at 330 p.m. and Monday at 10 a.m. ____________

7. Companies that plan to expand in China should be aware of several important factors for example regulatory environment cultural differences and technologies in use. ____________

8. Large and small companies have an important reason for expanding in China that is by 2025 China is predicted to be the world's largest economy. ____________

9. Franca Santin enjoyed her current position as sales representative very much but when a competing company offered her a substantial increase in salary she found it very tempting. ____________

10. Stories circulated about Henry Ford founder of the Ford Motor Company Lee Iacocca former CEO Chrysler Motor Company and Shoichiro Toyoda former chief Toyota Motor Company. ____________

C. Optional Writing. Your instructor may ask you to complete this exercise on a separate sheet.

According to the instructions that follow, write eight sentences about using the Internet or email. For example: *I generally use the Internet for email; however, I plan to get better at using it for research.*

Write three original sentences illustrating basic uses of semicolons. Then write one sentence using *namely* with a semicolon preceding it. Write three original sentences illustrating basic uses of colons. Compose a list arranged vertically, and write an introduction to it using an independent clause that requires a colon. Label each of the eight items.

Editor's Challenge

The following memos contain intentional errors. Use proofreader's marks to indicate corrections.

LONEWOLF PRODUCTIONS

TO: Patrick M. Young
FROM: Kellie Whitford
DATE: May 2, 200x
SUBJECT: SITES FOR *BODEGA BAY* TELEFILM

This memo describes the progress of my search for a appropriate rustic home, villa, or farmhouse. To be used for the wine country sequences in the upcoming telefilm *Bodega Bay*. As you requested three sites has been selected for you to inspect on May 21.

Background. To prepare for this assignment I consulted Director Mario Polero who gave me his preferences for the sight. He wants a picturesque home, that is located near vineyards, moreover he would like woods in the background. I also consulted Producer Tucker Setterberg who told me that the site must accommodate 55 to 70 production crew members for approximately three weeks' of filming. Jocelyn Garcia who is our telefilm accountant requested that the cost of the site not exceed $24,000, for a three week lease.

Work Completed. For the past eight days I have searched the Niagara Peninsula in the southern Ontario wine country. Since this area is rich with history I was able to locate many possibilities including: turn-of-the-century estates, Victorian mansions and rustic farmhouses. One of the best sites are the Country Meadows Inn a 97 year old farmhouse, with a breathtaking view of vallies and woods. The most promising towns are the following Niagara-on-the-Lake, St. Catharines and Pelham.

Work to Be Completed. In the next few days I'll search the Ontario countryside, and inspect winerys such as: Jackson-Triggs, Hillebrand, and Inniskillin. Many of the older winerys has charming structures, however they also attract tourists, and crowds of people.

By May 14, you'll have my final report, that will describe the three better locations.

Software Unlimited

Interoffice Memo

DATE: February 3, 200x
TO: Doug Brent
FROM: Jennifer Tejada JT
SUBJECT: RECOMMENDED FREE EMAIL PROGRAMS

As you requested I am submitting this list of three of the best free email cites that I could find on the Web. All of the cites seems to provide basic email service with various features, however a few features are available only for a fee.

1. Gmail <www.gmail.com>

Gmail is quickly becoming one of the most popular free email programs on the Web. This program which has no pop-ups or banner ads offers many attractive features. In addition the number of features are growing everyday. The most-popular features are the following, 2500 megabytes of storage, spam protection, automatic forwarding and virus scanning.

Messages can even be sent and read in over 40 languages, some of which are: Arabic, Tagalog, Latvian and Portuguese. Gmail also offers an unique feature, that is, Gmail integrates instant messaging in to the email experience. In order to sign up for a Gmail account you must be invited by someone whom all ready has one.

2. Yahoo Mail <www.mail.yahoo.com>

Yahoo Mail is another free email service thats easy to use. In addition to email a Yahoo Mail account includes the following free features, spam protection, virus protection, 1 gigabyte of storage and access from anywhere a user has a web connection. For just $19.99 a year you can get a Yahoo Mail Plus account. This premium account offers: virus cleaning, SpamGuardPlus and 2 gigabytes of email storage.

3. Hotmail <www.hotmail.com>

Hotmail which is owned by Microsoft is a third free email program. This program offers: powerful spam filters, virus scanning and virus cleaning. When a user first enrols they receive 25 megabytes of storage, however, after 30 days this amount increases to 250 megabytes.

Gmail is the program I recommend, Yahoo Mail and Hotmail are not as robust. Be sure and check out these sites, and then let me know whether you have any question.

POSTTEST

Add appropriate semicolons, colons, and commas.

1. Gas prices have risen dramatically therefore more people are walking and riding their bikes.
2. The following instructors have been chosen to represent their schools at the professional meeting Ian Mason Cégep de Jonquière Patricia Parnall Sir Sandford Fleming College and Richard Almonte George Brown College.
3. All morning sessions begin at 9 a.m. all afternoon sessions begin at 1 p.m.
4. Because we have little time before the deadline we are forced to choose from among the leaders for example AT&T, Sprint, and WirelessWorld.
5. We feel however that more time should be allowed for major equipment purchase decisions.

learning.web.ways

You're now ready to hunt for a job, and you decide to start with online listings.

Goal: To learn to locate job listings.

1. With your web browser on the screen, key <**http://www.monster.ca**>.
2. Click on **Find Jobs** menu and bookmark **<http://jobsearch.monster.ca/>**.
3. In the **Find Jobs** panel, enter the job title of your choice in the **Keywords** box. Next, select the industry you are interested in from the drop-down menu under **Industries**.
4. Select the province, and enter the city where you would like to work. You can also specify the approximate area close to that city that would be acceptable to you. Finally, click the **Find Jobs** button.
5. Study the jobs listed and print this page. Click on one or more of the advertised vacancies, and print the page describing an open position you would like to apply for.

End your session and submit the two printed pages.

1. dramatically; therefore, 2. meeting: Mason, Jonquière; Parnall, College; Almonte, 3. 9 a.m.; 4. deadline, leaders; for example, 5. feel, however,

CHAPTER

Other Punctuation 18

OBJECTIVES When you have completed the materials in this chapter, you will be able to do the following:

LEVEL I

- *Use periods to correctly punctuate statements, commands, indirect questions, and polite requests.*
- *Use periods to correctly punctuate abbreviations, initials, and numerals.*
- *Use question marks and exclamation points correctly.*

LEVEL II

- *Recognize acceptable applications of dashes and parentheses.*
- *Explain when to use commas, dashes, or parentheses to set off non-essential material.*
- *Correctly punctuate and capitalize material set off by parentheses and dashes.*

LEVEL III

- *Use double and single quotation marks properly.*
- *Correctly place other punctuation marks in relation to quotation marks.*
- *Use brackets, underscores, and italics appropriately.*

PRETEST

Use proofreading marks to insert appropriate punctuation in the following sentences.

1. Will you please send certificates to Wanda Allenton and PM Brin
2. Dr Lee Ms Adams and Mr Simon have been appointed to the YMCA committee
3. Cellphones pagers personal organizers these are some of the most frequently used mobile communication devices.

continued

PRETEST

4. The chapter entitled Telecommunication Today was the best one in the book Current Office Technology
5. Did Professor Scholl say There will be no class Tuesday

This chapter teaches you how to use periods, question marks, and exclamation points correctly. It also includes guidelines for punctuating with dashes, parentheses, single and double quotation marks, brackets, and underscores or italics.

LEVEL I

▶ Uses for the Period

The period is used to punctuate sentences, abbreviations, and numerals. Guidelines for each use are covered in this section.

To Punctuate Statements, Commands, and Indirect Questions

Most sentences in business and professional writing end with periods. Use a period at the end of a statement, a command, or an indirect question.

> Ali Mazahri was promoted to a position with increased salary and responsibilities. (Statement)
> Send our latest catalogue and price list to them. (Command)
> Marilyn asked whether we had sent the price list. (Indirect question)

To Punctuate Polite Requests

Use a period, not a question mark, at the end of a command phrased as a polite request. Although such a request may have the appearance of a question, it asks the reader to perform a specific action instead of responding with a *yes* or a *no.*

> Could you please check the latest prices on MP3 players.
> May I suggest that you follow the instructions on page 6 of your manual.
> Will you be sure to lock the door when you leave.

If you are uncomfortable using a period at the end of a polite request, rephrase the sentence so that it is more clearly a command.

> Will you please mail your cheque in the enclosed envelope. (Polite request)
> Please mail your cheque in the enclosed envelope. (Polite request rephrased as a command)

Hotlink

If your learning style is visual, you may find the following Punctuation Pattern Sheet from University College of the Fraser Valley very helpful. Print it out from **<http://www.ucfv.ca/writing_centre/Resources/Punctuation.htm>**.

Study Tip

Never use more than one punctuation mark to end a sentence. If the sentence ends with an abbreviation, only one period is needed.

1. P.M. Brin. 2. Dr. Lee, Ms. Adams, Mr. committee. 3. Cellphones, pagers, personal organizers—these devices. 4. "Telecommunication Today" Current Office Technology. 5. say, "There Tuesday"?

To Punctuate Abbreviations

Because of their inconsistencies, abbreviations sometimes present problems to writers. The following suggestions will help you organize certain groups of abbreviations and will provide many models. In studying these models, note the spacing, capitalization, and use of periods. Always consult an up-to-date dictionary or style manual when in doubt.

Use periods after most abbreviations beginning with lower case letters.

a.m. (ante meridiem)	p.m. (post meridiem)
doz. (dozen)	i.e. (that is)
e.g. (for example)	in. (inch or inches)

Use periods for most abbreviations containing both capital and lower case letters.

Dr. (Doctor)	No. (Number)
Esq. (Esquire)	Rev. (Reverend)
Ms. (blend of Miss and Mrs.)	Sat. (Saturday)
Mr. (Mister)	

Use periods with abbreviations that represent academic degrees and initials of a person's first and middle names.

B.A. (bachelor of arts)	M.D. (doctor of medicine)
M.B.A. (master of business administration)	Ph.D. (doctor of philosophy)
	Mr. J. A. Jones (initials)

Do *not* use periods or internal spaces for most capitalized abbreviations.

CBC (Canadian Broadcasting Corporation)	MBE (Member of the Order of the British Empire)
CEO (chief executive officer)	RAM (random-access memory)
CFO (chief financial officer)	RRSP (Registered Retirement Savings Plan)
CPU (central processing unit)	SASE (self-addressed, stamped envelope)
EST (Eastern Standard Time)	SIDS (sudden infant death syndrome)
FYI (for your information)	SOP (standard operating procedure)
IBM (International Business Machines)	UNEF (United Nations Emergency Force)
ID (identification)	URL (Universal Resource Locator)

Study Tip

Most abbreviations fall into this group. Note capitalized letters, lack of periods, and tight spacing.

Do *not* confuse metric symbols with abbreviations. As symbols, they require no periods.

cm (centimetre/s)	km (kilometre/s)
g (gram/s)	m (metre/s)
kg (kilogram/s)	mm (millimetre/s)

To Punctuate Numerals

For a monetary sum use a period (decimal point) to separate dollars from cents.

The two items in question, $13.92 and $98.07, were both charged in the month of October.

Use a period (decimal point) to mark a decimal fraction.

Only 38.6 per cent of registered voters actually voted in Wednesday's election.

Hotlink

To review commas and master other punctuation rules, consult the University of Western Ontario's web page at **<http://instruct.uwo.ca/writing/wg/module3.htm>**.

▶ Uses for the Question Mark

To Punctuate Direct Questions

Use a question mark at the end of a direct question.

Have you sent the price list?
What can we do to improve communications among departments?

To Punctuate Questions Appended to Statements

Place a question mark after a question that is appended to a statement (a tag question). Use a comma to separate the statement from the question.

Starbucks offers wireless Internet networks in some locations, doesn't it?
This personnel announcement should be sent by email, don't you think?

To Indicate Doubt

A question mark within parentheses may be used to indicate a degree of doubt about some aspect of a statement.

After the dot-com was launched (2001?), it immediately experienced financial difficulties.

The position carries a substantial monthly salary ($3500?), but no candidates have applied.

Study Tip

Don't be tempted to punctuate statements as questions. For example, "I wonder whether he called" is a statement, not a question.

▶ Uses for the Exclamation Point

The exclamation point is an emphatic mark of punctuation reserved for strong feelings. It is seldom seen in professional or academic writing.

To Express Strong Emotion

After a word, phrase, or clause expressing strong emotion, use an exclamation point.

Impossible! We understood the deadline to be tomorrow.
What a day! It seems as though closing time will never come.
It is incredible that my watch is still working after such punishment!

Do not use an exclamation point after mild interjections such as *oh* and *well*.

Well, it seems we have little choice in the matter.

Complete the reinforcement exercises for Level I on pp. 354–355.

LEVEL II

▶ Uses for the Dash

The dash is a legitimate and effective mark of punctuation when used according to accepted conventions. As an emphatic punctuation mark, however, the dash loses effectiveness when it is overused. With a word processor, a dash is formed by typing two hyphens with no space before, between, or after the hyphens. In printed or desktop publishing–generated material, a dash appears as a solid line (an *em* dash). Study the following suggestions for and illustrations of appropriate uses of the dash.

To Set Off Parenthetical Elements and Appositives

Within a sentence parenthetical elements are usually set off by commas. If, however, the parenthetical element itself contains internal commas, use dashes (or parentheses) to set it off.

> Sources of raw materials—farming, mining, fishing, and forestry—are all dependent on energy.
>
> Four efficient administrative assistants—Priscilla Alvarez, Vicky Evans, Yoshiki Ono, and Edward Botsko—received cash bonuses for outstanding service.

Hotlink

The University of Victoria Writer's Guide at **<http://web.uvic.ca/wguide/Pages/MasterToc.html>** has separate sections on parentheses and dashes at the bottom of the page. Follow the links.

To Indicate an Interruption

An interruption or abrupt change of thought may be separated from the rest of a sentence by a dash.

> The shipment will be on its way—you have my word—by Wednesday.
>
> Send the disks by Friday—no, we must have them by Thursday at the latest.

Sentences with abrupt changes of thought or with appended afterthoughts can usually be improved through rewriting.

To Set Off a Summarizing Statement

Use a dash (not a colon) to separate an introductory list from a summarizing statement.

> Variety of tasks, contact with people, opportunity for advancement—these are what I seek in a job.
>
> Cross-country skiing, hiking, and reading—those are Rudy's favourite pastimes.

Spot the Blooper

From a box of Post cereal: "Everyday's a new adventure with Katy."

To Attribute a Quotation

Place a dash between a quotation and its source.

> "English is the language of men ever famous and foremost in the achievements of liberty." — John Milton
>
> "Live as if you were to die tomorrow. Learn as if you were to live forever." — Mahatma Gandhi

▶ Uses for Parentheses

Parentheses are generally used in pairs to set off non-essential sentence elements. Careful writers avoid overusing parentheses because they may distract readers.

Study Tip

Parentheses say to the reader, "This is not too important; you can wait until you finish the sentence to read it." Dashes say, "Hey, this is important; pay attention!"

To Set Off Non-Essential Sentence Elements

Generally, non-essential sentence elements may be punctuated in three ways: (1) with commas, to make the lightest possible break in the normal flow of a sentence; (2) with dashes, to emphasize the enclosed material; and (3) with parentheses, to de-emphasize the enclosed material.

> One of the blueprints, which appears on page 7, shows the internal structure of the engine clearly. (Normal punctuation)
>
> One of the blueprints—which appears on page 7—shows the internal structure of the engine clearly. (Dashes emphasize enclosed material.)
>
> One of the blueprints (which appears on page 7) shows the internal structure of the engine clearly. (Parentheses de-emphasize enclosed material.)

Explanations, references, and directions are usually enclosed in parentheses when used as non-essential sentence elements.

> The bank's current business hours (10 a.m. to 3 p.m.) will be extended in the near future (to 6 p.m.).
>
> We recommend that you use hearing protectors (see our comment on p. 618) when using this electric drill.

Hotlink

Another handful of tips on punctuation can be found in the Study Write! Tips file on this Brock University site **<http://www.brocku.ca/sdc/learning/study_write_manual.php>**.

Punctuating Around Parentheses

If the material enclosed by parentheses is embedded within another sentence, a question mark or exclamation point may be used where normally expected. Do not, however, use a period after a statement embedded within another sentence.

> I visited the new business travel website (have you seen it?) last night. (A question mark concludes a question enclosed by parentheses and embedded in another sentence.)
>
> The fire alarm sounded (but no one responded!) during the middle of our final exam. (An exclamation mark concludes an exclamation enclosed by parentheses and embedded in another sentence.)
>
> An air conditioner cools space (this will be discussed in detail in the next chapter) by removing heat from it. (A period is not used at the end of a statement enclosed by parentheses and embedded in another sentence.)

Spot the Blooper

From an ad for PageMaker, a computer program: "It is still the most easiest program to learn yet the most powerful."

If the material enclosed by parentheses is not embedded in another sentence, use whatever punctuation is required. Note that the item in parentheses begins with a capital letter in this case.

> Report writers must document all references. (See the appendix for a guide to current documentation formats.)
>
> In less than ten years, the price of that article has tripled. (Who would have thought it possible?)

In sentences involving expressions within parentheses, a comma, semicolon, or colon that would normally occupy the position occupied by the second parenthesis is then placed after that parenthesis.

> When I return from my trip (in late June), I will begin work on the feasibility study. (Comma follows parenthesis.)
>
> Your application for a credit card was received before the deadline (November 1); however, you did not supply two financial references. (Semicolon follows parenthesis.)

Complete the reinforcement exercises for Level II on pp. 356–357.

LEVEL III

▶ Uses for Quotation Marks

Quotation marks help readers understand what words were written or spoken by somebody else. They may also be used to enclose short expressions, definitions, and titles.

To Enclose Direct Quotations

Double quotation marks are used to enclose direct quotations. Unless the exact words of a writer or speaker are being repeated, however, quotation marks are not employed.

> "There is a world market for about five computers," said IBM founder Thomas J. Watson. (Direct quotation enclosed.)
>
> Dwight Moody said that character is what you are in the dark. (Indirect quotation requires no quotation marks.)

Capitalize only the first word of a direct quotation.

> "The office staff," said Mrs. Rogers, "has now reached its full complement." (Do not capitalize the word *has*.)

To Enclose Quotations Within Quotations

Single quotation marks (apostrophes on most keyboards) are used to enclose quoted passages cited within quoted passages.

> Sharon Miles remarked, "In business writing I totally agree with Aristotle, who said, 'A good style must, first of all, be clear.'" (Single quotation marks within double quotation marks)

Hotlink

For a really extensive overview of punctuation, go to the Grammar Tutorials at the University of Calgary **<http://www.ucalgary.ca/UofC/eduweb/grammar>**.

To Enclose Short Expressions

Slang, words used in a special sense, and words following *stamped* or *marked* are enclosed within quotation marks.

> Cheryl feared that her presentation would "bomb." (Slang)
>
> In web terminology robots are referred to as "bots." (Word used in a special sense)
>
> The package was stamped "Handle with Care." (Words following *stamped*)

To Enclose Definitions

Quotation marks are used to enclose formal definitions of words or expressions. The word or expression being defined should be underscored or set in italics.

> The Latin word *ergo* means "therefore" or "hence."
>
> Business people use the term *working capital* to indicate an "excess of current assets over current debts."

To Enclose Titles

Quotation marks are used to enclose titles of subdivisions of literary and artistic works such as magazine and newspaper articles, book chapters, poems, lectures, TV show episodes, and songs. However, titles of entire books, magazines, pamphlets, newspapers, plays, movies, music albums, and television series are set in italics (or underscored).

> Office administration students should familiarize themselves with the section of *The Gregg Reference Manual* entitled "Glossary of Computer and Internet Terms."
>
> One source of information for your term paper might be the magazine article "Cross-Training of Key Personnel," which appeared in *Newsweek*.
>
> In the episode of *The Office* titled "Diversity Day," the boss, played by Steve Carell, managed to offend everyone.

Spot the Blooper

Toilet tissue advertisement heard on the radio: "For less changes, double your Royale."

Study Tip

In North American style, periods and commas are always inside quotation marks. Semicolons and colons are always outside. Question marks and exclamation points depend on the material quoted.

Punctuating Around Quotation Marks

Periods and commas are always placed inside closing quotation marks, whether single or double. Semicolons and colons are, on the other hand, always placed outside quotation marks.

> Betty Pearman said, "I'm sure the package was marked 'Fragile.'"
> The article is entitled "Bad Business of Banks," but we can't locate the magazine in which it appeared.
> The contract stipulated that "both parties must accept arbitration as binding"; therefore, the decision reached by the arbitrators is final.
> Three dates have been scheduled for the seminar called "Successful E-Business": April 1, May 3, and June 5.

Question marks and exclamation points may go inside or outside closing quotation marks, as determined by the form of the quotation.

> Jeanette said, "How may I apply for that position?" (Quotation itself is a question; question mark goes inside quotation marks.)
> "The next time your cellphone rings," fumed Mr. Bradley, "we will ask you to leave!" (Quotation is an exclamation.)
> Do you know who it was who said, "Money is more trouble than it's worth"? (Incorporating sentence asks question; quotation does not.)
> I can't believe that the cheque was stamped "Insufficient Funds"! (Incorporating sentence is an exclamation; quotation is not.)
> When did the manager say, "Who wants to reserve a summer vacation?" (Both incorporating sentence and quotation are questions. Use only one question mark inside the quotation marks.)

Hotlink

Another thorough overview of punctuation comes in the PowerPoint Presentation you can download from St. Francis Xavier University at **<http://people.stfx.ca/nmarenic/>**.

▶ Uses for Brackets

Within quotations, brackets are used by writers to enclose their own inserted remarks. Such remarks may be corrective, illustrative, or explanatory. Brackets are also used within quotations to enclose the word *sic*, which means "thus" or "so." This Latin word is used to emphasize the fact that an obvious error actually appears *thus* in the quoted material.

> "A British imperial gallon," reported Miss Sedgewick, "is equal to 1.2 US gallons [4.54 litres]."
> "The company's reorganization program," wrote President Theodore Bailey, "will have its greatest affect [*sic*] on our immediate sales."

▶ Uses for Italics

Study Tip

With today's sophisticated software programs, you can, like professional printers, use italics instead of underscoring for titles and special words.

Italics (or underscore if italics are not accessible) are normally used for titles of books, magazines, newspapers, and other complete works published separately, as already mentioned. In addition, words under discussion in a sentence and used as nouns are italicized.

> *Creative Financing*, a book by Thomas Manley, was favourably reviewed in *The Wall Street Journal*.
> Two of the most frequently misspelled words are *calendar* and *separate*. (Words under discussion used as nouns.)

Complete the reinforcement exercises for Level III on pp. 358–359.

HOTLINE QUERIES

Question: We can't decide whether a period should go inside quotation marks or outside. At the end of a sentence, I have typed the title "Positive Vs. Negative Values." The author of the document I'm typing wants the period outside because she says the title does not have a period in it.

Answer: When a period or comma falls at the same place quotation marks would normally fall, the period or comma is always placed inside the quotation marks, regardless of the content of the quotation. (In Britain a different style is observed; a few Canadian writers may use that style.)

Question: I'm not sure where to place the question mark in this sentence: *His topic will be "What Is a Good Health Plan (?)"* Does the question mark go inside the quotation marks? Also, should a comma precede the title of the talk?

Answer: First, the question mark goes inside the quotation mark because the quoted material is in the form of a question. Be sure that you do not use another end punctuation mark after the quotation mark. Second, do not use a comma preceding the title because the sentence follows normal subject-verb-complement order. No comma is needed to separate the verb and the complement.

Question: Is it correct to say *Brad and myself were chosen ... ?*

Answer: No. Use the subjective-case pronoun *I* instead of *myself.*

Question: What salutation should I use when addressing a letter to Sister Mary Elizabeth?

Answer: The salutation of your letter should be *Dear Sister Mary Elizabeth.* For more information on forms of address, consult a good dictionary or reference manual.

Question: Is anything wrong with saying *someone else's car*?

Answer: Although it may sound somewhat awkward, this possessive form is acceptable. The apostrophe is correctly placed in *else's.*

Question: I've looked in the dictionary, but I'm still unsure about whether to hyphenate *stepsister.*

Answer: Do not hyphenate family terms containing the prefixes *step* or *grand* (*stepsister, stepdaughter, granddaughter*). Always hyphenate such terms involving the prefix *great* or the suffix *in-law* (*great-uncle, son-in-law, brother-in-law*). In reading your dictionary, notice that centred periods are used to indicate syllables (grand·moth·er); hyphens are used to show hyphenated syllables (*great-aunt*).

Question: Can you tell me what sounds strange in this sentence and why? *The building looks like it was redesigned.*

Answer: The word *like* should not be used as a conjunction, as has been done in your sentence. Substitute *as if* (*the building looks as if it was redesigned*).

Question: I have a phone extension at work, and I often want to tell people to call me at this extension. Can I abbreviate the word *extension*? If so, what is the proper abbreviation?

Answer: The abbreviation for extension is *Ext.* Notice that the abbreviation is capitalized and ends with a period. When you use this abbreviation in conjunction with a phone number, place a comma before and after *(To reserve your spot, please call me at 685-1230, Ext. 2306, before November 30.)*

NAME ______________________________

CHAPTER 18 **Reinforcement Exercises**

LEVEL I

A. (Self-check) In the spaces provided after each sentence, indicate whether a period, question mark, or exclamation point is needed. Use the symbol. If no additional punctuation is required, write *C*.

Example: May I please have your answer by return mail⊙ ____⊙____

1. Would you give me your latest price figure for a ream of 16-pound bond paper ________
2. What a fantastic presentation ________
3. The meeting is at 2 p.m., isn't it ________
4. Has anyone checked the FedEx site to see whether our package was delivered ________
5. Send for your complimentary brochure today ________
6. Help! Smoke is coming from my keyboard ________
7. Juanita asked if she should come in at 7 a.m. to complete the work for LaserPro Ltd. ________
8. Oh, I don't believe we should worry about it at this time ________
9. I wonder whether he received my email message ________
10. Will you please keep one copy and return the other to me ________

Check your answers.

B. In the following sentences all punctuation has been omitted. Insert commas, periods, question marks, colons, and exclamation points. The words have extra space between them so that punctuation may be inserted easily. Use a caret (^) to indicate most insertions. In the space at the right, indicate the number of punctuation marks inserted. Consult a dictionary or a reference manual for abbreviation style if necessary.

Example: Will you please add Mr⊙ T⊙ G⊙ Skaggs Jr⊙ to the address list⊙ ____5____

1. I wonder if William R Templeton was hired as C I O at Intel, Inc ________
2. Common abbreviations like a m and p m often appear in business correspondence ________
3. Dr Iva Jeffreys was recently named C E O at Laurentian Enterprises ________
4. He did list his résumé on the Monster.ca site didn't he ________
5. It was Miss Jenkins not Mrs Reed who was appointed educational consultant to the C N I B ________
6. What a dilemma the latest C R T C regulations have created ________

1. . 2. ! 3. ? 4. ? 5. . 6. ! 7. C 8. . 9. . 10. .

7. Stop That's an emergency exit ____________

8. Deliver the signed contracts to Mr C P Ryan before 5 p m ____________

9. If I B M offers a full-service contract we would be interested ____________

10. What a great story on the C B C news ____________

11. Darren asked if most automobiles were delivered f o b Windsor ____________

12. I sent my congratulations on the completion of Peter's M B A degree ____________

13. The Toronto office pipes in radio station C F R B because the manager Ms Buckley prefers that station ____________

14. Does he often use the abbreviations e g and i e in his email messages ____________

15. Will you please R S V P before Friday September 30 ____________

16. Some authorities wonder if the I Q of school-age children is affected by T V ____________

17. Has the erroneous charge of $45 95 been removed from my account ____________

18. The guest list includes the following individuals Dr Lyn Clark Ms Deborah Kitchin and Professor Marilyne Hudgens ____________

19. Dan wondered whether he had fulfilled the requirements for his certificate ____________

20. Why we have not heard from the C F O is a mystery to me ____________

21. You did change your P I N as the bank requested didn't you ____________

22. Among the speakers are Michael Hartman M D and Gail Nemire R N (*Don't forget the commas.*) ____________

23. Since the funds were earned in the U K I must consult my C A about paying Canadian taxes ____________

24. Virginia T Laws Ph D who is a well-known communications consultant will address the group at 10 a m ____________

25. Wow I have finally finished this exercise ____________

NAME ______________________________

LEVEL II

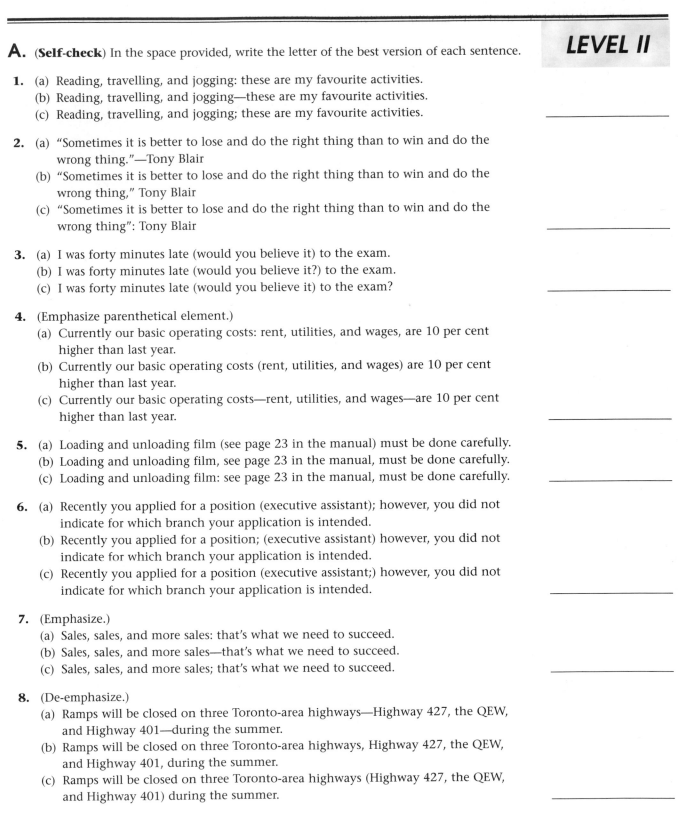

A. (**Self-check**) In the space provided, write the letter of the best version of each sentence.

1. (a) Reading, travelling, and jogging: these are my favourite activities.
(b) Reading, travelling, and jogging—these are my favourite activities.
(c) Reading, travelling, and jogging; these are my favourite activities. ______

2. (a) "Sometimes it is better to lose and do the right thing than to win and do the wrong thing."—Tony Blair
(b) "Sometimes it is better to lose and do the right thing than to win and do the wrong thing," Tony Blair
(c) "Sometimes it is better to lose and do the right thing than to win and do the wrong thing": Tony Blair ______

3. (a) I was forty minutes late (would you believe it) to the exam.
(b) I was forty minutes late (would you believe it?) to the exam.
(c) I was forty minutes late (would you believe it) to the exam? ______

4. (Emphasize parenthetical element.)
(a) Currently our basic operating costs: rent, utilities, and wages, are 10 per cent higher than last year.
(b) Currently our basic operating costs (rent, utilities, and wages) are 10 per cent higher than last year.
(c) Currently our basic operating costs—rent, utilities, and wages—are 10 per cent higher than last year. ______

5. (a) Loading and unloading film (see page 23 in the manual) must be done carefully.
(b) Loading and unloading film, see page 23 in the manual, must be done carefully.
(c) Loading and unloading film: see page 23 in the manual, must be done carefully. ______

6. (a) Recently you applied for a position (executive assistant); however, you did not indicate for which branch your application is intended.
(b) Recently you applied for a position; (executive assistant) however, you did not indicate for which branch your application is intended.
(c) Recently you applied for a position (executive assistant;) however, you did not indicate for which branch your application is intended. ______

7. (Emphasize.)
(a) Sales, sales, and more sales: that's what we need to succeed.
(b) Sales, sales, and more sales—that's what we need to succeed.
(c) Sales, sales, and more sales; that's what we need to succeed. ______

8. (De-emphasize.)
(a) Ramps will be closed on three Toronto-area highways—Highway 427, the QEW, and Highway 401—during the summer.
(b) Ramps will be closed on three Toronto-area highways, Highway 427, the QEW, and Highway 401, during the summer.
(c) Ramps will be closed on three Toronto-area highways (Highway 427, the QEW, and Highway 401) during the summer. ______

Check your answers.

1.b 2.a 3.b 4.c 5.a 6.a 7.b 8.c

B. Insert dashes or parentheses in the following sentences. In the space provided after each sentence, write the number of punctuation marks you inserted. Count each parenthesis and each dash as a single mark.

Example: (Emphasize.) Three of the biggest problems with email -- privacy, overuse, and etiquette -- will be discussed. 2

1. (De-emphasize.) The Tony-award-winning production of *The History Boys* have you seen the reviews will be opening here shortly. ______
2. Fingerprints, mug shots, and arrest records these are now stored on microforms by law enforcement officers. ______
3. "Over 60 per cent of management problems result from faulty communications." Peter Drucker ______
4. (Emphasize.) Three branch assistant managers Augusta Jones, James Redman, and Candi Herman will be promoted this month. ______
5. (De-emphasize.) Three branch assistant managers Augusta Jones, James Redman, and Candi Herman will be promoted this month. ______
6. (De-emphasize.) As soon as you are able to make an appointment try to do so before December 30, we will process your insurance forms. ______
7. Voice recorder, photo album, laser pointer, language translator these are just some of the ways an iPod can be used. ______
8. Funds for the project will be released on the following dates see Section 12.3 of the original grant : January 1, March 14, and June 30. ______
9. (De-emphasize.) Although one of the traditionally favoured teams England, Germany, Italy, or Brazil will probably win the World Cup, the host country is always a sentimental favourite. ______
10. The BlackBerry warranty contract is limited to sixty 60 days. ______

C. Using three different forms of punctuation, correctly punctuate the following sentence. In the space provided, explain how the three methods you have employed differ.

1. Numerous considerations all of which are fully described in our report prompted the closure of the outlet.
2. Numerous considerations all of which are fully described in our report prompted the closure of the outlet.
3. Numerous considerations all of which are fully described in our report prompted the closure of the outlet.

Explanation: ______

NAME ______________________________

LEVEL III

A. (**Self-check**) Indicate whether the following statements are true (*T*) or false (*F*).

1. Double quotation marks are used to enclose the exact words of a writer or speaker. ____________

2. The names of books, magazines, movies, and newspapers should be enclosed in quotation marks. ____________

3. Periods and commas are always placed inside closing quotation marks. ____________

4. Brackets are used by writers to enclose their own remarks inserted into a quotation. ____________

5. A quotation within a quotation is shown with single quotation marks. ____________

6. Semicolons and colons are always placed inside closing quotation marks. ____________

7. Titles of articles, book chapters, poems, and songs should be either italicized or underlined. ____________

8. If both a quotation and its introductory sentence are questions, use a question mark before the closing quotation marks. ____________

9. The word *sic* is used to show that a quotation is free of errors. ____________

10. A single quotation mark is typed by using the apostrophe key. ____________

Check your answers.

B. Many, but not all, of the following sentences contain direct quotations. Insert all necessary punctuation. Underlines may be used for words that would be italicized in print.

Example: (ital) The word asset means “an item of monetary value.”

1. I have yet to hear a man, said Gloria Steinem, ask for advice on how to combine marriage and a career

2. Careful speakers use the word mad to mean insane

3. Dr Graham’s chapter entitled Drawing the World Together appeared in the book Global Links

4. Did Donald Trump really say Anyone who thinks my story is anywhere near over is sadly mistaken

5. In his speech the software billionaire said Our goal is to link the world irregardless *sic* of national boundaries and restrictions

6. Oprah Winfrey said that the best jobs are those we’d do even if we didn’t get paid

7. When Garth began shouting during the argument his friend Kendra told him to chill

1.T 2.F 3.T 4.T 5.T 6.F 7.F 8.T 9.F 10.T

8. The postal worker said Shall I stamp your package Fragile

9. Did you see the article What People Earn in last week's Parade magazine

10. The expression persona non grata means one who is not acceptable

11. After banging on the elevator doors repeatedly Mrs Lowe shouted Please help us

12. Has anyone seen the extra copy of the sheet music for All You Need Is Love

13. The title of the article is Automation in the Office however the author may change the title later

14. In the arena of human life said Aristotle the honours and rewards fall to those who show their good qualities in action

15. In BusinessWeek I saw an article titled Communication for Global Markets

C. Insert all necessary punctuation. These sentences review Levels I, II, III.

1. Would you please send a copy of the current catalogue to Globex Ltd

2. Eating studying and working these are Mike's principal activities

3. Removing the back panel see the warning on page 1 should be done only by authorized repair staff

4. (Emphasize.) Two of our best researchers Darlene McClure and Judith Ehresman were hired by our competitor

5. (De-emphasize.) Four features maps, instant messaging, web searching, and email are what consumers want most on their cellphones

6. (Direct quote.) Was it President Martin who said What can't be cured must be endured

7. The word copyright literally means right to copy

8. Mary Gooderham's fascinating article on virtual reality in The Globe and Mail was entitled The Next Best Thing to Being

9. The envelope marked Confidential was delivered to the wrong office

10. (Direct quote.) Did Alicia say Where is our supply of printer cartridges

D. **Optional Writing.** On a separate sheet, type or write a paragraph describing your ideal job. Try to include as many of the punctuation marks you have studied as possible. Include commas, semicolons, periods, question marks, exclamation points, dashes, parentheses, quotation marks, italics, and possibly even brackets. Include a quotation from your boss. Make up the name of a book or article that you could publish about this job.

Editor's Challenge

The following letters contain intentional errors in concepts you have studied thus far. They also contain a few spelling errors. Use standard proofreading marks to show all necessary corrections. Notice that the first letter is addressed to a company; hence the writer doesn't know whom to address in the salutation. The simplified style avoids this problem.

GLOBAL IMPORTERS INC.
814 John Street, Suite 205
Kelowna, BC V1Y 5S7

May 15, 200x

West Coast Foods Ltd
729 Leland Street
Maple Ridge, BC. V2X 7L3

YOUR MAY 3 PURCHASE ORDER NO 14902

All the in stock items requested in your recent purchase order were ship to you Friday May 8 from our Vancouver warehouse.

Because of unseasonably wet weather in February; this springs supply of black teas from Sri Lanka are extremely limited. We have none of these fine tea on hand at present, however, we expect a small shipment to arrive by August 1.

We do have in our warehouse a stock of select black teas from the following sources, south China Japan and south India. Indian teas as you are well aware do not always meet some of our customers high standards. Which is why we hesitate to advice you to except the Indian tea as a substitute. Chinese and Japanese teas though are generally well regarded.

In fact one of our customers recently said "Our best sales are now from Chinese black tea. Another importer wrote "We are delighted with the recent shipment of Japanese black tea". Moreover an article in the January 8 issue of The Globe and Mail described the healthful affects of Japanese tea.

Please call us toll free at 1-800-321-8993 to tell us whether you wish to wait for the Sri Lankan black tea or whether you prefer the immediate supply of black tea from: China, Japan, or India.

BRIAN W. LEE, MANAGER

2419 Branch Lane SW
Calgary, AB T2W 3L1
August 23, 200x

Mr. Doug Young, Manager
Longhorn Grill
3210 South Homer Avenue SE
Calgary, AB T2P ON5

Dear Mr. Young,

Even when us servers has given good service some customers don't leave a tip. This is a serious problem for we servers at Longhorn Grill. Many of us has gotten together and decided to bring the problem—and a possible solution, to your attention in this letter. Please read our ideas carefully, then plan on meeting with us to discuss them.

Some restaurants (such as the Coach House in Toronto—now automatically adds a 15 per cent tip to the bill. Other restaurants are printing gratuity guideline's on checks. In fact American Express now provides a calculation feature on it's terminals so that restaurants can chose the tip levels they want printed. The following tip levels are included; 10, 15, or 20 per cent. You can read about these procedures in an article titled Forcing the Tip, which appeared recently in "The New York Times." Ive enclosed a copy.

A mandatory tip printed on checks would work good at Longhorn don't you think. We give good service and receive many complements, however, some customers forget to tip. By printing a suggested tip on the check we remind customers so that they won't forget. A printed mandatory tip also does the math for customers which is an advantage for those who are not to good with figures!

Printing mandatory tips on checks not only help customers but also prove to the staff that you support them in there goal to recieve decent wages for the hard work they do. A few customers might complain but these customers can always cross out the printed tip if they wish. If you have any doubts about the plan we could try it for a six month period and monitor customer's reactions.

We urge you to begin printing a mandatory 15 per cent tip on each customers bill. Our American Express terminals are already equipped to do this. Will you please let us know your feelings about this proposal as soon as possible. Its a serious concern to we servers.

Sincerely,

Brenda Stewart

Brenda Stewart
Server

Enclosure

POSTTEST

Use proofreading marks to insert necessary punctuation.

1. Will you please send me a copy of the article entitled Winning Negotiation Strategies
2. When did we receive this package marked Confidential
3. The only guests who have not sent RSVPs are Miss Lee Mrs Gold and Mr Sims
4. The word principal was misused in the chapter entitled Writing Persuasive Letters
5. Did Dr Simanic say "I'd like to put you on an exercise program"

learning.web.ways

More and more companies are beginning to require electronic résumés from job applicants. To prepare yourself for your job search, you decide to learn more about scannable résumés.

Goal: To learn about scannable résumés.

1. With your browser on the screen, go to the York University Career Centre guidelines for students and new graduates at **<http://www.yorku.ca/careers/jsm/resumesscannable.htm>**.
2. Read the information on scannable résumés. What guidelines should you observe in preparing one?
3. Bookmark this page, and print out the step-by-step instructions for creating a scannable résumé.
4. To download a sample scannable résumé, go to **<www.sass.uottawa.ca/careers/resources/resumes/scannable_resume_en.pdf>**.
5. Print it out. What is distinctive about the model you have downloaded?
6. Note the keywords used in the sample résumé. What keywords can you devise for your own résumé?
7. End your session and submit your printouts.

1. "Winning Negotiation Strategies." 2. "Confidential"? 3. Lee, Mrs. Gold, Mr. Sims.
4. principal "Writing Persuasive Letters." 5. Dr. say, "program"?

NAME ____________________

UNIT 5 REVIEW Chapters 16–18 (Self-Check)

First, review Chapters 16 through 18. Then, test your comprehension of those chapters by completing the exercises that follow and comparing your responses with those shown at the end of the book on p. 554.

LEVEL I

Insert necessary punctuation in the following sentences. Write *C* if the sentence is correct.

1. Under no circumstances Mr. Greenwood will your complaints be disregarded. ________

2. However the matter is resolved, the goodwill of the customer is paramount. ________

3. Tod Sizer a researcher at Bell Labs is developing ways to read cellphone signals bounced off the body. ________

4. A student who studies diligently and masters the principles will score well on the examination. ________

5. Our management team feels on the other hand that it must hold the line on benefits and salaries. ________

6. The sales representative Walter S. Anderson presented a thorough report. ________

7. Sears offers a discount of 10 per cent and also a cash rebate of more than $50 for each purchase. ________

8. The best time to ask for a raise is at 9 a.m. in the middle of the work week or at 1 p.m. after your boss has had lunch. ________

9. Because employers want to hire the right people many conduct web searches to learn more about job candidates. ________

Select (a), (b), or (c) to indicate the correctly punctuated sentence.

10. (a) Some of the equipment is stored in the warehouse other equipment is now in transit.
(b) Some of the equipment is stored in the warehouse, other equipment is now in transit.
(c) Some of the equipment is stored in the warehouse; other equipment is now in transit. ________

11. (a) Seminar participants are arriving from Calgary, Alberta, Regina, Saskatchewan, and Winnipeg, Manitoba.
(b) Seminar participants are arriving from Calgary, Alberta; Regina, Saskatchewan; and Winnipeg, Manitoba.
(c) Seminar participants are arriving from Calgary; Alberta; Regina; Saskatchewan; and Winnipeg; Manitoba. ________

12. (a) Investments should turn a profit; however, security is also important.
(b) Investments should turn a profit, however, security is also important.
(c) Investments should turn a profit; however security is also important. ________

13. (a) Would you please check the BBB website.
(b) Would you please check the B.B.B. website.
(c) Would you please check the BBB website? ________

LEVEL II

Select (a), (b), or (c) to indicate the best version of each sentence.

14. (a) When I last saw him (in late June?), he agreed to my salary increase.
(b) When I last saw him (in late June) he agreed to my salary increase.
(c) When I last saw him (in late June); he agreed to my salary increase. ________

15. (a) It was investigated by the R.C.M.P., wasn't it?
(b) It was investigated by the RCMP, wasn't it?
(c) It was investigated by the RCMP wasn't it? ________

16. (a) Wow! A total of 89.9 per cent of the voters approved!
(b) Wow, a total of 89 point 9 per cent of the voters approved!
(c) Wow. A total of 89.9 per cent of the voters approved! ________

17. (a) We are looking for three qualities in an employee; honesty, intelligence, and experience.
(b) We are looking for three qualities in an employee, honesty, intelligence, and experience.
(c) We are looking for three qualities in an employee: honesty, intelligence, and experience. ________

18. (a) Thus far, we have received brochures from Compaq, IBM, and Dell.
(b) Thus far, we have received brochures from, Compaq, IBM, and Dell.
(c) Thus far, we have received brochures from: Compaq, IBM, and Dell. ________

19. (a) Mr. Jenkins said, "We used to depend on fixed-rate mortgages."
(b) Mr. Jenkins said: "We used to depend on fixed-rate mortgages."
(c) Mr. Jenkins said; "We used to depend on fixed-rate mortgages." ________

20. (a) The spokesperson compared three other railways: Canadian National, Canadian Pacific, and Amtrak, with VIA Rail.
(b) The spokesperson compared three other railways—Canadian National, Canadian Pacific, and Amtrak—with VIA Rail.
(c) The spokesperson compared three other railways, Canadian National, Canadian Pacific, and Amtrak, with VIA Rail. ________

21. (a) Citigroup, General Electric, Bank of America, AIG, and HSBC—these are the five largest companies in the world.
(b) Citigroup, General Electric, Bank of America, AIG, and HSBC: these are the five largest companies in the world.
(c) Citigroup, General Electric, Bank of America, AIG, and HSBC, these are the five largest companies in the world. ________

22. (Emphasize.)
(a) Three airlines, Cathay Pacific, Singapore Airlines, and Thai Airways, offer the best first-class service.
(b) Three airlines: Cathay Pacific, Singapore Airlines, and Thai Airways, offer the best first-class service.
(c) Three airlines—Cathay Pacific, Singapore Airlines, and Thai Airways—offer the best first-class service. ________

23. (a) Notable members of the fund's honorary committee have been June Callwood, St. Clair Balfour, and Paul Beeston.
(b) Notable members of the fund's honorary committee have been: June Callwood, St. Clair Balfour, and Paul Beeston.
(c) Notable members of the fund's honorary committee have been—June Callwood, St. Clair Balfour, and Paul Beeston. ____________

24. (a) A pilot project—refer to page 6 of the report—may help us justify the new system.
(b) A pilot project, refer to page 6 of the report, may help us justify the new system.
(c) A pilot project (refer to page 6 of the report) may help us justify the new system. ____________

LEVEL III

Select (a), (b), or (c) to indicate the correctly punctuated sentence.

25. (a) In short: employees must be extremely courteous.
(b) In short—employees must be extremely courteous.
(c) In short, employees must be extremely courteous. ____________

26. (a) Our goal is to encourage, not hamper, good communication.
(b) Our goal is to encourage—not hamper, good communication.
(c) Our goal is to encourage, not hamper good communication. ____________

27. (a) Only one department submitted its report on time, namely the Legal Department.
(b) Only one department submitted its report on time, namely, the Legal Department.
(c) Only one department submitted its report on time: namely the Legal Department. ____________

28. (a) The location of the convention has been narrowed to three sites, namely, Victoria, Vancouver, and Seattle.
(b) The location of the convention has been narrowed to three sites; namely, Victoria, Vancouver, and Seattle.
(c) The location of the convention has been narrowed to three sites; namely Victoria, Vancouver, and Seattle. ____________

29. (a) The computer was producing "garbage," that is, the screen showed gibberish.
(b) The computer was producing "garbage"; that is, the screen showed gibberish.
(c) The computer was producing "garbage;" that is, the screen showed gibberish. ____________

30. (a) A cartel is defined as a "group of companies acting to control prices."
(b) A "cartel" is defined as a 'group of companies acting to control prices.'
(c) A *cartel* is defined as a "group of companies acting to control prices." ____________

31. (a) The Economist, a British magazine, featured an article called "Of Gambling, Grannies, and Good Sense."
(b) *The Economist,* a British magazine, featured an article called "Of Gambling, Grannies, and Good Sense."
(c) "The Economist," a British magazine, featured an article called *Of Gambling, Grannies, and Good Sense.* ____________

32. (a) "An ombudsman, said Sally Sirakides, is an individual hired by management to investigate and resolve employee complaints."
(b) "An ombudsman," said Sally Sirakides, "Is an individual hired by management to investigate and resolve employee complaints."
(c) "An ombudsman," said Sally Sirakides, "is an individual hired by management to investigate and resolve employee complaints." __________

33. (a) Who was it who said, "A penny saved is a penny earned."?
(b) Who was it who said, "A penny saved is a penny earned?"
(c) Who was it who said, "A penny saved is a penny earned"? __________

34. (a) J. Paul Buscher said, "I've never had a bad day; some days are just better than others."
(b) J. Paul Buscher said; "I've never had a bad day, some days are just better than others."
(c) J. Paul Buscher said, "I've never had a bad day some days are just better than others." __________

35. (a) Did the office manager really say, "Stamp this package 'Confidential'?"
(b) Did the office manager really say, "Stamp this package 'Confidential'"?
(c) Did the office manager really say, "Stamp this package "Confidential"? __________

Hotline Review

Write the letter of the word or phrase that correctly completes each sentence.

36. Every measure has been taken to (a) ensure, (b) insure your safety. __________

37. Because few shareholders were (a) appraised, (b) apprised of the CEO's total salary package, no complaints were heard. __________

38. My partner and (a) I, (b) me, (c) myself have signed an agreement. __________

39. The bulk of the estate was left to the woman's (a) stepdaughter, (b) step-daughter. __________

40. We give our web address to (a) whoever, (b) whomever requests it. __________

Informational Business Letters

Business letters are important forms of external communication. That is, they deliver information to individuals outside an organization. Although email has become incredibly successful for both internal and external communication, many important messages still require written letters. Business letters are necessary when a permanent record is required, when formality is significant, and when a message is sensitive and requires an organized, well-considered presentation. Business letters may request information, respond to requests, make claims, seek adjustments, order goods and services, sell goods and services, recommend individuals, develop goodwill, or achieve many other goals. All business people have to write business letters of various kinds, but a majority of those letters will be informational.

Characteristics of Business Letters

Writers of good business letters—whether the messages are informational, persuasive, or bad news—are guided by the four Cs: conciseness, clarity, correctness, and courtesy. In earlier Writer's Workshops, you learned techniques for making your writing concise and clear. You've also studied many guidelines for correct grammar and usage throughout this textbook. At this point we'll review some of these techniques briefly as they relate to business letters.

Conciseness. Concise letters save the reader's time by presenting information directly. You can make your letters concise by avoiding these writing faults: (a) wordy phrases (such as *in addition to the above* and *in view of the fact that*), (b) excessive use of expletives or fillers (such as *There are four reasons that explain . . .* or *It is a good plan*), (c) long lead-ins (such as *This message is to inform you that* or *I am writing this letter to*), (d) needless adverbs (such as *very, definitely, quite, extremely,* and *really*), and (e) old-fashioned expressions (such as *attached please find* and *pursuant to your request*).

Clarity. Business letters are clear when they are logically organized and when they present enough information for the reader to understand what the writer intended. Informational letters are usually organized directly with the main idea first. Clarity can be enhanced by including all the necessary information. Some authorities estimate that one-third of all business letters are written to clarify previous correspondence. To ensure that your letters are clear, put yourself in the reader's position and analyze what you have written. What questions may the reader ask? Does your information proceed logically from one point to another? Are your sentences and paragraphs coherent?

Correctness. Two aspects of correctness are accuracy of facts and accuracy of form. In regard to facts, good business writers prepare to write by gathering relevant information. They collect supporting documents (previous letters, memos, and reports), they make inquiries, they jot down facts, and they outline the message. Correct letters require thorough preparation. In the same manner, correct letters require careful proofreading and attention to form. Typographical errors, spelling irregularities, and grammatical faults distract the reader and damage the credibility of the writer. Correct business letters also follow one of the conventional formats, such as block or modified block, shown in Appendix C.

Courtesy. You develop courtesy in business letters by putting yourself in the place of the reader. Imagine how you would like to be treated, and show the same consideration and respect for the individual receiving your message. The ideas you express and the words used to convey those ideas create an impression on the reader. Be alert to words that may create a negative feeling, such as *you claim, unfortunately, you neglected, you forgot,* and *your complaint*. Create a positive feeling by presenting your message from the point of view of the reader. Try to use the word *you* more than the words *I* and *we*. Create a positive tone in business letters by using conversational language. How can you make your writing sound like conversation? Think of your reader as if he or she were sitting across from you having a friendly chat. Avoid formal, pretentious, and stuffy language, such as *the undersigned is pleased to grant your request*. In your business messages you can develop goodwill toward your company and toward yourself by putting yourself in the place of the reader, by developing a friendly tone, and by using conversational language.

Skill Check 5.1 Reviewing the Four Cs

1. Which of the following is most concise?
   (a) Due to the fact that we had a warehouse fire, your shipment is delayed.
   (b) This is to inform you that your shipment will be delayed.
   (c) Because of a warehouse fire, your shipment is delayed.
   (d) There was a warehouse fire, which explains why your shipment is delayed. ________
2. Which of the following is clear and logical?
   (a) If the strike is not settled quickly, it may last a while.
   (b) Flying over the rain forests of Indonesia, the trees form a solid and menacing green carpet.
   (c) This is not to suggest that Kingston, Oshawa, and London are not the most affordable areas for housing.
   (d) Prince Charles complained that the citizens of Britain speak and write their language poorly. ________
3. Which of the following is grammatically correct?
   (a) We hope that you and he will be in town for our next seminar.
   (b) A host of ethical issues involve business, including email privacy, whistleblowing, and mission statements.
   (c) We must develop a policy on returning merchandise. So that they know about it before they are made.
   (d) Jeffrey has 20 years experience in the software industry. ________
4. Which of the following is most courteous?
   (a) During your interview, I informed you that if we were not successful in finding a suitable candidate, I would contact you.
   (b) We appreciate receiving your letter describing your treatment by our store security personnel.
   (c) In your letter of June 1, you claim that you were harassed by our store security personnel.
   (d) Unfortunately, we are unable to complete your entire order because you neglected to provide a shirt size. ________
5. Which of the following sounds most conversational?
   (a) Attached herewith is the form you requested.
   (b) Pursuant to your request, we are forwarding the form you requested.
   (c) Under separate cover we are sending the form you requested.
   (d) You'll receive the form you requested in a separate mailing. ________

Writing Plan

Most business letters have three parts: opening, body, and closing. This three-part writing plan will help you organize the majority of your business messages quickly and effectively.

Opening. The opening of a business letter may include a subject line that refers to previous correspondence or summarizes the content of the message. A subject line should make sense but should not be a complete sentence; it is not followed by a period.

The first sentence of a business letter that requests or delivers information should begin directly with the main idea. If you are asking for information, use one of two approaches. Ask the most important question first, such as *Do you have a two-bedroom cottage on Devil's Lake available for the week of July 8–15?* A second approach involves beginning with a summary statement, such as *Please answer the following questions regarding* . . . . If the letter delivers information, begin with the most important information first, such as *Yes, we have a two-bedroom cottage on Devil's Lake available for* . . . or *Here is the information you requested regarding* . . . . Most informational business letters should *not* begin with an explanation of why the letter is being written.

Body. The body of the letter provides explanations and additional information to clarify the first sentence. Use a separate paragraph for each new idea, being careful to strive for concise writing.

If the message lends itself to enumeration, express the items in a bulleted or numbered list. Be certain, of course, to construct the list so that each item is parallel.

Think about the individual reading your message. Will that person understand what you are saying? Have you included enough information? What may seem clear to you may not be so evident to your reader. In responding to requests, don't hesitate to include more information than was requested—if you feel it would be helpful.

Maintain a friendly, conversational, and positive tone.

Closing. Business letters that demand action should conclude with a specific request, including end dating if appropriate. That is, tell the reader when you would like the request complied with, and, if possible, provide a reason (for example, *Please send me this information by June 1 so that I can arrange my vacation*).

Letters that provide information may end with a summary statement or a pleasant, forward-looking thought (for example, *I hope this information helps you plan your summer vacation*). Business organizations may also use the closing to promote products or services.

Avoid ending your letters with mechanical phrases such as *If I can be of further service, don't hesitate to call on me,* or *Thanks for any information you can provide.* Find a fresh way to express your desire to be of service or to show appreciation.

Figure 18.1 illustrates the application of the writing plan to an information request. Notice that the subject line summarizes the main topic of the letter, while the first paragraph provides more information about the reason for writing. The body of the letter explains the main idea and includes a list of questions so that the reader can see quickly what information is being requested. The closing includes an end date with a reason.

Skill Check 5.2 Reviewing the Writing Plan

In the space provided, write a, b, or c to identify the letter part where each of the following might logically be found.

(a) Opening (b) Body (c) Closing

1. Explanation and details ________
2. Subject line that summarizes main idea ________
3. End dating with reason ________
4. Enumerated or bulleted list ________
5. Main idea ________
6. Summary statement or forward-looking thought ________

Figure 18.1
Information Request

Summarizes main idea

Introduces purpose immediately

Explains need for information

Groups open-ended questions into list for quick comprehension and best feedback

Courteously provides end date and reason

GraphicPros
264 South Halsted Street
Mississauga, ON L5T 3K8
FAX (905) 568-2210 VOICE (905) 568-8319 INTERNET: http://www.graphicpros.com

March 5, 200x

Ms. Kesha Scott
Micro Supplies and Software
4671 Main Street
Saskatoon, SK S7K 3G3

Dear Ms. Scott:

SUBJECT: AVAILABILITY AND PRICE OF EQUIPMENT SECURITY DEVICES

Please provide information and recommendations regarding security equipment to prevent the theft of office computers, keyboards, monitors, faxes, and printers.

Our office now has 18 computer workstations and 6 printers that we must secure to desks or counters. Answers to the following questions will help us select the best devices for our purpose.

1. What device would you recommend to secure a workstation consisting of a computer, monitor, and keyboard?

2. What expertise and equipment are required to install and remove the security device?

3. How much is each device? Do you offer quantity discounts, and, if so, how much?

Because our insurance rates will be increased if the security devices are not installed before May 12, we would appreciate your response by March 26.

Sincerely,

Brent R. Barnwell

Brent R. Barnwell
Office Manager

Writing Application 5.1 At a computer or on a separate sheet of paper, revise the following poorly written letter. Use block style (every line starts at the left margin) and mixed punctuation. This is a personal business letter; follow the format shown in Figure C.2 in Appendix C (see page 466), inserting your own address in the return address block. Remember that the following letter is poorly written. Improve it!

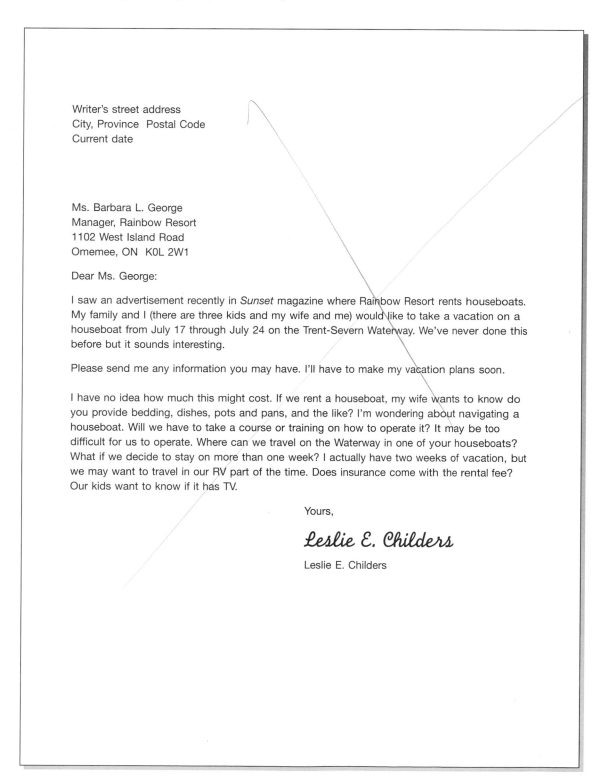

Writer's street address
City, Province Postal Code
Current date

Ms. Barbara L. George
Manager, Rainbow Resort
1102 West Island Road
Omemee, ON K0L 2W1

Dear Ms. George:

I saw an advertisement recently in *Sunset* magazine where Rainbow Resort rents houseboats. My family and I (there are three kids and my wife and me) would like to take a vacation on a houseboat from July 17 through July 24 on the Trent-Severn Waterway. We've never done this before but it sounds interesting.

Please send me any information you may have. I'll have to make my vacation plans soon.

I have no idea how much this might cost. If we rent a houseboat, my wife wants to know do you provide bedding, dishes, pots and pans, and the like? I'm wondering about navigating a houseboat. Will we have to take a course or training on how to operate it? It may be too difficult for us to operate. Where can we travel on the Waterway in one of your houseboats? What if we decide to stay on more than one week? I actually have two weeks of vacation, but we may want to travel in our RV part of the time. Does insurance come with the rental fee? Our kids want to know if it has TV.

Yours,

Leslie E. Childers

Leslie E. Childers

Writing Application 5.2 Assume you are Barbara George. Write a response to Mr. Childers' letter. Use modified block style and mixed punctuation. Tell Mr. Childers that the rental fee, which is $175 per day or $1000 per week, does include insurance. You have a houseboat available for July 17–24, but definite reservations must be made for that time and for the week following, if Mr. Childers decides to stay two weeks. Your houseboats can travel through 20 lakes, canals, and rivers. Rainbow Resort provides bedding, dishes, and kitchenware. Yes, each houseboat has a TV set. You also provide an AM/FM radio and a CD player. Your houseboats accommodate four to ten people, and you require a deposit of $500 for a one-week reservation. Reservations must be received by June 1 to ensure a July vacation. Your houseboats are easy to operate. No special training is required, but you do give each operator about 30 minutes of instruction. Send Mr. Childers a brochure describing Rainbow Resort and the memorable holiday he and his family can enjoy. The scenery and attractions are good.

Writing Application 5.3 Write a personal business letter in response to the following problem. For your home office you ordered a VoIP phone system called the VTech IP8100-2. This system comes with two cordless handsets, each with its own charging dock. It had many other attractive features and you were eager to try it. When it arrived, however, you installed it and discovered that an irritating static sound interfered with every telephone call you made or received. You don't know what caused the static, but the product description promised the following: "You'll experience excellent signal clarity with Frequency Hopping Digital Spread Spectrum (FHDSS) transmission, and a frequency of 5.8GHz. 95-channel auto-search ensures a clear signal." Because you must rely on clear calls for your business, you returned the VoIP phone system January 15 by UPS Next Business Day shipping service to ElectroWare Ltd., the supplier from whom you purchased the unit. You still have a copy of the invoice, which states that merchandise may be returned for any reason within 30 days after purchase. You also have the UPS receipt proving that you returned it. However, your MasterCard statement (Acct. No. 5390-3390-2219-0002) has not shown a credit for the return. Your last two monthly statements show no credit for $188.90. You're wondering what happened. Did ElectroWare receive the returned VoIP phone system? Why hasn't your account been credited? If the company did not receive the shipment, you want UPS to trace it. Write to ElectroWare Ltd., 22121 Crystal Creek Boulevard, Lethbridge, Alberta T9L 3T2. You have complied with ElectroWare's instructions regarding returning merchandise, and you want the company to credit your account. You do not want another phone system. Be sure to open your letter with a direct request for the action you want taken.

U N I T 6

Writing With Style

C H A P T E R

Capitalization 19

OBJECTIVES When you have completed the materials in this chapter, you will be able to do the following:

LEVEL I

- *Recognize proper nouns and proper adjectives for purposes of capitalization.*
- *Determine when to capitalize sentence beginnings, geographic locations, organization names, academic courses and degrees, and seasons.*

LEVEL II

- *Properly capitalize personal titles, numbered items, and points of the compass.*
- *Correctly capitalize departments, divisions, committees, government terms, product names, and literary titles.*

LEVEL III

- *Capitalize beginning words, celestial bodies, ethnic references, and words following* marked *and* stamped.
- *Apply special rules in capitalizing personal titles and terms.*

PRETEST

Use proofreading marks (≡) to show any letters that should be capitalized in the sentences below.

1. Last spring mother took classes in history, computer technology, english, and psychology.
2. The canadian medical association's executive will meet in the manitoba room of the hilton hotel on march 25.
3. After receiving a master's degree from york university, sharon became assistant to the human resources manager at general motors of canada.

continued

PRETEST

4. Our company president and vice-president met with several supervisors on the west coast to discuss how to compete against google's new online offerings.
5. The booklet provided by revenue canada explains the use of form T2202.

Rules governing capitalization reflect conventional practices; that is, they have been established by custom and usage. By following these conventions, a writer tells a reader, among other things, what words are important. In earlier times writers capitalized most nouns and many adjectives at will; few conventions of capitalization or punctuation were consistently observed. Today most capitalization follows definite rules that are fully accepted and practised at all times.

Within many large organizations, capitalization style is prescribed in a stylebook. Dictionaries are also helpful in determining capitalization practices, but they do not show all capitalized words. To develop skill in using capitals, study the rules and examples shown in this chapter.

LEVEL I

Career Tip

Many large companies publish style manuals showing their preferred capitalization and the spelling of frequently used terms. One of the first tasks of new employees is becoming familiar with the company style manual.

▶ Basic Rules of Capitalization

Proper Nouns

Capitalize proper nouns, including the *specific* names of persons, places, schools, streets, parks, buildings, religions, holidays, months, nicknames, agreements, websites, historical periods, and so forth. Do *not* capitalize common nouns that make *general* reference.

Proper Nouns	**Common Nouns**
Jackson Turner	a young man on the basketball team
Mexico, United States	neighbouring countries of Canada
Canadore College, University of British Columbia	a community college and a university
Grand Avenue Park	a park in town
Catholic, Moslem	representatives of two religions
Empire Room, Royal Inn	a room in the hotel
Canada Day, Easter	holidays
Humber River Bridge	a bridge over a river
Fairview Mall	a large shopping centre
Parliament, the Senate	components of government
January, February, March	first three months of the year
the Great One, the Big Apple	nicknames of people and places
Stipulation of Interest Agreement	an agreement between companies
The Online English Grammar Clinic	a website
Microsoft Word	a word processing program
Great Depression	a historical period

1. Mother English 2. Canadian Medical Association's Manitoba Room Hilton Hotel March 3. York University Sharon General Motors of Canada 4. West Coast Google's 5. Revenue Canada Form

Proper Adjectives

Capitalize most adjectives that are derived from proper nouns.

Arabic alphabet
British thermal unit
Danish pastry
Heimlich manoeuvre
Keynesian economics
Roman numeral
Richter scale
Victorian furniture

Study Tip

Most proper nouns retain their capital letters when they become adjectives—for example, French toast, Russian roulette, Persian cat, Spanish moss, Italian marble, and Swedish massage.

Do not capitalize those few adjectives originally derived from proper nouns that have become common adjectives (without capitals) through usage. Consult your dictionary when in doubt.

china dishes
diesel engine
french fries
homburg hat
italic type
mandarin collar
manila folder
venetian blinds

Beginning of Sentence

Capitalize the first letter of a word beginning a sentence.

Inventory and sales data are transmitted electronically.

Hotlink

For an enjoyable look at capitalization, go to the Red River College Writing Resources page at **<http://xnet.rrc.mb.ca/leshanson/Writing_Resources.htm>**.

Geographic Locations

Capitalize the names of *specific* places such as continents, provinces, cities, mountains, valleys, lakes, rivers, oceans, and geographic regions. Capitalize words like *county, state,* and *region* when they follow proper nouns.

South America, Asia
Ontario, British Columbia
Port Hood, Quebec City
Rocky Mountains
Lake Michigan, Labrador Sea
James Bay
Huron County, York Region
Manitoba Escarpment
Red River, Mississippi River
Rivière des Prairies
Atlantic Ocean, Indian Ocean
the Prairies, the Maritimes
New York State
Okanagan Valley

Organization Names

Capitalize the principal words in the names of all business, civic, educational, governmental, labour, military, philanthropic, political, professional, religious, social, and sports organizations.

Bank of Montreal
B'nai Brith
Business Development Bank of Canada
Canadian Red Cross
Canadian Union of Public Employees
Federation of Saskatchewan Indian Nations
Liberal Party, New Democrats
National Hockey League
Royal Canadian Legion
The Boeing Company*

Hotlink

Capitalization gets a thorough overview in the linked series of materials you can find at **<http://englishplus.com/grammar/captcont.htm>**.

* *Capitalize* the *only when it is part of an organization's official name (as it would appear on the organization's stationery).*

Hotlink

The Style Guide provided by the University of Victoria at **<http://communications.uvic.ca/publications/style/section-3.html>** will give you a thorough review of the rules of capitalization.

Generally, do not capitalize *company, association, board,* and other shortened name forms when they are used to replace full organization names. If these shortened names, however, are preceded by the word *the* and are used in formal or legal documents (contracts, bylaws, minutes, etc.), they may be capitalized.

> Did you know that the company will pay certain medical benefits? (Informal document)
>
> The Treasurer of the *Association* is herein authorized to disburse funds. (Formal document)

Academic Courses and Degrees

Capitalize the names of numbered courses and specific course titles. Do not capitalize the names of academic subject areas unless they contain a proper noun.

> Professor Rose Waxman is scheduled to offer Psychology 104 in the spring.
>
> All accounting majors must take business English and business law.
>
> Becky expects to enrol in Keyboarding 12, Office Administration 32, and Accounting 28.
>
> My most interesting classes are history, business management, and French.

Capitalize abbreviations of academic degrees whether they stand alone or follow individuals' names. Do not capitalize general references to degrees.

> Aleksandar hopes to earn B.Sc. and M.Sc. degrees.
>
> Sylvia Sasot, Ph.D., teaches psychology in the fall.
>
> New employees include Joanne Duncan, M.S.W., and Thomas Wong, R.P.N.
>
> The university offers bachelor's and master's degrees.

Study Tip

Course titles with numbers are usually capitalized (*Marketing 101*). Those without numbers usually are not capitalized (*marketing*).

Seasons

Do not capitalize seasons unless they are personified (referred to as if alive).

> Last winter we drew lots for summer vacations. (Usual reference)
>
> "Come, Winter, with thine angry howl ..."—Burns (Personification)

Complete the reinforcement exercises for Level I on pp. 384–385.

LEVEL II

▶ Special Rules of Capitalization

Titles of People

Many rules exist for capitalizing personal and professional titles of people.

a. Capitalize courtesy titles (such as *Mr., Mrs.,* and *Ms.*) and other personal titles when they precede names.

Mrs. Liane Goodale	Dr. Laurier Roberge
Aunt Gertrude	Budget Director Magee
Councillor Mendler	Mayor Rasmussen
Commander Howard Rogers	Chief Dan George
Rabbi David Cohen	Prince Charles

b. Capitalize titles in addresses and closing lines of correspondence.

Mr. Kenneth Miller	Very sincerely yours,
Executive Vice-President, Planning	
Energy Systems Technology	
112 Ellery Street	Patricia Barr
Victoria, BC V8W 3K5	Sales Supervisor

c. Generally, do not capitalize a title or an office appearing alone.

The president of that company was made chair of the board.
Refer the problem to the vice-president or to the human resources manager.

d. Do capitalize titles of high-ranking national or international officials.

the Prime Minister	the Chief Justice
the President of the United States	an audience with the Queen
the visit of the Pope	the Secretary of State

e. Do not capitalize titles or offices following names.

Leon Jones, president of Atlas Chemical Company
Rose Valenzuela, supervisor, Word Processing Centre
Davonne Adams, office manager

f. Do not capitalize titles when they precede or follow appositives (unless they represent special high rank, as in d).*

Our cost accountant, Mona Chase, submitted her revised figures.
Gary Bauer, vice-president, controls all hiring.
Reva Hillman discovered that her uncle, Paul Hillman, had named her his heir.

The capitalization of business titles can be summarized in one rule: Capitalize business titles *only* when they precede personal names and are not followed by appositives, as in this case: *Personnel Director Roslyn Katz.*

g. Do not capitalize family titles used with possessives or articles.

my mother	the aunt	Lee's uncle
his father	a cousin	Mike's dad

But do capitalize titles of close relatives when they are used without modifiers—as names are used.

Please call Father and Mother immediately.
This is Grandmother's brooch.

Numbered and Lettered Items

Capitalize nouns followed by numbers or letters (except in page, paragraph, line, and verse references).

Gate 69, Flight 238	Form 2900-4	Building I-63-B
Invoice No. 15891	Volume II, Appendix A	Supplement No. 3
page 6, line 12	County Road 56	Order 1034

Study Tip

Capitalize only the first word in salutations (*My dear Ms. Jones*) and complimentary closes (*Very truly yours*).

Study Tip

Notice that titles of high rank are capitalized whether they precede, follow, or replace a name.

Hotlink

Use this Capital Community College web page **<http://cctc.commnet.edu/grammar/powerpoint.htm>** and click on The PowerPoint® icon to access "A Capital Idea," a Microsoft® PowerPoint® presentation on the use of capital letters, a list of capitalization rules with examples, and an online quiz to help you test your mastery of this subject.

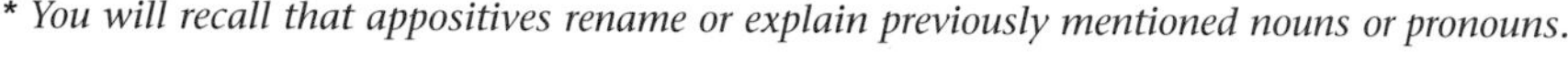
* *You will recall that appositives rename or explain previously mentioned nouns or pronouns.*

Points of the Compass

Capitalize *north, south, east, west,* and their derivatives when they represent *specific* regions. Do not capitalize the points of the compass when they are used in directions or in general references.

the Middle East, the Far East	heading east on Eglinton Avenue
the West, the Midwest (of the United States)	to the west of town
	eastern Ontario, western regions
the East, the West Coast	southern Manitoba

Study Tip

A clue to the capitalization of a region is the use of *the* preceding it: *the East Coast, the West, the Pacific Rim.*

Departments, Divisions, and Committees

Capitalize the names of departments, divisions, or committees within *your own* organization. Outside your organization capitalize only specific department, division, or committee names.

Send your employment application to their human resources department.
A steering committee has not yet been named.
Dr. Nguyen is director of the Northern Division of Barco. (Specific division)
Sue works in *our* Communication Services Department. (Insider reference)
Grievances are referred to *our* Personnel Practices Committee. (Insider reference)

Governmental Terms

Do not capitalize the words *federal, government, national, provincial,* or *state* unless they are part of a specific title.

Neither the provincial government nor the federal government would fund the proposal.
The legislative body in Quebec is called the National Assembly.

Product Names

Capitalize product names only when they represent trademarked items. Frequently used product names, like many in the following list, are shown in dictionaries and labelled as trademarked or proprietary terms. Common names following manufacturers' names are not capitalized, except in advertising.

BlackBerry	Formica counter	Plasticine
Coke, Coca-Cola	Jeep	Q-tip swab
Dell computer	Kleenex	Ritalin
Duo-Tang folder	Kodak camera	Styrofoam cup
DuPont Teflon	Magic Marker	Whirlpool washer

Hotlink

Natural Resources Canada offers additional examples of the proper use of capitalization at **<http://ess.nrcan.gc.ca/pubs/scipub/guide/gramm/caps_e.php>**.

Published and Artistic Titles

Capitalize the principal words in the titles of books, magazines, newspapers, articles, movies, plays, songs, poems, websites, and reports. Do *not* capitalize articles (*a, an, the*), short conjunctions (*and, but, or, etc.*), and prepositions of three or fewer letters (*in, to, by, for, etc.*) unless they begin or end the title.

John Robert Colombo's *A Little Book of Facts About a Really Big Country* (Book)
Ann Lee's *Financial Strategies You Can Bank On* (Book with preposition at end of title)
Andrew Cohen's *The Unfinished Canadian: The People We Are* (Book with title and subtitle)
The Globe and Mail (Newspaper)

"How to Get the Most From a Placement Service" in *Newsweek* (Magazine article)
Late Night with David Letterman (TV Series)
Life Is Beautiful (Movie)
Bob Dylan's "When the Ship Comes In" on *The Times They Are A-Changin'* (Song and album)

Complete the reinforcement exercises for Level II on pp. 386–387.

▶ Additional Rules of Capitalization

LEVEL III

Beginning Words

In addition to capitalizing the first word of a complete sentence, capitalize the first words in quoted sentences, independent phrases, bulleted or enumerated items, formal rules or principles following colons, and some components of business correspondence.

John F. Kennedy said, "Man is the most extraordinary computer of all." (Quoted sentence)

No, not at the present time. (Independent phrase)

Big utilities formed an alliance to sell the following:
1. Electricity
2. Natural gas
3. Energy management services (Enumerated items)

Our office manager responded with his favourite rule: Follow the company stylebook for correct capitalization. (Rule following colon)

Dear Mr. Steinbeck (First word and all nouns in a salutation)

Sincerely yours, (First word of a complimentary close)

Celestial Bodies

Capitalize the names of celestial bodies such as planets, stars, and constellations. Do not capitalize the terms *earth, sun,* or *moon* unless they appear in a context with other celestial bodies in the solar system.

Venus and Mars are the closest planets to Earth.
Global warming is changing the climate on earth.

Career Tip

Find a job you love, and you'll never have to work a day in your life.

Ethnic References

Terms that relate to a particular culture, language, or race are capitalized.

The Dene are the Athapaskan-speaking First Nations peoples, including the Chipewyan, Dogrib, Gwich'in, and Slavey groups.
In Hawaii, Asian and Western cultures merge.
Both English and Hebrew are spoken by Jews in Israel.
The politician wasn't popular with French-Canadian voters.

Words Following *marked* and *stamped*

Capitalize words that follow the words *marked* and *stamped.*

For greater care in transport, the package was stamped "Fragile."
That bill was marked "Paid in Full" on September 15.

Spot the Blooper

From a Wendy's International poster: "Be Cool in School! Good Grades Has Its Rewards!"

Special Uses of Personal Titles and Terms

a. Generally, titles are capitalized according to the specifications set forth earlier. However, when a title of an official appears in that organization's minutes, bylaws, or other such official documents, it is capitalized.

The Controller will have authority over college budgets. (Title appearing in bylaws)

By vote of the shareholders, the President is empowered to implement a stock split. (Title appearing in annual report)

b. When the terms *ex, elect, late,* and *former* are used with capitalized titles, these terms are not capitalized.

The projections of ex-Vice-President Baldwin have proven exceedingly accurate.

Mayor-elect Ross addressed the city council.

c. Titles are capitalized when used in direct address, except for the terms *sir, madam, ladies,* and *gentlemen.*

May I ask, Doctor, what my mother's prognosis is?

You'll soon learn, ladies and gentlemen, how this new procedure can reduce your workload.

Complete the reinforcement exercises for Level III on pp. 388–389.

HOTLINE QUERIES

Question: I don't know how to describe the copies made on our copy machine. Should I call them *Xerox* copies or something else?

Answer: They are *Xerox* copies only if made on a Xerox copier. Copies made on other machines may be called *xerographic* copies, *machine* copies, or *photocopies.*

Question: In the doctor's office where I work, I see the word *medicine* capitalized, as in *the field of Medicine.* Is this correct?

Answer: No. General references should not be capitalized. If it were part of a title, as in the Northwestern College of *Medicine,* it would be capitalized.

Question: I work for the National Therapy Association. When I talk about *the association* in a letter, should I capitalize it?

Answer: No. When a shortened form of an organization name is used alone, it is generally not capitalized. In formal or legal documents (contracts, bylaws, printed announcements), however, it may be capitalized.

Question: I work for a provincial agency, and I'm not sure what to capitalize or hyphenate in this sentence: *Provincial agencies must make forms available to* non-English-speaking *applicants.*

Answer: When a prefix is joined to a word that must be capitalized, the prefix is usually followed by a hyphen and the capital letter is retained, as in *anti-American, mid-July,* or *pre-Confederation.* In your example because the word *speaking* combines with *English* to form a single-unit adjective, it should be hyphenated. Thus the expression should be typed *non-English-speaking applicants.*

Question: When we use a person's title, such as *business manager,* in place of a person's name, shouldn't the title always be capitalized?

Answer: No. Business titles are capitalized only when they precede an individual's name, as in *Business Manager Smith.* Do not capitalize titles when they replace an individual's name: *Our business manager will direct the transaction.*

Question: How do you spell *marshal,* as in *Field Marshal Montgomery*?

Answer: The preferred spelling is with a single *l: marshal;* it may be confused with *Marshall,* a common surname spelled with double *l.* The noun *marshal* refers to a high military officer, a city law officer who carries out court orders, or a person who arranges a ceremony. As a verb, *marshal* means "to bring together" or "to order in an effective way" (*the lawyer marshalled convincing arguments*), and the preferred spelling is with a double *l* before the ending *-ing* or *-ed.* The similar-sounding word *martial* is an adjective and means "warlike" or "military" (*martial law was declared after the riot*).

Question: I'm writing a paper for my biology class on *in vitro fertilization.* Since this is a medical term, shouldn't I capitalize it?

Answer: Don't capitalize medical procedures unless they are named after individuals (*Tourette's syndrome*). *In vitro* means "outside the living body." Specialists in the field use the abbreviation *IVF* after the first introduction of the term.

NAME ______________________________

CHAPTER 19 Reinforcement Exercises

LEVEL I

A. **(Self-check)** In the following sentences, use standard proofreading marks to correct errors you find in capitalization. Use three short lines (≡) under a lower case letter to indicate that it is to be changed to a capital letter. Draw a diagonal (/) through a capital letter you wish to change to a lower case letter. Indicate at the right the total number of changes you have made in each sentence. If no changes are needed, write *0*.

Example: The Bandit Henry McCarthy was also known as Billy the kid. ____2____

1. One of the World's largest trading businesses is the japanese sumimoto corporation. ________
2. Born in Timiskaming county, Wilson grew up in the province of Manitoba. ________
3. All Ford Motor Company Cars and Light Trucks carry a Warranty. ________
4. In the fall Isaac Bantu plans to study italian, accounting, Management, and Marketing. ________
5. Use India ink to make dark headings on the manila folders. ________
6. Pelee island is located on the canadian side of lake erie. ________
7. Regulations of transport canada resulted in costly expenses for our Company. ________
8. Second Cup ensures high standards by training its Baristas in Coffee Preparation techniques and Customer Service. ________
9. All sales representatives of the Company met in the Sheraton room of the Red lion inn for a Training Session on Stress Management. ________
10. the winner in this year's dog show sponsored by the Westminster kennel club was a Doberman Pinscher from a german breeder. ________

Check your answers.

B. Use proofreading marks to correct any capitalization errors in these sentences. Indicate the total number of changes at the right. If no changes are needed, write *0*.

1. Because he was interested in Computer Technology, Craig took computer mathematics I, general physics I, and computer circuitry II. ________
2. Representatives from the methodist, presbyterian, baptist, and catholic faiths will take part in an International Conference in St. petersburg beach, florida. ________
3. Rex Mackey was sent to our port Dover branch office for the Month of August, but he hopes to return by Winter. ________

1. world's Japanese Sumimoto Corporation (4) 2. County (1) 3. cars light trucks warranty (4) 4. Italian management marketing (3) 5. (0) 6. Island Canadian Lake Erie (4) 7. Transport Canada company (3) 8. baristas coffee preparation customer service (5) 9. company Room Lion Inn training session stress management (8) 10. The winner Kennel Club pinscher German (5).

4. Members of the canadian wildlife federation lobby hard to protect the Gray Wolf, which makes its home in the northern rockies. ____________________

5. Expansion of the internet has seriously affected business at The Boeing Company. (The word *the* is part of the company name.) ____________________

6. Last Winter Tricia Adams took out a policy with the Prudential life insurance company. (The word *the* is part of the company name.) ____________________

7. Work schedules will have to be adjusted in november for remembrance day. ____________________

8. All company representatives gathered in quebec city in the champlain room of the holiday inn for the annual spring sales meeting. ____________________

9. The windy city is attractive to many American Tourists, as well as to increasing numbers of european and canadian visitors. ____________________

10. Professor Daruty employed the socratic method of questioning students to elicit answers about Business Management. ____________________

11. After driving through New York state, we stayed in New York city and visited the Empire State building. ____________________

12. Many nontraditional students face the herculean challenge of juggling full-time jobs while working on their Degrees or Diplomas. ____________________

13. Kay Randolph completed the requirements for a bachelor's degree at Simon Fraser university. ____________________

14. His report on diesel engines contained many greek symbols in the engineering equations. ____________________

15. The Hip-Hop music star's customized lincoln navigator sported big wheels, satellite radio, three dvd players, six tv screens, a sony playstation 3, and vibrating front seats. ____________________

NAME ______________________________

LEVEL II

A. (Self-check) Use proofreading marks to correct errors you find in capitalization. Indicate at the right the total number of changes you make.

Example: Project manager Harold Gross was promoted to Vice-President. ____3____

1. Henry Davis, supervisor of our legal department, travelled to the east coast over the holidays. (Note use of *our.*) ________
2. Please consult figure 52D in appendix B for instructions in computing the depreciation of equipment. ________
3. We will ask sales manager Sperazza to be chair of an investigative committee. ________
4. Both mother and aunt grace received Radio Shack Cellphones as Christmas gifts. ________
5. The Fishing Industry in the maritimes is reeling from the impact of recent Federal regulations. ________
6. Our business manager and our executive vice-president attended an e-business seminar in southern Alberta. ________
7. My Uncle recommended that I read the article titled "The 100 best companies to work for." ________
8. Address the envelope to Ms. Maris Sheaffer, director, employee services, Omega Corporation, 304 Hilyard Street, Edmonton, Alberta T6J 5G4. ________
9. The pope was reported in good condition after a fall in the Vatican. ________
10. Illy, a company founded in the Northern part of Italy during World war I, produces coffee made from pure arabica beans. ________

Check your answers.

B. Use proofreading marks to correct errors in the sentences below. Indicate the number of changes you make for each sentence.

1. Harley Lee, vice-president of Manufacturers trust company, asked his Executive Assistant to direct the united way office contributions. ________
2. My sister, my cousin, and I will fly to visit mother, father, and uncle Eduardo over the Spring holidays. ________
3. My Father suggested that I read the book *The Seven Habits Of Highly Successful People.* ________

---

1. Legal Department East Coast (4) 2. Figure Appendix (2) 3. Sales Manager (2) 4. Mother Aunt Grace cellphones (4) 5. fishing industry Maritimes federal (4) 6. (0) 7. uncle Best Companies Work For (5) 8. Director Employee Services (3) 9. Pope (1) 10. northern War (2)

4. When the prime minister entertained the queen, stringent security measures were effected. ____________________

5. To locate the exact amount of provincial funding, look on Line 7, Page 6 of supplement no. 4. ____________________

6. Akio Morita, the Founder of Sony Corporation, hurried to gate 16 to catch flight 263 to Vancouver. ____________________

7. The director of purchasing, Harvey Gross, ordered Victor Calculators and Sony Recorders. ____________________

8. The letter is addressed to Paul Jorgensen, director of research and development, blum corporation, p.o. box 58, gulfport, florida 33707. ____________________

9. May Co.'s ad featured Royal Manor Dishes and teflon-coated pans. ____________________

10. Overtime compensation for Carmen Corregas was referred to our workforce resources department. ____________________

11. Kristen shopped for kleenex tissues and kodak film at her local zellers. ____________________

12. Daphne Mainprize, curator, gave a talk in the stephen leacock museum on old brewery bay outside Orillia, Ontario. ____________________

13. Business Manager Edward Davis devised a procedure for expediting Purchase Orders from Area D Offices. ____________________

14. Douglas ordered a big mac, french fries, and a coca-cola for lunch. ____________________

15. David Kane is now supervising our entire west coast division. ____________________

16. As stated in Part II of the Contract, sun life assurance company pays claims related to injuries only. ____________________

17. Google was originally named googol; however, an Investor made a cheque out to "Google, Inc.," and this typo became the Company's name. ____________________

18. A winnipegger who enjoys warm weather, Mr. Difranco travels south each Winter to vacation in Southern Georgia. ____________________

NAME ____________________

LEVEL III

A. (Self-check) Use proofreading marks to indicate necessary changes. Write the total number of changes at the right.

Example: The Late Prime Minister Lester Pearson is remembered for his efforts to obtain world peace at the united nations. 3

1. Because the letter was marked "confidential," Sandy delivered it personally to the Boss. ________
2. The guiding principle of capitalization is this: capitalize *specific* names and references, but do not capitalize *general* references. ________
3. Members of both asian and hispanic cultures participated in the city's celebration. ________
4. Mercury, venus, earth, and mars are dense and solid. ________
5. The most frequently typed documents in a Lawyer's office are the following: ________
   1. affidavits
   2. wills and trusts
   3. briefs
6. How on Earth do you expect to get away with this? ________
7. Money traders watched carefully the relation of the canadian dollar to the american dollar, the japanese yen, the chinese yuan, and the european euro. ________
8. We have Ex-Councillor Lupus and Mayor-Elect Lanham scheduled for the Remembrance day ceremonies. ________
9. You, Sir, are in danger of being held in contempt of court. ________
10. Our Organization's bylaws state, "The Secretary of the Association will submit an agenda two weeks before each meeting." ________

Check your answers.

B. Use proofreading marks to indicate necessary changes. Write the total number of changes at the right.

1. As the Sun beat down on the crowd, the Vice-Chancellor continued his graduation address to the students of the university of Manitoba. ________
2. Would you like a ride home? yes, thank you very much. ________
3. Our Advertising Agency operates according to this rule: you must spend money to make money. ________

1. Confidential boss (2) 2. Capitalize (1) 3. Asian Hispanic (2) 4. Venus Earth Mars (3) 5. lawyer's Affidavits Wills Briefs (4) 6. earth (1) 7. Canadian American Japanese Chinese European (5) 8. ex-Councillor Mayor-elect Day (3) 9. sir (1) 10. organization's (1)

4. William noticed that the english spoken by asians in hong kong sounded quite british. ____________

5. The accountant marked the Invoice "paid." ____________

6. The Minutes of the last meeting show that the Vice-President, acting on behalf of the President, conducted the meeting despite the lack of a quorum. ____________

7. Mayor-Elect Hudson sat beside Ex-Mayor Benedict and councillor Waller at the morning Ceremony. ____________

8. How much, professor, does the Final Exam count? ____________

9. Three brands owned by the Coca-Cola company are the following: ____________
   1. canada dry
   2. minute maid
   3. nescafé

10. Benjamin Disraeli provided England with its National motto when he said, "something will turn up." ____________

C. Review of Levels I, II, and III.

Select (a) or (b) to indicate correct capitalization.

1. (a) a Television show on CBC (b) a television show on CBC ____________
2. (a) Roman empire (b) Roman Empire ____________
3. (a) awarded a Bachelor's degree (b) awarded a bachelor's degree ____________
4. (a) courses in English and sociology (b) courses in english and sociology ____________
5. (a) the Pacific Room at the Marriott (b) the pacific room at the Marriott ____________
6. (a) French fries and a pepsi-cola (b) french fries and a Pepsi-Cola ____________
7. (a) a file marked "urgent" (b) a file marked "Urgent" ____________
8. (a) avoid the sun's rays (b) avoid the Sun's rays ____________
9. (a) the prime minister's TV speech (b) the Prime Minister's TV speech ____________
10. (a) exit from highway 5 (b) exit from Highway 5 ____________

D. Optional Writing.

Your instructor may ask you to complete one or both of these exercises on a separate sheet.

(1) Write ten original sentences that contain at least 20 properly capitalized words, not counting the first word.

(2) Write one or two paragraphs summarizing an article from a local newspaper. Choose an article with as many capital letters as possible. Apply the rules of capitalization you learned in this chapter.

Editor's Challenge

The following letters contain intentional errors reflecting the concepts you have studied thus far, as well as a few spelling errors. Use standard proofreading marks to show all necessary corrections.

HOLST BROTHERS CONSTRUCTION

2230 DUNSMUIR AVE.
OTTAWA, ON K1A 2J7 **(613) 828-4493**

January 4, 200x

Ms. Danielle M. Forrester
President, Interior Design Institute
504 Richmond Street
Ottawa, ON K1N 7B7

Dear Ms. Forrester:

Here is a brief report about our work with the cheviot hills residence being prepared as the showcase house for the interior design institute. The renovation and remodelling is progressing on schedule, and should be ready for the photographers from metropolitan home magazine june 1.

Past Progress

During the Fall the work crew completed the following tasks, removal of all wood shingles, repair of the plywood roof base and installation of a permawear tile roof. In december we replaced damaged window facings we also repaired the plumbing in two baths and the kitchen. As you requested we investigated italian marble for the entry and spanish tiles for the patio. A price sheet for those items are enclosed.

Current Progress

At present we are concentrating on the Living Room which required ceiling repair and electrical rewiring, see page 6 of your blueprints. The pyramid skylight has been installed in the library, however, we had to alter two bookcases in doing so. After consulting the President and General Manager of our company, we decided to absorb some of the extra costs involved, however, other off budget items will be your responsibility.

Future Schedule

In February we expect to complete all the interior finish work, the painters will apply two coats of anderson no. 343 wall primer. I believe that Ms. Chin and Mr. Darwin whom you suggested would be decorating the downstairs, could begin there work february 15. Just have them call my Supervisor or I to arrange the exact date.

Sincerely yours,

Irena Overmeyer

Irena Overmeyer

National Association for Retail Marketing

540 Campus Place
Abbotsford, BC V2S 7Z8 **(604) 233-0948** **www.narm.ca**

January 5, 200x

Ms. Jamie Owens, President
Retail Group, Inc.
240 Pacific Avenue
Winnipeg, MB R3E 1G2

Dear Ms. Owens,

Please consider giving a presentation at the annual meeting of the National Association For Retail Marketing in the City of Abbotsford, British Columbia on April 6. Your presentation would proceed a lavishly-catered banquet.

In the passed you have said "retail has to feel relevant or its dead." Thats why were turning to you for guidance.

Many of we retailers have little experience in attracting Generation y shoppers and we realize that their going to represent 41 per cent of the canadian population in the next Decade. Its depressing for us to realize that only 15 per cent of this group shops in Department Stores. Attracting this segment of shoppers are critical to future profitability and that's why we are turning to you for help.

You have been the driving force behind a number of retail makeovers, including blockbuster video, nike, sears and tim hortons. Our members were especially impressed by your startling redesign of Mega Mart, making it one of the highest grossing sellers of consumer electronic's in north America. With your finger on the changing pulse of retail you were the first choice of our Committee to be keynote speaker at our annual meeting.

Will you be available to give our keynote address on April 6. Although our honorarium is only $3000 we can offer you the opportunity to share your expertise with 1500 of the top retailers in the Country. Many of them are struggling, and would enthusiastically welcome your presentation. In addition you may find that many would become future client's.

Enclosed is a brochure and pamphlets describing previous conferences. If you will call me at (604) 499-3928 I can provide details and answer questions. So that we may continue our conference planning procedures please let me know by November 10 whether you will become our Featured Speaker. This is you're chance to have a huge affect on future retailer's.

Sincerely Yours,

Douglas Eamon

Douglas Eamon
Events Coordinator

Enclosure

POSTTEST

Underline any letter that should be capitalized.

1. Our company president and marketing manager are fluent in french and spanish.
2. Judy studied english literature, accounting, and sociology at the university of alberta.
3. The engineers will meet in the algonquin room of the four points Sheraton next thursday.
4. Tell me, doctor, which hospital has the best cancer centre.
5. My mother, my father, and uncle michael will spend the easter holidays with us.

learning.web.ways

You have written a super résumé, and now you want to write a terrific application letter to introduce your résumé. You know that many websites offer tips on writing cover letters.

Goal: To improve your employment application letters.

1. With your web browser on the screen, first visit the Canadian Careers site **<http://www.canadiancareers.com/resandcl.html>**.
2. Read the **Cover Letter Guide** and print a copy.
3. In your browser's location box, enter the University of Waterloo's Career Services eManual URL **<http://www.cdm.uwaterloo.ca/steps.asp>**. Bookmark this site, and find the **Resumes & Letters** section of the manual.
4. Read this section, and jot down the tips you did not learn from the **Cover Letter Guide**.
5. End your session and submit your printout and tips.

---

1. French Spanish 2. English University of Alberta 3. Algonquin Room Four Points Thursday
4. Doctor 5. Uncle Michael Easter

C H A P T E R

Numbers

20

OBJECTIVES When you have completed the materials in this chapter, you will be able to do the following:

LEVEL I

- *Choose correctly between figure and word forms to express general numbers and numbers beginning sentences.*
- *Express money, dates, clock time, addresses, and telephone numbers appropriately.*

LEVEL II

- *Use the correct form in writing related numbers, consecutive numbers, periods of time, and ages.*
- *Use the correct form in expressing numbers with words, with abbreviations and symbols, and as round numbers.*

LEVEL III

- *Express correctly weights, measurements, and fractions.*
- *Use the correct form in expressing percentages, decimals, and ordinals.*

PRETEST

Examine the expression of numbers in the following sentences. Should word or figure form be used? Underline any incorrect form, and write an improved form in the blank provided. For example, which is preferred: *$10* or *ten dollars?*

1. Please plan to attend the 1st informational meeting on September 18th at ten a.m. ________________
2. When Roxanne reached 18 years of age, she assumed ownership of over fifty ha of property in two provinces. ________________
3. Please take twelve dollars to pick up 20 fifty-three-cent stamps at the post office. ________________

continued

PRETEST

4. Of the twenty cars we had available on May 2nd, we have only four cars left today. ______________

5. The art treasure measures only twenty-three cm by thirty cm, but it is said to be worth nearly two million dollars. ______________

Just as capitalization is governed by convention, so is the expression of numbers. Usage and custom determine whether numbers are to be expressed in the form of a figure (for example, *5*) or in the form of a word (for example, *five*). Numbers expressed as figures are shorter and easier to comprehend, yet numbers used as words are necessary in certain instances. The following guidelines are observed in expressing numbers that appear in written *sentences*. Numbers that appear in business documents such as invoices, statements, and purchase orders are always expressed in figures.

LEVEL I

▶ Basic Guidelines for Expressing Numbers

General Rules

The numbers *one* through *ten* are generally written as words. Numbers above *ten* are written as figures.

> The committee consisted of *nine* regular members and *one* chair.
> The *37* spoiled questionnaires were discarded.

Study Tip

To remember it better, some people call this the "Rule of Ten": Words for one through ten; figures for 11 and above.

Numbers that begin sentences are written as words. If a number involves more than two words, however, the sentence should be rewritten so that the number no longer falls at the beginning.

> *Twenty-three* investors provided capital for the down payment.
> A total of *320* distributors agreed to market the product. (Not *Three hundred twenty* distributors agreed to market the product.)

Money

Sums of money $1 or greater are expressed as figures. If a sum is a whole dollar amount, most business writers omit the decimal and zeros (whether or not the amount appears with fractional dollar amounts).

> Although he budgeted only *$25*, Mike spent *$34.50* for the gift.
> The statement showed purchases of *$7.13, $10, $43.50, $90,* and *$262.78.*

Sums less than $1 are written as figures that are followed by the word *cents*. If they appear with sums greater than $1, use a dollar sign and a decimal instead of the word *cents*.

> Lisa said that she had only *65 cents* with her.
> Our monthly petty cash statement showed purchases of *$7.13, $.99, $2.80, $1*, and *$.40*.

---

1. first 18 10 a.m. 2. eighteen 50 ha 3. $12 twenty 53-cent 4. 20 cars May 2 4 cars
5. 23 cm by 30 cm $2 million

Dates

In dates, numbers that appear after the name of the month are written in **cardinal figures** (*1, 2, 3,* etc.). Those that stand alone or appear before the name of a month are written in **ordinal figures** (*1st, 2nd, 3rd,* etc.).

> The meeting is scheduled for *October 5* in our office.
> On the *2nd* of January and again on the *18th,* we called for service.

Dates generally take the following form: month, day, year. An alternative form, used primarily in military and international correspondence, begins with the day of the month.

> By October 1, 2011, all construction on the subway must be completed. (General date format)
> The contract was originally signed *25 June 1999.* (Military and international format)

Some business organizations also prefer this international date style for its clarity since it separates the numerical date of the month from the year.

Career Tip

If your company has a style manual, check it for number preferences. Larger companies may prescribe the figure or word form they prefer for often-used numbers.

Clock Time

Figures are used when clock time is expressed with *a.m.* or *p.m.* Omit the colon and zeros with whole hours. When exact time is expressed with *o'clock,* either figures or words may be used. Note that phrases such as *in the afternoon* or *in the morning* may follow clock time expressed with *o'clock* but not time expressed with *a.m.* or *p.m.*

> The first shift starts at *8 a.m.*; the second, at *3:30 p.m.*
> At *four* (or *4*) *o'clock* in the afternoon, we'll announce the winner.

Addresses

Except for the number *One,* house and building numbers are expressed as figures. Apartment numbers, suite numbers, box numbers, and route numbers are also written in figure form.

805 Fiske Avenue	27321 Riverside Drive
One Victoria Boulevard	1762 Cone Street, Apt. 2B
PO Box 8935	Rural Route 19

If the officially designated form is unknown, street names that involve the number *ten* or a lower number are written as ordinal words (*First, Second*). In street names involving numbers greater than *ten,* the numeral portion is written as figures.

> 503 Second Street
> 11901 Ninth Avenue
> 2320 West 11 Street
> 613 North 102 Avenue

Spot the Blooper

From *The Suburban & Wayne Times:* "Cases of Lyme disease, which is transmitted by deer-carrying ticks, are on the rise." (What unintended meaning resulted from the unneeded hyphen?)

Telephone Numbers

Telephone and fax numbers are expressed with figures. When used, the area code is frequently placed in parentheses preceding the telephone number. In one common alternative form, the area code may be separated from the telephone number by a hyphen. A third and newer format is to separate the parts of the number with periods. When including an extension, separate it from the phone number with a comma.

> Please call us at *828-1100* for further information.
> You may reach me at *(306) 685-4321, Ext. 281,* after 9:30 a.m.

Call our toll-free number at 800-340-3281 for the latest sports updates.
Please fax your order to 902.937.5594.

Complete the reinforcement exercises for Level I on pp. 401–403.

LEVEL II

▶ Special Guidelines for Expressing Numbers

Related Numbers

Numbers used similarly in the same document are considered related and should be expressed as the largest number is expressed. Thus if the largest number is greater than *ten,* all the numbers should be expressed as figures.

Only *3* companies out of *147* failed to return the survey form.
Of the 98 email documents Casey received today, 19 were marked "Urgent" and 7 were marked "Confidential."
Nearly *20* employees will be expected to share the *15* computers, *8* printers, and *3* fax machines. (Note that items in a series are always considered to be related.)

Hotlink

This online handout downloadable from **<http://xnet.rrc.mb.ca/leshanson/Hot_Potato/Grammar_PPT/Numbers_or_Words.doc>** also links to a short quiz on expressing numbers.

Unrelated numbers within the same document are written as words or figures according to the general guidelines presented earlier in this chapter.

The *two* bridges carry at least *10,000* cars during the *four* peak traffic hours.
Twenty-three contract changes will be discussed by *89* employees working in *eight* departments.

Consecutive Numbers

When two numbers appear one after another and both modify a following noun, readers may misread the numbers because of their closeness. You should express one number in word form and the other in figure form. Use word form for the first number unless the second number would make a much shorter word.

We offered to publish *400 thirty*-page brochures. (Use figure form for the first and word form for the second number.)
The economist divided the era into *four 25*-year periods.
Erich purchased *two 512* MB memory cards for his digital camera.
We'll need at least *150 sixty*-watt bulbs. (Use word form for the second number as it is a significantly shorter word.)

Study Tip

Numbers included in a series (three or more items) are ALWAYS considered related.

Periods of Time

Periods of time such as seconds, hours, and years that can be expressed in one or two words are usually written in word form. However, figures may be used to achieve special emphasis in expressing business concepts such as discount rates, interest rates, warranty periods, credit terms, loan periods, and payment terms.

Word form
Mrs. Martino has been with our firm for *thirty-five* years.
We agreed to keep the book for only *fifteen* days.

Figure form (would require more than two words)
After a *183-day* strike, workers returned to their jobs.

Figure form (business concept)
For payment within *30* days, a cash discount is provided.
Higher interest rates are offered on *6-* to *9-*month certificates of deposit.

Note that in legal documents periods of time are usually expressed twice, first in words and then in figures enclosed in parentheses (*period of sixty (60) days*).

Study Tip

Figures are easier to understand and remember than words. That's why business terms, even for numbers under ten, are generally written as figures.

Ages and Anniversaries

Ages and anniversaries that can be written out in one or two words are generally expressed in word form. Those that require more than two words are written in figures. Figures are also used when an age (a) appears immediately after a name; (b) is expressed in exact years and months; or (c) is used in a technical, legal, or statistical sense.

When he was *forty-one,* Mr. Selnig became the company's president.
This year marks the *twenty-fifth* anniversary of the company's founding.
Grace Siebold, *63,* plans to retire in two years.
The child was adopted when he was *3* years and *8* months old.

Numbers Used With Words, With Abbreviations, and With Symbols

Numbers used with words are expressed as figures.

page 4	Policy 04-168315	Area Code 819
Room 14	Volume 5	Section 16
Option 3	Form 1040	Bylaw 96-221

Numbers used with abbreviations are also expressed as figures.

Apt. 16	Serial No. 265188440	Nos. 199 and 202
Ext. 245	Account No. 286-32-5891	Social Insurance No. 412 434 456

Notice that the word *number* is capitalized and abbreviated when it precedes a number. Notice, too, that no commas are used in serial, account, and policy numbers.

Symbols (such as #, %, ¢) are usually avoided in contextual business writing (sentences). In other business documents where space is limited, however, symbols are frequently used. Numbers appearing with symbols are expressed as figures.

15%   44¢   #10 nails   2/10, n/60

Spot the Blooper

From *The Denver Post*: "The Allied Jewish Federation, which overseas the fund drive, hopes to raise $5.5 million."

Round Numbers

Round numbers are approximations. They may be expressed in word or figure form, although figure form is shorter and easier to comprehend.

Approximately *400* (or *four hundred*) employees signed the petition.
At last count we had received about *20* (or *twenty*) reservations.

For ease of reading, round numbers in the millions or billions should be expressed with a combination of figures and words.

The Prime Minister asked for a budget cut of *$2 billion.*
In its lawsuit IBM made available to the government *69 million* documents.
Nearly *1.2 million* imported cars were sold last year.

Complete the reinforcement exercises for Level II on pp. 404–406.

LEVEL III

▶ Additional Guidelines for Expressing Numbers

Weights and Measurements

Weights and measurements, including temperatures, are expressed as figures.

> The truck needed *80* L of gasoline and *2* L of oil for the trip.
> A microfiche card measures *4* by *6* inches (about *10* by *15* cm).
> The announcement gave the baby's weight as *7* pounds *14* ounces.
> The highest temperature ever recorded was *134* degrees in 1922 in El Aziza, Libya.

In sentences the nouns following weights and measurements are spelled out if they refer to traditional units of measurement (for example, 7 *pounds* 14 *ounces*) but should not be spelled out if they refer to metric units of measure (10 by 15 *cm*). For business forms, charts, and technical writing, symbols or abbreviations are generally used.

> 57 kg   17°C   100 km   2 lb.   5 tbsp.   9′ × 12′   #10   7 oz.

Canada adopted SI (Système international d'unités, commonly referred to as the metric system) in 1971, but examples here include traditional forms such as *pound* and *foot* because they are still in common use.

Note that the metric/SI system uses symbols rather than abbreviations. No periods are used unless the symbol falls at the end of a sentence. Abbreviations for traditional units of measure are now commonly written without periods as well.

Fractions

Simple fractions are expressed as words and are hyphenated.

> Over *three-fourths* of the students attended the lecture.
> A *two-thirds* majority is needed to carry the measure.

Complex fractions appearing in sentences may be written either as figures or as a combination of figures and words.

> The computer will execute a command in *1 millionth* of a second. (Combination of words and figures is easier to comprehend.)
> Flight records revealed that the emergency system was activated *13/200* of a second after the pilot was notified. (Figure form is easier to comprehend.)

Hotlink

Here, at **<http://www.writersblock.ca/tips/monthtip/tipaug96.htm>**, are some additional tips on handling numbers.

Mixed fractions (whole numbers combined with fractions) are always expressed by figures.

> The office desks were expected to be *35¼* inches long, not *35½* inches. (Notice that no space follows a whole number when a keyboard fraction is used.)
> The envelope measured *3 5/8* inches by *6 1/2* inches. (Notice that fractions that must be keyed with diagonals are separated from their related whole numbers.)

When fractions that are constructed with diagonals appear with key fractions, be consistent by using the diagonal construction for all the fractions involved.

Percentages and Decimals

Percentages are expressed with figures that are followed by the expression *per cent*. The per cent sign (%) is used only on business forms or in statistical presentations.

Interest rates have been as low as *4 per cent* and as high as *19 per cent.*
The report states that *52 per cent* of the workers joined the union.

Decimals are expressed with figures. If a decimal does not contain a whole number (an integer) and does not begin with a zero, a zero should be placed before the decimal.

Daryl Thomas set a record when he ran the race in *9.86* seconds. (Contains a whole number)
Close examination revealed the settings to be *.005* of an inch off. (Begins with a zero)
Less than *0.1* per cent of the operating costs will be borne by taxpayers. (Zero placed before decimal that neither contains a whole number nor begins with a zero)

Hotlink

If you are still uncertain when to use numerals and when to use words, assistance is at hand with this PowerPoint, downloadable from **<http://xnet.rrc.mb.ca/leshanson/Hot_Potato/Numbers.htm>**.

Ordinals

Ordinal numbers are used to show position in an ordered sequence.

Although ordinal numbers are generally expressed in word form (*first, second, third,* etc.), three exceptions should be noted: (1) figure form is used for dates appearing before a month or appearing alone, (2) figure form is used for street names involving numbers greater than *ten,* and (3) figure form is used when the ordinal would require more than two words.

Most ordinals
The company is celebrating its *fortieth* anniversary.
Before the *eighteenth* century, spelling was not standardized.
Of 237 sales representatives, Joanna ranked *second* in total sales.
Jeanne Sauvé became the *twenty-third* Governor General in 1984.

Dates
Your payment must be received by the *30th* to qualify for the cash discount.
We experienced a power outage on the *2nd* of June.

Streets
A traffic light was installed on *Second* Street.
The customer service division has moved to *35th* Street.

Larger ordinals
Our bank ranks *103rd* in terms of capital investments.

Complete the reinforcement exercises for Level III on pp. 407–408.

HOTLINE QUERIES

Question: I recently saw the following format used by a business to publish its telephone number on its stationery and business cards: 647.582.0903. Is it now an option to use periods in telephone numbers?

Answer: Yes, this is now an acceptable option for writing telephone and fax numbers and may be reflecting European influences. To some, the style is upscale and chic; to others, it's just confusing. Telephone numbers written in the traditional formats are most readily recognized. That's why it's best to stick with parentheses or hyphens: (647) 582-0903 or 647-582-0903.

(Continued)

Question: I'm never sure when to hyphenate numbers, such as *thirty-one.* Is there some rule to follow?

Answer: When written in word form, the numbers *twenty-one* through *ninety-nine* are hyphenated. Numbers are also hyphenated when they form compound adjectives and precede nouns (*ten-year-old* child, *16-storey* building, *four-year* term, *30-day* lease).

Question: I've always been confused by *imply* and *infer.* Which is correct in this sentence: *We (imply* or *infer) from your message that the goods are lost.*

Answer: In your sentence use *infer. Infer* means "to draw a conclusion" or "to make a deduction based on facts." *Imply* means "to state indirectly." A listener or reader *infers.* A speaker or writer *implies.*

Question: Should I put quotation marks around figures to emphasize them? For example, *Your account has a balance of "$2,136.18."*

Answer: Certainly not! Quotation marks are properly used to indicate an exact quotation, or they may be used to enclose the definition of a word. They should not be used as a mechanical device for added emphasis.

Question: I'm an engineer, and we have just had a discussion in our office concerning spelling. I have checked the dictionary, and it shows *usage.* Isn't this word ever spelled *useage*?

Answer: No. The only spelling of *usage* is without the internal *e.* You are probably thinking of the word *usable,* which does have a variant spelling—*useable.* Both forms are correct, but *usable* is recommended for its simplicity. Incidentally, if the word *usage* can be replaced by the word *use,* the latter is preferred (*the use* (not *usage*) *of ink pens is declining*).

Question: How should I spell the word *lose* in this sentence? *The employee tripped over a (lose* or *loose) cord.*

Answer: In your sentence use the adjective *loose,* which means "not fastened," "not tight," or "having freedom of movement." Perhaps you can remember it by thinking of the common expression *loose change,* which suggests unattached, free coins jingling in your pocket. If you *lose (mislay)* some of those coins, you have less money and fewer *o*'s.

Question: My manager is preparing an advertisement for a charity event. She has written this: *Donors who give $100 dollars or more receive plaques.* I know this is not right, but I can't exactly put my finger on the problem.

Answer: The problem is in *$100 dollars.* That is like saying *dollars dollars.* Drop the word *dollars* and use only the dollar sign: *Donors who give $100 or more ....*

Question: A fellow team member wants to show dollar amounts in two forms, such as the following: *The consultant charges two hundred dollars ($200) an hour.* I think this is overkill. Do we have to show figures in two forms?

Answer: In formal legal documents, amounts of money may be expressed in words followed by figures in parentheses. However, business writers do not follow this practice because it is unnecessary, wordy, and pretentious. In fact, some readers are insulted because the practice suggests they are not bright enough to comprehend just one set of figures.

NAME ______________________

CHAPTER 20 Reinforcement Exercises

LEVEL I

A. (Self-check) Choose (a) or (b) to complete the following sentences.

1. We are able to finish only (a) 11, (b) eleven letters by noon. ______

2. (a) 15, (b) Fifteen applicants responded to the advertisement. ______

3. The office will reopen on the (a) 14th, (b) fourteenth of June. ______

4. Duplicating this brochure will cost (a) 4 cents, (b) \$.04 per page. ______

5. Ellen spends (a) \$30.00, (b) \$30 each month for her Internet-access service. ______

6. His address is listed as (a) Three, (b) 3 Meadowlark Drive. ______

7. Department mail is usually distributed at (a) 10, (b) ten a.m. ______

8. Organizers expect (a) 38,000, (b) 38000 to attend the Macworld Conference & Expo. ______

9. She said that a ream of paper would cost (a) \$6, (b) six dollars. ______

10. We plan to meet at (a) 9:00 a.m., (b) 9 a.m. Tuesday ______

Check your answers.

B. Assume that the following phrases appear within sentences (unless otherwise noted) in business correspondence. Write the preferred forms in the spaces provided. If a phrase is correct as shown, write *C*.

Example: twenty new blog entries <u>20 new blog entries</u>

1. fourteen clerks ______

2. on Tenth Street ______

3. \$.09 per issue ______

4. 7 email messages ______

5. June ninth ______

6. call 800/598-3459 ______

7. \$6.59, 98 cents, and \$30.00 ______

8. the eighteenth of September ______

9. meeting at 9:00 a.m. ______

10. eight o'clock breakfast meeting ______

11. thirty-three desks ______

12. January 22nd ______

13. a total of seventy-nine orders ______

14. costs \$49 dollars ______

15. two executives ______

16. exactly twenty-four dollars ______

17. 7 Hampton Square ______

18. 1 Hampton Square ______

19. (beginning of sentence) sixty-six rooms ______

1.a 2.b 3.a 4.a 5.b 6.b 7.a 8.a 9.a 10.b

20. at 7 o'clock ________________

21. (international style) May 15, 2002 ________________

22. at six thirty p.m. ________________

23. the fourth of May ________________

24. cheque for one hundred dollars ________________

25. exactly 90¢ ________________

26. before three p.m. ________________

27. 21 chapters ________________

28. 3 new laptops ________________

C. Rewrite these sentences, correcting any errors you note.

1. On January thirteenth Alex submitted the following petty cash disbursements: $2.80, 99 cents, $3.00, and 76 cents.

____

____

____

2. Elizabeth James moved from seventeen sixteen Sunset Drive to one Bellingham Court.

____

____

____

3. 22 pages of *The Gregg Reference Manual* are devoted to rules for expressing numbers.

____

____

____

4. On the 28 of January, I sent you 3 email messages about restricting Internet use.

____

____

____

5. If you have only thirty dollars, why are you considering the model that costs $49.99?

____

____

____

6. Regular work breaks are scheduled at 10:00 a.m. in the morning and again at 3:30 p.m. in the afternoon.

____

____

____

7. We want to continue operations through the thirtieth, but we may be forced to close by the twenty-second.

8. 1319 people visited our website when it launched July 1st.

9. 24 different wireless packages are available from our 3 local dealers.

10. Although McDonald's advertised a sandwich that cost only ninety-nine cents, most customers found that lunch cost between three dollars and three dollars and ninety-nine cents.

NAME ______________________

LEVEL II

A. (Self-check) Select (a) or (b) to complete each of the following sentences.

1. We are working on (a) three 16-page, (b) 3 sixteen-page booklets. ______
2. Elliot Walker has worked in Montreal for (a) twenty-seven, (b) 27 years. ______
3. The annual shareholders' meeting will be held in (a) Room Two, (b) Room 2. ______
4. Of the 235 emails sent, only (a) nine, (b) 9 bounced back. ______
5. Although she is only (a) 21, (b) twenty-one, Miss Love was appointed manager. ______
6. Google paid (a) $4.95 million, (b) $4,950,000 to settle a click-fraud case. ______
7. You can obtain Form (a) ten twenty, (b) 1020 by calling us. ______
8. Next week our company celebrates its (a) 25th, (b) twenty-fifth anniversary. ______
9. Your short-term loan covers a period of (a) 60, (b) sixty days. ______
10. The serial number on my monitor is (a) 85056170, (b) 85,056,170. ______

Check your answers.

B. For the following sentences underscore any numbers or words that are expressed inappropriately. Write the correct forms in the spaces provided. If a sentence is correct as written, write *C.*

Example: The documentation group has prepared 4 twenty-page reports. *four 20-page*

1. The advisory committee is composed of 17 members, of whom five are supervisors, three are consultants, and nine are technicians. ______
2. To qualify for the federal grant, we submitted 3 100-page proposals. ______
3. Protected by steel armour, today's undersea telephone cables are expected to last 25 years. ______
4. One spammer sent more than 825,000,000 unsolicited email messages. ______
5. The following policy Nos. are listed for John Daley: No. 1355801 and No. 1355802. ______
6. Model 8,400 costs $10,000 and can be leased for $275 a month. ______
7. Over 53,000,000 Chinese visit online forums regularly. ______
8. Of the 65 typed pages, nine pages need minor revisions and six pages require heavy revision. ______
9. John Edwards, forty-one, and Maria Gomez, thirty-three, were interviewed for the two executive positions. ______

1. a 2. a 3. b 4. b 5. b 6. a 7. b 8. b 9. a 10. a

10. On page twenty-two of Volume two, the total deficit is listed at nearly $34,000,000,000. ______________

11. Warranties on all flat-panel monitors are limited to ninety days. ______________

12. The total book club membership of eight hundred thousand received the four bonus books. ______________

13. Only 43 of the 57 staff members could attend the two training sessions. ______________

14. Bill Gates' Lake Washington mansion features a wall of twenty-four video screens, parking for twenty cars, and a reception hall for one hundred people. ______________

15. When the child was two years six months old, his parents established a trust fund for $1.6 million. ______________

16. It took 12 inspection teams to review and rewrite thirty thousand pages of deeds, options, leases, and bills of sale. ______________

17. The old man was 93 years old, but he said he felt as if he were fifty-three. ______________

18. With 4 pickups daily, the delivery service serves two thousand employees in 45 departments. ______________

C. Assume that the following phrases appear in business or professional correspondence. Write the preferred forms in the spaces provided. If a phrase is correct as shown, write *C*.

1. nine offices with eleven computers and fifteen desks

____

2. two twenty-five kg weights

____

3. loan period of sixty days

____

4. Martha Diamond, fifty-eight, and John Diamond, sixty-one

____

5. Account No. 362,486,012

____

6. three point two billion dollars

____

7. Gate Twenty-three

____

8. a period of seventeen years

____

9. 9 2-bedroom condos

____

10. about two hundred guests

____

11. four point four million people

____

12. Section three point two

____

13. insurance for 15 computers, 12 printers, and 3 scanners

____

14. fifty-nine customer comments

____

15. warranty period of two years

____

NAME ______________________________

LEVEL III

A. **(Self-check)** Choose (a) or (b) to complete the following sentences.

1. The rides are restricted to people taller than (a) 4'10", (b) 4 feet 10 inches. ________
2. Spam makes up more than (a) one-fifth, (b) one fifth, (c) 1/5 of all email messages sent. ________
3. Coca-Cola controls more than (a) 30 per cent, (b) thirty percent of the total soft-drink market in Japan. ________
4. Next year marks this company's (a) 40th, (b) fortieth anniversary. ________
5. Newspaper advertising accounts for about (a) one third, (b) one-third of all advertising dollars. ________
6. The company warehouses are now located on (a) Sixty-second, (b) 62nd Street. ________
7. We need a rug measuring (a) 3 by 4 m, (b) three by four m. ________
8. This year's maintenance costs are only (a) 0.5, (b) .5 per cent above last year's. ________
9. Did you order (a) five, (b) 5 L of oil? ________
10. Did you know that many high-rise buildings have no (a) 13th, (b) thirteenth floor? ________

Check your answers.

B. Rewrite the following sentences with special attention to appropriate number usage.

1. "Kingda Ka," which claims to be the world's fastest and tallest roller coaster, travels one hundred twenty eight miles per hour and is four hundred fifty six feet high.

____

____

2. Swiss engineers used precise instruments to ensure that Kingda Ka's three thousand one hundred eighteen feet of steel track were within 0.05 inches of specifications.

____

____

3. To ride Kingda Ka, one must be at least fifty-four inches but less than 6′5″ tall.

____

____

1.b 2.a 3.a 4.b 5.b 6.b 7.a 8.a 9.b 10.b

4. Travelling one hundred fifty km/h in an eighty km/h zone, the street racers caused a fatal crash.

5. Approximately 3/4 of every dollar contributed goes to charity.

6. Our company ranks one hundred seventh in terms of total exports.

7. Invoices that are paid before the tenth will receive a two per cent cash discount.

8. At least seven-tenths of the members attended the May tenth meeting when we approved the budget of thirty-five thousand dollars.

9. In the year 2,008 our nation celebrated its one hundred forty-first anniversary.

10. A stock that costs fifty dollars a share and pays four dollars in dividends will yield an eight per cent return.

C. Optional Writing. Your instructor may ask you to complete one or both of these exercises on a separate sheet.

(1) Select ten number rules from this chapter. Write one sentence illustrating each rule. Label each rule.

(2) In your local newspaper, find ten sentences with numbers. Write those sentences on a separate sheet. After each one explain what usage rule the number style represents. Strive to find examples illustrating different rules.

Editor's Challenge

The following messages contain intentional errors representing language principles covered thus far. Use standard proofreading marks to make corrections.

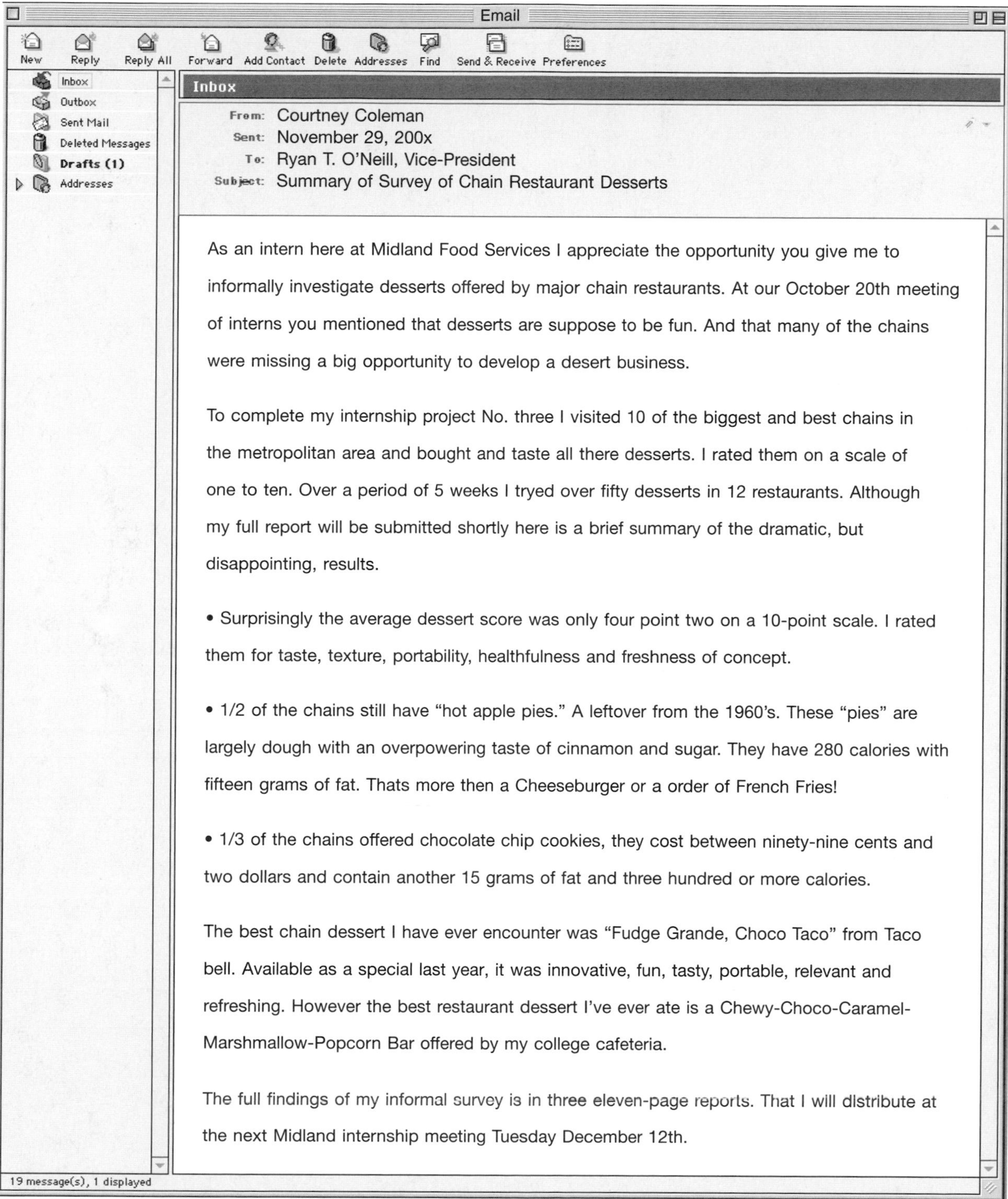

Inbox

From: Courtney Coleman
Sent: November 29, 200x
To: Ryan T. O'Neill, Vice-President
Subject: Summary of Survey of Chain Restaurant Desserts

As an intern here at Midland Food Services I appreciate the opportunity you give me to informally investigate desserts offered by major chain restaurants. At our October 20th meeting of interns you mentioned that desserts are suppose to be fun. And that many of the chains were missing a big opportunity to develop a desert business.

To complete my internship project No. three I visited 10 of the biggest and best chains in the metropolitan area and bought and taste all there desserts. I rated them on a scale of one to ten. Over a period of 5 weeks I tryed over fifty desserts in 12 restaurants. Although my full report will be submitted shortly here is a brief summary of the dramatic, but disappointing, results.

• Surprisingly the average dessert score was only four point two on a 10-point scale. I rated them for taste, texture, portability, healthfulness and freshness of concept.

• 1/2 of the chains still have "hot apple pies." A leftover from the 1960's. These "pies" are largely dough with an overpowering taste of cinnamon and sugar. They have 280 calories with fifteen grams of fat. Thats more then a Cheeseburger or a order of French Fries!

• 1/3 of the chains offered chocolate chip cookies, they cost between ninety-nine cents and two dollars and contain another 15 grams of fat and three hundred or more calories.

The best chain dessert I have ever encounter was "Fudge Grande, Choco Taco" from Taco bell. Available as a special last year, it was innovative, fun, tasty, portable, relevant and refreshing. However the best restaurant dessert I've ever ate is a Chewy-Choco-Caramel-Marshmallow-Popcorn Bar offered by my college cafeteria.

The full findings of my informal survey is in three eleven-page reports. That I will distribute at the next Midland internship meeting Tuesday December 12th.

October 1, 200x

CERTIFIED MAIL, RETURN RECEIPT REQUESTED

Mr. Charles Smith
Customer Relations
Sony Canada

115 Gordon Baker Road
Toronto, ON M2H 3R6

Dear Mr. Smith,

Pictures from a once in a lifetime trip are irreplaceable. Thats why I put my trust in Sonys Cyber-shot DSC-W100 Digital Camera, which I bought for a cruise I took to the french caribbean last Summer to celebrate my 40th birthday. Experience, dependability and customer service, these are the quality's that I associate with the name "Sony."

I took 100's of pictures on my twenty day trip. Although I checked some of the early shots using the lcd screen I didn't check any pictures for the last 1/2 of the trip in order to conserve my battery. When I come home however I learned that most of the pictures I took latter in the trip did not turn out because the camera had malfunctioned. 98 of the pictures I took the last week of my trip were faded to a near white colour. Enclosed is the camera, the memory card I used, the printed photos and my receipt for the camera.

As you must realize the value of these photographs are far greater then the cost of the printing, or the purchase price of the camera. The real loss is the complete record of a beautiful trip. Without pictures, I will not remember how I felt and looked standing in front of diamond rock in the Southern part of Martinique or shopping in the town of marigot in St. Martin. I will not remember dancing with children around a fire in a Guadalupe Village. 11 days of my dream vacation was essentially unrecorded. This represents more than 50% of my vacation.

Replacing the film or camera are not enough. Without pictures I feel like I never took the trip. I have suffered a tremendous emotional loss and I am requesting that sony pay me $7500 so that I may repeat my trip, and replace the pictures lost because of this faulty camera.

I know that Sony enjoys a excellent reputation with consumers, therefore, I trust that you will do the right thing in helping me replace my lost memories. Please contact me by October 30th so that I may begin making plans for a Spring cruise.

Sincerely,

Daniella Davidson

Daniella Davidson

Enclosures: Sony Cyber-shot camera, memory card, printed photos, receipt

POSTTEST

Underline numbers that are expressed inappropriately. Write corrected forms in the space provided.

1. It took Revenue Canada seven years to collect the 750,000 dollars owed by the 2 companies.

   ____

   ____

2. Before the third of the month, we had received seventeen calls regarding the bicycle we advertised for twenty dollars.

   ____

   ____

3. The department had eighteen employees; they shared four telephones, ten file cabinets, and seven computers.

   ____

   ____

4. If you save only five hundred dollars annually, you'll have fifty-four thousand dollars after twenty-five years if your savings earn an average of 10%.

   ____

   ____

5. We will need ten fifty-page booklets before December 1st.

   ____

   ____

1. $750,000 two 2. 3rd 17 $20 3. 18 4. $500 $54,000 25 10 per cent 5. 50-page December 1

learning.web.ways

You've sent out your résumés and landed a couple of promising interviews, but you'd like to learn more about what to expect and how to answer interview questions.

Goal: To learn how to be more successful in employment interviewing.

1. With your web browser on the screen, go to the Job-Interview website **<http://www.job-interview.net>**, and bookmark it.
2. Click **Interview Tips** (top of screen), and scroll down to identify the site recommended for further exploration.
3. Familiarize yourself with the material on the interview process, and print out the sections you find most useful or informative.
4. Use the browser Back button to return to Job-Interview.net. Explore other articles on interviewing.
5. Using your bookmarks, go to the University of Waterloo's Career Services eManual URL at **<http://www.cdm.uwaterloo.ca/steps.asp>**.
6. Select the link for **Interviews**. What two additional tips can you find on this site? Write them down.
7. End your session and submit your printout and answers.

C H A P T E R

Effective Sentences 21

OBJECTIVES When you have completed the materials in this chapter, you will be able to do the following:

LEVEL I

- *Eliminate wordy phrases and redundant words.*
- *Use the active voice of verbs in writing efficient sentences.*
- *Compose unified sentences by avoiding excessive detail and extraneous ideas.*

LEVEL II

- *Write clear sentences using parallel construction for similar ideas.*
- *Place words, phrases, and clauses close to the words they modify.*
- *Avoid ambiguous pronoun references when using pronouns such as* this, that, *and* which.

LEVEL III

- *Achieve emphasis by subordinating secondary ideas to primary ideas.*
- *Recognize and use concrete words instead of abstract words.*
- *Use transitional expressions (such as* therefore, however, *and* for example*) to develop coherence between thoughts.*

PRETEST

Rewrite the following sentences to eliminate problems in parallelism, redundancy, modification, reference, conciseness, and coherence.

1. In view of the fact that we are moving, we are not renewing the contract.

2. After illegally removing documents from his Toronto office, a jury convicted Conrad Black of obstruction of justice.

3. Lisa had to empty the cash register, count the cash, and the doors had to be locked.

4. I would like your final decision by June 1.

5. The new computer is for the desk in the outer office, which was delivered yesterday.

Business people value efficient, economical writing that is meaningful and coherent. Wordy communication wastes the reader's time; unclear messages confuse the reader and are counterproductive. In the business world, where time is valuable, efficient writing is demanded. You can improve your writing skills by emulating the practices of good writers. Most good writers begin with a rough draft that they revise to produce a final version. This chapter shows you how to revise your rough-draft sentences to make them efficient, clear, emphatic, and coherent.

1. Since we are moving, we are not renewing the contract. 2. After illegally removing documents from his Toronto office, Conrad Black was convicted of obstruction of justice. 3. Lisa had to empty the cash register, count the cash, and lock the doors. 4. I would like your decision by June 1. 5. The new computer, which was delivered yesterday, is for the outer office.

▶ Writing Efficient Sentences

LEVEL I

Revising Wordy Phrases

Sentences are efficient when they convey a thought directly and economically—that is, in the fewest possible words. Good writers excise all useless verbiage from their writing.

Wordy Phrases	Concise Substitutes
along the lines of	like
at all times	always
at the present time	now
at this point in time	now
by the name of	named
due to the fact that	because
for the purpose of	for
in all probability	probably
in connection with	about
in spite of the fact that	even though
in the amount of	for
in the event that	if
in the final analysis	finally
in the near future	soon
in the neighbourhood of	approximately
in terms of	regarding
in view of the fact that	since
until such time as	until
with a view to	to
with reference to	about
with regard to	about

Hotlink

The Capital Community College grammar materials are among the best on the Web. Don't miss sentences (basic parts), found at **<http://grammar.ccc.commnet.edu/grammar/powerpoint.htm>**.

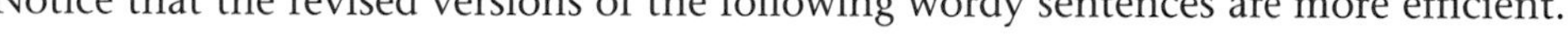

Notice that the revised versions of the following wordy sentences are more efficient.

Wordy: *Due to the fact that* fire damaged our warehouse, we must delay some shipments.
More efficient: *Because* fire damaged our warehouse, we must delay some shipments.

Wordy: Please send your cheque *in the amount of* $45.
More efficient: Please send your cheque *for* $45.

Wordy: We expected *in the neighbourhood of* 25 applicants.
More efficient: We expected *approximately* 25 applicants.

Eliminating Redundant Words

Words that are needlessly repetitive are said to be "redundant." Writers can achieve greater efficiency (and thus more effective sentences) by eliminating redundant words or phrases.

Redundant: The examples shown in Figure 2 illustrate letter styles.
More efficient: Figure 2 shows letter styles.

Redundant: The seminar covers only the fundamental basics.
More efficient: The seminar covers only the basics (or, only the fundamentals).

Hotlink

To learn how to avoid wordiness in your own writing, consult the Acadia University page at **<http://ace.acadiau.ca/english/grammar/wordiness.htm>**.

Hotlink

Passive voice clogs up sentences and paragraphs. For another look at the active vs. passive voice debate, see **<http://www.writersblock.ca/tips/monthtip/tipmar97.htm>**.

Redundant: As a rule, we generally approve all such requests.
More efficient: We generally approve all such requests.

Redundant: The committee co-operated together to settle the issue.
More efficient: The committee co-operated to settle the issue.

Using the Active Voice

Sentences that use active verbs are more economical—and, of course, more direct—than those using passive verbs. (See Chapter 8, Level II, for a review of passive and active voices.)

Passive: Your account *has been credited* with your recent payment.
Active: We *credited* your account with your recent payment.

Passive: At our next meeting your request *will be considered.*
Active: At our next meeting we *will consider* your request.

Passive: Our Products Division *was informed* by you that you want an office copier.

Active: You *informed* our Products Division that you want an office copier.

Writing Unified Sentences

A sentence is unified if it contains only closely related ideas. When extraneous or unrelated ideas appear in a sentence, they confuse the reader. Sentences lacking unity can be improved by clarifying the relationship between the ideas, by excising the extraneous ideas, or by shifting the unrelated ideas to separate sentences.

Lacks unity: It is easy for you to do your Christmas shopping, and we offer three unique catalogues.
Improved: Because we offer three unique catalogues, it is easy for you to do your Christmas shopping.

Lacks unity: I certainly appreciate the time you spent with me in our interview last week, and I am enrolling in a computer science course this summer.
Improved: I certainly appreciate the time you spent with me last week. Because of our interview, I am enrolling in a computer science course this summer.

Lacks unity: Retailers must have a system of inventory control, and they must keep current on reorders.
Improved: To be able to keep current on reorders, retailers must have a system of inventory control.

Hotlink

For additional insight on matters of clarity and good writing, download this handout on Improving Your Style, provided by the University of Guelph: **<http://www.lib.uoguelph.ca/assistance/writing_services//components/documents/style.pdf**

The inclusion of excessive detail can also damage sentence unity. If many details are necessary for overall clarity, put them in an additional sentence.

Excessive detail: One of the nation's leading suppliers of pure bottled water mails thousands of computerized statements every month, along with a variety of inserts including overdue payment notices and pieces that are meant to be advertising and promotions, which became very costly in terms of both cash flow and personnel time.

Improved: One of the nation's leading suppliers of pure bottled water mails thousands of monthly computerized statements, overdue notices, and promotional information. This mailing operation has become costly and time-consuming.

Excessive detail: A report can be important, but it may not be effective or be read because it is too long and bulky, which will also make it more difficult to distribute, to store, and to handle, as well as increasing its overall cost.

Improved: An important report may be ineffective because it is too long. Its bulk may increase its cost and make it difficult to read, handle, distribute, and store.

Spot the Blooper

Announcer's voice on a TV ad for Ford: "What is it about Ford cars that makes it the best-selling car in America?"

Complete the reinforcement exercises for Level I on pp. 422–424.

LEVEL II

▶ Writing Clear Sentences

Clear sentences immediately convey their central thought. Good writers achieve sentence clarity by the use of parallel construction, the avoidance of misplaced modifiers, and the use of unambiguous pronoun references.

Developing Parallel Construction

Clarity can be improved by using grammatically similar structures to express related parts of a sentence. For example, do not use *ing* words for two of the ideas in a list and a *to* verb for the third idea: *reading, eating, and studying* (not *to study*). Use nouns with nouns, verbs with verbs, phrases with phrases, and clauses with clauses. In the following list, use all verbs: *the machine sorted, stamped, and counted* (not *and had a counter*). For phrases, the wording for all parts of the list should be matched: *safety must be improved in the home, in the classroom, and on the job* (not *and for office workers*).

Hotlink

To learn how to write concisely, consult **<http://www.unc.edu/depts/wcweb/handouts/style.html>**.

Faulty: Steel filing cabinets are best for durability, ease of cleaning, and they resist fire better.

Improved: Steel filing cabinets are best for durability, ease of cleaning, and fire resistance. (Matches nouns.)

Faulty: Composing, revising, and then to retype—these are necessary steps in report writing.

Improved: Composing, revising, and retyping—these are necessary steps in report writing. (Matches *ing* nouns.)

Avoiding Misplaced Modifiers

As you will recall, modifiers are words, phrases, or clauses that limit or restrict other words, phrases, or clauses. To be clear, modifiers must be placed carefully, so that the words modified by them are obvious. When a modifier is placed so that it does not appear to be modifying the word or words intended to be modified, that modifier is said to be *misplaced.* In Chapter 11 introductory verbal modifiers were discussed. An introductory verbal modifier is sometimes misplaced simply by being at the beginning of the sentence. Consider how the introductory verbal modifier makes the following sentence nonsensical: *Walking down the street, the building was the tallest I had ever seen.*

Spot the Blooper

"The patient's pelvis was fractured by being thrown from a car."

Hotlink

You'll find a whole page on ambiguous modifiers (including misplaced modifiers) in the Sentence Elements section of the University of Calgary's online English Grammar Guide at **<http://www.ucalgary.ca/UofC/eduweb/grammar/>**. Click on "Sentence Elements" and follow the link to "Ambiguous Modifier."

Spot the Blooper

"Being moribund on arrival at the hospital, the doctor could do nothing for the patient."

Spot the Blooper

From *The Boston Globe*: "Then her hair caught fire while sitting in a front seat during a fireworks display."

After all, the building was not doing the walking. In positions other than the beginning of a sentence, misplaced modifiers may also interfere with sentence clarity.

Faulty:	We provide a map for all visitors *reduced to a one-inch scale.*
Improved:	For all visitors we provide a map *reduced to a one-inch scale.*
Faulty:	Employees did not hear the alarm *working busily on the rush printing job.*
Improved:	Employees *working busily on the rush printing job* did not hear the alarm.
Faulty:	You can install these wall pockets on flat surfaces *with screws or double-foam tape.*
Improved:	*With screws or double-foam tape,* you can install these wall pockets on flat surfaces.

Improving Pronoun References

Sentence confusion results from the use of pronouns without clear antecedents (refer to Chapter 7 for a discussion of *antecedent*). Be particularly careful with the pronouns *this, that, which,* and *it.* Confusion often results when these pronouns have as their antecedents an entire clause; such confusion can usually be avoided by substituting a noun for the pronoun or by following the pronoun with a clarifying noun (or nouns).

Faulty:	Installation of a computerized billing system has improved our cash flow and reduced our accounts receivable. *This* helps our entire operation run more efficiently and profitably.
Improved:	Installation of a computerized billing system has improved our cash flow and reduced our accounts receivable. *The new system* helps our entire operation run more efficiently and profitably.
Faulty:	We have a policy of responding to customer inquiries and orders on the same day they are received. *That* keeps us busy and keeps our customers satisfied.
Improved:	We have a policy of responding to customer inquiries and orders on the same day they are received. *That policy* keeps us busy and keeps our customers satisfied.
Faulty:	Our engineering projects require work on thousands of details that need constant updating and access to technical data, supplies, and references, *which* is why an open office design allowing team interaction is essential.
Improved:	Our engineering projects require work on thousands of details that need constant updating and access to technical data, supplies, and references. *These needs* explain why an open office design allowing team interaction is essential.

Complete the reinforcement exercises for Level II on pp. 425–427.

▶ Writing Emphatic and Coherent Sentences

LEVEL III

In your writing you can achieve emphasis and coherence by using clause subordination, concrete words, and effective transitions.

Emphasis Through Subordination

Subordination is a technique used by skilful writers to show the relationship between unequal ideas. Appropriate emphasis can be achieved by using subordinate conjunctions, such as *if, because, since,* and *when,* and relative pronouns, such as *who, which,* and *that,* to introduce secondary ideas or incidental information. Principal ideas should appear in independent clauses, and less important ideas should be expressed in subordinate or dependent clauses.

Principal idea: Compucorp recently entered the microcomputer market.
Secondary idea: Compucorp is a division of Intel.
Sentence: Compucorp, which is a division of Intel, recently entered the microcomputer market.

Principal idea: Your account is now three months overdue.
Secondary idea: You have been a good customer in the past.
Sentence: Although you have been a good customer in the past, your account is now three months overdue.

Principal idea: A credit card holder is not liable for more than $50 in unauthorized purchases.
Secondary idea: The credit card holder must give notice to the issuer of the card.
Sentence: If a credit card holder gives notice to the issuer of the card, the holder is not liable for more than $50 in unauthorized purchases.

Did You Know?

The language of the Information Age is English. More than 80 per cent of all the information stored in the millions of computers around the world is stored in English. And 85 per cent of all international telephone conversations are conducted in English.

Emphasis Through the Use of Concrete Words

As you know, concrete words (see Chapter 4, Level I) refer to specific persons, places, concepts, and actions. They bring to mind sharp images and arouse strong feelings. Abstract words, such as *honesty, freedom,* and *utilization,* because they refer to general ideas, do not call forth immediate sensory reactions or feelings. Use concrete words and constructions to make your writing emphatic, persuasive, and unambiguous.

Abstract: Your shipment will be sent *soon.*
Concrete: Your shipment will be sent *October 1.*

Abstract: Our candidate won by a *substantial margin.*
Concrete: Our candidate won by a *2-to-1 margin.*

Abstract: The utilization of *computer capabilities* helped us reduce costs.
Concrete: *Computerized filing* and *billing* helped us reduce costs.

Abstract: The Model DC-161 copier produces your first copy *quickly.*
Concrete: The Model DC-161 copier produces your first copy *in five seconds.*

Career Tip

Use concrete words when you wish to emphasize or promote an idea. Use abstract words to soften bad news.

When an abstract word is necessary, its meaning can often be enhanced by the addition of clarifying words.

Hotlink

For some basic advice on coherent, unified paragraphs, visit this Carleton University web page **<http://www.carleton.ca/wts/handouts/Paragraphs.htm>**.

Abstract: During the hearing, no one questioned Mr. Turner's *loyalty.*

Concrete: During the hearing, no one questioned Mr. Turner's *loyalty to the company.*

Coherence Through the Use of Transitional Words or Phrases

Orderly and consistent development of ideas leads to coherence. Coherence between sentences can be attained by the use of transitional expressions such as *therefore, in this way, in addition, for example, however, moreover, for this reason,* and *on the other hand.* Such words and phrases serve as flags to signal the reader that ideas are being contrasted or amplified. Notice that transitional words and phrases in the following sentences help the reader connect successive ideas.

We improved customer services as a result of spending less time on clerical chores. *Moreover,* we reduced storage charges for shipments held up because of incorrect documentation.

Our company stands ready to help you in the event of loss or damage to your microfilm records. *For example,* we have salvaged thousands of metres of muddied, tangled rolls of microfilm after floods.

A blank endorsement enables anyone in possession of a cheque to cash it. A special endorsement, *on the other hand,* enables only a specific person to negotiate the cheque.

When the federal government purchases goods on a cost-plus contract, it requires detailed accounting reports. *In this way,* it can monitor the production operations and costs.

Hotlink

Take this quiz on combining sentences, posted at **<http://web2uvcs.ca/ele/studyzone/410/reading/exercises/deathqz.htm>**.

Complete the reinforcement exercises for Level III on pp. 428–429.

HOTLINE QUERIES

Question: I just typed this sentence: *You will see in our manual where multiple bids must be obtained.* Somewhere from my distant past I seem to recall that *where* should not be used this way. Can you help me?

Answer: You're right. *Where* should not be substituted for the relative pronoun *that.* In your sentence, use *that.* A similar faulty construction to avoid is the use of *while* for *although* (*although* (not *while*) *I agree with his position, I disagree with his procedures*).

Question: When the company name *Halperin, Inc.,* appears in the middle of a sentence, is there a comma following *Inc.*?

Answer: Current authorities recommend the following practice in punctuating *Inc.* and *Ltd.:* Do not use commas to set off such expressions unless the company does so itself. Canadian companies, unlike American companies, seldom use commas in this position. If the company does use a comma before an expression like *Inc.,* however, then a comma also follows *Inc.* whenever it is followed by other words in a sentence (*we received from Kent, Inc., its latest catalogue*).

Question: Where should the word *sic* be placed when it is used?

Answer: *Sic* means "thus" or "so stated," and it is properly placed immediately following the word or phrase to which it refers. For example, *The kidnappers placed a newspaper advertisement that read, "Call Monna [sic] Lisa." Sic* is used within a quotation to indicate that a quoted word or phrase, though inaccurately spelled or used, appeared thus in the original. *Sic* is italicized and placed within brackets.

Question: Which is correct: *I feel* (*bad* or *badly*)?

Answer: *Bad* is an adjective meaning "not good," "ill," "regretful," etc. *Badly* is an adverb meaning "in a bad manner," "poorly," or "greatly." Your sentence appears to require *bad* (*I feel ill*), unless you mean that your sense of touch is impaired (*I feel poorly*).

Question: Should I capitalize *French* dressing?

Answer: Yes. Adjectives derived from proper nouns are capitalized (*French* dressing, *German* shepherd, *Danish* furniture). A few very well-known adjectives, however, are not capitalized (*pasteurized* milk, *china* plates).

Question: In a business report is it acceptable to write the following: *Most everyone agrees* ...?

Answer: In this construction *most* is a shortened form of *almost*. Although such contractions are heard in informal speech, they should not appear in business writing. Instead, use the longer form: *Almost everyone agrees* ....

Question: Everyone says "consensus of opinion," yet I understand that there is some objection to this expression.

Answer: Yes, the expression is widely used. However, since *consensus* means "collective opinion," adding the word *opinion* results in a redundancy.

NAME ________________________________

CHAPTER 21 Reinforcement Exercises

LEVEL I

A. **(Self-check)** In the following sentences, inefficient phrases have been underlined. In the space provided after each sentence, suggest a more efficient substitute for each underlined phrase.

Example: In the event that he is convicted, he could be sentenced to 20 years in prison. ___if___

1. In view of the fact that you have not responded to our letters, we have no alternative. ____________
2. We must at the present time send your account to our collection agency. ____________
3. Due to the fact that a strike has temporarily closed our factory, deliveries are delayed. ____________
4. We have to inform all customers with regard to our increased delivery charges. ____________
5. In the event that you are unable to attend, please notify us at once. ____________
6. We are attaching an invoice in the amount of $450. ____________
7. In spite of the fact that production costs are rising, we have tried to maintain our current pricing schedule. ____________
8. We find that we must at this point in time reconsider our prices. ____________
9. The lawyer refused to comment with regard to the charges against her client. ____________
10. We expected growth in the neighbourhood of 25 per cent. ____________

Check your answers.

B. Rewrite the following sentences to eliminate redundancies.

Example: This paragraph is exactly identical to that one.

This paragraph is identical to that one.

1. The reason why we are discussing the issue is to reach a consensus of opinion.

____

____

2. Our modern office equipment is up to date in every feature.

____

____

1. Since 2. now 3. Because 4. of/about 5. If 6. for 7. Even though/Although 8. now
9. about 10. of approximately/about

3. Any pages with corrections that are visible to the eye must be retyped.

4. In an explanation at the beginning of the article, the author explained his position.

C. Make the following sentences more efficient and more direct by using the active voice.

Example: The invoice was sent by our organization ten days ago.

We sent the invoice ten days ago.

1. Better service is received by our customers who read the instruction booklet.

2. Your order is now being processed by our Shipping Department.

3. Apparently my account was not credited by you with my cheque for $35.

4. The Employee of the Month award has been won by Robert Wedman.

D. The following sentences lack unity. Improve them by reorganizing the ideas or by shifting extra details to separate sentences.

Example: We are installing a centralized dictation system, and our current transcription production is days behind schedule.

Because we are installing a centralized dictation system, we are days behind in our current transcription production.

1. The keynote speaker will be Dr. Jay S. Cook, and vendors will display their products following the keynote address.

2. We have placed a lien on your property, and your payment is 60 days past due, which explains the lien.

3. We are one of the nation's largest office products distributors, and you can save 15 to 50 per cent on your word processing supplies for your office which we supply to our 260,000 customers who are satisfied from coast to coast because we have been in business for the past twenty years satisfying our customers.

4. Jeffrey Skilling had been CEO of Enron, and then he was convicted on 16 counts of fraud, conspiracy, and other charges and is now in a minimum-security US jail, where he is serving a 24-year sentence.

NAME ______________________________

LEVEL II

A. (Self-check) In the sentences below, the underlined words illustrate the following: (a) faulty parallel construction, (b) faulty phrase placement, or (c) faulty pronoun reference. After each sentence write the letter that best indicates the sentence fault.

Example: Our objectives are to increase production, reduce costs, and improving the quality of our work. ___a___

1. We use a four-part delivery ticket, with three copies made in various weights; this is the basis of our billing system. ________
2. Our visitor's package for Timmins includes one night's accommodation, continental breakfast, and you'll receive passes for the gold mine tour and the Shania Twain Centre. ________
3. A spokesperson for TD Banknorth indicated that the company is considering the appropriate next steps in an email message. ________
4. Our new billing system totals all balances, gives weekly reports, and statements are printed. ________
5. Centralized inspection in one area and floor inspection along the assembly line improve product quality; it is useful when precise standards must be met. ________
6. Automatic cash transfers can be made only on the written authority of the customer from a chequing account. ________
7. Computing, coding, recording, and storage—these are functions of data processing. ________
8. The three basic elements of a computer are input, processor, and output units, which can be obtained in a variety of configurations. ________
9. The next time you travel for business or for pleasure, charge everything to your credit card anywhere in the world. ________
10. Our objectives are to make our shares profitable, to operate efficiently, and developing good employee relations. ________

Check your answers.

B. Rewrite the following sentences so that they demonstrate parallel construction.

1. The job description lists these duties: answering the telephone, making appointments, and data must be collected for reports.

____

____

1.c 2.a 3.b 4.a 5.c 6.b 7.a 8.c 9.b 10.a

2. Tilley's travel shorts for men are lightweight, can be washed and dried overnight, and available in small to XXXL sizes.

3. Business letters should be written concisely, clearly, and with accuracy.

4. In filing, the use of colour can increase productivity significantly by providing faster retrieval, reducing the number of lost files, and improvement of employee morale.

C. Rewrite these sentences to remedy misplaced modifiers.

1. The customer wrote a cheque for his purchase with insufficient funds.

2. Any person may recover damages from the manufacturer of a product who is injured by a product.

3. Our coat resembles the original trenchcoat for the soldiers of the First World War designed by Englishman Thomas Burberry.

4. An instrument technician is needed for the Kensington Eye Institute with two years' recent experience.

D. Rewrite the following sentences to avoid faulty pronoun references.

1. Mrs. Valdez suggested that we try a four-day work week on an experimental basis for one month. *That* received considerable employee support.

2. As few as 5000 to 7000 wild tigers remain in the wild; *this* is a major concern for organizations like the World Wildlife Fund.

3. Our equipment is outmoded, production is costly, and orders are slow, *which* is why we are forced to cut back.

4. Kathleen speaks both French and Japanese fluently, *which* is why we are offering her a job.

NAME ______________________________

LEVEL III

A. (**Self-check**) After each of the following sentences, write *T* (true) or *F* (false).

1. Appropriate subordination of secondary ideas is a technique of skilful writers. ______
2. The word *however* might be used as a transition between related ideas. ______
3. *Transition* is an example of a concrete word. ______
4. The word *when* may be used to introduce a principal idea in an independent clause. ______
5. Transitional expressions serve as flags to signal changes in the presentation of ideas. ______
6. The use of concrete words makes writing more persuasive and emphatic. ______
7. Coherence is achieved when sentences and their parts are related logically. ______
8. Principal ideas should appear in independent clauses. ______
9. *Utilization* is an example of an abstract word. ______
10. Abstract words are as effective as concrete words. ______

Check your answers.

B. Shown below are sets of principal ideas and secondary ideas. For each set, write a sentence combining, with appropriate emphasis, both ideas.

	Principal Idea	Secondary Idea
1.	Ron Joyce and Tim Horton founded their coffee-and-doughnut business in Hamilton, Ontario, in the 1960s.	Tim Horton was a professional hockey player until his death in 1974.

____

____

	Principal Idea	Secondary Idea
2.	La Cité collégiale offers more than 80 post-secondary programs.	La Cité collégiale was the first French-language college of applied arts and technology in Ontario.

____

____

1.T 2.T 3.F 4.F 5.T 6.T 7.T 8.T 9.T 10.F

3. Critics say Barbie promotes unhealthy stereotypes. | Mattel has sold more than a billion dolls from its long-lived Barbie line.

4. Pierre Elliott Trudeau's *Memoirs* was on the bestseller list for several months. | *Memoirs* cost $35 in hardcover.

5. Alexander Shanks invented the first effective lawnmower in 1842. | Alexander Shanks was a Scot.

C. Rewrite the following sentences, making the italicized words concrete. Supply any information needed.

Example: The Bank of Canada's key rate was *increased.*

The Bank of Canada's key rate was increased by a quarter of a point.

1. We will send your order *as soon as possible.*

2. When we have further information, we will *contact* you.

3. Our daughter *is studying* at university.

4. Nancy Venables gave birth to a healthy *baby* in a *local hospital.*

D. Optional Writing. Your instructor may ask you to complete this exercise on a separate sheet.

Write four original sentences that use the following transitional expressions to develop coherence: *therefore, however, consequently,* and *in addition.* Write a sentence with a misplaced modifier; then show how it can be remedied. Label all five sentences.

Editor's Challenge

The following abstract and letter contain errors reflecting the concepts you have studied thus far. Use proofreading marks to show all necessary corrections. Be especially alert to wordy expressions that could be condensed.

ABSTRACT

On the date of November 10th Dennis W. Wilbur, Director, human resources development authorized a study for the purpose of learning whether or not employment equity guidelines for women is being met at Globex enterprises.

A research program was developed to make investigation into each divisions hiring practises. In the neighbourhood of twenty-three thousand employee records was searched to determine date of employment, division and gender. Statistics Canada data were examined by way of comparison.

The following findings in regard to the aforementioned study resulted;

- Halifax is five % above the numerical goals for the three year period
- Regina is seven % below the numerical goals for the three year period
- St. John's is two % above the numerical goals (but figures were available for only five hundred of 2,256 employees

On the basis of these findings the compliance committee recommend the development of (1) a intensive recruiting program to search for and bring qualified females into the Regina division and (2) the development of a training program to train females for drafting and design positions in Regina. The Regina Division should hire two females for every 1 male until such time as 16 extra females are hire. In view of the fact that a training program may cost as much as five hundred thousand dollars, we further recommend that a committee be established at this point in time to investigate funding.

580 East Leffels Street
Regina, SK S4S 3T5
November 7, 200X

Ms. Ellen Rabkin
Retail Credit Department
Union National Bank
PO Box 2051
Edmonton, AB T5W 4B3

Dear Ms. Rabkin:

Two years ago me and my wife became cardholders of your visa card, our account number is 4002-3422-8910-3299. We have been happy with the service until recent charges that we would like to discuss with you.

Between the period of August 7 and September 17, we made 12 small purchases. Ten of these purchases received telephone approval. When we received our October statement, a copy of which is enclosed we were surprised to see that we had been charged a penalty in the amount of ten dollars for each of these purchases due to the fact that our account was over the limit. The whole charge totalled $120.

Of course, we should of been more aware of the status of our account. In view of the fact that our purchases were approved however, we assumed that we were still within our credit limit.

Upon receipt of our October statement we immediately went to our bank branch and spoke with Mr Jonathan Walker, who listened patiently to our story. He was unable to wave the charges, and referred us to you.

Please examine our account, Ms. Radkin, and reconsider this penalty. Since we have never before exceeded our credit limit and having received telephone approval for most of the charge in question, we feel that the $120 charge should be removed. We appreciate Mr. Walkers attention and yours and look forward to a speedy resolution of this problem.

Sincerely,

Phillip M. Stevenson

Phillip M. Stevenson

Enclosure

POSTTEST

Rewrite the following sentences to correct problems in parallelism, redundancy, modification, reference, conciseness, and coherence.

1. Due to the fact that most Canadians are highly indebted, an increase in interest rates can have serious consequences.

   ___

   ___

2. Speeding down the highway, the brakes were suddenly applied.

   ___

   ___

3. First and foremost, you must reserve a meeting room.

   ___

   ___

4. All sales reports must be complete, concise, and written with accuracy.

   ___

   ___

5. Our benefit package is appealing to older employees with both dental and vision care services.

   ___

   ___

1. Because most Canadians . . .   2. Speeding down the highway, the driver suddenly applied the brakes.   3. First, you must reserve a meeting room.   4. All sales reports must be complete, concise, and accurate.   5. With both dental and vision care services, our benefit package is appealing to older employees.

learning.web.ways

Goal: To familiarize yourself with salary-negotiating techniques before your first job interview.

1. With your web browser on the screen, go to **<http://www.canadiancareers.com/salary.html>**.
2. Read the first section, and jot down three ways you can learn about the current salary scale in the job sector you're interested in.
3. Using the link provided, visit WetFeet.com. What other tips on how to negotiate a salary can you find there? Write down one of them and return to CanadianCareers.com.
4. Visit one of the websites listed on CanadianCareers.com for your salary research, and jot down the entry-level salaries in your field quoted there.
5. Using the **Back** button of your browser, return to CanadianCareers.com, and click on the link to the International Salary Calculator. Find out the salaries in your field in a couple of other cities in case you are offered an out-of-town job. Jot this information down.
6. End your session and submit your research results.

NAME ______________________

UNIT 6 REVIEW **Chapters 19–21 (Self-Check)**

First, review Chapters 19 through 21. Then test your comprehension of those chapters by completing the exercises that follow. Compare your responses with those shown at the end of the book.

LEVEL I

Select (a) or (b) to describe the group of words that is more acceptably expressed.

1. (a) courses in Business Law, Spanish, and Sociology (b) courses in business law, Spanish, and sociology ________

2. (a) living in York region (b) living in York Region ________

3. (a) the Province of Alberta (b) the province of Alberta ________

4. (a) during summer vacation (b) during Summer vacation ________

5. (a) a victorian home (b) a Victorian home ________

6. (a) the 22nd of June (b) the twenty-second of June ________

7. (a) twenty dollars (b) $20 ________

8. (a) on 11th Street (b) on Eleventh Street ________

9. (a) on November 28th (b) on November 28 ________

10. (a) in view of the fact that (b) because ________

11. (a) about (b) with reference to ________

12. (a) in the near future (b) soon ________

LEVEL II

Select (a) or (b) to describe the group of words that is more acceptably expressed.

13. (a) your Mom and Dad (b) your mom and dad ________

14. (a) travel north on Highway 10 (b) travel North on Highway 10 ________

15. (a) our manager, Joe Bertuccio (b) our Manager, Joe Bertuccio ________

16. (a) our Legal Department (b) our legal department ________

17. (a) a message from Mia Cook, Managing Director (b) a message from Mia Cook, managing director ________

18. (a) a message from Managing Director Cook (b) a message from managing director Cook ________

19. (a) for the next two years (b) for the next 2 years ____

20. (a) 2 twenty-five page booklets (b) two 25-page booklets ____

21. (a) nine computers serving 14 offices (b) 9 computers serving 14 offices ____

Each of the following sentences illustrates one of these sentence faults:

a = faulty parallel construction (such as *running, walking,* and *to ride*)

b = faulty phrase placement (phrase not close to word(s) it modifies)

c = faulty pronoun reference (pronoun such as *this, that, it* lacking clear antecedent)

Write the letter that describes the sentence fault in each of the next three sentences.

22. We installed fabric divider panels in the office to provide privacy, reduce sound, and they added colour to the office. ____

23. Michelle stood at the lectern on the stage looking at the audience with a blank mind and a dry mouth. ____

24. Poor ventilation, inadequate light, and hazardous working conditions were cited in the complaint. It must be improved before negotiations continue. ____

On a separate sheet of paper, rewrite the above sentences to rectify their faults.

LEVEL III

Select the correct group of words below, and write its letter in the space provided.

25. (a) Have a seat, sir (b) Have a seat, Sir. ____

26. (a) Mayor-Elect Joan White (b) Mayor-elect Joan White ____

27. (a) a package stamped "photographs" (b) a package stamped "Photographs" ____

28. (a) our 28th anniversary (b) our twenty-eighth anniversary ____

29. (a) less than 0.1 per cent (b) less than .1 per cent ____

30. (a) 4 L of ice cream (b) four L of ice cream ____

31. (a) a 10% return (b) a 10 per cent return ____

32. (a) when he became 21 (b) when he became twenty-one ____

33. (a) a 2/3 interest (b) a two-thirds interest ____

34. (a) the bright moon (b) the bright Moon ____

35. (a) South Asian and European cultures (b) south asian and european cultures ____

Hotline Review

Write the letter of the word or phrase that correctly completes each sentence.

36. May I (a) imply, (b) infer from your remark that you will not attend the meeting? __________

37. He made five (a) photocopies, (b) Xerox copies on the new Canon copier. __________

38. Ramona doesn't want to (a) loose, (b) lose her opportunity to travel abroad. __________

39. She paused to (a) marshal, (b) marshall, (c) martial her thoughts. __________

40. We felt (a) badly, (b) bad about missing the last meeting. __________

Short Reports

Reports are a fact of life in the business world today. They are important because they convey needed information, and they help decision makers solve problems. Organizing information into a meaningful report is an important skill you will want to acquire if your field is business.

Characteristics of Reports

As an introduction to report writing, this workshop focuses on the most important characteristics of reports. You'll learn valuable tips about the format, data, headings, and writing plan for short business reports and internal proposals.

Format. How should a business report look? Three formats are commonly used. *Letter format* is appropriate for short reports prepared by one organization for another. A letter report, as illustrated in Figure 21.1, is like a letter except that it is more carefully organized. It includes side headings and lists where appropriate. *Memo format* is common for reports written within an organization. These internal reports look like memos—with the addition of side headings. *Report format* is used for longer, more formal reports. Printed on plain paper (instead of letterhead or memo forms), these reports begin with a title followed by carefully displayed headings and subheadings.

Data. Where do you find the data for a business report? Many business reports begin with personal observation and experience. If you were writing a report on implementing flextime for employees, you might begin by observing current work schedules and by asking what schedules employees preferred. Other sources of data for business reports include company records, surveys, questionnaires, and interviews. If you want to see how others have solved a problem or collect background data on a topic, you can consult magazines, journals, and books. Much information is available electronically through online library indexes or from searching databases and the Web.

Headings. Good headings in a report highlight major ideas and categories. They guide the reader through a report. In longer reports they divide the text into inviting chunks, and they provide resting places for the eyes. Short reports often use *functional heads* (such as *Problem, Summary, and Recommendations*). Longer reports may employ *talking heads* (such as *Short-Term Parking Solutions*) because they provide more information to the reader. Whether your heads are functional or talking, be sure they are clear and parallel. For example, use *Visible Costs* and *Invisible Costs* rather than *Visible Costs* and *Costs That Don't Show.* Don't enclose headings in quotation marks, and avoid using headings as antecedents for pronouns. For example, if your heading is *Laser Printers,* don't begin the next sentence with *These produce high-quality output ....*

Figure 21.1
Short Report—Letter Format

Liberty Environmental Inc.
2593 North Glebe Road
Calgary, AB T2T 4T1 (403) 356-1094

October 9, 200x

Ms. Sharon J. Goode
Richmond Realty Inc.
3390 Chester Avenue
Calgary, Alberta T3S 1K7

Dear Ms. Goode:

Explains purpose, outlines sources of information

At the request of Richmond Realty, I have completed a preliminary investigation of its Mountain Park property listing. The following findings and recommendations are based on my physical inspection of the site, official records, and interviews with officials and persons knowledgeable about the site.

Includes headings to show report organization

Findings and Analyses

Describes findings and explains their significance

My preliminary assessment of the Mountain Park listing and its immediate vicinity revealed rooms with damaged floor tiles on the first and second floors of 2539 Mountain View Drive. Apparently, in recent remodelling efforts, these tiles had been cracked and broken. Examination of the ceiling and attic revealed possible contamination from asbestos. The insulation material surrounding the hot-water storage tank was in poor condition.

Located on the property is Mountain Technology, a possible hazardous waste generator. Although I could not examine its interior, this company has the potential for producing hazardous material contamination. Moreover, several large dumpsters in the parking area collect trash and debris from surrounding businesses. Because these dumpsters were uncovered, they pose a risk to the general public.

Concludes with recommendations for solving the problem

Recommendations

To reduce its potential environmental liability, Richmond Realty should take the following steps in regard to its Mountain Park listing:

Uses bulleted list to improve readability and comprehension

Begins each recommendation with a verb for consistency

- Conduct an immediate asbestos survey at the site, including inspection of ceiling insulation material, floor tiles, and insulation around a gas-fired heater vent pipe at 2539 Mountain View Drive.
- Prepare an environmental audit of the generators of hazardous waste currently operating at the site, including Mountain Technology.
- Obtain lids for the dumpsters situated in the parking areas, and ensure that the lids are kept closed.

If you would like to discuss the findings or recommendations in this report, please call me and I will be glad to answer your questions.

Sincerely,

Scott R. Evans

Scott R. Evans

Skill Check 6.1 Reviewing the Characteristics of Short Reports

Select a letter to indicate the best format for the report described.

(a) Memo format (b) Letter format (c) Report format

1. A short report to a company from an outside consultant ________
2. A short report from a product manager to her boss ________
3. A long report describing a company's diversity program ________
4. If you were writing a report to persuade management to purchase more computers, the best way to begin collecting data would be to
   a. observe current use
   b. consult books and journals
   c. search the Internet ________
5. Which combination of report headings is best?
   a. Delivery costs, Suppliers
   b. Reduction of delivery costs, Recommendations
   c. "Delivery costs," "Supply Costs"
   d. Reducing delivery costs, Finding new suppliers ________

Writing Plan for a Short Report

Short reports often have three parts: introduction, findings, and summary or recommendations. If the report is purely informational, a summary may be made instead of recommendations.

Introduction. This part of a report may also be called *Background.* In this section, you'll want to explain why you are writing. You may also (a) describe what methods and sources were used to gather information and why they are credible, (b) provide any special background information that may be necessary, and (c) offer a preview of your findings.

Findings. This section may also be called *Observations, Facts, Results,* or *Discussion.* Important points to consider in this section are organization and display. You may wish to organize the findings (a) chronologically (for example, to describe the history of a problem), (b) alphabetically (if you were, for example, evaluating candidates for a position), (c) topically (for example, discussing sales by regions), or (d) from most to least important (such as listing criteria for evaluating equipment). To display the findings effectively, you could (a) use side headings, (b) number each finding, (c) underline or boldface the key words, or (d) merely indent the paragraphs.

Summary or Recommendations. Some reports just offer information. Such reports may conclude with an impartial summary. Other reports are more analytical, and they generally conclude with recommendations. These recommendations tell readers how to solve the problem and may even suggest ways to implement the necessary actions. To display recommendations, number each one and place it on a separate line.

Notice that the letter report in Figure 21.1 includes an introduction, findings and analyses, and recommendations.

Writing Plan for an Internal Proposal

Both managers and employees must occasionally write reports that justify or recommend something such as buying equipment, changing a procedure, hiring an employee, consolidating departments, or investing funds. Here is a writing plan for an internal proposal that recommends a course of action.

Introduction. In this section identify the problem briefly. Use specific examples, supporting statistics, and authoritative quotes to lend credibility to the seriousness of the problem. If you think your audience will be receptive, announce your recommendation, solution, or action immediately and concisely. If you think your audience will need to be persuaded or educated, do not announce your solution until after you have explained its advantages.

Body. In writing the body of an internal proposal, you may want to include all or some of the following elements. Explain more fully the benefits of the recommendations or steps to be taken to solve the problem. Include a discussion of pros, cons, and costs. If appropriate, describe the factual and ethical negative consequences of the current situation. For example, if your internal proposal recommends purchasing new equipment, explain how much time, effort, money, and morale are being lost by continuing to use outdated equipment that needs constant repairs. Quantification through accurate facts and examples builds credibility and persuasive appeal. Explain the benefits of your proposal. A bulleted list improves readability and emphasis. Anticipate objections to your proposal and discuss ways to counter those objections. The body should also provide a plan and schedule for implementing your proposal. If many people will be included in implementing the proposal, prepare a staffing section. Describe who will be doing what. You may also describe alternative solutions and show how they will not work as well as your proposal.

Conclusion. In the conclusion summarize your recommendation. Describe the specific action to be taken. Ask for authorization to proceed. To motivate the reader, you might include a date for the action to take place and a reason for the deadline.

An internal proposal is generally formatted as a memo such as the one shown in Figure 21.2. In this memo report, the writer expects the reader to be receptive to the recommendation of pilot-testing smart tires. Thus, the proposal begins immediately with the recommendations. The body discusses how the recommendations would work, and it itemizes benefits. It anticipates objections and counters them. The closing summarizes what action is to be taken and presents a deadline.

Figure 21.2
Internal Proposal—Memo Format

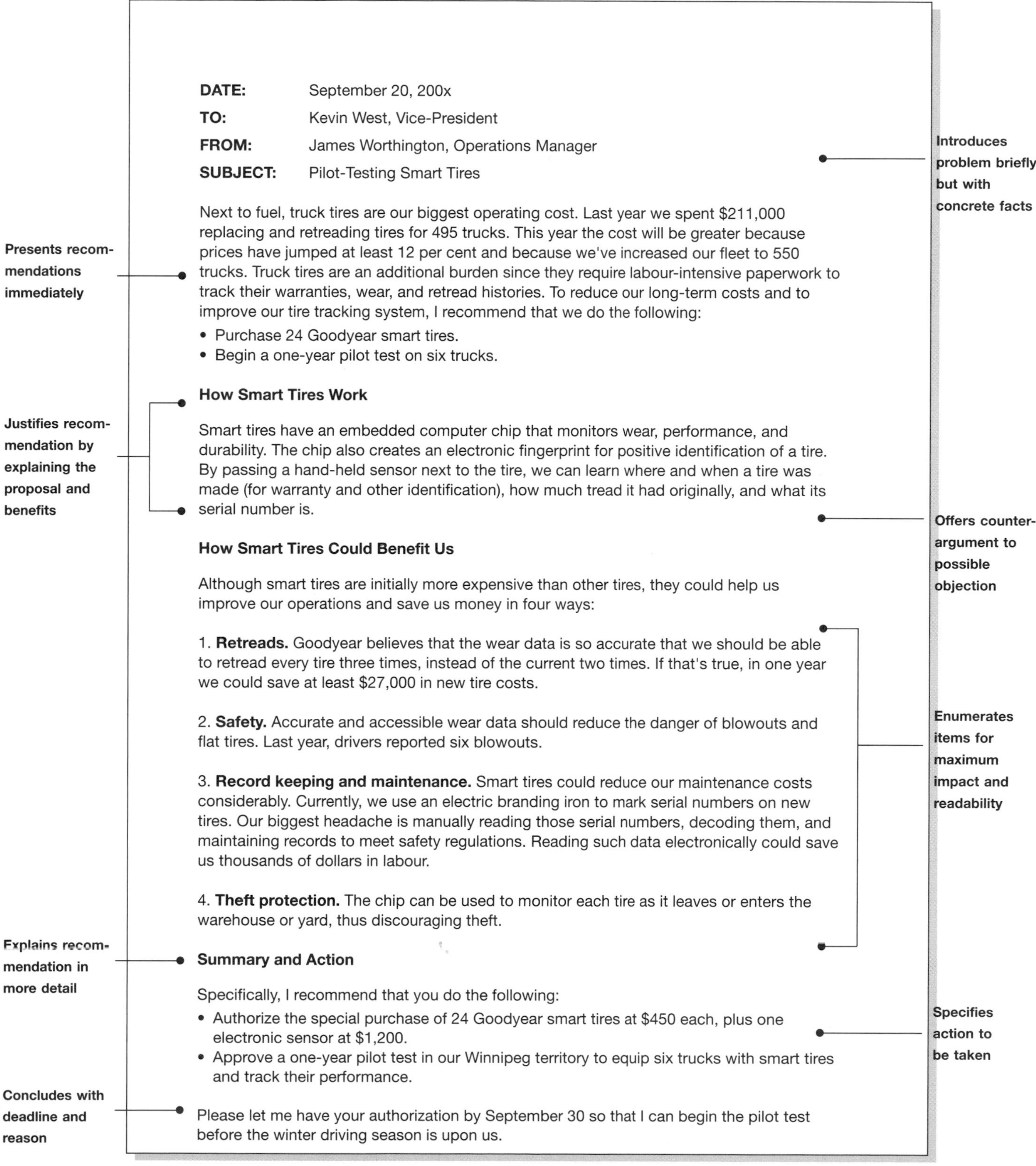

DATE: September 20, 200x
TO: Kevin West, Vice-President
FROM: James Worthington, Operations Manager
SUBJECT: Pilot-Testing Smart Tires

Next to fuel, truck tires are our biggest operating cost. Last year we spent $211,000 replacing and retreading tires for 495 trucks. This year the cost will be greater because prices have jumped at least 12 per cent and because we've increased our fleet to 550 trucks. Truck tires are an additional burden since they require labour-intensive paperwork to track their warranties, wear, and retread histories. To reduce our long-term costs and to improve our tire tracking system, I recommend that we do the following:

- Purchase 24 Goodyear smart tires.
- Begin a one-year pilot test on six trucks.

How Smart Tires Work

Smart tires have an embedded computer chip that monitors wear, performance, and durability. The chip also creates an electronic fingerprint for positive identification of a tire. By passing a hand-held sensor next to the tire, we can learn where and when a tire was made (for warranty and other identification), how much tread it had originally, and what its serial number is.

How Smart Tires Could Benefit Us

Although smart tires are initially more expensive than other tires, they could help us improve our operations and save us money in four ways:

1. **Retreads.** Goodyear believes that the wear data is so accurate that we should be able to retread every tire three times, instead of the current two times. If that's true, in one year we could save at least $27,000 in new tire costs.

2. **Safety.** Accurate and accessible wear data should reduce the danger of blowouts and flat tires. Last year, drivers reported six blowouts.

3. **Record keeping and maintenance.** Smart tires could reduce our maintenance costs considerably. Currently, we use an electric branding iron to mark serial numbers on new tires. Our biggest headache is manually reading those serial numbers, decoding them, and maintaining records to meet safety regulations. Reading such data electronically could save us thousands of dollars in labour.

4. **Theft protection.** The chip can be used to monitor each tire as it leaves or enters the warehouse or yard, thus discouraging theft.

Summary and Action

Specifically, I recommend that you do the following:

- Authorize the special purchase of 24 Goodyear smart tires at $450 each, plus one electronic sensor at $1,200.
- Approve a one-year pilot test in our Winnipeg territory to equip six trucks with smart tires and track their performance.

Please let me have your authorization by September 30 so that I can begin the pilot test before the winter driving season is upon us.

Introduces problem briefly but with concrete facts
Presents recommendations immediately
Justifies recommendation by explaining the proposal and benefits
Offers counter-argument to possible objection
Enumerates items for maximum impact and readability
Explains recommendation in more detail
Specifies action to be taken
Concludes with deadline and reason

Writing Application 6.1 Organize the following information into a short letter report. As Cynthia M. Chavez, president, Chavez and Associates, you have been hired as a consultant to advise the St. Catharines City Council. The City Council has asked you and your associates to investigate a problem with Willow Park Beachway.

In 1979 St. Catharines constructed a 4-metre pathway, now called the Willow Park Beachway. It was meant originally for bicycle riders, but today it has become very popular for joggers, walkers, bikers, in-line skaters, skateboarders, sightseers, and people walking their dogs. In fact, it's become so popular that it is dangerous. Last year the St. Catharines Police Department reported an amazing 65 collisions in the area. And this does not count the close calls and minor accidents that no one reported. The City Council wants your organization to identify the problem and come up with some workable recommendations for improving safety.

As you look into the matter, you immediately decide that the council is right. A problem definitely exists! In addition to the many pedestrians and riders, you see that families with rented pedal-powered surreys clog the beachway. Sometimes they even operate these vehicles on the wrong side. Your investigation further reveals that bicyclists with rental bikes do not always have bells to alert walkers. And poor lighting makes nighttime use extremely dangerous. You've noticed that conditions seem to be worst on Sundays. This congestion results from nearby art and crafts fairs and sales, attracting even more people to the crowded area.

Your investigation confirms that the beachway is dangerous, but what to do about it? In a brainstorming session, your associates make a number of suggestions for reducing the dangers to users. By the way, the council is particularly interested in lessening the threat of liability to the city. One of your associates thinks that the beachway should be made at least 5 or more metres wide. Another suggests that the beachway be lighted at night. Someone thinks that a new path should be built on the beach side of the existing beachway; this path would be for pedestrians only. Educating users about safety rules and etiquette would certainly be wise for everyone. One suggestion involves better striping or applying colours to designate different uses for the beachway. And why not require that all rental bicycles be equipped with bells? One of the best recommendations involves hiring uniformed "beach hosts" who would monitor the beachway, give advice, offer directions, and generally patrol the area.

In a short report, outline the problem and list your recommendations. Naturally, you would be happy to discuss your findings and recommendations with the St. Catharines City Council.

Writing Application 6.2 Assume that your office needs a piece of equipment such as a photocopier, fax, digital camera, computer, printer, scanner, shredder, or the like. Do the research necessary to write a convincing internal proposal to your boss. You feel that your boss will be receptive to your request, so you can use the direct approach.

A P P E N D I X

Developing Spelling Skills

A

▶ Why Is English Spelling So Difficult?

No one would dispute the complaint that many English words are difficult to spell. Why is spelling in our language so perplexing? For one thing, our language has borrowed many of its words from other languages. English has a Germanic base upon which a superstructure of words borrowed from French, Latin, Greek, and other languages of the world has been erected. For this reason, its words are not always formed by regular patterns of letter combinations. In addition, spelling is made difficult because the pronunciation of English words is constantly changing. Today's spelling was standardized nearly 300 years ago, but many words are pronounced differently today than they were then. Therefore, pronunciation often provides little help in spelling. Consider, for example, the words *sew, dough, hoe,* and *row*.

Canadian writers, unlike US and British writers, have a choice of spelling styles. Currently, most Canadians use a primarily British spelling style (the *our* and *re* endings for words like *honour* and *centre,* for example); others use a primarily US style (*or* and *er* for *honor* and *center*). This text uses British forms, but *The Canadian Oxford Dictionary* and *Gage Canadian Dictionary* indicate that both styles are acceptable in most cases. The spelling style chosen depends on custom and on the preference of the individual or on the requirements of the workplace. Above all, consistency within any single piece of writing is important. If you choose *our* and *re* spellings, you must use these throughout a document; it is incorrect to have, for example, both *honour* and *valor* in the same piece.

▶ What Can Be Done to Improve One's Spelling?

Spelling is a skill that can be developed, just as arithmetic, keyboarding, swimming, and other skills can be developed. Because the ability to spell is a prerequisite for success in business and in many other activities, effort expended to acquire this skill is effort well spent.

Three traditional approaches to improving spelling have met with varying degrees of success.

1. Rules or Guidelines

The spelling of English words is consistent enough to justify the formulation of a few spelling rules, perhaps more appropriately called guidelines since the generalizations in question have exceptions. Such guidelines are, in other words, helpful but not infallible.

2. Mnemonics

Another approach to improving your ability to spell involves the use of mnemonics or memory devices. For example, you might associate the word *principle* with the word *rule*, to form in your mind a link between the meaning and the spelling of *principle*. Mnemonics can be an effective device for the improvement of spelling only if the speller makes a real effort to develop the necessary memory hooks.

3. Rote Learning

A third approach to the improvement of spelling centres on memorization. Study the word until you can readily reproduce it in your mind's eye. Writing the word several times will also help you memorize its correct spelling.

▶ The 1-2-3 Spelling Plan

Proficiency in spelling is not attained without concentrated effort. Here's a plan for mastering the correct spelling of the 400 commonly misspelled words and word pairs included in this appendix. For each word, try this 1-2-3 approach.

1. Is a spelling guideline applicable? If so, select the appropriate guideline and study the word in relation to that guideline.
2. If no guideline applies, can a memory device be created to aid in the recall of the word?
3. If neither a guideline nor a memory device will work, the word must be memorized. Look at the word carefully. Pronounce it. Write it or repeat it until you can visualize all its letters in your mind's eye.

Before you try the 1-2-3 plan, become familiar with the six spelling guidelines that follow. These spelling guidelines are not intended to represent all the possible spelling rules appearing in the various available spelling books. These six guidelines are, however, among the most effective and helpful of the recognized spelling rules.

Guideline 1: Words Containing *ie* or *ei*

Although there are exceptions to it, the following familiar rhyme can be helpful.

(a) Write *i* before *e*
(b) Except after *c*,
(c) Or when sounded like *ay*
As in *neighbour* and *weigh*.

Study these three lists of words illustrating the three parts of the rhyme.

(a) *i* Before *e*		(b) Except After *c*	(c) or When Sounded Like *ay*
achieve	ingredient	ceiling	beige
belief	mischief	conceit	eight
believe	niece	conceive	freight
brief	piece	deceit	heir
cashier	relief	deceive	neighbour
chief	shield	perceive	reign
convenient	sufficient	receipt	sleigh
field	thief	receive	their
friend	view		vein
grief	yield		weight

Exceptions: These exceptional *ei* and *ie* words must be learned by rote or with the use of a mnemonic device. Note that many of them contain the long *e* sound.

ancient	foreign	neither
caffeine	forfeit	protein
either	height	seize
financier	leisure	weird

Guideline 2: Words Ending in *e*

For most words ending in an *e*, the final *e* is dropped when the word is joined to a suffix that begins with a vowel (such as *ing, able,* or *al*). The final *e* is retained when a suffix that begins with a consonant (such as *ment, less, ly,* or *ful*) is joined to such a word.

Final *e* Dropped	**Final *e* Retained**
advise, advisable	approximate, approximately
arrive, arrival	arrange, arrangement
believe, believing	care, careless
care, caring	definite, definitely
cure, curable	hope, hopeless
desire, desirable	like, likely
disperse, dispersal	require, requirement
hope, hoping	safe, safely
move, movable	sincere, sincerely
receive, receiving	time, timeless
value, valuable	use, useful

Exceptions: The few exceptions to this spelling guideline are among the most frequently misspelled words. As such, they deserve special attention. Notice that they all involve a dropped final *e.*

argument	ninth	wholly
judgment	truly	

Guideline 3: Words Ending in *ce* or *ge*

When *able* or *ous* is added to words ending in *ce* or *ge*, the final *e* is retained if the *c* or *g* is pronounced softly (as in *service* or *change*).

advantage, advantageous	change, changeable
courage, courageous	service, serviceable
outrage, outrageous	manage, manageable

Guideline 4: Words Ending in *y*

Words ending in a *y* that is preceded by a consonant normally change the *y* to *i* before all suffixes except those beginning with an *i.*

Change *y* to *i* Because *y* Is Preceded by a Consonant

accompany, accompaniment
apply, appliance
carry, carried, carriage
company, companies
dry, drier, driest
duty, dutiful
empty, emptiness
forty, fortieth
hurry, hurries
industry, industrious
secretary, secretaries
study, studied, studious
try, tried

Do Not Change *y* to *i* Because *y* is Preceded by a Vowel

annoy, annoying, annoyance
attorney, attorneys
employ, employer, employs
stay, staying, stayed
valley, valleys

Do Not Change *y* to *i* When Adding *ing*

accompany, accompanying
apply, applying
satisfy, satisfying
study, studying
try, trying

Exceptions: day, daily; gay, gaily; mislay, mislaid; pay, paid; shy, shyly.

Guideline 5: Doubling a Final Consonant

If one-syllable words or two-syllable words accented on the second syllable end in a single consonant preceded by a single vowel, the final consonant is doubled before a suffix beginning with a vowel is added.

Although complex, this spelling guideline is extremely useful and therefore well worth mastering. Many spelling errors can be avoided by applying this guideline.

One-Syllable Words

bag, baggage
can, canned
drop, dropped
fit, fitted
get, getting
man, manned
plan, planned
run, running
shut, shutting
slip, slipped
swim, swimming
ton, tonnage

Two-Syllable Words

acquit, acquitting, acquittal
admit, admitted, admitting
begin, beginner, beginning
commit, committed, committing
control, controller, controlling
defer, deferred (BUT deference*)
excel, excelled, excelling
occur, occurrence, occurring
prefer, preferring (BUT preferable*)
recur, recurred, recurrence
refer, referring (BUT reference*)
regret, regrettable

Here is a summary of conditions necessary for application of this guideline:

1. The word must end in a single consonant.
2. The final consonant must be preceded by a single vowel.
3. The word must be accented on the second syllable (if it has two syllables).

Words derived from *offer, differ, suffer, widen, deepen,* and *benefit* are not governed by this guideline because they are accented on the first syllable. The same is true of *cancel, equal,* and *travel*; however, since British spelling doubles the final *l* in these words (e.g., *travelled, travelling, traveller*), most Canadians make exceptions to the guideline in these cases.

* *Because the accent shifts to the first syllable, the final consonant is not doubled.*

Guideline 6: Prefixes and Suffixes

For words in which the letter that ends the prefix is the same as the letter that begins the main word (such as in *dissimilar*), both letters must be included. For words in which a suffix begins with the same letter that ends the main word (such as in *coolly*), both letters must also be included.

Prefix	**Main Word**
dis	satisfied
il	literate
ir	responsible
mis	spell
mis	state
un	necessary

Main Word	**Suffix**
accidental	ly
clean	ness
cool	ly
even	ness
incidental	ly
mean	ness

On the other hand, do not supply additional letters when adding prefixes to main words.

Prefix	**Main Word**
dis	appearance (not di*ss*appearance)
dis	appoint
mis	take

Probably the most important guideline you can follow in spelling correctly is to use the dictionary whenever in doubt.

400 Most Frequently Misspelled Words and Word Pairs*
(Divided into 20 lists of 20 words each)

List 1
absence
acceptance
accessible
accidentally
accommodate
accompaniment
accurately
accustom
achievement
acknowledgement/
acknowledgment**
acquaintance
acquire
across
actually
adequately
admitted
adolescence
advantageous
advertising
advice, advise†

List 2
afraid
against
aggressive
all right
almost
alphabetical
already
although
amateur
among
amount
analysis
analyze/analyse
angel, angle
annoyance
annual
answer
apologized
apparent
appliance

List 3
applying
approaches
appropriate
approximately
arguing
argument
arrangement
article
athlete
attack
attendance, attendants
attitude
attorneys
auxiliary
basically
beautiful
before
beginning
believing
benefited

* *Compiled from lists of words most frequently misspelled by students and business people.*

** *This type of listing (with a slash) indicates that British and American versions are both accepted in Canada. The first of each pair is the version more frequently used, according to* The Canadian Oxford Dictionary.

† *Pairs listed in this manner (separated by commas) are homonyms or commonly confused word pairs. Consult your dictionary for meanings.*

List 4
biggest
breath, breathe
brief
business
calendar
capital
career
careless
carrying
cashier
ceiling
certain
challenge
changeable
chief
choose, chose
cloths, clothes
column
coming
committee

List 5
companies
competition
completely
conceive
conscience
conscientious
conscious
considerably
consistent
continuous
controlling
controversial
convenience
council, counsel
cylinder
daily
deceive
decision
define
dependent

List 6
description
desirable
destroy
development
difference
dining
disappearance
disappoint
disastrous
discipline
discussion
disease
dissatisfied
distinction
divide
doesn't
dominant
dropped
due
during

List 7
efficient
eligible
embarrass
encourage
enough
environment
equipped
especially
exaggerate
exceed
excellence
except
exercise
existence
experience
explanation
extremely
familiar
fascinate
favourite/favorite

List 8
February
fictitious
field
finally
financially
foreigner
fortieth
forty
forward, foreword
freight
friend
fulfill/fulfil
fundamentally
further
generally
government
governor
grammar
grateful
guard

List 9
happiness
hear, here
height
heroes
hopeless
hoping
huge
humorous
hungry
ignorance
imaginary
imagine
immediately
immense
importance
incidentally
independent
indispensable
industrious
inevitable

List 10
influential
ingredient
initiative
intelligence
interest
interference
interpretation
interrupt
involve
irrelevant
irresponsible
island
jealous
judgment/judgement
kindergarten
knowledge
laboratory
labourer/laborer
laid
led, lead

List 11
leisurely
library
licence/license (noun)
license (verb)
likely
literature
lives
loneliness
loose, lose
losing
luxury
magazine
magnificence
maintenance
manageable
manoeuvre/maneuver
manner
manufacturer
marriage
mathematics

List 12
meant
mechanics
medicine
medieval
mere
miniature
minutes
mischief
misspell
mistake
muscle
mysterious
naturally
necessary
neighbour/neighbor
neither
nickel
niece
ninety
ninth

List 13
noticeable
numerous
obstacle
occasionally
occurrence
offered
official
omitted
operate
opinion
opportunity
opposite
ordinance
organization
origin
original
paid
pamphlet
parallel
particular

List 14
passed, past
pastime
peaceable
peculiar
perceive
performance
permanent
permitted
persistent
personal, personnel
persuading
phase, faze
philosophy
physical
piece
planned
pleasant
poison
political
possession

List 15
possible
practical
precede
preferred
prejudice
preparation
prevalent
principal, principle
privilege
probably
proceed
professor
prominent
proving
psychology
pursuing
quantity
quiet, quite
really
receipt

List 16
receiving
recognize
recommend
reference
referring
regard
relative
relieving
religious
reminiscent
repetition
representative
requirement
resistance
responsible
restaurant
rhythm
ridiculous
sacrifice
safety

List 17
satisfying
scenery
schedule
science
secretaries
seize
sense, since
sentence
separation
sergeant
serviceable
several
shining
shoulder
sight, site, cite
significance
similar
simply
sincerely
source

List 18
speak, speech
specimen
stationary, stationery
stopped
stories, storeys
straight, strait
strenuous
stretch
strict
studying
substantial
subtle
succeed
success
sufficient
summary
supposed
surprise
suspense
swimming

List 19
syllable
symbol
symmetrical
synonymous
technique
temperament
temperature
tendency
than, then
their, there, they're
themselves
theories
therefore
thorough
though
through
together
tomorrow
tragedies
transferred

List 20
tremendous
tried
truly
undoubtedly
unnecessary
until
unusual
useful
using
vacuum
valuable
varies
vegetable
view
weather, whether
weird
were, where
wholly, holy
writing
yield

APPENDIX

Developing Vocabulary Skills

B

If you understand the meanings of many words, you can be said to have a "good vocabulary." Words are the basis of thought. We think with words, we understand with words, and we communicate with words.

A large working vocabulary is a significant asset. It allows us to use precise words that say exactly what we intend. In addition, we understand more effectively what we hear and read. A large vocabulary also enables us to score well on employment and intelligence tests. Lewis M. Terman, who developed the Stanford-Binet IQ tests, believes that vocabulary is the single best indicator of intelligence.

In the business world, where precise communication is extremely important, surveys show a definite correlation between vocabulary size and job performance. Skilled workers, in the majority of cases, have larger vocabularies than unskilled workers. Supervisors know more words than the workers they direct, and executives have larger vocabularies than employees working for them.

Having a good vocabulary at our command doesn't necessarily ensure our success in life, but it certainly gives us an advantage. Improving your vocabulary will help you expand your options in an increasingly complex world.

Vocabulary can be acquired in three ways: accidentally, incidentally, and intentionally. Setting out intentionally to expand your word power is, of course, the most efficient vocabulary-building method. One of the best means of increasing your vocabulary involves the use of index cards: when you encounter an unfamiliar word, write it on a card and put the definition of the word on the reverse side of the card. Just five to ten minutes of practice each day with such cards can significantly increase your vocabulary.

Your campaign to increase your vocabulary can begin with the 20 lists of selected business terms and words of general interest included in this appendix. You may already know partial definitions for some of these words. Take this opportunity to develop more precise definitions for them. Follow these steps in using the word lists:

1. Record the word on an index card.

2. Look up the word in your dictionary. Compare the dictionary definitions of the word with the definition alternatives shown after the word in your copy of *Canadian Business English*. Select the correct definition, and write its letter in the space provided in your textbook. (The definitions provided in your textbook are quite concise but should help you remember the word's most common meaning.)

3. On the reverse side of your card, write the phonetic spelling of the word and the word's part of speech. Then write its definition, using as much of the dictionary definition as you find helpful. Try also to add a phrase or sentence illustrating the word.

4. Study your index cards often.

5. Try to find ways to use your vocabulary words in your speech and writing.

List 1

1. adjacent = (a) previous, (b) similar, (c) overdue, (d) nearby ________
2. ambivalence = having (a) uncertainty, (b) ambition,(c) compassion, (d) intelligence ________
3. belligerent = (a) overweight, (b) quarrelsome, (c) likable, (d) believable ________
4. cusp = (a) peak, (b) molar, (c) curse, (d) drinking vessel ________
5. decadent = in a state of (a) repair, (b) happiness, (c) decline, (d) extreme patriotism ________
6. entitlement = (a) label, (b) tax refund, (c) screen credit, (d) legal right ________
7. equivalent = (a) subsequent, (b) identical, (c) self-controlled, (d) plentiful ________
8. paramount = (a) foremost, (b) high mountain, (c) film company, (d) insignificant ________
9. plausible = (a) quiet, (b) believable, (c) notorious, (d) negative ________
10. unilateral = (a) powerful, (b) harmonious, (c) one-sided, (d) indelible ________

List 2

1. affluent = (a) rich, (b) slippery, (c) persistent, (d) rebellious ________
2. autocrat = one who (a) owns many cars, (b) is self-centred, (c) has absolute power, (d) collects signatures ________
3. benevolent = for the purpose of (a) religion, (b) doing good, (c) healing, (d) violence ________
4. entrepreneur = (a) business owner, (b) traveller, (c) salesperson, (d) gambler ________
5. impertinent = (a) stationary, (b) bound to happen, (c) obsolete, (d) rude or insolent ________
6. imprudent = (a) unwise, (b) crude, (c) vulnerable, (d) lifeless ________
7. mediator = one who seeks (a) overseas trade, (b) profits, (c) safe investment, (d) peaceful settlement ________
8. preponderance = (a) thoughtfulness, (b) exclusive right, (c) superiority, (d) forethought ________
9. recipient = (a) receiver, (b) respondent, (c) voter, (d) giver ________
10. reprehensible = (a) disobedient, (b) independent, (c) blameworthy, (d) following ________

List 3

1. affable = (a) cheap, (b) pleasant, (c) strange, (d) competent ________
2. consensus = (a) population count, (b) attendance, (c) tabulation, (d) agreement ________
3. criterion = (a) standard, (b) command, (c) pardon, (d) law ________
4. diligent = (a) gentle, (b) industrious, (c) prominent, (d) intelligent ________

5. hydraulic = operated by means of (a) air, (b) gasoline, (c) liquid, (d) mechanical parts ________

6. hypothesis = (a) triangle, (b) prologue, (c) highest point, (d) theory ________

7. phenomenon = (a) imagination, (b) rare event, (c) appointment, (d) clever saying ________

8. reticent = (a) reserved, (b) strong-willed, (c) inflexible, (d) disagreeable ________

9. sanctuary = a place of (a) healing, (b) refuge, (c) rest, (d) learning ________

10. stimulus = something that causes (a) response, (b) light, (c) pain, (d) movement ________

List 4

1. beneficiary = one who (a) receives a licence, (b) creates goodwill, (c) receives proceeds, (d) makes friends ________

2. constrain = (a) restrict, (b) filter, (c) use, (d) inform ________

3. corroborate = (a) contradict, (b) recall, (c) erode, (d) confirm ________

4. dun = a demand for (a) legal action, (b) payment, (c) credit information, (d) dividends ________

5. equitable = (a) fair, (b) profitable, (c) similar, (d) clear ________

6. fluctuate = (a) rinse out, (b) magnetize, (c) violate, (d) rise and fall ________

7. indolent = (a) self-indulgent, (b) lazy, (c) pampered, (d) uncertain ________

8. nullify = (a) disappear, (b) imitate, (c) invalidate, (d) enhance ________

9. obsolete = (a) ugly, (b) outmoded, (c) audible, (d) scant ________

10. stabilize = to make (a) pleasant, (b) congenial, (c) traditional, (d) firm ________

List 5

1. arbitrate = (a) decide, (b) construct, (c) conquer, (d) ratify ________

2. coalition = (a) deliberation, (b) allegiance, (c) adherence, (d) alliance ________

3. collate = (a) assemble, (b) denounce, (c) supersede, (d) discuss ________

4. conglomerate = combination of (a) executives, (b) companies, (c) investments, (d) countries ________

5. franchise = (a) fictitious reason, (b) right, (c) obligation, (d) official announcement ________

6. logistics = (a) speculations, (b) analytic philosophy, (c) reasonable outcome, (d) details of operation ________

7. proxy = authority to (a) act for another, (b) write cheques, (c) submit nominations, (d) explain ________

8. subsidiary = (a) performance below expectations, (b) country dominated by another, (c) company controlled by another, (d) depressed financial condition ________

9. termination = (a) end, (b) inception, (c) identification,(d) evasive action ________

10. virtually = (a) absolutely, (b) precisely, (c) almost entirely, (d) strictly ________

List 6

1. affiliate = (a) trust, (b) attract, (c) effect, (d) join ________
2. alter = (a) perform religious ceremony, (b) isolate, (c) attribute, (d) modify ________
3. boisterous = (a) noisily exuberant, (b) masculine, (c) cheerful, (d) rotund ________
4. configuration = (a) stratagem, (b) foreign currency, (c) form, (d) comprehension ________
5. conveyance = (a) vehicle, (b) transformation, (c) baggage, (d) consortium ________
6. infringe = (a) ravel, (b) embroider, (c) encroach, (d) margin ________
7. jurisdiction = (a) science of law, (b) enunciation, (c) justice, (d) authority ________
8. non-partisan = (a) unbiased, (b) antisocial, (c) ineffective, (d) untenable ________
9. parity = (a) price index, (b) justice under law, (c) plenitude, (d) equality of purchasing power ________
10. usury = (a) method of operation, (b) implementation, (c) illegal interest, (d) customary ________

List 7

1. anonymous = (a) multiplex, (b) powerless, (c) vexing, (d) nameless ________
2. cartel = (a) combination to fix prices, (b) ammunition belt, (c) partnership to promote competition, (d) placard ________
3. conjecture = (a) coagulation, (b) gesticulation, (c) guesswork, (d) connection ________
4. disparity = (a) unlikeness, (b) separation, (c) lack of emotion, (d) repudiation ________
5. environment = (a) urban area, (b) zenith, (c) surroundings, (d) latitude ________
6. impetus = (a) oversight, (b) stimulus, (c) hindrance, (d) imminence ________
7. portfolio = a list of (a) books, (b) security analysts, (c) corporations, (d) investments ________
8. quiescent = (a) presumptuous, (b) latent, (c) immoderate, (d) volatile ________
9. surrogate = (a) substitute, (b) accused, (c) authentic, (d) suspended ________
10. tariff = (a) marsupial, (b) announcement, (c) ship, (d) duty ________

List 8

1. accrue = (a) conform, (b) accumulate, (c) diminish, (d) multiply ________
2. amortize = (a) pay off, (b) reduce, (c) romance, (d) kill ________
3. commensurate = (a) infinitesimal, (b) erroneous, (c) reliable, (d) proportional ________
4. consortium = (a) configuration, (b) partnership or association, (c) royal offspring, (d) rental property ________
5. discernible = (a) perceptive, (b) pretentious, (c) recognizable, (d) dissident ________
6. frugal = (a) thrifty, (b) wasteful, (c) judicious, (d) profligate ________

7. pecuniary = (a) rudimentary, (b) eccentric, (c) financial, (d) distinctive ________

8. retract = (a) disavow, (b) reorganize, (c) reciprocate, (d) hide ________

9. scrutinize = (a) cheerfully admit, (b) baffle, (c) persist, (d) examine carefully ________

10. tenacious = (a) falling apart, (b) persistent, (c) immobile, (d) chagrined ________

List 9

1. amiable = (a) brusque, (b) impetuous, (c) feasible, (d) likeable ________

2. credible = (a) plausible, (b) deceitful, (c) religious, (d) financially sound ________

3. defendant = one who (a) sues, (b) answers suit, (c) judges, (d) protects ________

4. dissipate = (a) accumulate, (b) partition, (c) liquefy, (d) scatter or waste ________

5. incentive = (a) impediment, (b) support, (c) motive, (d) remuneration ________

6. innocuous = (a) harmless, (b) injectable, (c) facetious, (d) frightening ________

7. oust = (a) install, (b) instigate, (c) shout, (d) expel ________

8. pittance = (a) tiny amount, (b) tithe, (c) abyss, (d) pestilence ________

9. plaintiff = one who (a) defends, (b) is sad, (c) sues, (d) responds ________

10. superfluous = (a) extraordinary, (b) very slippery, (c) shallow, (d) redundant ________

List 10

1. adroit = (a) ideal, (b) resilient, (c) witty, (d) skilful ________

2. derogatory = (a) minimal, (b) degrading, (c) originating from, (d) devious ________

3. escrow = (a) international treaty, (b) public registration, (c) reprobate, (d) type of deposit ________

4. facsimile = (a) principle, (b) prototype, (c) exact copy, (d) counterfeit ________

5. inordinate = (a) unwholesome, (b) excessive, (c) unimportant, (d) treacherous ________

6. logical = (a) reasoned, (b) irrelevant, (c) lofty, (d) intricate ________

7. malfeasance = (a) prevarication, (b) injury, (c) superstition, (d) misconduct ________

8. noxious = (a) pernicious, (b) unusual, (c) pleasant, (d) inconsequential ________

9. résumé = (a) budget report, (b) minutes of meeting, (c) photo album, (d) summary of qualifications ________

10. spasmodic = (a) paralyzing, (b) intermittent, (c) internal, (d) painful ________

List 11

1. animosity = (a) happiness, (b) deep sadness, (c) hatred, (d) study of animals ________

2. caveat = (a) headwear, (b) warning, (c) neckwear, (d) prerogative ________

3. conscientious = (a) meticulous, (b) productive, (c) cognizant, (d) sophisticated ________

4. cosmopolitan = (a) provincial, (b) multicoloured, (c) intoxicating, (d) worldly ________

5. decipher = (a) preclude, (b) decode, (c) demise, (d) reproach ________

6. euphemism = (a) religious discourse, (b) grimace, (c) figure of speech, (d) mild or indirect expression ________

7. fraudulent = (a) loquacious, (b) candid, (c) deceitful, (d) despotic ________

8. peripheral = (a) marginal, (b) imaginary, (c) visionary, (d) supernatural ________

9. pungent = (a) knowledgeable, (b) uncouth, (c) acrid, (d) vulnerable ________

10. requisite = (a) essential, (b) demanding, (c) skilful, (d) discreet ________

List 12

1. ad valorem = (a) esteemed, (b) genuine, (c) precious, (d) proportional ________

2. carte blanche = (a) white carriage, (b) credit terms, (c) full permission, (d) geographical expression ________

3. de facto = (a) prejudicial, (b) actual, (c) routine, (d) unlawful ________

4. esprit de corps = (a) group enthusiasm, (b) strong coffee, (c) central authority, (d) government overturn ________

5. modus operandi = (a) method of procedure, (b) practical compromise, (c) business transaction, (d) flexible arbitration ________

6. per capita = per unit of (a) income, (b) population, (c) birth, (d) household ________

7. per diem = (a) daily, (b) weekly, (c) yearly, (d) individually ________

8. prima facie = (a) self-taught, (b) apparent, (c) principal, (d) artificial ________

9. status quo = (a) haughty demeanour, (b) steadfast opinion, (c) position of importance, (d) existing condition ________

10. tort = (a) rich cake, (b) extended dream, (c) wrongful act, (d) lawful remedy ________

List 13

1. acquit = (a) discharge, (b) pursue, (c) interfere, (d) impede ________

2. annuity = (a) yearly report, (b) insurance premium, (c) tuition refund, (d) annual payment ________

3. complacent = (a) appealing, (b) self-satisfied, (c) sympathetic, (d) scrupulous ________

4. contraband = (a) discrepancy, (b) opposing opinion, (c) smuggled goods, (d) ammunition ________

5. insolvent = (a) uncleanable, (b) inexplicable, (c) bankrupt, (d) unjustifiable ________

6. malicious = marked by (a) good humour, (b) ill will, (c) great pleasure, (d) injurious tumour ________

7. negligent = (a) careless, (b) fraudulent, (c) unlawful, (d) weak ________

8. nominal = (a) enumerated, (b) beneficial, (c) extravagant, (d) insignificant ________

9. rescind = (a) consign, (b) oppose, (c) repeal, (d) censure ________

10. stringent = (a) rigid, (b) expedient, (c) compliant, (d) resilient ________

List 14

1. affirm = (a) make secure, (b) assert strongly, (c) elevate, (d) encircle ________
2. exonerate = (a) commend, (b) declare blameless, (c) banish, (d) emigrate ________
3. expedite = (a) elucidate, (b) get rid of, (c) amplify, (d) rush ________
4. hamper = (a) impede, (b) delineate, (c) release, (d) assuage ________
5. implement = (a) suppress, (b) ameliorate, (c) carry out, (d) attribute ________
6. induce = (a) teach, (b) construe, (c) persuade, (d) copy ________
7. obliterate = (a) obstruct, (b) prevent, (c) minimize, (d) erase ________
8. quandary = a state of (a) doubt, (b) certainty, (c) depression, (d) apprehension ________
9. surmount = (a) hike, (b) overcome, (c) interpret, (d) specify ________
10. veracity = (a) truthfulness, (b) swiftness, (c) efficiency, (d) persistence ________

List 15

1. aggregate = a collection of (a) hostile individuals, (b) foreign words, (c) disparate elements, (d) sticky liquids ________
2. ambiguous = (a) peripatetic, (b) uncertain, (c) enterprising, (d) deceptive ________
3. amend = (a) alter, (b) pray, (c) praise, (d) utter ________
4. apportion = (a) sanction, (b) ratify, (c) estimate, (d) divide ________
5. collaborate = (a) scrutinize, (b) co-operate, (c) surrender, (d) accumulate ________
6. ingenuity = (a) innocence, (b) torpor, (c) cleverness, (d) self-composure ________
7. irretrievable = not capable of being (a) sold, (b) identified, (c) explained, (d) recovered ________
8. lenient = (a) liberal, (b) crooked, (c) benevolent, (d) explicit ________
9. retrench = (a) dig repeatedly, (b) reduce, (c) reiterate, (d) enlighten ________
10. trivial = (a) composed of three parts, (b) momentous, (c) paltry, (d) economical ________

List 16

1. audit = (a) examine, (b) speak, (c) exchange, (d) expunge ________
2. arrears = (a) retreat, (b) gratuity, (c) overdue debt, (d) option ________
3. curtail = (a) obstruct, (b) restore, (c) rejuvenate, (d) cut short ________
4. encumber = (a) grow, (b) substantiate, (c) burden, (d) illustrate ________
5. exemplify = (a) segregate, (b) divulge, (c) illustrate, (d) condone ________

6. extension = (a) unusual request, (b) prolonged journey, (c) haphazard results, (d) extra time ________

7. fortuitous = (a) accidental, (b) courageous, (c) radical, (d) assiduous ________

8. innovation = (a) reorganization, (b) occupancy, (c) introduction, (d) solution ________

9. syndicate = (a) union of writers, (b) council of lawmakers, (c) group of symptoms, (d) association of people ________

10. venture = (a) speculative business transaction, (b) unsecured loan, (c) stock split, (d) gambling debt ________

List 17

1. acquiesce = (a) gain possession of, (b) confront, (c) implore, (d) comply ________

2. enumerate = (a) articulate, (b) list, (c) enunciate, (d) see clearly ________

3. erratic = (a) pleasurable, (b) wandering, (c) exotic, (d) serene ________

4. expedient = serving to promote (a) fellowship, (b) one's own interests, (c) good of others, (d) speedy delivery ________

5. feasible = (a) authentic, (b) profuse, (c) practicable, (d) extraneous ________

6. literal = (a) exact, (b) devout, (c) apropos, (d) noticeable ________

7. lucrative = (a) providential, (b) swift, (c) pleasant, (d) profitable ________

8. negotiable = (a) essential, (b) adequate, (c) transferable, (d) economical ________

9. nonchalant = (a) dull, (b) cool, (c) unintelligent, (d) sagacious ________

10. reconcile = (a) settle or resolve, (b) calculate, (c) modify, (d) remunerate ________

List 18

1. byte = (a) dental occlusion, (b) computer storage, (c) digits processed as a unit, (d) type font ________

2. encrypt = (a) convert into code, (b) print, (c) commit fraud, (d) inter ________

3. execute = (a) eradicate, (b) inquire, (c) oppose, (d) carry out ________

4. memory = (a) printer logic, (b) computer information-storage capacity, (c) automatic printout, (d) software ________

5. menu = list of (a) parts, (b) options, (c) serial numbers, (d) vendors ________

6. morph = (a) combine, (b) alter by computer, (c) scan, (d) exchange data ________

7. program = (a) alphabetical list, (b) computer log, (c) coded instructions, (d) microprocessor ________

8. prompt = (a) reminder, (b) code, (c) function, (d) format ________

9. retrieve = (a) acquiesce, (b) instruct, (c) remove code, (d) recover information ________

10. tentative = (a) sporting, (b) hesitant, (c) permanent, (d) repetitive ________

List 19

1. apprehensive = (a) knowledgeable, (b) fearful, (c) reticent, (d) autonomous ________
2. circumspect = (a) cautious, (b) uncertain, (c) co-operative, (d) frugal ________
3. collateral = (a) revenue, (b) secret agreement, (c) book value, (d) security for a loan ________
4. insinuation = (a) disagreeable proposal, (b) indirect suggestion, (c) elucidating glimpse, (d) flagrant insult ________
5. liaison = (a) legal obligation, (b) treaty, (c) connection between groups, (d) quarantine ________
6. procrastinate = (a) predict, (b) reproduce, (c) postpone, (d) advance ________
7. ratification = the act of (a) confirming, (b) reviewing, (c) evaluating, (d) inscribing ________
8. renovate = (a) renegotiate, (b) restore, (c) supply, (d) deliver ________
9. saturate = to fill (a) slowly, (b) dangerously, (c) as expected, (d) to excess ________
10. vendor = (a) seller, (b) manufacturer, (c) tradesperson, (d) coin collector ________

List 20

1. abhorrent = (a) extremely disagreeable, (b) attractive, (c) valueless, (d) addictive ________
2. appraisal = (a) general information, (b) certification, (c) estimation, (d) approval ________
3. collusion = (a) secret agreement, (b) direct conflict, (c) partial exclusion, (d) original artwork ________
4. commingle = (a) swindle, (b) mix, (c) separate, (d) communicate ________
5. dissolution = (a) intemperance, (b) solubility, (c) subversion, (d) separation ________
6. ensue = (a) change subtly, (b) relinquish, (c) track down, (d) follow ________
7. rejuvenate = to make (a) youthful, (b) slender, (c) sturdy, (d) impregnable ________
8. stipulation = (a) permission, (b) requirement, (c) rejection, (d) concurrence ________
9. subsidy = (a) scholarship, (b) financial assistance, (c) payment due, (d) unacknowledged payment ________
10. tenuous = (a) flimsy, (b) indecisive, (c) cautious, (d) firm ________

APPENDIX

Reference Guide to Document Formats

C

Business documents carry two kinds of messages. Verbal messages are conveyed by the words chosen to express the writer's ideas. Non-verbal messages are conveyed largely by the appearance of a document. If you compare an assortment of letters and memos from various organizations, you will notice immediately that some look more attractive and more professional than others. The non-verbal message of professional-looking documents suggests that they were sent by people who are careful, informed, intelligent, and successful. Understandably, you're more likely to take seriously documents that use attractive stationery and professional formatting techniques.

Over the years certain practices and conventions have arisen regarding the appearance and formatting of documents. Although these conventions offer some choices (such as letter and punctuation styles), most business documents follow standardized formats. To ensure that your documents carry favourable non-verbal messages about you and your organization, you'll want to give special attention to the appearance and formatting of your letters, envelopes, memos, email messages, and fax cover sheets.

▶ Appearance

To ensure that a message is read and valued, you need to give it a professional appearance. Two important elements in achieving a professional appearance are stationery and placement of the message on the page.

Stationery

Most organizations use high-quality stationery for printed business documents. This stationery is printed on select paper that meets two qualifications: weight and cotton-fibre content.

Paper is measured by weight and may range from 9 pounds (thin onionskin paper) to 32 pounds (thick card and cover stock). Most office stationery is in the 16- to 24-pound range. Lighter 16-pound paper is generally sufficient for internal documents including memos. Heavier 20- to 24-pound paper is used for printed letterhead stationery.

Paper is also judged by its cotton-fibre content. Cotton fibre makes paper stronger, softer in texture, and less likely to yellow. Good-quality stationery contains 25 per cent or more cotton fibre.

Letter Placement

The easiest way to place letters on the page is to use the defaults of your word processing program. These are usually set for side margins of 1 inch to 1.25 inches. Many companies today find these margins acceptable.

If you want to adjust your margins to better balance shorter letters, use the following chart:

Words in Body of Letter	Side Margins	Blank Lines After Date
Under 200	$1\frac{1}{2}$ inches	4 to 10
Over 200	1 inch	2 to 3

Experts say that a "ragged" right margin is easier to read than a justified (even) margin. You might want to turn off the justification feature of your word processing program if it automatically justifies the right margin.

▶ Letter Parts

Professional-looking business letters are arranged in a conventional sequence with standard parts. Following is a discussion of how to use these letter parts properly. Figure C.1 illustrates the parts in a block-style letter.

Letterhead

Most business organizations use 8 1/2- by 11-inch paper printed with a letterhead displaying their official name, street address, email address, and telephone and fax numbers.

Dateline

On letterhead paper you should place the date two blank lines below the last line of the letterhead or 2 inches from the top edge of the paper (line 13). On plain paper place the date immediately below your return address. Since the date appears 2 inches from the top, start the return address an appropriate number of lines above it. The most common dateline format is as follows: *June 9, 2009.* Don't use *th,* etc., when the date is written this way. For European or military correspondence, use the following dateline format: *9 June 2009.* Notice that no commas are used.

Addressee and Delivery Notations

Delivery notations such as *FAX TRANSMISSION, MESSENGER DELIVERY, CONFIDENTIAL,* or *CERTIFIED MAIL* are typed in all capital letters two blank lines above the inside address.

In block-style letters, as shown in Figure C.1, all lines begin at the left margin. In modified block-style letters, as shown at the right, the date is centred or aligned with the complimentary close and signature block, which start at the centre. The date may also be backspaced from the right margin. Paragraphs may be blocked or indented. Mixed punctuation includes a colon after the salutation and a comma after the complimentary close.

Inside Address

Type the inside address—that is, the address of the organization or person receiving the letter—single-spaced, starting at the left margin. The number of lines between the dateline and the inside address depends on the size of the letter body, the font size, and the length of the typing lines. Generally, one to nine blank lines are appropriate.

Be careful to duplicate the exact wording and spelling of the recipient's name and address on your documents. Usually, you can copy this information from the letterhead of the correspondence you are answering. If, for example, you are responding to

Figure C.1
Letter and Punctuation Styles

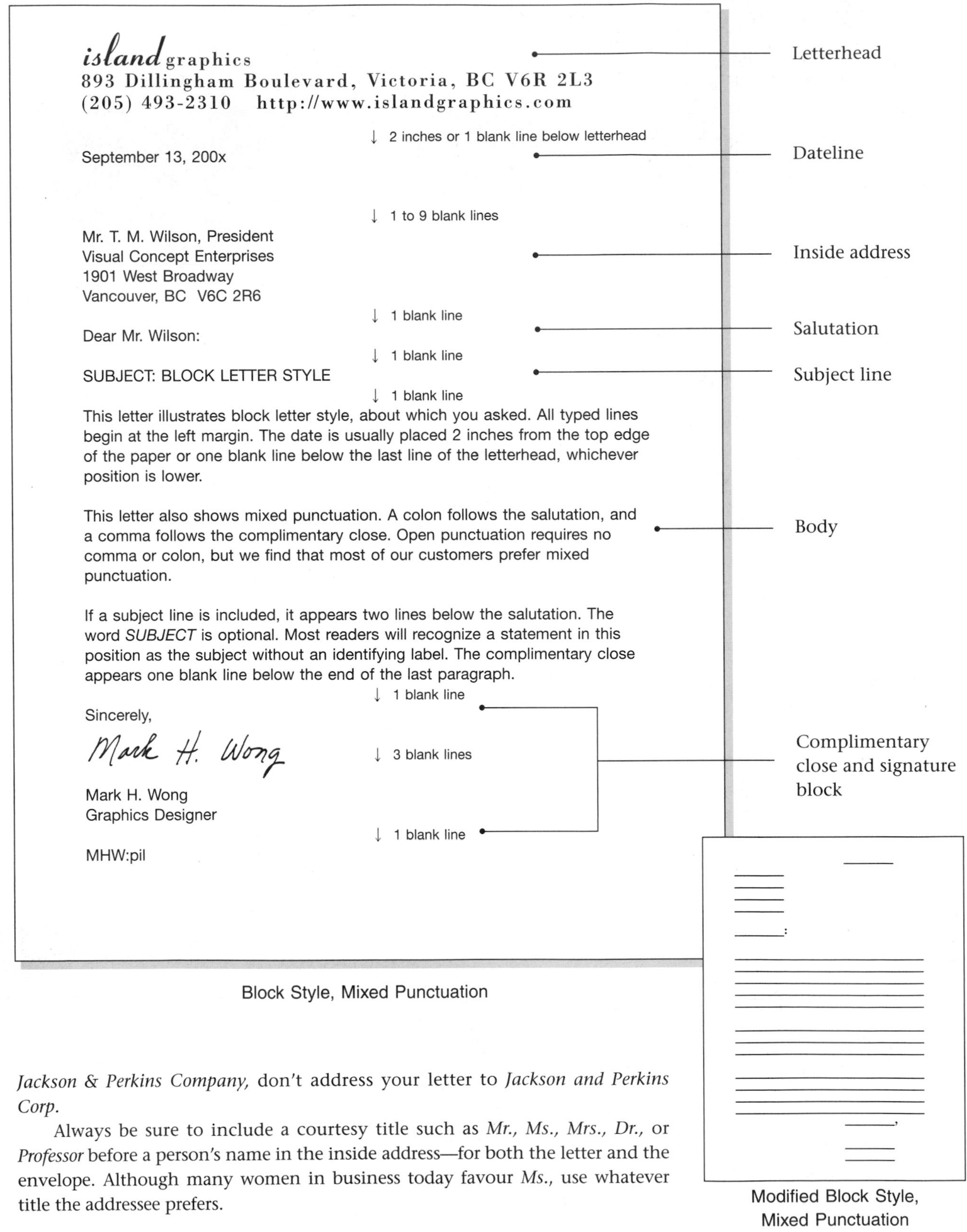

island graphics
893 Dillingham Boulevard, Victoria, BC V6R 2L3
(205) 493-2310 http://www.islandgraphics.com

September 13, 200x

Mr. T. M. Wilson, President
Visual Concept Enterprises
1901 West Broadway
Vancouver, BC V6C 2R6

Dear Mr. Wilson:

SUBJECT: BLOCK LETTER STYLE

This letter illustrates block letter style, about which you asked. All typed lines begin at the left margin. The date is usually placed 2 inches from the top edge of the paper or one blank line below the last line of the letterhead, whichever position is lower.

This letter also shows mixed punctuation. A colon follows the salutation, and a comma follows the complimentary close. Open punctuation requires no comma or colon, but we find that most of our customers prefer mixed punctuation.

If a subject line is included, it appears two lines below the salutation. The word *SUBJECT* is optional. Most readers will recognize a statement in this position as the subject without an identifying label. The complimentary close appears one blank line below the end of the last paragraph.

Sincerely,

Mark H. Wong

Mark H. Wong
Graphics Designer

MHW:pil

Block Style, Mixed Punctuation

Modified Block Style, Mixed Punctuation

Jackson & Perkins Company, don't address your letter to *Jackson and Perkins Corp.*

Always be sure to include a courtesy title such as *Mr., Ms., Mrs., Dr.,* or *Professor* before a person's name in the inside address—for both the letter and the envelope. Although many women in business today favour *Ms.,* use whatever title the addressee prefers.

Remember that the inside address is not included for readers (who already know who and where they are). It's there to help writers accurately file a copy of the message.

Attention Line

An attention line allows you to send your message officially to an organization but to direct it to a specific individual, office, or department. However, if you know an individual's complete name, it's always better to use it as the first line of the inside address and avoid an attention line. Here are two common formats for attention lines:

MultiMedia Enterprises
2931 St. Laurent
Montreal, QC H2F 3C2

ATTENTION MARKETING DIRECTOR

MultiMedia Enterprises
Attention: Marketing Director
2931 St. Laurent
Montreal, QC H2F 3C2

Attention lines may be typed in all caps or with upper and lower case letters. The colon following *Attention* is optional. Notice that an attention line may be placed two lines below the address block or printed as the second line of the inside address. You'll want to use the latter format if you're composing on a word processor because the address block may be copied to the envelope and the attention line will not interfere with the last-line placement of the postal code. (Mail can be sorted more easily if the postal code appears in the last line of a typed address.)

Whenever possible, use a person's name as the first line of an address instead of putting that name in an attention line. Some writers use an attention line because they fear that letters addressed to individuals at companies may be considered private. They worry that if the addressee is no longer with the company, the letter may be forwarded or not opened. Actually, unless a letter is marked "Personal" or "Confidential," it will very likely be opened as business mail.

Salutation

For most letter styles, place the letter greeting, or salutation, one blank line below the last line of the inside address or the attention line (if used). If the letter is addressed to an individual, use that person's courtesy title and last name (*Dear Mr. Lanham*). Even if you are on a first-name basis (*Dear Leslie*), be sure to add a colon (not a comma or a semicolon) after the salutation. Do not use an individual's full name in the salutation (not *Dear Mr. Leslie Lanham*) unless you are unsure of gender (*Dear Leslie Lanham*).

For letters with attention lines or those addressed to organizations, the selection of an appropriate salutation has become more difficult. Formerly, *Gentlemen* was used generically for all organizations. With increasing numbers of women in business management, however, *Gentlemen* became problematic. Because no universally acceptable salutation has emerged as yet, you'll probably be safest with *Ladies and Gentlemen* or *Gentlemen and Ladies*. The best way to avoid the salutation dilemma is to address a document to a specific person.

Subject and Reference Lines

Although experts suggest placing the subject line one blank line below the salutation, many organizations actually place it above the salutation. Use whatever style your organization prefers. Reference lines often show policy or file numbers; they generally appear one blank line above the salutation. Use initial capital letters as in a title, or use all capital letters.

Body

Most business letters and memoranda are single-spaced, with double-spacing between paragraphs. Very short messages may be double-spaced with indented paragraphs.

Complimentary Close

Typed one blank line below the last line of the letter, the complimentary close may be formal (*Very truly yours*) or informal (*Sincerely yours* or *Cordially*).

Signature Block

In most letter styles, the writer's typed name and optional identification appear two to three blank lines below the complimentary close. The combination of name, title, and organization information should be arranged to achieve a balanced look. The name and title may appear on the same line or on separate lines, depending on the length of each. Use commas to separate categories within the same line, but not to conclude a line.

Sincerely,
Jeremy M. Wood
Jeremy M. Wood, Manager
Technical Sales and Services

Cordially yours,
Casandra Baker-Murillo
Casandra Baker-Murillo
Executive Vice-President

Courtesy titles (*Ms., Mrs.,* or *Mr.*) should be used before names that are not readily distinguishable as male or female. They should also be used before names containing only initials and international names. The title is usually placed in parentheses, but it may appear without them.

Yours truly,
Ms. K. C. Tripton
(Ms.) K. C. Tripton
Project Manager

Sincerely,
Mr. Leslie Hill
(Mr.) Leslie Hill
Public Policy Department

Some organizations include their names in the signature block. In such cases the organization name appears in all caps one blank line below the complimentary close, as shown here:

Cordially,

LITTON COMPUTER SERVICES
Ms. Shelina A. Simpson
(Ms.) Shelina A. Simpson
Executive Assistant

Reference Initials

Reference initials identify who typed and formatted the letter. If used, the initials of the typist and writer are typed one blank line below the writer's name and title. Generally, the writer's initials are capitalised and the typist's are lower case, but this format varies. Today the writer's initials are usually omitted.

Enclosure Notation

When an enclosure or attachment accompanies a document, a notation to that effect appears one blank line below the reference initials. This notation reminds the typist to insert the enclosure in the envelope, and it reminds the recipient to look for the enclosure or attachment. The notation may be spelled out (*Enclosure, Attachment*), or it may be abbreviated (*Enc., Att.*). It may indicate the number of enclosures or attachments, and it may also identify a specific enclosure (*Enclosure: Form 1099*).

Copy Notation

If you make copies of correspondence for other individuals, you may use *cc* to indicate courtesy copy or carbon copy or merely *c* for any kind of copy. A colon following the initial(s) is optional.

Second-Page Heading

When a letter extends beyond one page, use plain paper of the same quality and colour as the first page. Identify the second and succeeding pages with a heading consisting of the name of the addressee, the page number, and the date. Use either of the following two formats:

Ms. Rachel Lawson   2   May 3, 200x

Ms. Rachel Lawson
Page 2
May 3, 200x

Both headings appear 1 inch from the top of the paper, followed by two blank lines to separate them from the continuing text. Avoid using a second page if you have only one line or the complimentary close and signature block to fill that page.

▶ Letter Styles

Business letters are generally prepared in one of two formats. The more popular is the block style.

Block Style

In the block style, shown in Figure C.1, all lines begin at the left margin. This style is a favourite because it is easy to format.

Modified Block Style

The modified block style differs from block style in that the date and closing lines appear in the centre, as shown at the bottom of Figure C.1. The date may be (1) centred, (2) begun at the centre of the page (to align with the closing lines), or (3) backspaced from the right margin. The signature block—including the complimentary close, writer's name and title, or organization identification—begins at the centre. The first line of each paragraph may begin at the left margin or may be indented five or ten spaces. All other lines begin at the left margin.

Personal Business Style

When business and professional writers prepare letters on plain paper, they often use the personal business style. It includes the writer's street and city address on two lines above the date, as shown in Figure C.2. Notice that the writer's name does not appear here; it is typed and signed at the end of the letter. The personal business letter may be formatted in (a) full block style with all lines starting at the left margin, (b) modified

Figure C.2
Personal Business Style

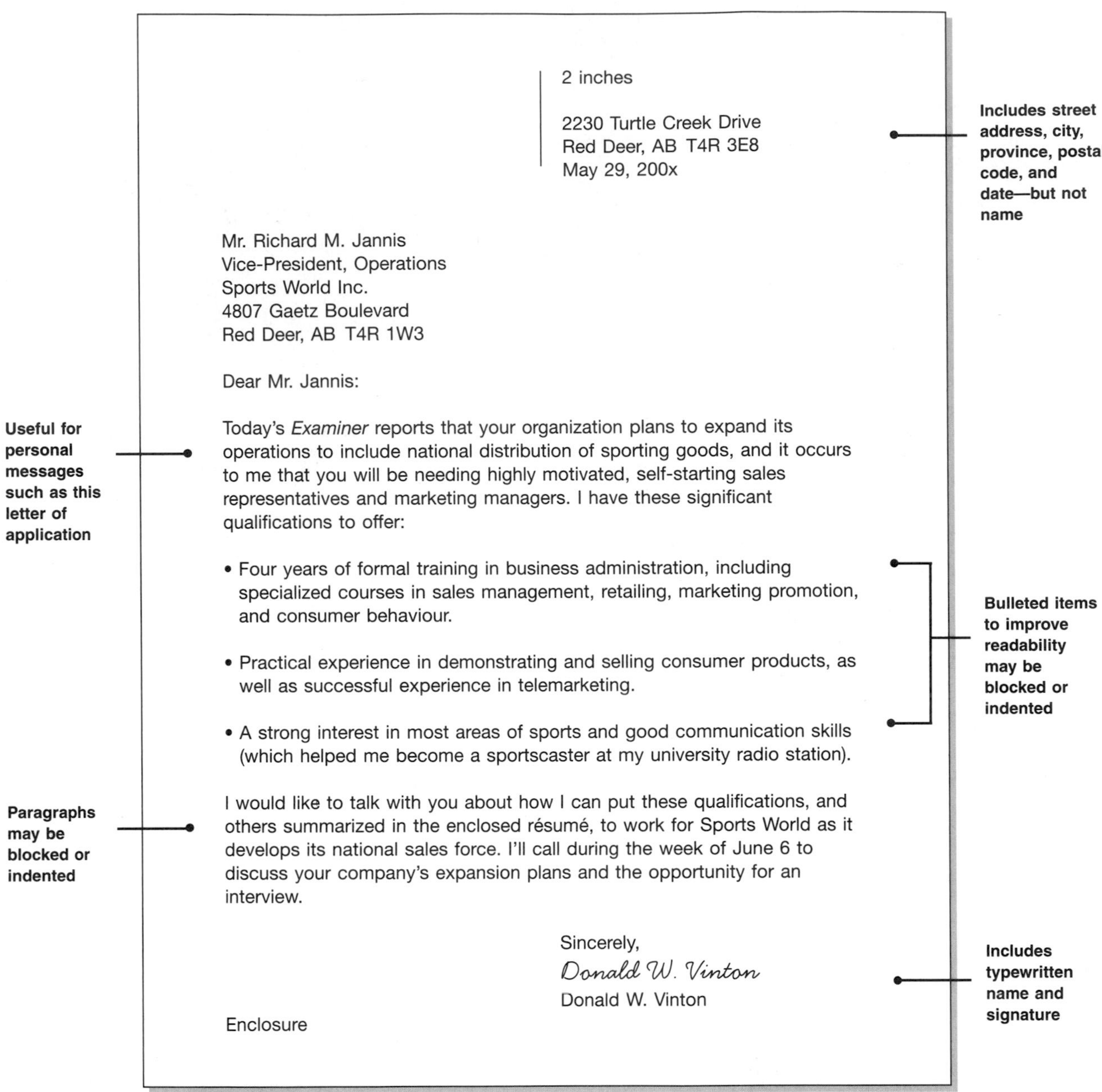
2 inches

2230 Turtle Creek Drive
Red Deer, AB T4R 3E8
May 29, 200x

Mr. Richard M. Jannis
Vice-President, Operations
Sports World Inc.
4807 Gaetz Boulevard
Red Deer, AB T4R 1W3

Dear Mr. Jannis:

Today's *Examiner* reports that your organization plans to expand its operations to include national distribution of sporting goods, and it occurs to me that you will be needing highly motivated, self-starting sales representatives and marketing managers. I have these significant qualifications to offer:

- Four years of formal training in business administration, including specialized courses in sales management, retailing, marketing promotion, and consumer behaviour.
- Practical experience in demonstrating and selling consumer products, as well as successful experience in telemarketing.
- A strong interest in most areas of sports and good communication skills (which helped me become a sportscaster at my university radio station).

I would like to talk with you about how I can put these qualifications, and others summarized in the enclosed résumé, to work for Sports World as it develops its national sales force. I'll call during the week of June 6 to discuss your company's expansion plans and the opportunity for an interview.

Sincerely,
Donald W. Vinton
Donald W. Vinton

Enclosure

Includes street address, city, province, postal code, and date—but not name
Useful for personal messages such as this letter of application
Bulleted items to improve readability may be blocked or indented
Paragraphs may be blocked or indented
Includes typewritten name and signature

block with blocked paragraphs, or (c) modified block style with indented paragraphs. In the modified block style, notice that the date and closing lines both start at the centre of the page.

▶ Punctuation Styles

Two punctuation styles are commonly used for letters. *Mixed* punctuation, shown in Figure C.1, requires a colon after the salutation and a comma after the complimentary close. *Open* punctuation contains no punctuation after the salutation or complimentary close.

With mixed punctuation, be sure to use a colon—not a comma or semicolon—after the salutation. Even when the salutation is a first name, the colon is appropriate.

▶ Envelopes

An envelope should be of the same quality and colour of stationery as the letter it carries. Because the envelope introduces your message and makes the first impression, you need to be especially careful in addressing it. Moreover, how you fold the letter is important.

Return Address

The return address is usually printed in the upper left corner of an envelope, as shown in Figure C.3. In large companies some form of identification (the writer's initials, name, or location) may be typed above the company name and return address. This identification helps return the letter to the sender in case of non-delivery.

On an envelope without a printed return address, single-space the return address in the upper left corner. Beginning 1/4 inch from the top and 1/2 inch from the left edge, type the writer's name, title, company, and mailing address.

Mailing Address

On legal-sized No. 10 envelopes (4 1/8 by 9 1/2 inches), begin the address 2 1/4 inches from the top and about 1/2 inch left of centre, as shown in Figure C.3. For small envelopes (3 5/8 by 6 1/2 inches), begin typing about 2 1/2 inches from the left edge. The easiest way to correctly position the mailing address on the envelope is to use your word processor's envelope feature.

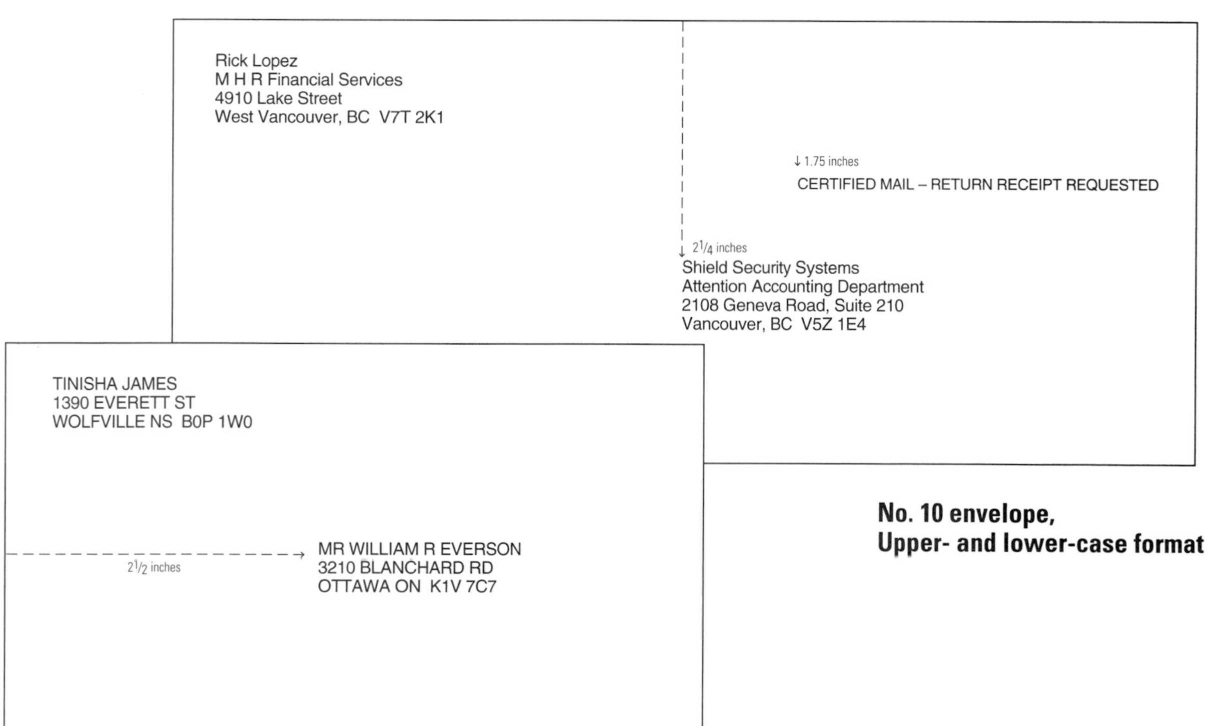

Rick Lopez
M H R Financial Services
4910 Lake Street
West Vancouver, BC V7T 2K1
1.75 inches
CERTIFIED MAIL – RETURN RECEIPT REQUESTED
2 1/4 inches
Shield Security Systems
Attention Accounting Department
2108 Geneva Road, Suite 210
Vancouver, BC V5Z 1E4
TINISHA JAMES
1390 EVERETT ST
WOLFVILLE NS B0P 1W0
2 1/2 inches
MR WILLIAM R EVERSON
3210 BLANCHARD RD
OTTAWA ON K1V 7C7

No. 10 envelope, Upper- and lower-case format

No. 6¾ envelope, CPC upper-case format

Figure C.3
Envelope Formats

Canada Post Corporation recommends that addresses be typed in all caps without any punctuation. This CPC style, shown in the small envelope in Figure C.3, was originally developed to facilitate scanning by optical character readers. Today's OCRs, however, are so sophisticated that they scan upper and lower case letters easily. Many companies today do not follow the CPC format because they prefer to use the same format for the envelope as for the inside address. If the same format is used, writers can take advantage of word processing programs to "copy" the inside address to the envelope, thus saving keystrokes and reducing errors. Having the same format on both the inside address and the envelope also looks more professional and consistent. For these reasons you may choose to use the familiar upper- and lower-case combination format. But you will want to check with your organization to learn its preference.

In addressing your envelopes for delivery in this country or in the United States, use the two-letter province and state abbreviations as shown in Figure C.4. Notice that these abbreviations are in capital letters without periods.

Figure C.4
Abbreviations of Provinces, Territories, and States

Province or Territory	Two-Letter Abbreviation
Alberta	AB
British Columbia	BC
Manitoba	MB
New Brunswick	NB
Newfoundland and Labrador	NL
Northwest Territories	NT
Nova Scotia	NS
Nunavut	NU
Ontario	ON
Prince Edward Island	PE
Quebec	QC
Saskatchewan	SK
Yukon Territory	YT

State or Territory	Two-Letter Abbreviation
Alabama	AL
Alaska	AK
Arizona	AZ
Arkansas	AR
California	CA
Canal Zone	CZ
Colorado	CO
Connecticut	CT
Delaware	DE
District of Columbia	DC
Florida	FL
Georgia	GA
Guam	GU
Hawaii	HI
Idaho	ID
Illinois	IL
Indiana	IN
Iowa	IA
Kansas	KS

State or Territory	Two-Letter Abbreviation
Kentucky	KY
Louisiana	LA
Maine	ME
Maryland	MD
Massachusetts	MA
Michigan	MI
Minnesota	MN
Mississippi	MS
Missouri	MO
Montana	MT
Nebraska	NE
Nevada	NV
New Hampshire	NH
New Jersey	NJ
New Mexico	NM
New York	NY
North Carolina	NC
North Dakota	ND
Ohio	OH
Oklahoma	OK
Oregon	OR
Pennsylvania	PA
Puerto Rico	PR
Rhode Island	RI
South Carolina	SC
South Dakota	SD
Tennessee	TN
Texas	TX
Utah	UT
Vermont	VT
Virgin Islands	VI
Virginia	VA
Washington	WA
West Virginia	WV
Wisconsin	WI
Wyoming	WY

Folding

The way a letter is folded and inserted into an envelope sends additional non-verbal messages about a writer's professionalism and carefulness. Most business people follow the procedures shown here, which produce the least number of creases to distract readers.

For large No. 10 envelopes, begin with the letter face up. Fold slightly less than one-third of the sheet toward the top, as shown below. Then fold down the top third to within 1/4 inch of the bottom fold. Insert the letter into the envelope with the last fold toward the bottom of the envelope.

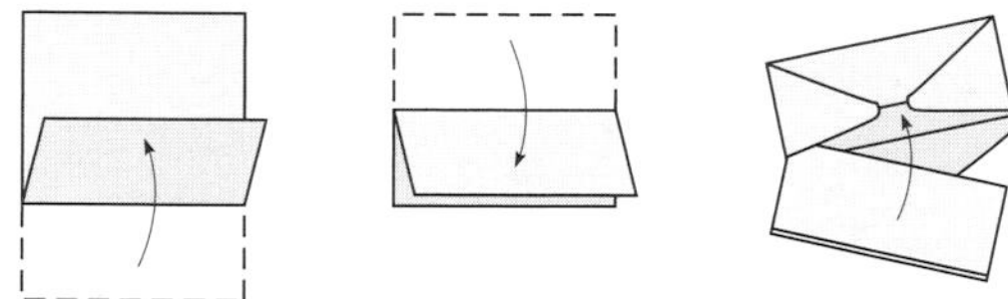

For small No. 6 3/4 envelopes, begin by folding the bottom up to within 1/2 inch of the top edge. Then fold the right third over to the left. Fold the left third to within 1/2 inch of the last fold. Insert the last fold into the envelope first.

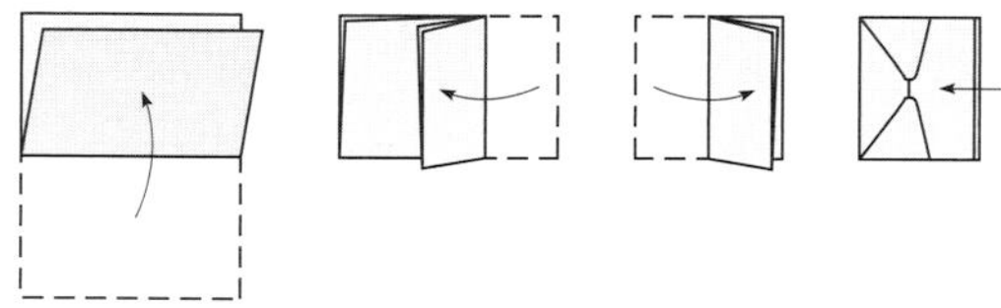

▶ Memoranda

Memoranda deliver messages within organizations, although email is replacing the use of printed memos in many places. Some offices use memo forms imprinted with the organization name and, optionally, the department or division names. Although the design and arrangement of memo forms vary, they usually include the basic elements of *TO, FROM, DATE,* and *SUBJECT*. Large organizations may include other identifying headings, such as *FILE NUMBER, FLOOR, EXTENSION, LOCATION,* and *DISTRIBUTION*.

Because of the difficulty of aligning computer printers with preprinted forms, many business writers use a standardized memo template (sometimes called a "wizard"). This template automatically provides attractive headings with appropriate spacing and formatting. Other writers store their own preferred memo formats. Either method eliminates alignment problems.

If no printed or stored computer forms are available, memos may be typed on company letterhead or on plain paper, as shown in Figure C.5. On a full sheet of paper, leave a 1 1/2-inch top margin; on a half sheet, leave a 1-inch top margin. Double-space and type in all caps the guide words: *TO:, FROM:, DATE:, SUBJECT:*. Align all the fill-in information two spaces after the longest guide word (*SUBJECT:*). Leave two blank lines after the last line of the heading, and begin typing the body of the memo. Like business letters, memos are single-spaced.

Memos are generally formatted with side margins of 1 1/4 inches, or they may conform to the printed memo form.

↓ 1 1/2 inches
MEMO

DATE: February 3, 200x

TO: Dawn Stewart, Manager
Sales and Marketing

FROM: Jay Murray, Vice-President
Operations

SUBJECT: TELEPHONE SERVICE REQUEST FORMS
↓ 2 blank lines

To speed telephone installation and improve service within the Bremerton facility, we are starting a new application procedure.

Service request forms will be available at various locations within the three buildings. When you require telephone service, obtain a request form at one of the locations that is convenient for you. Fill in the pertinent facts, obtain approval from your division head, and send the form to Brent White. Request forms are available at the following locations:

Figure C.5
Memo on Plain Paper

▶ Email Messages

Email has become the most popular form of communication in today's workplace. The following suggestions, illustrated in Figure C.6, may guide you in setting up the parts of an email message, but always check with your organization so that you can follow its practices.

To Line

Include the receiver's email address after *To*. If the receiver's address is recorded in your address book, you just have to click on it. Be sure to enter all addresses very carefully since one mistyped character prevents delivery.

From Line

Most systems automatically include your name and email address after *From*.

Cc

Insert the email address of anyone who is to receive a copy of the message. *Cc* stands for *carbon copy* or *courtesy copy*. Don't be tempted, though, to send needless copies just because it's so easy.

Bcc

Include here the email address of anyone who is to receive a copy of the message without the receiver's knowledge. *Bcc* stands for *blind carbon copy*. Writers are also using the *bcc* line for mailing lists. When a message is being sent to a number of people and their email addresses should not be revealed, the *bcc* line works well to conceal the names and addresses of all receivers.

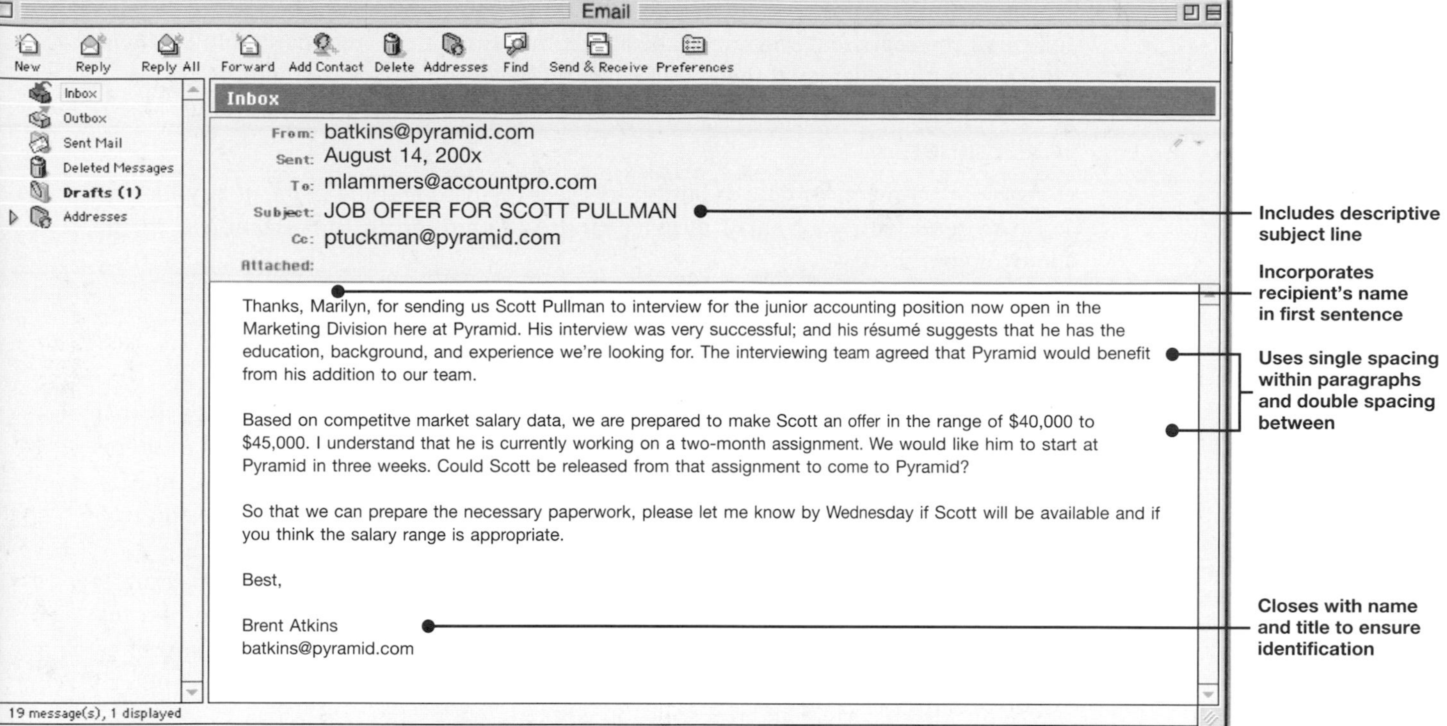
From: batkins@pyramid.com
Sent: August 14, 200x
To: mlammers@accountpro.com
Subject: JOB OFFER FOR SCOTT PULLMAN
Cc: ptuckman@pyramid.com
Attached:

Thanks, Marilyn, for sending us Scott Pullman to interview for the junior accounting position now open in the Marketing Division here at Pyramid. His interview was very successful; and his résumé suggests that he has the education, background, and experience we're looking for. The interviewing team agreed that Pyramid would benefit from his addition to our team.

Based on competitve market salary data, we are prepared to make Scott an offer in the range of $40,000 to $45,000. I understand that he is currently working on a two-month assignment. We would like him to start at Pyramid in three weeks. Could Scott be released from that assignment to come to Pyramid?

So that we can prepare the necessary paperwork, please let me know by Wednesday if Scott will be available and if you think the salary range is appropriate.

Best,

Brent Atkins
batkins@pyramid.com

Figure C.6
Typical Email Message

Subject

Identify the subject with a brief but descriptive summary of the topic. Be sure to include enough information to be clear and compelling. Capitalize the subject line as you would a title, or capitalize the entire line if space permits. Subject lines in all lower case letters look unimportant and unprofessional. Most important, never leave a subject line blank.

Salutation

Include a brief greeting, if you like. Some writers use a salutation such as *Dear Sondra* followed by a comma or a colon. Others are more informal with *Hi, Sondra!*, or *Good morning* or *Greetings*. Some writers simulate a salutation by including the name of the receiver in the first line, as shown in Figure C.6. Other writers treat an email message like a memo and skip the salutation entirely.

Message

Cover just one topic in your message, and try to keep your total message under two screens in length. Single space and be sure to use both upper and lower case letters. Double space between paragraphs.

Closing

Conclude an external message, if you like, with *Sincerely, Best wishes,* or *Warm regards*, followed by your name. If the recipient is unlikely to know you, it's a good idea to include your title and organization. Some email users include a *signature file* with identifying information that is automatically inserted at the end of each message. Writers of email messages sent within organizations may omit a closing but should still type at least their first names at the end of email messages to personalize them.

Attachment

Use the attachment window or button to select the path and file name of any file you wish to send with your email message, and call attention to the attachment in the body of your message.

▶ Fax Cover Sheet

Documents transmitted by fax are usually introduced by a cover sheet, such as that shown in Figure C.7. As with memos, the format varies considerably. Important items to include are (1) the name and fax number of the receiver, (2) the name and fax number of the sender, (3) the number of pages being sent, and (4) the name and telephone number of the person to notify in case of unsatisfactory transmission.

When the document being transmitted requires little explanation, you may prefer to attach an adhesive note (such as a Post-it™ fax transmittal form) instead of a full cover sheet. These notes carry essentially the same information as shown in our printed fax cover sheet. They are perfectly acceptable in most business organizations and can save considerable paper and transmission costs.

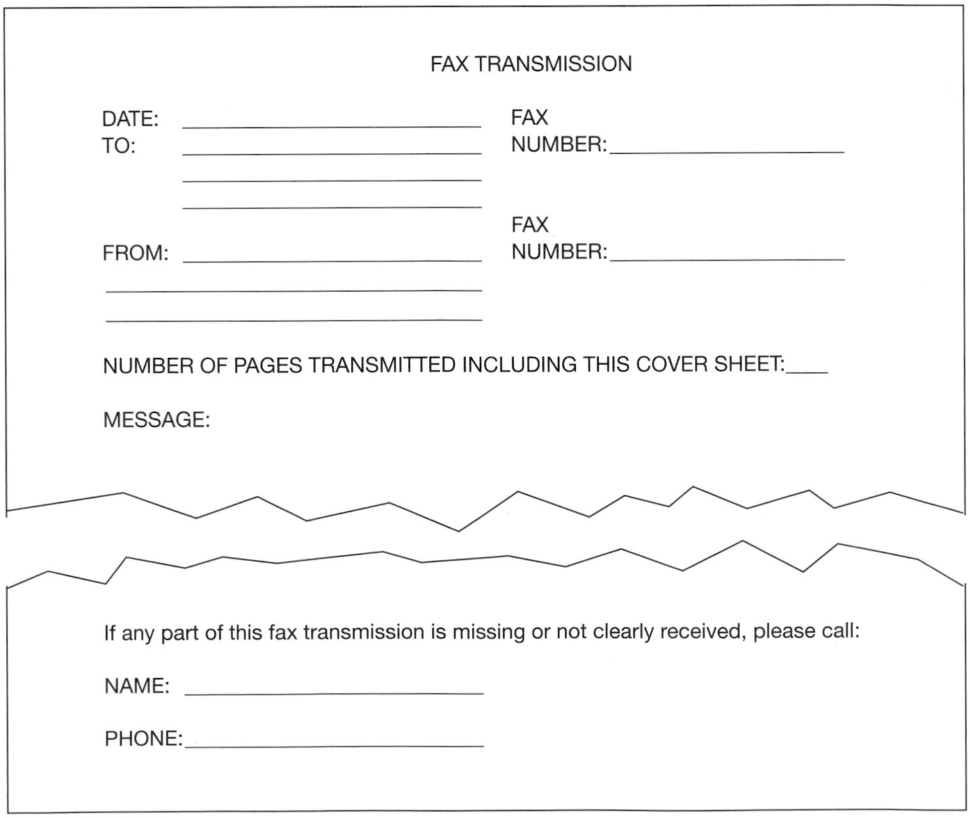

FAX TRANSMISSION

DATE: ____________________ FAX
TO: ____________________ NUMBER: ____________________
____
____

FAX
FROM: ____________________ NUMBER: ____________________
____
____

NUMBER OF PAGES TRANSMITTED INCLUDING THIS COVER SHEET: ____

MESSAGE:

If any part of this fax transmission is missing or not clearly received, please call:

NAME: ____________________

PHONE: ____________________

Figure C.7
Fax Cover Sheet

Self-Help Exercises

CONTENTS

NAME ______________________________

Nearly every student who takes this English course says, "I wish I had more exercises to try my skills on." Because of the many requests, we provide this set of self-help exercises for extra reinforcement. Immediate feedback is an important ingredient in successful learning. Therefore, a key to these exercises begins on p. 547. Don't check the key, of course, until you complete each exercise.

Use a current dictionary to complete the following exercise.

1. *Amanuensis* originally meant
(a) deterioration of sight (b) coarse herbs including pigweeds
(c) a servant with secretarial duties (d) a female warrior ____________

2. An *autocrat* is one who enjoys
(a) owning many cars (b) ruling by himself or herself
(c) democratic relationships (d) racing automobiles ____________

3. The words *in so much as* should be written
(a) in so much as (b) in somuchas
(c) insomuch as (d) in somuch as ____________

4. The abbreviation *MST* stands for
(a) master in statistical technology (b) manual or standard transmission
(c) Mountain Standard Time (d) master ____________

5. The abbreviation *Mme* stands for
(a) madame (b) mademoiselle
(c) master in mechanical engineering (d) monsieur ____________

6. In grammar the word *neuter* means
(a) asexual (b) neutral
(c) neither feminine nor masculine (d) both feminine and masculine ____________

7. The word *(non)productive* should be written
(a) non-productive (b) nonproductive
(c) non productive (d) non-Productive ____________

8. When the word *notwithstanding* is used to mean "nevertheless," it functions as what part of speech?
(a) conjunction (b) adverb
(c) preposition (d) adjective ____________

9. The plural of the word *proxy* is
(a) proxies' (b) proxys
(c) proxy's (d) proxies ____________

10. In Sri Lanka a *rupee* is a monetary unit equal to
(a) 10 cents (b) 100 cents
(c) 50 cents (d) $2 ____________

NAME ______________________

Worksheet 1

A. This exercise is designed to help you develop a better understanding of the parts of speech. Using Chapter 2, write a brief definition or description of the eight parts of speech listed here. Then list three words as examples of each part of speech.

	Brief Definition	Three Examples		
1. noun	names person, place, thing, concept	Anthony	paper	truth
2. pronoun	______	______	______	______
3. verb	______	______	______	______
4. adjective	______	______	______	______
5. adverb	______	______	______	______
6. preposition	______	______	______	______
7. conjunction	______	______	______	______
8. interjection	______	______	______	______

B. Fill in the parts of speech for all the words in these sentences. Use a dictionary if necessary.

We sent an email message to Jennifer, but she was very busy.

1. We ______
2. sent ______
3. an ______
4. email ______
5. message ______
6. to ______
7. Jennifer ______
8. but ______
9. she ______
10. was ______
11. very ______
12. busy ______

Gosh, the computer and printer processed this lengthy report in twenty seconds!

13. Gosh ______
14. the ______
15. computer ______
16. and ______
17. printer ______
18. processed ______
19. this ______
20. lengthy ______
21. report ______
22. in ______
23. twenty ______
24. seconds ______

We arrived promptly, but the committee meeting started late.

25. We ______
26. arrived ______
27. promptly ______
28. but ______
29. the ______
30. committee ______
31. meeting ______
32. started ______
33. late ______

NAME ___________________________

Worksheet 2

Fill in the parts of speech for all the words in these sentences. Use a dictionary if necessary.

I sold property in Fredericton, but one transaction may not clear escrow.

1. I ____________
2. sold ____________
3. property ____________
4. in ____________
5. Fredericton ____________
6. but ____________
7. one ____________
8. transaction ____________
9. may ____________
10. not ____________
11. clear ____________
12. escrow ____________

Oh, did Lee really think he could change that method of operation?

13. Oh ____________
14. did ____________
15. Lee ____________
16. really ____________
17. think ____________
18. he ____________
19. could ____________
20. change ____________
21. that ____________
22. method ____________
23. of ____________
24. operation ____________

The old accounting system was not accurate or efficient, but one company had used it faithfully for the past forty years.

25. The ____________
26. old ____________
27. accounting ____________
28. system ____________
29. was ____________
30. not ____________
31. accurate ____________
32. or ____________
33. efficient ____________
34. but ____________
35. one ____________
36. company ____________
37. had ____________
38. used ____________
39. it ____________
40. faithfully ____________
41. for ____________
42. the ____________
43. past ____________
44. forty ____________
45. years ____________

Kerry quietly slipped into an empty seat during the long class film.

46. Kerry ____________
47. quietly ____________
48. slipped ____________
49. into ____________
50. an ____________
51. empty ____________
52. seat ____________
53. during ____________
54. the ____________
55. long ____________
56. class ____________
57. film ____________

NAME ________________________________

Worksheet 1

Locating Subjects and Verbs

Action verbs tell what the subject is doing or what is being done to the subject. For each of the following sentences, locate the action verb and underline it twice. Then locate the subject of the verb and underline it once.

To locate the subject, use the verb preceded by *who?* or *what?* In the example the verb is *answered.* To help you find the subject, ask *who answered?*

Example: A group of applicants answered the advertisement.

1. One of our top salespeople sold $2 million worth of life insurance.
2. In the afternoon session, the speaker made a dynamic presentation.
3. Our telephones rang constantly during the sales campaign.
4. In the winter we will hire four new workers for this department.
5. Our management team built a strong program of sales and service.
6. The most successful salespeople received trips to Cuba.
7. In the meantime, our human resources manager will send you an application form.
8. Last week we released our new line of upscale, stylish cellphones.
9. One of the vice-presidents was given a promotion recently.
10. A committee consisting of 11 employees plus the manager was appointed to investigate.
11. The applicant with the best qualifications received the first interview.
12. Everything except labour and parts is covered by your warranty.

Linking verbs (such as *am, is, are, was, were, be, being,* and *been*) often join to the sentence words that describe or rename the subject. In the following sentences, underline the linking verbs twice and the subjects once.

Examples: E.J. Todd was president of the organization last year.
In the morning the air is cool.

13. Mr. Thomas is the office manager for Ryerson Metals Corporation.
14. The new copiers are very dependable.
15. Mrs. Seymour is the best person for the job.
16. Dul Youn Hu has been office manager for nine years.
17. Our new offices are much brighter than our previous ones.

NAME ____________________

Worksheet 2

Sentence Patterns

Finish the sentences below in the patterns indicated.

Subject–Verb

Example: Birds ___sing___.

1. The audience ____________.
2. Rain ____________.
3. Employees ____________.
4. The security alarm ____________.
5. In 1945 World War II ____________.
6. Last year's sales ____________.

Subject–Action Verb–Object

Example: The sales director made ___a call___.

7. Our salesperson sold a ____________.
8. The assistant sent ____________.
9. Ricky mailed the ____________.
10. I telephoned ____________.
11. Someone locked ____________.
12. The clerk filed all the ____________.

Subject–Linking Verb–Complement

Example: She is very ___friendly___.

Jim could have been the ___manager___.

13. Sales have been ____________.
14. Susan is the new ____________.
15. Last year the owner was ____________.
16. I am ____________.
17. The writer could have been ____________.
18. The caller was ____________.

Compose original sentences in the following patterns.

19. (Subject–verb) ____________
20. (Subject–verb) ____________
21. (Subject–action verb–object) ____________
22. (Subject–action verb–object) ____________
23. (Subject–linking verb–complement) ____________

NAME ________________________

Worksheet 3

Sentence Faults

From the list below select the letter that accurately describes each of the following groups of words.

a = correctly punctuated sentence
b = fragment
c = comma splice
d = run-on sentence

1. The management of a multinational corporation with branch offices in several cities. ________
2. Send me a brochure and a price list for your latest camping equipment. ________
3. For a generous return on your funds, invest in second trust deeds. ________
4. Brazil, Chile, and Australia are located in the southern hemisphere their summers and winters are the opposite of ours. ________
5. A training session on our new email program will be held Monday, January 14, all employees should plan to attend. ________
6. Because it is difficult to improve your language skills on your own. ________
7. Individuals and families who may have hereditary conditions such as a predisposition to certain cancers. ________
8. Queen Elizabeth and Prince Philip celebrated 60 years of marriage in 2007, they were married November 20, 1947. ________
9. Successful candidates for the positions will be motivated and energetic good communication skills will be essential. ________
10. I'll have the answer soon, first I must make a telephone call. ________
11. If you consider all the pros and cons before you make a decision. ________
12. We have no idea what to order only Dunia Sanchez can do that. ________
13. Your entire department is entitled to overtime compensation. ________
14. You check the current address list, and I'll check the old one. ________
15. You check the current address list, I'll check the old one. ________
16. You check the current address list I'll check the old one. ________
17. Although we have complete confidence in our products and prices. ________
18. When you return from the conference, please submit a brief report describing what you learned. ________
19. We must focus our charitable contributions on areas that directly relate to our business, therefore, we are unable to send a cheque this year. ________
20. If you agree that this memo accurately reflects our conversation. ________

NAME ______________________

LEVEL I

Write the preferred plural forms of the nouns shown below. Use a dictionary if necessary.

1. giraffe ____________
2. foot ____________
3. switch ____________
4. Bush ____________
5. box ____________
6. language ____________
7. fax ____________
8. sandwich ____________
9. income tax ____________
10. child ____________
11. success ____________
12. value ____________
13. dress ____________
14. branch ____________
15. recommendation ____________
16. woman ____________
17. mismatch ____________
18. taxi ____________
19. loaf (of bread) ____________
20. annex ____________
21. belief ____________
22. Ross ____________
23. storm ____________
24. ranch ____________
25. Jones ____________
26. Chavez ____________
27. letter ____________
28. business ____________
29. computer ____________
30. wish ____________

LEVEL II

Write the preferred plural forms of the nouns shown below. Use a dictionary if necessary.

1. wharf ____________
2. chief of police ____________
3. 2000 ____________
4. Wolf ____________
5. embargo ____________
6. cm ____________
7. size 10 ____________
8. amt. ____________
9. faculty ____________
10. by-product ____________
11. entry ____________
12. looker-on ____________
13. company ____________
14. knife ____________

15. court-martial ____________

16. A ____________

17. Sherman ____________

18. memo ____________

19. valley ____________

20. zero ____________

21. life ____________

22. yr. ____________

23. Mistry ____________

24. runner-up ____________

25. oz. ____________

26. journey ____________

27. M.B.A. ____________

28. wolf ____________

29. Kelly ____________

30. minority ____________

LEVEL III

Write the preferred plural forms of the nouns shown below. Use a dictionary if necessary.

1. datum ____________

2. thesis ____________

3. bacterium ____________

4. Chinese ____________

5. parenthesis ____________

6. Miss Soltan (informal) ____________

7. alumna ____________

8. Mr. West and Mr. Turner (formal) ____________

9. genus ____________

10. news ____________

11. p. (page) ____________

12. f. (and following page) ____________

13. larva ____________

14. Mrs. Smythe and Mrs. Webb (formal) ____________

15. criterion ____________

Select the correct word in parentheses, and complete the sentences in your own words.

16. The goods produced in that factory (is, are) ____________

17. Politics in Ottawa (is, are) ____________

18. Several (formula, formulas) ____________

19. Four separate (analysis, analyses) ____________

20. In the business curriculum economics (is, are) ____________

NAME ______________________________

Worksheet 1

LEVEL I

Before you begin this exercise, review the five-step plan for placing apostrophes:

1. Look for possessive construction. (Usually two nouns appear together.)
2. Reverse the nouns. (Use a prepositional phrase, such as *interest of three years*.)
3. Examine the ownership word. (Is it singular or plural?)
4. If the ownership word is singular, add an apostrophe and *s*.
5. (a) If the ownership word is plural and ends in *s*, add only an apostrophe.
   (b) If the ownership word is plural but does not end in *s*, add both an apostrophe and an *s*.

Using apostrophes, change the following prepositional phrases into possessive constructions.

Example: interest of three years — three years' interest

1. books of all students — students' books
2. office of this company — company's office
3. uniforms of the women — women's uniforms
4. rent of two months — two months' rent
5. mansion of the movie star — movie star's mansion
6. feelings of all the neighbours — neighbours' feelings
7. the landing of the pilot — pilot's landing
8. agreement of both partners — ____________
9. notebook of Jeffrey — ____________
10. strengths of the department — ____________
11. time of two years — ____________
12. customs of those people — ____________
13. merger of last week — ____________
14. credit from the bank — ____________
15. savings of citizens — ____________
16. mountains of Canada — ____________
17. requirements of the employer — ____________
18. résumés of all candidates — ____________
19. policies of the government — ____________
20. fees of both lawyers — ____________

NAME ____________________

Worksheet 2

Write the correct possessive form of the word in parentheses in the space provided.

1. Applicants will have at least a (year) wait for an apartment. ____________
2. Several (drivers) inquiries prompted the posting of a better sign. ____________
3. We found the (carpenter) tools after he left the building. ____________
4. The electronics store installed a hidden video camera to observe a suspected (thief) activities. ____________
5. We catch up on the (day) news by watching CBC Newsworld every night at 9. ____________
6. Our new (employees) cafeteria is particularly busy from 11 a.m. to 1 p.m. ____________
7. Only the (CEO) car may be parked in the special zone. ____________
8. Most (readers) letters supported the magazine's editorial position. ____________
9. Where is the (caller) message? ____________
10. All (authors) rights are protected by copyright law. ____________

Correct any errors in the following sentences by underlining the errors and writing the correct forms in the spaces provided. If a sentence is correct as written, write *C*.

11. The Gaps headquarters are as simple, clean, and comfortable as the company's clothing. ____________
12. The names of these customers are not alphabetized. ____________
13. Some of the countrys biggest manufacturers are being investigated. ____________
14. This account has been credited with four months interest. ____________
15. Your organizations voice mail system is excellent. ____________
16. The vice-presidents resignation left a vital position unfilled. ____________
17. Are you researching your familys genealogy? ____________
18. I am prepared to protest the bill of my lawyer, William Glass. ____________
19. In three years time, the software paid for itself. ____________
20. Not a single farmers crop was undamaged by the storm. ____________
21. A citizens committee was formed to address parking problems. ____________
22. One years interest on the account amounted to $120. ____________
23. Each customers complimentary game tickets were mailed today. ____________
24. Childrens clothing is on the first floor. ____________
25. New benefits for employees were announced in the supervisors memo. ____________

NAME ______________________________

LEVEL II

Correct any errors in the following sentences by underlining the errors and writing the correct forms in the spaces provided. If the sentence is correct as written, write *C*.

1. The document required the notary publics signature and seal. ____________

2. At least one companies' records are up to date. ____________

3. After school Juan stopped at the stationers for supplies. ____________

4. My uncle's lawyer's suggestions in this matter were excellent. ____________

5. The desk's top had to be refinished by a skilled woodworker. ____________

6. We borrowed my aunt's and uncle's motor home. ____________

7. All RNs' uniforms must now be identical. ____________

8. This month's expenses are somewhat less than last months. ____________

9. Debbie's and Julie's iPods have similar song lists. ____________

10. The president's secretary's telephone number has been changed. ____________

11. Have you called the new sales' representative? ____________

12. My two brothers-in-law's beards are neat and well trimmed. ____________

13. The committee meeting will be held at Larrys. ____________

14. We spent our vacation enjoying Quebecs' historical sights. ____________

15. I'm going over to Ricks to pick him up. ____________

16. The CBC's report on the vote was better than any other network's. ____________

17. Clark's and Clark's reference manual is outstanding. ____________

18. The Los Angeles' symphony planned an evening of Beethoven. ____________

19. The two architects licences were issued together. ____________

20. Our sales this year are greater than last years. ____________

21. All RCMP agents must pass rigorous security investigations. ____________

22. Diana's and Graham's marriage licence was lost. ____________

23. The Prime Minister answered all the reporters questions carefully. ____________

24. Workers said they expected a days pay for an honest days work. ____________

25. Robin and John's new car came with a five-year warranty. ____________

NAME ______________________________

LEVEL III

Write the correct possessive forms of the words shown in parentheses.

Example: The (Jarvis) cat is missing. Jarvises'

1. I see that (someone else) books also got wet. Someone else's
2. Lee (Ross) office is on the south side of the campus. Ross'
3. Both (class) test results were misplaced. Classes'
4. Beth (Saunders) home is farther away than anyone else's. ______
5. The bank is reconsidering the (Rodriguez) loan application. Rodriguezes'
6. I have no idea where (Les) car is parked. ______
7. Only my (boss) desk is cluttered. ______
8. The other (boss) desks are rather neat. ______
9. Did you hear that the (Abramovich) are moving? ______
10. Several (actress) costumes were so valuable that insurance policies were taken out to insure them. ______
11. I think that was Mr. (Harris) parking spot you just took. Harris'
12. Mrs. (Burns) history class met outside on that balmy day. ______
13. Who is (James) partner for the laboratory experiment? ______
14. That (waitress) station consists of four tables. ______
15. None of the (Garvey) belongings were missing. ______
16. Have you visited the (Morris) vacation home? ______
17. Only Mrs. (Betz) car remained in the parking lot. Betz's
18. It looks as if the (Walker) home is getting a new roof. ______
19. Miss (Simons) new Internet connection provides better access. ______
20. Mr. (Jones) property is on Kelton Avenue. ______
21. Professor (White) lecture was well organized and informative. ______
22. Have you seen the (Williams) four-room tent that they took camping last weekend? ______
23. We heard that the (Kimball) house may be sold. ______
24. Visitors at Graceland swore they saw (Elvis) ghost. ______

NAME ______________________________

Worksheet 1

LEVEL I

List seven pronouns that could be used as subjects of verbs.

1. ____________ **4.** ____________ **7.** ____________

2. ____________ **5.** ____________

3. ____________ **6.** ____________

List seven pronouns that could be used as objects of verbs or objects of prepositions.

8. ____________ **11.** ____________ **14.** ____________

9. ____________ **12.** ____________

10. ____________ **13.** ____________

Pronouns as Subjects

Select the correct pronoun to complete each sentence below. All the omitted pronouns function as subjects of verbs.

15. Mrs. Georges and (I, me) submitted purchase requisitions. ____________

16. In the afternoon training session, the manager and (she, her) will make presentations. ____________

17. Will you and (he, him) be going to the sales meeting? ____________

18. Mr. North and (they, them) expect to see you Saturday. ____________

19. It is difficult to explain why Bob and (her, she) decided to move. ____________

20. Of all the applicants, only (we, us) agreed to be tested now. ____________

21. We believe that Rudolf and (she, her) deserve raises. ____________

22. After Ms. Barko and (he, him) had returned, customers were handled more rapidly. ____________

23. Only you and (her, she) will participate in the demonstration. ____________

24. After the spring sales campaign, the sales manager and (he, him) will be promoted. ____________

25. Because we are most familiar with the project, you and (I, me) must complete the report. ____________

NAME

Worksheet 2

Personal Pronouns as Objects

Select the correct pronoun to complete each sentence below. All the omitted pronouns function as objects of verbs or prepositions. Prepositions have been underlined to help you identify them.

1. Just between you and (I, me), our branch won the sales trophy.

2. Michelle said that she had seen you and (he, him) at the airport.

3. We hope to show (they, them) the billing procedure this afternoon.

4. Everybody but (I, me) is ready to leave.

5. Have you talked with Brad and (her, she) about this change?

6. We need more workers like Maria and (him, he) to finish the job.

7. All supervisors except Mrs. Young and (her, she) approved the plan.

8. This insurance program provides you and (they, them) with equal benefits.

9. Terms of the settlement were satisfactory to (we, us).

10. Every operator but Molly and (I, me) had an opportunity for overtime.

Possessive-Case Pronouns

Remember that possessive-case pronouns (*yours, his, hers, its, whose, theirs,* etc.) do not contain apostrophes. Do not confuse these pronouns with the following contractions: *it's* (it is), *there's* (there is), *who's* (who is), and *you're* (you are). In the following sentences, select the correct word.

11. Do you think (its, it's) necessary for us to sign in?

12. Is (theirs, their's) the white house at the end of the street?

13. The contract and all (its, it's) provisions must be examined.

14. (There's, Theirs) a set of guidelines for us to follow.

15. Jack's car and (hers, her's) are the only ones left in the lot.

16. The cheque is good only if (its, it's) signed.

17. I was told that Sue's and (yours, your's) were the best departments.

18. (Who's, Whose) umbrella is that lying in the corner?

19. Most car registrations were sent April 1, but (our's, ours) was delayed.

20. (You're, Your) taking Don's place, aren't you?

NAME ______________________

LEVEL II

Select the correct pronoun to complete these sentences.

1. Do you expect Mr. Jefferson and (they, them) to meet you? them
2. No one could regret the error more than (I, me, myself). ____
3. These photocopies were prepared by Charles and (she, her). ____
4. (We, Us) policyholders are entitled to group discounts. ____
5. Procrastination disturbs Steven as much as (I, me, myself). ____
6. Universal Parcel is hiring James and (I, me, myself) for the summer. ____
7. Have you corresponded with the authors, Dr. Lee and (she, her)? ____
8. On that project no one works as hard as (he, him, himself). ____
9. Everyone but Mr. Foster and (he, him) can help customers if necessary. ____
10. Do you know whether Gary and (I, me, myself) signed it? ____
11. Only Erik (he, himself, hisself) knows what is best for him. ____
12. We asked two women, Denise and (she, her), to come along. ____
13. The proceeds are to be divided among Mr. Shelby, Mrs. Huerra, and (she, her). ____
14. Miss Greerson thinks that Mr. Campbell is a better salesperson than (she, her). ____
15. All property claims must be submitted to my lawyer or (I, me, myself) before April 15. ____
16. The new contract is acceptable to both management and (us, we, ourselves). ____
17. When reconciling bank statements, no one is more accurate than (she, her). ____
18. The best time for you and (he, him) to enrol is in January. ____
19. The president and (I, me, myself) will inspect the facility. ____
20. Everyone except Kevin and (I, me, myself) was able to join the program. ____
21. Send an application to Human Resources or (I, me, myself) immediately. me
22. (She and I, Her and me, Her and I) are among the best-qualified candidates. ____
23. Have you invited Jon and (she, her, herself) to our picnic? ____
24. Most of the email messages sent to (us, we) employees are considered spam. ____
25. Only Gurpreet and (I, me, myself) were given company cellphones. ____

NAME ______________________________

Worksheet 1

LEVEL III

Remember that pronouns that rename the subject and that follow linking verbs must be in the subjective (nominative) case (*It was he who placed the order*). When the infinitive *to be* has no subject (and that subject must immediately precede the infinitive *to be*), the pronoun that follows must be in the nominative case (*My sister is often taken to be I*). *No* subject = *no*minative.

In the following sentences, select the correct word.

1. It must have been (her, she) who called this morning. ____________

2. I certainly would not like to be (he, him). ____________

3. Do you think that it was (they, them) who complained? ____________

4. Tram answered the telephone by saying, "This is (her, she)." ____________

5. Mrs. Richards thought the salesperson to be (he, him). ____________

6. If you were (she, her), would you take the job? ____________

7. Cecile is sometimes taken to be (her, she). ____________

8. Jim said that yesterday's driver could have been (he, him). ____________

9. Miss Soriano asked Frank and (I, me, myself) to help her. ____________

10. Was it (they, them) who made the contribution? ____________

11. The most accurate proofreader seems to be (he, him). ____________

12. Producer Edwards would not allow me to be (he, him) in the production. ____________

13. Mr. Fox wants to assign you and (her, she) the project. ____________

14. Are you sure it was (I, me) who was called to the phone? ____________

15. The visitor was thought to be (she, her). ____________

16. If it had not been (she, her) who made the announcement, I would not have believed it. ____________

17. How could anyone have thought that Margaret was (I, me)? ____________

18. I do not wish to discourage either you or (he, him). ____________

19. If anyone is disappointed, it will be (I, me, myself). ____________

20. What makes Joan wish to be (she, her)? ____________

21. Do you think it was (he, him) who made the large contribution? ____________

22. Mr. Egal selected you and (he, him) because of his confidence in your abilities. ____________

23. If it had been (she, her), we would have recognized her immediately. ____________

24. Everyone thought the new manager would be (she, her). ____________

NAME ______________________________

Worksheet 2

Select the correct word to complete the following sentences.

1. Only the president and (he, him) can grant leaves of absence. ____________
2. The manager mistook Danielle to be (I, me). ____________
3. The body of the manuscript is followed by (its, it's) endnotes. ____________
4. Our staff agreed that you and (she, her) should represent us. ____________
5. How can you believe (us, we) to be guilty? ____________
6. I'm not sure (their's, there's) enough time left. ____________
7. Everyone thought the new manager would be (he, him). ____________
8. My friend and (I, me) looked for jobs together. ____________
9. This matter will be kept strictly between you and (I, me). ____________
10. Good students like you and (she, her) are always prepared. ____________
11. Judge Waxman is fully supported by (we, us) consumers. ____________
12. We agreed that (your, you're) the best person for the job. ____________
13. Send the announcement to Ms. Nguyen and (she, her) today. ____________
14. All employees except Kim and (he, him) will be evaluated. ____________
15. Many locker combinations are listed, but (your's, yours) is missing. ____________
16. Apparently the message was intended for you and (I, me, myself). ____________
17. Was it (he, him, himself) who sent the mystery email message? ____________
18. The bank is closed, but (it's, its) ATM is open. ____________
19. Please submit the report to (him or me, he or I) before May 1. ____________
20. (There's, Theirs) only one path for us to follow. ____________
21. For you and (he, him), I would suggest careers in marketing. ____________
22. These personnel changes affect you and (I, me, myself) directly. ____________
23. My friend and (I, me, myself) are thinking of a trip to Cuba. ____________
24. Only two branches plan to expand (they're, their) display rooms. ____________
25. The operator thought it was (she, her) calling for assistance. ____________
26. Because you are a member of the audit review team, you have a better overall picture of the operations than (I, me, myself). ____________
27. Though you may not agree with our decision, I hope you'll support Todd and (I, me, myself) in our effort to get the job done. ____________

NAME ______________________________

LEVEL I

Pronouns must agree with the words for which they substitute. Don't let words and phrases that come between a pronoun and its antecedent confuse you.

Examples: Every one of the women had *her* forms ready. (Not *their.*)
The supervisor, along with four assistants, offered *his* support. (Not *their.*)

Select the correct word(s) to complete these sentences.

1. Mrs. Kennedy, in addition to many other members of the staff, sent (her, their) best wishes. ______________

2. Every employee must have (his, her, his or her, their) physical examination completed by December 31. ______________

3. After a job well done, everyone appreciates (his, her, his or her, their) share of credit. ______________

4. Several office workers, along with the manager, announced (his or her, their) intention to vote for the settlement. ______________

5. Individuals like Mr. Herndon can always be depended on to do (his, his or her, their) best in all assignments. ______________

6. If a policyholder has a legitimate claim, (he, she, he or she, they) should contact us immediately. ______________

7. Every one of the employees brought (his or her lunch, their lunches) to the outdoor event. ______________

8. When a customer walks into our store, treat (him, her, him or her, them) as you would an honoured guest in your home. ______________

9. Carolyn Davis, along with several other company representatives, volunteered to demonstrate (her, his or her, their) latest software. ______________

10. A few members of the touring group, in addition to the guide, wanted (his or her picture, their pictures) taken. ______________

11. Any female member of the project could arrange (her, their) own accommodations if desired. ______________

12. Every player on the men's team complained about (his, his or her, their) uniform. ______________

Rewrite this sentence to avoid the use of a common-gender pronoun. Show three versions.

Every employee must obtain his parking permit in the personnel office.

13. ____

14. ____

15. ____

NAME ______________________________

LEVEL II

Underline any pronoun–antecedent errors in the following sentences. Then write a corrected form in the space provided. If a sentence is correct, write *C*.

1. Last Friday either Miss Monahan or Miss Chavez left their machine on. ____________

2. The Canadian Medical Association has not yet published it's opinion of the therapy. ____________

3. Every clerk, every manager, and every executive will be expected to do their part in making the carpooling program a success. ____________

4. Somebody left his cellphone in the tray at the airport security check. ____________

5. Neither one of the men wanted to have their remarks quoted. ____________

6. Every one of the delegates to the women's conference was wearing their name tag. ____________

7. The vice-president and the marketing director had already made their reservations. ____________

8. Each of the pieces of equipment came with their own software. ____________

9. The firm of Higgins, Thomas & Keene is moving their offices to Warner Plaza. ____________

10. Every manager expects the employees who report to them to be willing to earn their salaries. ____________

11. Neither of the women had her driver's licence in the car. ____________

12. We hoped that someone in the office could find their copy of the program. ____________

13. Either the first caller or the second one did not leave their phone number. ____________

14. If everybody will please take their seats, we can get started. ____________

15. The faculty agreed to publicize their position on budget cuts. ____________

16. We saw that HomeCo reduced their prices on lawn mowers. ____________

17. Few of the colour printers had the sale price marked on it. ____________

18. Every one of the male employees agreed to be more careful in protecting their computer password. ____________

19. Each bridesmaid will pay for their own gown. ____________

20. All managers and employees know that she or he must boost productivity. ____________

NAME ______________________________

Worksheet 1

LEVEL III

In selecting *who* or *whom* to complete the sentences below, follow these five steps:

he = who
him = whom

Example: We do not know (who, whom) the contract names.

1. Isolate the *who* clause: (*who, whom*) the contract names
2. Invert to normal subject–verb order: the contract names (*who, whom*)
3. Substitute pronouns: the contract names *him*/the contract names *her*
4. Equate: the contract names *whom*
5. Complete: We do not know *whom* the contract names.

1. (Who, Whom) will you invite to your party? ______________

2. Rick Nash is the employee (who, whom) the CEO asked to present to the board. ______________

3. Do you know (who, whom) will be taking your place? ______________

4. To (who, whom) did she refer in her letter? ______________

5. Did Mr. Glade say (who, whom) he wanted to see? ______________

6. Dr. Truong is a man (who, whom) everyone respects. ______________

7. (Who, Whom) was president of your organization last year? ______________

8. (Who, Whom) do you want to work with? ______________

9. (Who, Whom) has the best chance to be elected? ______________

10. I know of no one else (who, whom) plays so well. ______________

In choosing *who* or *whom* to complete these sentences, ignore parenthetical phrases such as *I think, we know, you feel,* and *I believe.*

11. Julie is a person (who, whom) I know will be successful on the job. ______________

12. The human resources director hired an individual (who, whom) he thought would be the best performer. ______________

13. Is Freda Hastings the dealer (who, whom) you think I should call? ______________

14. Major Kirby, (who, whom) I think will be elected, is running in the next election. ______________

15. (Who, Whom) do you believe will be given the job? ______________

NAME ______________________

Worksheet 2

In the following sentences, selecting *who, whom, whoever,* or *whomever* first requires isolating the clause within which the pronoun appears. Then, within the clause, determine whether a subjective- or objective-case pronoun is required.

Example: Give the package to (whoever, whomever) opens the door. (*He* or *she* opens the door = *whoever* opens the door.) whoever

1. A bonus will be given to (whoever, whomever) sells over $100,000. ______
2. Discuss the problem with (whoever, whomever) is in charge of the program. ______
3. We will interview (whoever, whomever) you recommend. ______
4. You may give the tickets to (whoever, whomever) you wish. ______
5. Johnson said to give the parking pass to (whoever, whomever) asked for it. ______
6. The committee members have promised to co-operate with (whoever, whomever) is selected to chair the committee. ______
7. Please call (whoever, whomever) you believe can repair the machine. ______
8. (Whoever, Whomever) is nominated for the position must be approved by the full membership. ______
9. Reservations have been made for (whoever, whomever) requested them in advance. ______
10. (Whoever, Whomever) is chosen to lead the delegation will command attention at the convention. ______

In choosing *who* or *whom* to complete these sentences, be especially alert to pronouns following the linking verbs. Remember that the subjective *who* is required as a subject complement.

Example: Was it (who, whom) I thought it was? (It was *he* = *who*.) who

11. (Who, Whom) is the customer who wanted a replacement? ______
12. The visitor who asked for me was (who, whom)? ______
13. Was the new CEO (who, whom) we thought it would be? ______
14. The winner will be (whoever, whomever) is tops in sales. ______
15. For (who, whom) was this new printer ordered? ______

NAME ______________________

Worksheet 3

In the following sentences, select the correct word.

1. (Who, Whom) did you call for assistance? Whom
2. Edward Lincoln, (who, whom) we thought would never be hired, did well in his first assignment. who
3. By (who, whom) are you currently employed? whom
4. You should hire (whoever, whomever) you feel has the best qualifications. whoever
5. Did the caller say (who, whom) he wanted to see? whom
6. The man (who, whom) I saw yesterday walked by today. whom
7. (Whoever, Whomever) is first on the list will be called next. whoever
8. The sales rep sent notices to customers (who, whom) she felt should be notified. who
9. Is the manager (who, whom) we thought it would be? Who
10. The manager praised the clerk (who, whom) worked late. who
11. She is the one (who, whom) Jenny helped yesterday. whom
12. Many of us thought Jamie Alison was a nice person with (who, whom) to work. whom
13. (Who, Whom) is Stacy often mistaken to be? Who
14. (Who, Whom) did you say to call for reservations? whom
15. Please make an appointment with (whoever, whomever) you consider to be the best internist. ______
16. Here is a list of satisfied customers (who, whom) you may wish to contact. ______
17. (Whoever, Whomever) is suggested by Mr. Arthur must be interviewed. ______
18. The candidate (who, whom) the party supports will win. ______
19. Jas is one on (who, whom) I have come to depend. ______
20. For (who, whom) are these contracts? ______
21. Do you know (whose, who's) jacket this is? ______
22. Do you know (who, whom) their sales representative is? ______
23. We're not sure (whose, who's) signed up for Friday's seminar. ______
24. Rodney Wilson, (who, whom) was our first choice, was appointed. ______
25. You'll never guess (whose, who's) running for president! ______

NAME ______________________

LEVEL I

Fill in the answers to the following questions with information found in your text.

1. What kind of action verb directs action toward a person or thing? ____________
2. What kind of action verb does not require an object to complete its action? ____________
3. What kind of verb links to the subject words that rename or describe the subject? ____________
4. What do we call the nouns, pronouns, and adjectives that complete the meaning of a sentence by renaming or describing the subject? ____________

In each of the following sentences, indicate whether the underlined verb is transitive (*T*), intransitive (*I*), or linking (*L*). In addition, if the verb is transitive, write its object. If the verb is linking, write its complement. The first two sentences are followed by explanations to assist you.

5. James ran along the dirt path back to his home. (The verb *ran* is intransitive. It has no object to complete its meaning. The prepositional phrase *along the dirt path* tells where James ran; it does not receive the action of the verb.) I
6. It might have been Fran who called yesterday. (The verb phrase ends with the linking verb *been.* The complement is *Fran,* which renames the subject *it.*) L – Fran
7. Jane filed the address cards of our most recent customers. ____________
8. Customers crowded into the store at the beginning of the sale. ____________
9. Sherry was a consultant on the software conversion project. ____________
10. Levi Strauss first sold pants to miners in San Francisco in the 1800s. ____________
11. The bank mailed your cancelled cheques last week. ____________
12. Chocolate fudge ice cream tastes better than chocolate mint. ____________
13. Do you think it was he who suggested the improvement? ____________
14. We walked around the shopping mall on our lunch hour. ____________
15. Our company recruiter asks the same questions of every candidate. ____________
16. Many corporations present gifts to important foreign clients. ____________
17. This dictionary is the best on the market for office workers. ____________
18. All employees listened intently as the CEO discussed annual profits. ____________
19. Ellen feels justified in asking for a raise. ____________
20. Customers have high expectations from most advertised products. ____________

NAME ______________________________

Worksheet 1

LEVEL II

Transitive verbs that direct action toward an object are in the active voice. Transitive verbs that direct action toward a subject are in the passive voice. Writing that incorporates active-voice verbs is more vigorous and more efficient than writing that contains many passive-voice verbs. To convert a passive-voice verb to the active voice, look for the doer of the action. (Generally the agent of the action is contained in a *by* phrase.) In the active voice, the agent becomes the subject.

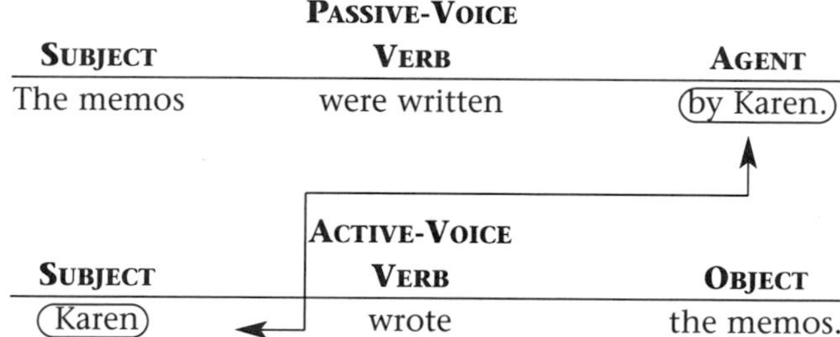

For each of the following sentences, underline the agent (doer of the action). Write that word in the space provided. Then rewrite the sentence changing the passive-voice verb to active voice. Your rewritten version should begin with the word (and its modifiers) that you identified as the agent.

Agent

1. The text message was not picked up by Mariam until Monday morning. ______________

____

____

2. Our order was shipped last week by Mattel. ______________

____

____

3. Withdrawals must be authorized by Mrs. Bradford beginning next week. ______________

____

____

4. Bill was asked by Mr. Stern to be responsible for turning out the lights at the end of the day. ______________

____

____

5. Employees who travel a great deal were forced by management to surrender their frequent-flyer awards. ______________

____

____

NAME ___________________________

Worksheet 2

Some sentences with passive-voice verbs do not identify the doer of the action. Before these sentences can be converted, a subject must be provided. Use your imagination to supply subjects, and rewrite the sentences in the spaces provided.

Passive: Interest will be paid on all deposits. (*By whom?* By First Federal.)
Active: First Federal will pay interest on all deposits.

By Whom?

1. The letters must be completed before 5 p.m. ___________
Mostafa must complete the letter before 5 p.m.

2. Cheques were written on an account with insufficient funds. ___________

3. Our computer was programmed to total account balances. ___________

4. Decisions were made in the courts that affected the daily lives of all Canadians. ___________

5. When home video games were first introduced, it was thought that they were too expensive to sell in mass quantities. ___________

6. Cash discounts are given only when orders are paid immediately with cash. ___________

7. Employees working with computers were warned to change their passwords frequently. ___________

8. For shipments sent in our packaging materials, the value is limited to $500. ___________

NAME ______________________________

LEVEL III

Write the correct answers in the spaces provided.

1. If I (was, were) you, I would complete my degree first. ____________
2. The personnel director recommended that Jeff (be, is) hired with the condition that he continue college courses at night. ____________
3. If Mr. Greer (was, were) in the office yesterday, he did not sign the cheques. ____________
4. One of the shareholders moved that a committee (be, is) constituted to study the problem immediately. ____________
5. If the manager were here, he (will, would) sign the work order and we could proceed. ____________
6. Government officials recommend that all homes (are, be) stocked with an emergency supply of food and water. ____________
7. Joyce said that if she (was, were) the travel agent, she would plan the trip differently. ____________
8. It is important that you (are, be) vaccinated. ____________
9. Dr. Washington suggested that the patient (rest, rests) for the next two days. ____________
10. Angela wished that she (was, were) able to fly to Vancouver to visit her sister. ____________
11. If Mrs. Balfour (was, were) in my position, she would probably do the same thing. ____________
12. Hendricks suggested that the cafeteria (is, be) opened earlier so that swing-shift employees could use it. ____________
13. Under the circumstances, even if the voter registration drive (was, were) successful, we might lose the election. ____________
14. The professor recommended that everyone (meet, meets) in the parking lot before the field trip. ____________
15. He acts as though he (was, were) the only employee who wants the weekend off. ____________
16. After consulting management, our manager suggested that all employees (are, be) given three-week vacations. ____________
17. If the fax machine (was, were) working, you could have the figures immediately. ____________
18. If Ron (was, were) at the sales meeting, I missed him. ____________
19. Laurie uses credit cards as if she (was, were) an heiress. ____________
20. It has been moved and seconded that the meeting (is, be) adjourned. ____________

NAME ______________________________

LEVEL I

Select the correct verb.

1. Did you tell me that your brother's name (is, was) Martin? ______ is
2. The accident (occured, occurred) late last evening. ______
3. Mr. Anderson said that the car you are driving (is, was) red. ______
4. Are your sure that her maiden name (is, was) Spitnale? ______
5. We were taught that an ounce of prevention (is, was) worth a pound of cure. ______

In the space provided, write the correct form of the verb indicated in parentheses.

Example: Joan (carry) a heavy workload every day. (present tense) ______ carries

6. Canadian firms (plan) to expand their markets abroad. (present) ______ plans
7. A Kentucky Fried Chicken franchise (sell) American-style fast food in Japan. (future) ______ will sell
8. The giant Mitsubishi conglomerate (supply) the Colonel with chicken in Japan. (past) ______ supplied
9. The marketing director (study) possible sales sites in foreign countries. (past) ______ studied
10. We (analyze) such factors as real estate, construction costs, and local attitudes toward fast food. (future) ______ will analyze
11. Management (apply) a complex formula to forecast the profitability of the new business. (past) ______ applied
12. We (consider) the vast differences between the two cultures. (past) ______ considered
13. Each local franchise (vary) the side dishes to accommodate cultural preferences. (present) ______ varies
14. Kentucky Fried Chicken (insist) on retaining its original recipe in foreign stores. (present) ______ insists
15. It (appeal) to the average customer in Japan. (future) ______ will appeal
16. Doing business in Japan (require) appreciation of rituals and formalities. (present) ______ requires
17. In East Asia the presentation of business cards (demand) special attention to ceremony. (future) ______ will demand
18. Western business people (try) to observe local customs. (past) ______ tried

NAME ____________________

Worksheet 1

LEVEL II

Select the correct verb.

1. The condition of the streets has (became, become) intolerable. become
2. Ice (froze, freezed) in the pipes last night. Froze
3. Before leaving on her vacation, Mrs. Stanton (hid, hide) her silver and other valuables. hid
4. Have you (chose, chosen) a location for the new equipment? Chosen
5. Three new homes were recently (builded, built) on Fairfax Avenue. built
6. After he had (drank, drunk) two glasses of milk, he asked for more. drunk
7. We must have (forgot, forgotten) the keys. Forgotten
8. Are you sure you have (gave, given) him the correct combination? given
9. André and the others had (went, gone) on the hike earlier. gone
10. The smaller dog was (bit, bitten) by a larger neighbourhood dog. bitten

Underline any errors in the following sentences. Write the correct form in the space provided. Write *C* if the sentence is correct as written. Do not add helping verbs.

Example: After we <u>run</u> out of food, we had to return to camp headquarters. ran

11. We had ate a small snack before we ordered dinner. Sung
12. The TV commercial was sang by an actress whose lips didn't match the soundtrack. ________
13. Mr. Gazdik was stricken just as he left the witness stand. ________
14. Hundreds of mushrooms sprung up after the rain. ________
15. Many people were shook by the minor earthquake yesterday. ________
16. Tracy had wore her stylish new boots only twice. ________
17. He had wrote a large portion of his report before leaving. ________
18. Their car was stole from its parking place overnight. ________
19. Because of a threatening storm, she should have took a cab. ________
20. If we had went to the movie premiere, we would have seen the stars. ________

NAME ______________________________

Worksheet 2

Lie–Lay

Use the chart below to help you select the correct form of *lie* or *lay* in these sentences.

Present	**Past**	**Past Participle**	**Present Participle**
lie (rest)	lay (rested)	lain (have, has, or had rested)	lying (resting)
lay (place)	laid (placed)	laid (have, has, or had placed)	laying (placing)

Example: This afternoon I must (rest) down before dinner. lie

1. I am sure that I (placed) the book on the desk yesterday. ______
2. Andrea angrily told her dog to (rest) down. ______
3. This month's bills have been (resting) in the drawer for weeks. ______
4. Bill has (placed) his books on the desk near the entrance. ______
5. The worker was (placing) concrete blocks for the foundation. ______
6. This evening I must (rest) down before we leave. ______
7. Yesterday I (rested) on my bed for an hour before dinner. ______
8. (Place) the papers in a stack over there. ______
9. That old candy has (rested) on the shelf for several weeks. ______
10. Let the fabric (rest) there for several hours until it dries. ______

Now try these sentences to test your skill in using the forms of *lie* and *lay.*

11. Will you be able to (lie, lay) down before dinner? ______
12. How long have these papers been (laying, lying) here? ______
13. Please tell your very friendly dog to (lay, lie) down. ______
14. Will the mason (lay, lie) bricks over the concrete patio? ______
15. The contract has (laid, lain) on his desk for over two months. ______
16. Yesterday I (laid, lay) down in the afternoon. ______
17. Mothers complain about clothes that are left (laying, lying) around. ______
18. Returned books (lie, lay) in a pile at the library until the staff can return them to the stacks. ______
19. I'm sure I (laid, layed, lied) my keys on this counter. ______
20. When you were (lying, laying) the new carpet, did you remove the baseboards? ______

NAME ______________________________

LEVEL III

Keep your textbook handy so that you can look up the verb forms required in the following sentences.

Example: By June 1 you (employ) here one full year. (future perfect, passive) *will have been employed*

1. McDonald's (open) many restaurants in foreign countries. (present perfect) ________
2. McDonald's (plan) to launch a franchise program. (present progressive) ________
3. We (call) for service at least three times before a technician arrived. (past perfect) ________
4. She (work) on that project for the past six months. (present perfect) ________
5. We (see) the very first screening of the documentary. (past progressive) ________
6. The mayor (sign) the proclamation at this afternoon's public ceremony. (future progressive) ________
7. The water main (broke) by the bulldozer working on street repairs. (past perfect, passive) ________
8. I (see) two good movies recently. (present perfect) ________
9. We (consider) the installation of a new email system. (present progressive) ________
10. The Queen's message (hear) all across Canada. (past progressive, passive) ________

The next sentences review Level II.

11. The alarm had (rang, rung) three times before we responded. ________
12. Yesterday we (drank, drunk) more water than usual because of the heat. ________
13. You must (chose, choose) new stationery for the office. ________
14. The car has been (drove, driven) many kilometres. ________
15. Steve claims he (saw, seen) the report yesterday. ________
16. If Chris had (went, gone) earlier, he would have told us. ________
17. Sue said she (seen, saw) an accident on her way to work. ________
18. The tour guide asked if everyone had (ate, eaten). ________
19. Dr. White had (wrote, written) four letters about his new car. ________
20. The price of our shares (raised, rose) again yesterday. ________
21. Witnesses had (swear, swore, sworn) to tell the truth during the trial. ________
22. If we had (began, begun) the report earlier, we could have met the deadline. ________

NAME ______________________

Worksheet 1

LEVEL I

For each of the following sentences, cross out any phrase that comes between a verb and its subject. Then select the correct verb and write it in the space provided.

Example: One ~~of the most interesting books on all the lists~~ (is, are) *Becoming a Millionaire at 21.* is

1. Many websites on the prohibited list (provide, provides) games or amusement that employees may not access. ______
2. The supervisor, together with two technicians, (is, are) working on the faulty circuit. ______
3. This company's supply of raw materials (come, comes) from South America. ______
4. A good many workers in addition to Martha (think, thinks) the work shifts should be rearranged. ______
5. Everyone except you and John (is, are) to repeat the test. ______
6. The table as well as two chairs (was, were) damaged. ______
7. A list with all the customers' names and addresses (is, are) being sent. ______
8. Other equipment, such as our terminals and printers, (need, needs) to be re-evaluated. ______
9. One of the online shopping sites (has, have) a section devoted to clearance items. ______
10. Several copies of the report (is, are) being prepared for distribution. ______
11. The furniture, as well as all the printers and computers, (is, are) for sale. ______
12. Effects of the disease (is, are) not known immediately. ______
13. Three salespeople, in addition to their district sales manager, (has, have) voiced the same suggestion. ______
14. Profits from his home business (is, are) surprising. ______
15. Every one of the potential businesses that you mention (sounds, sound) good. ______
16. A shipment of 8000 drill sets (was, were) sent to four warehouses. ______
17. Everyone except the evening employees (is, are) coming. ______
18. We learned that two subsidiaries of the corporation (is, are) successful. ______
19. Officials in several levels of government (has, have) to be consulted. ______
20. A letter together with several enclosures (was, were) mailed yesterday. ______

NAME ______________________________

Worksheet 2

For each of the following sentences, underline the subject. Then select the correct verb and write it in the space provided.

Example: Here (is, are) a copy of the findings for your files. is

Suggestion: If you know that a subject is singular, temporarily substitute *he, she,* or *it* to help you select the proper verb. If you know that a subject is plural, temporarily substitute *they* for the subject.

1. The flow of industrial goods (travel, travels) through different distribution channels than does the flow of consumer goods. ______

2. Here (is, are) the newspaper and magazines you ordered. ______

3. Coleman, Harris & Juarez, Inc., one of the leading management consultant firms, (is, are) able to accept our business. ______

4. The books on the open shelves of our company's library (is, are) available to all employees. ______

5. There (appear, appears) to be many significant points omitted from the report. ______

6. The various stages in the life cycle of a product (is, are) instrumental in determining profits for that product. ______

7. No one except the Cunninghams (was, were) able to volunteer. ______

8. A member of the organization of painters and plasterers (is, are) unhappy about the recent settlement. ______

9. The size and design of its container (is, are) influential in the appeal of a product. ______

10. Just one governmental unit from the local, provincial, or national levels (is, are) all we need to initiate the project. ______

11. American Airlines (has, have) been able to increase service while cutting costs. ______

12. Only two seasons of the year (provide, provides) weather that is suitable for gliding. ______

13. (Has, Have) the Wongs' moving van arrived yet? ______

14. At present the condition of the company's finances (is, are) extremely strong as a result of the recent bond sale. ______

15. Incoming mail from three flights (is, are) now being sorted. ______

16. The salary of Marie Ouellette, along with the earnings of several other employees, (has, have) been increased. ______

17. One of the best designs (appear, appears) to have been submitted by your student. ______

18. Aggressiveness and delinquency in boys (is, are) linked to high levels of lead in their bones, according to a recent study. ______

NAME ________________________________

LEVEL II

For each of the following sentences, underline the subject. Then select the correct word and write it in the space provided.

1. Most of the salary compensation to which he referred (is, are) beyond basic pay schedules. ________
2. The Committee on Youth Activities (has, have) enlisted the aid of several well-known athletes. ________
3. Each of the young men and women (deserve, deserves) an opportunity to participate in local athletics. ________
4. Either your company or one of your two competitors (is, are) going to win the government contract. ________
5. All the work for our Special Products Division (is, are) yet to be assigned. ________
6. Either of the two small businesses (is, are) able to secure a loan. ________
7. City council members (was, were) sharply divided along partisan lines. ________
8. Neither the packing list nor the two invoices (mention, mentions) the missing ottoman. ________
9. Every one of your suggestions (merit, merits) consideration. ________
10. Our survey shows that (everyone, every one) of the owner-managed businesses was turning a profit. ________
11. Either Steven or you (is, are) expected to return the call. ________
12. Each of the machines (has, have) capabilities that are suitable for our needs. ________
13. Mrs. Roberts said that most of the credit for our increased sales (belong, belongs) to you. ________
14. First on the program (is, are) the group of Indo-European folk dancers. ________
15. Some of the enthusiasm (is, are) due to the coming holiday. ________
16. After 10 p.m. the staff (has, have) to use the front entrance only. ________
17. (Was, Were) any of the supervisors absent after the holiday? ________
18. Many a young clerk and assistant (has, have) been helped by our in-service training programs. ________
19. We were informed that neither management nor the employees (has, have) special privileges. ________
20. Most of the work that was delivered to us four days ago (is, are) completed. ________

NAME ______________________

LEVEL III

Select the correct word for each sentence.

1. Reed says that 25 metres of plastic pipe (has, have) been ordered. ______________
2. The number of women in the labour force (is, are) steadily increasing. ______________
3. Phillip said that he is one of those individuals who (enjoy, enjoys) a real challenge. ______________
4. Over two-thirds of the stock issue (was, were) sold immediately after it was released. ______________
5. Gerald is the only one of the four applicants who (was, were) prepared to complete the application form during the interview. ______________
6. That most offices are closed on weekends (is, are) a factor that totally escaped Mr. Brotherton. ______________
7. The majority of the employees (favour, favours) the reorganization plan. ______________
8. Telephones (is, are) one item that we must install immediately. ______________
9. At least four-fifths of the women in the audience (is, are) willing to participate in the show. ______________
10. How could it be I who (am, is) responsible, when I had no knowledge of the agreement until yesterday? ______________
11. Let it be recorded that on the second vote the number of members in favour of the proposal (is, are) less than on the first vote. ______________
12. Only half of the box of disks (is, are) left in the supply cabinet. ______________
13. Are you one of those people who (like, likes) to sleep late? ______________
14. I'm sure that it is you who (is, are) next on the list. ______________
15. It looks as if 50 centimetres of extra cord (is, are) what we need. ______________
16. Our office manager reports that a number of printers (need, needs) repair. ______________
17. At least one-third of the desserts purchased for the party (was, were) uneaten. ______________
18. Hiking in Europe and sailing to Scandinavia (is, are) what I plan for my future vacations. ______________
19. Rajina Paramanathan is one of our email users who (complain, complains) about the system. ______________
20. Whoever submitted an application earliest (has, have) the right to be interviewed first. ______________

NAME ______________________________

LEVEL I

A verb form ending in *ing* and used as a noun is a gerund.

> *Passing* the examination is important. (Gerund used as a subject.)

A noun or pronoun modifying a gerund should be possessive.

> *Your* passing the examination is important.

Don't confuse verbals acting as nouns with those acting as adjectives.

> The man *passing* the test received his licence. (*Passing* functions as an adjective describing *man*.)

> The man's *passing* the test is important. (Verbal noun *passing* functions as the subject of the verb *is*.)

In the following sentences, underline any gerunds and write their modifiers in the space provided. If a sentence contains no gerund, write *None*.

Example: It is your smoking that disturbs the others. ______your______

1. This job offer is contingent on your passing our physical examination. ______________
2. Our office certainly did not approve of his investing in high-risk securities. ______________
3. It was Mr. Cortina's gambling that caused him to lose his job. ______________
4. The increase in sales is directly related to our placing the staff on commission. ______________

Some of the remaining sentences contain gerunds. If any error appears in the modifier, underline the error and write the correct form in the space provided. If the sentence is correct, write *C*.

Example: Mrs. Feng was instrumental in us acquiring the Collins account. ______our______

5. His recent award is directly related to Mr. Frank receiving a promotion. ______________
6. The individual receiving the award could not be present to accept it. ______________
7. Do you think you criticizing the manager had anything to do with your transfer? ______________
8. We deeply appreciate you calling us to give us this news. ______________
9. Is it Mr. Davidson writing that makes the message illegible? ______________
10. It appears that us faxing the company is the only logical action to take at this time. ______________
11. An employee taking a message must write clearly. ______________
12. Mrs. Fackler said that me working overtime was unnecessary this weekend. ______________
13. The employees working overtime this week will receive their overtime pay in next month's cheques. ______________

NAME ______________________

LEVEL II

A verbal form used as an adjective (to describe or modify nouns and pronouns) is a participle. When a participle, either as a separate word or as part of a phrase, introduces an independent clause, the participle or its phrase should be followed by a comma. When a phrase containing a participle interrupts the flow of a sentence with non-essential information, it should be set off with commas. The following sentences are punctuated correctly. Underline the participles and participial phrases.

1. While preparing the report, Isabelle verified all calculations.
2. Surrounded, the enemy troops raised a white flag.
3. Mr. Wilson, seeing his opportunity, brought up the subject of employee fringe benefits.
4. Our new records management system, installed just two months ago, is saving us money.
5. Miss Strawn, rereading the article several times, could not believe her eyes.
6. Opening a new account, Mr. and Mrs. Sams both filled out signature cards.
7. Irritated, the manager raised his voice.
8. A person opening a new account is required to have a valid signature card on file.

For each of the following sentences, add any commas necessary to punctuate verbal forms or phrases. In the space provided, write the comma(s) and preceding words. If a sentence is correct, write *C*.

Example: Comptroller Duffy, restricted by federal guidelines, revised many budget procedures. Duffy, guidelines,

9. After choosing a model, we placed our equipment order. ______
10. Mr. Dallas, consulting his local stockbroker opened an account. ______
11. Reading a stock market ticker tape requires some training. C
12. Displaying security transactions large tickertape screens may be found in most brokerage houses. ______
13. An executive representing a local brokerage firm called me. ______
14. Terry Sanderson representing a local brokerage firm called me. ______
15. Acting on her own behalf Miss Delgado placed an order for 100 shares of stock. ______
16. Growing in popularity the Global Positioning System (GPS) is a satellite-based navigation system. ______
17. Using GPS is becoming important to drivers, boaters, and even hikers. ______
18. Circling the earth twice a day GPS satellites transmit precise information. ______

NAME ____________________

LEVEL III

From the pairs of sentences that follow, select the sentence that is more logically stated. Write its letter in the space provided.

1. (a) Hurriedly proofreading the report, three errors were found by Minako. ____________
(b) Hurriedly proofreading the report, Minako found three errors.

2. (a) To get to the meeting quickly, a shortcut was taken by Mike. ____________
(b) To get to the meeting quickly, Mike took a shortcut.

3. (a) In investing money in the stock market, one must expect risks. ____________
(b) In investing money in the stock market, risks must be expected.

4. (a) While looking for Ann's number, the telephone rang and I heard Ann's voice. ____________
(b) While looking for Ann's number, I answered the phone and heard Ann's voice.

5. (a) After filling out an application, the personnel manager gave me an interview. ____________
(b) After filling out an application, I was given an interview by the personnel manager.

6. (a) Driving erratically down the street, the driver was stopped by the officer. ____________
(b) Driving erratically down the street, the officer stopped the driver.

7. (a) To receive a certificate, 30 hours of training must be completed. ____________
(b) To receive a certificate, a student must complete 30 hours of training.

Check your answers. Using the better versions of the above sentence pairs as models, rewrite the following sentences to make them logical. Add words as necessary, but retain the verbal expressions as sentence openers.

8. Completing the examination in only 20 minutes, a perfect score was earned by Maria. ____________

____

____

9. To locate the members' names and addresses, a current directory was used. ____________

____

____

10. Driving through the desert, the highway seemed endless. ____________

____

11. To stay in touch with customers, telephone contacts were made by sales representatives. ____________

____

____

12. Addressing an audience for the first time, my knees shook and my voice wavered. ____________

____

NAME ______________________

LEVEL I

Write the correct comparative or superlative form of the adjective shown in parentheses.

Example: Carmen is (neat) than her sister. neater

1. We hope that the new procedures prove to be (effective) than previous procedures. ______
2. Of all the suggestions made, Mr. Bradley's suggestion is the (bad). ______
3. Mrs. Schrillo's daughter is certainly (friendly) than she is. ______
4. Of the three individuals who volunteered, Ted is the one about whom I am (less) certain. ______
5. I don't believe I've ever seen a (beautiful) sunset than this one. ______
6. We make many printers, but the Model SX6 is the (fast). ______
7. No restaurant makes (good) hamburgers than Tommy's. ______
8. Located next to the airport, Malton is probably the (noisy) area in the city. ______
9. Living in the suburbs usually provides (quiet) surroundings than in the city. ______
10. Of all the letters we have received, this one seems the (sincere). ______
11. For this job we need the (skilled) employee in the department. ______
12. I'm afraid Andrea has the (less) chance of being selected for the position. ______
13. No one at work is (slow) than Bob. ______
14. DataSource is (likely) to be awarded the contract than CompuPro. ______
15. This is probably the (unusual) request I've ever received. ______
16. Pierre has had (few) citations than any other driver. ______
17. The office is certainly looking (good) today than yesterday. ______
18. Everyone watching the video thought that Yong looked (credible) than any other actor. ______
19. It was the (bad) accident I've ever seen. ______
20. Sharon's report had the (few) errors of all those submitted. ______

NAME ______________________________

LEVEL II

If the underlined word or words in the sentences below are correctly expressed, write *C*. If they are incorrect, write a corrected form in the space provided.

Example: Because less people made contributions, we failed to reach our goal. fewer

1. He played his Internet music so loud that we couldn't work. ________
2. We have decided to increase our point-of-purchase advertising. ________
3. How much further will we proceed in our study of business ethics? ________
4. Less opportunities exist in that field; therefore, I'm transferring to computer science. ________
5. The machine is running quieter since we installed a hood. ________
6. Gerald and I felt badly about Ken's accident. ________
7. The general manager should not become involved in this conflict-of-interest issue. ________
8. Ms. Edelstein was dressed neatly for the interview. ________
9. At present we're searching for a source of inexpensive, accessible raw materials. ________
10. My organization has selected the later of the two proposals you submitted. ________
11. Kurt said he was sure he did good on his examination. ________
12. Most candidates completed the examinations satisfactory. ________
13. We are conducting the campaign from house-to-house. ________
14. Mrs. Wharton appeared to be looking quite well despite her recent illness. ________
15. You can sure depend on my help whenever you need it. ________
16. The children were playing quiet when the guests arrived. ________
17. We employees are real concerned about the new parking fee. ________
18. You are a preferred charge-account customer at our store. ________
19. We expect a signed contract in the not-too-distant future. ________
20. Unfortunately, we've had less applications this year than ever before. ________

NAME ______________________________

LEVEL III

In the following sentences, select the correct word(s).

1. Only the (a) two last, (b) last two speakers made relevant comments. ______
2. No one could be more (a) perfect, (b) nearly perfect for the job. ______
3. Don is more stubborn than (a) anyone else, (b) anyone I know. ______
4. He is the most (a) nearly stubborn, (b) stubborn of all my friends. ______
5. (a) Mrs. Karim reports that she has only one volunteer.
   (b) Mrs. Karim only reports that she has one volunteer. ______
6. Applications will be given to the (a) first five, (b) five first job candidates. ______
7. Los Angeles is larger than (a) any other city, (b) any city in Calfornia. ______
8. I recommend this reference manual because it is (a) more nearly complete, (b) more complete than other reference manuals. ______

For each of the following sentences, underline any errors in the use of adjectives and adverbs. Then write the correct form. Mark *C* if the sentence is correct as written.

9. He can be counted on to paint the room as neat as a professional would do the job. ______
10. The uniform you are required to wear certainly fits you good. ______
11. Because we have less work to do this week, we should finish soon. ______
12. The recently-enacted law has received great support. ______
13. Apparently we have picked the worse time of the year to list an office for rent. ______
14. Although it is a honorary position, the chairmanship is important. ______
15. We hadn't hardly reached shelter when it began to rain. ______
16. The Andersons made a round the world tour last year. ______
17. Because of their many kindnesses to us, I feel badly that we cannot reciprocate in some way. ______
18. If less people were involved, the new procedures could have been implemented earlier. ______
19. He only said that he would work hard to complete the contract. ______
20. Festival promoters rented a 840 acre farm in Ulster County. ______

NAME ______________________

LEVEL I

Underline any errors in the following sentences. Then write the correct form. If the sentence is correct as written, write *C*.

1. You should of seen the looks on their faces! ____________

2. No one except Mr. Levine and he had access to the company records. ____________

3. I read the book and plan to attend the lecture too. ____________

4. Just between you and I, this engine has never run more smoothly. ____________

5. We borrowed some of the magazines off of Mrs. Kelsey. ____________

6. If you will address your inquiry too our Customer Relations Department, you will surely receive a response. ____________

7. The director of human resources, along with the office manager and she, is planning to improve hiring procedures. ____________

8. You could of done something about the error if you had known earlier. ____________

9. Because we have to many machines, we are planning a sale. ____________

10. All salespeople except Ms. Berk and he were reassigned. ____________

11. Did you obtain your copy of the proposal off him? ____________

12. Please get your passes from either Mrs. Bowman or he. ____________

13. See if you can get some change for the machine off of her. ____________

14. Both the project coordinator and he should have verified the totals before submitting the bid. ____________

15. The commission for the sale has to be divided between Ms. Carpenter and he. ____________

16. Because to few spaces are available, additional parking must be found on nearby streets. ____________

17. If you and he could of come yesterday, we might have been able to help you. ____________

18. So that we may better evaluate your application, please supply references too. ____________

19. You could of had complimentary tickets if you had called her. ____________

20. The marketing manager assigned too many customers to Anwar and I. ____________

NAME ______________________________

LEVEL II

For each of the following sentences, underline any errors in the use of prepositions. Then write a correct form. Mark *C* if the sentence is correct as written.

1. We think that beside salary the major issue is working conditions. ____________
2. Your support and participation in this new web program will be greatly appreciated. ____________
3. The warranty period was over with two months ago. ____________
4. Please come into see me when you are ready for employment. ____________
5. Just inside of the office entrance is the receptionist. ____________
6. The senior Mr. Wiggins left $3 million to be divided between three heirs. ____________
7. Will you be able to deliver the goods like you said you would? ____________
8. For most of us, very few opportunities like this ever arise. ____________
9. Exactly what type shingles did you have in mind? ____________
10. Some of the trucks were moved in to the garage at dusk. ____________
11. When can we accept delivery of the electrical components ordered from Hellman Ltd.? ____________
12. Because of your concern and involvement in our community action campaign, we have received thousands of dollars in contributions. ____________
13. I know the time and date of our next committee meeting, but I do not know where it will be held at. ____________
14. If you were willing to accept further responsibility, I would assign you the committee chairmanship. ____________
15. Joanna could not help from laughing when she saw her email. ____________
16. Please hurry up so that we may submit our proposal quickly. ____________
17. What style furniture is most functional for the waiting room? ____________
18. After going into meet the supervisor, Carla was hired. ____________
19. All parking lots opposite to the corporate headquarters will be cleaned. ____________
20. Immediately after Kathy graduated high school, she started college. ____________

NAME ______________________________

LEVEL III

In the following sentences, select the correct word.

1. Mrs. Shelton found that her voice was rising as she became angrier and angrier (a) at, (b) with the caller. ____________

2. We know of no one who is more expert (a) in, (b) with cellphone technology than Dr. France. ____________

3. If you concur (a) with, (b) in this action, please notify your representative. ____________

4. After corresponding (a) to, (b) with their home office, I was able to clear up the error in my account. ____________

5. The houses in that subdivision are identical (a) to, (b) with each other. ____________

6. If you (a) plan to attend, (b) plan on attending the summer session, you'd better register immediately. ____________

7. A few of the provisions are retroactive (a) for, (b) to January 1. ____________

8. Jeff talked (a) to, (b) with his boss about the company's future plans. ____________

9. Standing (a) on, (b) in line is not my favorite activity. ____________

10. She made every effort to reason (a) to, (b) with the unhappy customer. ____________

11. Apparently the letters on the screen do not sufficiently contrast (a) with, (b) to the background. ____________

12. The courses, facilities, and students in this school are certainly different (a) from, (b) than those at other schools. ____________

13. Do you dare to disagree (a) to, (b) with him? ____________

14. Being the leader of a business team is similar (a) with, (b) to coaching a sports team. ____________

15. I am angry (a) at, (b) with the proposal that we share offices. ____________

16. Mr. Reese insisted that he was completely independent (a) of, (b) from his campaign contributors. ____________

17. He went on working oblivious (a) from, (b) to the surrounding chaos. ____________

18. The figures on the balance sheet could not be reconciled (a) to, (b) with the actual account totals. ____________

19. A number of individuals agreed (a) to, (b) with the plan. ____________

20. If you are desirous (a) about, (b) of taking a June vacation, you had better speak with the office manager soon. ____________

14 CONJUNCTIONS TO JOIN EQUALS Self-Help Exercises

NAME ______________________________

LEVEL I

Name four coordinating conjunctions:

1. ______________________ **2.** ______________________

3. ______________________ **4.** ______________________

When coordinating conjunctions connect independent clauses (groups of words that could stand alone as sentences), the conjunctions are preceded by commas. The two independent clauses form a compound sentence.

COMPOUND SENTENCE: We hope to increase sales in the East, *but* we need additional sales personnel.

Use a comma only if the sentence is compound. When the words preceding or following the coordinating conjunction do not form an independent clause, no comma is used.

SIMPLE SENTENCE: The bank will include the cheque with your monthly statement *or* will send the cheque to you immediately.

In the following sentences, selected coordinating conjunctions are italicized. Mark (a) or (b) for each sentence.

a = No punctuation needed b = Insert a comma before the italicized conjunction.

5. Mr. Green is a specialist in information systems *and* he will be responsible for advising and assisting all our divisions. ______

6. Mr. Green is a specialist in information systems *and* will be responsible for advising and assisting all our divisions. ______

7. This is a sales meeting *but* other topics of interest may also be discussed. ______

8. I have studied the plan you are developing *and* feel that it has real merit. ______

9. We seek the reaction of the council *and* of others who have studied the plan. ______

10. Our executive vice-president will make the presentation in Toronto *or* he will unveil the plan in London. ______

11. I think that the plan will be effective *and* that it will save us time and money. ______

12. This new benefit plan will cost the employee more money *but* the expanded benefits will more than offset the increased costs. ______

13. We are taking over a portion of the fourteenth floor *but* we will not be moving into that area until March. ______

14. Send me your latest price list for all digital camera equipment *and* place my name on your mailing list for future mailings. ______

15. Our international telephone costs are very high *and* may become even more exorbitant if we don't use email more extensively. ______

NAME ____________________

LEVEL II

1. Name six conjunctive adverbs:

(a) ____________ (c) ____________ (e) ____________

(b) ____________ (d) ____________ (f) ____________

2. When a conjunctive adverb joins independent clauses, what punctuation mark precedes the conjunctive adverb? ____________

3. Many words that serve as conjunctive adverbs can also function as parenthetical adverbs. When used parenthetically, adverbs are set off by what punctuation marks? ____________

In the following sentences, words acting as conjunctive or parenthetical adverbs are underlined. Add necessary commas and semicolons to punctuate the sentences.

4. The company is planning <u>nevertheless</u> to proceed with its expansion.
5. The price of the tour is contingent upon double occupancy <u>that is</u> two people must share accommodations.
6. This organization <u>on the other hand</u> is quite small in the industry.
7. Our bank is extending its service until 6 p.m. <u>hence</u> we are better able to accommodate your banking needs.
8. Stationery and supplies are stored on open shelves <u>however</u> printed forms are kept in filing cabinets.
9. Our group will travel first to New York <u>then</u> we will proceed to Paris.
10. The manager has <u>consequently</u> requested a leave of absence.
11. We have few summer jobs available in our organization <u>consequently</u> we have to tell young people to look elsewhere.
12. When they graduate <u>on the other hand</u> these same young people will find a different employment picture with our organization.
13. We are <u>nevertheless</u> sending you samples of our principal products.
14. Profits were poor last year <u>on the other hand</u> profits this year are much better.
15. Today's job market is very competitive <u>however</u> recent graduates can find jobs if they are well trained and persistent.
16. Job candidates <u>consequently</u> often prepare different résumés for each opening.
17. Most recruiters prefer chronological résumés <u>consequently</u> we advise our graduates to follow the traditional résumé format.
18. Personnel professionals spend little time reading a cover letter <u>therefore</u> it is wise to keep your letter short.
19. A résumé emphasizes what you have done <u>however</u> a cover letter stresses what you can do for an employer.
20. During an employment interview, recruiters try to uncover negative information <u>however</u> job candidates try to minimize faults and weaknesses.

NAME ______________________

LEVEL III

The correlative conjunctions *both … and, either … or, neither … nor,* and *not only … but (also)* should be used in parallel constructions. That is, the words these conjunctions join should be similarly patterned. Compare the words that *follow* the conjunctions. For example, if a verb follows *either*, a verb should follow *or*. If the active voice is used with *neither*, then the active voice should be used with *nor*. Study the following examples.

Parallel: Suk Ying is *either* typing the Collins report *or* proofreading it. (Both conjunctions are followed by verbs.)

Not Parallel: *Either* Suk Ying is typing the Collins report *or* proofreading it. (A subject and verb follow *either,* but only a verb follows *or.*)

Parallel: I have *neither* pumped the gas *nor* checked the oil.

Not Parallel: *Neither* have I pumped the gas, *nor* was the oil checked. (An active-voice construction follows *neither* while a passive-voice construction follows *nor.*)

In the following pairs, write the letters of the sentences that are constructed in parallel form.

1. (a) We have neither the energy to pursue this litigation, nor do we have the finances. ____________
(b) To pursue this litigation, we have neither the energy nor the finances.

2. (a) You may either write a research report, or a book report can be made. ____________
(b) You may either write a research report or make a book report.

3. (a) He is not only clever but also witty. ____________
(b) Not only is he clever, but he is also witty.

4. (a) The website contains both information, and it has an application form. ____________
(b) The website contains both information and an application form.

Revise the following sentences so that the correlative conjunctions are used in efficient parallel constructions.

5. You can either fax him your response, or you can send him an email message. ____________

6. Our goals are both to educate motorists, and also lives may be saved. ____________

7. Neither does Tony have a job offer, nor does he even have an interview lined up. ____________

8. We knew either that we had to raise more money or begin selling stock. ____________

NAME ______________________________

LEVEL I

Use *T* or *F* to indicate whether the following statements are true or false.

1. A phrase is a group of related words without both a subject and a verb. ________

2. A clause is a group of related words containing both a subject and a verb. ________

3. An independent clause has a subject and a verb and makes sense by itself. ________

4. A dependent clause contains a subject and a verb but depends for its meaning on another clause. ________

5. Words such as *after, if,* and *when* are used preceding independent clauses. ________

Indicate whether the following groups of words are phrases (*P*), independent clauses (*I*), or dependent clauses (*D*). If you indicate that a group of words is an independent clause, capitalize the first word (use ≡) and place a period at the end of the group of words.

Example: he stood in a very long line⊙ ____I____

6. in the past year ________

7. although she came to every meeting ________

8. she came to every meeting ________

9. during the period from April to October ________

10. if sales continue to climb as they have for the past four months ________

11. the director asked for additional personnel ________

12. as soon as we can increase our production ________

13. we can increase our production ________

14. because your organization has financial strength ________

15. in the future ________

16. satellite telephone service is now available ________

17. in order that we may improve service to our customers ________

18. we will compute your average monthly gas consumption ________

19. when he returns to the office ________

20. fill out and mail the enclosed card ________

21. by next fall ________

22. we are reworking our original plans ________

NAME ______________________

23. since a good résumé has five essential parts

24. because your old résumé listed your work history and then went on to describe previous jobs in grim and boring detail disregarding their current relevance

25. A good résumé is a breath of fresh air to an employer

LEVEL II

Add necessary commas to the following sentences. If a sentence requires no punctuation, write *C* next to it.

1. If you follow my suggestions you will help to improve the efficiency of our department.
2. You will if you follow my suggestions help to improve the efficiency of our department.
3. You will help to improve the efficiency of our department if you follow my suggestions.
4. When completed the renovation should make the seventh floor much more attractive.
5. Let's discuss the problem when Ms. Gardner returns.
6. The motorist who parked his car in the restricted area is in danger of being ticketed.
7. Our latest company safety booklet which was submitted over six weeks ago is finally ready for distribution.
8. As you may know we have paid dividends regularly for over seventy years.
9. These payments provided there is no interruption in profits should continue for many years to come.
10. If necessary you may charge this purchase to your credit card.
11. Any employee who wishes to participate may contact our Human Resources Department.
12. James Gilroy who volunteered to head the program will be organizing our campaign.
13. I assure you that you will hear from Ms. Habib as soon as she returns.
14. Before you send in the order may I see the catalogue?
15. May I see the catalogue before you send in the order?
16. The additional premium you were charged which amounted to $175.12 was issued because of your recent accident.
17. As expected the proposal should help us more clearly define long-term objectives.
18. We will submit the proposal within four working days if that schedule meets with your approval.
19. Before we sign any contract we must make site visits and verify all information.
20. In this proposal I have outlined a seven-step purchasing program that meets all the objectives you indicated were important to you.

NAME ______________________________

LEVEL III

Use the information provided within parentheses to construct dependent clauses for the following sentences. Add subordinators such as *who, which, although,* and *since.*

Example: Dr. Cushman recently moved his practice to Victoria. (Dr. Cushman specializes in pediatrics.)
Dr. Cushman, who specializes in pediatrics, recently moved his practice to Victoria.

1. The original agreement was drawn between Mr. Hightower and Columbia Communications. (The agreement was never properly signed.) ______________________________

2. Atlantic Insurance Company services not only individuals but also communities. (Atlantic Insurance Company is a company of people rather than statistics.) ______________________________

3. Thank you for informing us that your credit card is missing. (This credit has an expiration date of April 30.)

Combine the following clauses into single sentences.

4. (Your account is four months past due.) We will be forced to take legal action. We must hear from you within seven days. ______________________________

5. Sally Horton won an award as this month's outstanding employee. (She works in our Quality Control Department.) Ms. Horton is secretary to the manager in that department. ______________________________

6. Pam Eichorn recently received her business diploma. Now she is looking for a job near Windsor. (Windsor is Pam's hometown.) ______________________________

NAME ______________________________

7. We are sending you four poster advertisements. They will appear in magazines in April. (April marks the beginning of a national campaign featuring our sports clothes.) ______________________________

____

____

8. Mr. Girard plans to retire at the end of this year. (Mr. Girard has worked at Rocketwell for thirty-seven years.) After he retires, Mr. Girard plans to devote more time to his orchid collection. ______________________________

____

____

NAME ______________________________

LEVEL I

Add necessary commas to the following sentences. For each sentence indicate the number of commas that you have added. If a sentence is correct, write *C*.

1. Your present insurance Mr. Isaq does not cover the care and custody of property belonging to others. ______
2. By the way have you updated the fire insurance coverage on your home and its contents? ______
3. When the matter is resolved however we hope to continue our mutually profitable business relationship. ______
4. Our team leader is from Calgary Alberta but is now working in Edmonton. ______
5. The CEO's son Mark will be joining our team for the summer. ______
6. The alternative plan on the other hand will not improve employee profit-sharing benefits. ______
7. Send the shipment to MicroTech Systems 750 Grant Road Burnaby British Columbia V5E 4B2 as soon as possible. ______
8. It appears sir that an error has been made in your billing. ______
9. You have until Friday April 30 to make complete payment on your past-due account. ______
10. Mr. Franklin T. Molloy who is an advertising executive has been elected chairman of the council. ______
11. Anyone who is interested in applying for the job should see Mrs. Isfahani. ______
12. I hope that your brother Gary will be able to join us. ______
13. You will in addition receive a free brochure outlining our wireless devices. ______
14. Our latest wireless technology provides support for high-traffic areas such as airports shopping centres and college campuses. ______
15. All things considered the company will be obligated to pay only those expenses directly related to the installation. ______
16. Only Mr. Hudson who is a specialist in information systems is qualified to write that report. ______
17. You can avoid patent trademark and copyright problems by working with a lawyer. ______
18. We are convinced incidentally that our lawyer's fees are most reasonable. ______
19. Mr. Van Alstyne developed the policy Ms. Thorson worked on the budget and Mr. Seibert handled compensation issues. ______
20. Sasha will travel to Italy Greece and Croatia next summer. ______

NAME ______________________________

LEVEL II

Add necessary commas to the following sentences. For each sentence indicate the number of commas that you have added. If a sentence is correct, write *C*.

1. We must find a practical permanent solution to our Internet access problems. ________

2. For a period of about six months it will be necessary to reduce all expenditures. ________

3. Melissa Meyer speaking on behalf of all classified employees gave a welcoming address. ________

4. We held a marketing meeting last week and we included representatives from all divisions. ________

5. I am looking forward to getting together with you when you are again in Halifax. ________

6. We do appreciate as I have told you often your continuing efforts to increase our sales. ________

7. Consumer patterns for the past five years are being studied carefully by our marketing experts. ________

8. For some time we have been studying the growth in the number of working women and minorities. ________

9. After you have examined my calculations please send the report to Bill Thompson. ________

10. Please send the report to Bill Thompson after you have examined my calculations. ________

11. Would you please after examining my calculations send the report to Bill Thompson. ________

12. Our personnel director is looking for intelligent articulate young people who desire an opportunity to grow with a start-up company. ________

13. Call me as soon as you return or send me an email message within the next week. ________

14. Beginning on the 15th of June Dell is slashing prices on laptop computers. ________

15. I mentioned to him at that time that we could not locate the monitor. ________

16. As soon as I can check the inventory we will place an order. ________

17. On October 25 the president and I visited Sandra Goodell who is president of Sandra Goodell Public Relations. ________

18. You may at your convenience submit a report describing when where and how we should proceed. ________

19. To begin the purchase process we will need your request by Thursday June 1 at the latest. ________

20. Any student who has not signed up for a team by this time must see the instructor. ________

NAME ______________________

LEVEL III

Add necessary commas to the following sentences. For each sentence indicate the number of commas that you have added. If a sentence is correct, write *C*.

1. Michael Ferrari Ph.D. has written another book on consumer buying. ______
2. In 2004 our company expanded its marketing to include the United Kingdom. ______
3. By 2008 12 of our competitors were also selling in Great Britain. ______
4. In 2004 our staff numbered 87; in 2008 103. ______
5. It was a large manila envelope not a white folder in which the contract was placed. ______
6. Long before our president conducted his own research into marketing trends among youthful consumers. (Tricky!) ______
7. "We prefer not to include your name" said the auditor "when we publish the list of inactive accounts." ______
8. You may sign your name at the bottom of this sheet and return it to us as acknowledgment of this letter. ______
9. The provisions of your Policy No. 85000611 should be reviewed every five years. ______
10. Irving Feinstein M.D. will be the speaker at our next meeting. ______
11. Dr. Feinstein received both an M.D. and a Ph.D. from the University of Toronto. ______
12. Ever since we have been very careful to count the number of boxes in each shipment. ______
13. In her lecture Dr. Hawkins said "One species of catfish reproduces by hatching eggs in its mouth and growing them to about three inches before releasing them." ______
14. Did you say it was Mr. Chong not Mrs. Lambert who made the sale? ______
15. Ten computers were sold in January; nine in February. ______
16. Our figures show that 17365000 separate rental units were occupied in September. ______
17. "The function of a supervisor" remarked Sid Stern "is to analyze results not to try to control how the job is done." ______
18. By the way it was the president not the vice-president who ordered the cutback. ______
19. "A diamond" said the therapist "is a chunk of coal that made good under pressure." ______
20. Whoever signs signs at her own risk. ______

NAME ____________________

LEVEL I

Punctuate the following groups of words as single sentences. Add commas and semicolons. Do not add words or periods to create new sentences.

Example: Come in to see our new branch office; meet our friendly manager and customer service representatives.

1. Our principal function is to help management make profits however we can offer advice on staffing problems as well.
2. Delegates came from as far away as Charlottetown Prince Edward Island Mount Pearl Newfoundland and Fort McMurray Alberta.
3. Jerry looked up names Andrea addressed envelopes and Janelle stuffed envelopes.
4. Thank you for your order it will be filled immediately.
5. Employees often complain about lack of parking space on the other hand little interest was shown in a proposed carpooling program.
6. Computers are remarkable however they are only as accurate as the people who program them.
7. This sale is not open to the general public we are opening the store to preferred customers only.
8. Some of the employees being promoted are Jill Roberts secretary Legal Department Lea Lim clerk Human Resources and Mark Cameron dispatcher Transportation Department.
9. We will be happy to co-operate with you and your lawyers in settling the estate however several matters must be reviewed.
10. In the morning I am free at 10 a.m. in the afternoon I have already scheduled an appointment.
11. The book was recently selected for a national award thus its sales are soaring.
12. Look over our online catalogue make your selections and click to submit your order.
13. We hope that we will not have to sell the property but selling may be our only option.
14. The film that you requested is now being shown to law students in Ontario it will be shown during June in Manitoba and it will be used during July and August in the provinces of Alberta and British Columbia.
15. We do not sell airline seats we sell customer service.
16. Our convention committee is considering the Hyatt Regency Hotel Vancouver British Columbia the Hotel Halifax Halifax Nova Scotia and The Valhalla Inn Toronto Ontario.
17. As requested the committee will meet Thursday May 4 however it is unable to meet Friday May 5.
18. Market research involves the systematic gathering recording and analyzing of data about consumer and product issues.

NAME ____________________

LEVEL II

Add colons, semicolons, or commas to the following sentences. Do not add words or periods. Write *C* after the sentence if it is correct.

1. Three phases of our business operation must be scrutinized purchasing, production, and shipping.

2. The candidates being considered for supervisor are Ned Bingham, Sean Davis, and Anna Donato.

3. Senator Zoubek was quoted as saying "The economy can continue its recovery only if prices are controlled. In addition, inflation must remain below 7 per cent."

4. Following are four dates reserved for counselling. Sign up soon.

September 28	January 4
September 30	January 6

5. At its next meeting, the board of directors must make a critical decision should the chief executive officer be retained or replaced?

6. This year's seminar has been organized to give delegates an opportunity to exchange ideas, plans, techniques, and goals.

7. The three Cs of credit are the following character, capacity, and capital.

8. Our Boston Massachusetts tour package included visits to these interesting historical sites the House of Seven Gables, Bunker Hill, the Boston Tea Party Ship and Museum, and Paul Revere's home.

9. I recommend that you take at least three courses to develop your language arts skills Essentials of College English 31, Business Communication 32, and Report Writing 35.

10. The speaker said that "membership is voluntary" but that contributions would be greatly appreciated.

11. Several of the tax specialists on the panel were concerned with the same thought government spending continues to rise while taxes are being reduced.

12. For each individual the credit bureau keeps the following information on file credit history, payment history, outstanding debt, and types of credit in use.

13. Scholarships will be awarded to Jill Hofer Jeremy Stone and Carolena Garay.

14. Our favourite Alberta resort is noted for fly fishing, mountain biking, tennis, and hiking.

15. Our favourite Alberta resort is noted for the following fly fishing, mountain biking, tennis, and hiking.

NAME ______________________________

LEVEL III

Add colons, semicolons, dashes, or commas as needed. If a word following a colon should not be capitalized, use a proofreading mark (/) to indicate lower case. Show words to be capitalized with a capitalization mark (≡). Mark *C* if a sentence is correct as it stands.

1. There are three primary ways to make a credit check namely by email, by Canada Post, or by telephone.

2. Please order the following supplies Cartridges, paper, and staples.

3. Although we are expanding our services we continue to do business according to our original philosophy that is we want to provide you with flexible and professional investment services on a highly personal basis.

4. Word processing specialists are taught this rule Never turn the power off at a workstation unless a document has been stored.

5. Dr. Ruglio's plane departed at 2 15 and should arrive at 6 45.

6. We invited Damon, Kevin, Tony, and Tom but Tony was unable to come.

7. Three of our top executives namely Mr. Gabereau, Mr. Wright, and Mrs. Stranahan are being transferred to the Winnipeg office.

8. On our list of recommended reading is *Investment an Introduction to Analysis*.

9. The library, as you are already aware, needs space for additional books, particularly in the non-fiction field and even greater space will be required within the next five years.

10. Our airline is improving service in several vital areas for example baggage handling, food service, and weather forecasts.

11. Julie Schumacher was hired by a brokerage house and given the title of "registered representative" that is she is able to buy and sell securities.

12. Professor Wilson listed five types of advertising Product, institutional, national, local, and corrective.

13. We considered only one location for our fall convention namely Montreal.

14. Many important questions are yet to be asked concerning our program for instance how can we meet our competitor's low prices on the West Coast?

15. If possible call him as soon as you return to the office however I doubt that he is still at his desk.

NAME ____________________

LEVEL I

Add any necessary punctuation to the following sentences.

1. Will you please review the F A Q s (frequently asked questions) posted on our website
2. You did say the meeting is at 10 a m didn't you
3. Mrs Kephart is a C A working for Berman Ltd
4. Do you know whether Donald L Cullens, Jr. applied for the job
5. Help The door is jammed
6. Will you please Miss Juarez visit our website and register for your gift
7. What a day this has been
8. Although most candidates had B A degrees two applicants had M A degrees
9. Our C E O and C F O normally make all budget decisions
10. Cynthia asked if invitations had been sent to Miss Tan Mr Roe and Ms Rich
11. All calls made before 9 a m E S T are billed at a reduced rate
12. Alan Bennett M D and Gina Hawtin Ph D were our keynote speakers
13. Because Susanne typed 80 w p m she was hired as a word processing specialist for C I D A
14. We're expanding marketing efforts in China France and the U K
15. The C P U of this computer is made entirely of parts from the U S A
16. The sales representative did say that the price of the car was f o b Windsor didn't he
17. Would you please check Policy Nos 44657001 and 44657002 to see if each includes $50 000 comprehensive coverage
18. Did you say the order was received at 5 p m P S T
19. Wow How much was the lottery prize
20. After Mike completed his M A he was hired to develop scripts for movie D V Ds

LEVEL II

Write *T* (true) or *F* (false) after the following statements.

1. In typewritten or simple word processing–generated material, a dash is formed by typing two successive underscores. ____________
2. Parentheses are often used to enclose explanations, references, and directions. ____________

NAME ______________________________

3. Dashes must be avoided in business writing since they have no legitimate uses. ____________

4. Question marks and exclamation points may be used to punctuate parenthetical statements (enclosed within parentheses) within other sentences. ____________

5. If a comma falls at the same point where words enclosed by parentheses appear, the comma should follow the final parenthesis. ____________

Circle the letter of the correctly punctuated sentence.

6. (a) I am busy on all those dates—oh, perhaps October 18 is free.
   (b) I am busy on all those dates: oh, perhaps October 18 is free.
   (c) I am busy on all those dates, oh, perhaps October 18 is free.

7. (De-emphasize)
   (a) Directions for assembly, see page 15, are quite simple.
   (b) Directions for assembly—see page 15—are quite simple.
   (c) Directions for assembly (see page 15) are quite simple.

8. (a) Eat, sleep, and read: that's what I plan to do on my vacation.
   (b) Eat, sleep, and read—that's what I plan to do on my vacation.
   (c) Eat, sleep, and read, that's what I plan to do on my vacation.

9. (a) To file a complaint with the Better Business Bureau (BBB), call during regular business hours.
   (b) To file a complaint with the Better Business Bureau, (BBB) call during regular business hours.
   (c) To file a complaint with the Better Business Bureau (BBB) call during regular business hours.

10. (Normal emphasis)
   (a) Mrs. Hemphill (who is an excellent manager) may be promoted.
   (b) Mrs. Hemphill, who is an excellent manager, may be promoted.
   (c) Mrs. Hemphill—who is an excellent manager—may be promoted.

11. (a) "What is needed for learning is a humble mind." (Confucius)
   (b) "What is needed for learning is a humble mind.": Confucius
   (c) "What is needed for learning is a humble mind." —Confucius

12. (a) The due date is past (July 1;) however, your payment is welcome.
   (b) The due date is past; (July 1) however, your payment is welcome.
   (c) The due date is past (July 1); however, your payment is welcome.

13. (a) Only one person knows my password—Denise Powell, and I have confidence in her.
   (b) Only one person knows my password (Denise Powell), and I have confidence in her.
   (c) Only one person knows my password; Denise Powell, and I have confidence in her.

14. (Emphasize)
   (a) Our current mortgage rates: see page 10 of the enclosed booklet—are the lowest in years.
   (b) Our current mortgage rates (see page 10 of the enclosed booklet) are the lowest in years.
   (c) Our current mortgage rates—see page 10 of the enclosed booklet—are the lowest in years.

NAME ______________________________

LEVEL III

W... (true) or *F* (false) for each of the following statements.

1. When the exact words of a speaker are repeated, regular (double) quotation marks are used to enclose the words. ____________
2. To indicate a quotation within another quotation, single quotation marks (apostrophes on most keyboards) are used. ____________
3. When a word is defined, its definition should be underscored. ____________
4. The titles of books, magazines, newspapers, and other complete works published separately may be either underscored or italicized. ____________
5. The titles of book chapters and of magazine articles may be underscored or enclosed in quotation marks. ____________
6. Periods and commas are always placed inside closing quotation marks. ____________
7. Brackets are used when a writer inserts his or her own remarks inside a quotation. ____________
8. The Latin world *sic* may be used to call attention to an error in quoted material. ____________
9. Semicolons and colons are always placed outside closing quotation marks. ____________
10. Question marks and exclamation points may be placed inside or outside closing quotation marks. ____________

Write the letter of the correctly punctuated statement.

11. (a) "Jobs," said Mr. Steele, "will be plentiful this summer."
    (b) "Jobs, said Mr. Steele, will be plentiful this summer."
    (c) "Jobs", said Mr. Steele, "will be plentiful this summer." ____________
12. (a) The manager said, "This memo is clearly marked Confidential."
    (b) The manager said, "This memo is clearly marked 'Confidential'."
    (c) The manager said, "This memo is clearly marked 'Confidential.' " ____________
13. (a) A *chattel* is defined as a "piece of movable property."
    (b) A "chattel" is defined as a *piece of movable property*.
    (c) A "chattel" is defined as a "piece of movable property." ____________
14. (a) Do you know who it was who said, "Forewarned is forearmed."
    (b) Do you know who it was who said, "Forewarned is forearmed"?
    (c) Do you know who it was who said, "Forewarned is forearmed."? ____________
15. (a) "We warn all email users to avoid messages that are 'flaming,'" said the CEO.
    (b) "We warn all email users to avoid messages that are "flaming," said the CEO.
    (c) "We warn all email users to avoid messages that are 'flaming'", said the CEO. ____________

NAME ______________________________

COMPLETE PUNCTUATION REVIEW

Insert all necessary punctuation in the following sentences. Correct any incorrect punctuation. Do not break any sentences into two sentences.

1. Did you see the article entitled Soaring Salaries of C E O s that appeared in The New York Times
2. This years budget costs are much higher than last years, therefore I will approve overtime only on a case by case basis.
3. The board has three new members Dr. Carla Chang Professor Mark Rousso and Robert Price Esq
4. Needless to say all contract bids must be received before 5 pm E S T
5. We formerly depended on fixed-rate not variable rate mortgages.
6. The following representatives have been invited Christine Lenski DataCom Industries, Mark Grant LaserPro Inc., and Ivan Weiner Image Builders.
7. Last year we moved corporate headquarters to Vancouver British Columbia but maintained production facilities in Calgary Alberta.
8. (Quotation) Did Dr. Tran say We will have no class Friday.
9. Graduation ceremonies for B A candidates are at 11 a m, graduation ceremonies for M B A candidates are at 2 p m.
10. As we previously discussed the reorganization will take effect on Monday August 8.
11. We feel however that the cars electrical system should be fully warranted for five years.
12. Will you please send copies of our annual report to Anna Golan and D A Rusterholz?
13. Although he had prepared carefully Mitchell feared that his presentation would bomb.
14. In the event of inclement weather we will close the base and notify the following radio stations CFRB CHIN and CHUM.
15. (Emphasize) Three excellent employees Gregorio Morales, Dawna Capps, and DaVonne Williams will be honoured at a ceremony Friday June 5.
16. (Quotation) "Your attitude not your aptitude will determine your altitude, said Zig Ziglar.
17. By May 15 our goal is to sell 15 cars, by June 15 20 additional cars.
18. The full impact of the C R T C ruling is being studied you will receive information as it becomes available.
19. If the fax comes before 9 pm we can still meet our June 1 deadline.
20. Send the contract to Ms Courtney Phillips Administrative Assistant Globex Industries 7600 Normandale Boulevard Scarborough ON M1K 5G4 as soon as possible.
21. (De-emphasize) Please return the amended budget proposal see page 2 for a summary of the report to the presidents office by Friday March 4.
22. Prospective entrepreneurs were told to read a Success magazine article entitled A Venture Expert's Advice.

NAME ________________________________

23. Larry Zuckerman our former manager now has a similar position with I B M.

24. Employees are concerned primarily with three job issues namely wages, security, and working conditions.

25. As expected this years expenses have been heavy, consequently we may have to freeze hiring for the next six months.

26. Would you please send the parcel to Lori Lofchik 1021 Dearness Drive London Ontario N6E 1N7

NAME_______________________________

LEVEL I

Write the letter of the group of words that is correctly capitalized.

	(a)	(b)	
1.	(a) a case of german measles	(b) a case of German measles	______
2.	(a) in the field of marketing	(b) in the field of Marketing	______
3.	(a) the Richardson Building	(b) the Richardson building	______
4.	(a) for all Catholics and Protestants	(b) for all catholics and protestants	______
5.	(a) an order for china and crystal	(b) an order for China and crystal	______
6.	(a) both Master's and Doctor's degrees	(b) both master's and doctor's degrees	______
7.	(a) Welland Canal	(b) Welland canal	______
8.	(a) a class in conversational French	(b) a class in Conversational French	______
9.	(a) a memo from our Edmonton Office	(b) a memo from our Edmonton office	______
10.	(a) a salad with French dressing	(b) a salad with french dressing	______
11.	(a) the Russian revolution	(b) the Russian Revolution	______
12.	(a) traffic in the big apple	(b) traffic in the Big Apple	______
13.	(a) the King Edward room	(b) the King Edward Room	______
14.	(a) the Remembrance Day holiday	(b) the Remembrance day holiday	______
15.	(a) the waters of the bay of Fundy	(b) the waters of the Bay of Fundy	______

Use proofreading marks to capitalize (≡) or to show lower-case (/) letters in the following sentences.

16. Bob's Esso Station is located on Speedway Avenue in the next County.

17. Many employees of the Meredith Corporation plan to participate in the Company's profit-sharing plan.

18. Over 3600 supporters attended a gala benefit for the AIDS committee of Toronto at the metro toronto convention centre.

19. During the Winter I will enrol in management, business english, and accounting.

20. The American Association Of Nurses will open its annual meeting in the Pacific ballroom of the Regency hotel in San Francisco.

21. Our persian cat and russian wolfhound cohabit quite peacefully.

22. Last Summer my family and I visited epcot center in orlando, florida.

23. The two companies signed a stipulation of interest agreement last april.

24. Interior designers recommended italian marble for the entry and mexican tiles for the patio.

25. A limousine will take guests from pearson international airport directly to the royal york hotel.

NAME ______________________________

LEVEL II

Write the letter of the group of words that is correctly capitalized.

1.	(a) my uncle and my aunt	(b) my Uncle and my Aunt	________
2.	(a) Very sincerely yours,	(b) Very Sincerely Yours,	________
3.	(a) Send it to Vice-President Lee	(b) Send it to vice-president Lee	________
4.	(a) Volume II, Page 37	(b) Volume II, page 37	________
5.	(a) located in northern Saskatchewan	(b) located in Northern Saskatchewan	________
6.	(a) stored in building 44	(b) stored in Building 44	________
7.	(a) within our Human Resources Department	(b) within our human resources department	________
8.	(a) the World Wildlife Federation	(b) the world wildlife federation	________
9.	(a) in appendix III	(b) in Appendix III	________
10.	(a) heading South on Highway 5	(b) heading south on Highway 5	________
11.	(a) the book *Love and Will*	(b) the book *Love And Will*	________
12.	(a) both federal and provincial laws	(b) both Federal and Provincial laws	________
13.	(a) Q-tips and kleenexes	(b) Q-tips and Kleenexes	________
14.	(a) orders from Sales Director Ali	(b) orders from sales director Ali	________
15.	(a) a trip to the east coast	(b) a trip to the East Coast	________

Use proofreading marks to capitalize (≡) or to show lower-case letters (/) in the following sentences.

16. We received a directive from Ruth MacVean, Supervisor, Administrative Services Division.

17. The President of our Company gave an address entitled "Leadership: What Effective Managers do and how They do it."

18. Gina Schmidt, customer service representative, attended a convention in the Eastern part of the province.

19. To reach my home, proceed north on highway 10 until you reach exit 7.

20. Mayor Bruno visited the Capital in an attempt to increase the city's share of Provincial funding.

21. The best article is "Does your training measure up?" by Leslie Brokaw.

22. John placed his ray-ban sunglasses on the formica counter.

23. Sue's Mother and Father were scheduled to leave on flight 37 from gate 6 at phoenix sky harbor international airport.

24. Taxicab, Bus, and Limousine service is available from the Airport to the ritz-carlton hotel.

NAME________________________________

Write the letter of the group of words that is correctly capitalized.

LEVEL III

	(a)	(b)	
1.	(a) photographs sent from Venus to Earth	(b) photographs sent from Venus to earth	______
2.	(a) a room marked "private"	(b) a room marked "Private"	______
3.	(a) the Egyptian Room and the Sahara Room	(b) the Egyptian room and the Sahara room	______
4.	(a) the finest production on earth	(b) the finest production on Earth	______
5.	(a) from President-Elect Ross	(b) from President-elect Ross	______
6.	(a) When, sir, are you free?	(b) When, Sir, are you free?	______
7.	(a) some asian cultures	(b) some Asian cultures	______
8.	(a) an envelope stamped "confidential"	(b) an envelope stamped "Confidential"	______
9.	(a) our sales director, Joe Hines	(b) our Sales Director, Joe Hines	______
10.	(a) to ex-Premier Davis	(b) to Ex-Premier Davis	______

Use proofreading marks to capitalize (≡) or to show lower-case letters (/) in the following sentences.

11. The returned cheque was stamped "Insufficient funds."

12. A paddleboat travelled south down the Mississippi river.

13. No one recognized ex-minister Thurston when he toured the Okanagan valley.

14. We wonder, professor, if the gravity of Mars might be similar to that of earth.

15. The Organization's bylaws state: "On the third Monday of every month the Club's Treasurer will prepare the financial report."

16. The President of our Company has travelled to Pacific Rim Countries to expand foreign markets.

17. The Minister of foreign affairs met with the prime minister to discuss this country's National policy toward african nations.

18. Have you any sheets of bond paper left? only a few.

19. In malaysia we soon learned that muslims do not eat pork and that buddhists and hindus do not eat beef.

20. Although he was known as a "banker's banker," Mr. Wong specialized in Mortgage Financing.

NAME ______________________

LEVEL I

In the space provided, write the letter of the correctly expressed group of words.

1. (a) for 24 employees (b) for twenty-four employees ________

2. (a) only 9 pens left (b) only nine pens left ________

3. (a) twenty-five dollars (b) $25 ________

4. (a) on the thirtieth of May (b) on the 30th of May ________

5. (a) it cost 20 cents (b) it cost twenty cents ________

6. (a) (military style) 5 April 2005 (b) April 5, 2005 ________

7. (a) $2.05, 85¢, and $5.00 (b) $2.05, $.85, and $5 ________

8. (a) we started at 9 a.m. (b) we started at nine a.m. ________

9. (a) 2 Highland Avenue (b) Two Highland Avenue ________

10. (a) 226 Sixth Street (b) 226 6th Street ________

Underline any errors in the expression of numbers in the following sentences. Write the correct forms.

11. 194 businesses were sent the ethics survey December 1st. ________

12. 2 companies have moved their corporate offices to twenty-fifth Avenue. ________

13. Three of the least expensive items were priced at $5.00, $3.29, and 99 cents. ________

14. If your payment of $100.00 is received before the 2 of the month, you will receive a discount. ________

15. On February 1st the guidelines for all fifteen departments went into effect. ________

16. Our office, formerly located at Two Ford Place, is now located at One Kent Avenue. ________

17. Please call me at 815-611-9292, Ext. Three, before 4 p.m. ________

18. On May 15th 2 performances will be given: two p.m. and eight p.m. ________

19. 3 of our employees start at 8:00 a.m., and 5 start at 8:30 a.m. ________

20. If reservations are made before the fifteenth of the month, the fare will be 204 dollars. ________

21. Grossmont College offers a fifteen-hour training course that costs one hundred twenty-five dollars. ________

22. Classes meet Monday through Thursday from 11:45 a.m. until one p.m. ________

23. The Werners moved from 1,762 Milburn Avenue to 140 East 14th Street. ________

24. Lisa had only $.25 left after she purchased supplies for forty-four dollars. ________

25. On the third of January and again on the 18th, our machine needed service. ________

NAME ____________________

LEVEL II

Write the letter of the correctly expressed group of words.

	(a)	(b)	
1.	(a) for 82 students in 3 classes	(b) for 82 students in three classes	________
2.	(a) an interest period of ninety days	(b) an interest period of 90 days	________
3.	(a) over the past thirty years	(b) over the past 30 years	________
4.	(a) two 35-day contracts	(b) 2 thirty-five-day contracts	________
5.	(a) he is 45 years old	(b) he is forty-five years old	________
6.	(a) line three	(b) line 3	________
7.	(a) nearly 2.6 billion units	(b) nearly 2,600,000,000 units	________
8.	(a) 26 ten-page pamphlets	(b) twenty-six 10-page pamphlets	________
9.	(a) Lois Lamb, 65, and John Lamb, 66	(b) Lois Lamb, sixty-five, and John Lamb, sixty-six	________
10.	(a) exactly two years and seven months ago	(b) exactly 2 years and 7 months ago	________

Underline any errors in the expression of numbers in the following sentences. Write the corrected forms.

11. We have received 50 reservations over the past 14 days. ________

12. Please order twenty-five two-ring binders large enough to hold 100 pages each. ________

13. 33 of the corporations had operating budgets that exceeded one million dollars. ________

14. Only 10 telephones are available for the forty-eight employees in 5 offices. ________

15. Chapter eight in Volume two provides at least three references to pumps. ________

16. About 100 chairs are stored in Room Four, and another eight chairs are in Room 14. ________

17. We ordered two thirty-inch desks and three chairs. ________

18. Of the twenty requests we received, five were acted on immediately and three had to be tabled. ________

19. The 2 loans must be repaid within 90 days. ________

20. When she was only 24 years old, Mrs. Ibrahim supervised more than 120 employees. ________

21. Only two of the 125 mailed surveys were undeliverable. ________

22. Frank Morris, sixty-four, plans to retire in one year. ________

23. Linda Hannan and her fifteen-person company signed a four million dollar contract. ________

24. She purchased new equipment to beam fifty-two World Cup games from nine locations to forty million avid soccer fans in Pacific Rim countries. ________

25. The thirty-year mortgage carries an interest rate of eight per cent. ________

NAME ______________________________

LEVEL III

Assume that all the following phrases appear in complete sentences. Write the letter of the phrase that is appropriately expressed.

1. (a) the tank holds just 9 gallons (b) the tank holds just nine gallons ______

2. (a) only a three per cent gain (b) only a 3 per cent gain ______

3. (a) 4/5 of the voters (b) four-fifths of the voters ______

4. (a) a 50% markup (b) a 50 per cent markup ______

5. (a) a one-half share (b) a one half share ______

6. (a) a decline of .5 per cent (b) a decline of 0.5 per cent ______

7. (a) he placed 3rd in the province (b) he placed third in the province ______

8. (a) in the nineteenth century (b) in the 19th century ______

9. (a) a 5-pound box of candy (b) a five-pound box of candy ______

10. (a) at least 95% of the shareholders (b) at least 95 per cent of the shareholders ______

Underline any errors in the expression of numbers. Write the corrected forms.

11. A No. Ten envelope actually measures four and a half by nine and a half inches. ______

12. All the drivers in the 33rd Grand Prix finished the race. ______

13. Tests show that the driver responded in less than seven two hundredths of a second. ______

14. Great strides in communication technology have made made in the 21st century. ______

15. The desk top measured thirty and three-fourths inches by sixty and a half inches. ______

16. Payment must be received by the thirtieth to qualify for a three per cent discount. ______

17. The office was moved about fifty blocks on the tenth of December. ______

18. Place the date of a business letter on line 13, which is two inches from the top edge of the paper. ______

19. The computer weighs thirty-one pounds and is seventeen and a half inches wide. ______

20. Appropriation measures must be passed by a 2/3 majority. ______

21. She ordered a nine by twelve rug to cover two thirds of the floor. ______

22. After completing Form Ten Forty, the accountant submitted his bill for 800 dollars. ______

23. By the year 2,010, the number of employees over the age of 55 will have increased by 52%. ______

24. Nine different airlines carry over one hundred thousand passengers daily. ______

25. The company car was filled with twenty-five litres of gasoline and one litre of oil. ______

NAME ____________________

LEVEL I

Revise the following sentences to eliminate wordy phrases and needless repetition.

1. In the event that the shares rise, please sell my holdings.____________________

2. In a summary at the end of her report, Catherine Perkins reported increased service costs. ____________________

3. At this point in time, please sign your name in the space provided for your signature. ____________________

4. In spite of the fact that a tall fence surrounded the parking lot on all sides, security was a problem.

5. As a rule in the contemporary workplace of today, we generally expect all employees to have good computer skills.

Revise the following sentences to avoid passive-voice verbs.

6. Apparently this letter was written by an employee from your office. ____________________

7. The lights were left on by the last person who used the room. ____________________

8. We were informed by your electronics division that your prices will be raised. ____________________

9. Credit cannot be extended because your bills have not been paid. ____________________

10. A nine-person intervention team was trained by Canada Post. ____________________

NAME ________________________________

Revise the following sentences to make them more unified.

11. Phil will be taking a two-week vacation, and your work assignment has been changed. ____________

____

12. We need to land some new accounts, and each of us must do what we can to save funds. ____________

____

LEVEL II

Revise the following sentences to avoid faulty parallel construction.

1. Figures were checked, corrections were made, and we sent the report. ____________

____

2. Mrs. Ralston had to supervise office workers, order supplies, and all salespeople were contacted daily by her.

____

____

3. Our administrative assistant should be proficient in keyboarding, computer applications, and writing reports is also required.

____

____

4. Consumer activists seek to ensure that products perform as advertised, they are safe, and the physical environment is not harmed.

____

____

5. The policy affected all vendors, suppliers, and those involved with consulting. ____________

____

Revise the following sentences to avoid misplaced modifiers.

6. The busy personnel director interviewed only candidates who had excellent computer skills in the morning.

____

____

7. You and your staff will have no trouble in any of the 21 countries you visit with exchange rates and red tape.

____

____

NAME ____________________

8. Our placement service is in constant touch with industry in placing our graduates located on the eighteenth floor.

____

____

Revise the following sentences to avoid unclear pronoun references. Be particularly careful with the pronouns *this, that, which,* and *it.* Be sure they refer to clear antecedents.

9. Computers and new software helped us reduce personnel costs, increase productivity, and improve quality. That justifies the cost of this investment.

____

____

10. An initial registration fee is required of all new members, which is due on the 1st of the month. ____________________

____

11. Both data and word processing functions are performed with the new software; therefore, this should reduce overall costs.

____

____

NAME ____________________

LEVEL III

Use subordinate conjunctions (such as *if, because, although,* and *since*) or relative pronouns (such as *who, that,* and *which*) to create one sentence from the two ideas shown below.

	Primary Idea	**Secondary Idea**
1.	The Time Book Club will send you a free bestseller if you join now.	We have given over $30 million worth of books to our members.
2.	Electricity is the most powerful servant ever made available to man.	Electricity can be dangerous if used carelessly.
3.	Business executives have difficulty forecasting future sales and profits.	Complex variables such as income, unemployment, and taxes influence buying power.
4.	The RCMP has more than 20,000 members and handles problems of national significance.	The force began as the North-West Mounted Police in 1873.

Improve the coherence of the following sentences by adding appropriate transitional expressions (such as *therefore, however, for example,* and other expressions discussed in the chapter).

5. Our bank has experienced unprecedented growth in the past five years; ____________, we plan to expand our facilities to meet the growing demand for our services.

6. You could be enjoying the many conveniences that Imperial Credit Card holders enjoy; ____________, to do so, you must first complete the enclosed application to receive one of our cards.

7. We are sending you a new Imperial Credit Card Directory; ____________, we are sending you a handy form for ordering other directories for your use.

8. Only a few of our salespeople have made reservations for the April 10 seminar; ____________, we are sending this reminder of the seminar.

9. Our college savings plan will help you finance more than your children's tuition costs; ____________, fees for room, board, books, and other expenses may be included.

Chapter 1 Self-Help Answers

1. c 2. b 3. c 4. c 5. a 6. c 7. a 8. b 9. d 10. b

Chapter 2 Self-Help Answers

Worksheet 1

A. *Answers will vary.* 2. substitutes for a noun he she it 3. shows action or joins words that describe the subject jumps works is 4. describes nouns or pronouns tall soft five 5. modifies verbs, adjectives, or other adverbs hurriedly very nicely 6. joins nouns and pronouns to the sentence to for at 7. connects words or groups of words and but or 8. shows strong feelings Wow! Gosh! No!
B. 1. pronoun 2. verb 3. adj 4. adj 5. noun 6. prep 7. noun 8. conj 9. pronoun 10. verb 11. adv 12. adj 13. interj 14. adj 15. noun 16. conj 17. noun 18. verb 19. adj 20. adj 21. noun 22. prep 23. adj 24. noun 25. pronoun 26. verb 27. adverb 28. conj 29. adj 30. adj 31. noun 32. verb 33. adv

Worksheet 2

1. pronoun 2. verb 3. noun 4. prep 5. noun 6. conj 7. adj 8. noun 9. verb 10. adv 11. verb 12. noun 13. interj 14. verb 15. noun 16. adv 17. verb 18. pronoun 19. verb 20. verb 21. adj 22. noun 23. prep 24. noun 25. adj 26. adj 27. adj 28. noun 29. verb 30. adv 31. adj 32 conj 33. adj 34. conj 35. adj 36. noun 37. verb 38. verb 39. pronoun 40. adv 41. prep 42. adj 43. adj 44. adj 45. noun 46. noun 47. adv 48. verb 49. prep 50. adj 51. adj 52. noun 53. prep 54. adj 55. adj 56. adj 57. noun

Chapter 3 Self-Help Answers

Worksheet 1

1. (S) one (V) sold 2. (S) speaker (V) made 3. (S) telephones (V) rang 4. (S) we (V) will hire 5. (S) team (V) built 6. (S) salespeople (V) received 7. (S) manager (V) will send 8. (S) we (V) released 9. (S) one (V) was given 10. (S) committee (V) was appointed 11. (S) applicant (V) received 12. (S) Everything (V) is covered 13. (S) Mr. Thomas (V) is 14. (S) copiers (V) are 15. (S) Mrs. Seymour (V) is 16. (S) Dul Youn Hu (V) has been 17. (S) offices (V) are

Worksheet 2

Answers will vary. 1. applauded 2. fell 3. arrived 4. rang 5. ended 6. dropped 7. policy 8. an email 9. letter 10. him 11. the door 12. letters 13. good 14. manager 15. Mr. Jones 16. Mary 17. Mr. Smith 18. John 19–23. *Answers will vary.*

Worksheet 3

1. b 2. a 3. a 4. d 5. c 6. b 7. b 8. c 9. d 10. c 11. b 12. d 13. a 14. a 15. c 16. d 17. b 18. a 19. c 20. b

Chapter 4 Self-Help Answers

LEVEL I

1. giraffes 2. feet 3. switches 4. Bushes 5. boxes 6. languages 7. faxes 8. sandwiches 9. income taxes 10. children 11. successes 12. values 13. dresses 14. branches 15. recommendations 16. women 17. mismatches 18. taxis 19. loaves 20. annexes 21. beliefs 22. Rosses 23. storms 24. ranches 25. Joneses 26. Chavezes 27. letters 28. businesses 29. computers 30. wishes

LEVEL II

1. wharves 2. chiefs of police 3. 2000s 4. Wolfs 5. embargoes 6. cm 7. size 10s 8. amts. 9. faculties 10. by-products 11. entries 12. lookers-on 13. companies 14. knives 15. courts-martial 16. A's 17. Shermans 18. memos 19. valleys 20. zeros 21. lives 22. yrs. 23. Mistrys 24. runners-up 25. oz. 26. journeys 27. M.B.A.s 28. wolves 29. Kellys 30. minorities

LEVEL III

1. data 2. theses 3. bacteria 4. Chinese 5. parentheses 6. the Miss Soltans 7. alumnae 8. Messrs. West and Turner 9. genera 10. news 11. pp. 12. ff. 13. larvae 14. Mmes. Smythe and Webb 15. criteria or criterions 16. are 17. is or are 18. formulas 19. analyses 20. is

Chapter 5 Self-Help Answers

LEVEL I

Worksheet 1

1. students' books 2. company's office 3. women's uniforms 4. two months' rent 5. movie star's mansion 6. neighbours' feelings 7. pilot's landing 8. partners' agreement 9. Jeffrey's notebook 10. department's strengths 11. two years' time 12. people's customs 13. week's merger 14. bank's credit 15. citizens' savings 16. Canada's mountains 17. employer's requirements 18. all candidates' résumés 19. government's policies 20. both lawyers' fees

Worksheet 2

1. year's 2. drivers' 3. carpenter's 4. thief's 5. day's 6. employees' 7. CEO's 8. readers' 9. caller's 10. authors' 11. Gap's 12. C 13. country's 14. months'

15. organization's 16. vice-president's 17. family's 18. C 19. years' 20. farmer's 21. citizens' 22. year's 23. customer's 24. Children's 25. supervisor's

LEVEL II

1. public's 2. company's 3. stationer's 4. The suggestions of my uncle's lawyer 5. desk top or top of the desk 6. aunt and uncle's 7. C 8. last month's 9. C 10. telephone number of the president's secretary 11. sales 12. beards of my two brothers-in-law 13. Larry's 14. Quebec's 15. Rick's 16. C 17. Clark and Clark's 18. Angeles 19. architects' 20. last year's 21. C 22. Diana and Graham's 23. reporters' 24. day's day's 25. C

LEVEL III

1. someone else's 2. Ross' or Ross's 3. classes' 4. Saunders' or Saunders's 5. Rodriguezes' 6. Les' or Les's 7. boss's 8. bosses' 9. Abramoviches 10. actresses' 11. Harris' or Harris's 12. Burns' or Burns's 13. James' or James's 14. waitress's 15. Garveys' 16. Morrises' 17. Betz' or Betz's 18. Walkers' 19. Simons' or Simons's 20. Jones' or Jones's 21. White's 22. Williamses' 23. Kimballs' 24. Elvis' or Elvis's

Chapter 6 Self-Help Answers

LEVEL I

Worksheet 1

1–14. *Order of answers may vary.* 1–7. I, you, he, she, it, we, they 8–14. me, you, him, her, it, us, them 15. I 16. she 17. he 18. they 19. she 20. we 21. she 22. he 23. she 24. he 25. I

Worksheet 2

1. me. 2. him 3. them 4. me 5. her 6. him 7. her 8. them 9. us 10. me 11. it's 12. theirs 13. its 14. There's 15. hers 16. it's 17. yours 18. Whose 19. ours 20. You're

LEVEL II

1. them 2. I 3. her 4. We 5. me 6. me 7. her 8. he 9. him 10. I 11. himself 12. her 13. her 14. she 15. me 16. us 17. she 18. him 19. I 20. me 21. me 22. She and I 23. her 24. us 25. I

LEVEL III

Worksheet 1

1. she 2. he 3. they 4. she 5. him 6. she 7. she 8. he 9. me 10. they 11. he 12. him 13. her 14. I 15. she 16. she 17. I 18. him 19. I 20. she 21. he 22. him 23. she 24. she

Worksheet 2

1. he 2. me 3. its 4. she 5. us 6. there's 7. he 8. I 9. me 10. her 11. us 12. you're 13. her 14. him 15. yours 16. me 17. he 18. its 19. him or me 20. There's 21. him 22. me 23. I 24. their 25. she

Chapter 7 Self-Help Answers

LEVEL I

1. her 2. his or her 3. his or her 4. their 5. their 6. he or she 7. his or her lunch 8. him or her 9. her 10. their pictures 11. her 12. his 13. Every employee must obtain his or her ... 14. Every employee must obtain a parking permit ... 15. All employees must obtain their parking permits ...

LEVEL II

1. use *her* instead of *their* 2. *its* instead of *it's* 3. *his or her* instead of *their* 4. *his or her* for *his* 5. *his* for *their* 6. *her* for *their* 7. C 8. *its* for *their* 9. *its* for *their* 10. *him or her* for *them* 11. C 12. *his or her* for *their* 13. *his or her* for *their* 14. *his or her seat* for *their seats.* 15. *its* for *their* 16. *its* for *their* 17. *them* for *it* 18. *his* for *their* 19. *her* for *their* 20. *they* for *she or he*

LEVEL III

Worksheet 1

1. Whom 2. whom 3. who 4. whom 5. whom 6. whom 7. Who 8. Whom 9. Who 10. who 11. who 12. who 13. whom 14. who 15. Who

Worksheet 2

1. whoever 2. whoever 3. whomever 4. whomever 5. whoever 6. whoever 7. whoever 8. Whoever 9. whoever 10. Whoever 11. Who 12. who 13. who 14. whoever 15. whom

Worksheet 3

1. Whom 2. who 3. whom 4. whoever 5. whom 6. whom 7. Whoever 8. who 9. who 10. who 11. whom 12. whom 13. Who 14. Whom 15. whomever 16. whom 17. Whoever 18. whom 19. whom 20. whom 21. whose 22. who 23. who's 24. who 25. who's

Chapter 8 Self-Help Answers

LEVEL I

1. transitive 2. intransitive 3. linking 4. complements 5. I 6. L—Fran 7. T—cards 8. I 9. L—lifeguard 10. T—pants 11. T—cheques 12. L—better 13. L—he 14. I 15. T—questions 16. T—gifts 17. L—best 18. I 19. L—justified 20. T—expectations

LEVEL II

Worksheet 1

1. Mariam (Mariam did not pick up the text message ...)
2. Mattel (Mattel shipped our order last week.)
3. Mrs. Bradford (Mrs. Bradford must authorize withdrawals ...)
4. Mr. Stern (Mr. Stern asked Bill to be responsible ...)
5. management (Management forced employees who ...)

Worksheet 2

Revised sentences will vary. 1. Clerks must complete ... 2. Mr. Smith wrote cheques ... 3. John programmed ... 4. Judges made decisions ... 5. When manufacturers first introduced ... 6. We give cash ... 7. Management warned employees ... 8. We limit the value ...

LEVEL III

1. were 2. be 3. was 4. be 5. would 6. be 7. were 8. be 9. rest 10. were 11. were 12. be 13. were 14. meet 15. were 16. be 17. were 18. was 19. were 20. be

Chapter 9 Self-Help Answers

LEVEL I

1. is 2. occurred 3. is 4. is 5. is 6. plan 7. will sell 8. supplied 9. studied 10. will analyze 11. applied 12. considered 13. varies 14. insists 15. will appeal 16. requires 17. will demand 18. tried

LEVEL II

Worksheet 1

1. become 2. froze 3. hid 4. chosen 5. built 6. drunk 7. forgotten or forgot 8. given 9. gone 10. bitten 11. eaten 12. sung 13. C or struck (meaning?) 14. sprang 15. shaken 16. worn 17. written 18. stolen 19. taken 20. gone

Worksheet 2

1. laid 2. lie 3. lying 4. laid 5. laying 6. lie 7. lay 8. lay 9. lain 10. lie 11. lie 12. lying 13. lie 14. lay 15. lain 16. lay 17. lying 18. lie 19. laid 20. laying

LEVEL III

1. has opened 2. is planning 3. had called 4. has worked 5. were seeing 6. will be signing 7. had been broken 8. have seen 9. are considering 10. was being heard 11. rung 12. drank 13. choose 14. driven 15. saw 16. gone 17. saw 18. eaten 19. written 20. rose 21. sworn 22. begun

Chapter 10 Self-Help Answers

LEVEL I

Worksheet 1

1. provide 2. is 3. comes 4. think 5. is 6. was 7. is 8. needs 9. has 10. are 11. is 12. are 13. have 14. are 15. sounds 16. was 17. is 18. are 19. have 20. was

Worksheet 2

1. travels 2. are 3. is 4. are 5. appear 6. are 7. was 8. is 9. are 10. is 11. has 12. provide 13. Has 14. is 15. is 16. has 17. appears 18. are

LEVEL II

1. is 2. has 3. deserves 4. is 5. is 6. is 7. were 8. mention 9. merits 10. every one 11. are 12. has 13. belongs 14. is 15. is 16. has 17. Were 18. has 19. have 20. is

LEVEL III

1. has 2. is 3. enjoy 4. was 5. was 6. is 7. favour 8. are 9. are 10. am 11. is 12. is 13. like 14. are 15. is 16. need 17. were 18. are 19. complain 20. has

Chapter 11 Self-Help Answers

LEVEL I

1. your 2. his 3. Mr. Cortina's 4. our 5. Mr. Frank's 6. C 7. your criticizing 8. your calling 9. Mr. Davidson's 10. our faxing 11. C 12. my working 13. C

LEVEL II

1. While preparing the report 2. Surrounded 3. seeing his opportunity 4. installed just two months ago 5. rereading the article several times 6. Opening a new account 7. Irritated 8. opening a new account 9. model, 10. Dallas, stockbroker, 11. C 12. transactions, 13. C 14. Sanderson, firm, 15. behalf, 16. popularity, 17. C 18. day,

LEVEL III

1. b 2. b 3. a 4. b 5. b 6. a 7. b

8. Completing the examination in only 20 minutes, Maria earned a perfect score.
9. To locate the members' names and addresses, we used a current directory.
10. Driving through the desert, we thought the highway seemed endless.
11. To stay in touch with customers, sales representatives made telephone contacts.
12. Addressing an audience for the first time, I felt my knees shake and my voice wavered.

Chapter 12 Self-Help Answers

LEVEL I

1. more effective 2. worst 3. friendlier 4. least certain 5. more beautiful 6. fastest 7. better 8. noisiest 9. quieter 10. most sincere 11. most skilled 12. least 13. slower 14. more likely 15. most unusual 16. fewer 17. better 18. more credible 19. worst 20. least

LEVEL II

1. loudly 2. C 3. C 4. Fewer 5. more quietly 6. bad 7. conflict-of-interest 8. C 9. C 10. latter 11. well 12. satisfactorily 13. house to house 14. C 15. surely 16. quietly 17. really 18. charge account 19. not-too-distant 20. fewer

LEVEL III

1. b 2. b 3. a 4. b 5. a 6. a 7. a 8. a 9. neatly 10. well (for *good*) 11. C 12. recently enacted 13. worst (for *worse*) 14. an (for *a*) 15. had hardly 16. round-the-world 17. bad (for *badly*) 18. fewer people 19. said only 20. an 840-acre

Chapter 13 Self-Help Answers

LEVEL I

1. should have (for *should of*) 2. him (for *he*) 3. C 4. me (for *I*) 5. from (for *off of*) 6. to (for *too*) 7. her (for *she*) 8. could have (for *could of*) 9. too (for *to*) 10. him (for *he*) 11. from (for *off*) 12. him (for *he*) 13. from (for *off of*) 14. C 15. him (for *he*) 16. too (for *to*) 17. could have (for *could of*) 18. C 19. could have (for *could of*) 20. me (for *I*)

LEVEL II

1. besides (for *beside*) 2. support *of* 3. omit *with* 4. in to (for *into*) 5. omit *of* 6. among (for *between*) 7. as (for *like*) 8. C 9. type *of* shingles 10. into (for *in to*) 11. C 12. concern *for* 13. omit *at* 14. C 15. omit *from* 16. omit *up* 17. style *of* 18. going *in to* meet 19. omit *to* 20. graduated *from*

LEVEL III

1. b 2. a 3. b 4. b 5. b 6. a 7. b 8. b 9. b 10. b 11. a 12. a 13. b 14. b 15. a 16. a 17. b 18. b 19. a 20. b

Chapter 14 Self-Help Answers

LEVEL I

The order of Answers 1–4 may vary. 1. and 2. or 3. nor 4. but (also acceptable for 1–4: for, so, yet) 5. b 6. a 7. b 8. a 9. a 10. b 11. a 12. b 13. b 14. b 15. a

LEVEL II

1. *Answers for this item may vary.* therefore, however, consequently, moreover, then, hence, thus 2. semicolon 3. commas 4. planning, nevertheless, 5. occupancy; that is, 6. organization, on the other hand, 7. 6 p.m.; hence 8. shelves; however, 9. York; then 10. has, consequently, 11. organization; consequently, 12. graduate, on the other hand, 13. are, nevertheless, 14. year; on the other hand, 15. competitive; however, 16. candidates, consequently, 17. résumés; consequently, 18. letter; therefore, 19. done; however, 20. information; however,

LEVEL III

1. b 2. b 3. a 4. b
5. You can either fax him your response or send him an email message.
6. Our goals are both to educate motorists and also to save lives.
7. Tony has neither a job offer nor even an interview lined up.
8. We knew that we had to either raise more money or begin selling stock.

Chapter 15 Self-Help Answers

LEVEL I

1. T 2. T 3. T 4. T 5. F 6. P 7. D 8. I 9. P 10. D 11. I 12. D 13. I 14. D 15. P 16. I 17. D 18. I 19. D 20. I 21. P 22. I 23. D 24. D 25. I

LEVEL II

1. suggestions, 2. will, if you follow my suggestions, 3. C 4. completed, 5. C 6. C 7. booklet, which was submitted over six weeks ago, 8. know, 9. payments, provided there is no interruption in profits, 10. necessary, 11. C 12. Gilroy, who volunteered to head the program, 13. C 14. order, 15. C 16. charged, which amounted to $176.12, 17. expected, 18. days, 19. contract, 20. C

LEVEL III

Answers may vary.

1. Although it was never properly signed, the original agreement was drawn between Mr. Hightower and Columbia Communications.
2. Atlantic Insurance Company, which is a company of people rather than statistics, serves not only individuals but also communities.
3. Thank you for informing us that your credit card, which has an expiration date of April 30, is missing.
4. Because your account is four months past due, we will be forced to take legal action unless we hear from you within seven days.
5. Sally Horton, who works as secretary to the manager in our Quality Control Department, won an award as this month's outstanding employee.

6. Pam Eichorn recently received her business diploma, and now she is looking for a job near Windsor, which is her hometown.
7. We are sending you four poster advertisements that will appear in magazines in April, which marks the beginning of a national campaign featuring our sports clothes.
8. Mr. Girard, who has worked at Rocketwell for thirty-seven years, plans to retire at the end of this year and devote more time to his orchid collection.

Chapter 16 Self-Help Answers

LEVEL I

1. (2) insurance, Mr. Isaq, 2. (1) By the way, 3. (2) resolved, however, 4. (2) Calgary, Alberta, 5. C 6. (2) plan, on the other hand, 7. (4) Systems, 750 Grant Road, Burnaby, British Columbia V5E 4B2, 8. (2) appears, sir, 9. (2) Friday, April 30, 10. (2) Molloy, who is an advertising executive, 11. C 12. C 13. (2) will, in addition, 14. (2) airports, centres, 15. (1) considered, 16. (2) Hudson, who is a specialist in information systems, 17. (2) patent, trademark, 18. (2) convinced, incidentally, 19. (2) policy, budget, 20. (2) Italy, Greece,

LEVEL II

1. (1) practical, 2. (1) months, 3. (2) Meyer, employees, 4. (1) week, 5. C 6. (2) appreciate, often, 7. C 8. C 9. (1) calculations, 10. C 11. (2) please, calculations, 12. (1) intelligent, 13. (1) return, 14. (1) June, 15. C 16. (1) inventory, 17. (1) Goodell, 18. (2) when, where, 19. (3) process, Thursday, June 1, 20. C

LEVEL III

1. (2) Ferrari, Ph.D., 2. C 3. (1) 2008, 4. (1) 2008, 5. (2) envelope, not a white folder, 6. (1) before, 7. (2) name," said the auditor, 8. C 9. C 10. (2) Feinstein, M.D., 11. C 12. (1) since, 13. (1) said, 14. (2) Chong, not Mrs. Lambert, 15. (1) nine, 16. (2) 17,365,000 (or 17 365 000) 17. (3) supervisor," remarked Sid Stern, results, 18. (3) way, president, vice-president, 19. (2) diamond," said the therapist, 20 (1) signs, signs

Chapter 17 Self-Help Answers

LEVEL I

1. profits; however, 2. Charlottetown, Prince Edward Island; Mount Pearl, Newfoundland; and Fort McMurray, 3. names, envelopes, 4. order; 5. space; on the other hand, 6. remarkable; however, 7. public; 8. Roberts, secretary, Legal Department; Lea Lim, clerk, Human Resources; and Mark Cameron, dispatcher, 9. estate; however, 10. 10 a.m.; 11. award; 12. catalogue, selections, 13. property, 14. Ontario; Manitoba; 15. seats; 16. Hyatt Regency Hotel, Vancouver, British Columbia; the Hotel Halifax, Halifax, Nova Scotia; and the Valhalla Inn, Toronto, 17. requested, Thursday, May 4; however, Friday, 18. gathering, recording,

LEVEL II

1. scrutinized: 2. C 3. saying: 4. C 5. decision: 6. C 7. following: 8. Boston, Massachusetts, sites: 9. skills: 10. C 11. thought: 12. file: 13. Hofer, Stone, 14. C 15. following:

LEVEL III

1. check; namely, 2. supplies: cartridges, 3. services, philosophy; that is, 4. rule: 5. 2:15 6:45 6. Tom; 7. executives—namely, Mr. Gabereau, Mr. Wright, and Mrs. Stranahan— 8. *Investment: An* 9. field; 10. areas; for example, 11. representative"; that is, 12. advertising: product, 13. convention, namely, 14. program; for instance, 15. possible, office; however,

Chapter 18 Self-Help Answers

LEVEL I

1. FAQs website. 2. 10 a.m., didn't you? 3. Mrs. C.A. Ltd. 4. Donald L. Cullens, Jr., job? 5. Help! jammed! 6. please, Miss Juarez, gift. 7. been! 8. B.A. degrees, M.A. degrees. 9. CEO CFO decisions. 10. Tan, Mr. Roe, and Ms. Rich. 11. 9 a.m. EST rate. 12. Bennett, M.D., Hawtin, Ph.D., speakers. 13. 80 w.p.m. CIDA. 14. China, France, and the UK. 15. CPU USA. 16. f.o.b. Windsor, didn't he? 17. Nos. $50,000 coverage. 18. 5 p.m. PST? 19. Wow! prize? 20. M.A., DVDs.

LEVEL II

1. F (use two hyphens) 2. T 3. F 4. T 5. T 6. a 7. c 8. b 9. a 10. b 11. c 12. c 13. b 14. c

LEVEL III

1. T 2. T 3. F 4. T 5. F 6. T 7. T 8. T 9. T 10. T 11. a 12. c 13. a 14. b 15. a

Chapter 18 Review

1. "Soaring Salaries of CEOs" The New York Times? 2. This year's last year's; therefore, case-by-case 3. members. Dr. Carla Chang, Professor Mark Rousso, and Robert Price, Esq. 4. say, 5 p.m. EST. 5. fixed-rate , not variable-rate, 6. invited: Christine Lenski, DataCom Industries; Mark Grant, LaserPro Inc.; and Ivan Weiner, 7. Vancouver, British Columbia, Calgary, 8. say, "We Friday"? 9. B.A. 11 a.m.; M.B.A. 2 p.m. 10. discussed, Monday, August 8. 11. feel, however, car's 12. D.A. Rusterholz. 13. carefully, "bomb." 14. weather, stations: CFRB, CHIN, and CHUM. 15. employees—Gregorio ... Williams—Friday, June 5. 16. attitude, aptitude, altitude," 17. cars; by June 15,

18. CRTC studied; 19. 9 p.m., 20. Ms. Courtney Phillips, Administrative Assistant, Globex Industries, 7600 Normandale Boulevard, Scarborough, ON M1K 5G4, 21. (see page 2 for a summary of the report) to the president's Friday, 22. <u>Success</u> "A Venture Expert's Advice." 23. Zuckerman, our former manager, IBM. 24. issues; namely, 25. expected, this year's heavy; consequently, 26. Lofchik, Drive, London, N6E 1N7.

Chapter 19 Self-Help Answers

LEVEL I

1. b 2. a 3. a 4. a 5. a 6. b 7. a 8. a 9. b 10. a 11. b 12. b 13. b 14. a 15. b 16. station county 17. company's 18. Committee Metro Toronto Convention Centre 19. winter English 20. of Ballroom Hotel 21. Persian Russian 22. summer Epcot Center Orlando, Florida 23. Stipulation of Interest Agreement April 24. Italian Mexican 25. Pearson International Airport Royal York Hotel

LEVEL II

1. a 2. a 3. a 4. b 5. a 6. b 7. a 8. a 9. b 10. b 11. a 12. a 13. b 14. a 15. b 16. supervisor 17. president company Do How Do It 18. eastern 19. Highway Exit 20. capital provincial 21. "Does Your Training Measure Up?" 22. Ray-Ban Formica 23. mother and father Flight 37 Gate 6 Phoenix Sky Harbor International Airport 24. bus limousine airport Ritz-Carlton Hotel

LEVEL III

1. a 2. b 3. a 4. a 5. b 6. a 7. b 8. b 9. a 10. a 11. Funds 12. River 13. Minister Valley 14. Professor Earth 15. organization's 16. president company countries 17. Foreign Affairs Prime Minister national African 18. Only 19. Malaysia Muslims Buddhists Hindus 20. mortgage financing

Chapter 20 Self-Help Answers

LEVEL I

1. a 2. b 3. b 4. b 5. a 6. a 7. b 8. a 9. a 10. a 11. (Answers will vary.) A total of 194 December 1 12. Two 25th Avenue 13. $5 $.99 14. $100 2nd 15. February 1 15 departments 16. 2 Ford Place 17. (815) 611-9292, Ext. 3 18. May 15 two 2 p.m. 8 p.m. 19. Three 8 a.m. five 20. 15th $204 21. 15-hour $125 22. 1 p.m. 23. 1762 14 24. 25 cents $44 25. 3rd

LEVEL II

1. b 2. b (preferred) 3. a 4. a 5. b 6. b 7. a 8. a 9. a 10. b 11. fourteen 12. 25 two-ring 13. Thirty-three $1 million 14. ten 48 five 15. Chapter 8 Volume 2 16. Room 4 8 chairs 17. 30-inch 18. 20 requests 5 3 19. two loans 20. twenty-four years 21. Only 2 22. 64 23. 15-person $3 million 24. 52 40 million 25. thirty-year or 30-year 8 per cent

LEVEL III

1. a 2. b 3. b 4. b 5. a 6. b 7. b 8. a 9. a 10. b 11. No. 10 4 1/2 by 9 1/2 inches 12. thirty-third 13. 7/200 14. twenty-first 15. 30 3/4 inches by 60 1/2 inches 16. 30th 3 percent 17. 50 blocks 10th 18. 2 inches 19. 31 pounds 17 1/2 inches 20. two-thirds 21. 9 by 12 two-thirds 22. Form 1040 $800 23. 2010 fifty-five 52 per cent 24. 100,000 or 100 000 25. 25 litres 1 litre

Chapter 21 Self-Help Answers

LEVEL I

Answers will vary.

1. If the shares rise, please sell my holdings.
2. In her summary, Catherine Perkins reported increased service costs.
3. Now please sign your name in the space provided.
4. Although a tall fence surrounded the parking lot, security was a problem.
5. In today's workplace we generally expect all employees to have good computer skills.
6. An employee from your office apparently wrote this letter.
7. The last person who used the room left the lights on.
8. Your electronics division informed us that you are going to raise your prices.
9. We cannot extend credit because you have not paid your bills.
10. Canada Post trained a nine-person intervention team.
11. Because Phil will be taking a two-week vacation, your work assignment has been changed.
12. Until we land some new accounts, each of us must do what we can to save funds.

LEVEL II

Answers will vary.

1. We checked figures, made corrections, and sent the report.
2. Mrs. Ralston had to supervise office workers, order supplies, and contact all salespeople daily.
3. Our administrative assistant should be proficient in keyboarding, computer applications, and report writing.
4. Consumer activists seek to ensure that products perform as advertised, are safe, and do not harm the environment.
5. The policy affected all vendors, suppliers, and consultants.
6. In the morning the busy personnel director interviewed only candidates ...
7. You and your staff will have no trouble with exchange rates and red tape in any of the ...

8. Our placement service, located on the eighteenth floor, is in constant touch with industry ...
9. Computers and new software helped us reduce personnel costs, increase productivity, and improve quality. These results justify the cost of this investment.
10. An initial registration fee is required of all new members. That fee is due on the 1st of the month.
11. Both data and word processing functions are performed with the new software; therefore, this software should reduce overall costs.

LEVEL III

Answers will vary.

1. The Time Book Club, which has given over $30 million worth of books to members, will send you a free bestseller if you join now.
2. Although dangerous if used carelessly, electricity is the most powerful servant ever made available to man.
3. Because complex variables such as income, unemployment, and taxes influence buying power, business executives have difficulty forecasting future sales and profits.
4. The RCMP, which began as the North-West Mounted Police in 1873, has more than 20,000 members and handles problems of national significance.
5. therefore (*or* consequently) 6. however 7. in addition (*or* moreover) 8. consequently (*or* therefore) 9. for example (*or* in fact)

Unit 1 Review Chapters 1–3

1. F 2. T 3. F 4. F 5. T 6. F 7. T 8. F 9. T 10. T 11. b 12. c 13. d 14. b 15. a 16. c 17. b 18. a 19. b 20. a 21. c 22. c 23. a 24. b 25. c 26. b 27. a 28. d 29. a 30. b 31. a 32. c 33. d 34. c 35. a 36. c 37. a 38. b 39. b 40. c

Unit 2 Review Chapters 4–7

LEVEL I

1. a 2. b 3. b 4. c 5. a 6. b 7. b 8. a 9. b 10. d 11. c

LEVEL II

12. a 13. c 14. a 15. a 16. b 17. b 18. b 19. a 20. b 21. c 22. b

LEVEL III

23. b 24. b 25. d 26. b 27. a 28. a 29. b 30. b 31. a 32. a 33. b 34. b 35. b

Hotline

36. b 37. a 38. b 39. b 40. b

Unit 3 Review Chapters 8–11

LEVEL I

1. a 2. c 3. b 4. b 5. a 6. b 7. b 8. a 9. a 10. b 11. b 12. b

LEVEL II

13. a 14. b 15. b 16. b 17. b 18. b 19. b 20. 2 21. 0 22. 1

LEVEL III

23. b 24. a 25. a 26. b 27. b 28. a 29. b 30. b 31. b 32. b 33. b

Hotline

34. a 35. b 36. a 37. b 38. b

Unit 4 Review Chapters 12–15

LEVEL I

1. a 2. a 3. b 4. a 5. b 6. a 7. b 8. c 9. 0 10. 1 11. 0 12. 0 13. 1

LEVEL II

14. a 15. a 16. b 17. a 18. a 19. a 20. d 21. c 22. e 23. a 24. c 25. b 26. e 27. e

LEVEL III

28. a 29. b 30. a 31. b 32. a 33. c 34. e 35. d

Hotline

36. b 37. b 38. b 39. b 40. a

Unit 5 Review Chapters 16–18

LEVEL I

1. circumstances, Greenwood, 2. C 3. Sizer, Labs, 4. C 5. feels, hand, 6. representative, Anderson, 7. c 8. c 9. people, 10. c 11. b 12. a 13. a

LEVEL II

14. a 15. b 16. a 17. c 18. a 19. a 20. b 21. a 22. c 23. a 24. c

LEVEL III

25. c 26. a 27. b 28. b 29. b 30. c 31. b 32. c 33. c 34. a 35. b

Hotline

36. a 37. b 38. a 39. a 40. a

Unit 6 Review Chapters 19–21

LEVEL I

1. b 2. b 3. b 4. a 5. b 6. a 7. b 8. a 9. b 10. b 11. a 12. b

LEVEL II

13. b 14. a 15. a 16. a 17. b 18. a 19. a 20. b 21. a 22. a (... sound, and add colour.) 23. b (With a blank mind and a dry mouth, Michelle ...) 24. c (... complaint. These problems must be addressed ...)

LEVEL III

25. a 26. b 27. b 28. b 29. a 30. a 31. b 32. b 33. b 34. a 35. a 36. b 37. a 38. b 39. a 40. b

Index